Outward Foreign Direct Investment (FDI) in Emerging Market Economies

Tomasz Dorożyński
University of Lodz, Poland

Anetta Kuna-Marszałek
University of Lodz, Poland

A volume in the Advances in Finance, Accounting, and Economics (AFAE) Book Series

IGI GLOBAL
DISSEMINATOR OF KNOWLEDGE

www.igi-global.com

Published in the United States of America by
IGI Global
Business Science Reference (an imprint of IGI Global)
701 E. Chocolate Avenue
Hershey PA, USA 17033
Tel: 717-533-8845
Fax: 717-533-8661
E-mail: cust@igi-global.com
Web site: http://www.igi-global.com

Library of Congress Cataloging-in-Publication Data

CIP Data Pending
ISBN: 978-1-5225-2345-1
eISBN: 978-1-5225-2346-8

This book is published in the IGI Global book series Advances in Finance, Accounting, and Economics (AFAE) (ISSN: 2327-5677; eISSN: 2327-5685)

British Cataloguing in Publication Data
A Cataloguing in Publication record for this book is available from the British Library.

Advances in Finance, Accounting, and Economics (AFAE) Book Series

Ahmed Driouchi
Al Akhawayn University, Morocco

ISSN:2327-5677
EISSN:2327-5685

Mission

In our changing economic and business environment, it is important to consider the financial changes occurring internationally as well as within individual organizations and business environments. Understanding these changes as well as the factors that influence them is crucial in preparing for our financial future and ensuring economic sustainability and growth.

The **Advances in Finance, Accounting, and Economics (AFAE)** book series aims to publish comprehensive and informative titles in all areas of economics and economic theory, finance, and accounting to assist in advancing the available knowledge and providing for further research development in these dynamic fields.

Coverage

- Environmental and Social Accounting
- Banking
- Economic Policy
- Economics of Innovation and Knowledge
- Economic Indices and Quantitative Economic Methods
- Statistical Analysis
- Fiscal Policy
- Finance
- Public Finance
- Investments and Derivatives

IGI Global is currently accepting manuscripts for publication within this series. To submit a proposal for a volume in this series, please contact our Acquisition Editors at Acquisitions@igi-global.com or visit: http://www.igi-global.com/publish/.

The Advances in Finance, Accounting, and Economics (AFAE) Book Series (ISSN 2327-5677) is published by IGI Global, 701 E. Chocolate Avenue, Hershey, PA 17033-1240, USA, www.igi-global.com. This series is composed of titles available for purchase individually; each title is edited to be contextually exclusive from any other title within the series. For pricing and ordering information please visit http://www.igi-global.com/book-series/advances-finance-accounting-economics/73685. Postmaster: Send all address changes to above address.

Titles in this Series

For a list of additional titles in this series, please visit: www.igi-global.com

Measuring Sustainable Development and Green Investments in Contemporary Economies
Mihai Mieila (Valahia University of Târgoviște, Romania)
Business Science Reference • copyright 2017 • 250pp • H/C (ISBN: 9781522520818) • US $170.00 (our price)

Handbook of Research on Unemployment and Labor Market Sustainability in the Era of Globalization
Füsun Yenilmez (Eskişehir Osmangazi University, Turkey) and Esin Kılıç (Eskişehir Osmangazi University, Turkey)
Business Science Reference • copyright 2017 • 474pp • H/C (ISBN: 9781522520085) • US $245.00 (our price)

Business Infrastructure for Sustainability in Developing Economies
Nilanjan Ray (Netaji Mahavidyalaya, India)
Business Science Reference • copyright 2017 • 343pp • H/C (ISBN: 9781522520412) • US $190.00 (our price)

Applied Behavioral Economics Research and Trends
Rodica Ianole (University of Bucharest, Romania)
Business Science Reference • copyright 2017 • 255pp • H/C (ISBN: 9781522518266) • US $160.00 (our price)

Value Relevance of Accounting Information in Capital Markets
Marianne Ojo (George Mason University, USA) and Jeanette Van Akkeren (QUT School of Accountancy, Australia)
Business Science Reference • copyright 2017 • 323pp • H/C (ISBN: 9781522519003) • US $205.00 (our price)

Handbook of Research on the EU's Role and Representation in the G20 Political and Economic Climate
Abdulkadir Isik (Namik Kemal University, Turkey)
Business Science Reference • copyright 2017 • 429pp • H/C (ISBN: 9781522508564) • US $310.00 (our price)

Examining the Role of National Promotional Banks in the European Economy Emerging Research and Opportunities
Iustina Alina Boitan (Bucharest University of Economic Studies, Romania)
Business Science Reference • copyright 2017 • 184pp • H/C (ISBN: 9781522518457) • US $120.00 (our price)

Tools and Techniques for Economic Decision Analysis
Jelena Stanković (University of Niš, Serbia) Pavlos Delias (Eastern Macedonia and Thrace Institute of Technology, Greece) Srđan Marinković (University of Niš, Serbia) and Sylvie Rochhia (Université Côte d'Azur, CNRS, GREDEG, France)
Business Science Reference • copyright 2017 • 305pp • H/C (ISBN: 9781522509592) • US $205.00 (our price)

Corporate Espionage, Geopolitics, and Diplomacy Issues in International Business
Bryan Christiansen (PryMarke, LLC, USA) and Fatmanur Kasarcı (PryMarke Business Academy, Turkey)
Business Science Reference • copyright 2017 • 374pp • H/C (ISBN: 9781522510314) • US $210.00 (our price)

Table of Contents

Detailed Table of Contents

The purpose of the chapter is to present recent theoretical developments in FDI theories with an emphasis on sourcing strategies of firms. It is stated that economic theory explains the existence of the so called vertical FDI as the result of market failures or transaction costs and incomplete contracts. Firms engage in foreign sourcing due to lower costs or an access to unique resources but that sourcing takes place within firms' boundaries in order to benefit from internalization advantages. Although recent theories have been developed in the context of FDI from developed countries, those new insights can be easily applied to the case of outward FDI from emerging economies as well.

Corporate Social Responsibility has developed rapidly in the last decades, and its role has increased due to the new challenges of the global economy, as companies need a positive reputation in order to obtain a "social license to operate". The aims of this study are: (1) to describe the concepts of corporate social responsibility and Outward Foreign Direct Investment (OFDI), focusing on the relationship between them, (2) to introduce the main CSR risks and opportunities of OFDI, and (3) to summarize the possible solutions for addressing CSR-related risks in OFDI activities. Our study indicates that zero tolerance of corruption is a strategic objective of investing companies. Prevention and mitigation of human rights violations are ethical obligations and in the business interest of corporations. Companies face significant social, environmental, and economic risks, as well as risks to their reputations, because of their supply chains.

Foreign direct investments (FDI) seem to have been thoroughly studied in specialised literature. However the scope of available statistical data often significantly hampers or even prevents any in-depth analysis of the phenomenon. The dynamic economic processes lead to the formation of new linkages, new organisational solutions in international enterprises that co-exist with well described and recognised forms of FDI but escape proper monitoring of statistical institutions. The chapter discusses the different concepts of measuring and interpreting FDI to provide researchers helpful guidelines how to deal with the problems of different methodological dilemmas. A main conclusion is that data provided by official statistics are insufficient and incoherent, and analysis of the scale of OFDI engagement of enterprises (especially from emerging countries) carries some risk and its results should be approached with caution. The case study of Poland's statistics has been used to portray the most significant discrepancies and problems.

The outward foreign direct investments of developing economies have showed significant increase in recent years. Rising outward foreign direct investment stock of developing economies makes its determinants and consequences crucial. The aim of this study is to determine the home country specific determinants of outward FDI. For this purpose, a panel data analysis is performed with the data of BRICS and Next Eleven countries for the period from 1994 to 2014. The analysis results reveal that inward foreign direct investment, interest rates and technological capability of home country have positive influence and total labor force of home country has negative effect on outward FDI of developing economies.

Emerging market economies have clear deficit in governance infrastructure and also have an increasing trend in the amount of foreign direct investment (FDI) outflows compared with advanced countries. Hence the main issue of the study is to identify the determinants leading to the increase in FDI outflows with special emphasize given to the role of governance infrastructure. Thus, the aim of the study is to analyze the effect of governance infrastructure together with other control variables on FDI outflows in emerging market economies. It is found that improvement in all measured aspects of governance infrastructure leads to increase in FDI outflows from emerging market economies and governance infrastructure, human capital and physical infrastructure are base factors for MNCs taking outward FDI decision from emerging market economies. It is also found that FDI outflows from emerging market economies are not market or efficiency seeking; instead they are resource, labor or finance seeking.

Intense internationalisation of an economy is usually perceived as a positive process, which – in general – gives an opportunity to accelerate growth and strengthen competitiveness. Therefore the authorities of an economy try to support FDI flows by implementing different incentives. The main goal of the chapter is to show the scale and scope of outward foreign direct investments (OFDI) of Polish companies in the light of economic transformation experience and authorities support. The chapter is organized as follows: first it presents Poland's path from centrally planned state to developed, competitive economy. Secondly, the focus is laid on support offered to companies undertaking OFDI ventures and finally on the scale and scope of Poland's outward investments.

The chapter explores FDI trends and patterns in Russia. FDI global framework includes multiple stakeholders with diverse interests, expectations, and political attitudes toward foreign investment. Conceptual RDI framework in the chapter is supported by examining Russia's FDI profile, patterns, and dynamics across major economic sectors and regions. Russia's performance in the Global Competitiveness Report 2015-2016 is used to analyze the nation's FDI attractiveness compared to other countries. Further discussion focuses on Russia's macro-economic structure in the FDI context that includes sectorial and regional aspects. Specifically, the chapter concentrates on examining FDI in the Greater Moscow and Greater St. Petersburg, Russia's leading economic regions. These regions receive significant FDI inflows and make substantial contribution to the nation's economic output and trade. The chapter culminates in exploring FDI dynamics in Russia under the current economic crisis and strategies for survival and revival on the regional, sectorial, and company level.

With the collapse of communism, some former communist States of Eastern Europe managed to muddle through their way to a market economy and entered the European Union. This brought about the acceleration of Foreign Direct Investment (FDI) among the European economies and accelerated the globalization process. Although there is plenty of research on FDI and trade among countries, the aim of this chapter is to analyze how trade between Portugal and the Czech Republic have evolved over form 2000 until 2015. The chapter seeks to complement previous studies on FDI and trade as Portugal and the Czech Republic are part of the European Union, but have had different historical, cultural, and economic paths. The main conclusion of the chapter is that trade between both countries has grown significantly. The main reason affecting trade between both countries is the economic unrest Portugal has been through since 2008.

Section 3
OFDI in Emerging Economies: Case Studies from Asia

Chinese SMEs' investment into the North East of England: 1) resource-based factors; 2) home and host institutional factors; 3) network factors; and 4) international entrepreneurial factors. The findings have policy implications for both the governments of the UK and China, as well as managerial implications for future Chinese investors. This chapter provides fresh explanation of Chinese SMEs' investment into a developed economy.

Preface

There is a vast array of studies, which thoroughly discuss the effects of FDI on highly developed economies at the macro-economic level. Due to the abundance of potential motives, determinants and various ways of interpreting the FDI, conclusions drawn by individual researchers depend on the context and analytical method applied. Unsurprisingly, evaluation of these effects is ambiguous or sometimes even contradictory, which explains why further attempts are made to provide clear explanation of dependences in this area.

Theoretical interpretations of the course of active internationalization in the emerging economies, including Central and Eastern Europe and Asia, are suffering from the cognitive gap. The specificity of emerging economies makes some researchers believe that MNEs in these countries "diverge from the standard behavior" the MNEs exhibit in developed economies; as a result, they advocate developing a separate line in international business theory. However, there are others, who maintain that the existing research framework perfectly suffices for analytical purposes as the MNEs in the emerging economies are still in their infancy and differ from the "model" in developed countries only with a shorter history and less mature market approach.

If we wish to fill in the cognitive gap, we need to, inter alia, identify how the economic performance of mother companies in emerging economies evolves as a result of FDI. In most cases, the success or failure of a foreign investment critically impacts the fate of a particular investor but it may also influence the economic performance of his domestic business partners, competitors and even the situation of the local community where jobs are either created or lost. That is why we want to know, which factors are decisive, perhaps not so much for the economic performance of the affiliate, but for the effects on the competitiveness of the multinational enterprise and changes in its domestic economic environment. This knowledge is crucial for managers and politicians responsible for international economics especially in the light of a rather common global practice of offering government support to domestic FDI.

The main goal of the book is to identify, evaluate and describe the effects of international expansion in the form of foreign direct investment for the enterprises involved, and for the economy of the home country. Detailed research topics covered in this book are divided into 4 main groups.

The first group of topics aims at assessing if and how the enterprises involved in foreign direct investment influence the economy of their home country.

The second group concerns the scale, structure, motivation, incentives, barriers and strategies involved in foreign direct investment of investors.

The third group of issues is designed to assess the relevance of internal factors within an enterprise for its overseas investment activities.

Finally, the fourth group is connected with social problems arising from the outward foreign direct investment (OFDI). In particular, we are interested in its effects on the MNEs' approach to corporate social responsibility (CSR) actions undertaken by the affiliates and headquarters, consequences for the local communities in the home country, and possibilities of holding a dialogue among the stakeholders.

Until now, the effects of OFDI for the home countries have been relatively thoroughly discussed and researched at the macro-economic level in highly developed countries; developing and emerging economies have attracted much less attention in this regard. Moreover, so far much less effort has been focused on studying the effects of investing abroad observed at the micro level. We believe this book will, at least partly, fill in this gap by contributing to debates over active internationalization of enterprises. Explaining the scale of the phenomenon, how the consequences of investment expansion emerge and how they impact the parent enterprises and the rest of the economy is also vital for economic policy recommendations in investors' home countries. Hopefully, it will also enable the assessment of economic rationale of such expansion and the sense of state support to it (incentives to attract OFDI).

Our book consists of 3 sections and 16 chapters.

The first section is the most general one. It is dedicated to theoretical, methodological and social aspects. In the first chapter: *Sourcing strategies of firms. Recent theoretical developments*, Tomasz Serwach from the University of Lodz (Poland) attempts to present recent theoretical developments in FDI theories highlighting the sourcing strategies of firms. The main aim of the chapter is to present the reasons why firms engage in vertical FDI (and it is equivalent to the reasons why firms source inputs using their own organizations). It starts with an overview of the neoclassical theory and its ability to explain this tendency. The second part focuses on market failures referred to by economists to justify vertical FDI within neoclassical theory framework. The third part presents the most popular alternative theories of FDI while the fourth one comments on the development of FDI theory.

Outward Foreign Direct Investment as a Corporate Social Responsibility Challenge is a chapter by Krisztina Szegedi, Gyula Fülöp & Adam Bereczk from the University of Miskolc (Hungary). The authors wanted to accomplish three main goals: (1) to describe the concepts of corporate social responsibility and OFDI, focusing on the relationship between them, (2) to introduce the main CSR risks and opportunities involved in OFDI, and (3) to summarize possible solutions for addressing CSR-related risks in OFDI activities. They concluded that zero tolerance of corruption is a strategic objective of investing companies. Prevention and mitigation of human rights violations are ethical obligations, which serve the best interest of international corporations. Companies face significant social, environmental, and economic risks, as well as risks to their reputations, because of their supply chains.

The chapter *Dilemmas on OFDI Measuring and Interpreting: The case of Poland* by Agnieszka Kłysik-Uryszek & Anetta Kuna-Marszałek from the University of Lodz (Poland) discusses the different concepts of measuring and interpreting FDI to provide researchers with helpful guidelines on how to deal with different methodological dilemmas. The main conclusion of the chapter is that data provided by official statistics are insufficient and incoherent, which is why the analysis of the scale of OFDI engagement of enterprises (especially from the emerging economies) carries some risk and its results should be approached with caution. The case study of Poland's statistics has been used to portray the most significant discrepancies and problems.

Rıfat Karakuş from the Çankırı Karatekin University (Turkey) presents the chapter *Home Country-Specific Determinants of Outward Foreign Direct Investment in Developing Economies.* The aim of this study is to identify the home country specific determinants of OFDI. For this purpose, a panel data analysis has been performed on data from BRICS and other 11 countries for the period from 1994 to 2014. Results of the analysis reveal that inward foreign direct investment, interest rates and technological capabilities of the home country have positive influence on OFDI originating from developing economies while total labor force of the home country has negative effect on the phenomenon.

Next chapter in the first section of the book, *The Role of Governance on Outward Foreign Direct Investment in Emerging Market Economies,* has been written by Adem Gök from the Kırklareli University (Turkey). Its aim is to explore the effect of governance infrastructure together with other control-related variables on FDI outflows in emerging market economies. Its findings show that improvement across all measured aspects of governance infrastructure leads to the increase in FDI outflows from emerging market economies and governance infrastructure, human capital and physical infrastructure are basic factors considered by MNCs from emerging market economies in making decisions on outward FDI. It has also been found out that FDI outflows from emerging market economies are not market or efficiency seeking but rather resource, labor or finance seeking.

The last chapter in this section is *Political Economy of Foreign Direct Investment: The Complexity of Linking Theory with Practice* by Esra LaGro from the CIRP (Turkey). The main objective of this chapter is to link the theory and practice of FDI through the lens of global political economy while simultaneously presenting examples from Europe and Turkey, which also reflect its inherent complexity.

The second section of the book consists of 4 case-studies from the European countries. Marta Anna Götz from the Vistula University (Poland) & Barbara Jankowska from the Poznan University of Economics and Business (Poland) in their chapter *On Some Aspects of State-owned Enterprises' Foreign Direct Investments (SOEs' FDI): The case of Polish SOEs' FDI* discuss the rationale for examining foreign direct investment made by SOEs and outline the challenges which need to be addressed in this respect. The authors applied the qualitative methodology of critical literature review and descriptive analysis of internationalization of Polish state-controlled firms. This chapter may provide a valid contribution into the current studies devoted mainly to Chinese or other Asian emerging state-controlled multinationals by adding the Central and Eastern European, or - more precisely -Polish, perspective.

Tomasz Dorożyński, Agnieszka Kłysik-Uryszek & Anetta Kuna-Marszałek from the University of Lodz (Poland) in the chapter *Outward Foreign Direct Investment In Post-Transition Economy: Poland's Experience* have tried to examine the scale and scope of outward foreign direct investments of Polish companies in the light of economic transformation experience and support offered by the state authorities. The chapter is organized as follows: first it presents Poland's path from a centrally planned to a developed, competitive market economy. Secondly, the focus of this work is on support available to companies who undertake OFDI ventures and finally on the scale and scope of Poland's outward investments.

In the next chapter *The Role of Inward FDI for Economic Growth at the Time of Downturn: The Case of Russia* Anatoly Zhuplev from the Loyola Marymount University (USA) & Mikhail Kuznetsov from the National Association of Corporate Directors (Russian Federation) explore FDI trends and patterns in Russia. The main goal of the chapter is to investigate the role of FDI in economic growth and transformation of the Russian economy in the context of the current socio - economic and political turbulence, as well as to outline scenarios for change in the national economy. Discussion in the chapter develops around an array of empirical supporting evidence and factual illustrations from the national, sectoral, and regional level interpreted in international comparative context.

Last chapter in the second section of the book entitled *Trade and FDI between the Czech Republic and Portugal: Analysis of the 2000-2015 period* has been drafted by a team of researchers from the University of Aveiro (Portugal). Lenka Novotná, Inês Martins & António Carrizo Moreira analyze how trade between Portugal and the Czech Republic has evolved over the period 2000 - 2015. The chapter seeks to complement previous studies on FDI and trade as Portugal and the Czech Republic are part of the European Union, but have had different historical, cultural, and economic paths.

The third section of the book is devoted to 6 case-studies of OFDI in Asia. The chapter *The determinants of foreign direct investment outflows from Turkey* by Raif Cergibozan & Caner Demir from the Kırklareli University (Turkey) shows that the destination country's market size, similarly to the home country's development level, trade openness and wage index are positively related to OFDI from Turkey while the home country's interest rate shows a negative relationship. Turkey's OFDI is significantly determined by the opportunities offered by the foreign markets, as well as the outstanding home country factors. In order to observe the possible relation between OFDI flows and define potential factors that might have an effect on them the authors used the ARDL Bounds Test.

Ahmet Oğuz Demir & Muhammad Moiz from the Istanbul Commerce University (Turkey) present the chapter *Outward Foreign Direct Investment in Emerging Economies: A Case of Turkey*. In their study they use the Global Competitiveness Index to find host and home country factors which have driven OFDI from Turkey to their top 10 investment destinations for the past 10 years. The following host country factors have been found to significantly correlate with Turkey's OFDI: innovation, technological readiness, labor market efficiency, infrastructure, domestic market size, and exports but they differ when it comes to the country of destination. Infrastructure and domestic competition are the two home country factors, which turned out to be significantly correlated with Turkey's OFDI.

Foreign Direct Investment in Indian Market is a chapter by Manoj Kumar from the Mother Parwati Education Services (India). The author investigates the effect of the institutional framework upon the nature of technology spillovers over the years 2004 - 2013. Study results suggest a mixed success of industrial promotion policies. Tariffs on final goods, as well as input tariffs are negatively associated with productivity at the company level. However, the evidence shows that stronger productivity spillovers associated with firms that received tax breaks are statistically significant, suggesting that tax holidays were more successful than tariffs as an instrument to promote productivity growth in India.

Next chapter *Incentives to attract foreign direct investment in emerging economies: a causality analysis for the Indian case* by Ishita Ghosh & Ishita Ghoshal from the Symbiosis International University (India) focuses on macroeconomic factors that may explain FDI flows into India. The analysis of the seventeen countries top investors in India in the years 2008-14 reveals that the overall FDI outflows, inflation, exchange rate and growth of the economy affect FDI flows into India in the long run while only the exchange rate has a causal effect on the same.

Mohammad Ashraful Ferdous Chowdhury from the Shahjalal University of Science & Technology (Bangladesh) is the author of the chapter *The Nexus between Institutional Quality and Foreign Direct Investments (FDI) in South Asia: Dynamic Heterogeneous Panel Approach*. The objective of his study has been to identify the impact of institutional quality on FDI (both inward and outward) of the 3 countries in South Asia (Bangladesh, India, and Pakistan).

The final chapter in the book has been written by Rose Quan & Zhibin Lin from the Northumbria University (UK). Its purpose is to identify the key factors that explain decisions made by the Chinese small and medium-sized enterprises (SMEs) to invest in the North East of England. The authors conducted 23 semi-structured interviews with the key decision makers in the Chinese SMEs sector who pursue business operations in the North East of England.

We wish you a pleasant reading.

Tomasz Dorożyński
University of Lodz, Poland

Anetta Kuna-Marszałek
University of Lodz, Poland

REFERENCES

Damijan, J., Kostevc, Č., & Rojec, M. (2014). Outward FDI and company performance in CEECs. *GRINCOH Working Paper Series Papers 2.08*, 1-24.

Desai, M., Foley, F., & Hines, J., Jr. (2005). Foreign Direct Investment and the Domestic Capital Stock. *NBER Working Paper 11075*, from www.nber.org/papers/w11075

Globerman, S. (2012). Canadian Outward Foreign Direct Investment and Its Implications for the Canadian Economy. The Conference Board of Canada. Report. May.

Globerman, S., & Shapiro, D. M. (2008). Outward FDI and the economic performance of emerging markets. In K. P. Sauvant (Ed.), *The Rise of Transnational Corporations from Emerging Markets. Threat or Opportunity?* (pp. 229–271). Cheltenham: Edward Elgar. doi:10.4337/9781848441460.00023

Gorynia, M., & Trąpczyński, P. (2014). Determinanty efektywności zagranicznych inwestycji bezpośrednich. *Ekonomista*, *5*, 663–684.

Sunesen, E., Jespersen, S., & Thelle, M. (2010). Impacts of EU Outward FDI. *Copenhagen Economics Final Report*. 20 May.

Trąpczyński, P. (2014). *Determinants of foreign direct investment performance in the internationalization of Polish companies*. unpublished doctoral thesis. Poznań: Uniwersytet Ekonomiczny w Poznaniu.

Wiliński, W. (2013). *Polityka gospodarcza państw wysoko rozwiniętych i rozwijających się w zakresie wspierania krajowych spółek inwestujących poza granicami kraju*. Warszawa: Oficyna Wydawnicza SGH.

Section 1

OFDI in Emerging Economies:
Theoretical, Methodological, and Social Aspects

Chapter 1
Sourcing Strategies of Firms: Recent Theoretical Developments

Tomasz Serwach
University of Lodz, Poland

ABSTRACT

The purpose of the chapter is to present recent theoretical developments in FDI theories with an emphasis on sourcing strategies of firms. It is stated that economic theory explains the existence of the so called vertical FDI as the result of market failures or transaction costs and incomplete contracts. Firms engage in foreign sourcing due to lower costs or an access to unique resources but that sourcing takes place within firms' boundaries in order to benefit from internalization advantages. Although recent theories have been developed in the context of FDI from developed countries, those new insights can be easily applied to the case of outward FDI from emerging economies as well.

INTRODUCTION

Foreign Direct Investment (FDI) has become one of the most popular forms of the internationalization of firms and an integral part of the global economy. In 2010 about a quarter of the world output was generated by transnational corporations and 10% of that output was produced by FDI entities in host countries (UNCTAD, 2011, p. 25). It is also estimated that one third of the world trade is intrafirm and in 1994 more than 40% (36%) of the US imports (exports) was made within the same organization (Antras, 2003, p.1375). Regarding emerging markets, in 2003 more than 55% of Chinese exports was shipped by FDI entities (Goldstein, Lardy, 2005, p. 11-12). Cravino and Levchenko (in press, appendix: Table A1), using ORBIS database for 2004-2012 period, document that, for example, the ratio of foreign multinationals' revenue to total sales was between 20% and 30% in countries like Mexico, Ukraine or Serbia. Those figures suggest that the impact of FDI on economic activity around the world has become profound.

It is worth stressing that FDI as a mode of internationalization may both decrease or increase the volume of international trade. In case of the so called horizontal FDI that type of investment is a substitute for exports. The motive behind such an investment is market seeking and that goal may be achieved by exporting or presence on the foreign market (FDI). If that kind of FDI was prevalent, then we would

DOI: 10.4018/978-1-5225-2345-1.ch001

observe FDI and trade flows going in the opposite directions. However, the world economy has been characterized by increasing both FDI activities and international trade. It means that the other (vertical) type of FDI must be dominant in the global economy. Vertical FDI can be seen as fragmentation of the production process and locating some stages abroad. It is connected with the movements of inputs and intermediate goods across borders, hence that type of FDI leads to an increase in the volume of international trade.

The main aim of the article is to present the reasons why firms engage in vertical FDI (and it is equivalent to the reasons why firms source inputs using their own organizations). The first section overviews the abilities of neoclassical theory to explain such a phenomenon. The second part focuses on market failures which enable economists to justify vertical FDI within neoclassical theory framework. The third section presents the most popular alternative theories of FDI. The fourth part includes the authors commentary on the development of FDI theory.

BACKGROUND

The dynamic growth of FDI activities has been observed especially since mid-1980's with the noticeable acceleration since mid-1990's. It seems that the empirics goes in tandem with the theory. The first models of vertical FDI were formalized in the mid-1980's (Helpman 1984 and 1985, Ethier 1986). Additionally, the so called eclectic theory of international production (OLI paradigm) was introduced. That theory suggests that a firm investing abroad must exploit three kinds of advantages:

- **Ownership Advantages:** Associated with the competitive edge of a company (due to, for example, market power or size),
- **Location Advantages:** Related to beneficial characteristics of the host country/region (like a significant pool of cheap labor or an easy access to natural resources, technology etc.),
- **Internalization Advantages:** Stemming from keeping certain operations within firm's organization.

According to Gattai (2006, p. 227), the literature from the 1980's and 1990's was mainly focused on the first two types of advantages and the issue of internalization was underestimated, although Rugman (1980, s. 370) stated then that *existing FDI theories are really subcases of the theory of internalization*. However, since then that aspect of FDI has become an important research topic. One of the reasons has been the availability of huge firm-level datasets. It became clear that firms are heavily engaged in outward FDI. For example, Antras (2014, p. 32) presented the share of intrafirm imports in total imports for various industries in the United States (see Figure 1). In many of them that share was higher than 80% (in vehicle-related industries). Even in the so called light industries intrafirm imports was observed. It seems that many firm are willing to organize sourcing from abroad, but within their own organization. That observation makes internalization as one of the most vital aspects of FDI researchers should investigate.

It seems that economists have tried to enrich the FDI theory by modelling the decisions of firms to engage in international investment. Firms sourcing inputs in other countries may do so by contracting independent suppliers (international outsourcing) or by vertical FDI (offshoring). When such a decision is not trivial (FDI or not) but it is possible to organize sourcing in different ways, it is especially important to specify why some companies try to keep supplies within their own boundaries. Having

Figure 1. Share of US intrafirm imports for top 25 importing industries (NAICS6) in 2010
Antras, 2014, p. 32.

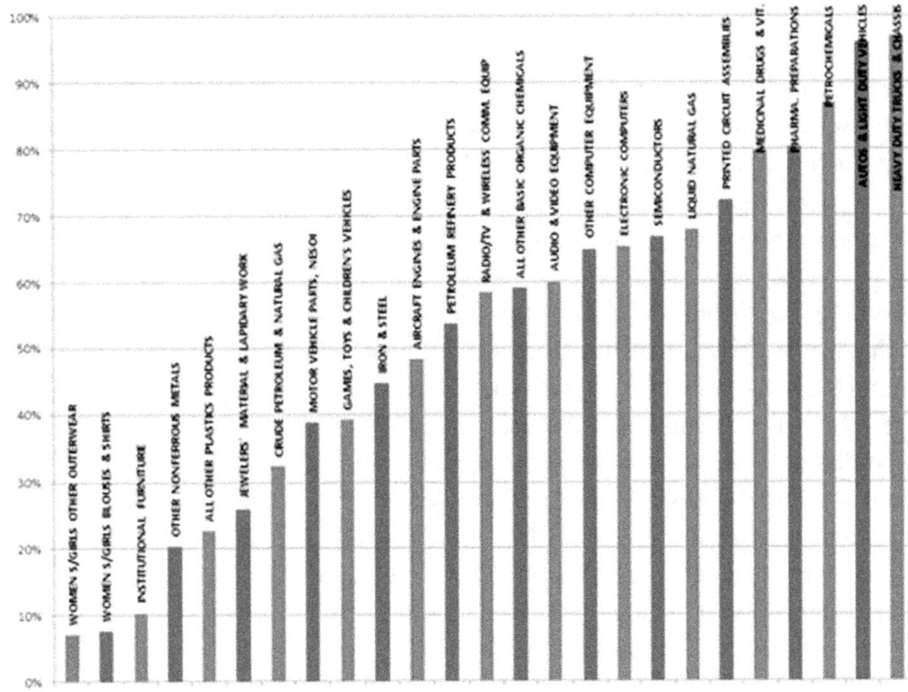

that in mind, Ethier (1986, p. 805) wrote that *internalization appears to be emerging as the Caesar of the OLI triumvirate*.

Moreover, it should become evident that FDI theory is inextricably linked to the branch of economics called industrial organization. Since Coase (1937) economists have been raising the question about the boundaries of the firm. Many answers have been given and it seems that neoclassical theory – at least within perfect competition framework – cannot successfully explain the phenomenon of vertical integration and – as a consequence – vertical FDI.

FDI AND THE NEOCLASSICAL THEORY OF THE FIRM

The main problem of the neoclassical theory of the firm is its inability to explain why the firm exists. Such an odd statement was first presented by Coase in his seminal 1937 paper. That inability stems from the fact that the neoclassical theory is based on two contradictory premises:

- The existence of the firm – as the object of the analysis,
- The efficiency of the market.

If the market if efficient, then it is the cheapest way of sourcing. All necessary inputs and intermediate goods should be supplied by independent entities. What is more, even a firm would be unnecessary and we should observe only the loose forms of cooperation between independent people. In other words, there should be only market transaction instead of the formal organization in the form of the firm. Quoting Coase (1937, s. 388),

... outside the firm, price movements direct production, which is co-ordinated through a series of exchange transactions on the market. Within a firm, these market transactions are eliminated and in place of the complicated market structure with exchange transactions is substituted the entrepreneur-co-ordinator, who directs production. It is clear that these are alternative methods of co-ordinating production. Yet, having regard to the fact that if production is regulated by price movements, production could be carried out without any organization at all, well might we ask, why is there any organization?

The next weakness of the neoclassical theory is its inability to define the boundaries of the firm. In other words, that theory does not answer the question: which stages of the production process will be conducted within the firm, and which ones will be outsourced? Assuming the existence of the firm, one should be surprised that such a unit in many cases is supplied by related entities and not by independent suppliers. According to the neoclassical theory, market – when it is not monopolized – is efficient and other firms should offer all necessary intermediate goods at the cheapest price. In the context of international production it means that when markets are efficient the production should take form of the cooperation of different and autonomous firms. Vertical FDI should not be observed or at least such a mode of internationalization should not be very common.

It is evident that in such circumstances there are two ways of explaining vertical FDI:

- Introducing market inefficiency by incorporating market failures,
- Using alternative theoretical frameworks.

Both ways are presented in the next sections.

FDI AND MARKET FAILURES

There are many examples of market failures which can be used to model vertical FDI. In this section, due to limited length of the paper, I present only several of them – those most commonly seen in the literature.

One of the most obvious market failure is linked to monopolization. When supplying sector is heavily concentrated, then a firm may engage in vertical integration. As Stuckey and White (1993) put it,

... companies sometimes integrate because a company in an adjacent stage of the industry chain has more market power. If one stage of an industry chain exerts market power over another and thereby achieves abnormally high returns, it may be attractive for participants in the dominated industry to enter the dominating industry.

Such a situation may be described as follows. Assume that there are two monopolists – downstream and upstream. The former produces final goods and the latter – intermediate goods. A downstream monopolist charges price in a typical profit-maximizing way – it is its marginal cost with a markup. At the same time, that marginal cost is equal to the price charged by an upstream monopolist which is also marginal cost of that firm with its markup. Hence, the price of final good is equal to upstream monopolist's marginal cost with double markup (it is an example of the so called double marginalization problem). When both firms integrate, their profit will be higher than the sum of profits in case of separate functioning (see Church and Ware, 2000, p. 685-686). Therefore there are reasons why downstream monopolist may start its own operations in supplying sector or even take over its current supplier (an upstream monopolist). In both situations it may take the form of vertical FDI. In the former case it would be greenfield FDI (especially when cost of production abroad are lower than at home) and in the latter – brownfield FDI (if upstream monopolist is located abroad).

Generally, when a supplying sector charges high prices, it may encourage companies to seek sourcing abroad. It may stem from market concentration or high costs of the production of intermediate goods and inputs (including knowledge). That is why firms from emerging markets may be willing to invest in other developing countries (with even lower unit labor costs) or developed countries (with lower costs of technology and knowledge creation). An observation confirming such a statement can be seen in Penn World Tables (9.0 version) data. It seems that in many emerging economies costs of sourcing are high: for example, in 2002 the composite price of investment goods was equal to 35% of the US level in Russia, 30% in China and 24% in India. At the same time the price level of consumption goods was comparable to only 26%, 24% and 20% of the US level in those countries respectively. Structural factors in mentioned economies may inflate prices of sourcing, giving rise to outward FDI.

Another examples of market failure are linked to imperfect information. It may lead to problems with monitoring the quality of goods and technology diffusion. When information is imperfect, a firm may be unable to satisfactory monitor the quality of its supplies and it may take costly steps to attract customers (who are also subject to imperfect information). In such a case supplier may lower the quality of intermediate goods. To avoid that a purchaser may pay higher price for supplies – when the quality of intermediate goods is unsatisfactory, then the cooperation is ceased and the supplier is punished by losing abnormal profits (hence, high prices act like the disciplinary device). However, a buyer must also save resources to promote its product, hence if the price paid to supplier is too high, purchaser may start producing intermediate good by its own. When such a production takes place abroad, vertical FDI is made.

Similar situation happens when it is impossible for a firm to observe whether other entities appropriate its – sophisticated and extraordinary – technology. In order to discourage supplier to do so, a firm pays high prices. However, when those prices are too high, again it may motivate purchaser to start its own operation is cooperating sectors. It may take the form of FDI, when those operations take place abroad.

Antras, Desai and Foley (2009) combine information-related issues of technology appropriateness with imperfectness of financial market. In their model a firm develops technology which may be used in another country. Financial sector organizes funding of the cooperation between mentioned firm and its foreign partner. However, it is impossible to perfectly monitor whether foreign entity will act to achieve common goal (the model touches on the principal-agent problem). The pressure from financial market motivates a firm to make an FDI to gain control over foreign operations.

All those theoretical findings suggest that outward FDI from emerging markets will be observed when it is hard to monitor the quality of sourcing, technology and know-how cannot be successfully appropriated and there are frictions in the financial system. Those factors can be measured by the World Bank's Rule of Law Index. It is a matter of fact that emerging markets place low in the rank of countries with regard to that indicator. It means that firms from those countries may invest abroad, because they have difficulties with finding a reliable supplier who could provide them with intermediate goods of satisfactory quality or would not pose as a threat of technology expropriation.

Another World Bank's study – Doing Business – may shed light on the costs of monitoring activities of potential partners. According to the 2016 issue of the study, emerging and developing countries are characterized by low value of the Depth of credit information index (0-8 scale with the higher value, the deeper information). The average for the East Asian & Pacific region was 4.2, Latin America & Caribbean – 4.8 and South Asia – 3.9, whereas for the OECD high income countries – 6.5. Presented figures indicate that emerging countries experience some financial frictions and (when one uses those values as a proxy for general monitoring costs, because they reflect transparency in business) are affected by information imperfectness.

FDI AND ALTERNATIVE THEORIES OF THE FIRM

It seems that currently the most popular explanation of vertical FDI is based on contract incompleteness. The most vigorous proponent of that theory is Pol Antras (see Antras, 2003 and 2005, Antras and Helpman, 2004 and 2008). The key role in that analysis is played by a hold-up problem. It means that two parties are held up within a particular transaction. That problem can be seen when one investigates two crucial assumption of that theory:

- Asset specificity,
- Contractual frictions.

The first one can be seen as follows. Intermediate goods must be adapted to the specificity of final goods, hence they also must be specific to a particular transaction. Buyers define characteristics of intermediate goods and sellers decide whether to conform to that specification. If so, intermediate goods become adapted and they are valuable for a particular buyer but not by other possible purchasers who have their own requirements. It means that in case of unsatisfactory cooperation it will be difficult for a producer of intermediate goods to sell them to another firm. In other words, those goods (called assets) become specific – sometimes it is said that they are illiquid.

Stuckey and White (1993) defines three types of asset specificity:

- **Site Specificity:** It happens when buyers and sellers locate fixed assets in close proximity,
- **Technical Specificity:** It occurs when at least one party to a transaction invests in equipment that can only be used only within that transaction and that has low value in alternative uses.
- **Human Capital Specificity:** It relates to situations when employees develop skills that are specific to a particular relationship.

The next assumption is the presence of contractual frictions. According to Church and Ware (2000, p. 73),

... a complete contract is one that will never need to be revised or changed and is enforceable. It specifies precisely what each party is to do in every possible circumstance and for every circumstance the corresponding distribution of the gains from trade. And regardless of the circumstances a court will be able to enforce the contract – it is capable of requiring compliance and imposing damages such that both parties to the contract will honor the terms of the contract. This type of contract would provide no opportunities for renegotiation or holdup since it would contain no gaps, or missing provisions. However circumstances unfolded, the contract would unambiguously govern the exchange.

Yet, in real world contracts are imperfect. As Lyons (2005, p.2) stated *the reason for this failure might be due to bounded rationality such that some contingencies cannot be imagined, or to the cost of writing complex contracts*. Contracts are incomplete due to the costs associated with writing and enforcing them which include (Church and Ware, 2000, p. 73-74):

- The costs of determining or anticipating all of the possible contingencies,
- The costs of reaching an agreement for each of the relevant contingencies,
- The costs of writing the contract in sufficiently precise terms that the contract can be understood and interpreted as intended by a court,
- The costs of monitoring,
- The costs of enforcement.

Contract incompleteness leads to an increase in costs and results in future renegotiations. For instance, after some unforeseen events occur, parties must renegotiate to define the way how to split the surplus resulting from the transaction. However, if independent supplier invested heavily in adapting intermediate goods to specificity of the transaction, those goods become illiquid and it lowers that supplier's bargaining power (because intermediate goods are less valued outside that transaction). If a supplier is forward-looking, then such an outcome is anticipated by that firm and supplier underinvests in adaptation of its intermediate goods, making them less suitable for the buyer.

A buyers may avoid such a situation by engaging in vertical integration. It results in gaining control over assets and makes dependent units (not independent ones) responsible for the supply of highly specific intermediate goods. Due to better conditions (generally, lower costs of production) such a vertical integration takes a form of FDI. According to Stockey and White (1993) vertical integration should be especially seen in industries with high asset specificity and high transaction frequency – in other cases other organizational forms may arise (see Figure 2).

Figure 2. Transaction-asset matrix
Stockey and White, 1993.

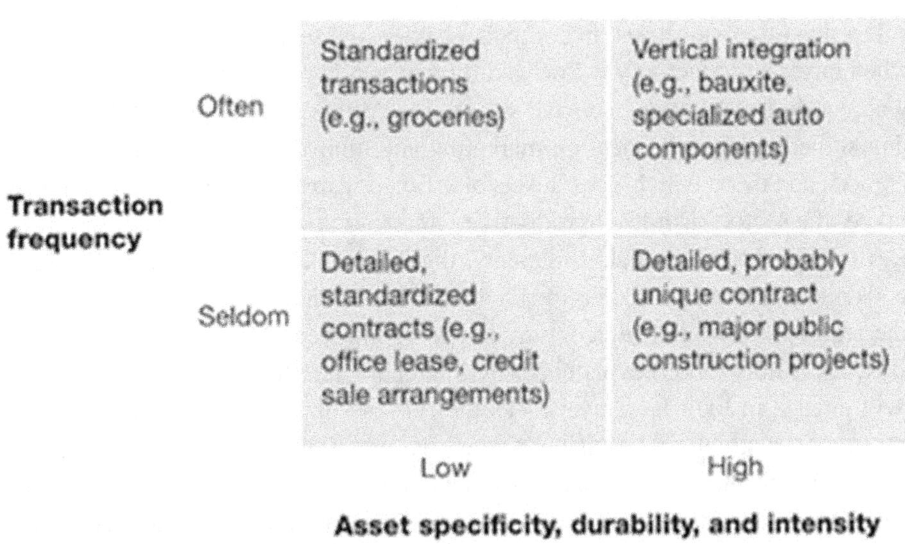

Figure 3. The effect of contractibility on the share of US intrafirm imports
Antras, 2014, p. 43.

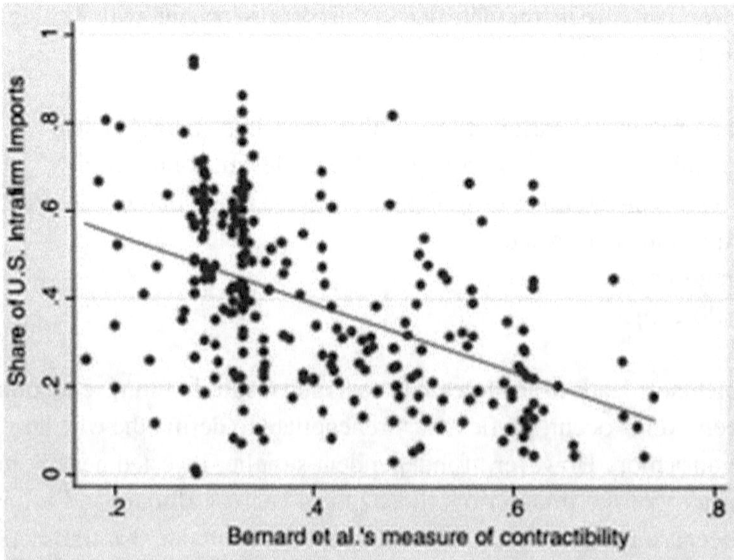

Weak contractual environment may increase the likelihood that a firm will engage in FDI instead of outsourcing. The link between contractibility and intrafirm imports is shown in Figure 3.

Carluccio and Fally (2010) extended Antras' models by including imperfect financial market. They suggest that FDI helps firms overcome the problem of not having an access to external funding. It means that firms engage in FDI in countries with relatively weak financial development. Applying that finding to the case of outward FDI from emerging markets, it is obvious that the level of financial development is especially important when such an investment takes place in even more underdeveloped countries. In other words, conclusions from Carluccio and Fally (2010) apply to the South-South FDI.

Antras and Helpman (2004) introduced in their model heterogeneity of firms in terms of their productivity. They showed different modes of sourcing depending on firm-level efficiency and type of a sector. They described two industries. In component-intensive sectors a buyer depends on outsourcing (domestic, when buyer's productivity is low, and foreign, when productivity is high).

FDI may appear in headquarter-intensive sector. For Antras and Helpman those are industries intensively using skilled labor, dependent on marketing and innovation. Highly productive firms import intermediate goods and those with highest levels of efficiency invest abroad. Figure 4 presents the links between the type of a sector, firm-level productivity and sourcing patterns.

Generally, the higher R&D and skill intensity, the more headquarter-intensive a sector is and the more it depends on intrafirm imports. Figures 5 and 6 support that view.

One of the features of the global economy is the dominance of FDI over outsourcing in capital-intensive industries. Antas (2003) explained why that characteristic of industry increases the chances that a firm will engage in FDI. If a buyer faces the risk of supplier's underinvestment in adaptation, that firm may support a supplier by – using Antras' words – investment sharing (activities mitigating hold-up problem). When the scale of that investment sharing is high, a buyer may cease cooperation with independent supplier and start producing intermediate goods (with substantial differences between

Figure 4. Organizational forms
Based on Antras and Helpman, 2004, p. 565.

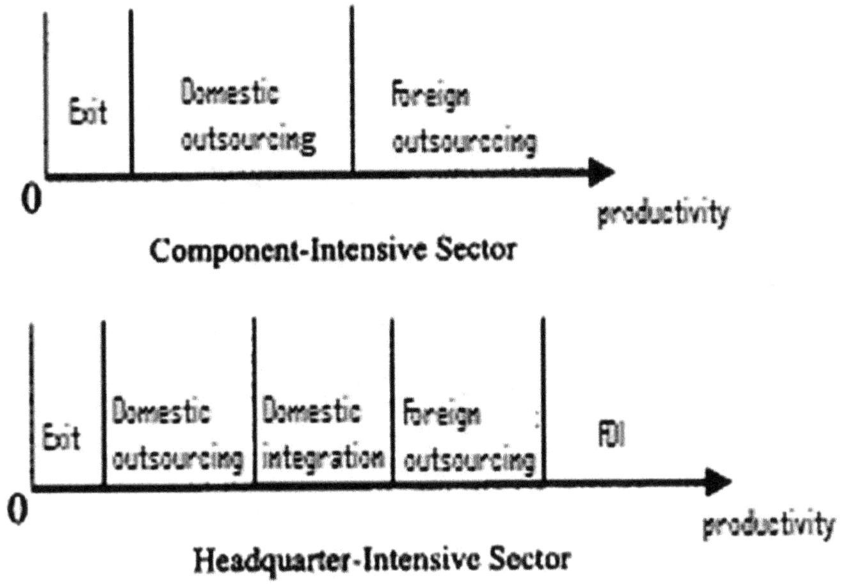

Figure 5. The effect of R&D intensity on the share of US intrafirm imports
Antras, 2014, p. 39.

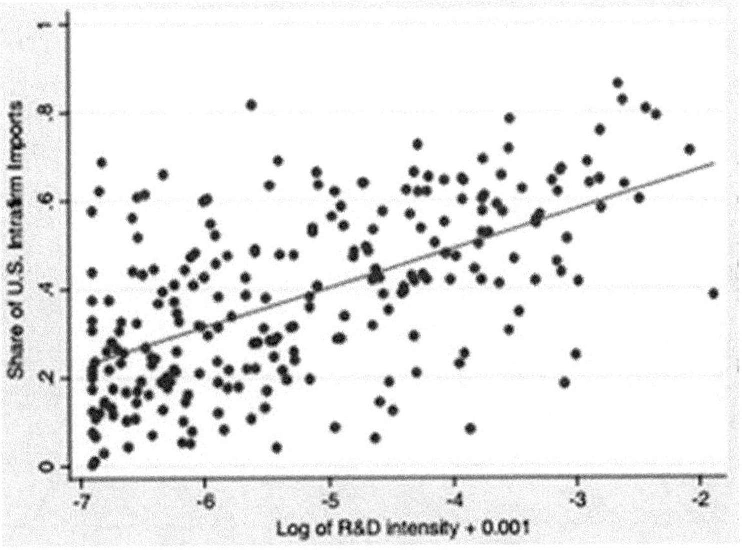

countries in terms of production costs, availability of resources or other important characteristics it may take place abroad – vertical FDI). Since capital is much more mobile internationally than labor, investment sharing is expected to be easier in capital-intensive industries and in those sectors vertical FDI would be more common. In other words, the higher capital intensity, the higher the share of intrafirm trade, as reflected in Figure 7.

Figure 6. The effect of skill intensity on the share of US intrafirm imports
Antras, 2014, p. 39.

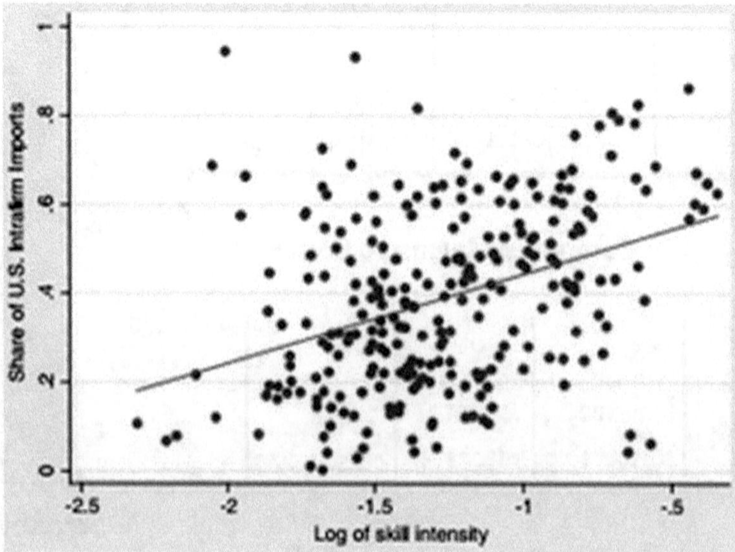

Figure 7. The effect of capital intensity on the share of US intrafirm imports
Antras, 2014, p. 38.

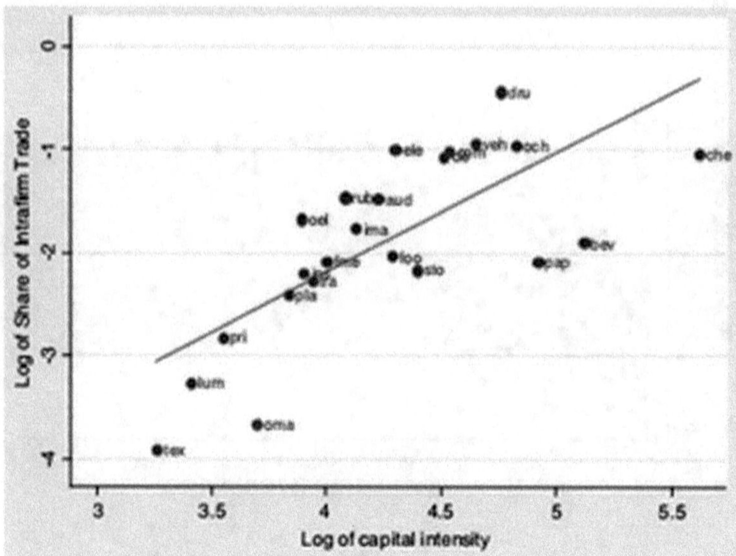

Theory of incomplete contracts is also able to describe the phenomenon of international life cycle of a product. By doing so, it shows how standardization of production affects sourcing decisions of firms. Antras (2005) presents a model which leads to following conclusions:

- **Low Standardization of Production:** Final good depends heavily on R&D, marketing etc., hence hold-up problem is a serious obstacle and a firm decides to source all intermediate goods and inputs domestically,
- **Intermediate Standardization of Production:** A firm tends to lower costs by moving production abroad; however, a hold-up problem still exists and makes a firm willing to keep production under control (hence, a firm decides to make a vertical FDI),
- **High Standardization of Production:** There appears a possibility to lower costs and a hold-up problem is no longer a serious challenge, so a firm contracts independent foreign supplier.

A little bit different analysis was conducted by Costinot, Oldenski and Rauch (2011). They showed that sourcing of firms depends on the routineness of the sector. In their model contractual frictions are the result of the impossibility to specify many nonroutine activities a supplier must undertake. They present several reasons why integration lowers the costs of dealing with nonroutine problems:

- **Opportunism:** When an unforeseen problem occurs, it is easier to exert power over internal supplier than over an external one;
- **Renegotiation:** Integration eliminates (or at least reduces) costs (such as delays) resulting from the necessity to renegotiate when problems occur;
- **Communication:** It is easier to solve problems within the firm due to a common corporate culture.

The main conclusion of the paper is similar to that from Antras (2005). Firms decide to engage in FDI when the level of routineness of a sector is intermediate. The link between that characteristic of an industry and sourcing pattern can be presented as follows:

- **Low Routineness:** Domestic sourcing,
- **Intermediate Routineness:** Vertical FDI,
- **High Routineness:** Foreign outsourcing.

The authors estimated the impact of routineness of various US sectos and the share of intrafirm imports. To assess how routine activities within a particular industry is they used O*NET (*Occupational Information Network*) database which includes information on the importance of decision making and problem solving in occupations associated with an industry. According to the estimates (see Table 1) the share of intrafirm imports rises with the increase in routineness.

Although presented theories were developed mainly with the aim to explain FDI conducted by firms from advanced economies, it is possible to use those models to describe foreign investment conducted by players from emerging markets. Firstly, there are studies proving that even in emerging economies firms with higher productivity are more likely to engage in outward FDI (see, for example, Tian and Yu, 2015, for the analysis of Chinese companies). Secondly, at least Chinese firms mirror the pattern seen advanced economies and invest abroad in non-labor-intensive industries (in skill-intensive sectors in skill-abundant countries, but in capital-intensive sectors in capital-scarce countries; see Chen, Dol-

Table 1. The effect of routineness on the share of US intrafirm imports

Model:	1	2	3	4	5
N:	29,645	29,645	29,645	29,645	27,775
Routine	−0.183***	−0.082**	−0.086**	−0.090***	−0.083**
	(−6.75)	(−2.21)	(−2.47)	(−2.59)	(−2.48)
Ln(K/L)		0.012	0.058*	0.07*	0.064*
		(0.38)	(1.66)	(1.75)	(1.65)
Ln(S/L)		0.016	0.003	0.005	−0.024
		(0.42)	(0.08)	(0.13)	(−0.67)
Ln(R&D)		0.165***	0.127***	0.136***	0.111***
		(4.22)	(2.88)	(3.06)	(2.70)
Specificity			0.082**	0.084**	0.067
			(2.17)	(2.13)	(1.63)
Intermediation				0.032	0.015
				(0.88)	(0.41)
Dispersion					0.073*
					(1.92)
Fixed effects	Ctry-year	Ctry-year	Ctry-year	Ctry-year	Ctry-year
R^2	0.261	0.281	0.285	0.285	0.292

The dependent variable is the share of intrafirm imports. Standardized beta coefficients reported for pooled data from 2000 to 2006. *, **, and *** indicate significance at the 10%, 5%, and 1% levels. Standard errors are clustered by industry. *T*-statistics are in parentheses.

Costinot, Oldenski and Rauch, 2011, p. 306.

lar and Tang, 2015). It indicates that such investment projects do not take place in highly routine and standardized sectors. What is more, that finding is supported by many anecdotal evidences of FDI from emerging markets conducted with the aim of technology seeking. Arnott (2010) described the case of Geely's (China) acquisition of Volvo Car stating that *the group plans to use vast Chinese demand to double Volvo sales, while using the Swedish group's technology, dealership network and global brand to push Geely outside China*. Alon, Hale and Santos (2010) wrote that *Chinese companies engage in vertical integration mainly by buying producers of specialized machinery and equipment.* That pattern is backed by the incomplete contract theory with its focus on asset specificity. They used several examples of such a behavior of Chinese investors, like the purchase of American producer of metal production machinery (Mesta Engineering) by Shoudu Iron and Steel Company and – in the context of an access to foreign technology – the purchase of radio equipment maker from the US, Quorum Systems, by Spreadtrum Communications. Authors concluded that Chinese *vertical deals can be viewed as resource-seeking, with machinery being the target resource, or as strategic acquisitions of technology. The United States, Europe, and Japan are primary destinations for such transactions.*

FUTURE RESEARCH DIRECTIONS

All mentioned theories make economist more able to explain various microeconomic FDI-related phenomena. Specifically they may be a basis for the analyzes of the reasons behind firms' sourcing decisions. By doing so, they enable researchers to find out why some firms do not consider the markets as an efficient source of intermediate goods but prefer supplies from dependent units (for example, in the form of FDI). It seems that firms investing abroad have some unique features:

- They are dependent on intermediate goods which are produced by relatively highly concentrated sectors,
- The quality of their goods depend substantially on the quality of intermediate goods,
- They possess sophisticated technology and know-how and are more productive than other firms within their industry,
- They require highly specific intermediate goods,
- They operate in the sector of intermediate level of standardization and routineness.

Those theories can be put in the broader context of attempting to give some microeconomic (specifically, firm-level) foundations to international flows of goods, services and production factors. Apart from vertical FDI, the same phenomenon has been observed in the theories of horizontal FDI (see Helpman, Melitz and Yeaple, 2004) and international trade (see Melitz, 2003, Bernard, Eaton, Jensen and Kortum, 2003, Melitz and Ottaviano, 2008).

Despite all the advantages, recent theoretical developments have some weaknesses. Generally, they focus on firms from advanced economies willing to locate production in countries with lower costs. At the same time, they do not explicitly show why some firms from developing countries invest abroad. When a company from emerging market invests in even less advanced economy, that decision may be explained by existing theories. However, the problem arises when a firm from developing country makes and FDI in an advanced economy. Cost-cutting is then no longer the motive researchers should focus on when they try to find an explanation. It seems that all new theories are still applicable but with minor modification that in such a case firms try to benefit from better technology, more renowned brands etc.

Moreover, some features of mentioned models remain problematic. One of them is the fact that some characteristics of firms are unexplained (they are seen as exogenous). If high sectoral concentration leads firms to make an FDI, why do not all firms engage in that form of internationalization? The obvious answer is that firm are differently exposed to that concentration – they may have different share of outlays on an intermediate good from monopolized sector in the whole spending on intermediate goods. If so, when why? What hampers the switching from technology using over-priced intermediate goods to more cost-efficient one?

What is more, while international trade theory ceased to treat firm-level productivity as exogenous (see, for instance, Yeaple, 2005), FDI theorists still see that characteristic of firms as a fixed one. However, firm's efficiency may vary in time and the will to increase that efficiency may be one of the main reasons why companies engage in FDI, especially when one considers decisions of firms from developing countries investing in more sophisticated economies.

Another controversy is connected with the issue of concentration of an upstream sector. An example of double marginalization suggests that high concentration of intermediate-goods sector may stimulate FDI made by downstream industry due to too high prices. However, when there are only few firms in supplying sector (oligopoly) and Bertrand competition prevails, they may charge prices similar to those that would be quoted on highly competitive market. Hence, in such a case there would be no double marginalization and the cost of intermediate goods would not be inflated. It means that the more nuanced analysis of the impact of concentration of supplying sector on price competitiveness of a final-good producer (and the decision whether to form an FDI) is needed.

Mentioned theories also suggest that a firm engages in sequential process of internationalization. When its sector is not standardized and routine, then there are no foreign operation. The next stage is FDI which enables a firm to save resourced with keeping control over foreign activities. When a sector becomes standard and routine, a firm switches its mode of internationalization (it engages in foreign outsourcing). However, the production of highly specific, unique and innovative intermediate goods may also be localized abroad (one of the examples is manufacturing of various parts of smartphones). What is more, when the pace of technological progress is fast, the benefits of integration may be too small compared to cooperation with independent supplier as presented by Bartel, Lach and Sicherman (2005) in the context of domestic production. Combining all those insights leads to conclusion that FDI may not be observed in some cases, especially when technology changes rapidly.

Despite all those drawbacks recent theoretical developments have enriched economists' knowledge about the motives behind firms' sourcing decisions. It should be clear, however, that it is extremely difficult to present a theory which would embrace all the factors affecting such decisions and explain different patterns of sourcing. Firms are highly heterogeneous, so they are their decisions.

CONCLUSION

FDI theory has been developing rapidly, mainly by incorporating various insights from the industrial organization theory. Recent developments focus mainly on the issue of internalization. That is why they enable economists to explain why some firms outsource the production of intermediate goods to foreign subcontractors, while others decide to make an FDI. It became obvious that neoclassical theory of the firm – at least within perfect competition framework – is not applicable to FDI, hence some forms of market failures or even other theories must be used to specify the motives behind firm's investment decisions.

It seems that foreign investors differ substantially from other firms and that matters for their sourcing patterns. However, even those investors are highly heterogeneous and it make almost impossible to present unified theory of multinational firm. That is why different theoretical concepts has been constantly emerging.

REFERENCES

Alon, T., Hale, G., & Santos, J. (2010). *What Is China's Capital Seeking in a Global Environment?* Retrieved September 30, 2016, from http://www.frbsf.org/economic-research/files/el2010-09.pdf

Antras, P. (2003). Trade, Contracts, and Trade Structure. *The Quarterly Journal of Economics*, *118*(4), 1375–1418. doi:10.1162/003355303322552829

Antras, P. (2005). Incomplete Contracts and the Product Cycle. *The American Economic Review*, *95*(4), 1054–1073. doi:10.1257/0002828054825600

Antras, P. (2013). Grossman-Hart (1986) Goes Global: Incomplete Contracts, Property Rights, and the International Organization of Production. *Journal of Law Economics and Organization*, *30*(1), 1–58.

Antras, P., Desai, M., & Foley, F. C. (2009). Multinational Firms, FDI Flows and Imperfect Capital Markets. *The Quarterly Journal of Economics*, *125*(3), 1171–1219. doi:10.1162/qjec.2009.124.3.1171

Antras, P., & Helpman, E. (2004). Global Sourcing. *Journal of Political Economy*, *112*(3), 552–580. doi:10.1086/383099

Antras, P., & Helpman, E. (2008). Contractual Frictions and Global Sourcing. In E. Helpman, T. Verdier, & D. Marin (Eds.), *The Organization of Firms in a Global Economy* (pp. 9–54). Harvard University Press. doi:10.4159/9780674038547-001

Arnott, S. (2010). *China's Geely buys Volvo for $1.5bn*. Retrieved September 20, 2016, from http://www.independent.co.uk/news/business/news/chinas-geely-buys-volvo-for-15bn-2041772.html

Bartel, A., Lach, S., & Sicherman, N. (2005). *Outsourcing and Technological Change (National Bureau of Economic Research No. 11158)*. Cambridge, MA: National Bureau of Economic Research. doi:10.3386/w11158

Bernard, A. B., Eaton, J., Jensen, J. B., & Kortum, S. (2003). Plants and Productivity in International Trade. *The American Economic Review*, *93*(4), 1268–1290. doi:10.1257/000282803769206296

Chen, W., Dollar, D., & Tand, H. (2015). *Why is China investing in Africa? Evidence from the firm level.* Retrieved September 25, 2016 from http://www.hwtang.com/uploads/3/0/7/2/3072318/odi_chen_dollar_tang_abstract.pdf

Church, J., & Ware, R. (2000). *Industrial Organization: A Strategic Approach.* New York: Irwin McGraw-Hill.

Coase, R. H. (1937). The Nature of the Firm. *Economica*, *4*(16), 386–405. doi:10.1111/j.1468-0335.1937.tb00002.x

Costinot, A., Oldenski, L., & Rauch, J. (2011). Adaptation and the Boundary of Multinational Firms. *The Review of Economics and Statistics*, *93*(1), 298–308. doi:10.1162/REST_a_00072

Cravino, J., & Levchenko, A. (in press). Multinational firms and international business cycle transmission. *The Quarterly Journal of Economics.*

Ethier, W. J. (1986). Multinational Firm. *The Quarterly Journal of Economics*, *101*(4), 805–833. doi:10.2307/1884179

Goldstein, M., & Lardy, N. R. (2005). *China's Role in the Revived Bretton Woods System: Case of Mistaken Identity (Peterson Institute for International Economics No. 05-2).* Washington, DC: Peterson Institute for International Economics.

Helpman, E. (1984). A Simple Theory of International Trade with Multinational Corporations. *Journal of Political Economy*, *92*(3), 451–471. doi:10.1086/261236

Helpman, E. (1985). Multinational Corporations and Trade Structure. *The Review of Economic Studies*, *52*(3), 443–457. doi:10.2307/2297663

Helpman, E., Melitz, M. J., & Yeaple, S. R. (2004). Export Versus FDI with Heterogeneous Firms. *The American Economic Review*, *94*(1), 300–316. doi:10.1257/000282804322970814

Kohler, W., & Smolka, M. (2009). *Global Sourcing Decisions and Firm Productivity: Evidence from Spain* (CESifo No. 2903). Munich: CESifo.

Lyons, B. R. (2005). *Incomplete Contracts Theory and Contracts between Firms: A Preliminary Empirical Study (City College Norwich No. 01-1)*. Norwich: City College Norwich.

Melitz, M. J. (2003). The Impact of Trade on Intra-industry Reallocations and Aggregate Industry Productivity. *Econometrica*, *71*(6), 1695–1725. doi:10.1111/1468-0262.00467

Melitz, M. J., & Ottaviano, G. (2008). Market Size, Trade, and Productivity. *The Review of Economic Studies*, *75*(1), 295–316. doi:10.1111/j.1467-937X.2007.00463.x

Rugman, A. M. (1980). Internalisation as a general theory of foreign direct investment. *Weltwirtschaftliches Archiv*, *116*(2), 365–279. doi:10.1007/BF02696864

Stuckey, J., & White, D. (1993). *When and when not to vertically integrate*. Retrieved August 20, 2016, from http://www.mckinsey.com/business-functions/strategy-and-corporate-finance/our-insights/when-and-when-not-to-vertically-integrate

Tian, W., & Yu, M. (2015). *Distribution Outward FDI and Productivity Heterogeneity: Evidence from Chinese Firms*. Retrieved September 30, 2016, from http://www.econ.hit-u.ac.jp/~cces/HIAS_HP/paper/Miaojie_Yu.pdf

UNCTAD. (2011). *World Investment Report 2011. Non-Equity Modes of International Production and Development*. New York, NY: UNCTAD.

Yeaple, S. R. (2005). A simple model of firm heterogeneity, international trade, and wages. *Journal of International Economics*, *65*(1), 1–20. doi:10.1016/j.jinteco.2004.01.001

KEY TERMS AND DEFINITIONS

Asset Specificity: A feature of an asset that makes it valuable within a particular transaction or relationship but with lower value or even meaningless for any third party.

Hold-Up Problem: A situation when parties involved in a transaction do not cooperate in the most efficient way because of the risk of giving the other party increased bargaining power.

Incomplete Contracts: A contract that does not specify all possible future contingencies. That feature leads to renegotiations due to problems with contract enforcement.

Internalization: A process of conducting transactions and/or certain operations within the boundaries of a firm.

Market Failure: A case of inefficient market allocation of resources.

Transaction Costs: All costs of participation in a market. In the context of sourcing transaction costs stem from searching a reliable supplier, contract enforcement etc.

Vertical Integration: A firm strategy that means keeping at least some of the other stages of the production process within firm boundaries.

Chapter 2
Outward Foreign Direct Investment as a Corporate Social Responsibility Challenge

Krisztina Szegedi
University of Miskolc, Hungary

Gyula Fülöp
University of Miskolc, Hungary

Ádám Bereczk
University of Miskolc, Hungary

ABSTRACT

Corporate Social Responsibility has developed rapidly in the last decades, and its role has increased due to the new challenges of the global economy, as companies need a positive reputation in order to obtain a "social license to operate". The aims of this study are: (1) to describe the concepts of corporate social responsibility and Outward Foreign Direct Investment (OFDI), focusing on the relationship between them, (2) to introduce the main CSR risks and opportunities of OFDI, and (3) to summarize the possible solutions for addressing CSR-related risks in OFDI activities. Our study indicates that zero tolerance of corruption is a strategic objective of investing companies. Prevention and mitigation of human rights violations are ethical obligations and in the business interest of corporations. Companies face significant social, environmental, and economic risks, as well as risks to their reputations, because of their supply chains.

INTRODUCTION

In the last few decades Corporate Social Responsibility (CSR) has emerged, and one reason for its increased role is new challenges of the global economy, in which a positive reputation is required for a company to obtain a "social license to operate". As a result of Outward Foreign Direct Investment (OFDI), companies face many CSR-related risks and opportunities. In spite of this, the topic of Corporate Social Responsibility does not appear in the majority of books and articles about foreign direct investment. The role of emerging economies concerning Corporate Social Responsibility is special. On the one hand,

DOI: 10.4018/978-1-5225-2345-1.ch002

in emerging economies companies are less aware of the importance of risks related to corporate social responsibility. This issue is either considered to be less significant than in the developed countries or they just lack CSR knowledge. On the other hand, CSR-related risks are much higher in the emerging economies; let us just think of environmental pollution, the violation of human rights or extensive corruption.

These reasons led to corporate social responsibility being treated in a separate chapter in the book about outward foreign investment of emerging countries. Although both corporate social responsibility and outward foreign direct investment have their own literature, there are few works where these two topics are interrelated. This is particularly relevant in case of emerging countries, so this chapter can be considered new. Here the authors examine the CSR-related challenges that companies experience. Regarding these challenges, the authors aim to introduce the main CSR-related risks and opportunities of outward foreign direct investment. A further objective of the chapter is to describe innovative solutions which can be considered as effective best practice in solving social and environmental problems and developing a more responsible business culture and operation.

BACKGROUND

The relations between Outward Foreign Direct Investment and Corporate Social Responsibility cannot be clear without knowing these two concepts; therefore, this section introduces different approaches to corporate social responsibility and their theoretical and practical aspects. Following this, the main points of foreign direct investment are briefly introduced, as well as corporate motivation and determining factors, through a micro-economic perspective (OFDI approach). The determining factors and characteristics of OFDI activities naturally depend greatly on the characteristics of the company and its operating conditions, leading to large variation. Here the focus is primarily on the features and factors influencing OFDI in companies in developing nations, briefly referring to features of companies of emerging economies appearing in foreign markets.

Approaches to Corporate Social Responsibility

The topic of corporate social responsibility has a history stretching back several decades. Although the first mentions in the economic literature referred to the responsibility of corporate leaders, it has become clear that CSR relates to the basic objectives of companies. This leads to the question of who has the responsibility in companies, and why them. Various answers can be given to this question, and thus there are a number of different approaches and definitions of CSR. However, it is clear that this has become an unavoidable/essential topic, and is not related just to theory but has also become – to various degrees and in different forms – part of the day-to-day practices of firms.

In order to understand the concept of corporate social responsibility, it is necessary to review its development. The conventional – neoclassical – corporate conception can be considered the beginning; a company is a legal entity whose fundamental purpose is the maximization of profit for its owner(s). Since the owners and the management tended to become separate over time, the principle-agent approach took precedence, casting light on the information asymmetry and conflict of interests between owners and management. The responsibility of the leadership first appeared in connection with this approach, since the ownership can ensure that the company management keeps the interests of the owner(s) in mind (Chikán, 2003).

A question raised in the 1930s was whether the leadership of a company has a responsibility not just towards the owners, but also towards society (Dodd, 1932). In the 1950s, social responsibility emerged not just as an opportunity, rather as a duty towards society on the part of the company leadership to make decisions that fulfill the aims and values of society (Bowen, 1953). The concept of CSR became the focus of debate in corporate theory in the 1970s, when the renowned economist Milton Freidman emphasized that social responsibility of a company is pursuing profits and nothing else, of course while not breaking any laws. If a company's leaders were to do anything else, then their responsibility to the owners would be at risk of being ignored. (Friedman, 1970).

The emergence of corporate social responsibility was aided by various social movements, bringing issues such as civil rights, women's rights, consumer rights, and environmental protection to the fore. It is also partially due to these movements that stakeholders – such as employees, consumers, and even society in general – have raised their expectations towards companies (Carroll, 2015). Thus the concept of CSR that exists today no longer concerns just the responsibility of leadership, but also the legitimacy of companies, raising again the question of what the fundamental aims of the firm are, and leading to the conclusion that the traditional business model is not in balance, and requires reconsideration.

Although there is no uniform definition of corporate social responsibility, it is characteristic of each definition that people understand the company to be a kind of community that operates in a social and natural environment, which can have positive or negative effects, and this must be taken into consideration during its operation (Szegedi, 2010). One of the best known definitions is that of Carroll (1991), according to which corporate social responsibility includes four areas of responsibility – economic, legal, ethical, and philanthropic – which build upon each other, and that reflect expectations of the society (interpreted as stakeholders in a wide meaning) towards an enterprise. Economic responsibility is embodies as the responsibility due to the owners, focusing upon successful operation and long-term return on investment. Legal responsibility refers to complying with the laws and regulations, while ethical responsibility involves other legitimate expectations of stakeholders. Philanthropic responsibility covers programs contributing to well being and better quality of life, such as supporting the arts, education, or communities. According to the European Union's definition, CSR is "the responsibility of enterprises for their impacts on society" (European Commission, 2011, p. 6).

These days corporate social responsibility has a close connection with the topic of sustainable development, classically defined as development "that meets the needs of the present without compromising the ability of future generations to meet their own needs" (World Commission on Environment and Development, 1987, p. 41). The authors accept the approach that treats CSR as the ethical behavior of an enterprise towards its stakeholders, which can be comprised of economic, environmental, and social responsibilities at the same time (Watts & Holme, 2000); corporate responsibility also means corporate sustainability (United Nations Global Compact, 2013).

CSR appears in many forms in corporate practice. It has been observed that one of the determining factors is the size of the enterprise, and that large companies are more likely to deal with the topic, considering it a strategic issue (Chiu & Sharfman, 2016). The small and medium-sized sector puts less emphasis on CSR, although progress is seen here as well (United Nations Global Compact, 2013; Williamson, Stampe-Knippel, & Weber, 2014). The majority of companies take part in philanthropic activities, a considerable number of them aim at improving operational effectiveness, while a genuine intention to transform their business model is observed in only a small part of them (Rangan, Chase & Karim, 2015).

An important point in the integration of CSR into corporate practice is the "business case", or to what degree CSR will pay off, in an economic and financial ('bottom-line') sense. Kurucz, Colbert and Wheeler (2008) pointed out, that the business case for CSR can be derived from cost and risk reduction, competitive advantage, reputation and legitimacy and creating win–win situations through synergistic value creation. Numerous studies have shown a relationship between CSR and long-term returns (Carroll, 2015). The authors are of the viewpoint that CSR is an ethical responsibility of enterprises, regardless of whether it leads to financial returns. At the same time, such growing expectations of stakeholders and market recognition increasingly tend to lead to returns on CSR, thus moving in a positive direction for integration of this approach in practice.

Features of Outward Foreign Direct Investment

A significant amount of the foreign investments of companies can be characterized as foreign direct investment (FDI). "Foreign direct investment is a category of investment that reflects the objective of establishing a lasting interest by a resident enterprise in one economy in an enterprise that is resident in an economy other than that of the direct investor. The direct or indirect ownership of 10% or more of the voting power is evidence of such a relationship" (OECD, 2015a, p. 76). From a macroeconomic perspective, there is capital flow between the home and host country, which can be traced in the balance of payments of both countries. From a microeconomic perspective, investments are examined at a corporate level. The realized investments made by foreign companies are referred to as IFDI (inward foreign direct investment), while the foreign investments of domestic companies are referred to as OFDI (outward foreign direct investment) (Denisia, 2010).

The corporate motives for FDI activities have been researched from different perspectives and at different levels since the 1960s. Dunning (2001) provided an excellent summary of the earlier trends and created the defining theoretical framework of this area. The concept is known as the OLI Model or OLI Framework, which stands for ownership, location and internalization. In his work the author relies on three building blocks. He integrates the concept of Bain (1956), which focuses on the intention to acquire superior technologies and knowledge, economies of scale and distribution channels (ownership advantages). Simultaneously, the transaction cost theory introduced in the 1930s can explain the motives behind FDI, as it can be used to reduce information, contractual, and other kinds of costs. The third theoretical element focuses on the role of different locations in the international production chain (Dunning, 1977). The specific advantages that each country offers can be natural or human resources, proximity to markets, or new technologies. The importance of the model is that it integrates the advantages of expanding a company's current assets to foreign countries with the opportunities provided by these countries, while also taking into account the potential strategic benefits of market presence, efficiency and obtaining natural resources (Huang & Zhu, 2016).

The OFDI theories were primarily based on the characteristics of developed countries. As a result of globalization the majority of outward foreign direct investments (OFDI) were provided by companies located in developing countries (primarily in BRICS countries); therefore, a new approach was necessary to precisely explain these phenomena. In his paper, Knoerich (2012) showed that for companies in developing countries the most positive result of OFDI is the reverse spillover effect. This concept means the flow of knowledge, technical abilities, and efficiency from the host country to the corporate headquarters. Transferring profits to the home country is favorable for the home country, while the companies take advantage of access to resources that would be unavailable to them in their home countries.

It is important to note that these resources not only include natural resources but also technological knowledge and the acquisition of certain brands (Caseiro & Masiero, 2014).

The emergence of companies located in developing countries in foreign markets can be attributed to both "pull" and "push" factors. As a result of the free movement of capital and goods, competition has become more intensive and diverse in their traditional markets. Economic weakness or political features of their home countries had a similar effect on these companies. Changes in conditions forced the companies to obtain new technologies and to be present in foreign markets to increase their chances of survival. This had to be achieved even though they seriously lacked both information and capital, and their competitors in developed countries had already gained experience and established their positions on the international market (hence the terms "latecomer" and "newcomer"). On the other hand, the increasing international extension of corporate networks (in which the development of information and communication technologies played a significant role) still provides opportunities for newcomers to connect to the global production chain and to gain access to the necessary markets and professional knowledge (Li, 2015).

The determining factors of OFDI activities include institutional factors, government subsidies and restrictions, the level of economic freedom, political transparency, cultural relations, the liberalization of capital movement, privatization processes, the level of industrialization, modernization efforts, expansion of trade and state associations, and the typical entry modes of companies. The influence of these factors depends on the development level of the home and host countries (Contessi, 2009; Stoian, 2013). Empirical studies have confirmed that institutional factors such as economic freedom, political influence and FDI restrictions have a strong influence on the direction of the flow of investments (Kang & Jiang, 2012). Furthermore, government subsidies and the industrial structure of the home country can also influence foreign investments (Peng, Wang & Jiang, 2008). There are differences between developing countries regarding the importance of factors resulting from their size, geographical location, and political and economic traditions. The differences are most obvious for Central and Eastern European and BRIC countries. According to Svetlicic (2004), in the case of companies in transition economies the characteristics of both developing and developed countries are present (Stoian, 2013).

THE RELATIONSHIP BETWEEN CSR AND OFDI

This chapter introduces the effects of globalization on corporate social responsibility (CSR) and analyzes the CSR-related risks and opportunities of Outward Foreign Direct Investment.

The Effect of Globalization on Corporate Social Responsibility

Globalization has had a significant impact on the concept of corporate social responsibility from several aspects. Globalization amplified the voice of critics who questioned whether companies are interested in the balance between their interest in profit and social values. It became obvious that besides its positive impact, globalization can also have controversial or negative effects and companies can influence their local and global environments both positively and negatively (Epstein, 2007). The significant problems of globalization such as pollution, human rights issues, financial inequality, insecurity, unemployment, and crises have also highlighted the controversial role of companies. It is no coincidence that more and more people argue against this form of globalization and aim to develop a more humane and ethical way.

In addition, the behavior of the business world has recently received a great deal of attention due to the internet and improvements in communication technology. The expectations of certain pressure groups (consumers, environmentalists, employees, political activists, non-governmental organizations) and their increased sensitivity to environmental and social issues cannot be ignored. As a result, demands for transparency in companies' business activities and their consequences have increased. These demands originate not only from those typically called stakeholders in the wider sense, but also particularly from shareholders, since they claim access to ever more information from companies in order to more accurately identify the potential benefits or risks of prospective investments.

Reputational risk has become an increasingly significant aspect recently. Any mistake or error can cause the company to lose prestige or may result in financial loss for the company. There are several instances of loss of corporate reputation. Clothing manufacturers such as Nike were accused of child labor and inadequate working conditions, which forced the company to make efforts toward transparency (Dorey, 2011). Corporate scandals (e.g. Enron, WorldCom, Parmalat) show that fraud was made possible by malpractice, inadequate control mechanisms, problems in corporate governance, management and auditor deficiencies, and unclear ethical guidelines (Soltani, 2014). Shell was prosecuted repeatedly for pollution in Nigeria and for violating human rights, and also indicted (Hennchen, 2015). The latest Volkswagen scandal caused also considerable damage to customers, shareholders, employees, and competitors.

In many cases, irresponsible behavior cannot be narrowed down to one company or industry. The best-known example is the selfish and irresponsible conduct of the financial institutions that became one of the causes of the economic crisis in 2008 due to the significance of their activities and global network. It is no coincidence that the resulting crisis in confidence strengthened the need for CSR in both the public and private banking sector (Lentner, Szegedi & Tatay, 2015). Based on the new, normative approach to legitimacy, companies in each sector need to obtain a "social license to operate" (Demuijnck & Fasterling, 2016). With this background it is understandable that global issues and the companies' role in their development have led to negative feelings against these companies, requiring the companies to rebuild trust and to develop genuine corporate social responsibility in its wider sense.

CSR-Related Risks of Outward Foreign Direct Investment

One of the economic effects of FDI – one of the main driving forces of globalization – is that it has helped developing countries. However, there are huge differences between each country. Chinese companies aim to acquire strategic assets through investments in developed countries. Many third world countries have become more internationalized than the transition countries in Central and Eastern Europe (CEE). Nonetheless, the economic and political institutions of CEE countries are more advanced as a result of the EU accession, which has had a great influence on OFDI possibilities. Globalization can support OFDI through liberalization processes and developing institutions and regulations, as in the case of Russia or Malaysia (Goh & Wong, 2011; Kalotay & Sulstarova, 2010; Stoian, 2013). In the transition countries there is a positive correlation between economic freedom, political transparency and OFDI (Li, 2015; Stoian, 2013).

The internal stakeholders of a company are its owners and the employees, while the external stakeholders are the customers, suppliers, competitors, the government, local communities and non-governmental organizations. The CSR-related risks can be understood through the violation of the legitimate expectations of each group of stakeholders, shown in Table 1.

Table 1. CSR risks

Stakeholder	CSR Risk
Shareholders	Endangering long-range return on investment, Theft, Fraud, Endangering company assets, Money laundering, Insider dealing, Conflicts of interest
Employees	Poor working conditions, Discrimination, Harassment, Privacy right violation, Unfair labor practices
Customers	Low quality/dangerous product or service, Inadequate/false information to customers, Corruption & bribery, Unethical advertising, Misuse of customer information
Suppliers	Unethical contract terms & conditions, Non-payment, Corruption & bribery, Discrimination, Harassment
Competitors	Anti-competitive practices
Governments	Tax evasion, Fraud, Corruption & bribery, Political activity
Local communities	Human rights violations, Endangering jobs, Endangering healthy environment
Civil organizations	Civil rights violations
Natural environment	Environmental pollution, Endangering biodiversity, Animal testing

Authors' compilation.

While the available research on 1,015 CSR-related penalties of 2,522 companies (Vigeo, 2015) does not provide an overall picture of the situation, it illustrates the seriousness of the risks well. Results showed that 55% of the sanctions were issued for the violation of business behavior rules, which includes corruption, anti-competitive practices and violations of customer rights. A further 9% of the CSR-related sanctions were issued for inappropriate health and safety work conditions and 4% because of discrimination (Vigeo, 2015).

Outward foreign direct investment significantly increases the number of stakeholders, while making the corporate stakeholder network more complex. New groups of stakeholders might appear through foreign investment (e.g. indigenous and tribal people) that have different characteristics than traditional stakeholders, and about whom the companies do not always have the necessary information. From a CSR perspective the existing cultural and ethical differences between the home and the host country are a particularly important factor. They pose a risk in any stakeholder group, but especially with employees, management, suppliers, business partners, local communities and government officials.

There is a special relationship between OFDI and CSR. Developed countries have a more advanced CSR culture than developing or emerging countries due to a stricter regulatory environment and the higher expectations of the stakeholders. Surroca, Tribó & Zahra, (2013) studied 110 multinational companies in 22 countries and found that advanced regulations and pressure from the stakeholders encourage "window-dressing" in the home country and to irresponsible practices in foreign countries, especially when institutional control is high in the home country but low in the host country or in the case of highly competitive, technology-intensive industries. At the same time the strengthening of international non-governmental organizations helps control irresponsible behavior.

In the following paragraphs the authors summarize the most typical CSR risks of outward foreign direct investment: corruption, human rights violations, and supply chain risks.

Case Study: Corporate Social Responsibility in Chinese Companies

In connection with China we can read about a lot of negative issues related to CSR: faulty consumer products, overworked and underpaid employees, child work, worker suicides, toxic emissions and broken safety rules. However, recently CSR has started to develop. This can be traced back to several factors. The most important of them is accepting rules that encourage national and foreign, state and non-state companies to carry out obligatory or voluntary CSR activities. The other important factor is increased foreign direct investment. Private firms started to be considerably more engaged with solving social problems. As a result of criticism concerning companies starting up business in China, the expectations related to CSR activities have increased towards companies and now has now progressed well beyond charity (Vermander, 2014; Huang & Zhao, 2016).

The judgement of CSR effects of Outward Foreign Investment activities at Chinese companies is dissimilar. Studies on the CSR practices of Chinese companies in Africa showed that several companies focused on short-term financial performance, regardless of ecological and social performance, unless a scandal occurred (Timokhina, 2014). According to other opinions, foreign investments increased the social responsibility of Chinese companies and their commitment to ethical standards (Cheung, Kong, Tan & Wang, 2014; Hasegawa & Noonha, 2014). There are several examples of the public relations efforts of Chinese companies, but successful companies are integrating CSR into their business processes proactively, particularly the companies operating internationally (Timokhina, 2014).

Corruption

"Corruption is the abuse of entrusted power for private gain" (Transparency International, 2015a). Corruption can take many different forms both in the private and public spheres, such as bribery, giving and receiving gifts, offering entertainment, facilitation payment, fraud, embezzlement, money laundering, tax evasion, and nepotism. The amount of estimated corruption comes to more than 5% of global GDP (World Economic Forum, 2014). The International Monetary Fund (2016) highlights that the cost of corruption is also very significant, about 1.5–2 trillion USD (approximately 2% of global GDP). Corruption raises the cost of doing business by 10–25% (OECD, 2015b). As a consequence, corruption is not only an ethical issue but also has huge economic significance.

Corruption has always been present in societies and probably cannot be erased completely, but its extent does make a difference. The more widespread corruption is, the bigger the damage it can cause. When corruption is present, it is not the most effective solution that is chosen, competition is not fair and equality of chances is not ensured either. Besides, corruption also contributes to sustaining human rights problems and economic instability, hindering social and economic development. In foreign working capital investments, where obtaining natural resources or taking competitive advantage of a cheap labor force can often be an aim, there is a real danger that capital investments will go to a country with a high corruption level.

The level of corruption cannot be defined exactly, but estimates exist. The corruption perception index (CPI) of Transparency International provides estimates for the corruption level of the public sector based on different surveys and evaluations. Evaluations are made on a 0-100 scale, where 0 means a very high corruption level and 100 means a country that is free of corruption. Data prove that corruption is a global problem; 68% of the 168 countries evaluated in 2015 had very serious problems with corruption, which directly affects more than 6 billion people worldwide. It is thought provoking that among countries with high corruption level there are not only underdeveloped countries but G20 countries as well (the latter account for half of the high-level corruption countries countries). Even some companies of the most corruption-free countries occasionally apply bribery in order to gain foreign business (Transparency International, 2015b). However, the extent of corruption is definitely larger in emerging markets, as Figure 1 shows. According to the latest survey of EY (2016), 39% of its global respondents think bribery is widespread in their countries, while the numbers are 51% in developing countries and 21% in developed countries. Transparency International (2016) also emphasizes that in emerging economies the level of company transparency is really low, thus promoting corruption.

Figure 1. Corruption Perceptions Index 2015
Source: Transparency International (2015b).

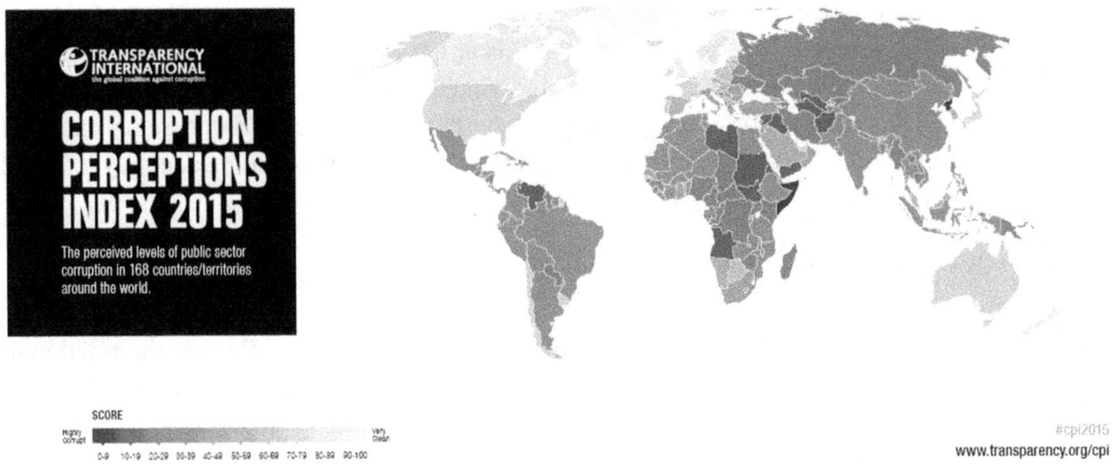

In outward foreign direct investment, the bribery of central or local governmental officials poses an especially high risk. The intention of corruption may be to win a state tender, influence contractual conditions, or overlook a breach of contract. Through bribery these companies intend to get subsidies, lower taxes or exclusive licenses to pursue certain activities, e.g. utilizing natural resources. There are cases of corruption that attempt to influence the outcome of lawsuits or legal procedures, for instance in arguments between competitors or concerning environment pollution (The World Bank, 1997).

Bribing a foreign official is mostly committed by large companies (60%), in many cases indirectly through agents, relatives, lawyers, or accountants (OECD, 2015b). Corruption, however, is a risk not only related to governments. Business consultants, suppliers, sub-suppliers, contractors, sub-contractors, sales and customs agents and other third parties also pose risks. Panalpina World Transport Holding Ltd., a Swiss freight forwarding company, gave facilitation payments and gifts to customs officials on behalf of their customers in order to circumvent local rules relating to imports into African, South American and Asian countries. Panalpina and their customers, such as Royal Dutch Shell Plc. and five oil services companies paid penalties of USD 236.5 million (The Wall Street Journal, 2010).

Corruption is not exclusive to a single industry, but the extractive, engineering, construction, real estate, transportation, and storage and communication sectors are considered especially risky in terms of bribery and corruption (OECD, 2015b; World Economic Forum, 2015). A recent analysis showed that government officials are bribed not only in developing countries and that bribery happens also in developed countries in the same ratio (OECD, 2015). More than 20 countries were involved in the corruption scandal of Siemens that resulted in a fine of USD 1.6 billion, including Nigeria, a country with a high level of corruption, and Norway, which is considered clean of corruption (Pro Publica, 2008).

In emerging markets, the high level of corruption can be found not only due to the fact that investing companies face the bribability of local officials, entrepreneurs and the expectations related to corruption. It is also clear that in the outward foreign direct investment activities of emerging countries the investing countries can start active company corruption activities due to their tolerance of the culture of national high-level corruption. If the intention of active corruption can be recognized in the investing company, the firms and officials of the receiving countries will tolerate or even expect it. Thus, the risk of corruption is increasingly present, causing even more serious economic and social damage and hindering the development of the emerging or developing country.

Corruption can have serious consequences for a company too. The investigation of corruption cases usually lasts more than seven years and carries significant costs (OECD, 2015b). Companies found guilty of corruption can face severe punishment and individual consequences may include fines or even imprisonment. Self-reporting is considered a mitigating circumstance. Being found guilty can put the company on a blacklist, lead to a loss of reputation, and the participants of the market may lose confidence in the company – thus making corruption a risk of strategic importance.

Human Rights Violations

Human rights mean the rights to which a person is inherently entitled regardless of their nationality, gender or other status, and they are applicable everywhere in the world. Human rights are diverse and include, among other, labor rights, political rights or the right to a healthy and good life or the right to a clean environment. The basic human rights are summarized in Table 2. Human rights not only consist of rights but also obligations. Each person has to respect the rights of others. It is the duty of the states to respect and enforce human rights (United Nations Human Rights Office of the High Commissioner, 2016).

Respecting and enforcing human rights is not only the duty of individuals and states, but also of companies as well (United Nations Human Rights Office of the High Commissioner, 2011). However, it is not enough for the companies to only respect human rights and express a commitment towards them. They should encourage the same behavior in the stakeholders of the company, and if such a right is violated then the necessary remedial measures have to be taken. For companies this refers to ethical obligations related to the "do the right thing" principle. Furthermore, this behavior is also in the economic interest of the company, as it can decrease regulatory and operational risk and has significant reputational advantages (United Nations Global Compact, 2015a).

Human rights issues in the business sector are often associated with child labor or discrimination, although there are several other relevant areas of importance. The most important human rights violations are listed below, as based on the Business & Human Rights Resource Centre (2016) website, where specific examples can be found for each topic and the data can be filtered by countries or companies.

- **Abuses:** Abduction, Arbitrary detention, Beatings & violence, Complicity, Death penalty, Death threats, Deaths, Denial of freedom of expression, Denial of freedom of movement, "Disappearances", Displacement, Genocide, Human trafficking, Injuries, Intimidation & threats, Killings, Rape & sexual abuse, Sexual harassment, Slavery, Torture & ill-treatment, Unfair trial
- **Discrimination:** Age discrimination, Disability discrimination, Gender discrimination, HIV/AIDS discrimination, Marital status discrimination, Political opinion discrimination, Pregnancy discrimination, Racial/ethnic/caste/origin discrimination, Religious discrimination, Sexual orientation & gender identity (LGBT) discrimination
- **Environment:** Climate change, Environmental discrimination
- **Labor:** Freedom of association, Prison labor, Export processing zones, Forced labor & modern slavery, Living wage, Child labor
- **Security:** Security issues & conflict zones: General, Conflict prevention & resolution

The topics of health, safety, security and environment (HSSE) are seldom thought of as human rights issues. These areas, however, always affect individuals and the current or next generation, whether the HSSE issue itself relates to employees, suppliers, or local communities. This area has been in the focus of NGOs for years. Perhaps the most well-known example is the Shell incident in Nigeria, which still generates new complications. In 2008, two oil spills destroyed the livelihood of the Bodo community in Ogoniland, Nigeria. After legal action was taken in the UK at the end of 2014, the outcome achieved by the community together with NGOs was a compensation of GBP 55 million paid out by Shell. However, the site of the incident still has not been cleared up properly (Amnesty International, 2016).

Several HSSE-related topics are among the highest global risks. Failure of climate-change mitigation and adaptation ranks as the most impactful risk to society and ranks third in terms of probability. The risk of biodiversity loss and ecosystem collapse and the spread of infectious diseases are also among the top 10 risks based on their impact. The top 10 risks in terms of probability include extreme weather events and natural catastrophes, while man-made environmental catastrophes are also considered as a significant risk (World Economic Forum, 2016). In countries with a lower level of HSSE culture, the impact and likelihood of these risks is increasing due to factors such as conflict zones, war zones or religion.

Table 2. Shortened version of Universal Declaration of Human Rights

- **We Are All Born Free and Equal**- All human beings are born free and equal in dignity and rights.
- **Don't Discriminate** - Everyone has all human rights regardless of race, sex, language, religion, political or other opinion, national or social origin, property, birth or other status.
- **The Right to Life** - Everyone has the right to life, liberty and security of person.
- **No Slavery** - Slavery and the slave trade are prohibited.
- **No Torture** - No one shall be subjected to torture or to cruel, inhuman or degrading treatment or punishment.
- **You Have Rights No Matter Where You Go** - Everyone has the right to recognition everywhere as a person before the law.
- **We're All Equal before the Law** - All are equal before the law and are entitled without any discrimination to equal protection of the law.
- **Your Human Rights Are Protected by Law** - Everyone has the right to an effective remedy when not treated fairly.
- **No Unfair Detainment** - No one shall be subjected to arbitrary arrest, detention or exile.
- **The Right to Trial** - Every person is entitled to an impartial hearing.
- **We're Always Innocent until Proven Guilty** - Every person shall be considered innocent until proven guilty.
- **The Right to Privacy** - Every person has the right to protection of his or her privacy.
- **Freedom to Move** - Every person has the right to freedom of movement within a country and to leave and return to his or her country.
- **The Right to Asylum** - Every person has the right to asylum from persecution.
- **Right to a Nationality** - Everyone has the right to a nationality.
- **Marriage and Family** - All adults have the right to marry of their own free will and found a family.
- **The Right to Ownership** - Every person has the right to own property.
- **Freedom of Thought** - Everyone has the right to freedom of thought, conscience and religion.
- **Freedom of Expression** - Every person has the right to freedom of opinion and expression.
- **The Right to Public Assembly** - Everyone has the right to freedom of peaceful assembly and association.
- **The Right to Democracy** - Every person has the right to take part in the government of his or her country.
- **Social Security** - Every person has economic, social and cultural rights.
- **Workers' Rights** - Every person has the right to work, to receive just pay, and to form and join trade unions.
- **The Right to Play** - Every person has the right to rest and leisure.
- **Food and Shelter for All** - Every person has the right to an adequate standard of living.
- **The Right to Education** - Every person has the right to education.
- **Copyright** - Every person has the right to participate in cultural activities and benefit from scientific advancement.
- **A Fair and Free World** - Everyone is entitled to a social order in which these human rights can be realized.
- **Responsibility** - Every person has duties to the democratic society according to the law.
- **No One Can Take Away Your Human Rights** - No person can take away these rights and freedoms.

Author's compilation based on United Nations General Assembly, 1948.

Case Study: MOL Group's Human Rights Efforts

MOL Group is one of the largest companies headquartered in Hungary, operating in the oil and gas industry in over 30 countries. MOL Group is committed to respecting fundamental human rights and strives to protect them. Within its comprehensive Ethics Management System, the company has identified vulnerable groups: workers, business partners/contractors' staff, local communities and special vulnerable groups (women and minorities). Based on secondary external information the MOL Group Human Rights Map was created, containing all the countries where MOL Group operates. In the map the countries are assessed, based upon external evaluation, as Low, Medium, High and Critical risk countries from a human rights point of view. Furthermore, a Human Rights Pyramid was created based on external human rights assessments and self-assessment. The pyramid contains human rights issues that can occur in its everyday business, and which the company pays attention to. MOL Group focuses on health, safety and environmental protection as the highest priority. The employees have obligatory human rights training courses and annual managerial presentations include human rights issues. Remediation plays an important role as well: based on the human rights risk assessment and complaints, subsidiaries elaborate mitigation plans and make significant mitigation efforts. Human rights issues are only one aspect of the Dow Jones Sustainability Assessment, in which MOL Group was ranked in the top 15 percent of the Dow Jones World Sustainability Index in 2016 (MOL Group, 2016).

Supply Chain Risks

Global companies have complex and constantly changing networks of suppliers. Global supply chains have expanded considerably in recent decades. According to data from the International Labor Organization (2015), more than 450 million jobs are in global supply chains, making up 20.6% of total employment. Taiwan and China are particularly affected, with half of all employees working in the global supply chain, while in the Republic of Korea and the European Union the proportion stands at 33%.

It is difficult and often impossible to review the entire complex supply chain, as it often involves large numbers of suppliers or subcontractors, including some who are part of the informal sector. There are different laws or a lack of legislation, and different ethical values in different countries. Companies face significant social, environmental, reputational and economic risks because of their supply chain. Human rights problems and labor rights abuses may occur, as vulnerable groups such as women workers, migrant workers, child laborers, or poor people are typical in the supply chain (Human Rights Watch, 2016).

News about supply chain is becoming more frequent. Problems in the Apple supply chain were said to include 60-hour working weeks, worker suicides, child labor, pay being withheld, discrimination against women and minorities, and beatings and harassment. Nike was strongly criticized for production in sweatshops, Siemens got mixed up with price fixing cartels, and in 2014 Samsung agreed to compensate former semiconductor workers who suffered from cancer due to chemical exposure (International Trade Union Confederation, 2016). The value chain is put at risk not only through violating human rights, but also through corruption and other CSR risks. The Global Compact benchmarking report points to supplier sustainability as the top barrier for large companies (United Nations Global Compact, 2013).

CSR-Related Opportunities of OFDI

CSR offers not only risks in outward foreign direct investment situations, but also a number of opportunities, some of which are introduced below.

Philanthropy

Many people still mistakenly consider philanthropy as the sole area of corporate social responsibility. The reason behind this misunderstanding is probably the inclusion of 'social' in the term. For this reason, the term 'corporate responsibility' (CR) is becoming more widespread among corporations and other

Case Study: BP's Corporate Social Responsibility in Russia

BP has a commitment to having corporate social responsibility as an integral part of its business in Russia. As one of the largest foreign companies, BP has many local social, cultural, educational and charity projects in Russia. Within its education program BP supports nine universities in Russia providing support for students, professors and scientific research projects. Extended charity characterizes BP's operations in Russia, which focusses on supplying sick children with medicine, the diagnosis of complex illnesses, and distance learning for school-age patients. The company supports the cultural life of Russia, too, sponsoring The Polytechnical Museum, the Mariinsky Theatre, the Tretyakov Gallery, the State Hermitage, the Moscow Tchaikovsky Conservatory, the Stanislavsky and Nemirovich-Danchenko Moscow Music Theatre (BP, 2016).

organizations, as it is considered to be broader and refer to the responsibility due to all stakeholders. Neither concept – CSR or CR – excludes philanthropy, but it needs to be more than simply 'window dressing' substituting for a commitment to true economic, legal and ethical responsibility.

Corporate philanthropy takes on many forms in practice. It may focus on sponsoring education, health care, culture or sports, but can also be targeted at a particular group or community. Often the employees of a company take part in their own voluntary activities as a form of support. 'Good corporate citizenship', besides being of use to society, also may reduce social and environmental risks, prevent scandals, or decrease criticism from civil organizations and others by enhancing corporate reputations. In the outward foreign investment process of Chinese companies, philanthropy can be viewed as a key component of their CSR program. The target of their CSR is promoting their legitimacy, reputation, and competitive advantage, in an effort to overcome the companies' "liability of foreignness" (Timokhina, 2014).

Improving Operational Effectiveness

The aim of CSR is to deliver social or environmental benefits and support a company's operations across the value chain, often improving efficiency and effectiveness. It may increase revenue or decrease costs, for example initiatives that reduce resource use, waste, or emissions. Investments in employee working conditions, health care, or education, may enhance productivity. CSR can improve morale and conditions at work, resulting in a more committed, productive, innovative, loyal and content workforce and a company that is more attractive to a well-qualified and well-trained labor force.

Transforming the Business Model

Key elements of this approach are improved business performance and achieving social or environmental results. Unilever's Project Shakti ("empowerment") in India provides a good example. The company recruits village women, provides them with access to microfinance loans, and trains them in selling soaps, detergents, and other products door-to-door. As a result of the initiative more than 65,000 women entrepreneurs found jobs, while increasing rural access to hygiene products contributing to public health. From a financial point of view, as of 2012 Project Shakti had achieved more than GBP 100 million in sales and Unilever decided to roll out similar programs in other parts of the world (Rangan et al., 2015).

This new model has many benefits for stakeholders: increasing transparency for customers by means of responsible trade, upgrading corporate brands, attracting loyal and responsible customers, and developing mutually beneficial partnership collaborations based on trust and common scales of values. This results in new business opportunities, new markets and an increase in innovation productivity. Greater transparency of corporate processes leads to an increase in the feelings of satisfaction of stakeholders and investors, and also results in greater interest in the company. CSR helps develop good relationships with government, regulators, authorities, and the public, contributing to the development of a more stable global market, creating corporate and social values at the same time (Szegedi, 2010).

This CSR approach can be considered as corporate social innovation (CSI), the basis of which is that, nowadays, many businesses realize that they can make a powerful contribution to the solution of social and environmental problems by providing creative, innovative and profitable possibilities. Corporate social innovation has three basic principles: it is part of the core business strategy, it leverages market forces to create positive impacts, and it is unleashed by strategic collaboration (KPMG, 2014). When considered in this light, CSR can even be considered as social enterprise, since the purpose of the existence of the company is to carry out some sort of social mission or endeavor so that business expectations can also be met. Every enterprise should be at the same time a social enterprise, keeping the balance among economic, environmental and social objectives and thus contributing to sustainable development (Szegedi, Fülöp & Bereczk, 2016).

SOLUTIONS AND RECOMMENDATIONS

The policies and regulations of CSR and the voluntary assumption of responsibility by companies offer assistance in meeting the challenges of outward foreign direct investment corporate social responsibility.

Guidelines

Numerous CSR standards have been elaborated as "soft law". Some are widely recognized international standards but there are also international multi-stakeholder initiatives and industry association initiatives providing standards for the social and environmental practices of firms at home and abroad. CSR standards such as the ILO Conventions, UN Declaration on Human Rights, OECD Guidelines for Multinationals, UN Global Compact, GRI Guidelines, AA1000 Framework, ISO 26000, the United Nations' "Protect, Respect and Remedy" Framework, and Principles for Responsible Investment are increasingly recognized and appreciated. The majority of CSR standards typically focus on the operations of multinational enterprises and, as such, are significant for international investment (United Nations Conference on Trade and Development, 2015).

International investment agreements indicate increased attention to sustainable development considerations. "New generation" investment policies strive to create synergies with wider economic development goals or industrial policies and achieve seamless integration in development strategies; foster responsible investor behavior and incorporate principles of CSR; ensure policy effectiveness in their design and implementation and in the institutional environment within which they operate (United Nations Conference on Trade and Development, 2012).

One effective tool for publishing CSR-related information is CSR/CR reporting. During this process a company can gather data and analyze environmental, social and corporate governance (ESG) risks in order to create long-term value and resilience to environmental and social change. The rate of CR reporting is high worldwide, and has become standard business practice: 93% of the world's largest 250 companies report their CR activities. CR reporting is essential to convince investors about the future success potential of the business (KPMG, 2013).

Laws

Although CSR traditionally meant voluntary commitment, as a result of the scandals of large corporations and the 2008 crisis triggered by problems of ethics and responsibility, legal regulation has increased. Most of the problems arose not with legal acceptance of the principles of human rights but with compliance with the existing laws. Several examples can be given of the legal regulation of and incentives for CSR in various countries. It is mandatory to submit reports on the social and environmental impacts of large corporations in, for instance, France, the United Kingdom, China, and South Africa. Spain was the first to pass a sustainable economy act, while the first corporate social responsibility law was made in India (Mélypataki & Szegedi, in press).

The corporation law of China obliges corporations to take social responsibility. Apart from it, guidelines for Central State-Owned-Enterprises require the establishment of necessary mechanisms to carry out CSR. The Shanghai Stock Exchange and the Shenzhen Stock Exchange mandated certain listed firms to disclose environmental, social and governance (ESG) information starting from 2008 (Ioannou & Serafeim, 2014). As of 2015, 113 Chinese, 30 Polish and only 4 Hungarian companies have joined (UN Global Compact 2015b). Seven Chinese financial institutions – but no Hungarian or Polish ones – have joined the UNEP Finance Initiative on sustainable banking (UNEP Finance Initiative, 2015).

The OECD had urged the imposition of severe penalties for foreign bribery as early as 1999 in order to suppress corruption. This convention was accepted by every OECD member and many non-member nations, as well. Strict laws for the suppression of corruption were made in the United Kingdom, similar to the Foreign Corrupt Practices Act of the United States. Under the UK Bribery Act companies represented in the United Kingdom are held responsible for bribery occurring in any nation in the world (International Monetary Fund, 2016). The initiative of the OECD was significant, as the 41 signatory countries represent approximately two-thirds of world exports and almost 90% of total foreign direct investment outflows. However, active enforcement is carried out in only four countries, and in 20 counties with 20.5% of world exports there is no or little enforcement (Transparency International, 2015c). The enforcement status is shown in Table 3.

Table 3. Enforcement of the OECD Convention on Combating Foreign Bribery

Enforcement Level	Countries	Export Share
Active enforcement	Germany, Switzerland, United Kingdom, United States	4 counties with 22.8% of world exports
Moderate enforcement	Austria, Australia, Canada, Finland, Italy, Norway	6 counties with 8.9% of world exports
Limited enforcement	France, Greece, Hungary, Netherlands, New Zealand, Portugal, South Africa, South Korea, Sweden	9 counties with 12.6% of world exports
Little or no enforcement	Argentina, Belgium, Brazil, Bulgaria, Chile, Colombia, Czech Republic, Denmark, Estonia, Ireland, Israel, Luxembourg, Japan, Mexico, Poland, Russia, Slovak Republic, Slovenia, Spain, Turkey	20 counties with 20.5% of world exports

Authors' compilation based on Transparency International, 2015c.

Corporate Self-Regulation

As a consequence of globalization, multinational corporations have gathered considerable economic influence, and the full regulation of their activities by the legal instruments of each nation is not possible. Thus the emphasis has moved to self-regulation. The business sphere volunteers to play a role in environmental protection and in solving various social problems. As a result of the recent economic crisis and the crisis of confidence brought on by it, responsible business conduct has become even more important. Corporations voluntarily set down the values and ethical standards by which they do business. In an ideal case, these norms do not remain within the walls of the company, but spread along the whole value chain, involving also suppliers.

CSR risks can cause severe harm due to legal impact (e.g. fines, penalties, imprisonment, product seizure, debarment), financial impact (e.g. decrease of the bottom line, share prices, potential future earnings, loss of investor confidence), business impact (e.g. embargoes, plant shutdowns, inability to operate in key markets), reputational impact (e.g. bad press or social media discussion, loss of customer trust, decreased employee morale) if ethical misconduct or a legal violation occurs. In order to handle CSR risks and prevent CSR-related problems, investing companies should analyze the risks and integrate CSR issues into their investment during development planning and the decision-making process. They should initiate proper CSR actions, comply with CSR standards, and facilitate dialog between stakeholders. The institution of a grievance mechanism available to both internal and external stakeholders is vital.

It has been found that in practice, companies deal more with environmental protection and employment issues than, for instance, human rights and anti-corruption measures. Only the largest companies carry out dialogs with stakeholders. Activities related to sustainability are a challenge when it comes to suppliers. However, the supply chain development of multinational companies can impact both the environment and local economies, especially in emerging markets (UN Global Compact, 2013). More typically, voluntary initiatives are unable to prevent problems such as human rights violations in the supply chain, and therefore mandatory legal regulation is needed (Human Rights Watch, 2016).

Case Study: Corporate Social Responsibility of the Largest Companies in Poland

An empirical research study examined the 227 most important companies operating in Poland based on the following 12 CSR-related indicators: CSR on the website, Person in charge of CSR at the company, CSR policy, Code of ethics/Code of conduct, Social report, Social report based on GRI standards, References to CSR in their annual report, Ecology, Supply chain, Human rights, Fighting against corruption and Results confirmed by the company. They wanted to find out how developed the CSR activities of the companies are. The findings have revealed a number of problems. Many companies still believe that CSR is sponsorship and philanthropy. Some international corporations – including Accor, BSH, Jabil, Fiat, Ikea Industry and Whirlpool – received lower scores because they did not translate all information into Polish. From an economic point of view very significant sectors, such as the metal, machinery and motor industry or the electrical appliances sector, did not achieve good CSR results. Environmental issues are more highly prioritized than human rights issues. Only 37% of the largest Polish companies cared about CSR in their supply chain, just 22.4% have an employee responsible for CSR, and an even lower rate of 15.4% have a CSR report available on the company webpage. This poor result was surprising, as non-financial reporting is obligatory for selected large companies in Poland as of 2016 in Poland based on an EU directive (Piskalski, 2015).

FUTURE RESEARCH DIRECTIONS

The new sustainable development goals set by the United Nations in 2015 include numerous themes: no poverty, zero hunger, good health and well-being, quality education, gender equality, clean water and sanitation, affordable and clean energy, decent work and economic growth, industry, innovation and infrastructure, reduced inequalities, sustainable cities and communities, responsible consumptions and production, climate action, life below water, peace, justice and strong institutions, and partnership for the goals (Sustainable Development Knowledge Platform, 2015). Work towards meeting these goals has to be shared among governments, corporations, the civil sphere, and individuals. The goals and the responsibility are shared, and everyone needs to contribute in order to achieve these aims. How this can take place is a topic requiring further research.

Among the inevitable effects of OFDI are CSR-related risks and possibilities, which can be major challenges for the companies of the home countries. Main tasks are reducing compliance costs, diminishing business risks and taking part in the development of other countries. These require new points of view, new skills and knowledge, and taking proper initiatives and actions. For the companies involved it can be a real learning process.

In order to form a new business model, the evaluation of foreign investors should take into consideration not only financial capabilities but also social aspects. Social outcomes – both positive and negative – need to be assessed and integrated into a complex evaluation. A wide interpretation of profit should be taken, including aspects such as lowering energy consumption, managing to mitigate social problems, or meeting needs of society.

It is not sufficient to integrate social aspects into operations of the business sphere; for a world that works responsibly and sustainably, business aspects also need to be integrated into operations in the public and civil sphere. Further research can offer methods for carrying out such integration.

CONCLUSION

Companies seeking a "social license to operate" are interested in creating a positive reputation through corporate social responsibility (CSR). This trend has been promoted by challenges brought about due to the increasingly globalized economy. Foreign direct investment is considered to be one of the main drivers of globalization, and one of its economic impacts has been to aid developing nations. In transitional economies, a positive relationship has been found between economic liberalization, political transparency, and outward foreign direct investment.

As a result of Outward Foreign Direct Investment (OFDI) companies face many CSR-related risks. OFDI significantly increases the complexity of the stakeholder system and the regulatory and cultural environment. The major risks of corporate social responsibility in relation to OFDI include corruption, anti-competitive practices, violations of customer rights, inappropriate health and safety work conditions, and discrimination. Companies face significant social, environmental, reputational and economic risks from their supply chains. In order to avoid corruption, human right violations due diligence, risk assessment, and effective programs are required.

Corporate social responsibility does not only create a risk in outward foreign investment; it also offers a number of positive opportunities. In addition to being of use to society, "good corporate citizenship" may reduce social and environmental risks, prevent scandals, and decrease criticism from civil organizations and others concerned, thus enhancing the corporate reputation. The aim of CSR is to deliver social or environmental benefits, support a company's operations across the value chain, often improving efficiency and effectiveness within existing business models. Transforming the business model approach improves business performance and the chance of positive social or environmental outcomes. CSR can be considered as Corporate Social Innovation (CSI) when it is part of the core business strategy. CSI leverages market forces to create positive impacts, and is unleashed by strategic collaboration. In this sense, CSR can also be suitable for social enterprises.

When dealing with the challenges faced by corporate social responsibility in outward foreign direct investment, assistance can be found in CSR policies and legal regulation, as well as the voluntary acceptance of responsibility by companies.

REFERENCES

Amnesty International. (2016). *Niger Delta: Government clean-up does not let Shell off the hook*. Retrieved July 12, 2016 from https://www.amnesty.org/en/latest/news/2016/06/niger-delta-government-clean-up-does-not-let-shell-off-the-hook/

Bain, J. S. (1956). Advantages of the large firm: Production, distribution, and sales promotion. *Journal of Marketing*, *20*(4), 336–346. doi:10.2307/1248235

Bowen, H. R. (1953). *Social responsibilities of the businessman*. New York: Harper & Row.

BP. (2016). *Corporate Social Responsibility*. Retrieved October 13, 2016 from http://www.bp.com/en_ru/russia/csr.html

Business & Human Rights Resource Centre. (2016). *Search Topics*. Retrieved July 12, 2016 from https://business-humanrights.org/en/search-topics

Byus, K., Deis, D., & Ouyang, B. (2010). Doing well by doing good: Corporate social responsibility and profitability. *SAM Advanced Management Journal*, *75*(1), 44–55.

Carroll, A. B. (1991, July-August). The Pyramid of Corporate Social Responsibility: Toward the Moral Management of Organizational Stakeholders. *Business Horizons*.

Carroll, A. B. (2015). Corporate social responsibility: The centerpiece of competing and complementary frameworks. *Organizational Dynamics*, *44*(2), 87–96. doi:10.1016/j.orgdyn.2015.02.002

Caseiro, L. C. Z., & Masiero, G. (2014). OFDI Promotion Policy in Emerging Economies: The Brazilian and Chinese Strategies. *Critical Perspectives on International Business*, *10*(4), 237–255. doi:10.1108/cpoib-03-2014-0023

Cheung, Y.-L., Kong, D., Tan, W., & Wang, W. (2014). Being Good When Being International in an Emerging Economy: The Case of China. *Journal of Business Ethics*, *130*(4), 805–817. doi:10.1007/s10551-014-2268-7

Chikán, A. (2003). *Vállalatgazdaságtan*. Budapest: Aula Kiadó.

Chiu, S. C., & Sharfman, M. (2016). Corporate Social Irresponsibility and Executive Succession: An Empirical Examination. *Journal of Business Ethics*, *17*(February), 1–17.

Contessi, S. (2009). Foreign direct investment, productivity, and country growth: an overview. *Federal Reserve Bank of St. Louis Review,* (91), 61-78

Demuijnck, G., & Fasterling, B. (2016). The Social License to Operate. *Journal of Business Ethics*, *136*(4), 675–685. doi:10.1007/s10551-015-2976-7

Denisia, V. (2010). Foreign direct investment theories: An overview of the main FDI theories. *European Journal of Interdisciplinary Studies*, *2*(2), 104–110.

Dodd, E. M. Jr. (1932). For Whom Are Corporate Managers Trustees? *Harvard Law Review*, *45*(7), 1145–1163. doi:10.2307/1331697

Dorey, D. J. (2011). The Transparent Supply Chain: From Resistance to Implementation at Nike and Levi-Strauss. *Journal of Business Ethics*, *103*(4), 587–603. doi:10.1007/s10551-011-0882-1

Dunning, J. H. (1977). Trade, location of economic activity and the MNE: A search for an eclectic approach. In B. Ohlin, P. O. Hesselborn, & P. M. Wijkman (Eds.), *The international allocation of economic activity* (pp. 395–418). London: Macmillan. doi:10.1007/978-1-349-03196-2_38

Dunning, J. H. (2001). The eclectic (OLI) paradigm of international production: Past, present and future. *International Journal of the Economics of Business*, *8*(2), 173–190. doi:10.1080/13571510110051441

Epstein, E. M. (2007). The Good Company. Rhetoric or Reality? Corporate Social Responsibility and Business Ethics Redux. *American Business Law Journal*, *44*(2), 207–222. doi:10.1111/j.1744-1714.2007.00035.x

European Commission. (2011). *A renewed EU strategy 2011-14 for Corporate Social Responsibility*. Brussels: European Commission.

EY. (2016). *Corporate misconduct. Individual consequences. 14th Global Fraud Survey*. London: EYGM Limited.

Friedman, M. (1970, September 13). The Social Responsibility of Business is to Increase its Profits. *The New York Times Magazine*.

Goh, S. K., & Wong, K. N. (2011). Malaysias outward FDI: The effects of market size and government policy. *Journal of Policy Modeling*, *33*(3), 497–510. doi:10.1016/j.jpolmod.2010.12.008

Hasegawa, H., & Noonha, C. (Eds.). (2014). *Asian Business and Management. Theory, Practice and Perspectives* (2nd ed.). London: Palgrave Macmillen.

Hennchen, E. (2015). Royal Dutch Shell in Nigeria: Where Do Responsibilities End? *Journal of Business Ethics*, *129*(1), 1–25. doi:10.1007/s10551-014-2142-7

Huang, H., & Zhao, Z. (2016). The influence of political connection on corporate social responsibility - evidence from Listed private companies in China. *International Journal of Corporate Social Responsibility*, *1*(9), 1–19.

Huang, X., & Zhu, Y. (2016). *Managing Chinese Outward Foreign Direct Investment: From Entry Strategy to Sustainable Development in Australia*. London: Palgrave Macmillan UK. doi:10.1057/9781137394606

Human Rights Watch. (2016). *Make Rules on Rights Binding for Businesses. ILO Should Create Treaty to Protect Workers.* Retrieved July 12, 2016 from https://www.hrw.org/news/2016/05/30/make-rules-rights-binding-businesses

International Labor Organization. (2015). *World Employement Social Outlook. The Changing Nature of Jobs*. Geneva: International Labour Office.

International Monetary Fund. (2016). *Corruption: Cost and Mitigating Strategies*. Washington, DC: International Monetary Fund.

International Trade Union Confederation (2016). *Scandal Inside the Global Supply Chains of 50 Top Companies. Frontlines Report 2016.* Brussels: International Trade Union Confederation.

Ioannou, I., & Serafeim, G. (2014). *The Consequences of Mandatory Corporate Sustainability Reporting: Evidence from Four Countries*. Harvard Business School, Working Paper, 11-100, August 20, 2014. Retrieved July 12, 2016 from http://www.hbs.edu/faculty/Publication%20Files/11-100_7f383b79-8dad-462d-90df-324e298acb49.pdf

Kalotay, K., & Sulstarova, A. (2010). Modelling Russian outward FDI. *Journal of International Management*, *2*(16), 131–142. doi:10.1016/j.intman.2010.03.004

Kang, Y., & Jiang, F. (2012). FDI location choice of Chinese multinationals in East and Southeast Asia: Traditional economic factors and institutional perspective. *Journal of World Business*, *47*(1), 45–53. doi:10.1016/j.jwb.2010.10.019

Knoerich, J. (2012) *The development dimension of outward foreign direct investment*. The Third Copenhagen Conference on Emerging Multinationals: OFDI from Emerging Economies, 25-26 October 2012, Copenhagen Business School, Denmark.

KPMG. (2013). *The KPMG Survey of Corporate Responsibility Reporting 2013*. Retrieved July 12, 2016 from https://www.kpmg.com/Global/en/IssuesAndInsights/ArticlesPublications/corporate-responsibility/Documents/corporate-responsibility-reporting-survey-2013-exec-summary.pdf

KPMG. (2014). *Breaking Through - How Corporate Social Innovation Creates Business Opportunity.* Retrieved July 12, 2016 from http://www.kpmg.com/Ca/en/IssuesAndInsights/ArticlesPublications/Documents/5441-KPMG-Social-Innovation-Report-FY14-web-Final.pdf

Kurucz, E., Colbert, B., & Wheeler, D. (2008). The business case for corporate social responsibility. In A. Crane, A. McWilliams, D. Matten, J. Moon, & D. Siegel (Eds.), *The Oxford handbook of corporate social responsibility* (pp. 83–112). Oxford, UK: Oxford University Press.

Lentner, C., Szegedi, K., & Tatay, T. (2015). Corporate Social Responsibility in the Banking Sector. *Public Finance Quarterly*, *2015*(1), 95–103.

Li, D. (2015). *The compressed development of Chinese OFDI and its impact on Chinese government investment policies*. Retrieved July 12, 2016 from http://www.victoria.ac.nz/chinaresearchcentre/publications/papers/The-Compressed-Development-of-Chinese-OFDI.pdf

Mélypataki, G. & Szegedi, K. (in press). A vállalati társadalmi felelősségvállalás (CSR) és a jog kapcsolata. *Miskolci Jogi Szemle*. XI. évfolyam 2016 1. szám.

MOL Group. (2016). *About MOL Group*. Retrieved October 13, 2016 from https://molgroup.info/en/about-mol-group

OECD. (2015a). *OECD Factbook 2015-2016 Economic, Environmental and Social Statistics*. Paris: OECD Publishing.

OECD. (2015b). *OECD Foreign Bribery Report: An Analysis of the Crime of Bribery of a Foreign Official*. Paris: Holman Fenwick Willan LLP.

Peng, M. W., Wang, D. Y. L., & Jiang, Y. (2008). An institution-based view of international business strategy: A focus on emerging economies. *Journal of International Business Studies*, *39*(5), 920–936. doi:10.1057/palgrave.jibs.8400377

Piskalski, G. (2015): Corporate Social Responsibility in the Polish Reality. Theory and Practice. Warsaw: CentrumCSR.PL Foundation

Publica, P. (2008). *The World Wide Web of Siemens's Corruption*. Retrieved July 12, 2016 from https://www.propublica.org/special/the-world-wide-web-of-siemenss-corruption

Rangan, V. K., Chase, L., & Karim, S. (2015). The Truth About CSR. *Harvard Business Review*, (January–February): 40–49.

Soltani, B. (2014). The Anatomy of Corporate Fraud: A Comparative Analysis of High Profile American and European Corporate Scandals. *Journal of Business Ethics*, *120*(2), 251–274. doi:10.1007/s10551-013-1660-z

Stoian, C. (2013). Extending Dunnings Investment Development Path: The role of home country institutional determinants in explaining outward foreign direct investment. *International Business Review*, *22*(3), 615–637. doi:10.1016/j.ibusrev.2012.09.003

Surroca, J., Tribó, J. A., & Zahra, S. A. (2013). Stakeholder Pressure On MNEs and the Transfer of Socially Irresponsible Practices to Subsidiaries. *Academy of Management Journal*, *56*(2), 549–572. doi:10.5465/amj.2010.0962

Sustainable Development Knowledge Platform. (2015). *Sustainable Development Goals*. Retrieved July 12, 2016 from https://sustainabledevelopment.un.org/sdgs

Svetlicic, M. (2004). Transition economies multinationals – are they different from Third World multinationals? In C. Chakraborty (Ed.), *Proceedings of the 8th International Conference on Global Business and Economic Development*. Montclair State University.

Szegedi, K. (2010). The Concept and Development Tendencies of Corporate Social Responsibility. *Club of Economics in Miskolc. TMP*, *5*, 67–74.

Szegedi, K., Fülöp, G., & Bereczk, Á. (2016). Relationships between Social Entrepreneurship, CSR and Social Innovation. *Theory and Practice. World Academy of Science, Engineering and Technology International Journal of Social, Behavioral, Educational, Economic. Business and Industrial Engineering, 10*(5), 1470–1475.

The Wall Street Journal. (2010). *Panalpina Settlements Announced, With $236.5 Million in Penalties.* Retrieved July 12, 2016 from http://blogs.wsj.com/corruption-currents/2010/11/04/panalpina-settlements-announced-with-2365-million-in-penalties/

The World Bank. (1997). *Helping Countries Combat Corruption. The Role of the World Bank.* Washington, DC: World Bank Group.

Timokhina, O. (2014). *Chinese foreign direct investment in Africa in corporate social responsibility context.* Maastricht School of Management, Working Paper No.2014/29. Retrieved July 12, 2016 from http://www.msm.nl/resources/uploads/2014/09/MSM-WP2014-29.pdf

Transparency International. (2015a). *What is Corruption?* Retrieved July 12, 2016 from http://www.transparency.org/what-is-corruption/#define

Transparency International. (2015b). *Corruption Perception Index 2015.* Retrieved July 12, 2016 from http://www.transparency.org/cpi2015#downloads

Transparency International. (2015c). *Exporting Corruption. Assessing Enforcement of the OECD convention on Combating Foreign Bribery.* Retrieved July 12, 2016 from http://www.transparency.org/exporting_corruption

Transparency International. (2016). *Emerging market companies show low levels of transparency, allowing corruption to thrive.* Retrieved October 13, 2016 from http://www.transparency.org/news/pressrelease/emerging_market_companies_show_low_levels_of_transparency_allowing_corrupti

UNEP Finance Initiative. (2015). *UNEP FI Membership around the world.* Retrieved August 28, 2015 http://www.unepfi.org/signatories/?tx_phpadd_pi1[sortby]=country

United Nations Conference on Trade and Development. (2012). *World Investment Report. Towards a New Generation of Investment Policies.* New York: United Nations.

United Nations Conference on Trade and Development. (2015). *World Investment Report. Reforming International Investment Governance.* New York: United Nations.

United Nations General Assembly. (1948). *The Universal Declaration of Human Rights.* Paris: United Nations General Assembly.

United Nations Global Compact. (2013). *Global Corporate Sustainability Report.* New York: United Nations Global Compact Office.

United Nations Global Compact. (2015a). *A Guide for Business How to Develop a Human Rights Policy* (2nd ed.). New York: United Nations Global Compact Office.

United Nations Global Compact. (2015b). *Our Participants.* Retrieved August 28, 2015 from https://www.unglobalcompact.org/what-is-gc/participants

United Nations Human Rights Office of the High Commissioner. (2011). *Guiding Principles on Business and Human Rights. Implementing the United Nations „Protect, Respect and Remedy" Framework.* New York: United Nations Human Rights Office of the High Commissioner.

United Nations Human Rights Office of the High Commissioner. (2016). *What are human rights?* Retrieved July 12, 2016 from http://www.ohchr.org/EN/Issues/Pages/WhatareHumanRights.aspx

Vermander, B. (2014): The Development of CSR in China. In The American Chamber of Commerce (Ed.), Shanghai Corporate Social Responsibility Ten Years Report 2004-2014. The American Chamber of Commerce.

Vigeo. (2015). *Paying the Penalty: The Cost of CSR Misconduct.* Paris: Vigeo. Retrieved July 12, 2016 from http://www.vigeo.com/csr-rating-agency/images/stories/formulaires/2015_05_Related_Sanctions_version_finale_ENG.pdf

Watts, P., & Holme, L. (2000). *Meeting changing expectations. Corporate Social responsibility.* World Business Council for Sustainable Development.

Williamson, N., Stampe-Knippel, A., & Weber, T. (2014). *Corporate Social Responsibility National Public Policies in the European Union.*Luxembourg: Publications Office of the European Union.

World Commission on Environment and Development. (1987). *Our Common Future.* Oxford, UK: Oxford University Press.

World Economic Forum. (2014). *White Paper on Business Sustainability: What it is and why it matters.* Geneva: World Economic Forum.

World Economic Forum. (2015). *Building Foundations Against Corruption. Recommendations on Anti-Corruption in the Infrastructure & Urban Development Industries.* Geneva: World Economic Forum.

World Economic Forum. (2016). *The Global Risks Report 2016* (11th ed.). Geneva: World Economic Forum.

KEY TERMS AND DEFINITIONS

Corporate Social Responsibility: A business model for interests beyond profit that takes the legitimate needs of stakeholders into consideration.

Corporate Sustainability: A business model based on the balance of economic, environmental and social factors.

Corruption: Abuse of power for personal gain.

Human Rights: Inalienable fundamental rights to which every person is entitled.

Outward Foreign Direct Investment: Direct investments of companies in a foreign country.

Responsible Supply Chain: A network ensuring ethical and responsible conduct throughout the entire value chain.

Stakeholder: An individual or group influencing or being influenced by a company.

Sustainable Development: A lifestyle taking into account the needs of future generations.

Chapter 3
Dilemmas on OFDI Measuring and Interpreting:
The Case of Poland

Agnieszka Kłysik-Uryszek
University of Lodz, Poland

Anetta Kuna-Marszałek
University of Lodz, Poland

ABSTRACT

Foreign direct investments (FDI) seem to have been thoroughly studied in specialised literature. However the scope of available statistical data often significantly hampers or even prevents any in-depth analysis of the phenomenon. The dynamic economic processes lead to the formation of new linkages, new organisational solutions in international enterprises that co-exist with well described and recognised forms of FDI but escape proper monitoring of statistical institutions. The chapter discusses the different concepts of measuring and interpreting FDI to provide researchers helpful guidelines how to deal with the problems of different methodological dilemmas. A main conclusion is that data provided by official statistics are insufficient and incoherent, and analysis of the scale of OFDI engagement of enterprises (especially from emerging countries) carries some risk and its results should be approached with caution. The case study of Poland's statistics has been used to portray the most significant discrepancies and problems.

INTRODUCTION

Foreign direct investment plays crucial role in contemporary economy; however, despite abundant theoretical and empirical writings on the subject many issues have still remained unclear or unclassified. Additionally, rapidly changing economic reality generates new business relationships in connection with international capital flows. These new flows not always fit already existing FDI classification framework and thus cannot be reflected in theoretical considerations. Yet, they take place at significant scale and should be explored when it comes to their motives and economic effects. Hence, attention needs to be paid to indicators that measure and evaluate contemporary FDI.

DOI: 10.4018/978-1-5225-2345-1.ch003

Methodological difficulties connected with FDI analysis can be divided into two groups: statistical and formal. The first ones refer to inconsistencies between available statistical data (at national and international levels) and classifications described in official documents of international organisations (OECD, World Bank, UNCTAD, IMF) and in specialised literature, which provide the basis for analysing motives and assessing effects of investment. Despite many publications that offer detailed description and categories of international flows of capital (OECD 1999, OECD 2005, IMF 2004), national and international statistics often prevent any precise analysis of the phenomena due to over-aggregation of indicators or interpretation discrepancies.

Second group of difficulties results from the absence of theoretical considerations and in-depth cognitive surveys of different types of FDI (especially non-manufacturing ones). Numerous theoretical concepts that discuss FDI at micro scale focus predominantly on relocation of industrial operations and leave services, support to export or financial sector out. The main research problem concerns the interpretation of financial flows, which account for a growing share of FDI flows. And it is not just about establishing special purpose entities abroad to achieve tax optimisation but also about large scale investments made by investment funds (i.e. M&A). On top of that, balance of payments-based macroeconomic statistics classify as FDIs not only primary investment (in foreign affiliate equity and reinvested profit) but also intra-corporate loans used to support related companies. These FDIs are also out of the mainstream of theoretical considerations but they significantly impact overall FDI amount (in particular OFDI from countries such as Poland) and investment position of countries.

The goal of the chapter is to put in order all FDI-related lack of clarity at micro and macro levels; it also draws attention to serious inconsistencies between theoretical considerations that explain FDI specificity and the reality revealed by available statistical data.

The chapter is composed of the following parts: the Background gives a general outlook at selected methodological problems connected with FDI analysis. It identifies difficulties and discrepancies in definitions, collection and presentation of statistical data, as well as main problems of how theoretical concepts of FDI (motives, investment modes and effects) translate into real position of investors and countries.

Main focus of the chapter has been laid on the exemplification of the above mentioned problems and inconsistencies using the case of OFDI from Poland. The authors provide a general outlook at the available sources of data and discuss individual challenges faced by researchers who wish to explore reasons and effects of Poland's OFDI. Then, propose solutions and recommendations, as well as future research directions. Main findings are summarized in Conclusions.

BACKGROUND

FDI is an important category in international accounts, and one of the five functional categories used as the primary basis for classifying data on financial transactions, positions, and income (Kozlow 2011, p. 27). Unfortunately, the quality of FDI data remains unsatisfactory and apparently the collection of high quality data on inward and outward FDI is a challenge to statisticians and researchers, which has been raised as an issue since the 1990s (Cantwell 1992). The problem becomes particularly clear when we compare FDI in international and national economic accounts. The lack of reliable statistical information and inconsistency in data collection and reporting methods of many countries complicate studies and make impact assessment difficult. Besides, it limits the ability of policymakers to formulate appropriate

Table 1. Imbalance between global (world) FDI inflows and outflows, 2010-2015 (millions of USD)

Year	FDI Inflows	FDI Outflows	FDI Inflows - FDI Outflows
2010	1 388 821	1 391 918	-3 097
2011	1 566 839	1 557 640	9 199
2012	1 510 918	1 308 820	202 098
2013	1 427 181	1 310 618	116 563
2014	1 276 999	1 318 470	-41 471
2015	1 762 155	1 474 242	287 913

UNCTAD, WIR 2016, p. 196.

FDI policies and strategies (Fujita 2008, p. 108). Timely and reliable statistics are the key if they are to be used as tools by decision makers and potential investors.

For example, in principle inward FDI and outward FDI across the world should balance. However, due to differences in the interpretation of FDI definition, various ways of calculating and the compilation and reporting of statistics, they rarely do (Table 1). Lack of balance between global inward FDI (IFDI) and outward FDI (OFDI) flows is also due to the so called "capital in transit", treated as a separate category by very few countries, which does not improve the transparency of generally available statistics.

Many studies highlight the "problem of limited generalizability due to the idiosyncratic and country-specific nature of the subject" (Bellak 1998, p. 253).

At microeconomic level FDI analysis relates to the theory of international manufacturing and it focuses on the investing enterprise. FDIs are undertaken in order to conduct a long-term control over an enterprise located abroad. This "lasting interest" is usually defined as direct or indirect ownership of equity that entitles it to the minimum of 10% voting rights (i.e. of ordinary or voting shares) in the direct investment enterprise.

Investors may create independent economic entities from scratch (*greenfield* investments) or by taking over the control of an already existing enterprise (*cross-border acquisitions and mergers)*[1]. Sometimes *joint-ventures*, where the new entity is created together with a national partner may be isolated out of a *greenfield* investments. Among the acquisitions there are *brownfield* investments. Their aim is to modernize and restructure an acquired enterprise into a competitive entity through its development, replacement of equipment and technology and often also human resources and assortment. In transformation economies, including Poland, *brownfield* investments are most often connected with the privatization of state enterprises.

Referring to main definitions, FDI capital flows are made up of three basic components: (Navaretii, Venables 2004, p. 285):

1. Equity capital, which comprises equity in branches, all shares in subsidiaries and associates (except non-participating, preferred shares that are treated as debt securities and are included under other direct investment capital) and other capital contributions such as provisions of machinery, etc.;
2. Reinvested earnings consisting of the direct investor's share (in proportion to direct equity participation) of earnings, no distributed, as dividends by subsidiaries or associates and earnings of branches not remitted to the direct investor;

3. Other direct investment capital or intercompany debt transactions, meaning capital involved in debt-generating transactions within a multinational corporation; these are debt securities and trade loans between parent company and its foreign affiliate. It should be stressed that need to stress that these long-term loans may be provided at lower than current market rates.

However, in many cases non-financial involvement (such as participation in management process, membership in advisory board, technical, know-how or organizational support) is decisive for the effects and success of an investment. Unfortunately, while financial engagement of an investor in a foreign entity is quantifiable and, to a certain extent, reflected in national and international statistics, there are no statistics or measures that would describe other (non-financial) engagement of an investor (although theoretically, e.g., the value of available technology or know-how could be calculated).

At macroeconomic scale FDIs are one among types of international capital flows and belong to the balance of payments. Earnings on FDI are often a major component of property income from abroad in the distribution of income accounts. FDI stocks are reflected in current and financial accounts. In the first case they include income of foreign direct investors that can be divided into income from shares in corporate equity and income from other debts. FDI on financial account comprises: capital inflows from cash purchases of shares and stock, in-kind capital, injections of capital, reinvested profits and the balance of other receivables and liabilities (Golejowska 2008, p. 13). There are various ways in which countries collect and process statistical data pertaining to FDI flow and stock. The most important of them include: 1) international transactions reporting system (ITRS) that uses records of bank transactions of foreign economic operators – most often used by central financial institutions (e.g. central banks) to produce the statistics of the balance of payments, 2) enterprise surveys, most often deployed by central statistical offices, and 3) administrative sources such as investment promotion agencies, tax revenue offices, security exchange offices.

Incompatibility of presented data is, unfortunately, the main obstacle. With respect to FDI value, the fullest picture can be obtained from balance of payments statistics as they include all transactions within a given economy. However, the level of aggregation (adequate for data in the balance of payment) totally ignores data relating to decisions and outcomes of investments made by individual enterprises, the element highlighted in data from enterprise surveys. Other sources of data cannot be unambiguously classified and they usually limit themselves to, e.g., data on the biggest investments made in cooperation with a particular entity (promotion agencies). Additional research problem may also consist in lack of access to specific data (e.g. originating from tax agencies) – some institutions that do not manage statistical data but have access to them within the scope of their operations, do not present data in collective reports and do not make them available to external entities even upon special request.

To sum up, a number of difficulties associated with measuring FDI could be indicated. The most relevant of them include (Bürgi-Schmelz et al. 2010, p. 7; Kozlow 2011, p. 31)

1. Identifying the units that meet the definition of a direct investor, direct investment enterprise, and fellow enterprise;
2. Differences in the level of consolidation between business registers, particularly where different registers are used in international and national accounts. It often happens when separate agencies are responsible for compiling data. For example, for national accounts, countries often include each individual enterprise into national registers, while for international economic accounts countries often consolidate domestic units that are under common control for statistical purposes. That may

produce inconsistencies in how direct investors, direct investment enterprises and fellow enterprises are classified by industry sector in national and international economic accounts;
3. Conducting a survey, in which respondents provide data according to the concepts used in direct investment;
4. Ensuring that direct investment equity position data reported by the direct investor are based on information from the books of the direct investment enterprise abroad. In other words, information on equity holdings is often not recorded on the same basis by the direct investor and its direct investment enterprise;
5. Estimating reinvested earnings of direct investment enterprises, especially on a timely quarterly basis. On many occasions, information on reinvested earnings is available only after a very long delay, and then sometimes only for annual data.

Despite attempts to master statistical systems on FDI they are still full of gaps and their quality is questioned by many researchers. According to Bellak (1998), international standards are often either neglected by those who collect data on FDI or they are too complex to fulfil. Harmonisation of various FDI-related definitions and statistical systems for collection and presentation of FDI data is going on. The same can be said about what international corporations are doing but important discrepancies remain, even among developed countries (Fujita 2008, p. 108). Measuring FDI is a difficult task especially in transition economies. These difficulties are also reinforced by the transformation of statistical systems (von Westernhagen 2002, p. 208).

According to UNCTAD (2006), in some developing and transitional economies additional difficulties emerge. Much FDI are transactions referred to as "round tripping". They consist in capital exports by domestic agents and their return as FDI, which results from, e.g., bureaucratic and tax difficulties faced by enterprises in their home countries. Investment abroad gives them some freedom to continue investing domestically or abroad. The practice is the result of financial incentives intended exclusively to foreign investors, lack of effectively operating institutions that could intermediate the funds domestically and better protect ownership rights abroad. "Round-tripping" is quite a widespread phenomenon (Borga 2016), it can be witnessed, e.g., in China (Geng 2004; Garcia-Herrero, Xia, Casanova 2015) or Russia (Ledyaeva, Karhunen, Whalley 2013).

SELECTED "ORGANIZATIONAL" ISSUES

Although FDI account for a large portion of international investment, not all investments are really "direct". Hence, to analyse it, we first of all need to study types of transactions and entities that conclude them. Against this background, identification of investor's motivation is also important as that is the initial criterion that distinguishes direct investment from other types of international investment (e.g. portfolio investment). As it has been already mentioned, FDI include both initial transactions between two operators and any later capital transactions between them and related companies, whether they are legal persons or not.

Sometimes enterprises from different countries establish relations that carry some FDI characteristics, even when formally they are not related (two enterprises in two different countries that have the same Management Board, units responsible for the strategy and joint funds but none has got the minimum 10% share in the other). Under such circumstances enterprises are tied not with any direct investment but rather with broadly understood capital links. In some countries FDI statistics cover just loan-based relationships between a parent and a daughter company while in other all links among entities within a capital group. On the international scale this problem had been discussed and solved in Benchmark Definition of Foreign Direct Investment 4th ed. (OECD 2008), but the guidelines have not been implemented into all the national statistics yet.

Nonetheless, at this point attention should be paid to general FDI breakdown on organisational side. An enterprise Embarking on FDI may hold shares abroad in:

- Independent economic operators (legal entities) as
  - Subsidiary companies with more than 50% of investor's share in equity capital,
  - Associate companies with up to 50% (but more than 10%) of investor's share in equity capital,
- Operators who formally belong to the investor (i.e. without legal personality) as
  - **Branches:** Units authorised to conduct the same activities as the parent company,
  - **Representations:** Unit whose responsibilities are limited to representation, promotion, marketing and trade activities performed for the parent company.

Sometimes FDI may be a simple and straightforward structure but it may also be a maze of very complex relationships. In accordance with international standards, statistics on outgoing and incoming direct investment should cover all enterprises owned directly and indirectly, with and without legal person that meet certain criteria (i.e. all dependent and related companies, as well as their affiliates). Full scope of direct investment relations allows to use the so called „*Fully Consolidated System*" (FCS) recommended by international organisations (e.g. OECD, IMF, and UNCTAD). This subject has been extensively discussed in literature (OECD 2005, IMF BOPCOM-04/32). Examples of its practical applications are presented in Fig. 1.

Figure 1. Application of the Fully Consolidated System
OECD 2005, p. 52.

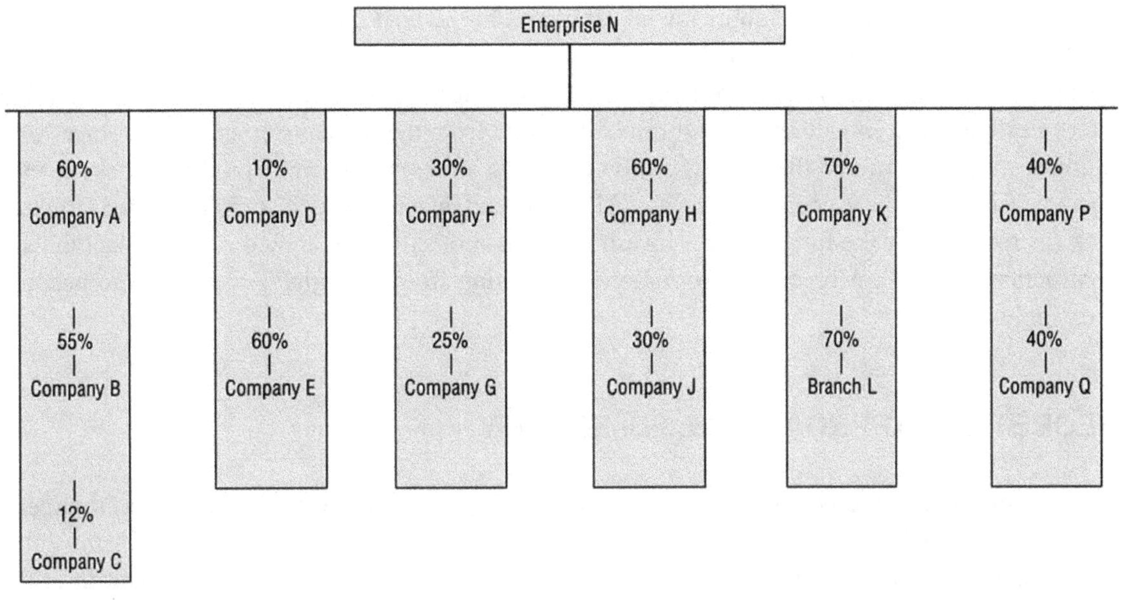

According to the FCS the example presented in Figure 1 could be analysed as follows (OECD 2005, pp. 51-52):

- Company A is a subsidiary of N. Company B is a subsidiary of A and thus a subsidiary of N even though only 33% of B is indirectly attributable to N.
- Company C is an associate of B and, through the chain of subsidiaries A and B, of N as well, even though only 4%of C is indirectly attributable to N.
- Company D is an associate of N, Company E is a subsidiary of D and thus an associate of N even though only 6% of E is indirectly attributable to N.
- Company F is an associate of N and G is an associate of F, but G is not an associate of N.
- Company H is a subsidiary of N and Company J is an associate of H and thus an associate of N.
- Company K is a subsidiary of N and L is a branch of K and thus of N.
- Company P is an associate of N and Q is an associate of P, but Q is not an associate of N.

The above analysis shows that FCS-based FDI statistics would cover enterprises A, B, C, D, E, F, H, J, K, L and P but would exclude G and Q. The method is neither easy for researchers (Gregorová 2005) nor is it free of disadvantages (IMF 2004), however, it is often recommended in practice to identify an indirectly owned direct investment relationship. As an alternative, the "*US Method*" (USM) could be used. The USM excludes (the FCS may include) foreign enterprises in which the direct investor has less than a 10% equity interest but it includes (and the FCS excludes) associates of associates in which the direct investor has 10% or more equity interest. In the example in Figure 1 the USM would exclude companies C and E but include Q.

In this context, the problem of overlapping investment is also very important. If that is enough to have more than 10% of equity capital of an affiliate to establish a FDI relationship, therefore one FDI venture can become a FDI of several direct investors. Thus, firstly we may not unambiguously identify investor's home country, which prevents precise analyses that would consider geographical distribution of FDI (directions of capital flows, motives and effects of investments undertaken by investors from one country in another, etc.); and, secondly, at international scale we will have statistical inconsistencies. Investors declare their affiliated entities while statistics in the host country will show only one entity with the involvement of foreign capital.

The above described problems are largely true of transition economies (including the Central and Eastern Europe countries) although most direct investors from these countries are at first stages of active internationalisation and they develop little extensive structures where capital relations are easily detectable. However, these countries also host MNE-dependent entities with complex capital structures, which (as residents) make further direct investment (chain ones). Thus, they directly impact the scale and structure of OFDI. Moreover, corporations originating from emerging economies are becoming increasingly stronger.

THEORETICAL APPROACH VS. FDI REALITY

Relocation of economic activities (i.e. FDI) is economically justified as the market experiences numerous distortions, such as (Witkowska 1996, p. 37): market imbalances, distortions generated by government and international institutions, imperfect market structure and market inefficiencies that perpetuate differences in availability (and prices) of production factors at international level. That is why rationally operating enterprises decide to engage in foreign direct investment in order to discount potential benefits of having a network of enterprises or affiliates in various market and business environments and to optimise the performance. Improved efficiency, the fundamental goal of foreign investment, may be achieved, inter alia, by reducing the costs of manufacturing and distribution, expansion of the scope of operation (increased sales), risk reduction through geographic and sectoral diversification of activities. Literature identifies two main types of foreign direct investment, depending on global strategy of a given enterprise:

- Vertical investment,
- Horizontal investment.

They have been distinguished based on empirical observations and theoretical studies. The starting point comes from theories of multinational enterprise and foreign direct investment[2] initially based on neoclassical assumptions and then on the assumptions of new trade theory[3]. Unfortunately, despite extensive theoretical writings on potential consequences of specific types of investment, we have no indications as to how allocate investments to specific types. Ability to precisely examine vertical and horizontal FDI relations could importantly help to identify relationships between FDI and trade, crucial for wider studies of economic growth. It is even more important because vertical and horizontal investments produce different effects not only in host countries but also in home economies. Vertical investment generates international trade flows between the parent company (or at least related companies) and a foreign entity. Under favourable circumstances, it may not just prevent the reduction of capacity output and employment in the home country (caused by capital exports) but stimulate increased production of goods that are further used as components in the production of a foreign affiliate. Similar scenario may develop when an investor establishes a representative office abroad to assist export.

Totally new effects can be produced by horizontal investment intended to substitute export. The situation is much less favourable for investor's economy as it limits production in the home country and may reduce employment and income. M&A in new sectors of economy undertaken to diversify risk have relatively the least impact upon the home economy. Such foreign investments can be treated as lost investment opportunities at home.

Obviously, it should be stressed that the problem consists not only in developing appropriate measures to identify production relations between an investor and a foreign entity (where the scale of vertical trade relations between the parent company and related companies within capital group can be used as an approximant) but also in the difficulty to identify dominant nature of a concrete investment. In practice, extensive production structures of MNEs unable simple classification of performed on operations they actually pursue.

Investments made by investment funds pose another interpretation problem in particular in the context of FDI analysis as a type of international production pattern. These funds often acquire enterprises operating at international level and as such they count as FDI flows. However, their motives and, first of all, investment directions go beyond FDI concepts that can be found in literature. Their actions more often coincide with conclusions of portfolio investment theory. Similar things can be said about big financial holdings – their investments, although often classified as FDI (since they exceed the 10% threshold), result from macroeconomic mechanisms of the financial market rather than from production location abroad.

A relatively new phenomenon in MNEs growth is the expansion of organisational structure with geographically dispersed special purpose entities. Usually they are established to optimise financial effect of assets management (e.g. when a given economy offers favourable tax arrangements connected with a particular business profile), tax optimisation or, e.g., seeking financial resources in international markets (e.g. stock issued in international stock exchanges). Such operations are especially easy within integration groupings where there are no legal limitations in establishing a new entity abroad or where difficulties are reduced to minimum. At theoretical level, such operations can be attributed to "efficiency seeking" motivation, however, they are hard to explain with international production concepts or models of stage or network internationalisation.

Deepened analyses of investment operations are seriously impeded by chain investment made by MNEs' affiliates, which are formally residents of a given economy. Their investment operations result from decisions, resources and competitive advantages of the corporation, not just the affiliate based in a given economy, which can be analysed in the light of internationalisation of enterprises. Yet, these operations hinder the life of researchers who explore investment operations of companies from transition economies. Their investments are often much bigger and more "advanced" than it would be expected from economic development of the home economy. Thus, by trying to anchor the analysis in macroeconomic FDI concepts (models of Ozawa, Investment Development Path by J.H. Dunning or even R. Vernon's international product life cycle) we may draw erroneous conclusions as to the general level (stage) of economic development and advantages of an economy.

METHODOLOGICAL PROBLEMS OF OFDI STUDIES IN POLAND

Despite increasing interest in Poland's OFDI, access to complete and reliable statistical data about companies engaged in internationalisation is very limited. Analysis of the methodology used to collect and process published data calls for a cautious assessment of reality. It is not possible to directly compare data in available statistical sources.

Data on foreign direct investments undertaken by Polish enterprises under the Polish reporting system come, in principle, from two sources: the National Bank of Poland (NBP) and the Central Statistical Office of Poland (GUS). General comparison of the data provided by the two is presented in Table 2. All international sources, such as Eurostat, IMF, UNCTAD, OECD use data supplied by the Polish reporting system, i.e., effectively by NBP and GUS.

NBP data – due to the specificity of how data are collected from the balance of payments statistics – give information about the values of all financial flows (i.e. initial equity investment, intra-group loans, reinvested profits and other income of direct investors) broken down by geographic regions, industries and sectors. Moreover, they provide both stock values and yearly flows. Nevertheless, we should be careful when combining these values as the sum of flows in subsequent years does not add up to the overall stock value. It connects, inter alia, with the present market evaluation of assets held by Polish investors and the changing exchange rate.

The second source of information, not necessarily about FDI but about investors with holdings in foreign entities, is periodical publications of the Central Statistical Office of Poland. These data are collected and made available since 2009. They come from annual statements of economic operators that must be submitted by all operators active in Poland. This method of data collection helps to analyse the effects of foreign subsidiaries' operations (employment, revenue from sales, foreign trade, including trade with related operators within capital group). However, they do not provide any information about the value of investments (neither about the initial investment nor later capital flows between the parent company and its related entities). We also need to bear in mind that GUS is not able to require statistical data from companies who do not comply with the reporting requirement and it cannot verify the accuracy of provided data. As a result, it has got data concerning companies that voluntarily provided them. Hence, data published in individual years and reports differ and generally may somehow be underestimated. That is due to the unwillingness of economic operators, in particular small ones (to whom the need to fill in long questionnaires means a considerable time burden) to provide data.

Another serious inconsistency in NBP and GUS data, which makes direct comparison of the two sources impossible results from the scope of entities obliged to submit statements. The NBP data include all operators within the national economy while the GUS area of competence excludes the financial sector. Therefore, in order to realise the scale of Poland's OFDI one should rather use NBP data. Figure 2 presents cumulated value of Poland's OFDI. It can be clearly seen that significant intensification of international involvement of enterprises took place after 2004. In the record-breaking 2012 cumulated investment amounted to ca. 12% GDP.

Still, closer analysis of Poland's OFDI shows the need of sceptical/cautious assessment of these significant values. Firstly, subsidiaries and associates of multinational enterprises located in Poland also enjoy resident status in Polish economy. Thus, their investments, which are in fact chain investments, are reflected in NBP and GUS statistics as Poland's OFDI. It may slightly complicate the examination of regulations governing Polish foreign direct investments since not all of these investments result from the competitive merits of affiliates operating in Poland but from ownership advantages and the strategy of the corporation. Hence, they may be independent of the economic development and current economic

Table 2. Comparison of the scope of statistical data on OFDI: GUS and NBP

Measure		GUS	NBP
Value of OFDI (Position)	Of which: • Equity capital investment • Reinvested earnings • Other capital (intracompany loans)	-	+
OFDI yearly outflows		-	+
Data in PLN		+	+
Data in other currencies (USD, EUR)		-	+
No. of investing entities		+	-
No. of foreign affiliates		+	-
Investment directions (countries)		+ (by no. of foreign entities in a given economy)	+ (by amount of capital invested in a given economy)
Type of investment (no. of greenfield investments)		-	-
Investor's share % in equity of a foreign affiliate (without branches and representation offices)		+	-
Revenue in foreign affiliates (including revenue from exports)		+	-
Income from foreign affiliates		-	+
Vertical links with the parent company (trade)		+	-
In-kind outlays on fixed assets in foreign affiliates		+	-

Authors' own compilation.

Figure 2. Poland's OFDI according to NBP (in bln PLN)
Authors' own compilation based on NBP data.

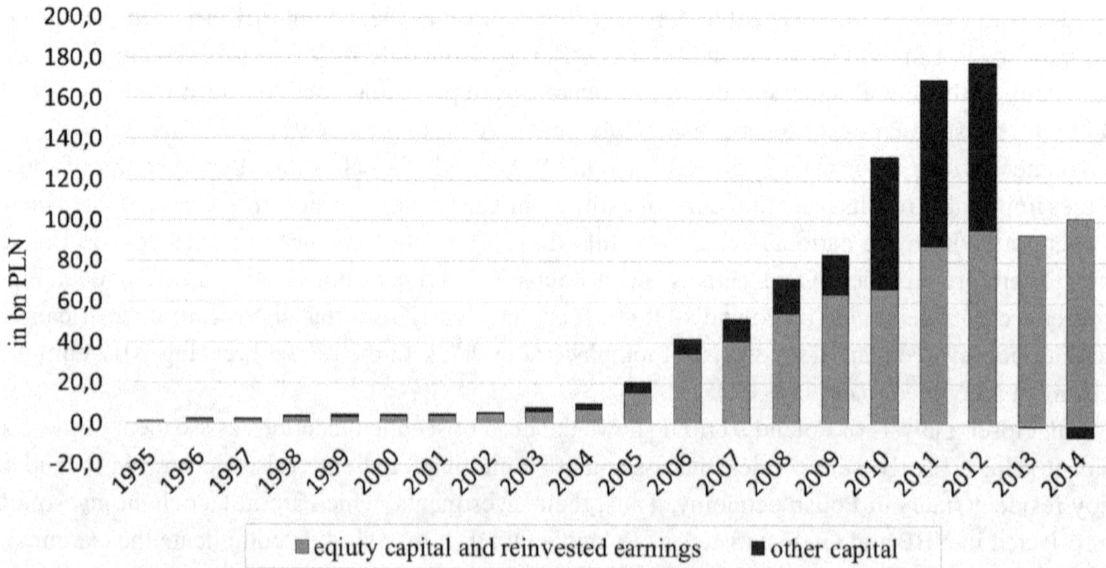

performance of the country. Unfortunately, neither NBP nor GUS give information about the direct scale of engagement of Polish affiliates of multinational corporations in FDI.

Secondly, a large part of OFDI represents „other capital", meaning intra-corporate loans. Studies demonstrate that to a large extent the loans were granted by affiliates of multinational enterprises to parent companies based in Western Europe. In the times of crisis Polish subsidies were the source of capital to the "Western economy".

More attention should be paid to methodological problem with the continuity of data (in data for the years 2010-2012). In 2010 the approach to "other capital" changed and started to include not only net loans granted directly to parent companies but all other forms of support made available to related entities within capital group, i.e. also those where non-resident was a dominant entity. This change produced significant increase in "other capital". Three years later this interpretation was given up and loan-based relationships with non-resident as a dominant party and entities operating within a capital group were transferred to IFDI account. Considerable drop in „other capital" may also be attributed to partial repayment of debt incurred earlier or to big liabilities of Polish companies vis-a-vis their „daughter" companies based abroad through which investors raise capital from bonds issued in the European market (NBP 2016). In connection with this change, NBP made available a new time series reviewed since 2010 in accordance with new guidelines – see Figure 3.

Summing up, while amounts in statistics are significant, most of them are dedicated to support exports, investment in financial sector or chain investment of multinational enterprises (including intra-corporate loans). Therefore, there are many OFDIs but in reality they do not stem from advantages referred to in theoretical FDI concepts.

Comparison of GUS and NBP data in sectoral (Table 3.) and geographical (Table 4.) breakdown provide interesting information about the structure of Poland's OFDI. Of course, different scopes of

Figure 3. Reviewed Poland's OFDI according to NBP
Authors' own compilation based on NBP data.

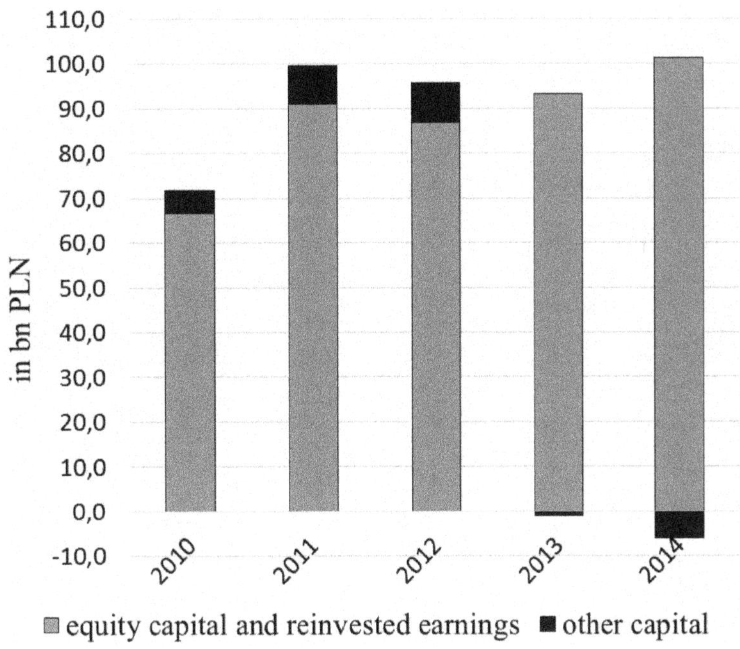

data are very important: GUS provides information about investors' economic activity while NBP gives the value of investment.

The comparison of sectoral OFDI structure applied by GUS and NBP reveals two principal issues. Half of Polish foreign investments are made by operators from the financial sector and thus are completely ignored by GUS. As it has been already mentioned, the mechanism of such investments is totally different than for investments of non-financial sector. Considering general development level of Polish economy and the structure of entities from the financial sector (largely based on foreign capital) one may assume that to a large extent these investments result from decisions of international financial operators (banks, capital or insurance funds). Hence, we should not attach to much importance to this component of Polish foreign investment in the context of macroeconomic assessment of Poland's development (e.g. to calculate NOI indicator in accordance with the concept of IDP J. H. Dunning).

By excluding investments of the financial sector from comparative analysis one should, in principle, bring sectoral investment structure (according to NBP) to the structure of investors and their foreign entities (according to GUS). Relative shares of investments of individual non-financial sectors according to NBP would then be twice as high as those presented in Table 2. Assuming, with some caution, that populations of entities based on which GUS and NBP organised their statistics are similar, one may try to identify how much capital-intensive are investments in individual sectors. For example, manufacturing companies account for 1/3rd of all investors from non-financial sector and they invested ca.30% of total Poland's non-financial OFDI. Entities from mining and extraction sector represented only 0.7% of all investor but value of their investment is almost 10% of all OFDI. That is indicative of high capital-intensity of their ventures. The same can be said about the section "Professional, scientific and technical activities". Operators in this section account for ca. 8% investors but their investments exceed 28% of

Table 3. Sectoral structure of Poland's OFDI in 2014 according to GUS and NBP

	GUS	NBP
Total	1645 Investors	95 237.9 bn PLN
Mining and extraction	0.7%	5.1%
Industrial manufacturing	35.1%	14.1%
Manufacture of food products, beverage and tobacco products	3.3%	1.0%
Manufacture of coke and refined petroleum products	1.8%	2.9%
Manufacture of pharmaceuticals	4.0%	0.9%
Manufacture of metals and fabricated metal products	7.5%	2.4%
Manufacture of electric devices	3.0%	-
Manufacture of cars, trailers and semi-trailers	0.5%	3.4%
Manufacture and distribution of electricity, gas, steam and air	1.0%	-5.4%
Construction	10.8%	-1.0%
Wholesale and retail trade; repair of cars and motorcycles	20.7%	6.5%
Transport and warehousing	3.9%	1.2%
Information and communication	5.5%	-11.0%
Activities connected with production of films, video recording and TV shows, other entertainment activities	-	-4.8%
Telecommunications	-	-7.9%
Finance and insurance	4.5%	50.4%
Operations of financial holdings	-	39.0%
Services to real estate market	3.6%	1.2%
Professional, scientific and technical activities	8.1%	14.4%
Head offices operations	-	9.8%
Management consultancy	-	4.2%
Administration and support services	3.6%	14.1%

Authors' own compilation based on GUS and NBP data.

all Polish non-financial investment. Of course, these conclusions are very general and carry high risk of error. Significant differences in the methodology of data collection do not allow formulating universal conclusions even if the structures are compared.

Analysis of investment directions according to standards applied by GUS and NBP also reveal serious differences. In this case, any comparison is even more difficult as we may not remove the financial sector from the analysis of NBP data because the NBP does not inform where these investments are directed. Based on general knowledge and external data we may expect that large portion of these flow to financial centres in Europe: Luxembourg, Switzerland, and United Kingdom (London). These locations dominate in NBP reports but they are not indicated in GUS statistics.

If we omit investments in countries perceived as financial centres or offering preferential financial terms (e.g., in taxation such as Cyprus), we can clearly see Polish investors' interest focusing mainly on

Table 4. Geographic structure of Poland's OFDI in 2014 according to NBP

	GUS (No. of Foreign Entities)	NBP (Invested Amount)
Total	3,703 entities	95 237.9 (in bn PLN)
Europe	-	**92.4%**
European Union (27 countries)	-	**71.4%**
Euro zone (17 countries)	-	**75.0%**
Cyprus	4.8%	**31.7%**
Luxembourg	1.8%	**26.9%**
Switzerland	1.0%	**12.0%**
the Netherlands	1.9%	**11.1%**
Czech Republic	**7.1%**	6.4%
Slovakia	3.8%	1.0%
Germany	**13.4%**	4.2%
Lithuania	3.1%	3.5%
Hungary	3.3%	1.5%
United Kingdom	2.9%	3.6%
France	2.5%	-1.1%
Romania	4.9%	2.1%
Russian Federation	**7.3%**	2.7%
Ukraine	**9.0%**	0.2%
USA	**2.9%**	**2.3%**
Asia	-	**3.6%**
India	-	1.0%

Authors' own compilation based on GUS and NBP data.

neighbouring countries. They are interested in German, Czech, and Lithuanian markets. Many affiliates have been established also in Ukraine and Russia, however, the value of these investments is small.

To complete the picture, it should be mentioned two more issues that hinder studying investment-related activities of Polish investors based on data originating from GUS and NBP. The first is the problem with access to panel data. Confidentiality of statistical data introduced by virtue of binding legislation in Poland forbids publishing data when aggregated in a way that would enable the identification of data concerning a particular company. In practical terms, it means that the statistical office (GUS) may not make sectoral or sectional data available when there are fewer than 4 entities or when an operator's dominant position is strong enough to determine indicators for all of the group. NBP does not publish any data disaggregated to the level of groups of enterprises. It seriously impedes studying FDI in Poland using econometric methods since to do that, in most cases, we need panel data, and in Poland building such a time series is impossible.

The second problem consists in the absence of possibilities to trace investors' activities in foreign entities. Generally available GUS statistics organise company-related data by investor or foreign entity's PKD (Polish classification of economic activities), however, it is not possible to directly trace whether an investor in his foreign affiliate replicates his principal activities or whether he focuses on other business activities (industries). Thus, one does not know if, e.g., manufacturing companies manufacture the same products in their dependent entities or if they deal with manufacturing at all (or perhaps just trade or act as special purpose vehicles established to acquire additional funds or for tax optimisation purposes).

SOLUTIONS AND RECOMMENDATIONS

Identified inconsistencies and gaps in available statistical data make us approach all results of studies with caution and require good knowledge about the basis on which conclusions have been drawn. The scope of data and potential exclusions may considerably impact the picture. Hence, the attention is to be paid to the methodology of data collecting used in particular studies and avoid direct comparisons.

Dynamically changing international business relations, expanded activities of international corporations, and globalisation favour new organisational and financial solutions between economic operators. Many of them are close to internationalisation, which forces out changes in the approach to definition and classification of FDI, as well as notions used to describe firms involved in direct investment. Theoretical achievements connected with the analysis of the phenomenon should be the closest possible to what actually happens in economy.

Besides, it seems justified to collect data for the same time, i.e. data on business activities in different countries should reflect the situation as at the end of calendar year. Data collected either for the beginning or for the end of fiscal year (which may be different for each country) may impact their comparability at international level. Besides, for many enterprises, information on reinvested earnings is available only after a very long delay and thus early estimates are subject to considerable change when more complete data become available. Uniform time, for which data are collected facilitates comparisons not only at international but also at national level.

It is also important to collect data for the same degree of consolidation of accounts in multinational enterprises (e.g., if in a given country data on the number of dependent entities are collected based on consolidated accounts while other data are taken from non-consolidated accounts we are not able to compare the variable which is subject to analysis) and to distinguish between direct and indirect control. Some countries do not treat all investments on an equal footing that is why we need to harmonise the rules.

It is also worth mentioning that statistical data must be allocated to places where investor's business actually takes place, not to his headquarters (Domański 2002) – but this postulate seems the most difficult to comply with. In most cases it is impossible to unequivocally identify the location where business takes place, especially when we deal with investment in the financial sector.

FUTURE RESEARCH DIRECTIONS

Insufficiencies with respect to the scale and structure of published data on foreign investors' activities seriously hinder (or even prevent) any reliable assessment of investors, as well as the impact of OFDI on both home and host economy. OFDI is important enough for the economy to justify its in-depth studies aimed at developing the best rules of FDI policy. All parties are interested in achieving maximum benefits.

Two main directions of action can be suggested: firstly, we should try to conduct as much research as possible based on available data and try to work out new indicators that would help learn more about the specificity of Poland's OFDI. On top of that, studies could be supported with other research methods, e.g., questionnaire-based studies in enterprises or, to a certain extent only, econometric analysis. (Świerkocki et al. 2015; Kłysik-Uryszek, Kuna- Marszałek 2015, 2016). On the other hand, we should identify gaps in available data to mobilise reporting organisations (GUS and NBP) to go more in-depth in their OFDI related research and to provide increasingly more detailed data. It seems necessary to improve interpretation and classification of terms and to unify the collection and presentation of statistical data by different institutions.

Since most issues discussed in this chapter are universal, it would be advisable to reporting institutions from other countries to expand their statistics to achieve the most complete and coherent internationally available data (from international institutions) and to enable the widest possible international comparative studies.

CONCLUSION

Over twenty five years of economic transformation in Poland, including radical stabilisation, liberalisation and institutional reconstruction, have widened the scope of economic freedom, promulgated private ownership and rationalised economic operations. Foreign direct investments, both IFDI (Kłysik-Uryszek 2010; Świerkocki ed. 2011; Michałek, Brzozowski, Cieślik 2012; Wydmus, Bombińska, Pera 2012), as well as OFDI, especially after EU accession, (Karaszewski ed. 2013, Gorynia, Nowak, Wolniak 2010, Kłysik-Uryszek 2013a, 2013b; Gorynia et al. 2014; Buczkowski et al. 2015) played fundamental role in the process.

However, despite many discussions, interest of international organisations and broad literature concerning FDI, the data provided by official statistics are still insufficient and incoherent. Two sources of data about Poland's OFDI – GUS and NBP provide divergent data about investments and, unfortunately, cannot be freely combined or used in joint studies. Analyses conducted based on NBP data show the value and scale of investments, sectors from which capital has been exported and countries, to which it has flown. GUS, in turn, provides data on investors' activities rather than on the value of investment. However, it should be stressed that GUS data come from statements submitted by companies and data included in them are not verified. Moreover, not all enterprises comply with the reporting requirement thus we may expect that statistics published by GUS are largely underestimated. Analysis of the scale of OFDI engagement of Polish enterprises carries some risk and its results should be approached with caution. On top of that, many aspects relevant from the viewpoint of the specificity of Poland's OFDI are missing from these reports. We mean here types and forms of foreign investments and their importance to parent companies, as well as the scope of ties between investors and MNEs, which may impact the scale of chain investments.

REFERENCES

Bellak, Ch. (1998). The measurement of foreign direct investment: A critical review. *The International Trade Journal*, *12*(2), 227–257. doi:10.1080/08853909808523905

Borga, M. (2016). Not all foreign direct investment is foreign: the extent of round-tripping. *Columbia FDI Perspectives, 172*, 1-3.

Buczkowski, B., Kłysik-Uryszek, A., Kuna-Marszałek, A., & Świerkocki, J. (2015). *Poland,s Outward Foreign Direct Investment. Experiences of enterprises from the Łódź region*. Łódź: Łódź University Press.

Bürgi-Schmelz, A., Kozlow, R., Kitili, A., van Wersch, M., & Joisce, J. (2010). *Recent Progress in Measuring FDI in the Wake of Globalization*. Paper Prepared for the 31st General Conference of The International Association for Research in Income and Wealth, St. Gallen, Switzerland.

Cantwell, J. (1992). The Methodological Problems Raised by the Collection of Foreign Direct Investment Data. *Scandinavian International Business Review, 1*(1), 86–102. doi:10.1016/0962-9262(92)90038-8

Cieślik, A. (2000). *Nowa teoria handlu zagranicznego w świetle badań empirycznych*. Warsaw: PWN.

Cieślik, A. (2005). *Geografia inwestycji zagranicznych, przyczyny i skutki lokalizacji spółek z udziałem kapitału zagranicznego w Polsce*. Warsaw: Wyd. UW.

Fujita, M. (2008). A critical assessment of FDI data and policy implications. *Transnational Corporations, 17*(2), 107–126.

Garcia-Herrero, A., Xia, L., & Casanova, C. (2015). *China's Outbound Foreign Direct Investment: How much goes where after round-tripping and offshoring?* BBVA Research, Working Paper 15/17.

Geng, X. (2004). *Round-Tripping Foreign Direct Investment and the People's Republic of China*. ADB Institute Research Paper Series 58.

Główny Urząd Statystyczny. (2016). *Statistics Database*. Retrieved June 30, 2016, from www.stat.gov.pl

Golejowska, A. (2008). *Bezpośrednie inwestycje zagraniczne a procesy restrukturyzacji gospodarki*. Gdańsk: Wydawnictwo Uniwersytetu Gdańskiego.

Gorynia, M. (Ed.). (2005). *Strategie firm polskich wobec ekspansji inwestorów zagranicznych*. Warsaw: PWE.

Gorynia, M., Nowak, J., Trąpczyński, P., & Wolniak, R. (2014). The internationalization of Polish firms: Evidence from a qualitative study of FDI behaviour. In *Internationalization of Firms from Economies in Transition* (pp. 39–68). Cheltenham, UK: Edward Elgar. doi:10.4337/9781783474707.00009

Gorynia, M., Nowak, J., & Wolniak, R. (2010). Investment Development Paths of Central European Countries: A Comparative Analysis. *Argumenta Oeconomica, 1*, 65–87.

Gregorová, L. (2005). Foreign Direct Investment Statistics in the Czech Republic. Description of system and methodology. Balance of Payments Division. Czech National Bank.

IMF. (2004). *Indirect FDI Relationships and Alternatives to the Fully Consolidated System*. BOP-COM-04/32. IMF.

Karaszewski, W., Jaworek, M., Kuzel, M., Szałucka, M., Szóstek, A., & Kuczmarska, M. (2013). *Aktywność inwestycyjna polskich przedsiębiorstw za granicą. Czynniki i skutki*. Warsaw: PWN.

Kłysik-Uryszek, A. (2010). *Bezpośrednie inwestycje zagraniczne w gospodarce regionu. Teoria i praktyka*. Warsaw: CeDeWu.pl.

Kłysik-Uryszek, A. (2013a). Skala i kierunki polskich bezpośrednich inwestycji zagranicznych. *Journal of Management and Finance*, *11*(1), 293–305.

Kłysik-Uryszek, A. (2013b). Zagraniczna ekspansja kapitałowa polskich przedsiębiorstw. *Journal of Management and Finance*, *11*(2), 161–173.

Kozlow, R. (2011). Multinational enterprises, foreign direct investment and related income flows. In *The Impact of Globalization on National Accounts* (pp. 27–38). New York: United Nations Economic Commission for Europe.

Ledyaeva, S., Karhunen, P., & Whalley, J. (2013). *Foreign Investment Is Not Foreign: Round-Trip Versus Genuine Foreign Investment In Russia*. CEPII Working Paper 2013-05.

Michałek, J. J., Brzozowski, M., & Cieślik, A. (Eds.). (2012). *Wpływ Rozwoju Społecznego na Handel i Inwestycje Zagraniczne*. Warsaw: PWE.

Navaretti, G. B., Venables, A., & Barry, F. (2004). *Multinational Firms in the World Economy*. Princeton, NJ: Princeton University Press.

OECD. (1999). *OECD Benchmark Definition of Foreign Direct Investment* (3rd ed.). OECD.

OECD. (2005). *Podręcznik wskaźników globalizacji ekonomicznej*. OECD.

OECD. (2008). *OECD Benchmark Definition of Foreign Direct Investment* (4th ed.). OECD.

Statystyka bilansu płatniczego. Uwagi metodyczne. (2015). Departament Statystyki NBP. Warsaw.

Świerkocki, J. (Ed.). (2011). *Foreign Direct Investment. The Case of Lodz Region*. Łódź: Łódzkie Towarzystwo Naukowe.

UNCTAD. (2006). *World Investment Report 2006. FDI from Developing and Transition Economies: Implications for Development*. New York: United Nations.

UNCTAD. (2016). World Investment Report. Investor Nationality: Policy Challenges. Geneva: UNCTAD.

von Westernhagen, N. (2002). *Systemic Transformation, Trade and Economic Growth: Developments Theoretical Analysis and Empirical Results*. Berlin: Springer-Verlag. doi:10.1007/978-3-642-57483-2

Witkowska, J. (1996). *Bezpośrednie inwestycje zagraniczne w Europie Środkowowschodniej. Próba interpretacji na gruncie teorii bezpośrednich inwestycji zagranicznych i teorii integracji*. Łódź: Wyd. UŁ.

Wydmus, S., Bombińska, E., & Pera, B. (2012). *Bezpośrednie Inwestycje Zagraniczne a Konkurencyjność Eksportu Polski*. Warsaw: CEDEWU.

KEY TERMS AND DEFINITIONS

Balance of Payments (BoP): A statement that summarizes all economic transactions between the residents of the country and the rest of the world in a particular period (over a quarter of a year or more commonly over a year). It encompasses all transactions involving: goods, services and income; financial claims on and liabilities to the rest of the world; and transfers such as gifts.

Economic Transformation: Change of an economic system, in particular shifting from a centrally-planned to a market economy, based on a functioning free market, competition, and private business.

FDI: Foreign direct investment (outward – OFDI; inward – IFDI), the most advanced form of internationalisation of companies; FDI are undertaken to exercise a long-term capital supervision over an entity located abroad (branches or subsidiaries). Investors may create independent economic enterprises from scratch (*greenfield* investments) or take control over an already existing company (acquisitions and mergers).

Foreign Entity: An entity (affiliate company or a branch/representation) located in host economy in which a foreign investor has a long term capital supervision.

Foreign Investor: An enterprise (legal person) located in home economy that sets up an OFDI abroad in the form of independent entity, i.e. affiliate company (subsidiary or associate company) or branch/representation.

GUS: Main Statistic Office in Poland.

Internationalisation of a Company: Process, through which a firm moves from operating in a domestic marketplace to international markets.

NBP: National Bank of Poland.

ENDNOTES

1. It is not the only division present in literature. An extensive discussion of other classifications of FDI is included in: *Strategie firm polskich wobec ekspansji inwestorów zagranicznych*, Gorynia (2005).
2. Overview of studies on the subject can be found in: Cieślik (2005).
3. The theory includes elements of market organisation, imperfect competition, product diversification and increasing revenues from scale. For new trade theory see: Cieślik (2000).

Chapter 4
Home Country-Specific Determinants of Outward Foreign Direct Investment in Developing Economies

Rıfat Karakuş
Çankırı Karatekin University, Turkey

ABSTRACT

The outward foreign direct investments of developing economies have showed significant increase in recent years. Rising outward foreign direct investment stock of developing economies makes its determinants and consequences crucial. The aim of this study is to determine the home country specific determinants of outward FDI. For this purpose, a panel data analysis is performed with the data of BRICS and Next Eleven countries for the period from 1994 to 2014. The analysis results reveal that inward foreign direct investment, interest rates and technological capability of home country have positive influence and total labor force of home country has negative effect on outward FDI of developing economies.

INTRODUCTION

Foreign direct investment (FDI) is defined as "a category of cross-border investment made by a resident entity in one economy (the direct investor) with the objective of establishing a lasting interest in an enterprise (the direct investment enterprise) that is resident in an economy other than that of the direct investor" (OECD, 2008). The lasting interest implies the existence of a long-term relationship between the direct investor and the enterprise and a significant degree of influence by the direct investor on the management of the enterprise. Ownership of at least 10% of the voting power is generally accepted that the investor has enough influence on management of the enterprise although in some examples less than 10% of the voting power can provide active management ability or more than this voting power cannot be enough for creating a direct management authorization.

FDI can be classified in two forms from point of a reporting economy. Inward FDI indicates the all direct investments by the non-residents in the reporting economy and outward FDI refers to investments

DOI: 10.4018/978-1-5225-2345-1.ch004

which made to another economy by reporting economy residents. When FDI of whole world economy is handled, superiority of developed countries attracts the attention as expected. Naturally FDI flows from more industrialized to less-industrialized countries, or from capital-rich to capital-scarce developing countries. However, in recent years reverse flow of FDI from developing economies to other economies have showed increase with the effect of globalization process. (Bano & Tabbada, 2015) As shown in the Figure 1, total outward FDI stock of world economy has had a tendency to increase from 1980 to 2014 except the years 2001 and 2008. Also percentage of developing and transition economies outward FDI has been ever-growing from 2003 to 2014 although the percentage of developed economies has revealed a downward spiral. Besides when outward FDI stock growth rate of economies is observed, developing and transition economies have given an outstanding performance from 2004 to 2014 except the year 2009.

Developed economies have nearly 80 percent of world outward FDI stocks. Their existing operations support this weight on total of FDI thanks to reinvested earnings. Developed-economy multinational enterprises (MNEs) have operated in other countries for long time and they have advantage of these operations profits. They can invest with the profit of existing operations as outward FDI, so their dominance on outward FDI of world proceeds. When the top 20 home economy of outward FDI is observed, the density of the developed economies is perceived. Respectively, United States, Hong Kong, China, Japan, Germany, Russian Federation, Canada, France, Netherlands, Singapore, Ireland, Spain, Republic of Korea, Italy, Norway, Switzerland, Malaysia, Kuwait, Chile, Taiwan Province of China are the top 20 economy which have outward FDI around the world. 11 economies in top 20 and 10 economies in top 15 are the developed economies. (UNCTAD, 2015) Although the dominance of developed economies is shown in total, capacity of the developing economies is non-negligible. Developed-economy MNEs make their invested in other economies with reinvested earnings ever-increasingly, however the developing-economy MNEs mostly use equity for outward FDI and with these equity investments they increase share on world outward FDI stocks. Also future expectations about the outward FDI predicts that developing MNEs investments in other countries will gradually increase with the effect of investments that is currently made and will create reinvested earnings in the future.

Figure 1. Outward FDI of whole world economy: 1980-2014
UNCTAD, 2015.

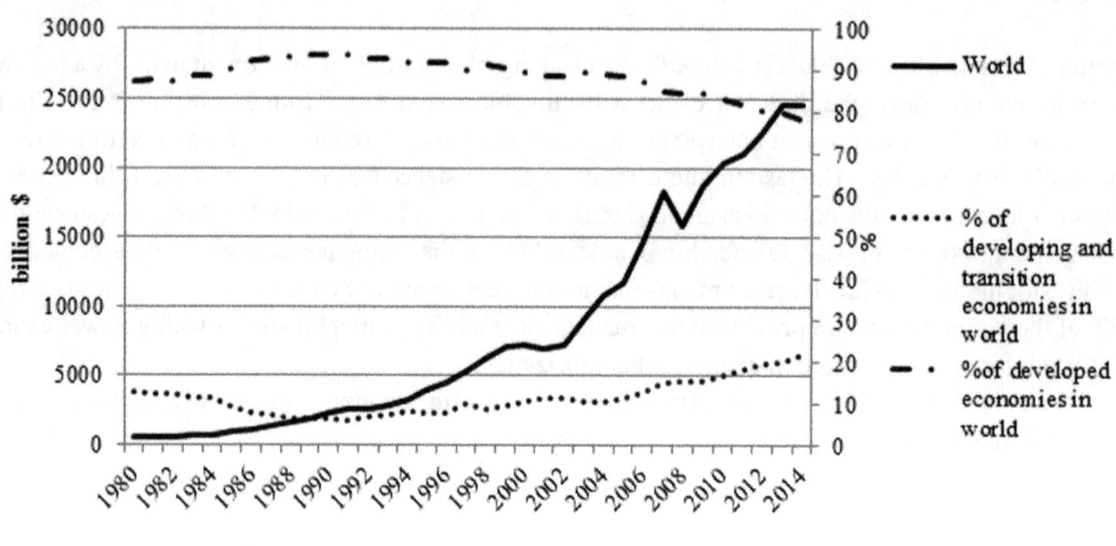

Figure 2. Capital source of outward FDI from developed and developing economies
UNCTAD, 2015.

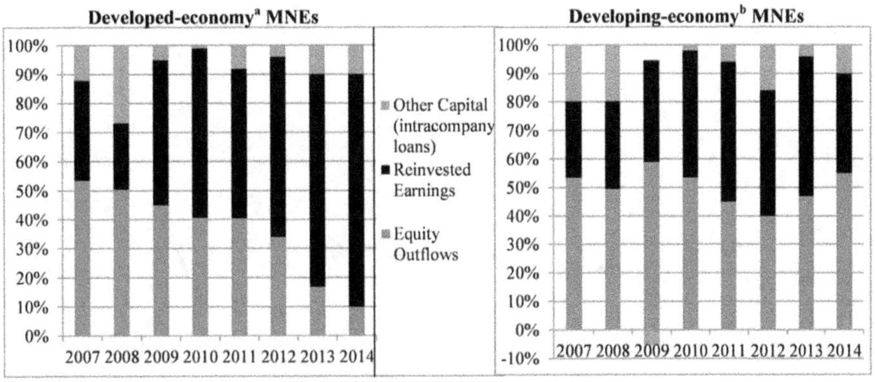

[a] Economies included are Australia, Belgium, Bulgaria, Canada, Croatia, Cyprus, the Czech Republic, Denmark, Estonia, Finland, Germany, Greece, Hungary, Iceland, Ireland, Israel, Latvia, Lithuania, Luxembourg, Malta, the Netherlands, Norway, Portugal, Slovakia, Slovenia, Spain, Sweden, Switzerland, the United Kingdom and the United States.
[b] Economies included are Algeria, Anguilla, Antigua and Barbuda, Aruba, the Bahamas, Bahrain, Bangladesh, Barbados, Belize, the Plurinational State of Bolivia, Botswana, Brazil, Cambodia, Cabo Verde, Chile, Costa Rica, Curaçao, Dominica, El Salvador, Fiji, Grenada, Guatemala, Honduras, Hong Kong (China), India, Indonesia, the Republic of Korea, Kuwait, Lesotho, Malawi, Mexico, Mongolia, Montserrat, Morocco, Namibia, Nicaragua, Nigeria, Pakistan, Panama, the Philippines, Saint Kitts and Nevis, Saint Lucia, Saint Vincent and the Grenadines, Samoa, Sao Tome and Principe, Seychelles, Singapore, Sint Maarten, South Africa, Sri Lanka, the State of Palestine, Suriname, Swaziland, Taiwan Province of China, Thailand, Trinidad and Tobago, Turkey, Uganda, Uruguay, the Bolivarian Republic of Venezuela and Viet Nam.

The outward FDI stock of developing economies and their share versus developed economies is growing. Also developing-economy MNEs are hot prospect for the future. Hence the affecting factors and consequences of developing-economy FDI outflows become significant. For this reason, this study aims to determine the relationship between FDI outflow of developing economies and selected home country specific determinants namely income, trade openness, exchange rate, interest rate, technological capability and labor force. By using data of BRICS and Next Eleven countries between 1994 and 2014, a panel data analysis will be performed and effects of home country specific factors on outward FDI of developing economies will be analyzed. In the chapter, firstly the outward FDI from developing economies will be investigated, and then related literature will be reviewed. Finally to determine the effects of home country specific factors on outflow FDI, a panel data analysis will be performed and the results will be discussed.

BACKGROUND

Although developed economies keep the leading position for outward FDI around the world, cross-border investment activities from developing economies have continued to rise from 1980s until today. Outward FDI of developing economies which was only about 70 billion $ in 1980 had reached to 5.320 billion $ in 2014. Cross-border investment activities of the developing economies have delivered great performance in comparison with developed economies. Parallel to increasing volume of outward FDI, share of developing economies on world FDI outflows have improved perpetually during the recent years. While the developing economies FDI outflows in world economy is only 6 percent in 1991, their share approximated to 22 percent in 2014. Also the growth rate reveals the performance of developing-

Figure 3. Outward FDI from developing economies: 1980-2014
UNCTAD, 2015.

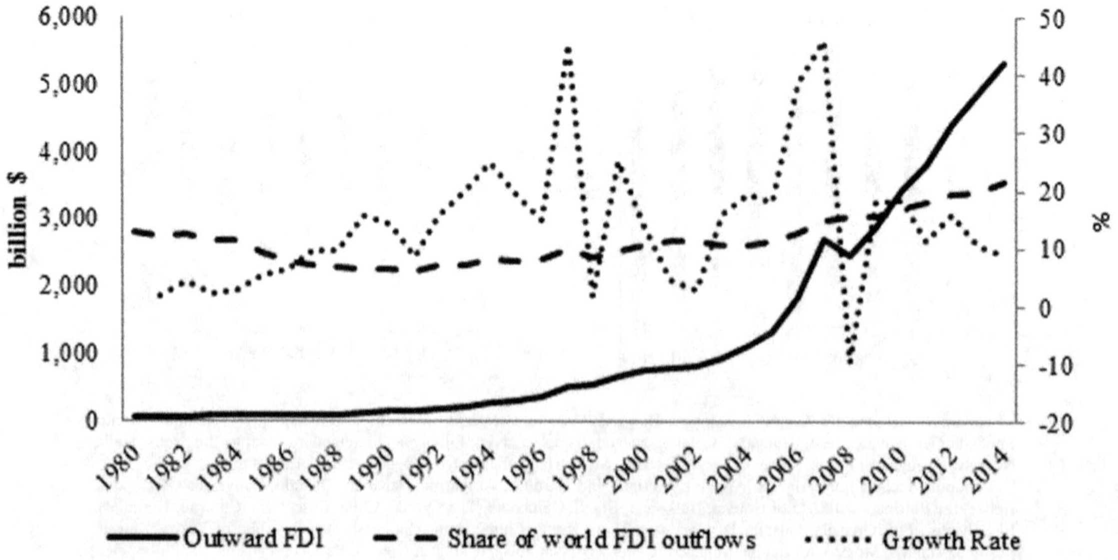

country MNEs according to cross-border investments. Although there is a fluctuant growth rate in recent years, it is almost always positive and implies that the outward FDI stock of the developing economies continues to rise.

When FDI outflows of developing countries are examined regionally, the impact of the Asia economies is felt during the recent years. In 2014, nearly 82 percent of the developing economies outward FDI belonged to Asia economies. In developing Asian economies, Eastern Asia economies have the biggest portion of the outward FDI with a nearly 69 percent of whole Asia. Countries such as China, Hong Kong, South Korea, Taiwan become prominent the Eastern Asia. Other big part of the Asia outward FDI (about 21 percent) belongs to South-Eastern Asia economies which contain Indonesia, Malaysia, Philippines, Singapore, Thailand and Vietnam as developing countries. Subsequent to Asia economies, American economies have the second big part of the developing economies outward FDI. Although in 1980s outward FDI of American economies have had the three times more than Asia economies, in recent years their investments have become only one fifth of Asian economies. In America region, developing economies of South America (Brazil, Chile, Uruguay, Bolivia, Venezuela, etc.) step forward with about 78 percent of outward FDI of whole America. Another region that outward FDI share in developing economies have declined is Africa and the large part of this little share appertains to Southern Africa developing economies.

The developing country MNEs can make cross-border investments in not only developing countries but also developed countries. As shown in Graph 5, some of the developing economies have investments in developed economies more than developing or transition economies. For example, in 2012, outward FDI stock of Republic of Korea is mostly presence in the developed countries by 75, 4 percent. On the other hand, some developing economies FDI stocks abroad are mostly presence in developing economies such as China, Malaysia, Pakistan and Taiwan. As a conclusion, it is easily seen that developing-economy MNEs can attempt to new investments around the world regardless of where. They are able to make cross-border investments as well as in developing countries, as long as they find opportunity for high-yield investments.

Figure 4. Regional FDI outflows as a share of developing country outflows
UNCTAD, 2015.

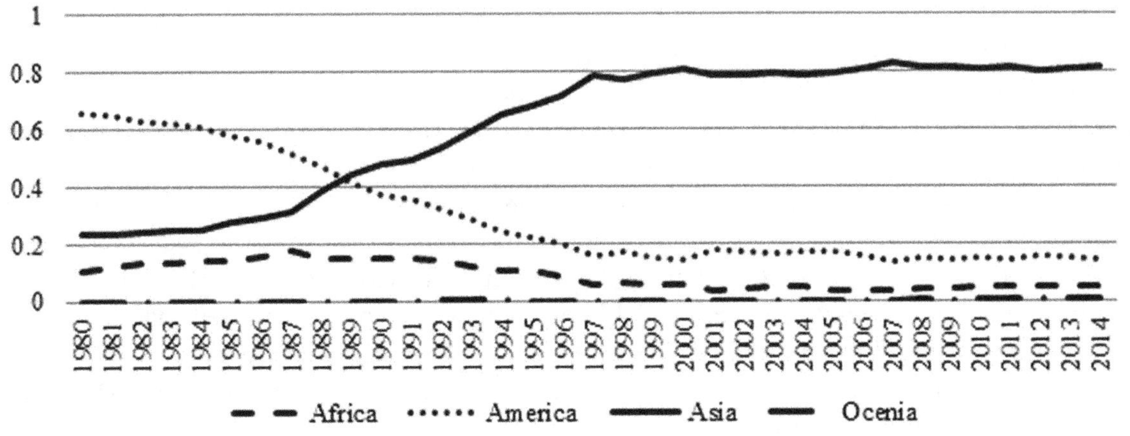

Figure 5. Outward FDI stock of selected developing countries by host economy development class: 2012
UNCTAD, 2014.

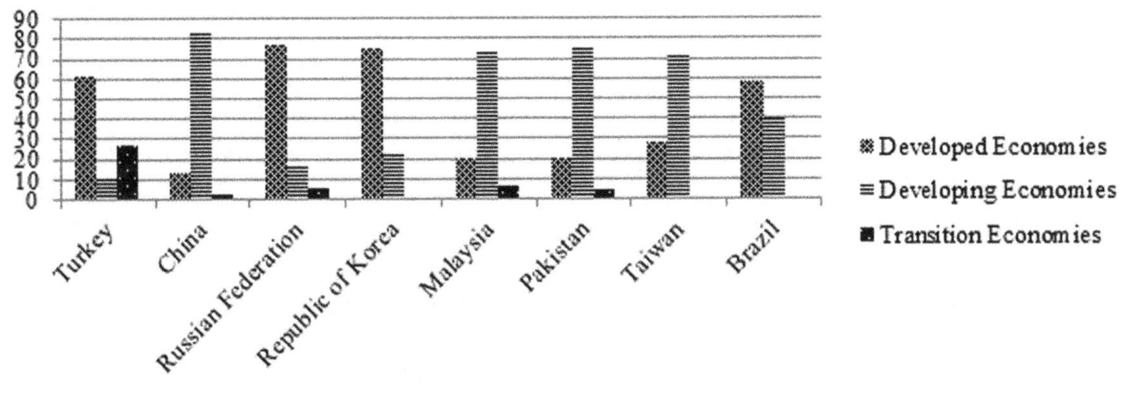

Developing-economy MNEs make cross-border investments in the form of both merger and acquisitions (M&As) and greenfield projects. MNEs from developing and transition economies are consolidating their role as investors in cross-border M&A operations. The share of these MNEs in the total (net) value of cross-border M&As rose from about 10 per cent in 2003 to almost 40 per cent in 2012 and has remained stable since then. Also developing economies have gained 10 percentage points in the global value of announced greenfield FDI projects, from 20 per cent in 2005 to 30 per cent in 2014. Developing-economy MNEs make investments abroad in three main sectors: primary, manufacturing and services. In recent years, services sector especially finance and construction investments are remarkable. (UNCTAD, 2015)

There are several home country specific factors which may affect the outward FDI of a country. Mainly income level, openness to trade, exchange rate, interest rate, inflation rate, human capital and technological capability are discussed with their effects on outward FDI.

Income level of countries may be evaluated as one of the main factors that can affect FDI outflows. Investment Development Path (IDP) theory, that was originally introduced by Dunning in 1981 and improved by this author and others (Dunning 1986, 1988, 1993, 1997; Dunning & Narula 1996; Narula

1996; Duran & Ubeda 2001, 2005) is well-known theory about the economic development and FDI outflows of the countries. According to IDP theory, net outward investment position (the difference between outward direct investment stock and inward direct investment stock of a country) follows a five stage path in relation to level of economic development which is denoted by the Gross Domestic Product (GDP) or GDP per capita. In the first two and last stages of the path net outward investment of the countries decline while GDP or GDP per capita increase. However, in the third and fourth stage of the path net outward investment and GDP or GDP per capita of countries rise concurrently. So income level of countries is decisive on FDI outflows. There are also other reasons to predict the effect of income level on FDI outflows. Developed economies can create available financial markets that lead to entrepreneurial development. (Alfaro et al., 2004) In addition increasing GDP or GDP per capita has a significant effect on savings (Gersovitz, 1988). More entrepreneurs can reach required financial resources easily when economic development is achieved. This situation makes companies more capital intensive and so more competitive. Consequently more entrepreneurs become multinational and FDI outflows increase with the effect of increasing income level.

Trade openness is another important factor that can affect the FDI outflows of countries. Imports and exports of countries are the core indicator of trade openness. More liberalized economies gain knowledge about foreign markets and this valuable knowledge provide opportunity to operate or manage production abroad (Kueh et al., 2010). Also importing economy multinationals become market-favorable when they make investments in the home markets of the import producing companies (Kyrkilis & Pantelidis, 2003). For this reasons, a higher degree of openness is expected to provide a higher level of outward FDI activity.

Exchange rate influences the import and export of countries as well as inward and outward FDI. Appreciation of currencies support import and hinder export. In a similar way, appreciation of currencies encourages the FDI outflows and depreciation of currencies discourages the FDI outflows because capital requirement of foreign investment in domestic currency is pushed up (Aliber, 1970). Theoretically a positive relationship between exchange rate and FDI outflows is expected.

Interest rates create opportunity cost for investments. In the same time, higher interest rates affect the cost of capital. So lower interest rates reduce opportunity cost of foreign investment and enable capital abundance to investment (Kueh et al., 2010; Kyrkilis & Pantelidis, 2003). Likewise increasing inflation has negative effects on outward FDI because it results increase in interest rates and depreciation in currency (Buckley et al., 2007). The excepted influence of interest and inflation rates is similar and negatively correlated with outward FDI.

Quality, delivery time and production costs of goods and services are critical factors for companies that want to remain competitive. These factors become more significant with competitive pressure in the world. The technological knowledge of companies allows improvement in quality, decreasing in delivery time and production costs (Giardini & Ceretti, 2005). The technological capability of whole economy can be measured by patent applications and high technology exports and a positive relationship is expected between these variables and FDI outflows of countries.

The countries' ability to create, acquire and organize human skills adds value MNEs as well as technological capability. This ability attracts inward FDI and encourages outward FDI. Knowledge capital in other words skilled labor force of countries can contribute FDI outflows (Narula, 1996). On the other hand companies direct their investments abroad to minimize their production costs. Labor costs are one big part of the production costs and lower labor cost becomes attractive for MNEs (Svetlicic, 2007). When considered from this point of view increasing labor force keeps labor cost lower in home country and companies do not need to invest abroad. So effect of human capital on FDI outflows can differ by countries.

Also the question of what affect the outward FDI of economies have been subject to many empirical studies. Parallel to volume of outward FDI, the studies mainly focused on developed countries. However, in recent years along with the popularity of developing-economy MNEs empirical studies for these economies stand in the literature. Studies that analyze the effect of home country specific factors on outward FDI of developing economies are summarized below.

Williams (2009) examined the effect of GDP per capita, GDP per capita growth rate, interest rate, literacy rate, level of corruption, current account balance on outward FDI of 15 small island developing economies. A five year panel data for the years 1998-2002 was used to estimate the model. The results reveal that per capita income, per capita income growth rate (i.e., economic growth) and the level of corruption in the home market are the factors that influence local firms to invest in foreign market through foreign direct investment. Per capita income has a negative effect on outward FDI, however per capita income growth rate and level of corruption influences the outward FDI positively. Converse effects of per income capita and its growth rate are remarkable. Increase in per income capita is evaluated as consumer richness and consumers in home market become richer, there is no need to go abroad. So a negative relationship between per income capita and FDI outflows occurs. However increase in per income capita growth rate is expressed as growing of home economy. When home economy becomes larger, but market size is small, firms will seek customers in other markets and this leads to more FDI outflows.

Verma and Brennan (2013) investigated the selected macroeconomic determinants of Indian outward FDI. By using data between 1981 and 2009, time series analysis was applied. Analysis results revealed that GDP, human capital (approximated by the number of enrollments of students in tertiary education) and openness of the economy (approximated by the ratio of exports plus imports to GDP) had a positive influence on FDI outflows. The positive effect of human capital is also seen in type of outward FDI of India. There has been a tremendous increase in service outward FDI from India in recent years. In addition, export activities of the country enable MNEs to obtain information regarding foreign markets and knowledge as well as skills in establishing operations abroad. So export level makes positive contribution to FDI outflows. On the other hand, contrary to expectations any statistical effect of exchange rate, interest rate and technology capability on outward FDI could not be detected.

Saad et al. (2014) to determine the push factors of Malaysia outward FDI performed a multiple regression analysis by using data between 1981 and 2011. In the study, exchange rate, exports, GDP, inward FDI, natural resources availability, patent numbers and labor productivity of home country were used as independent variables and their effect on outward FDI was researched. Results of the analysis revealed that there is a statistically significant and positive relationship between export level, GDP, inward FDI and outward FDI, and also negative relationship between exchange rate, labor productivity, patent numbers and outward FDI. The result on labor productivity level indicates the requirements of technical capabilities cannot be met thus pushing MNEs to involve in overseas production.

In recent years, Asian developing economies have gained importance on world FDI outflows. Bano and Tabbada (2015) tried to answer the question that what drives outward FDI in developing countries and more specifically, what are the home-country determinants of outward FDI? By using data of China, India, Indonesia, Malaysia, the Philippines and Thailand between 1990 and 2010, the effect of savings rate (as percent of GDP), GDP, foreign reserves, exports and FDI inflow on FDI outflows was researched. According to analysis results, there is a statistically significant and positive relationship between GDP, foreign reserves and outward FDI and negative relationship between savings and FDI outflows for these six economies. The findings suggest that for a developing country to aspire to be a capital exporter through FDI, it must possess all or most of the high domestic savings rate, an export-oriented economy, a GDP that is growing rapidly and substantial international reserves.

Determinants and motives of outward foreign direct investment from China's provincial firms are investigated by Chen (2015). Data of 30 provinces for the period from 2003 to 2012 are used to determine the relationship between OFDI and the home-side variables of China's provinces. Per capita GDP, patent numbers, FDI inflows, export to GDP ratio, import the GDP ratio and GDP are selected as home country specific independent variables. The results of the study reveals that provincial economic development (GDP per capita), innovation and technology (patent numbers), and export to GDP ratio are statistically significant determinants and positively affect the outward FDI, while FDI inflows, import to GDP ratio and provincial market size (GDP) are not statistically significant.

EFFECTS OF HOME COUNTRY SPECIFIC FACTORS ON OUTWARD FDI

Data Set

To determine the relationship between outward FDI and home country specific factors, BRICS (Brazil, Russia, India, China and South Africa) and Next Eleven countries (Bangladesh, Egypt, Indonesia, Iran, Mexico, Nigeria, Pakistan, the Philippines, Turkey, South Korea and Vietnam) selected as the sample that represents the developing countries. Yearly data for the period of 1994-2014 is used in the study. Outward FDI stock US Dollars at current prices and current exchange rates in millions (OFDI) is the dependent variable of the analysis and used as logarithm. The data source for outward FDI is data center of UNCTAD. The effect of home-country specific factors on outward FDI is determined with the model that is formulated as Equation 1:

$$\log OFDI_{i,t} = \beta_1 + \beta_2 \log IFDI_{i,t} + \beta_3 \log GNI_{i,t} + \beta_4 \log CPI_{i,t} + \beta_5 \log ECXR_{i,t} \\ + \beta_6 \log_{i,t} TLF + \beta_7 \log_{i,t} TIE + \beta_8 \log IR_{i,t} + \beta_9 \log PN_{i,t} + \beta_{10} \log HTE_{i,t} + u_{i,t} \tag{1}$$

In the equation, "i" refers to the countries; "t" represents the period t; "log" reveals the logarithm of related variable and $OFDI_{i,t}$ expresses the outward FDI of i country for t period. Independent variables being located in the equation are explained in Table 1.

For all-time series variables, the stationary of the series is essential. When the variables in a regression are nonstationary, correct R-square values and t-statistics cannot be generated by the analysis. (Greene, 2012) For preventing spurious relations between the variables, unit root tests are applied and nonstationary series are included the model with first or second differences which provides stationary series. For the variables of this analysis, Levin, Lin and Chu (2002) unit root test is performed and stationary of the series is determined. (Table 2) According to unit root test results, only logEXCR and logHTE series are stationary at the I(0) level. However all of the other variables are stationary at the I(0) level and series generated by first difference of these variables are included to analysis.

Table 1. The explanation of the independent variables

Independent Variable	Description	Source
$logIFDI_{i,t}$	The logarithm of the inward FDI stock (US Dollars at current prices and current exchange rates in millions) of home country i for period t. This variable is selected to express foreign investments made by non-residents in country i.	UNCTAD
logGNI	The logarithm of GNI (current international $) of home country i for period t. GNI variable refers to economic size of the countries for related period.	WORLDBANK
logCPI	The logarithm of annual consumer price indices Index Base 2005 of home country i for period t. Consumer price index is added to equation as inflation measurement.	UNCTAD
logEXCR	The logarithm of the annual currency exchange rate (1.00 USD) of home country i for the period t.	UNCTAD
logTLF	The logarithm of the total labour force annually (absolute value in thousands) of home country i for the period t. This variable represents the workforce of the home countries.	UNCTAD
logTIE	The logarithm of the total export and import of goods and services (current US$) of home country i for the period t. Total of the export and import is added to model to exhibit the openness of home country to global economy.	WORLDBANK
logIR	The logarithm of the lending interest rate (%) of home country i for the period t. Lending rate is the bank rate that usually meets the short- and medium-term financing needs of the private sector.	WORLDBANK
logPN	The logarithm of the patent applications that are worldwide patent applications filed through the Patent Cooperation Treaty procedure or with a national patent office for exclusive rights for an invention of home country i for the period t. This variable refers to the technological capacity of the countries.	WORLDBANK
logHTE	The logarithm of the high-technology exports (current US$) of home country i for the period t. This variable also refers to the technological capacity of the countries.	WORLDBANK

Table 2. Unit root test results

Variables	I(0) Level		I(1) Level	
	Statistic	Probability	Statistic	Probability
logOFDI	4.1960	1.00	-4.2912	0.00
logIFDI	2.4084	0.9920	-4.3468	0.00
logGNI	5.2407	1.00	-3.3223	0.0004
logCPI	0.5268	0.7008	-3.1115	0.0009
logEXCR	-2.3292	0.0099		
logTLF	1.4416	0.9253	-5.4586	0.00
logTIE	3.2975	0.9995	-7.4347	0.00
logIR	0.7456	0.7720	-8.2907	0.00
logPN	2.2535	0.9879	-7.2716	0.00
logHTE	-2.6284	0.0043		

Panel Data Analysis

By using 16 countries data for the period 1994-2014, to identify home-country specific determinants of outward FDI of developing countries is aim of this study. Using a panel data regression analysis for these aim and data set is appropriate. With panel data, it is possible to bring together the regression data and time-series data. With panel data, observation of subjects over time unlike regression data and observation of many subjects unlike time-series data are possible. (Frees, 2004) For the data set of this analysis, 16 cross-section and 20 time-series for each cross section, using panel regression analysis is necessary and brings along the advantages of panel data.

In this analysis, it is endeavoured to determine the effect of nine independent variables (logIFDI, logGNI, logCPI, logEXCR, logTLF, logTIE, logIR, logPN, logHTE) on dependent variable (logOFDI). However, there may exist exogenous variables, excluded due to data availability or difficulty of measuring, which should be included for obvious effects on the outcomes. The existence of correlation between these excluded variables and explaining variables cause the correlation between the error term of the regression model and independent variables and induce biased results and estimation. To avoid biased results and estimation in other words to create precise analysis results identification of individual and/or time effects in the model is crucial. After identifying individual and/or time effects in the model best suitable panel model will be selected. (Bozkurt & Akman, 2016)

Individual and/or time effects in the model may be investigated with different tests. If related test results reveal that there is individual and/or time effects in the model, type of the effects should be specified. By using Hausman (1978) tests, it is decided that fixed or random effects model is more appropriate for the panel data analysis. However, if according to tests results there is no individual and/or time effects in the model, pooled ordinary least square should be used as the most suitable model.

Panel Data Model Selection

As mentioned above, determination of individual and/or time effects in the model is crucial to select precise panel data model. To determine the individual and/or time effects, seven tests are used and their results are reported in Table 3.

LR Test (1) examines H_0 which argues that standard errors of the individual and time effects are zero. According to this test result there is no individual or time effects. LR Test (7) also retests the time effect in the model and reveals that there is no time effect identically. So it is concluded that the model is free from time effect.

H_0 of F Test (2) examines that all individual effects are zero, H_0 of LR Test (3) and Score Test (6) examines that standard errors of individual effects are zero and H_0 of LM Test (4) and ALM Test (5) examines that variances of individual effects are zero. According to LR Test (3) and LM Test (4) there is no individual effects and pooled OLS is appropriate model for this analysis. However F Test (2), ALM Test (5) and Score Test (6) results reveal that individual effects exist in the model. When all test results are discussed together, whether individual effects in the model exist or not is irresolute. For this reason, panel data analysis will be performed by pooled OLS model, also according to Hausman Test results fixed or random effects model is used as an alternative.

If there is individual and/or time effects are in the model, fixed or random effect models will be used. To determine the appropriate model, Hausman (1978) Test should be performed. H_0 of Hausman Test is that difference in coefficients is not systematic. If null hypothesis of Hausman Test is accepted, random

Table 3. Individual and/or time effects test results

Tests	(1) LR Test	(2) F Test	(3) LR Test	(4) LM Test	(5) ALM Test	(6) Score Test	(7) LR Test
Regression Models	**Random Individual and Period Effects.**	**Fixed Effects Model**	**Random-Effects ML Model**	**Random Effects GLS Model**	**Random Effects GLS Model**	**Random Effects ML Model**	**Random Period Effects ML Model.**
Test Statistics							
F or Chi^2 Sat.	1.40	1.84	1.40	0.00	10.07	3.68	0.00
Probability	0.4967	0.0441	0.118	1.00	0.00	0.055	1.00
H_0:	Accept	Reject	Accept	Accept	Reject	Reject	Accept
Results							
Individual Effect	NO	YES	NO	NO	YES	YES	-
Time Effect	NO	-	-	-	-	-	NO
Pooled OLS	YES	NO	YES	YES	NO	NO	YES

Table 4. Hausman test result

Chi2 Sat.	Probability
1.45	0.9193

effect model should be chosen. If null hypothesis of this test is rejected, fixed effect model is suitable for the analysis. Hausman Test result for this study is shown in Table 4. According to test results, null hypothesis is accepted and so random effect model is suitable fır the analysis. After this results panel data analysis is performed with both pooled OLS and random effect models.

Heteroscedasticity and Autocorrelation Tests

If the error terms in a regression equation do not have a constant variance, the heteroscedasticity occurs. When heteroscedasticity problem is current in an equation, the OLS estimator remains unbiased. However, the estimated standard errors are biased, so the usual t statistics or F statistics cannot be used properly. Even if standard errors could be correctly measured, the OLS estimator is no longer BLUE (unbiased and efficient). Also if the error terms in a regression are serially dependent, there is autocorrelation which cause same problems with heteroscedasticity.

To determine whether heteroscedasticity and autocorrelation problems exist in panel regression models, varied tests are applied and their results are represented in Table 5. According to test results heteroscedasticity and autocorrelation problems occur for pooled OLS model. Random effect model is free from autocorrelation, but heteroscedasticity is also in effect. To avoid the consequences of heteroscedasticity and autocorrelation, robust standard error estimators of Newey and West (1987; 1994) and Driscoll and Kraay (1998) are employed for pooled OLS model. To present the effect of heteroscedasticity on results in random effect model robust standard error estimators of Huber, Eicker and White (1967; 1967; 1980) and Rogers (1993) are preferred.

Table 5. Heteroscedasticity and autocorrelation tests results

Tests	For Pooled OLS			For Random Effect Model	
	(1) Breusch-Pagan and Cook-Weisberg Test	(2) White Test	(3) Wooldridge Test	(4) Levene and Brown-Forsythe Test	(5) aLM Test for Autocorrelation
Test Statistics					
F stat.	-	-	11.199	7.935	1.35
Chi² Sat.	8.56	114.42	-		
Probability	0.0034	0.0002	0.0065	0.00	0.2445
H_0:	Reject	Reject	Reject	Reject	Accept
Results					
Heteroscedasticity	YES	YES	-	YES	-
Autocorrelation	-	-	YES	-	NO

Note: For (1) Breusch-Pagan (1979) and Cook-Weisberg (1983) Test, (2) White (1980) test and (4) Levene (1960) and Brown-Forsythe (1974)Test H_0: No heteroscedasticity and for (3) Wooldridge (2002) test and (5) aLM test for autocorrelation H_0: No autocorrelation.

Estimation Results

The results of the correlation matrix between dependent variable (OFDI) and all variables used in the model are revealed in Table 6. The highest positive correlation (0.79) occurs between outward FDI and inward FDI. Besides, the lowest positive correlation (0.09) appears between outward FDI and total labor force. The highest negative correlation (0.13) is attained between outward FDI and currency exchange rates and the lowest negative correlation (0.01) occurs between outward FDI and interest rates. Although there is high correlation between some independent variables, variance inflation factors (VIF) for these variables are smaller than 10, so there is no question about collinearity in regressions.

Table 6. Correlation matrix

	logOFDI	logIFDI	logGNI	logCPI	logTLF	logTIE	logIR	logPN	logEXCR	logHTE
logOFDI	1									
logIFDI	0.7897	1								
logGNI	0.4865	0.3469	1							
logCPI	-0.0839	-0.0774	-0.0971	1						
logTLF	0.0926	0.1046	0.5288	-0.1124	1					
logTIE	0.3069	0.1828	0.6783	-0.0842	0.2798	1				
logIR	-0.0092	-0.0198	0.0007	0.0294	0.0486	0.0153	1			
logPN	0.5529	0.3771	0.783	-0.0911	0.2469	0.5491	0.0014	1		
logEXCR	-0.1311	-0.1207	-0.1648	0.2206	-0.0826	-0.0931	0.0372	-0.0925	1	
logHTE	0.3165	0.23	0.4338	-0.0867	0.2374	0.338	-0.0174	0.3141	-0.0789	1

Table 7 presents the main results of panel data analyses. Firstly, all of the models (F and Chi^2 statistics) are statistically significant at 1% level which means that the set of independent variables have the ability of explaining dependent variable logOFDI. Explanatory power of the models is 71%. In other words R^2 statistics reveal that the independent variables used in the model can explain the 71% of the movements in dependent variable.

According to pooled OLS regression with Newey-West standard errors, there is a statistically significant relationship between outward FDI and inward FDI, total labor force (TLF), patent numbers (PN) and high technology exports (HTE) for developing economies. Any effect of other variables on outward FDI cannot be proven. Except HTE, other three independent variables (IFDI, TLF and PN) have statistically significant effect on outward FDI according to pooled OLS regression with Driscoll-Kraay standard errors. Both random effect models show that there is a statistically significant relationship between outward FDI and inward FDI, interest rates, patent numbers and high technology exports for countries creating the model sample. However, effect of other variables on outward FDI is found as insignificant.

Table 7. Estimation results

	Pooled OLS		**Random Effect Model**	
	Regression with Newey-West Standard Errors (1)	**Regression with Driscoll-Kraay Standard Errors (2)**	**Regression with Heteroskedasticity-Robust Standard Errors (Eicker-Huber-White) (3)**	**Regression with Robust Std. Error (Rogers) (4)**
logIFDI	0.378213 (0.001)*	0.378213 (0.00)*	0.377728 (0.007)*	0.377728 (0.007)*
logGNI	1.01E-08 (0.318)	1.01E-08 (0.179)	8.84E-09 (0.493)	8.84E-09 (0.493)
logCPI	-10.4539 (0.719)	-10.4539 (0.636)	-19.219 (0.405)	-19.219 (0.405)
logEXCR	-116.009 (0.581)	-116.009 (0.554)	-70.9396 (0.786)	-70.9396 (0.786)
logTLF	-0.97268 (0.015)**	-0.97268 (0.004)*	-0.90615 (0.127)	-0.90615 (0.127)
logTIE	-1.77E-09 (0.888)	-1.77E-09 (0.88)	-2.59E-09 (0.731)	-2.59E-09 (0.731)
logIR	13.65217 (0.202)	13.65217 (0.236)	17.98413 (0.00)*	17.98413 (0.00)*
logPN	0.313046 (0.014)**	0.313046 (0.022)**	0.334541 (0.007)*	0.334541 (0.007)*
logHTE	479.7446 (0.019)**	479.7446 (0.179)	489.6148 (0.078)***	489.6148 (0.078)***
Constant	-7450.83 (0.032)**	-7450.83 (0.16)	-7767.28 (0.136)	-7767.28 (0.136)
F-Statistic	49.48*	385.33*		
Wald Chi^2			51175.38*	51175.38*
R^2		0.71	0.71	0.71
Number of observation: 320 Number of Groups:16				

*, ** and *** indicates that the coefficient estimations are statistically significant at 1%, 5% and 10% level, respectively.

Firstly, both pooled OLS and random effect models indicate that inward FDI of developing economies has a positive influence on outward FDI of these countries. Too close coefficients of the models point that 1% increase in inward FDI creates respectively 0.37-0.38% increase in outward FDI. Patent numbers is another independent variable that its influence on outward FDI is found as significant. Outward FDI of developing economies is positively associated with patent numbers, with a 1% increase in the patent numbers increasing outward FDI by 0.31% and 0.33% according to pooled OLS and random effect models respectively. Effect of high technology exports on outward FDI is determined as significant by three methods. Its effect on outward FDI is the highest in all. 1% increasing in high technology exports results 479.74% and 489.61% increase in outward FDI in other of different methods. Total labor force variable is detected by pooled OLS model and interest rate is determined by random effect model as significant. Although the total labor force has a negative influence on outward FDI, interest rate has a positive impact on outward FDI. If total labor force increases 1%, outward FDI will decrease 0.97% and if interest rate increases 1%, outward FDI will increase 17.98%.

SOLUTIONS AND RECOMMENDATIONS

The results of the analysis reveal that inward FDI, interest rate and technological capability (approximated by patent applications and high technology exports) of home countries have positive influence on outward FDI of developing economies. Influence of inward FDI and technological capability is coherent with theoretical expectations. Inward FDI supports economic level, know-how and liberalization of countries and positive effect of inward FDI on FDI outflows makes sense. Similarly technological capability by creating competitive advantages is anticipated to contribute MNEs. On the other hand, positive relationship between interest rates and outward FDI is surprising. Increasing interest rates creates higher opportunity cost and cost of capital and discourages companies from investments. However empirical results exhibit a reverse situation. Companies can reach lower cost financial instruments in countries where they invest and they may invest abroad when interest rates increase in home country. This alternative is compatible with the analysis results. The negative effect of total labor force on outward FDI is another result of the study. More labor force in home country dissuades companies from investing abroad.

The findings of this analysis may have some practical implications for developing country policy makers. After evaluating the consequences of FDI outflows, policy makers may use related factors as a tool to support FDI outflows or discourage from FDI outflows. To support the outward FDI, countries can promote technological capability and encourage inward FDI by support packages. On the other hand the effect of interest rates on outward FDI is not ignored. Mainly rising interest rates is a useful tool to attract foreign funds to country. However analysis results reveal that interest rates have a positive effect on FDI outflows and rising interest rates results to increase in FDI outflows. This contradictious effect of interest rates on fund inflow and outflow should be examined closely by policy makers.

This study contributes to general understanding of the determinants of developing economies' outward FDI. By using a wide country set and a large current data period respectable results for companies and policy makers are generated. However there are some limitations. Firstly effect human capital is measured only from the point of total labor force because the data representing the skills of labor force is not available for whole data set. Future studies can use more independent variables such as corporate tax rate and investment policy of the home countries. Also host country and firm level determinants of the outward FDI can be added to analysis in future studies and limitations of this study will be eliminated.

FUTURE RESEARCH DIRECTIONS

This study contributes to general understanding of the determinants of developing economies' outward FDI. By using a wide country set and a large current data period respectable results for companies and policy makers are generated. However there are some limitations. Firstly effect human capital is measured only from the point of total labor force because the data representing the skills of labor force is not available for whole data set. Future studies can use more independent variables such as corporate tax rate and investment policy of the home countries. Also host country and firm level determinants of the outward FDI can be added to analysis in future studies and limitations of this study will be eliminated.

CONCLUSION

In this chapter, the effects of home country specific factors on outward FDI of developing countries are discussed. Cross-border investment activities from developing economies have continued to rise from 1980s until today and outward FDI stocks of developing countries reach a significant volume as of today. So the factors affecting the outward FDI of these countries have importance. In accordance with this purpose, panel data analysis is performed with the data of BRICS and Next Eleven countries for the period from 1994 to 2014. Inward FDI, GNI, consumer price indices, currency exchange rate, total labour force, total export and import of goods and services, lending interest rate, patent applications and high-technology exports are used as independent variables of the analysis. The results of the analysis reveal that inward FDI, interest rate and technological capability (approximated by patent applications and high technology exports) of home countries have positive influence on outward FDI of developing economies.

REFERENCES

Alfaro, L., Chandab, A., Kalemli-Ozcanc, Ş., & Sayek, S. (2004). FDI and economic growth: The role of local financial markets. *Journal of International Economics*, *64*(1), 89112. doi:10.1016/S0022-1996(03)00081-3

Aliber, R. Z. (1970). A theory of direct foreign investment. In C. P. Kindleberger (Ed.), *The International Corporation*. Cambridge, MA: MIT Press.

Bano, S., & Tabbada, J. (2015). Foreign Direct Investment Outflows: Asian Developing Countries. *Journal of Economic Integration*, *30*(2), 359–398. doi:10.11130/jei.2015.30.2.359

Bozkurt, I., & Akman, E. (2016). Financial Integration Into EU: The Romanian Case. *Amfiteatru Economic*, *18*(42), 269–285.

Breusch, T. S., & Pagan, A. R. (1980). The Lagrange multiplier test and its applications to model specification in econometrics. *The Review of Economic Studies*, *47*(1), 239–253. doi:10.2307/2297111

Brown, M. B., & Forsythe, A. B. (1974). Robust tests for equality of variances. *Journal of the American Statistical Association*, *69*(346), 364–367. doi:10.1080/01621459.1974.10482955

Buckley, P. J., Clegg, L. J., Cross, A. R., Liu, X., Voss, H., & Zheng, P. (2007). The Determinants of Chinese Outward Foreign Direct Investment. *Journal of International Business Studies*, *38*(4), 499–518. doi:10.1057/palgrave.jibs.8400277

Chen, C. (2015). Determinants and motives of outward foreign direct investment from Chinas provincial firms. *Transnational Corporations*, *23*(1), 1–28. doi:10.18356/6ba5ab37-en

Cook, R. D., & Weisberg, S. (1983). Diagnostics for heteroscedasticity in regression. *Biometrika*, *70*(1), 1–10. doi:10.1093/biomet/70.1.1

Driscoll, J., & Kraay, A. C. (1998). Consistent covariance matrix estimation with spatially dependent data. *The Review of Economics and Statistics*, *80*(4), 549–560. doi:10.1162/003465398557825

Dunning, J. H. (1981). Explaining the International Direct Investment Position of Countries: Towards a dynamic and development approach. *Weltwirtschaftliches Archiv*, *117*(1), 30–64. doi:10.1007/BF02696577

Dunning, J. H. (1986). The Investment Development Cycle Revisited. *Weltwirtschaftliches Archiv*, *122*(4), 667–677. doi:10.1007/BF02707854

Dunning, J. H. (1988). The eclectic paradigm of international production: A restatement and some possible extensions. *Journal of International Business Studies*, *19*(1), 1–31. doi:10.1057/palgrave.jibs.8490372

Dunning, J. H. (1993). *Multinational Enterprises and the Global Economy*. Addison-Wesley Publishing.

Dunning, J. H. (1997). *Alliance Capitalism and Global Business*. London: Routledge.

Dunning, J. H., & Narula, R. (1996). The Investment Development Path Revisited: Some emerging issues. In J. H. Dunning & R. Narula (Eds.), *Foreign Direct Investment and Governments: Catalysts for economic restructuring*. London: Routledge.

Duran, J. J., & Ubeda, F. (2001). The Investment Development Path: A new empirical approach and some theoretical issues. *Transnational Corporations*, *10*(2), 1–34.

Duran, J. J., & Ubeda, F. (2005). The Investment Development Path of Newly Developed Countries. *International Journal of the Economics of Business*, *12*(1), 123–137. doi:10.1080/1357151042000323076

Eicker, F. (1967). Limit theorems for regressions with unequal and dependent errors. In *Proceedings of the Fifth Berkeley Symposium on Mathematical Statistics and Probability*, (vol. 1, pp. 59–82). Berkeley, CA: University of California Press.

Frees, E. W. (2004). *Longitudinal and Panel Data: Analysis and Applications in the Social Sciences*. New York: Cambridge University Press.

Gersovitz, M. (1988). Saving and Development. In H. Chenery & T. N. Srinivasan (Eds.), *Handbook of Development Economics*. Amsterdam: Elsevier.

Giardini, C., & Ceretti, E. (2005). Implementation of an On-line Supervision System for Scheduling and Controlling a Production Plant. In *AMST'05 Advanced Manufacturing Systems and Technology: Proceedings of the Seventh International Conference* (*vol. 486*, pp. 347-356). Vienna: Springer. doi:10.1007/3-211-38053-1_33

Greene, W. H. (2012). *Econometric Analysis*. Upper Saddle River, NJ: Pearson Education.

Hausman, J. A. (1978). Specification tests in econometrics. *Econometrica, 46*(6), 1251–1271. doi:10.2307/1913827

Huber, P. J. (1967). The behavior of maximum likelihood estimates under nonstandard conditions. In *Proceedings of the Fifth Berkeley Symposium on Mathematical Statistics and Probability* (vol. 1, pp. 221–233). Berkeley, CA: University of California Press.

Kueh, J.S.H., Puah, C.H. & Liew, K.S. (2010). *Selected Macroeconomic Determinants of Foreign Direct Investment Outflow of Singapore.* MPRA Paper No.25940.

Kyrkilis, D., & Pantelidis, P. (2003). Macroeconomic determinants of outward foreign direct investment. *International Journal of Social Economics, 30*(7), 827–836. doi:10.1108/03068290310478766

Levene, H. (1960). Robust tests for equality of variances. In I. Olkin, S. G. Ghurye, W. Hoeffding, W. G. Madow, & H. B. Mann (Eds.), *Contributions to Probability and Statistics: Essays in Honor of Harold Hotelling* (pp. 278–292). Menlo Park, CA: Stanford University Press.

Levin, A., Lin, C., & Chu, C. J. (2002). Unit Root Tests In Panel Data: Asymptotic And Finite-Sample Properties. *Journal of Econometrics, 108*(1), 1–24. doi:10.1016/S0304-4076(01)00098-7

Narula, R. (1996). *Multinational Investment and Economic Structure: Globalisation and Competitiveness.* London: Routledge.

Newey, W. K., & West, K. D. (1987). A Simple, Positive Semi-Definite, Heteroskedasticity and Autocorrelation Consistent Covariance Matrix. *Econometrica, 55*(3), 703–708. doi:10.2307/1913610

Newey, W. K., & West, K. D. (1994). Automatic Lag Selection in Covariance Matrix Estimation. *The Review of Economic Studies, 61*(4), 631–653. doi:10.2307/2297912

OECD. (2008). *Benchmark Definition of Foreign Direct Investment* (4th ed.). Retrieved from https://www.oecd.org/daf/inv/investmentstatisticsandanalysis/40193734.pdf

Rogers, W. H. (1993). sg17: Regression standard errors in clustered samples. Stata Technical Bulletin, 13, 19-23.

Saad, R. M., Noor, A. H. M., & Nor, A. H. S. M. (2014). Developing Countries Outward Investment: Push Factors for Malaysia. *Procedia: Social and Behavioral Sciences, 130*, 237–246. doi:10.1016/j.sbspro.2014.04.028

Svetlicic, M. (2007). Outward foreign direct investment by enterprises from Slovenia. *Transnational Corporations, 16*(1), 55-87.

UNCTAD. (2014). *Bilateral FDI Statistics.* Retrieved from http://unctad.org/en/Pages/DIAE/FDI%20Statistics/FDI-Statistics-Bilateral.aspx

UNCTAD. (2015). *World Investment Report 2015: Reforming International Investment Governance.* Retrieved from http://unctad.org/en/PublicationsLibrary/wir2015_en.pdf

Verma, R., & Brennan, L. (2013). An Analysis of the Macroeconomic Determinants of Indian Outward Foreign Direct Investment. In M. A. Marinov & S. T. Marinova (Eds.), *Emerging Economies and Firms in the Global Crisis* (pp. 137–153). New York: Palgrave Macmillan. doi:10.1057/9781137277473_6

White, H. (1980). A heteroskedasticity-consistent covariance matrix estimator and a direct test for heteroskedasticity. *Econometrica, 48*(4), 817–838. doi:10.2307/1912934

Williams, D. A. (2009). Determinants of Outward Foreign Direct Investments from Small Island Developing States. *American Journal of Economics and Business Administration, 1*(2), 47–56. doi:10.3844/ajebasp.2009.47.56

Wooldridge, J. M. (2002). *Econometric Analysis of Cross Section and Panel Data*. Cambridge, MA: MIT Press.

KEY TERMS AND DEFINITIONS

BRICS: An acronym for the combined economies of Brazil, Russia, India, China and South Africa.

Greenfield Investment: A form of foreign direct investment where a parent company builds its operations in a foreign market from the ground up.

Human Capital: A collection of resources—all the knowledge, talents, skills, abilities, experience, intelligence, training, judgment, and wisdom possessed individually and collectively by individuals in a population.

Investment Development Path: A theory that was originally introduced by Dunning in 1981 and explains the relationship between national income and net outward foreign direct investment in a five stage path.

Next Eleven: A term to represent eleven countries - Bangladesh, Egypt, Indonesia, Iran, Mexico, Nigeria, Pakistan, the Philippines, Turkey, South Korea and Vietnam.

Panel Data Analysis: A statistical model which enables the data sets containing cross section and time series together.

Trade Openness: A measure of economic policies that either restrict or invite trade between countries.

UNCTAD: The United Nations body responsible for dealing with development issues, particularly international trade – the main driver of development by its 194 member States.

Chapter 5
The Role of Governance on Outward Foreign Direct Investment in Emerging Market Economies

Adem Gök
Kırklareli University, Turkey

ABSTRACT

Emerging market economies have clear deficit in governance infrastructure and also have an increasing trend in the amount of foreign direct investment (FDI) outflows compared with advanced countries. Hence the main issue of the study is to identify the determinants leading to the increase in FDI outflows with special emphasize given to the role of governance infrastructure. Thus, the aim of the study is to analyze the effect of governance infrastructure together with other control variables on FDI outflows in emerging market economies. It is found that improvement in all measured aspects of governance infrastructure leads to increase in FDI outflows from emerging market economies and governance infrastructure, human capital and physical infrastructure are base factors for MNCs taking outward FDI decision from emerging market economies. It is also found that FDI outflows from emerging market economies are not market or efficiency seeking; instead they are resource, labor or finance seeking.

INTRODUCTION

There are several benefits that the home countries derive from outward FDI. First, and most distinctive, is that the stream of income, mainly in the form of repatriated profits, from foreign earnings through affiliates in host countries. Second, it creates employment and contributes to growth in home country if outward FDI complements home country production as such as affiliates in host country import intermediate products or inputs from the parent company in home country. Third, MNCs may learn new skills and technics from exposure to host countries through outward FDI. (Nourbakhshian et.al., 2012; Behbehani and Al Hallaq, 2013), Fourth, outward FDI allows MNCs to explore new global markets, to

DOI: 10.4018/978-1-5225-2345-1.ch005

generate higher profits and incomes through the production and sales in host country markets (Bukari, 2016). Fifth, efficiently utilized and managed abundant natural resources in host countries decrease costs and increase the price competency of MNCs (Bukari, 2016). Finally, affiliates in host countries generally use production techniques that are developed and patented in home country R&D base; hence it is another stream of income for home country.

Governance infrastructure of a country may affect outward FDI in two ways. First, and most distinctive, is the positive impact of quality of governance on outward FDI both in the short and long run. The effect of governance on FDI is through the effect of institutions on investment environment of a country and through the decreasing transaction costs, production costs and uncertainty (Bellos and Subasat, 2012). Second effect is the negative short run effect of governance infrastructure on outward FDI mainly referred as escape response of outward FDI due to low quality of governance in home countries (Klimek, 2015; Witt and Lewin, 2007).

The main issue of the study is to identify the determinants leading to the increase in FDI outflows with special emphasize given to the role of governance infrastructure. Thus, the aim of the study is to analyze the effect of governance infrastructure together with other control variables on FDI outflows in emerging market economies.

The study claims that governance infrastructure as a base factor has positive significant effect on outward FDI in contrast to studies maintaining escape response argument. Hence, the study builds a new theoretical perspective for the outward FDI before delving into the empirical analysis.

Next section presents background for the study. A new theoretical perspective for FDI theory is developed in third section. Fourth section explains how governance is measured in thesis. Fifth section presents data, variables and methodology used in thesis. Statistical analysis is carried out in sixth section. Seventh section presents empirical analysis. Last section provides concluding remarks.

BACKGROUND

There are numerous studies in the literature that have concentrated on the role of governance on inward FDI. The studies examining the role of governance on outward FDI or considering governance as a determinant of outward FDI are limited (Globerman et. al., 2006; Witt and Lewin, 2007; Kayam, 2009; Das, 2013; Subasat and Bellos, 2013; Klimek, 2015). Also, there are other studies in the literature analyzing the effect of host country governance on outward FDI of home countries such as Mishra and Daly (2007). This type of studies is not included in the empirical survey.

Globerman et. al. (2006) found statistically significant positive effect of governance on outward FDI in both emerging and transition European economies and emerging markets for the period 1995-2001. They used principal component analysis of six main WGI governance variables as a proxy for overall governance performance of the countries. They had only three-year data for each governance indicator, hence they extrapolated them which may lead to biased results since 57% of governance data were extrapolated.

Witt and Lewin (2007) argued that outward FDI is an escape response from perceived misalignments between firms' needs and home country institutional environment in advanced industrialized nations in the context of societal coordination. The main drawback of their study is that the conclusion they reached does not base on an empirical analysis. Instead they reviewed the literature on IB without even employing meta-analysis based on the selected studies.

Although Kayam (2009) concluded that improvement in government stability, investment profile and bureaucracy quality decreases outward FDI as an escape response, her estimation results do not support. In total of sixty five developing and transition economies in four regional clusters for the period 2000-2006, bureaucracy quality has no statistically significant effect on outward FDI in any cluster, investment profile has statistically significant negative effect on outward FDI only in two regions and finally government stability has statistically significant negative effect on outward FDI only in one region. Hence only three out of twelve regression supports her conclusion.

Das (2013) found that increase in home country political risk leads to increase in outward FDI as an escape response in his analysis of fifty-six developing economies for the period 1996-2010 with panel random effect estimation technique.

In a bilateral panel regression analysis, Subasat and Bellos (2013) found that high corruption, improvement in bureaucratic quality and democratic accountability in home countries leads to increase in outward FDI directed to fifteen Latin American countries for the period 1980-1996.

Klimek (2015) found that deterioration of governance in home countries increases outward FDI in developing countries for the period 1996-2010.

All studies above except Witt and Lewin (2007) used fixed or random effect panel regression technique, hence they all have endogeneity problem resulting from reverse causality problem or multicollinearity issue between governance variables and control variables used in the regression. Also, the studies analyzing developing countries include least developed countries leading to biased results for the analysis since the governance infrastructure in least developed countries are totally different from developing countries and takes the lowest values compared to all countries.

MAIN FOCUS OF THE STUDY AND PROBLEMS ENCOUNTERED

Emerging market economies have clear deficit in governance infrastructure and also have an increasing trend in the amount of foreign direct investment (FDI) outflows compared with advanced countries. The main issue of the study is to identify the determinants leading to the increase in FDI outflows with special emphasize given to the role of governance infrastructure. Thus, the aim of the study is to analyze the effect of governance infrastructure together with other control variables on FDI outflows in emerging market economies. The study claims that governance infrastructure as a base factor has positive significant effect on outward FDI in contrast to studies maintaining escape response argument. Hence, the study builds a new theoretical perspective for the outward FDI before delving into the empirical analysis.

There are numerous studies in the literature that have concentrated on the role of governance on inward FDI. The studies examining the role of governance on outward FDI or considering governance as a determinant of outward FDI are limited.

This limited literature analyzing the role of governance on outward FDI has following drawbacks as;

- All of them employ fixed or random effect panel regression technique, hence they all have endogeneity problem resulting from reverse causality problem or multicollinearity issue between governance variables and control variables used in the regression.
- None of the studies consider lag of outward FDI as a potential determinant of outward FDI. Hence all of the analyses employed are static panels, not dynamic panels.

- The studies analyzing developing countries include least developed countries leading to biased results for the analysis since the governance infrastructure in least developed countries are totally different from developing countries and takes the lowest values compared to all countries.
- Most of the studies use WGI (2016) governance variables that are mainly devised for inquiring the role of governance on growth, rather than role of governance on outward FDI. Another problem with these indices is that they encompass 31 different datasets with sub indices under same name or similar indices from different databases. Hence there exists a high multicollinearity. Also, another disadvantage is that some datasets do not include same indices for all countries; some specific only to African countries or the datasets do not contain all the years. Hence there is a high asymmetry when all countries involved.

SOLUTIONS AND RECOMMENDATIONS

How the study tackles those drawbacks in the previous section is as follows;

The study employs System GMM analysis that allows both overcoming endogeneity problem and including lag of FDI outflows as a possible determinant of FDI outflows. Hence it is not static but dynamic panel analysis.

- The study excludes least developed countries from the analysis based on difference in governance infrastructure that developed in the historical context. Least developed countries are generally ex-colonies, did not find a chance to establish their own governance structures since they are ruled by the regimes of colonizers for many years. When they thought they won their independence, they were ruled by totalitarian regimes left behind and supported by advanced countries of today for sustaining political stability of the region or securing their economic interests (Beyer, 2008; Etzioni, 2008). The colonial state and extractive institutions persisted even after independence (Acemoglu et.al, 2001). Developing countries generally are not colonized as in the case of least developed countries; they are just occupied. They are not extractive states; most of them are either founder or part of great civilizations in the past. Main problem is that most of them could not adapt their historical and cultural inheritance, customs, economic practices, belief and legal system with modern practices and standards of advanced countries, but they have made an effort to catch up advanced countries, hence they have better governance infrastructure compared with least developed countries. Thus including least developed countries into the analysis leads to biased results.
- Four governance indices are created in the study based on two different databases as ICRG (2011) and FRH (2011). All the sub-indices are totally distinct from each other; hence there is less multicollinearity issue. All of the sub-indices are available for all countries starting from 1996. Hence the governance clusters are symmetrical in the sense that, any sub-indices used for any country will be used for other countries too. Kaufman et al. (2011) recognizes the fact that other definitions of governance may of course be relevant for other purposes and encourages users with different objectives to combine their sub-indices in different ways more suited to their needs. Hence, four aspects of governance are determined that have potential to influence FDI decision of MNCs. Hence, the aim of the study is to measure the role of governance on FDI outflows just based on these aspects of governance. It is more clearly in this way, which sub-indices are used for aggregate indices for which purposes.

Figure 1. Determinants of outward FDI

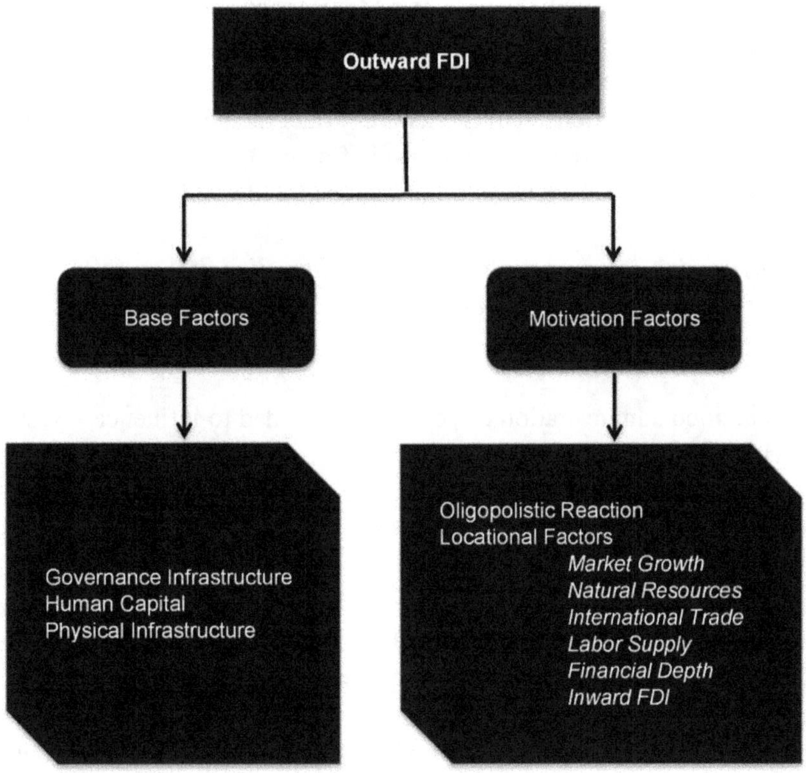

THEORETICAL PERSPECTIVE

Figure 1 presents that any outward FDI decision taken by individual investor or MNC depends on two factors as base and motivation. Without the base that the home country offers to investors, any motivation behind the outward FDI decision may not put into practice. FDI theories in the literature has either totally excluded the base factor or partially included it as other determinants of FDI. Most of the studies in the literature have concentrated on the motivation factor behind the FDI decision.

Base Factors

Base factors include governance infrastructure, physical infrastructure and human capital that the home countries offer to investors.

Governance Infrastructure

Governance infrastructure of a country may affect outward FDI in two ways. First, and most distinctive, is the positive impact of quality of governance on outward FDI both in the short and long run.

The effect of governance on FDI is firstly through the effect of institutions on investment environment of a country and secondly through the decreasing transaction and production costs, and uncertainty (Bellos and Subasat, 2012).

Formal institutions such as constitutions, prudential laws, regulations, government policies and informal institutions such as traditions, habits, customs affect the perception and willingness of investors, they limit opportunism, build transactional trust in financial transactions, and ultimately influence international players to engage in cross border transactions (North, 1990).

Governance helps determine policy formulation and implementation that, in turn, determine whether or not there is a sound, attractive business environment for investment and production. (World Bank, 2003, p.10)

Good policies and good administration of policies are needed to influence investment climate of a country and one without the other would be ineffective (World Bank, 2003).

High quality of governance infrastructure offers domestic enterprises favorable conditions to become strong and competitive for foreign expansion by allowing them to close deals with host countries' administration (Klimek, 2015).

Klimek (2015) also argues that governance infrastructure of home countries may significantly influence development opportunities of its multinationals abroad if the acquirers were operating in a more transparent and reliable institutional framework, especially to overcome the obstacles that are mainly raised by the national security of the host countries.

Second effect is the negative short run effect of governance infrastructure on outward FDI mainly referred as escape response of outward FDI due to low quality of governance in home countries (Klimek, 2015; Witt and Lewin, 2007).

Witt and Lewin (2007) argue that in times of rapid changes in the extra-institutional environment, slower rate of institutional change due to higher levels of societal coordination increases the probability of misalignments between firms' needs and home country's institutional environment that leads the increased propensity of firms to take outward FDI decision as a means of escape to other (host) countries in which institutional environment is perceived to be in closer alignment with firms' needs (Witt and Lewin, 2007).

Institutions may propel or even force the outflow of capital from particular locations. Poor institutions may induce home country capital to look for better and safer conditions in a host country. In this case, the low quality of institutions in the home country will be positively correlated with high level of outflows...Corporations headquartered in a risky location will consider opportunities to transfer some of its assets abroad. (Klimek, 2015, p.102)

The risk of expropriation, expectation of unlawful acts by the government, inhospitable conditions for new entrants, possible consequences of financial crises or difficult conditions in a home country are other factors that may encourage firms to relocate some of its assets abroad as an escape reason (Klimek, 2015)

It is claimed that this second effect of governance infrastructure on outward FDI may only occur in the short run since after a point, these MNCs will eventually move their parent company to another country where there exists a well established governance infrastructure and after that point is reached, it is no more possible to talk about outward FDI for the initial home country. Hence the long run relationship between governance infrastructure and outward FDI is still positive; low quality of governance is a structural impediment for flourishing of MNCs to increase outward FDI to affiliates in host countries.

Human Capital

The quality of human capital in home country determines the skill level of management, workers and innovation capabilities of research personnel in R&D bases of the parent company. Since innovation capabilities of parent company determines the extent of outward FDI by protected knowledge and management capabilities determine marketing, advertising, communication and transportation costs through internalization of MNCs, high level of human capital is a base factor that increases outward FDI through foreign operations of the parent firm.

Physical Infrastructure

Not only the quality of physical infrastructure in host countries, but also the quality of physical infrastructure in home countries where FDI is originated matters since the quality of physical infrastructure are associated with greater accessibility and reduction in transportation costs. (Khadaroo and Seetanah, 2007)

Erenburg (1993) argues that if physical infrastructure were not extended to local and multinational enterprises publicly, then these enterprises would be operating with less efficiency, as they would have to build their own infrastructure leading to duplication and wasting of resources.

Motivation Factors

FDI decision of a typical foreign investor is taken at least considering one motivation factor as;

Oligopolistic Reaction

According to Knickerbocker (1973), FDI is an interactive kind of corporate behavior by which rival firms in an industry composed of a few large firms countering one another's moves by making similar moves themselves.

Either the countering firms acquire about the same advantages as the firm that made the initial move, so that a new competitive balance is established in the industry, or the countering firms force the firm with the advantage to forego exploiting it by the threat of intensifying competition in the industry to the point where all rivals suffer. In this case the old competitive balance is restored. (Knickerbocker, 1973, p.6)

Locational Factors

Market Growth

The literature has mainly focused on the negative effect of market growth on outward FDI decision of MNCs based on market seeking motive. Low level of growth is considered as a sign of weaker performance of home economy leading investors to interest in locations offering better prospects by allowing diversification with higher returns (Klimek, 2015). Also, high level of growth not only attracts investors from abroad, but also encourages domestic firms to invest locally, hence leading to decreasing amount of outward FDI (Globerman et.al., 2006).

But, it is claimed that high growth rate in home country increases investment opportunities of parent company in the form of outward FDI due to the higher amount of abundant capital ready to invest in locations that bring higher returns (Klimek, 2015).

Given the higher growth and structural transformation of many developing countries, we can expect further expansion of outward FDI as these countries aspire to become significant regional or global players. (Das, 2013, p.9)

Natural Resources

High level of available natural resources not only attracts investors from abroad as in the form of inward FDI, but also encourages domestic firms to invest locally, hence leading to decreasing amount of outward FDI according to resource seeking motive. Thus, low level of available natural resources in home countries leads to increase in FDI outflows.

International Trade

International operations of MNCs are generally established to replace exports or to produce imports and in some cases, international operations occur only because there is actual or potential trade. International trade brings enterprises of one country into contact with enterprises of another country, which often causes conflict. International operations are one means of resolving this conflict. Not only advantages lead to trade but also trade leads to advantages. A firm may establish distribution channels or may establish differentiated product through its export activities, which improves its advantages leading to foreign operations (Hymer, 1960).

Labor Supply

Low level of labor supply in home country both leads to higher wages and lower quality of human capital unable to meet the necessary skill set for domestic operations of parent company. Hence MNCs established in home country will seek foreign markets with available or abundant labor supply that results in increase in FDI outflows based on labor seeking motive.

Financial Depth

Tight regulations on financial markets, uneasy access to financial capital in the form of credits and liquid assets in home country makes parent company hard to borrow locally in order to finance its investments. Hence MNCs established in home country will seek foreign markets where well-established financial markets exist, leading to increase in FDI outflows based on finance seeking motive.

Inward FDI

Increasing level of FDI inflows in a country indicates that as a host country, it is an attraction center for foreign investors, hence domestic firms and MNCs that established their parent company in that home country are less inclined to take outward investment decision in foreign locations, instead they try to expand their operations in their home market first. Hence the trend in FDI inflows should be the first indicator for home country MNCs to expand their international operations.

Since FDI inflows in transition countries are generally market or resource seeking, MNCs investing in these countries do not establish R&D centers since it is not technology intensive FDI as in developed countries, instead the knowledge embedded in the production process are protected by patents. Hence MNCs established in transition countries cannot increase their FDI outflows because there are no or few spillover effects from FDI inflows.

MEASURING GOVERNANCE

Reviewing the literature, all the studies examining role of governance on FDI based on either just one index like corruption, political stability, etc. or aggregate indices as Kaufman et al. (2011), La Porta et al. (1997), etc.

Different authors led to different conclusions based on countries included, data span, estimation techniques and governance indices used. There are both similar and contrasting results with respect to these differences.

Aggregate indicators drawn from a variety of sources should provide more precise measures of governance than individual indicators (Globerman and Shapiro, 2002). It is possible to measure the effect of different aspects of governance on outward FDI by this way. That's why four aggregate governance indicators created by sub-indices taken from ICRG and FRH databases used in the study.

The three governance indicators; political stability, administrative quality and public voice are based on governance indicators developed by Aysan et.al. (2006). But, the reason to include these indicators, the motivation behind using them and the sub-indices of the indicators differ from Aysan et.al. (2006). Governance indicators used in the study are as follows:

Political Stability Index (PSI)

This index is constructed to measure the safety of political environment in home countries. This index is the average of three indices from ICRG (2011); government stability, external conflict and internal conflict.

Since the FDI decision of MNCs based on motivations and concerns different than short-term capital flows, politically unstable countries are not preferred as home countries to initiate outward FDI.

If the home country of the MNCs, which initially is politically stable, turns into unstable either because of internal and external conflict, or the impaired government, MNCs either decreases their size on the home country by increasing outward FDI or shifts their bases to politically more stable countries.

Government stability is the most important aspect of political stability. Since MNCs initiate foreign operations from home country, based on current government policies, they want home country governments to be stable and realizing promised policies in order to earn profits based on those outward FDI decisions initiated before.

The internal conflict is the indicator of how the public in the home country reacts against government; it is the outcome of policies of current and past governments. MNCs do not want operate in home countries that lack of internal peace, with conflict and civil warfare in everyday life.

Due to external conflict, MNCs do not want to establish their operation bases in home countries that are under the high probability of constant warfare or conflicts with neighbor countries.

Economic Stability Index (ESI)

This index is constructed to measure the sustainability of FDI due to economic stability of the home countries. This index is the average of six indices from ICRG (2011); risk for budget balance, risk for current account, risk for exchange rate stability, risk for foreign debt, risk for inflation and risk for international liquidity.

Economic stability is another important aspect of governance, since MNCs consider the costs and returns on outward FDI projects. If an economy is governed by inadequate and inconsistent economic policies and turns into unstable one, it constitutes the major cause of unpredictable high costs. Returns on FDI projects, which seems profitable at the beginning turn into losses mainly due to exchange rate risks and inflation. Bad economic governance increases uncertainty and risks, which are detrimental to foreign operations. Hence MNCs either relocate its operation base to economically more stable home country or just make outward FDI if they predicted that the time required to exploit full return on FDI comes before the time of the economy in the home country becomes unstable.

Administrative Quality Index (AQI)

This index is constructed to measure the quality of the relationship between investor and the administrative / bureaucratic institutions of the home country, and the protection of investor rights. This index is the average of three indices from ICRG (2011); investment profile, bureaucracy quality and corruption.

MNCs taking outward FDI decision in a home country evaluate the performance of bureaucracy based on how responsive is the system to the need of investors, does it take too much time and effort even to initiate simple steps of investment plans, do investor have to deal with lots of unnecessary formalities and red tape. The bad quality of bureaucracy is a detrimental factor for foreign operations, since it increases the time for implementation of investment plans; hence it increases the costs of investment due to time lags.

Another important factor is the role of corruption in carrying out investment plans of MNCs. It increases the cost of outward FDI; hence it is a detrimental factor.

MNCs also consider the protection against expropriation, contract viability by the risk of unilateral contract modification or cancellation, and payment delays by the extent that profits can be transferred out of the host country to home country bases. These sub factors define the investment profile of a home country and it constitutes an important role for MNCs taking outward FDI decision since they show the extent of protection of investor rights.

Public Voice Index (PVI)

This index is constructed to measure the protection of consumer rights against investors and investor rights against government. This index is the average of three indices; democratic accountability from ICRG (2011), political rights and civil liberties from FRH (2011).

MNCs internalize external markets through outward FDI and they import products from their own foreign affiliates in the host countries. The type of products and services supplied by MNCs to home country markets are highly sensitive to the preferences of consumers since the consumer rights in the home country are well protected. Any reduction in the quality of goods and services offered to domestic consumers or any harm given to environment or public health is confronted with public reaction either by the legal system which provides those rights to consumers through lawsuits or by democratic actions through boycott, rallies, assembly against MNCs. Since MNCs take this reality into account at the planning stage of their investment, increasing protection of consumer rights either through legal system or democratic rights of the public do not constitute a detrimental factor for FDI outflows in these countries. On the contrary, they enlarge the preference set of consumers, which lead to increased amount of FDI outflows by MNCs. This is the mechanism for the protection of consumer rights against investors in home country.

Democratic institutions provide checks and balances on elected officials, which in turn reduce arbitrary government intervention and lowers the risk of policy reversal and strengthen private property protection. (Asiedu and Lien, 2011, p.1)

Hence home countries governed by democratic regimes are preferred by MNCs to establish their bases of operation, which initiates outward FDI. This is the mechanism for the protection of investor rights against government of home country.

DATA AND VARIABLES

The study covers fifty-two emerging market economies by excluding all least developed countries for the period 1996-2010. See Table 3 in Appendix 1 for the list of emerging market economies covered in the study. See Table 4 in Appendix 2 for the source of the variables.

STATISTICAL ANALYSIS

Trend in FDI Outflows

Figure 2 both presents total FDI outflows from three different country clusters in million dollars and total FDI outflows from three different country clusters as a percentage of all FDI outflows in the world. Advanced, developing and least developed countries all have an increasing trend in total FDI outflows. While the FDI outflows from advanced countries had increased trefold, the FDI outflows from developing countries had increased sixfold during the period 1996-2010. Also, the share of total FDI outflows from developing and least developing countries had increased, the share of total FDI outflows from advanced countries had decreased as a percantage of all FDI outflows in the world.

According to Figure 3, average FDI outflows as a percentage of GDP from emerging market economies had doubled with an increasing trend. Inspecting one standard error bands indicate that emerging market economies had experienced divergence with respect to this indicator. Divergence is highest in 2003 and 2009; right after financial crises. Kuwait in 1998 and 2003, Bahrain in 2009 have the lowest, Bostwana in 2001, Bahrain in 2004, Kuwait in 2007 and 2009 have the highest level of FDI outflows as a percentage of GDP.

Figure 2. Total FDI outflows and FDI outflows as a percentage of world
Source: Author's own calculation based on UNCTAD (2016).
Note: The right axis for LDCs.

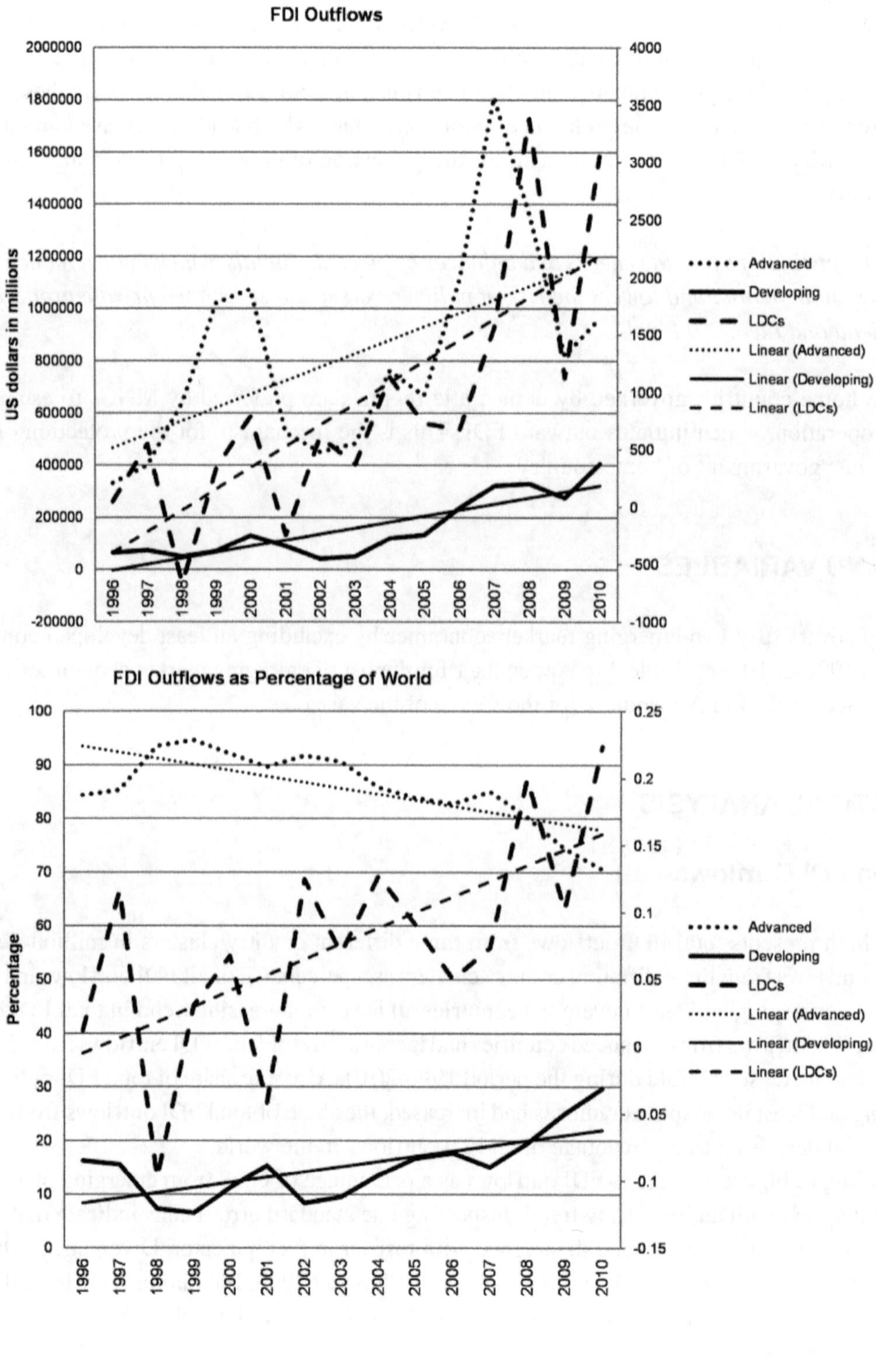

Figure 3. FDI outflows as a percentage of GDP
Source: Author's own calculation based on UNCTAD (2016).

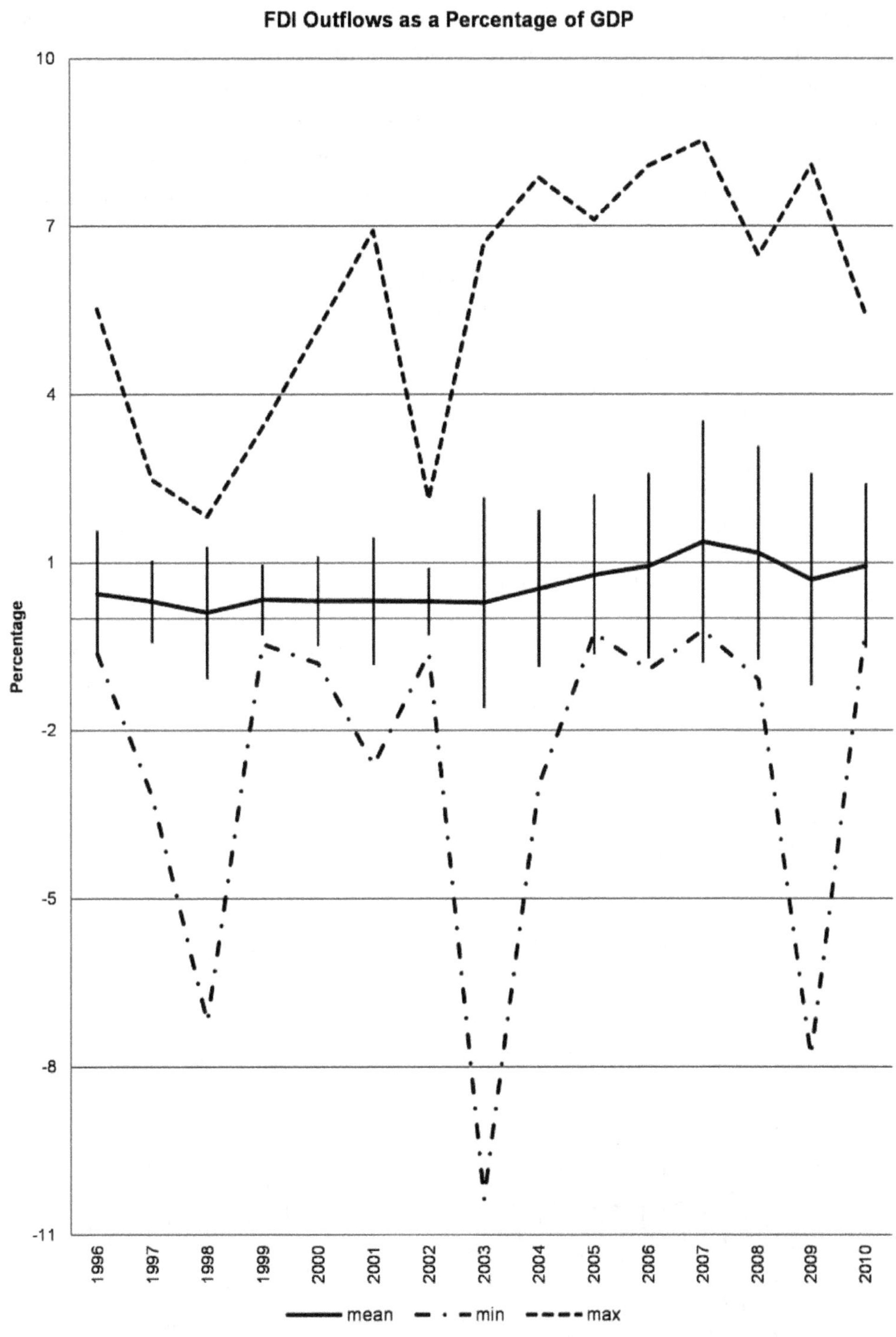

Trend in Governance Infrastructure

Figure 4 presents four different aspects of governance in emerging market economies as political stability (psi), economic stability (esi), administrative quality (aqi) and public voice (pvi). Emerging market economies have the highest performance in political stability compared with other governance variables. The economic stability of these countries has a clear increasing trend despite the financial crises experienced in this period. There is no increasing or decreasing trend in other governance variables. These countries have clear deficit in governance infrastructure especially in administrative quality and public voice.

Figure 4. Average governance performance for emerging market economies
Source: Author's own calculation based on ICRG (2011) and FRH (2011).

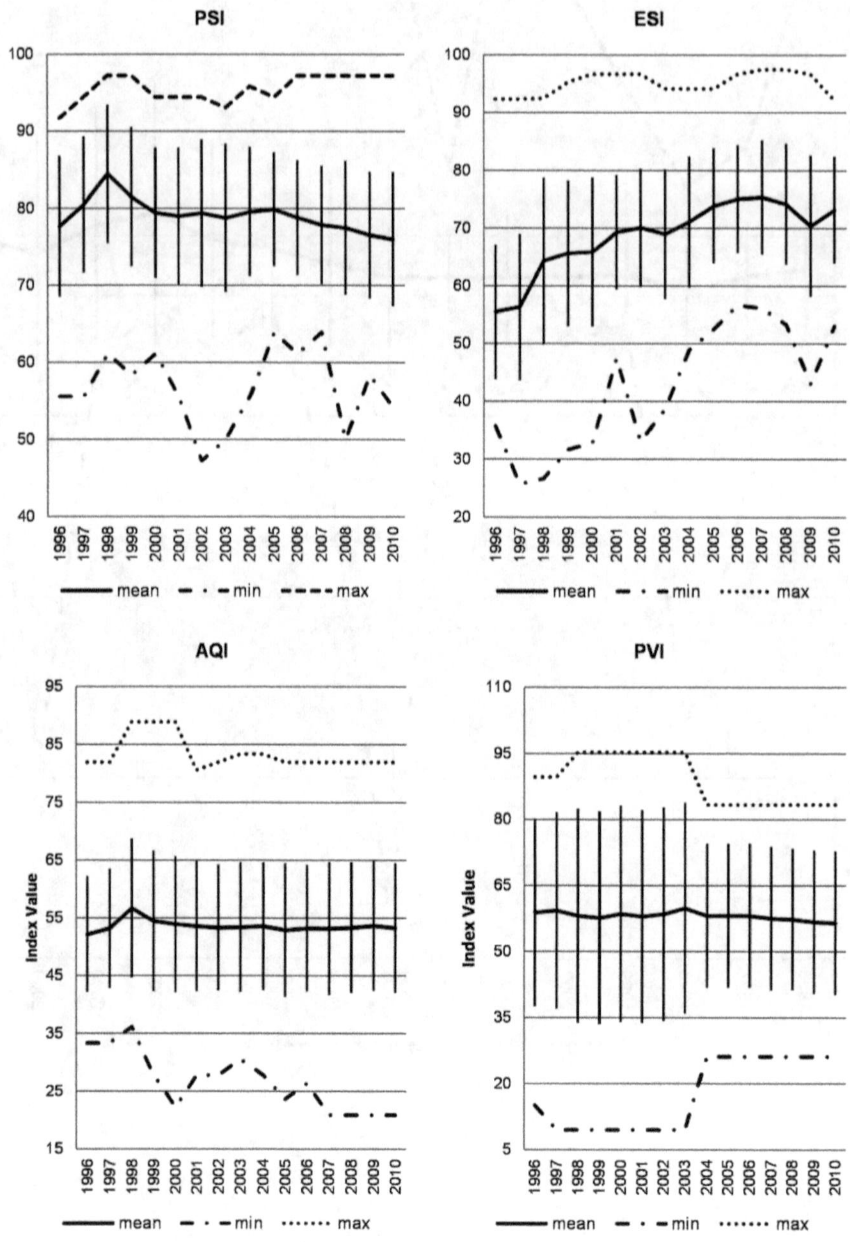

Figure 5 presents the comparison of governance indices of emerging market economies and developed market economies. Except for economic stability (esi), emerging market economies have performed worse than developed market economies for all other governance variables. It seems that emerging market economies have closed the gap in economic stability relative to the developed market economies.

Figure 5. Average governance performance for emerging and developed market economies
Source: Author's own calculation based on ICRG (2011) and FRH (2011).

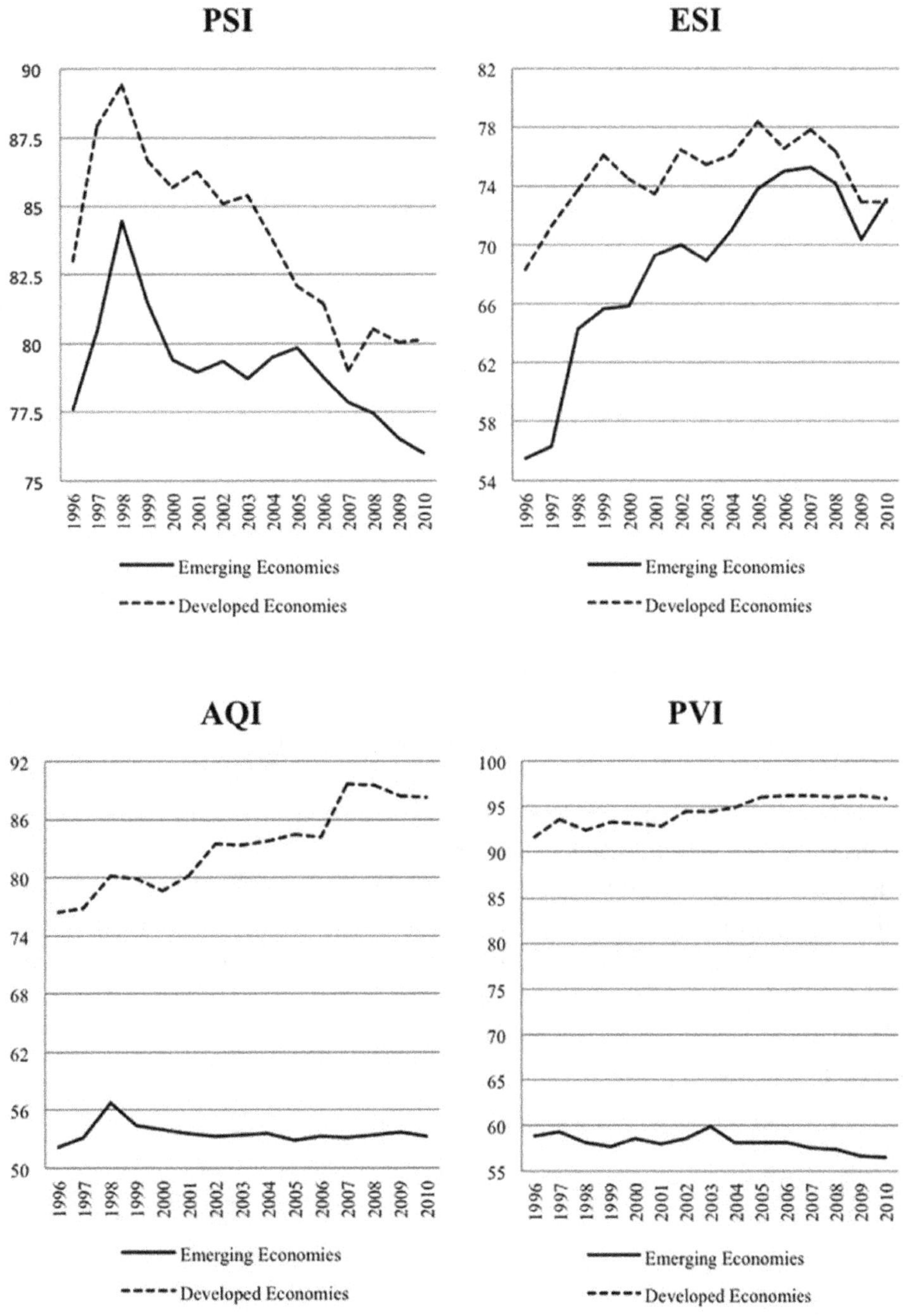

EMPIRICAL ANALYSIS

Empirical Model

The general model to be estimated with System GMM is as below;

$$y_{it} = \propto y_{i,t-1} + X'_{it}\beta + \varepsilon_{it} \tag{1}$$

$$\varepsilon_{it} = \mu_i + \nu_{it} \tag{2}$$

$$E(\mu_i) = E(\nu_{it}) = E(\mu_i \nu_{it}) = 0 \tag{3}$$

The disturbance term ε_{it} has two orthogonal components as the fixed effects, μ_i and idiosyncratic shocks, ν_{it}

$$\Delta y_{it} = (\propto - 1)\Delta y_{i,t-1} + \Delta X'_{it}\beta + \Delta \nu_{it} \tag{4}$$

Assuming that changes in any instrumenting variable w are uncorrelated with the fixed effects (Roodman, 2009).

$$E(\Delta w_{it}\mu_i) = 0 \tag{5}$$

The System GMM estimator that is developed by Arellano and Bover (1995), Blundell and Bond (1998) augments the Difference GMM estimator that is developed by Arellano and Bond (1991) by making an additional assumption of the first differences of instrument variables are uncorrelated with the fixed effects (5), which allows the introduction of more instruments. Hence it can dramatically improve efficiency by building a system of two equations; one is the original equation (1), the other is the transformed one (4). While Arellano and Bond (1991) instruments differences with levels, Blundell and Bond (1998) instruments levels with differences (Roodman, 2009).

Validity depends on the assumption that the v_{it} is not serially correlated. But if the v_{it} is serially correlated of order 1 then, for instance, $y_{i,t-2}$ is endogenous to the $v_{i,t-1}$ in the error term in differences, $\Delta\varepsilon_{it} = v_{it} - v_{i,t-1}$, making it a potentially invalid instrument. The researcher would need to restrict the instrument set starting with third lag or longer. If the researcher finds second order correlation, he or she would need to start with even longer lags (Roodman, 2009).

Reduced From Equation;

$$OFDI_{it} = \propto OFDI_{i,t-1} + \beta_1 BASE_{it} + \beta_2 MOT_{it} + \varepsilon_{it} \tag{1.1}$$

$$\varepsilon_{it} = \mu_i + \nu_{it} \tag{1.2}$$

$$E\left(\mu_i\right) = E(\nu_{it}) = E(\mu_i \nu_{it}) = 0 \tag{1.3}$$

$$\Delta OFDI_{it} = \delta \Delta OFDI_{i,t-1} + \phi \Delta BASE_{it} + \lambda \Delta MOT_{it} + \nu_{it} \tag{1.4}$$

$$E\left(\Delta w_{it} \mu_i\right) = 0 \tag{1.5}$$

$OFDI_{it}$ represents FDI outflows for country i in year t. $OFDI_{i,t-1}$ represents FDI outflows for country i in year t-1 to measure the oligopolistic reaction. $BASE_{it}$ represents governance indicators, human capital and physical infrastructure as base factors. MOT_{it} represents motivation factors for country i in year t. GDP growth is included as a motivation factor in all regressions since FDI, governance and growth are three concepts interact with each other according to literature.

Model 1 is the benchmark model including lag of FDI outflows, all governance indicators, human capital, physical infrastructure and FDI inflows.

Models 2-5 include governance infrastructure as the only base factor, GDP growth and all other motivation factors. All motivation factors other than lag of FDI outflows and GDP growth are regressed in separate models.

Estimation Results

According to our benchmark Models 1.1, 1.2, 1.3 and 1.4 in Table 1; improvement in all aspects of governance infrastructure leads to increase in FDI outflows in emerging market economies. Politically and economically more stable home countries with high administrative quality due to efficient and uncorrupted bureaucracies and more democratic institutions providing check and balances against arbitrary government intervention creates more investment friendly business environment and secure both investor and consumer rights, leading to increase in outward FDI. The results of the study support the findings of Globerman et.al. (2006) with respect to aggregate governance infrastructure and Subasat and Bellos (2013) with respect to administrative quality and public voice. The findings of the study are in contrast with the literature on outward FDI as an escape response to deterioration in governance infrastructure in home countries (Das, 2013; Witt and Lewin, 2007; Kayam, 2009; Klimek, 2015).

Model 1.2 in Table 1 suggests that improvement in human capital in home country increases FDI outflows by enhancing skill level of management, workers and technical staff by increasing innovative capabilities of the parent company and decreasing marketing, advertising, communication and transportation costs due to better management capabilities. Since there is a statistically significant positive relationship between human capital and FDI outflows, FDI outflows do not base on efficiency seeking motive; instead human capital is a base factor positively contributing to expanding foreign operations of MNCs.

Improvement in physical infrastructure leads to increase in FDI outflows from emerging market economies due to greater accessibility and reduction in communication and transportation costs according to Model 1.8 in Table 1. Hence it will not be a misleading conclusion that physical infrastructure is a base factor for outward FDI decision of MNCs.

All models in Table 1 reveal that there is a statistically significant negative relationship between FDI inflows and FDI outflows in emerging market economies. Increasing level of FDI inflows indicates that these countries are attraction center based on either resource or market seeking motive for MNCs established abroad, hence MNCs established in these countries first try to exploit these locational attractions by increasing domestic operations of parent company leading decrease in FDI outflows.

All of the estimation results in Table 1 and 2 reveal that lag of FDI outflows has statistically significant positive effect on current FDI outflows, which confirms the oligopolistic reaction by suggesting that outward FDI is an interactive corporate behavior in an industry where a few large firms counter one another's moves by making similar moves themselves (Knickerbocker, 1973)

According to the estimation results both in Table 1 and 2; statistically significant positive relationship between market growth and FDI outflows suggest that FDI outflows from emerging market economies do not base on market seeking motive. Higher growth rates in home countries increase investment opportunities of parent company in the form of outward FDI due to the higher amount of abundant capital ready to invest in locations that bring higher returns. The results of the study do not support Globerman et.al. (2006) who found no statistically significant effect of growth on outward FDI. But our result support Klimek (2015) in his estimation result with dependent variable of per capita FDI outflows instead of outward FDI stocks.

The estimation results of Model 2.1 in Table 2 present that there is a statistically significant negative relationship between available natural resources and FDI outflows in emerging market economies. Hence decreasing level of available natural resources in home countries leads to increase in FDI outflows based on resource seeking motive.

There is a statistically significant negative relationship between labor supply and FDI outflows in emerging market economies according to Model 3.2 in Table 2. Low level of labor supply in home countries both lead to higher wages and lower quality of human capital unable to meet the necessary skill set for domestic operations of parent company. Hence MNCs established in home country will seek foreign markets with available or abundant labor supply that result in increase in FDI outflows based on labor seeking motive.

Inspection of Model 4.3 in Table 2 reveals that international trade substitutes FDI outflows in emerging market economies due to statistically significant negative relationship between international trade and FDI outflows. Increasing amount of international trade due to higher amount of exports replace FDI outflows from home countries. The findings of the study contrast with Das (2013) who found that increase in trade openness proxied by our measure leads to increase in outward FDI and Globerman et.al. (2006) who found that international trade complements outward FDI.

The result of Model 5.4 in Table 2 presents that there is a statistically significant negative relationship between financial depth and FDI outflows in emerging market economies. Decreasing amount of financial depth due to tight regulations on financial markets, uneasy access to financial capital in the form of credits and liquid assets in home country makes parent company hard to borrow locally in order to finance its investments. Hence MNCs established in home country will seek foreign markets where well-established financial markets exist, leading to increase in FDI outflows based on finance seeking motive.

FUTURE RESEARCH DIRECTIONS

The main drawback of the study is that the analysis cover the period 1996-2010, hence the effect of deterioration in governance infrastructure in several Middle East emerging market economies on outward

Table 1. System GMM estimation results I

Dependent Variable: ofdi						
	Model 1.1	**Model 1.2**	**Model 1.3**	**Model 1.4**	**Model 1.5**	**Model 1.6**
l.ofdi	0.415***	0.616***	0.352**	0.417***	0.651***	0.612***
	(0.153)	(0.140)	(0.143)	(0.123)	(0.168)	(0.167)
psi	0.012*					
	(0.006)					
esi		0.005*				
		(0.003)				
aqi			0.022**			
			(0.009)			
pvi				0.020*		
				(0.011)		
humcap					0.005*	
					(0.003)	
infra						0.011*
						(0.006)
gdpgr	0.059**	0.060**	0.062**	0.059*	0.051**	0.061*
	(0.023)	(0.026)	(0.028)	(0.031)	(0.024)	(0.033)
ifdi	-0.086*	-0.084*	-0.097**	-0.136*	-0.069*	-0.089*
	(0.046)	(0.049)	(0.048)	(0.075)	(0.038)	(0.051)
Prob > F	0.000	0.000	0.000	0.000	0.000	0.000
Countries	52	52	52	52	52	52
Instruments	32	36	32	32	33	32
Hansen	0.390	0.307	0.237	0.372	0.743	0.376
AR(2)	0.467	0.389	0.485	0.441	0.401	0.397

Source: Author's Own Calculations.

Notes: The values in parenthesis are robust standard errors. ***, ** and * denote significance levels at % 1, % 5 and % 10 respectively. AR(#) is test for #-order serial correlation in the #-differenced residuals, under the null of no serial correlation. Hansen test of over-identification is under the null that all instruments are valid. All of the independent variables are treated endogenously. Appropriate lags of endogenous variables were instrumented according to AR(#) test of serial correlation.

FDI after 2010 could not have been analyzed due to data unavailability. A further study with available governance data covering 2010-2015 may be necessary to conclude that the relationship between governance infrastructure and FDI outflows changed or not in emerging market economies.

CONCLUSION

It is found that total FDI outflows in million dollars and total FDI outflows as a percentage of all countries in the world both have increasing trend in emerging market economies. Average FDI outflows as a percentage of home country GDP has doubled during the period under analysis. These countries gener-

Table 2. System GMM estimation results II

Dependent Variable: ofdi				
	Model 2.1	**Model 3.2**	**Model 4.3**	**Model 5.4**
ofdi	0.517**	0.382***	0.731***	0.616***
	(0.197)	(0.091)	(0.202)	(0.175)
psi	0.013*			
	(0.007)			
esi		0.015*		
		(0.008)		
aqi			0.014**	
			(0.007)	
pvi				0.009**
				(0.005)
gdpgr	0.099*	0.044*	0.068**	0.078***
	(0.052)	(0.026)	(0.031)	(0.027)
natural	-0.024*			
	(0.013)			
labsup		-0.012*		
		(0.007)		
trop			-0.008**	
			(0.003)	
findep				-0.008*
				(0.005)
Prob > F	0.000	0.000	0.000	0.000
Countries	52	52	52	52
Instruments	32	52	28	37
Hansen	0.468	0.435	0.748	0.283
AR(2)	0.477	0.485	0.434	0.421

Source: Author's Own Calculations.

Notes: The values in parenthesis are robust standard errors. ***, ** and * denote significance levels at % 1, % 5 and % 10 respectively. AR(#) is test for #-order serial correlation in the #-differenced residuals, under the null of no serial correlation. Hansen test of over-identification is under the null that all instruments are valid. All of the independent variables are treated endogenously. Appropriate lags of endogenous variables were instrumented according to AR(#) test of serial correlation.

ally have clear deficit in different aspects of governance infrastructure. Also on average, they have an increasing economic stability despite global financial crises occurred in this period.

According to the empirical findings, improvement in all aspects of governance infrastructure leads to increase in FDI outflows in emerging market economies. Politically and economically more stable home countries with high administrative quality due to efficient and uncorrupted bureaucracies and more democratic institutions providing check and balances against arbitrary government interventions create more investment friendly business environment and secure both investor and consumer rights, leading to increase in outward FDI. Hence governance infrastructure together with human capital and physical infrastructure are base factors for home country MNCs. It is also found that FDI outflows from emerging market economies are not market or efficiency seeking; instead they are resource, labor or finance seeking. And international trade, especially increase in exports, replaces FDI outflows. The results also support oligopolistic reaction behavior of MNCs in taking outward FDI decision. Finally, it is found that increase in FDI inflows leads to decrease in FDI outflows since MNCs established in emerging home country markets first try to exploit locational advantages before expanding their foreign operations.

REFERENCES

Acemoglu, D., Johnson, S., & Robinson, J. A. (2001). The colonial origins of comparative development: An empirical investigation. *The American Economic Review*, *91*(5), 1369–1401. doi:10.1257/aer.91.5.1369

Arellano, M., & Bond, S. (1991). Some tests of specification for panel data: Monte Carlo evidence and an application to employment equations. *The Review of Economic Studies*, *58*(2), 277–297. doi:10.2307/2297968

Arellano, M., & Bover, O. (1995). Another look at the instrumental variable estimation of error-components models. *Journal of Econometrics*, *68*(1), 29–51. doi:10.1016/0304-4076(94)01642-D

Asiedu, E., & Lien, D. (2011). Democracy, foreign direct investment and natural resources. *Journal of International Economics*, *84*(1), 99–111. doi:10.1016/j.jinteco.2010.12.001

Aysan, A. F., Nabli, M. K., & Véganzonès-Varoudakis, M. A. (2006). Governance and private investment in the Middle East and North Africa. *World Bank Policy Research Working Paper*, (3934), 1-65.

Behbehani, M., & Al Hallaq, S. S. (2013). Impact of home country outward foreign direct investment on its economic growth: A case of Kuwait. *Asian Journal of Business and Management Sciences*, *3*(3), 19–33.

Bellos, S., & Subasat, T. (2012). Governance and foreign direct investment: A panel gravity model approach. *International Review of Applied Economics*, *26*(3), 303–328. doi:10.1080/02692171.2011.587110

Beyer, C. (2008). *Violent globalisms: conflict in response to empire*. Ashgate Publishing, Ltd.

Blundell, R., & Bond, S. (1998). Initial conditions and moment restrictions in dynamic panel data models. *Journal of Econometrics*, *87*(1), 115–143. doi:10.1016/S0304-4076(98)00009-8

Bukari, P. A. (2016). *Foreign direct investment: How beneficial is it?* Retrieved May 5, 2016 from http://www.dundee.ac.uk/cepmlp/gateway/files.php?file=cepmlp_car17_36_983684938.pdf

Das, K. C. (2013). Home country determinants of outward FDI from developing countries. *Margin: The Journal of Applied Economic Research*, *7*(1), 93–116.

Erenburg, S. J. (1993). The real effects of public investment on private investment. *Applied Economics*, *25*(6), 831–837. doi:10.1080/00036849300000137

Etzioni, A. (2008). *Security first: for a muscular, moral foreign policy*. Yale University Press.

FRH. (2011). *Freedom in the world database*. New York: Freedom House.

Globerman, S., & Shapiro, D. (2002). Global foreign direct investment flows: The role of governance infrastructure. *World Development*, *30*(11), 1899–1919. doi:10.1016/S0305-750X(02)00110-9

Globerman, S., Shapiro, D., & Tang, Y. (2006). Foreign direct investment in emerging and transition European countries. *International Finance Review*, *6*(6), 431–459. doi:10.1016/S1569-3767(05)06017-6

Hymer, S. H. (1960). *The International Operation of National Firms: A Study of Direct Investment* (Ph.D. dissertation). M.I.T.

ICRG. (2011). *International country risk guide*. New York: PRS Group.

Kaufman, D., Kraay, A., & Mastruzzi, M. (2011). The worldwide governance indicators: Methodology and analytical issues. *Hague Journal on the Rule of Law*, *3*(2), 220–246. doi:10.1017/S1876404511200046

Kayam, S. S. (2009). Home market determinants of FDI outflows from developing and transition economies. *MPRA Paper*, *16781*, 1–19.

Khadaroo, A. J., & Seetanah, B. (2007, November). Transport Infrastructure and FDI: Lessons from Sub Saharan African Economies. In *African Economic Conference (AEC)* (pp. 15-17). Academic Press.

Klimek, A. (2015). Institutions and outward foreign direct investment. *International Journal of Management and Economics*, *46*(1), 101–119. doi:10.1515/ijme-2015-0023

Knickerbocker, F. T. (1973). *Oligopolistic reaction and the multinational enterprise*. Cambridge, MA: Harvard University Press.

La Porta, R., Lopez-de-Silanes, F., Shleifer, A., & Vishny, R. W. (1997). Legal determinants of external finance. *The Journal of Finance*, *52*(3), 1131–1150. doi:10.1111/j.1540-6261.1997.tb02727.x

North, D. C. (1990). *Institutions, institutional change and economic performance*. Cambridge University Press. doi:10.1017/CBO9780511808678

Nourbakhshian, M. R., Aghapour, A. H., & Gheshmi, R. (2012). The contribution of foreign direct investment into home country's development. *International Journal of Business and Social Science*, *3*(2), 275–287.

Roodman, D. (2009). How to do xtabond2: An introduction to difference and system GMM in Stata. *The Stata Journal*, *9*(1), 86–136.

Subasat, T., & Bellos, S. (2013). Governance and foreign direct investment in latin america: A panel gravity model approach. *Journal of Management and Sustainability*, *50*(1), 107–131.

UNCTAD. (2016). *UNCTAD statistics*. United Nations. Retrieved March 17, 2016, from http://unctadstat.unctad.org/wds/ReportFolders/reportFolders.aspx?IF_ActivePath=P,5

WDI. (2016). *World development indicators*. The World Bank. Retrieved March 17, 2016, from http://data.worldbank.org/data-catalog/world-development-indicators

WGI. (2016). *Worldwide governance indicators*. The World Bank. Retrieved March 17, 2016, from http://info.worldbank.org/governance/wgi/index.aspx#home

Witt, M. A., & Lewin, A. Y. (2007). Outward foreign direct investment as escape response to home country institutional constraints. *Journal of International Business Studies*, *38*(4), 579–594. doi:10.1057/palgrave.jibs.8400285

World Bank. (2003). *Better governance for development in the Middle East and North Africa. Mena Development Report*. Washington, DC: The World Bank.

KEY TERMS AND DEFINITIONS

Administrative Quality Index: The index value of administrative quality in home country taking values between 0 and 100.

Economic Stability Index: The index value of economic stability in home country taking values between 0 and 100.

Financial Depth: The ratio of liquid assets as a percentage of home country GDP.

Governance Infrastructure: The quality of home country institutional capabilities.

Human Capital: Availability of educated human resources in home country.

International Trade: Total volume of exports and imports as a percentage of home country GDP.

Labor Supply: Availability of population aged 15-65 that are currently employed or in search of a job in home country.

Natural Resources: Availability of total natural resource rents as a percentage of home country GDP.

Physical Infrastructure: Availability of energy, water, communication and transportation infrastructure in home country.

Political Stability Index: The index value of political stability in home country taking values between 0 and 100.

Public Voice Index: The index value of public voice in home country taking values between 0 and 100.

APPENDIX 1

Table 3. List of emerging market economies

Algeria	Gabon	Paraguay
Argentina	Guatemala	Philippines
Bahrain	Honduras	Poland
Bolivia	Hungary	Qatar
Botswana	India	Romania
Brazil	Iran	Russia
Brunei Darussalam	Jamaica	Saudi Arabia
Bulgaria	Jordan	South Africa
Cameroon	Kazakhstan	Sri Lanka
Chile	Kenya	Thailand
China	Kuwait	Tunisia
Colombia	Libya	Turkey
Congo Republic	Malaysia	Ukraine
Costa Rica	Mexico	United Arab Emirates
Croatia	Moldova	Uruguay
Dominican Republic	Morocco	Venezuela
Ecuador	Pakistan	
Egypt	Papua New Guinea	

APPENDIX 2

Table 4. Data source

Variable Name	Code	Indices\Sub Indices	Data Source
FDI Outflows	ofdi	FDI Outflows as a Percentage of GDP	UNCTAD (2016)
FDI Inflows	ifdi	FDI Inflows as a Percentage of GDP	UNCTAD (2016)
Political Stability	psi		
Index		Government Stability	ICRG (2011)
		Internal Conflict	ICRG (2011)
		External Conflict	ICRG (2011)
Economic Stability	esi		
Index		Risk for Budget Balance	ICRG (2011)
		Risk for Current Account as % of GDP	ICRG (2011)
		Risk for Exchange Rate Stability	ICRG (2011)
		Risk for Foreign Debt	ICRG (2011)
		Risk for Inflation	ICRG (2011)
		Risk for International Liquidity	ICRG (2011)
Administrative Quality	aqi		
Index		Investment Profile	ICRG (2011)
		Bureaucracy Quality	ICRG (2011)
		Corruption	ICRG (2011)
Public Voice Index	pvi		
		Democratic Accountability	ICRG (2011)
		Political Rights	FRH (2011)
		Civil Liberties	FRH (2011)
GDP Growth	gdpgr	GDP Growth (annual %)	WDI (2016)
Human Capital	humcap		
		Completed Primary	WDI (2016)
		Completed Secondary	WDI (2016)
		Completed Tertiary	WDI (2016)
Infrastructure	infra		
		Access to Electricity (% of population)	WDI (2016)
		Improved Water Source (% of population)	WDI (2016)
		Internet Users (per 100 people)	WDI (2016)
		Telephone Lines (per 100 people)	WDI (2016)
		Roads, Total Network / Population	WDI (2016)
		Rail Lines (total route-km) / Population	WDI (2016)
		Air Transport, Passengers Carried / Population	WDI (2016)
Labor Supply	labfor	Labor Force / Population * 100 / Population 15-64 (% of total)	WDI (2016)
Natural Resources	natural	Total Natural Resources Rents (% of GDP)	WDI (2016)
Financial Depth	findep	Money and Quasi Money (M2) as % of GDP	WDI (2016)
International Trade	trade	Trade (% of GDP)	WDI (2016)

Chapter 6
Political Economy of Foreign Direct Investment:
The Complexity of Linking Theory with Practice

Esra LaGro
CIRP, Turkey

ABSTRACT

The global political economy evolves around shifting theoretical and conceptual paradigms that simultaneously reflect the ongoing globalization process involving several actors and processes. Thus the complexity of linking the theory and practice of global political economy increases, and this, in return, accelerates further the in-depth inquiries in this interdisciplinary field of research such as discussions around global governance, international economic system, international trade, global value chains, and international development among several others. More specifically, in parallel with these developments, underlying trends in the global economy point to vast developments in both theory and practice of foreign direct investment (hereinafter FDI) across regions, countries and sectors as well, which form the main focus point of this chapter which will attempt to address the complexity of linking theory with actual practice through also involving global value chains with reference to FDI between EU member states and Turkey.

INTRODUCTION

As it is well-known, FDI has been pivotal point of research since the World War II in global economy with numerous studies and research pointing out its different aspects in both developing and developed countries. Moreover, several theoretical and/or conceptual frameworks have been brought into perspective analyzing FDI inflows and outflows in both economic and political perspectives, the patterns of FDI across the world, effects of FDI on economic development, competitiveness concerns, role of multinationals, role of international organizations, global value chains, and so on. Still, however, there is hardly any single agreed upon theoretical or conceptual framework concerning FDI but many. This

DOI: 10.4018/978-1-5225-2345-1.ch006

is partially because FDI requires further evidence from real world to sustain the mainstream theoretical framework associated with realism/economic nationalism, liberalism, critical theory of global political economy among others as well as the existing shifting theoretical paradigms on the FDI. Thus the main objective of this chapter is to attempt linking the theory and practice of FDI through the lens of global political economy while simultaneously presenting examples from Europe and Turkey reflecting also its inherent complexity.

While realizing this main objective, a multi-layered analysis will be used as the methodological framework towards reaching concrete results on FDI issues. Global level of analysis relates to a broad set of parameters such as global political developments in relation to FDI flows and even more specifically the global value chains among others. The interstate level of analysis relates to interactions between the states in relation to the FDI inflows and outflows as a subset of regional and global level.

In this chapter, first, the intersection of the mainstream GPE theories will be briefly presented both in general and specifically with reference to FDI through employment of the above-mentioned levels of analysis as the structural framework. Second, shifting paradigms of global political economy from liberalism to structural transformation, economic development, to tough international competition and to political regimes and policy environment for FDI will be points of emphasis next to several issues which form the basis of FDI decisions and processes across the world underlying further the state-market interactions as well. Third, the current work of international organizations such as UNCTAD, IFC, and OECD towards enhancement of global order vis-à-vis FDI will be briefly presented. Fourth, the FDI interactions between the European Union and Turkey will be brought into perspective as the main example. Fifth, the chapter will combine shifting global paradigms in FDI with actual FDI processes thus will attempt to link theory with practice. Finally, the chapter will briefly identify future research areas with reference to the political economy of FDI in line with the different perspectives and discussions that are presented throughout the chapter underlining the complexity of the overall process.

BACKGROUND

The mainstream GPE theories such as Realism (Economic Nationalism), Liberalism and Historical Structuralism (Marxism) provide a relatively clear analytical distinction while also covering a variety of sub-theories and hybrid paradigms in themselves or at times intersecting with one another in relation to the criticisms around the mainstream theories. This widely recognized analytical classification of the GPE theories owes to Cohn (2011). For the sake of clarity in relation to FDI, however, this section will not indulge in detailed definitions around these rather well-known GPE theories but instead will directly present an overview of more specific FDI theories that relate to the practice of FDI in an attempt to link the existing theoretical approaches with the practice for the better.

Prior to presentation of an overview of FDI theories, still, it is also important to present the internationally recognized definition of FDI. There are basically three internationally accepted definitions of FDI; one belongs to IMF (1993), the second one belongs to OECD (1996), and the third one is that of UNCTAD (2003). For the purposes of this chapter the OECD definition of FDI is taken into account which reads as below:

FDI is defined as cross-border investment by a resident entity in one economy with the objective of obtaining a lasting interest in an enterprise resident in another economy. The lasting interest implies the existence of a long-term relationship between the direct investor and the enterprise and a significant degree of influence by the direct investor on the management of the enterprise. (OECD, 1996)

Once having established the definition of FDI, it is also possible to say that the specific theories of FDI stemmed basically from the studies along the determinants of FDI and the attempts for conducting empirical studies around these specific determinants.

During the post-world war reconstruction of Europe, the investments to European countries from the USA initiated as to mend the destruction of European economy evolved in a way to associate FDI outflows and inflows eventually with Multinational Corporations (MNCs) mainly along the course of time whereby relations with home and host countries, the structure of the FDI, the social and employment effects of FDI, etc. are commonly examined. The important landmark on the FDI developments across the world occurred with the rise of neoliberalism as of 1980s until now. Although neoliberalism is usually accepted to be an economic issue, it constituted in itself the re-definition of right wing politics in both the USA and the UK at the time thus it carried heavy political connotations also reflected simultaneously on the economic recipes of the international organisations such as IMF and the World Bank. The globalization phenomenon also formed the enabling environment for the expansion of FDI flows further. International organizations eventually became more concerned with the assessment of FDI flows and its various technological, socio-cultural, development, and welfare aspects while also closely reviewing the activities of MNCs.

Conversely, FDI is not and should not be considered solely as a MNC activity, it is more than that. Currently also nations and individual local businesses which certainly cannot be classified as a MNC per se in its full sense also carry out FDI flows across the globe through joint ventures and mergers as well as complete acquisitions. In the recent years, several dimensions of FDI came into perspective and with that developing and developed country interaction across FDI issues; while policy makers were becoming more concerned with the regulatory environment for FDI or with the concern for a sound enabling environment for FDI towards investment promotion and facilitation both nationally and internationally. The establishment of WTO, and the ever increasing impact of free trade also brought expansion of FDI flows and with that the simultaneous discussions around the significance of global value chains and how possibly states could be involved in them successfully through trade and investment while increasing their competitiveness in global markets. In other words, in the new millennium, the global competitiveness challenge became tougher than ever for both states and businesses alike and FDI forms a significant component of this process along with international trade.

Against such a background, since the World War II, there have been several attempts to theorize FDI based on its evolution in the global economy through its economic and political and even social determinants, through economic modelling, through observation of its specific field applications and its consequences for host and home countries, its politics, etc. In line with these attempts, and following an overview of these, it is possible to say that there is not one single theoretical framework but many depending on the sector in question or region or country or individual firm. It is also important to remember that FDI theories are by definition interdisciplinary in nature covering macroeconomics, microeconomics, industrial organization, international trade, international business, law, finance, international development, politics, and international relations among others. Thus it is not surprising that it highly intersects with interdisciplinary field of GPE and its components.

Since there are several theoretical frameworks for explaining various different aspects of FDI from various perspectives, it is not possible to review them all here but a narrowed down focus would still be useful also in relation to conventional issue areas such as global capital markets, international trade, international development which are also directly relevant to GPE and its mainstream theories. It is also important to note that economic theories of FDI are more extensively put forth compared to political theoretical explanations by its very nature.

Economic Theories on FDI

In this context, the first group of FDI theories relate to those both at macroeconomic and institutional level. Among the macro level theories of FDI, capital markets theory, dynamic macroeconomic theory, FDI theories based on factors such as exchange rates, economic geography, the gravity approach to FDI, institutional theories can be considered among the many theories that are widely used to explain FDI phenomenon through the course of time. Capital Markets Theory, one of the oldest theories of FDI going back to 1960s postulates that FDI is determined by the interest rates. On the other hand, dynamic macroeconomic FDI theory postulates that FDI is a long term reflection of the MNC strategies and that nature and timing of the FDI depends on the changes in macroeconomic environment. Relating the FDI to factors of production and accepting innovation among the significant determinants of FDI is another theoretical paradigm which received considerable attention. The gravity approach postulates that the economic, socio-cultural proximity, etc. of two countries can increase FDI flows.

Another group of theories on FDI relate for example to international development which is also one of the issue areas of GPE. A well-known example is the Life Cycle Theory developed by Vernon (1966) in a seminal article that analyzed the relationship between product life cycle and possible FDI flows. The five stage theory of Dunning (1973) is also among the leading theories in this context where by each stage reflects a specific outcome in the FDI process in terms of attracting FDI and changes in the factors of production especially the labor in the host countries, mainly the developing countries. At the end of these five stages, this theoretical framework assumes equilibrium for incoming and outgoing FDI but whether theory meets the practice in terms of this projected equilibrium naturally remains as a point of debate.

The next group of theories is related to micro level issues such as specific markets and firms. In this context, the firm specific advantages paradigm developed by Hymer (1976) highlights, for example, the economies of scale and reduction in transaction costs in explaining the FDI processes. Another theoretical paradigm underlines the firm behavior in oligopolistic markets whereby game theoretical approach comes into the front. These two paradigms are followed by the well-known Theory of Internalization developed initially by Buckley and Casson (1976) and subsequently accelerated by Hennart (1982) and several others, which, in essence, postulate that market imperfections are challenged by creation of their own markets by the firms – the internalization.

Another significant theoretical framework is the OLI paradigm developed by Dunning (1980, 1988), in other words, what is known as the Eclectic FDI Theory. This theory takes into account a mixture of different levels of analyses into perspective including macroeconomics, international trade, microeconomics and industrial organization. The "O" signifies the ownership advantage that reduces the firm specific transaction costs in the shape of know-how, human capital, brand, etc. when operating in a different country than the home country. The "L" signifies the localization advantage whereby trade barriers, transport costs, economic input acquisition form the main assets. The "I" signifies finally the internalization advantages. The weight of O or L or I could vary depending on the firm, sector, market and country, and these in return would affect the market outcomes. OLI paradigm has also been useful in development of widely accepted typologies of FDI such as Resource seeking FDI, Market seeking FDI, Efficiency seeking FDI, Strategic asset seeking FDI.

Undoubtedly, the economic theories of FDI are not confined to those above and there are still several specific theoretical frameworks in their own right. However, what is presented here is a gist of ongoing mainstream work since the 1960s until now. The economic theories of FDI cover theories on MNCs, MNC decisions on FDI, implementation modalities of FDI, mergers and acquisitions, joint ventures, Greenfield investments, brownfield investments, etc. Further the host and home country relations, developing and developed country cases of FDI inflows and outflows are also part of the FDI theories. SMEs and their internationalization are also a concern in FDI theory and practice in the recent years, next to calls for sound industrial policies integrating trade policy, investment policy, social policy among others. Last but not least, specific FDI typologies have specific theoretical unpinnings underlying them.

Political Theories on FDI

Büthe and Millner (2008) argue that the political determinants of FDI are scarcely researched compared to the economic counterparts with a view to theorize them. However, there are a number of political determinants which received relative attention on FDI such as domestic level issues related to political stability and political institutions coupled by regime type in a given country. Accordingly, political stability is a definitive factor in attracting FDI while sound political system and institutions are considered among the accelerating factors for FDI attractiveness for a given country. Next, the regime type is also considered as an important political determinant of FDI. Government interventions of economic and legal nature are also among the political determinants. Further, international organisations and the dominance of powerful countries in them is another GPE related political concern especially when regulating international trade and investment is in the forefront.

As mentioned above, the discussions around the FDI theories are interdisciplinary in nature and there are both economic and political aspects followed by socio-cultural issues. However, it is not possible to present them all here as the linkages around international trade and FDI, international development and FDI, technology transfers and FDI, business culture and FDI are among the several issue areas which require further detailed attention and thus remain beyond the scope of the current chapter. However, in the upcoming section below some highly discussed issues around FDI will be brought into perspective to enable the readers to focus on contemporary discussion around the FDI issues.

FOREIGN DIRECT INVESTMENT IN CONTEXT

Most recently, FDI has received accelerated focus and interest both from economists and policymakers alike along with acceleration of globalization and the increasing interaction between developed and developing countries, different sectors, etc. The current outlook of FDI, however, points to policies and political risks along the FDI flows while highlighting the developing countries to be on the rise compared to conventional developed country dominance in receiving FDI. According to *World Investment Report 2015*, for example, global FDI flows in 2014

... declined by 16% to $1.23 trillion..., mostly because of the fragility of the global economy, policy uncertainty for investors and elevated geopolitical risks" "....Inward FDI flows to developing econo-

mies reached their highest level ever, at $681 billion with a 2 per cent rise. Developing economies thus extended their lead in global inflows. China became the world's largest recipient of FDI. Among the top 10 FDI recipients in the world, 5 are developing economies. (UNCTAD, 2015)

Again, 9 out of 20 largest investor countries are either developing or transition countries (UNCTAD, 2015) highlighting the direction of global developments in FDI flows. Comparative overview of the global FDI covering selected years can be observed through Table 1.

Table 1. FDI in context

Item	Value at current prices (Billions of dollars)				
	1990	2005–2007 (pre-crisis average)	2012	2013	2014
FDI inflows	205	1 397	1 403	1 467	1 228
FDI outflows	244	1 423	1 284	1 306	1 354
FDI inward stock	2 198	13 894	22 073	26 035	26 039
FDI outward stock	2 254	14 883	22 527	25 975	25 875
Income on inward FDI[a]	82	1 024	1 467	1 517	1 575
Rate of return on inward FDI[b]	4.4	7.6	7.0	6.1	6.4
Income on outward FDI[a]	128	1 105	1 445	1 453	1 486
Rate of return on outward FDI[b]	5.9	7.6	6.6	5.8	5.9
Cross-border M&As	98	729	328	313	399
Sales of foreign affiliates	4 723	21 469	31 687	33 775[c]	36 356[c]
Value-added (product) of foreign affiliates	881	4 878	7 105	7 562[c]	7 882[c]
Total assets of foreign affiliates	3 893	42 179	88 536	95 230[c]	102 040[c]
Exports of foreign affiliates	1 444	4 976	7 469	7 688[d]	7 803[d]
Employment by foreign affiliates (thousands)	20 625	53 306	69 359	71 297[c]	75 075[c]
Memorandum					
GDP[e]	22 327	51 799	73 457	75 453	77 283
Gross fixed capital formation[e]	5 592	12 219	17 650	18 279	18 784
Royalties and licence fee receipts	31	172	277	298	310
Exports of goods and services[e]	4 332	14 927	22 407	23 063	23 409

Source: UNCTAD.

UNCTAD, 2015.

Current Issues on FDI: Linkage of International Trade and Investment, Global Value Chains and Competitiveness, and Enabling Environment for FDI

This section provides emphasis on most recent outstanding issues on FDI flows whereby current discussions are simultaneously brought into perspective.

FDI, Global Value Chains, and Competitiveness

FDI is a major element of globalization process whereby, through internationalization, the production processes are increasingly fragmented and scattered across the world next to global financial flows and portfolio investments. The accelerated global development of FDI point to the fact that internationalization of business is becoming gradually more demanding, for example, FDI is often used to evade barriers to trade by businesses among other issues. Debates about the advantages, business or policy contexts of FDI are covering a wide range, and debates abound. However, the continuing debate does not change the realities of daily business transactions of MNCs, mergers and acquisitions, and cross-border investments. UNCTAD, OECD, IMF and IFC are trying to evaluate the global investment trends, and business practices through several surveys and data analyses while determinants of FDI are periodically transformed since 1990s owing to cumulative field experiences and transactions as well as changing international economic conditions.

Globalization empowers multi-country production location choices, through the activities of the MNCs. Among the strategic drivers of the multi-country location choices for business it is possible to define the differences in production costs, competitiveness factors, socio-cultural and environmental issues as well as geographic location among others. Accordingly, production takes place in local, national, regional and global scales owing to a variety of reasons. The drivers of multi-country production lead to global supply chains through business and economic transactions that create diverse value chains. Concurrently, these value chains indicate different phases of development either developed or newly developing. Irrespective of the complexity of the value chains, they are called global if the related activities are taking place at a global scale. The participation in global value chains is accepted to be a measure of competitiveness as a result of the work of international organizations, i.e. OECD, WTO and UNCTAD also. Consequently, a country is considered to be competitive if it has built in a capacity to join global value chains, or if it can remain as part of the global value chains, or if it can move up the ladder within the global value chains.

UNCTAD in its *World Investment Report 2013* focuses on the global value chains and the FDI as its main theme. UNCTAD reports that there is a significant correlation between inward FDI levels and participation in global value chains. This recent underlying trend of assessment of global value chains and FDI also forms the focus points of the current study with a view to provide a more thorough assessment regarding its main objective.

Global competitiveness rankings annually presented by World Economic Forum (WEF, 2014) include important FDI determinants while providing an overview of country performance on competitiveness which is increasingly measured through participation in global value chains. The 2013-2014 scores are presented below to indicate current performance, concentrating on the EU member states and Turkey as an example (see Figure 1).

At present, the question of global competitiveness coupled with the recent trend for becoming part of global value chains through international trade and investment are also increasing. These trends launched competition towards improving the economic standing of countries in order to attract FDI,

Figure 1. Global competitiveness of EU member states and Turkey 2013-2014
WEF, 2014.

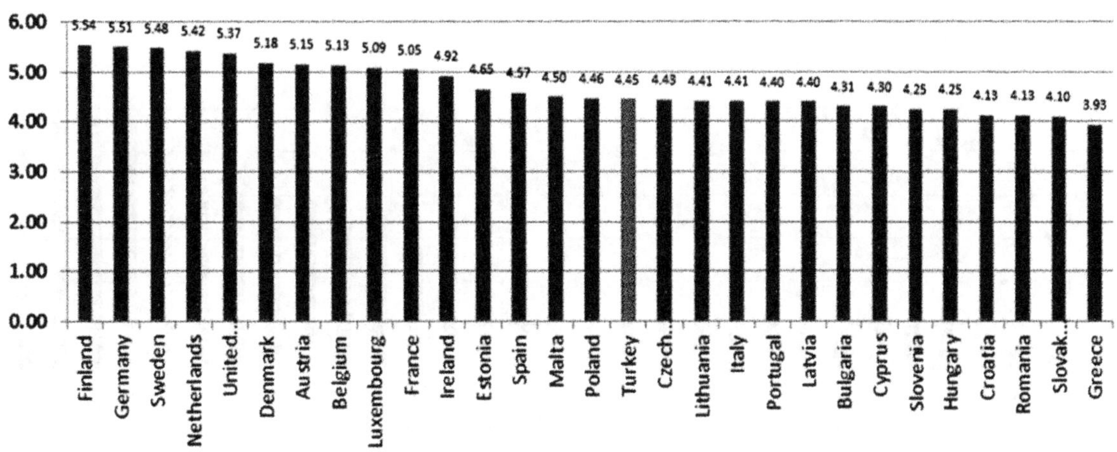

while simultaneously managing the domestic economic conditions. Subsequently, countries are competing for attracting FDI for a variety of reasons such as technology, employment, finance, R&D, growth, etc. Naturally, the EU member states are also part of the global trends. The EU is a major economic player with considerable weight in global FDI environment on the overall; while, Turkey, as a country within Pre-Accession process to the EU, is also a relatively dynamic economy in FDI context. As a recent trend, Turkish businesses are significant FDI partners for EU businesses with considerable outward FDI reaching out several EU member states.

Investment Climate (The Enabling Environment), Assessments of International Organisations, the Policy, and Institutional Contexts

- **Assessments of International Organisations in Relation to Enabling Environment:** International organisations such as UNCTAD, OECD and IFC have long been involved in the assessment of investment climate across countries and regions as well as globally. This, in return, brought the increased emphasis between assessment of the investment climate (the enabling environment) and the business perceptions analyses such as the one annually done by IFC, the *Doing Business Index.*

Doing Business Index is made up of several subcomponents towards examining the investment environment such as creation of new businesses, getting permits, etc., next to a dimension of entrepreneurship indicating the new business density in the countries concerned. These subcomponents also refer to determinants of attracting FDI. Therefore, the Index itself and its subcomponents are directly correlated to global competition for the FDI, and especially from view point of the business case of the FDI. Moreover, the indicators used in this Index will become even more important for countries in the years to come with reference to fast developing global value chins and locational choices for the FDI (see Figure 2).

According to the 2015 rankings of IFC, EU member states are generally high ranking in terms of ease of doing business thus provide a favorable investment climate for FDI also. Comparably, however, Turkey lags behind and is the last fifth in the regional European ranking just above Luxembourg, Greece,

Figure 2. Doing business index
IFC, 2015.

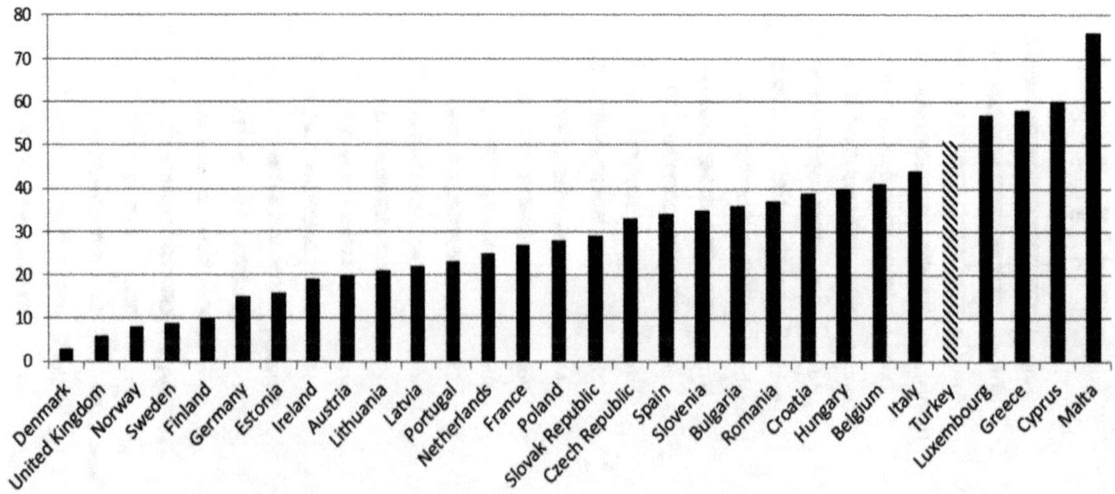

Cyprus and Malta. Again, for example, when the EU8, in other words, crisis struck economies of EU and the most recent EU member states are considered (Ireland, Portugal, Spain, Italy, Greece, Bulgaria, Romania, and Croatia) Turkey is 8th among only above Greece and after Italy.

Annual IFC Surveys are indicative of the enabling environment for the businesses and therefore the FDI especially when the sub-components of the Doing Business Index are taken into account as well. However, there also other surveys and studies conducted annually by multinationals such as E&Y which support and complement the findings of the IFC. For example, *2015 European Attractiveness Survey* of the E&Y confirms the IFC findings and indicates that Europe is among the prevalent destinations for FDI with %59 of the global investors voting for Europe as the most attractive destination. Europe is also an important FDI benchmark in its own right because it corresponds approximately 25% of the global FDI inflows annually. In the year 2015, "Europe attracted 4,341 projects (+10%) and 185,583 jobs (+12%)" compared to 2014 (E&Y, 2015), while global FDI has been shrinking.

There are also other international indices and available data to assess the enabling environment for FDI such the *OECD FDI Regulatory Restrictiveness Index* which focuses on four basic strands: Foreign equity limitations; Screening or approval mechanisms; Restrictions on the employment of foreigners as key personnel; Operational restrictions (OECD, 2013).

- **The Policy and Institutional Context for FDI:** The policy and institutional context for FDI is a vital aspect of successful integration into global economy for individual countries and businesses alike especially with reference to FDI as part of the enabling environment. The enabling environment is made up of critical aspects in FDI transactions. Recognizing the significance of enabling environment, this section will provide brief remarks with reference to the EU and Turkey as part of the attempt to link theory with the practice.

The institutional context focuses on mapping existing bilateral institutional structures between the business circles in Turkey and in the EU; providing an analysis of the effectiveness of such structures for business facilitation and market integration between the two sides towards providing recommendations for FDI. In parallel with this, the policy framework focuses on identifying the policy context as a benchmark towards most effective and successful bilateral economic relations between EU and Turkey in a way to facilitate policy entrepreneurship concerning the FDI.

The institutional dimension of FDI requires a holistic approach as a mixture of public and private sector involvement in the FDI processes. In this context, the fundamental international pillars are UNCTAD and OECD; and in national context, investment promotion agencies, business organizations, sectoral organizations and public sector institutions such as Ministries of Economy in individual countries.

With reference to the EU on investment promotion and the role of investment promotion agencies (hereinafter IPAs), there is a need for change to achieve success. This is basically because, partially due to rise of global value chains, only offering the merits of a specific country or region is not enough to attract investments. What is more needed is recognizing advantages of the country in question vis-à-vis sectors and sub-sectors; and to promote and market those. Moreover, another necessary step in investment promotion is to bring forth innovation and entrepreneurship in a given country or sector into perspective to attract FDI. This type of a specialization on part of the investment promotion agencies is considered to bring beneficial results compared to usual practices of investment promotion. These overall is entitled as "smart specialization" a recent terminology as it is coined by the EU. In return, smart specialization also mirrors on how the IPAs would or should approach international investors. In essence, while European countries and regions focus on "smart specialization", the IPAs need to focus on "smart targeting" as complementary to this process. It should be highlighted that what is called "smart targeting" is not just implementing best practice guides of international organizations such as UNCTAD or OECD regarding investment promotion, but IPAs should focus on strategic value chain participation channels to create additional value in attracting FDI.

Sectoral organizations are significant players in FDI and trade as they have existing international sectoral links to similar sectoral organizations in other countries and regions. Their significance also owes to the fact that these types of organizations have access to sectoral clusters, often representing them, and also they create an important potential for the internationalization of SMEs, next to also enabling participation in value chains. Consequently, their involvement in trade and investment facilitation needs to be enhanced through design of networking channels and other business schemes in a sustainable way.

The policy framework and the regulatory environment for investment and trade is arguably needing a new definition as opposed to its current scattered sets of bilateral investment treaties (BITs) between the countries. In broader view, within the current global environment increasingly webbed by GVCs, it is almost impossible to design implement industrial policies without taking them into account, and investment and trade policies are part of the industrial policies in general.

While the efforts towards integrated policies regarding investment and trade and on the overall for new industrial policies are continuing, and while calls for multilateral global investment governance is in the agenda, it is also important to note that the policy and regulatory framework can prove to be disastrous if they become tacit tools for protectionism. Hence a balance needs to be observed for the policy and regulatory side of investments. Countries increasingly design investment policies within the broader framework of industrial policies, while instantaneously both OECD and UNCTAD provide frameworks for improving the investment environment as guidance for the countries and to develop a multilateral investment framework under their mandate.

The European Union recently developed its own investment framework as well. The Lisbon Treaty provides mandate to the EU for contributing to a gradual removal of restrictions on the FDI and the EU intends to use this in an efficient manner. This, however, does not mean that the Union will define and enforce the investment liberalization measures. The mandate is still to be shared with the individual member states, and the real value of the EU mandate lies within the framework of the international investment negotiations, providing more leverage compared to individual countries' investment negotiation positions.

- **A Benchmark; FDI Case of Turkey and Europe:** Clearly as a benchmark, for example, investors from Turkey have also found Europe as an attractive FDI destination on a regular basis as indicated in Figure 3 below with emphasis on the years 2011, 2012 and 2015.

Turkish investors follow up business opportunities in European markets rather diligently through establishing new firms or through M&A. These investments usually aim new brand acquisition, market and product differentiation, and acquiring competitive advantage through know-how transfers into main firm in Turkey. In the year 2011, Turkish SMEs have bought more than 3000 firms in Europe either as acquisitions or joint ventures. The sectors where Turkish investors indicated interest are as follows; chemicals, food, health, energy, textiles, retail, automotive and construction. These also resulted in technology transfers. For example, some Turkish firms carried the factories with all their overall machinery, know-how, and patents into Turkey as well as experienced staff. Turkish companies have acquired 26 firms in the first ten months of 2013 with a volume of USD 730 million. Two top destinations for these acquisitions are Italy, and Greece; and the sectors are manufacturing, transport, food, energy, IT, services and automotive. The expectations point to an increase in FDI volume beyond USD 1 billion in the near future.

Figure 3. FDI from Turkey to Europe 2007-2015
Central Bank of Turkey, 2015; monthly frequency, million USD.

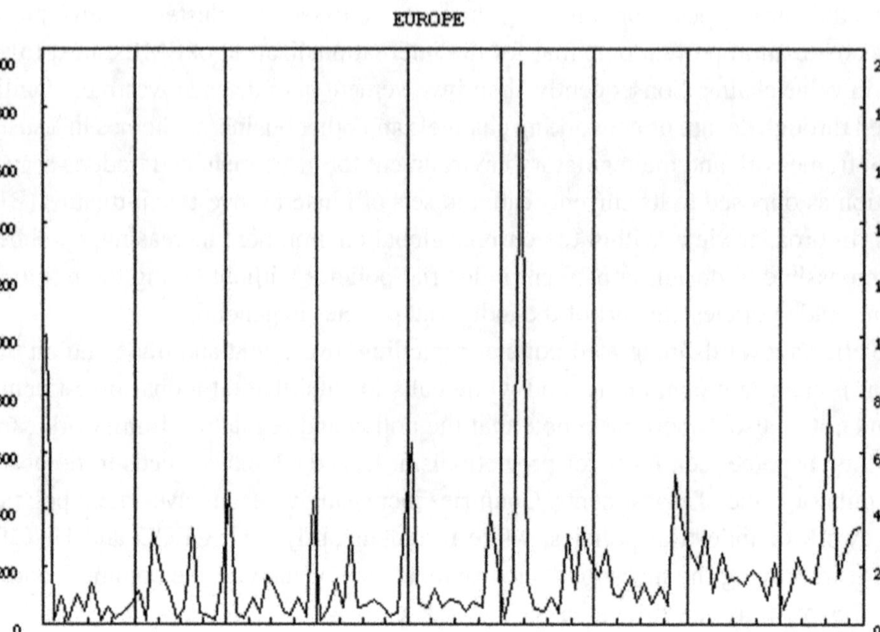

On the other hand, the source of the FDI projects in Turkey is primarily Europe with 46.3%, followed by North America with 14.7%, and Central and Eastern Europe with 2.1%. Business leaders consider the most significant assets of Turkey in attracting FDI as market opportunities, large domestic market, and reasonable labor cost. Turkey's EU member state competitors in attracting FDI are Spain, Portugal, Greece and Romania respectively. In essence, the FDI projects in Turkey spread across the overall global value chain. Leading sectors in FDI projects are business services, diversified industrial products, automotive, ICT, financial services, chemicals, mining and materials, life sciences.

RECOMMENDATIONS

FDI is a vast subject with several components and complementary issues relevant to GPE and it requires focus in terms of recommendations to be made to stay within viable boundaries. Consequently this section is limited to linkage of FDI with global value chains and competitiveness next to enabling environment and its international context.

1. **FDI, Global Value Chains, and Competitiveness:** There is a concrete link between international trade and FDI thus the global value chains. The countries that can increase and keep up their presence in global value chains especially with reference to strategic sectors with added value will have the possibility to increase their competitiveness. However, becoming part of value chains does not necessarily mean that the country or sector in question could stay there forever as the world is in flux. Therefore, the key recommendation in this regard is to have a strategic vision for global economic involvement and sectoral smart targeting based on a sound industrial policy. FDI in this context is to be considered as a facilitator only and should be supported by global and domestic political stability.
2. **Enabling Environment:** Once the enabling environment for FDI is well-defined, the country in question can possibly enhance its advantages within global investment framework. But, then, the sustainability of FDI comes into perspective; and sustainability of FDI further needs to be coupled with sound policy and institutional framework towards investment promotion and facilitation. While enabling environment is being created the multiple array of stakeholders are to be taken on board and capacitated such as investment promotion agencies, business and/or sectoral organisations among others.
3. **International Context:** Within a globalized world no country exists in a vacuum, therefore the economic interconnectedness of sectors and countries require an international order whereby a positive sum game could be created for all those involved in the FDI processes. This would not only mean protecting economic interests but it also has political connotations that require attention. Eventually, a model institution such as WTO is needed for investments in the long run such as a World Investment Agency to provide sound grounds for FDI interactions across the globe to regulate the existing and future bilateral investment treaties. This would also remedy the currently ongoing patch work of several international organisations and businesses alike. Another important aspect within such an institutionalization process would be regular and sound collection of FDI data which remains to be a problem in FDI assessments and empirical studies.

FUTURE RESEARCH

The future research on FDI can be enhanced on three fronts: economic, political, and socio-cultural embracing also the mainstream GPE theoretical framework through which theory can meet its reality. The economic front requires a number of important steps. The first one is enhanced empirical research on internationalization of SMEs as drivers of global economy and economic growth. The second one is applied research on industrial policy and FDI involving smart targeting framework. The third one is global financial transactions through asset seeking FDI. The fourth one is technology transfers that are made through FDI flows and their potential contribution to global economy. The fifth one is international development and the role of FDI given the current rising developing country MNCs.

The political front, on the other hand, requires extensive research behind the politically enabling environment for the FDI across different regions and countries in a comparative way involving also the regulatory and institutional environment in such a way to identify the gatekeepers of FDI and to measure their levels of influence.

The socio-cultural front demands understanding the differences of business culture and the subsequent population and employment trends in a given country with a view to enhance FDI. In brief, for future research both multidisciplinary and interdisciplinary empirical research is required to be able to theorize FDI in a way to meet its reality.

CONCLUSION

This chapter briefly reviewed the theoretical underpinnings of FDI in relation to its practice with reference to global competitiveness, value chains, enabling environment and the international organisations.

From view point of global economic relations, according to several indices such as Global Competitiveness Index, Doing Business Index, FDI Regulatory Restrictiveness Index that are considered as measures of competitiveness and participation in global value chains next to attractiveness for FDI, the current patch work of international organisations such as IFC, OECD and UNCTAD are prevalent but they do not provide a holistic approach. There is need for international standards, policy and institutional context as enabling environment for international investment. The Bretton Woods's institutional system is not following the fast changes in global economy any further.

In the international indices, when Europe and Turkey are benchmarked, the performance of Turkey is in the middle or low ranks among the EU member states whereby Turkey can benefit from the advances of the countries such as Ireland, Italy, Spain and Portugal and can engage in further partnerships with countries such as Croatia, Bulgaria, Romania and Greece also using the advantage of geographical proximity.

Currently there is an ongoing trend for FDI outflows from Turkey to Europe; however, this should not be taken as part of Pre-Accession process per se. It is more that individual businesses see windows of opportunity in investing in the EU businesses. The motivations for inward FDI to Turkey from the EU cover all the spectrum but market and strategic asset seeking FDI are more emphasized; same emphasis is true for outward FDI from Turkey to the EU. While the advantages cover a large spectrum, the weight and significance of these advantages vary across the invested sectors due to sectoral characteristics. For example, in financial services the ICT infrastructure and R&D capabilities in Turkey came to forefront together with skilled workforce. In niche sectors, participation in sectoral clusters is highlighted more, especially from view point of SME internationalization. There are also interesting cases in mining sector, which further created cross-sectoral spillovers in investments. In the manufacturing sector, next to market expansion, a strong motive is to enhance the already existing product value chains. On the overall, Turkey is perceived as a recommended investment hub by the existing investors due to several strengths and opportunities. For Turkish businesses investing in the EU, the main theme is market seeking FDI in most of the cases, followed by efficiency seeking FDI. Brand acquisition emerged also as a strong trend with a view to enhance market expansion.

Further, from view point of politics, the current political turmoil across the world and more specifically for example the in Middle East will likely be a point of concern in relation to regional FDI flows if not globally. Political instability, regime changes, and changes in regulatory environment are becoming more demanding than ever for the businesses while especially the global economy is leading towards stagnation. In the international context, international organisations are questioned for enhancement of FDI and therefore calls for such as the E15 Initiative of WEF are increasing towards a global investment regime which is not likely to be created anytime soon.

Next, international development is another issue that needs to be considered since it has both economic and political consequences globally.

Finally, when attempting to link the theory of FDI with its reality, economics is likely to prevail over politics and the inherent complexity will continue.

REFERENCES

Buckley, P. J., & Casson, M. C. (1976). *The Future of the Multinational Enterprise*. London: Homes and Meier. doi:10.1007/978-1-349-02899-3

Büthe, T., & Millner, H. V. (2008). The Politics of Foreign Direct Investment into Developing Countries: Increasing FDI through International Trade Agreements? *American Journal of Political Science*, *52*(4), 741–762. doi:10.1111/j.1540-5907.2008.00340.x

Cohn, T. H. (2011). *Global Political Economy* (6th ed.). Pearson.

Dunning, J. H. (1973). The determinants of international production. *Oxford Economic Papers*, *25*, 289–336.

Dunning, J. H. (1980). Toward an eclectic theory of international production: Some empirical tests. *Journal of International Business Studies*, *11*(1), 9–31. doi:10.1057/palgrave.jibs.8490593

Dunning, J. H. (1988). The Eclectic Paradigm of International Production: A restatement and some possible extensions. *Journal of International Business Studies*, *19*(1), 1–31. doi:10.1057/palgrave.jibs.8490372

E&Y. (2015) *European Attractiveness Survey 2015*. Retrieved January 22, 2016 from http://www.ey.com/GL/en/Issues/Business-environment/ey-european-attractiveness-survey-2015

Hennart, J. F. (1982). *A theory of multinational enterprise*. University of Michigan Press.

Hymer, S. (1976). The International Operations of Nation Firms: A Study of Foreign Direct Investment. Cambridge, MA: MIT Press.

IFC. (2015). *Doing Business Index 2015*. Retrieved from http://www.doingbusiness.org/reports/global-reports/doing-business-2015

OECD. (2013). *FDI Regulatory Restrictiveness Index*. Retrieved from http://www.oecd.org/investment/fdiindex.htm

UNCTAD. (2015). *World Investment Report 2015. Reforming International Investment Governance*. Retrieved from http://unctad.org/en/pages/PublicationWebflyer.aspx?publicationid=1245

Vernon, R. (1966). International investment and international trade in the product cycle. *The Quarterly Journal of Economics*, *80*(2), 190–207. doi:10.2307/1880689

KEY TERMS AND DEFINITIONS

Historical Structuralism: This is a theoretical perspective embracing Marxism and contemporary standing of Marxist thought in general and it also provides hybrid theories in explaining global economic relations since the predictions of Marx remained unresolved in relation to the evolution and current state of capitalism. This theoretical framework is still important in relation to its critical approach towards both realist and liberalist thinking in GPE.

IFC Doing Business Index: Like the Global Competiveness Index, it is considered as one of the measures of global value chain participation internationally while simultaneously providing a benchmark for FDI competitiveness of individual countries.

Investment Promotion: Is mainly a government activity covering a wide range of activities from facilitation of attracting FDI to provision of subsequent services to the existing investors and potential investors. Thus it is public sector services geared to FDI.

Liberalism: Unlike realism, liberalism centers on the freedom of economic activity regardless of political pursuits of individual states thus it considers international economic relations as a positive-sum game for all the actors involved. Liberalism advocates that the role of the state should be kept in minimum in relation to economic activities and that markets should remain free of state intervention unless there is a need for adjustment.

Realism: The main stream theoretical framework in GPE which assumes that international system is anarchical and a zero-sum game whereby states are the most powerful actors; and each state acts for its own survival. It advocates that politics determines economic activities of the state based on pursuit of national interest and national security. It can also be coined as "economic nationalism".

UNCTAD: Is acronym for United Nations Conference on Trade and Development. UNCTAD is one of the key international organisations in the field of FDI and provides a variety of services from collecting and maintaining data on FDI to provision of reports such as annual World Investment Report, organizing debates, interaction with civil society, etc. UNCTAD has 194 member states currently and its original focus is international trade and development.

Value Chain: In its most basic definition, a value chain is the term which covers the whole range of activities for a product or service from its very beginning until its reach to the final consumer. Hence it is made up of several components, in other words, it is a chain of fragmented production covering both manufacturing and services as a whole.

Section 2

OFDI in Emerging Economies:

Case Studies from Europe

Chapter 7
On Some Aspects of State-Owned Enterprises' Foreign Direct Investments (SOEs' FDI):
The Case of Polish SOEs' FDI

Marta Anna Götz
Vistula University, Poland

Barbara Jankowska
Poznan University of Economics and Business, Poland

ABSTRACT

This chapter seeks to enrich the existing literature by discussing the broader context of international engagement of state-owned enterprises (SOEs). It discusses the rationale for examining foreign direct investment (FDI) done by SOEs and outlines the challenges which need to be addressed in this respect. It provides a brief overview of FDI carried by Polish SOEs. The authors applied the qualitative methodology of critical literature review and descriptive analysis of internationalization of Polish state-controlled firms. This chapter can contribute to the current studies devoted mainly to Chinese or other Asian emerging state-controlled multinationals by adding the Central and Eastern European (CEE), in particular the Polish, perspective. It concludes that given the well-recognised peculiarities of such entities adequate framework needs to be adopted to explore their foreign activities. The Polish multi-case study encompassing nine entities demonstrates that the group can be pretty heterogeneous and indeed can combine the specificity of multinational enterprises (MNEs) and SOEs.

INTRODUCTION

The reasons for state ownership fluctuate over time, but state-controlled firms appear to be a constant feature of the economic landscape (PWC, 2015). SOEs are often granted privileges that are not available to competitors, which gives them the undue advantage over their rivals. There is a clear need to understand the behaviour and practices of SOEs in global context, beyond the borders, to identify the

DOI: 10.4018/978-1-5225-2345-1.ch007

key concerns and to develop the rules safeguarding fair conditions for public and private market participants (Cuervo-Cazurra et al., 2014). The topic is even more relevant taking into account the last global economic crisis 2008+. The crisis period was related to the growing importance of SOEs and according to some researchers their importance will grow in the next years (Flores-Macias & Musacchio, 2009; Bremmer, 2010; Augustynowicz & Kwiatkowski, 2013).

This chapter discusses the rationale for exploring SOEs' foreign activities in the current world setting. The authors deliberately skip the review of the extremely broad literature devoted to emerging markets and mainly Chinese SOEs as these cases seem to differ substantially from European firms, at least due to the peculiarities of varieties of capitalism models adopted (Nölke & Vliegenthart, 2009). The authors instead focus on the perspective of global coordination. They review the studies and international reports which identify the evolving international role of SOEs. They also outline the main features of internationalisation process of Polish SOEs in the most advanced form of foreign direct investment (FDI). Such entities are featuring high on the agenda of currently negotiated agreements such as Transatlantic Trade and Investment Partnership (TTIP), or classic bilateral investment treaties (BITs). Their activities, in particular foreign operations, are in the spotlight of many international institutions which recognise the growing need of monitoring of SOEs' development.

This chapter is structured as follows. First, the authors present the background briefly introducing the distinct traits of state-owned enterprises. Next, they move towards the main issues of this chapter and outline the basic facts about the international engagement of SOEs as retrieved from databases. Special attention is being paid to Polish SOEs and their FDI against SOE from other CEE countries. Challenges stemming from growing foreign presence of many previously domestic oriented SOEs are discussed in the next section. Then, before formulation of conclusion the authors highlight some recommendations and future research directions. Last but not least, the chapter provides some concluding remarks, summing up in a way the conducted study.

BACKGROUND: IDIOSYNCRASIES OF STATE-OWNED ENTERPRISES

The real-life phenomenon which are SOEs and their internationalization efforts call for the alteration within the varieties of capitalism. Some experts underline that e.g. the typology distinguishing between the liberal market economy (LME), capital market economy (CME), dependant market economy (DME) should be enriched with the fourth model of SME – the State-Permeated Capitalism (Nölke, 2015). This new version complements existing ones by accentuating the state influence on the economy also via nurturing domestic champions and their outward FDI. Though, even in Europe the traditional varieties of capitalism have been undergoing profound changes in the result of 2008 global financial crisis (Schweiger, 2014). Todays' approach seems to evolve towards more nuanced perception of state-owned or controlled companies away from simple dichotomy state or private which views SOEs as hybrid organizations, in which the levels of ownership and control by the state can vary significantly (Bruton et al., 2015). Modern state capitalism accommodating four new varieties - wholly owned state-owned enterprises, the state as a majority investor, the state as a minority investor, and the state as a strategic supporter of specific sectors - hence, challenges the conventional, very polarized view of state versus private ownership (Musacchio et al., 2015).

There are large discrepancies in SOEs reporting by national statistical offices and responsible ministries. In the OECD countries only 10% of SOEs are publicly listed (OECD, 2004). Despite these differences SOEs in most OECD members respect the same general rules for insolvency and bankruptcy as private companies do. Accounting and auditing standards apply to SOEs as they do to private companies, and SOEs may additionally undergo controls carried out by specific state audit entities. They also have to observe stringent financial disclosure and transparency standards. In fact, in some countries such as Denmark or Poland, they are even obliged to follow some additional requirements.

Contrary to the legacy of old common wisdom assuming inferior economic results of SOEs Musacchio (et al., 2015), argue

... that many of these firms following these new varieties of state capitalism are taking the stage in the global economy and are often performing at least equal to, if not better than, their private counterparts. 25 largest SOEs among the top 100 firms in the Fortune Global 500 have an average return on assets of 3.49% and an operating margin of 14%, which is comparable to the 3.44% and 5.7%, respectively, what can be found among the largest 75 private firms in the world. (Musacchio et al., 2015)

Musacchio (et al., 2015) pointed to the emergence of a new form of state capitalism that is related to the transformation in the nature of SOEs. Nowadays governments can hold majority or minority equity positions. Public listing of these firms called for improvement of the financial reporting and higher transparency of governance which was possible thanks to independent board members. This kind of reforms attracted minority private investors (Pargendler et al., 2013) and gave rise to profitable businesses that expand in foreign markets. Next to the firms with the majority stake of the state companies with the government as the minority shareholder exists (Inoue et al., 2013).

SOEs have been mainly researched with respect to their domestic performance and apparent disadvantages - inferior efficiency, agency problems, ineffectiveness, and weak corporate governance (Shapiro & Globerman, 2009). It has been argued, that SOEs are "less able to develop capabilities or ownership advantages" that would be transferable to be exploited abroad, and which are a key driver for international growth (Kirca et al, 2012). Though, there is also a widespread recognition of numerous benefits accruing to these enterprises. The empirical analysis conducted by Christiansen and Kim (2014) indicates that, in addition to any financing advantages, large state-invested enterprises also seem to benefit from an unusually favourable position in their home markets. Most frequently cited advantages include: outright subsidisation (tax exemptions, favourable tax regimes or other in-kind benefits); concessionary financing and guarantees like credit below market interest rate; other preferential treatment by government (less restrictions, softer disclosure regulations, not required compliance with certain standards); monopolies and advantages of incumbency; captive equity as SOEs' equity is generally "locked in" and their managers are not expected as much as in private firms to deliver in terms of dividends or other rate of return etc. and exemption from bankruptcy rules and information advantages (Christiansen & Kim, 2014). For these reasons SOEs are prone to engage in economically irrational behaviour such as excessive capital investments or anticompetitive business practices, and in consequence disrupting the order of fair international competition. Thus, the OECD has been calling for ensuring a level playing field, or competitive neutrality between SOEs and private-sector companies (Capobianco & Christiansen, 2011).

STATE-OWNED MULTINATIONAL ENTERPRISES: CONTRASTING CONCEPTUAL ISSUES WITH FACTS AND FIGURES

Conceptual Issues on the International Engagement of State-Owned Multinational Enterprises

The operations of SOMNEs being embedded in organizational settings that differ from the private sector and additionally in diversified institutional context – different countries expose the need to review and maybe revise the prevailing international business theories focused on internationalization of firms. There is a clear need of explanations why SOE internationalize (Bass & Chakrabarty, 2014; Choudhury & Khanna 2014; Götz & Jankowska, 2016).

When one takes into account the fact that SOEs operate to fulfil the governmental priorities there is the question which if any of the priorities can impede or facilitate the emergence of SOMNEs. The traditional justification for the existence of SOEs rather indicates the inhibitory mechanism to SOEs' internationalization. Since SOEs operations go in line with the ambitions and goals of the politicians one can presume, that only if these ambitions and goals have anything to do with foreign expansion this kind of entities will internationalize. OFDI on the side of SOEs can reduce the export opportunities for domestic firms. The substitution of export activities by the OFDI operations can lead to negative balance of payment in the domestic market of SOEs. These implications work rather as a kind of impediment to SOEs internationalization (Mazzolini, 1980). The establishment of SOEs in particular industries can be explained by some resource constraints in the country (Vernon, 1979). These can be industries not attractive for the private sector and at the same time often not prone to internationalization. Exploitation of state ownership to improve the employment rate in the domestic economy will impede the internationalization of SOEs through OFDI since this internationalization mode can have negative impact on the situation in the domestic labour market (Mazzolini, 1980).

Nevertheless, the internationalisation of SOEs can be fostered by the political priorities related to the ambitions of state governments to dominate in particular industries worldwide. These aspirations can be sometimes even far away from the conventional wisdom and logic in business that is based on the rules of risk mitigation and profit maximisation. Financial goals can be put into the background and the power and dominance goals can be in the forefront. The lack of profitability logic is sometimes reflected in the set of target markets SOEMNEs focus on. The choice of markets can be based on the foreign policy priorities and not on the country-specific advantages the markets provide to foreign investors. It is quite visible in the case of Chinese firms (Ramasamy et al., 2012). The internationalization ambitions of SOEs can be fostered by their higher resilience to risk. Governments providing budget, resources and possessing the power to influence regulatory framework can reduce the risk related to international business operations. It is possible especially when SOEs come from countries with strong governments (Knutsen et al., 2011).

The liberalization of trade, FDI inflows and outflows, removal of any market entry and exit barriers result often in the growing intensity of competitive rivalry within particular national markets thus exposing the necessity to find new competitive arena even among SOEs. Foreign expansion can be used to stabilize the position of SOEs (Clifton et. al., 2011; Dau, 2012; Witt & Lewin, 2007). The competitive pressure in the domestic market faced by SOEs forces the managers to focus more on market goals than just on political and social implications of their operations. Combining the internal – SOEs specific features with the changes in their external settings of operations one can indicate that the motivations to go international on the side of SOEs will work only if the regulatory framework is conducive. It means that the probability of SOEs internationalization is higher when the external circumstances they operate in resemble more the pure market economy conditions. With respect to internationalization processes, on the one hand SOEs can be the target of foreign takeover (IFDI), on the other hand they can themselves become a vehicle for carrying foreign investment abroad (OFDI), in which case their ownership matters much being either a liability or an asset.

As one of the pioneers in this area in 1979, Vernon identified likely challenges and problems to be expected due to internationalisation of SOEs (such as the inclination to use domestic inputs), which as it seems they have not materialised, perhaps also due to such early warning statements as these quoted in the Vernon's paper (1979). SOEs' engagement in internationalisation certainly reflects the political economy of home country (Dharwadkar, 2000). SOEs discussion has typically been framed around questions of efficiency, productivity or administrative bureaucracy. SOMNEs development requires new augmented approach which takes into account the fact that these firms are vehicles to exercise foreign policy and diplomacy goals. On the one hand, peculiarities of SOEs contribute to the traditional knowledge of MNEs by adding the "non-business argument, on the other hand studies on MNEs enhance the understanding of foreign expansion by SOEs by adding the "extraterritoriality" argument (Cuervo-Cazurra, 2014). Whereas the first assumes some irrationality with political objectives given priority over economic ones; the latter argument point to the extraterritorial dimension of the need to address market imperfection or export certain ideology. These extensions are further complemented with augmented versions of five theories. Agency theory focuses on the relationships between the agent who is tasked by the principal to perform an action in the principal's name and principal themselves himself (Holmstrom, 1979). SOEs typical dual agency problem needs to be extended in SOMNEs case into triple one including also the relations between headquarter and subsidiary managers. Transaction cost economics explains firm behaviour as deriving from the information asymmetries and imperfect contracting or opportunism (Williamson, 1985). In the case of SOMNEs, the perceptions of transaction costs differ mainly because the government has a different risk tolerance than private owners. Governments have larger budgets and resources that enable them to take more risks (Kaldor, 1980). The resource-based view focuses on how firms can develop own capabilities to achieve an advantage over competitors (Penrose, 1959). SOEs peculiar resources can be seen as an asset but also as a liability. If the earlier is true SOE would engage in larger riskier projects, when the latter is true SOEs would face some hostility in host country and hence prefer greenfield investments over acquisitions. Resource dependence theory analyses power relationships among two parties, where the one is able to exercise power over the other one which depends on the former. In case of SOMNEs a way to reduce the influence of politicians would be to depend less on government funds and support via internationalizing the firm (Noreng, 1994). Finally, the neo-institutional theory focuses on understanding of the legitimacy required to operate in a foreign country. Companies have to respond to various pressures and imitate practices that are perceived as legitimate (DiMaggio, Powell, 1991). A MNE faces two sets of such pressures on its legitimacy, from the home country headquarters and from the host country environment (Kostova & Zaheer, 1999). This conflict suggest that SOMNEs are more likely to select host countries in which their state ownership is perceived as more legitimate than these host countries in which there is less legitimacy of state ownership. Additionally, one may expect that regardless of the selected host country, SOMNEs are more likely than private MNEs to engage in legitimacy building actions under the umbrella of corporate social responsibility (CSR).

State-Owned Multinational Enterprises in the Cross-Country Perspective: Facts and Figures

SOMNC is a legally independent firm with direct ownership by the state that has value-adding activities outside its home country; be they downstream activities such as sales subsidiaries, or upstream activities such as R&D centers (Cuervo-Cazurra et al., 2014).[1] A SOMNE represents a hybrid organizational form with the dual characteristics of both the state-owned enterprise (SOE) and the multinational enterprise (MNE). When compared with private MNEs, SOMNEs are generally less profit-oriented and have a more complex corporate governance structure. They have less autonomy to establish their strategies, but also experience a lower level of uncertainty in their external environment. As a result, SOMNEs have more difficulty than private MNEs in developing strategies and making organizational changes.

The developments of SOMNEs can be attributed to different global trends. First, is the fact that due to globalization challenges and increased competition SOEs have been less able than in the past to depend on governments for protection, and compensation for significant losses from the increased foreign competition in their local markets (Tan & Tan, 2005). This less favourable settings have forced SOEs to engage in OFDI, to compensate for suffered changes. Second trend is the establishment of new codes and regulations by international institutions guiding the international capital flows. Thirdly, privatisation processes enabling turning SOEs into SOMNEs were accompanied particularly after the 2008 crisis with opposite trends of MNEs turning into SOMNEs via nationalisation and bail-outs mainly.

Of the 2000 largest companies "Forbes Global 2000" (2010-2011), 204 have been identified as majority SOEs with ownership spread across 37 different countries. The numbers vary significantly by country, with China leading the list (70 SOEs), followed by India (30), Russia (9), the United Arab Emirates (9) and Malaysia (8). Among OECD countries SOEs operate in Norway, France, Ireland, Greece, Finland, Korea, Belgium, Sweden, Austria and Turkey. Their numbers do not reflect the share of the state in the whole economy but might be a proxy for the relative importance of the state among a country's most international business players.[2] The proportion of SOEs among the Fortune Global 500 has grown from 9% in 2005 to 23% in 2014, driven particularly by the growth of Chinese firms. SOEs global proliferation and increasing significance worldwide also as vehicles for FDI is testified by the numbers. Among 100 thousands MNEs only 650 are state owned MNEs (44% from advanced economies), though, they have more than 8500 foreign affiliates and out of 100 largest MNEs as much as 19 are SOMNEs (World Investment Report, 2011).

Figures provided by the Dealogic database (comprehensive information on international deals with the industry, region and main characteristics of the deal) demonstrate that deals done by Chinese and Russian SOEs account for 45% of all international transactions of SOEs. Among OECD countries, the top five countries with large state-owned enterprises' international transactions are France (415 deals), Italy (216 deals), Norway (205 deals), Japan (155 deals) and Germany (137 deals) (Christiansen & Kim, 2014). Significant number of transactions which took place among European countries seemed to illustrate the cross-border consolidation processes/integration of EU market (Christiansen & Kim, 2014). Although the growing role of state enterprises in the international marketplace does not yet present a serious macroeconomic challenge (Christiansen & Kim, 2014). Their international investment can if then fall into three categories. The first category refers to SOEs, that located in sectors where all other private enterprises operate internationally (e.g. hydrocarbons). The second type has been a wave of cross-border consolidations in the public utilities sectors in the EU area, which in many cases has involved SOEs. The third category embraces Chinese SOEs that in particular have been encouraged by their government to expand abroad as part of the so-called "go global" strategy.

Firms from the OECD countries are the largest owners of foreign subsidiaries, however, just less of 2% of their parent companies are SOEs (Kowalski et al., 2013). This is considerably lower than the share of SOEs on the "Global 2000 list", suggesting that private firms tend to be overall more active internationally than SOEs. To assess the extent of FDI done by SOE Kowalski (et al., 2013) conducted regression analysis.[3] Obtained results show that the SOEs do not differ from private firms with regard to their number of domestic subsidiaries but their number of foreign subsidiaries and as such the ratio of foreign over domestic subsidiaries is significantly lower than for private firms. These findings suggest that the SOEs among the world's largest publically listed companies tend to be less internationally oriented than their private counterparts. Nevertheless, there are considerable differences with respect to the quantitative magnitude of this aspect as SOEs in OECD countries tend to be relatively more domestically oriented than in emerging economies. Despite such orientation international institutions stress the need to explore cross-border implications of SOEs activities.[4]

The comprehensive list of 15 largest SOMNEs encompasses four companies from China and one from France, Norway, Sweden, Malaysia, Japan, Singapore, Qatar, Brazil, Russia, Venezuela and India (Cahen, 2014). Their TNI index varies between 2.7 (China National Petroleum - CNPC), and 82.9 (Qatar Telecom - Ooredoo) whereas government control ranges from 38% (Gazprom) to 100% (Chinese - Sinochem Group, China National Offshore Oil Corp; China National Petroleum, CITIC; Petróleos de Venezuela SA (PDVSA) from Venezuela, Vattenfall AB from Sweden and Petronas from Malaysia).

Based on qualitative study of foreign direct investment conducted by Brazil's Petrobras Cahen (2014) claims that SOEs can be either risk-seeking or risk-averse agents depending on the risk level related to the entry to the particular country and on institutional transformations in their home countries. SOES international behaviour reflects also different stages of evolution these firms undergo. SOEs' motivation for internationalization evolved in reaction to changing environment, in particular to conducted reforms. Besides, as it seems greater SOE internationalization leads to more efforts to modernize SOE managers' approaches.

State-Owned Enterprises in Poland and Their Foreign Investments Against Other CEE Countries: Facts and Figures

Studies on OFDI by Polish firms are still relatively new research area and they often don't present the findings separately for state-owned firms (Ciesielska, 2014; Éltető et al, 2015; Gorynia, Nowak, Wolniak, 2010; Gorynia et al., 2015; Götz, 2014; Nowiński, 2015; Obłój, Wąsowska, 2012; Wąsowska, Obłój, 2013). Findings obtained by these authors to some extent confirm the classic theory developments, though, also stress the peculiarities of Polish emerging multinationals such as the relatively lower importance of psychological distance and political risk when expanding abroad.

According to "Forbes Global 2000" in 2011 Poland had 6 firms on the list all of them being SOEs (*The world's...*, 2012).[5] Such 100% dominance of SOEs in that ranking can be also spotted in Czech Republic. It is also high in Greece (25%) and Norway (20%). In other EU countries it is respectively: 10% in Austria, 13% in Belgium, 8% in Finland and France, 2% in Germany, 7% in Ireland, 3% in Italy, 4% in Sweden and 1% in UK. The high proportion of SOEs in Poland among largest companies additionally justifies the need to study this particular cohort of enterprises. These companies with the Ministry of Treasury as shareholder contribute to the economy by creating jobs, safeguarding tax incomes and generating considerably revenues particularly in strategic sectors such as energy (Baniak, 2015). Many of them thanks to their activity in the field of corporate social responsibility (CSR) are part of RESPECT index measuring other than purely economic performance of Warsaw Stock Exchange (WSE) listed firms. It shall be noted that out of 20 companies included in this ranking in 2013 almost 50% (9) are enterprises with state stake. Inspection of SOEs against the background of varieties of capitalism compiled by Musacchio (et al., 2015) revealed that Poland has some 498 firms with the central government as a majority shareholder and 691 firms with the central government as a minority investor (Musacchio et al., 2015, p. 117).

Besides scare lists and rankings which enable inferring some data on SOEs and their foreign activities in particular there are also other substitute dataset providing complementary information. OECD Indicators of Product Market Regulation (PMR), are a comprehensive and internationally-comparable set of indicators that measure the degree to which policies promote or inhibit competition in areas of the product market where competition is viable.[6] They measure the economy-wide regulatory and market environments and include also data on state control in particular public ownership - scope of SOEs and their governance.

Comprehensive data gathered and published by OECD with respect to PMR show the decreasing scope of public ownership in Polish economy as the value of index fall from 4.9 in 1998 to 4.3 in 2013. Likewise, the variable "state control" has declined in 2013 as compared to readings in 2008 and 2003. These figures can be enriched by insight on size, composition and outward orientation of the state sector (Christiansen, 2011). Comparison of the total number of all Polish SOEs in 2009 with most recent figures from 2012 points to significant drop from 1210 to 326 firms (OECD, 2013; 2014). Another source claims, that the number of such firms in Poland has decreased from 365 in 2010 to 198 in 2012 which means drop of more than 45% within relatively short period of time (Adamczyk, 2014). Due to the missing information on employment and value in 2009 it cannot be assessed how much this decline in number of SOEs translated into lower employment or value. Interestingly there is information only on two M&A deals done by listed SOEs in 2012 valued at USD 2896 million.

Following the transition commence for a long time, Polish OFDI was almost negligible and limited in fact to trade-supporting activities in selected key export markets (Zimny, 2013). It really took off after the EU accession in 2004. This year can be seen a symbolic watershed moment, but it has not been until then when Polish private sector had matured enough and first home-grown multinational enterprises (MNEs) and state owned enterprises (SOEs) also began investing abroad (Éltető et al., 2015). Transformation in early nineties induced several processes and triggered profound changes in economic landscape but foreign commercial expansion does not seem to be one of them. Although the ratio of OFDI stock from Poland to IFDI stock in Poland is still rather small and accounted for 25% in 2011, compared to 126% in the European Union, it has grown rapidly from 3% in 2000 and 7% in 2005. The recently observed in Poland wider approval for foreign expansion should be seen as the late result of long-term processes which started 25 years ago. So far, Polish governments have been running rather neutral policy towards OFDI or Polish MNEs. Notwithstanding, the natural conditions enabling firms to thrive, it seems Poland might adopt a more active approach in this respect, among others trying to turn SOEs into national champions and, eventually, into MNEs.

The low proportion of OFDI is not only a Polish feature, but shared with other countries of the region also among the Visegrad Group - V4 group which is presented in Figure 1.

Figure 1. OFDI stocks percentage of total world
Source: UNCTAD databases, http://unctadstat.unctad.org/wds/ReportFolders/reportFolders.aspx, retrieved January 2015.

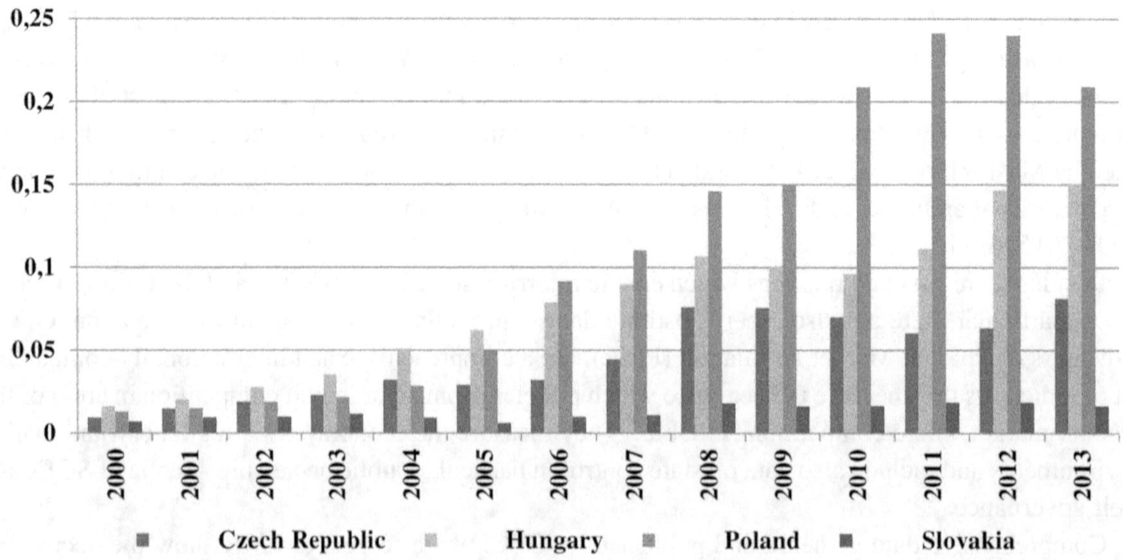

Some state-owned enterprises also began investing abroad, sometimes with the Government's encouragement. Actually, despite certain communist burden and inefficiency SOEs might have had it easier to internationalize as most of their private CEE firms were then occupied with privatization, and modernization, focusing on the domestic market which offered plenty of opportunities and facing significant scarcity of multiple resources when trying to penetrate foreign markets (Ferencikova & Hluskova, 2015).

CEE countries are hence rightly branded by Kalotay (2010) as dwarfs when it comes to OFDIs. However, the increasing OFDI stocks presented in Figure 2, implies that all V4 countries are continually expanding their presence abroad. Poland due to its sheer size naturally leads the group. Two dates stand out: 2004 and accession to the EU after which OFDI stocks have picked up and 2008 when the value accumulated stagnated.

Nevertheless, available statistics presented in Figure 3 reveal that flows from V4 countries represent maximum 0,8% of world flows, and usually range within some 0,001 and -0,4. Even Poland (the largest country of V4 group with seemingly highest potential although visible leading within the group) has once barely exceeded the 0,6% mark.

The negligible role CEE region plays in world as sources of FDI can be again confirmed by figures on V4 OFDI stocks as a percentage of world total. Even group's leader Poland cannot claim more than 0,25%. The authors' earlier study (Éltető et al, 2015) shows that here has been no clear trend in all V4 countries with respect to OFDI flows. Sudden formidable surge or plunge of such flows may suggest the possible significance of single contracts / deal / acquisition which may distort the whole stream volume.

In the VCC Report it has been stated that in Poland 5 of the 19 firms have a significant state stake in them, although only two – PGNiG (73%) and LOTOS (53%) – are majority-owned by the state (Zimny, 2013). In 2012, the Report found that "the ranking includes some state-controlled firms but is dominated by private ones" (Zimny, 2013). Major Polish MNEs included a number of state-owned (or state-controlled) enterprises in the petroleum (PKN Orlen, LOTOS), gas (PGNiG) and chemical (Ciech)

Figure 2. OFDI stocks USD at current prices and current exchange rates in millions
Source: UNCTAD databases, http://unctadstat.unctad.org/wds/ReportFolders/reportFolders.aspx, retrieved January 2015.

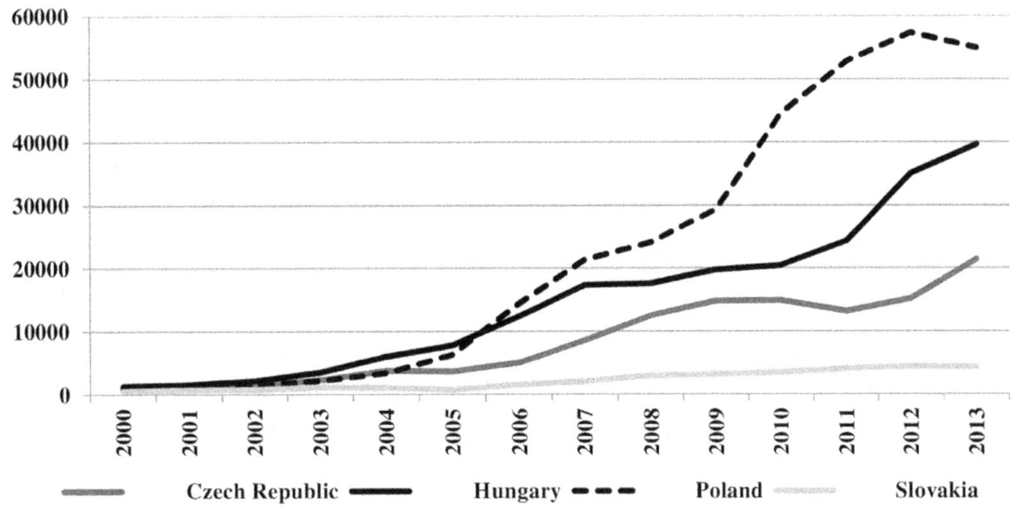

Figure 3. OFDI flows percentage of total world
Source: UNCTAD databases, http://unctadstat.unctad.org/wds/ReportFolders/reportFolders.aspx, retrieved January 2015.

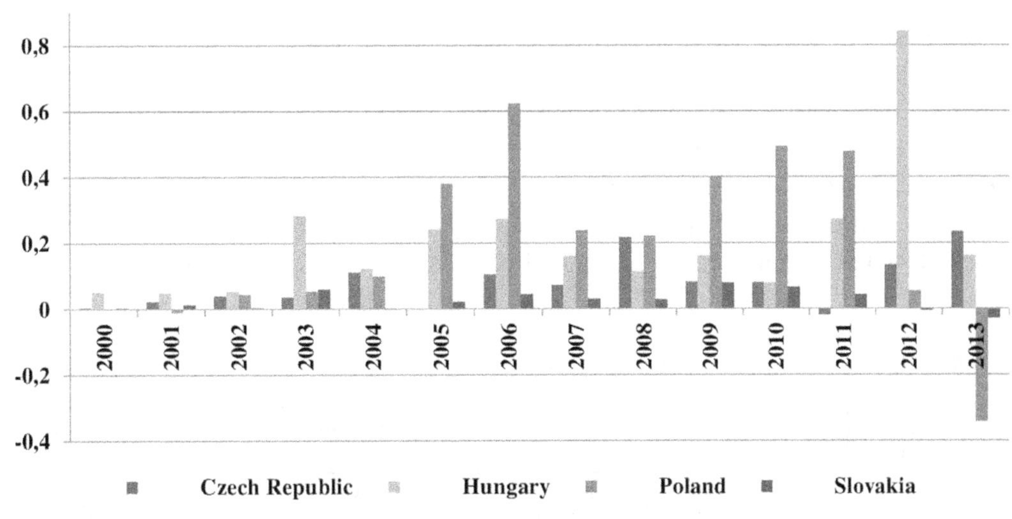

industries. In April 2015 the estimated value of foreign investment of key Polish SOEs totalled 30 billion PLN (Baniak, 2015).

Foreign acquisitions of Polish SOEs raised much controversies. Business media reported on that occasions of wider costs and losses for the whole society (Frączyk, 2014). Impairment losses and write-offs due to failed investment abroad have led to a decline in the share prices of investing enterprises. The largest state-owned companies seem to have a special talent for making losses abroad, losing a fortune, yet belonging to Polish taxpayers. Quoted are failed investments in Norwegian oil deposits by Lotos in 2008, PKN Orlen purchase of Lithuanian refinery Mozejki in 2006, KGHM acquisition of copper deposits in Kongo in late nineties. These fiascos to some extent reflect home-made own mismanagement, though, not only. Hostile approach faced by Orlen in Lithuania and hurdles multiplied by Russian pipelines operator or misleading preparation of oil rig by subcontractor in case of Lotos Norwegian venture indicate other "external" factors. Affected enterprises seek compensation, try to utilise available tools such as the tax shield and sue to the international arbitrage tribunals. Altogether, the losses due to failed foreign purchases make a considerable sum which by the fact of state ownership can be regarded as wealth reduction of the society and /or liability for country's budget (Irzyński, 2014). Apparently overly optimistic foreign acquisitions turned out to be miscalculated and brought about rather losses, write-offs and share prices' drop implying also the need to repay loans taken to finance the purchase. Write-offs do not mean of course a sudden outflow of money from firms' corporate bank accounts, though, they lead to the asset revaluation in balance sheets. Nevertheless, such investments can be also perceived as overdue internationalisation of Polish firms and an opportunity for the national economy and nation's wealth (Roguski & Furman, 2013). Geographic expansion is an important element of business strategy. And even when not smooth, it can enable to fail your way to success as it offers a chance to acquire know-how, built expertise, strengthen competences, and gain expertise. The media frenzy accompanying them may obviously be justified, though, one need to bear in mind that such firms are usual suspects and their moves are watched much more closely hence commented and criticised than those of private peers which might as well be unsuccessful.

Available insight on Polish FDI done by SOEs comes mainly from dedicated case studies and there is no single source providing exhaustive information on either MA or Greenfields by SOEs.[7] Hence, in order to assess the foreign expansion by Polish companies with the state as stakeholder first the list of such firms has been established. As the main reference serves Rzeczpospolita List of "2000 Polish firms" (Lista Polskich Przedsiębiorstw i Eksporterów, 2015). From all 2000 entities, have been selected companies with indicated state stake and simultaneously listed on WSE. In the first step 19 of such companies have been identified. Closer inspection of available data enables also excluding firms: with almost non-existent (reduced significantly recently following the privatisation processes), around/below 10% state stake or apparently not involved in foreign activity. This enabled setting up the final registry of nine Polish listed SOE conducting FDI. Table 1 offers synopsis of covered SOEs.

Table 1. Summary of Polish SOEs active abroad

SOE	State Stake (%)	Foreign Presence
PGNiG	72	7 foreign subsidiaries out of total 31. Located in Germany, Norway, Sweden, the Netherlands, Lebanon, United Arab Emirates and Ukraine. Operating branch in Pakistan, representative offices in Belgium, Belarus, Ukraine, Russia.
Lotos	53	15 out of 40 subsidiaries are hosted abroad, mainly in Lithuania, Cyprus, Norway and Curacao.
PZU	35	11 out of 55 Group subsidiaries are abroad, in Ukraine, Germany, Romania, Latvia, Lithuania and Sweden.
PKP Cargo / PKP SA	33	6 direct foreign subsidiaries, out of which 2 are in liquidation; in 2 PKP has more than 50% share and 7 indirect subsidiaries in Slovakia, Hungary, Czech Republic, Italy and the Netherlands.
Azoty	33	Companies run in Germany and in Africa in Senegal.
KGHM	32	9 subsidiaries supervised directly by KGHM out of 52 entities in the Group are located abroad, and 26 affiliates being part of KGHM International.
Tauron	30	2 subsidiaries out of 14 are located abroad along with 50% share in firms in Czech Republic and Sweden.
PKO BP	29	6 out of 46 subsidiaries within the Group are located abroad, among them 4 direct and 2 indirect subsidiaries in Ukraine and Sweden.
PKN Orlen	28	7 out of 36 entities constituting the group are located abroad – in Czech Republic, Lithuania, Germany, Sweden and Malta.

Source: Own elaboration (data as on November 2015).

The state stake varies in the examined group between some 27% and 72%. Lotos and PGNiG are only two firms where the state owns more than 50% of stake. Explored companies run abroad not only core business units (mining, extraction or trading) but also servicing units dealing with auxiliary functions – ships chartering, placing Eurobonds etc.). Comparing and contrasting the examined Polish SOEs enables some simple profiling of them with respect to their foreign presence. Assessing each firm against the background of its peers illuminates certain idiosyncrasies and allows to capture the dominating trait. The authors are aware that interested companies may not share our judgement and see their foreign involvement differently. Though, our opinion derives from evaluating each firm in wider context of its peers' engagement. Based on such exercises, the authors would suggest that:

- PGNiG, Lotos, PKN Orlen and KGHM can be indeed regarded as multinationals. Their complex structure and various modes of involvement abroad renders such name. They set up new businesses, purchase existing firms and conduct not only activities of core business such as resources exploration, processing but also establish firms tasked with global coordination of such spread presence – they manage and exercise control over other entities within the group, serve for marketing purposes and are representative offices. Their foreign presence is both geographically and operationally diversified.
- Azoty is a resource-seeking firm, venturing abroad with clear aim of tapping into foreign mineral resources and realising hence concrete acquisition projects.
- PZU and PKO BP are distinctly regional, market-driven ventures preferring close neighbouring locations with activities being extension and replication of operations carried at home and constituting the core business.
- Tuaron can be regarded as rather a small-scale timid investor gradually expanding presence abroad.
- PKP Cargo investments seem to fit into strategic-asset and indirectly a market-seeking FDI as it purchases foreign railway carriers in order to serve foreign markets.

Given the state stake and scope of foreign presence it seems justified to name investigated firms as rather quasi-SOMNEs/para-SOMNEs – as they are owned or controlled by the state to the limited extent (as compared to Chinese SOESs), their expansion abroad has begun relatively recently and has limited reach.

SOLUTIONS AND RECOMMENDATIONS

The dual nature and hybrid form of SOMNEs implies various challenges. This peculiarity is best summarised by He (et al., 2015) who stressed: the possible internal conflicts, management autonomy, varying expectations, perceived and tolerated uncertainty or readiness of risk taking and degree of flexibility.

In the current consensus view of many governments some rules of the game are required when state enterprises are engaged in commercial competition. This is mainly due to the fact that while governments have entered into numerous obligations with respect to international trade and investment, state-owned enterprises may frustrate the fulfilment of these commitments. Hence it must be stressed that it is not motives or efficiency of SOE what matter but trade- and investment-distorting effects with which these negotiators are concerned.

In respect of state-owned enterprises, the EU seeks to impose certain substantive and transparency requirements for the moment being not included in WTO agreements.[8] Efforts are being undertaken to set up a joint platform of state-owned enterprise-related disciplines, which can be used in subsequent international trade agreements and forums to address state capitalism concerns. For the EU, government ownership is not problematic in itself but certain advantages provided by governments must be addressed.[9]

The prominence of SOE as topic of public debate and policy-makers' interests is reflected in currently negotiated TTIP (Wooton, 2015) and features high on the agenda of recently concluded TTP (Hufbauer, 2015). Trans-Pacific Partnership members are committed to assure the level playing field between SOE and private firms by limiting, for example, the preferential access to finance or new markets. Obviously, certain transition periods before new rules take effect and possible carve-out are taken into account. Trans-Pacific Partnership launches some discipline on accounting practices and governing boards and a requirement that SOE open their procurement of goods and services to foreign firms. The treatment of SOE is also topic being covered during the negotiations of comprehensive bilateral investment agreement between the EU and China (Bickenbach, 2015). The Commission believes that this deal needs to address unfair advantages enjoyed by Chinese SOEs. Various privileges of such enterprises on the one hand, can be detrimental for European companies investing in China, on the other hand, may offer Chinese SOEs investing in Europe an unfair advantage. The likely remedies include first and foremost more transparency - "inter alia the timely publication of financial accounts according to international standards, the disclosure of leading managers' past and present connections to government offices, the publication of any exemptions of SOEs from any measure, regulation or law, and the disclosure of any tax preferences or subsidies for any SOEs" (Bickenbach, 2015, p. 23). New rules would be not only in interest of European about also Chinese companies who might in that way be freed from continuous prejudices and suspicions.

Existing regulatory frameworks that discipline some forms of anti-competitive behaviour of SOEs have been designed with domestic objectives in mind or were conceived at times when the state sector was oriented primarily towards domestic markets (Kowalski, 2013). In terms of international trade and investment, it is difficult to identify explicit strategies of OECD governments to expand the activity of their SOEs abroad. This does not mean that the authorities have no means of shielding an SOE or a national champion from foreign competition, or of helping facilitate their expansion abroad.

There is already in force law which regulates at the international level foreign activities of SOEs (Kawase, 2014). Regarding outward direct investments, some international investment agreements (IIAs) concluded between home and host countries contain provisions exempting subsidies. Other preferential treatment for SOEs that is discriminatory and anticompetitive in nature by host countries may be found to be in non-compliance, for instance, with the principle of national treatment or that of fair and equitable treatment. Furthermore, a foreign investor can bring a claim against the government of its host country for the reason of SOEs' misconduct under the investor-state dispute settlement (ISDS) provisions of the relevant IIA. On the other hand, regarding inward direct investments, when a host country deals with strategic investment activities and anticompetitive business practices by foreign SOEs, it is effective to apply within the purview of the OECD Code of Liberalisation of Current Invisible Operations, domestic investment review and blocking processes for the reason of protecting national security and public interests. Many IIAs basically do not restrict such investment reviews without liberalisation commitments on investment. And most IIAs provide for national security and public order exceptions. The IMF's Santiago Principles and the OECD Declaration on SWFs and Recipient Country Policies can be cited as relevant international soft law (WIR, 2009; Götz, Jankowska, 2016).

FUTURE RESEARCH DIRECTIONS

It is visible that there is no proper understanding of how institutions in the country of origin of SOEMNEs affect the strategies of outward investments (Kirca, 2010; Nielsen & Nielsen 2010, Wan, 2005, Wan & Hoskisson, 2003). Experts argue that attention should be paid to listed SOEs which display characteristics of both the state and private sectors. They may be motivated by objectives other than profits, and these are determined through a political process, on the other they are simultaneously subject to market forces.

There are however, many aspects missing form current international legal framework and the indication and characterization of these aspects could be the future focus of the study. It seems infeasible currently to require transparency of information such as the description of business and financial standing; to control outright government subsidies; to monitor person-oriented SOEs' strengths (like close relationships with influential politicians). Problems arise also in terms of how to quantify preferential treatment in environmental regulations for SOEs or SOEs' lax corporate governance. Even the definition of an SOE is another difficult issue to agree upon. Should the term 'state-owned' be taken literally as meaning 100% government ownership or more than 50% of its voting shares held by the government could be sufficient? What about "state-influenced enterprises"? (Shapiro & Globerman, 2009) Furthermore, treatment of enterprises owned by sub-national governments is seemingly another reason for splits among the negotiators.

Given the internationalisation processes of SOEs i.e. their higher involvement in trade and investment it seems inevitable to better monitor and asses these tendencies to help governments formulate informed and balanced policy responses. Existing law has mainly domestic inward perspective and does not seem adequate for international processes. National antitrust law can be used to deal with the abuse of dominant position by SOEs and to prevent anticompetitive effects associated with M&As by SOEs (Capobianco & Christiansen, 2011). Competitive neutrality arrangements in some OECD members aim to mitigate or eliminate competitive advantages of state-owned enterprises, with respect to taxation, or financing costs (OECD, 2012). In the EU, for example, the state interactions with other entities are governed by special rules in the areas of antitrust, state aid and transparency. WTO rules are generally ownership-neutral and the disciplines that they impose on government regulations and actions do not distinguish between situations where the provider of the goods or services is a public or a private. They can, nevertheless, discipline some government policies and actions involving state-owned enterprises, for example, when they receive trade-distorting state subsidies. Violation of national treatment or most-favoured nation principles, granting of subsidies or other forms of influencing trade by state-owned enterprises themselves can also be covered by WTO disciplines.

Yet, some of the definitional ambiguities have rendered application of these disciplines uncertain and some provisions allow countries to exempt state-owned enterprises' actions from certain WTO disciplines. Finally, many existing PTAs and BITs include specific provisions on state-owned enterprises, attempting to fill gaps in existing multilateral provisions.

The literature on SOMNEs is scant and mostly focused on Asia.[10] In fact what the authors know mostly come from the public administration, developmental economics and political economy literatures. Little is known about their international impacts and aspirations in the global arena and, in particular, about SOMNEs form CEECs.

CONCLUSION

This chapter has been inspired by the recognised and growing interest in international dimension of SOEs activity. As it seems SOEs cause more concerns due to their outward orientation. This issue is additionally compounded by the scare data available in this respect. There is still very little reliable information on the importance of state-owned enterprises in today's global markets and on the exact nature of the advantages they may be enjoying because of their ownership (Büge et al., 2013). Some 10% of the world's 2000 largest corporations are fully owned or partially controlled by governments (Krist & Benka, 2013).

Right now there are almost no rules governing how SOEs may operate in international trade, and SOEs can have unfair advantages in competition with privately-owned companies that must respond to market forces. Given the predicted growth tendency several issues need to be addressed which require enhanced policy coordination and information sharing to prevent or mitigate politicization of their operating and low efficiency and to assure that the international trade and investment environment remains open, non-discriminatory and offering a level playing field – so called competitive neutrality. Nevertheless, on the positive note it needs to be stressed that as found by OECD "SOEs are becoming more "international", but not necessarily more "political" and "host countries have often welcomed the contribution from foreign state-owned investors" (Christiansen & Kim, 2014). Twenty years ago, concerns about unfair competition between private companies and state-owned enterprises were minimal as most SOEs concentrated on home markets. However, today many SOEs are significant players in global markets. On a domestic level, countries can keep SOEs in check by anti-trust actions. Internationally, however, current rules are weak and do not adequately address the issue. In the EU itself, the member countries rely on SOEs to differing degrees and the EU has had to develop rules to ensure a level competitive playing field. TTP and TTIP negotiations, present an opportunity to develop rules to ensure fair competition. Without effective international rules on state-owned enterprises, free trade and investment are endangered. SOEs require an explicit and deliberate regulatory treatment due to their unique properties (Kawase, 2014). Given the controversies they initiate it seems that one coherent approach to their regulation is a preferred way than the piecemeal and overlapping rules currently considered.

Polish companies covered in this study are in fact partially state-owned enterprises given the not high (and diminishing) share of the Ministry of Treasury as stakeholder. It seems questionable if despite their significant foreign presences and the fact that their FDI are accounting for the bulk of total Poland's OFDI they deserve to be called the SOMNEs (or given the above – partially state-owned/para state-owned); if the scale and scope of their foreign engagement suffice for such name? This descriptive exercise may promote better understanding of foreign activities of Polish SOEs. It may enrich current literature on SOMNEs and in particular fill the current gap with respect to other than Chinese state-owned foreign activity. It synthesises the available knowledge on the internationalisation of Polish state-controlled and owned entities. Hence, it complements existing studies devoted mostly to single firm – case studies.

Literature review suggest the need of covering many legal aspects of SOEs international activity (e.g. Blyschak, 2016). Exploring SOMNEs in global context might include comprehensive comparison either to private domestic peers or other SOMNEs from a region or a given industry and sector. Such contextual embedded analysis would also yield some insight to the peculiarities of SOMNEs. In other words, it is not only the concrete topic which needs to be addressed with respect to SOMNEs' operations but also the research setting and design of investigation which can shed light on various so far not examined issues.

Based on the authors' investigation following general conclusions can be drawn. It might be expected that the future research agenda on SOEs' international activity would evolve around the aspect of their low (lack of) efficiency and worse performance due to managerial deficiencies, agency problems or other state-related labilities. On the other hand, most likely the further exploration would tackle the undue competitive advantages and other benefits which accrue to SOMNEs and which stem from the state protection. Given the aforementioned controversies and polarised opinions on SOMNEs rise the authors believe that it is of utmost importance to design the research properly. So it can better capture the SOEs peculiarities against the background of other entities. The contextualisation hence should not be underestimate. True picture of SOEs' foreign activity can be painted reliably only if contrasted with private peers from the sector or other SOMNEs from the region. The broader context would provide more detailed assessment. It would enable diagnosing if SOMNEs are indeed so special class of enterprises or their foreign investments actually do not deviate from the behaviours of their private peers.

As revealed by the close examination of articles published by the FT 45 top journals during the most recent 15-years period only 39 out of them actually focused on SOEs (30 of them exclusively on China!) and although, inquiry into SOEs is rising, the research on the topic continues to be scarce (Bruton et al, 2015). The authors believe that their research and presented discussion might contribute to the contemporary debate on SOEs and SOMNEs in particular and address the encouragement of Bruton, Peng, Ahlstrom, Stan, Xu (2015, p. 95) to "devote additional attention to (SOEs) this important, adaptive, and enduring organizational form that generates approximately 10% of global GDP and represents some of the world's largest firms".

ACKNOWLEDGMENT

Research has been undertaken within the project funded by the National Science Centre titled "State role in (post) crisis European economy – policy towards foreign direct investment" and allocated on the basis of decision number DEC-2014/13/B/HS4/00165.

REFERENCES

Adamczyk, J. (2014). *Ekonomiczne i społeczne efekty spółek z udziałem skarbu państwa, Studia i Materiały.* Wydział Zarządzania i Administracji Uniwersytetu Jana Kochanowskiego w Kielcach.

Augustynowicz, P., & Kwiatkowski, G. (2013). Przedsiębiorstwa państwowe na liście Fortune Global 500 w latach 2005–2012. *Przegląd Zachodniopomorski, 3*(1), 21–35.

Baniak, R. (2015). *Deputy of the Ministry of State Treasury.* Retrieved from http://www.polskatimes.pl/artykul/3813841,polskie-firmy-coraz-chetniej-inwestuja,id,t.html

Bass, A. E., & Chakrabarty, S. (2014). Resource security: Competition for global resources, strategic intent, and governments as owners. *Journal of International Business Studies, 45*(8), 961–979. doi:10.1057/jibs.2014.28

Bickenbach, F., Liu, W. H., & Li, G. (2015) The EU-China Bilateral Investment Agreement in Negotiation: Motivation, Conflicts and Perspectives. *Kiel Policy Brief,* 95. Retrieved June 17, 2016, from https://www.ifw-kiel.de/wirtschaftspolitik/zentrum-wirtschaftspolitik/kiel-policy-brief/kpb-2015/kiel-policy-brief-95

Blyschak, P. M. (2016). State-Owned Enterprises in International Investment. *ICSID Review*, *31*(1), 5–11. doi:10.1093/icsidreview/siv048

Bremmer, I. (2010). *The End of The Free Market. Who Wins the War Between States and Corporations.* New York, NY: Portfolio.

Bruton, G., Peng, V., Ahlstrom, D., Stan, C., & Xu, K. (2015). State-owned enterprises around the world as hybrid organizations. *The Academy of Management Perspectives*, *29*(1), 92–114. doi:10.5465/amp.2013.0069

Büge, M., Egeland, M., Kowalski, P., & Sztajerowska, M. (2013). *State-owned enterprises in the global economy: Reason for concern?* Retrieved June 17, 2016, from http://www.voxeu.org/article/state-owned-enterprises-global-economy-reason-concern

Cahen, F. R. (2014). Internationalization of state-owned enterprises through foreign direct investment. *Revista de Administração de Empresas*, *55*(6), 645–659. doi:10.1590/S0034-759020150604

Capobianco, A., & Christiansen, H. (2011). Competitive Neutrality and State-Owned Enterprises: Challenges and Policy Options. *OECD Corporate Governance Working Papers,* 1. 10.1787/5kg9xfgjdhg6-en

Choudhury, P., & Khanna, T. (2014). Toward resource independence - Why state-owned entities become multinationals: An empirical study of Indias public R&D laboratories. *Journal of International Business Studies*, *45*(8), 943–960. doi:10.1057/jibs.2014.20

Christiansen, H. (2011), The Size and Composition of the SOE Sector in OECD Countries, *OECD Corporate Governance Working Papers*, 5. 10.1787/5kg54cwps0s3-en

Christiansen, H., & Kim, Y. (2014), State-Invested Enterprises in the Global Marketplace: Implications for a Level Playing Field. *OECD Corporate Governance Working Papers*, 14. 10.1787/5jz0xvfvl6nw-en

Ciesielska, D. (2014). Polish Foreign Direct Investments – trends, patterns and determinants. *The Macrotheme Review*, *3*(1), 214-229.

Clifton, J., Comín, F., & Díaz-Fuentes, D. (2011). From national monopoly to multinational corporation: How regulation shaped the road towards telecommunications internationalisation. *Business History*, *53*(5), 761–781. doi:10.1080/00076791.2011.599588

Cuervo-Cazurra, A., Inkpen, A., Musacchio, A., & Ramaswamy, K. (2014). Governments as owners: State-owned multinational companies. *Journal of International Business Studies*, *45*(8), 919–942. doi:10.1057/jibs.2014.43

Database on National Practices and Regulations with Respect to State Enterprises. (n.d.). Retrieved November 2015 from http://qdd.oecd.org/subject.aspx?Subject=8f22ef7d-b780-4570-a4b1-7e0cb3ad7e04

Dau, L. (2012). Pro-market reforms and developing country multinational corporations. *Global Strategy Journal*, *2*(3), 262–276. doi:10.1111/j.2042-5805.2012.01033.x

Dharwadkar, R., George, G., & Brandes, P. (2000). Privatization in emerging economies: An agency theory perspective. *Academy of Management Review*, *25*, 650–669.

DiMaggio, P. J., & Powell, W. (1991). The new institutionalism in organizational analysis. Chicago: University of Chicago Press.

Éltető, A., Ferenčíková, S., Götz, M., Hlušková, T., Jankowska, B., Kříž, E., & Sass, M. (2015). Outward FDI Policies in Visegrad Countries. *IZ Policy Papers*, 16. Retrieved September 10, 2016, from: http://www.iz.poznan.pl/news/1179_pp_16.pdf

Ferencikova, S., & Hluskova, T. (2015). Internationalization of Central and Eastern European companies – theory and its implications in the Slovak IT sector. *Journal for East European Management Studies, 20*(4), 415–434.

Flores-Macias, F., & Musacchio, A. (2009). The Return of State-Owned Enterprises. *Harvard International Review*. Retrieved June 17, 2016, from http://hir.harvard.edu/the-return-of-state-ownedGuillén-enterprises

Frączyk, J. (2014). *Państwowe giganty tracą miliardy za granicą. Wszystko naszym kosztem*. Retrieved June 17, 2016, from http://finanse.wp.pl/kat,1033747

Gorynia, M., Nowak, J., Trąpczyński, P., & Wolniak, R. (2015). *The Investment Development Path of Poland: a Current Assessment*. Paper presented at the 41st Annual Conference of the European International Business Academy (EIBA), Rio de Janeiro.

Gorynia, M., Nowak, J., & Wolniak, R. (2010). Foreign direct investment of Central and Eastern European countries, and the investment development path revisited. *Eastern Journal of European Studies, 2*(1), 23–25.

Götz, M. (2014). *Polskie bezpośrednie inwestycje za granicą. Metodologia teorii ugruntowanej*. Poznań: Wydawnictwo Instytutu Zachodniego.

Götz, M., & Jankowska, B. (2016). Internationalization by State-owned Enterprises (SOEs) and Sovereign Wealth Funds (SWFs) after the 2008 Crisis. Looking for Generalizations. *International Journal of Management and Economics, 50*(1), 63–81. doi:10.1515/ijme-2016-0012

He, X., Eden, L., & Hitt, M. A. (2015). The Renaissance of State-Owned Multinationals. *Thunderbird International Business Review, 58*(2), 117–129. doi:10.1002/tie.21711

Holmstrom, B. (1979). Moral hazard and observability. *The Bell Journal of Economics, 10*(1), 74–91. doi:10.2307/3003320

Hufbauer, G. C., & Cimino-Isaacs, C. (2015). *What You Need to Know about the Trans-Pacific Partnership*. Retrieved July 05 2016, from https://piie.com/commentary/op-eds/what-you-need-know-about-trans-pacific-partnership

Inoue, C. F. K. V., Lazzarini, S. G., & Musacchio, A. (2013). Leviathan as a minority shareholder: Firm level performance implications of equity purchases by the government. *Academy of Management Journal, 56*(6), 1775–1801. doi:10.5465/amj.2012.0406

Irzyński, R. (2014). *Duże inwestycje mogą oznaczać duże straty. PKN Orlen i Lotos coś o tym wiedzą*. Retrieved July 05, 2016, from http://www.polskieradio.pl/42/1701/Artykul/1273885,Duze-inwestycje-moga-oznaczac-duze-straty-PKN-Orlen-i-Lotos-cos-o-tym-wiedza

Julien, C., & Sohlberg, M. (2015). *An unprecedented step – commission releases TTIP negotiation proposal*. Retrieved June 17, 2016, from http://www.internationallawoffice.com/Newsletters/International-Trade/European-Union/King-Spalding-LLP/An-unprecedented-step-commission-releases-TTIP-negotiation-proposals

Kaldor, N. (1980). Public or private enterprise – The issue to be considered. In W. J. Baumol (Ed.), *Public and private enterprises in a mixed economy* (pp. 1–12). New York: St. Martin's. doi:10.1007/978-1-349-16394-6_1

Kalotay, K. (2010). The future of Russian outward foreign direct investment and the eclectic paradigm: What changes after the crisis of 2008-2009? *Competitio (University of Debrecen), 9*(1), 31-54. Retrieved April 02, 2016, from http://ssrn.com/abstract=1702829

Kawase, T. (n.d.). *Trans-Pacific Partnership negotiations and rulemaking to regulate state-owned enterprises*. Retrieved July 05, 2016, from http://www.voxeu.org/article/trans-pacific-partnership-negotiations-and-rulemaking-regulate-state-owned-enterprises

Kirca, A. H., Hult, G. T. M., Roth, K., Cavusgil, S. T., Perryy, M. Z., Akdeniz, M. B., & White, R. C. et al. (2012). Firm-specific assets, multinationality, and firm performance: A meta-analytic review and theoretical integration. *Academy of Management Journal, 54*(1), 47–72. doi:10.5465/AMJ.2011.59215090

Knutsen, C. H., Rygh, A., & Hveem, H. (2011). Does state ownership matter? Institutions effect on foreign direct investment revisited. *Business and Politics, 13*(1), 1–33. doi:10.2202/1469-3569.1314

Kostova, T., & Zaheer, S. (1999). Organizational legitimacy under conditions of complexity: The case of the multinational enterprise. *Academy of Management Review, 24*(1), 64–81.

Kowalski, P., Büge, M., & Sztajerowska, M. (2013). State-Owned Enterprises, Trade Effects and Policy Implications. *OECD Trade Policy Papers*, 147. Retrieved July 05, 2016, from http://www.oecd-ilibrary.org/trade/state-owned-enterprises_5k4869ckqk7l-en

Krist, B., & Benka, S. (2013). *On a Collision Course: State Owned Enterprises and Free Trade*. Retrieved July 05, 2016, from http://americastradepolicy.com/new/#.ViJR5dZga9Y

Lista polskich przedsiębiorstw i eksporterów. (2015). Retrieved 13 July, 2016, from http://www.rp.pl/rankingi/lista_2000

Mazzolini, R. (1980). The international strategy of state-owned firms: An organizational process and politics perspective. *Strategic Management Journal, 1*(2), 101–118. doi:10.1002/smj.4250010202

Musacchio, A., Lazzarni, S. G., & Aguilera, R. V. (2015). New varieties of state capitalism: Strategic and governance implications. *The Academy of Management Perspectives, 29*(1), 115–131. doi:10.5465/amp.2013.0094

Nielsen, B. B., & Nielsen, S. (2010). A multilevel approach to understanding the multinationality–performance relationship. *Advances in International Management, 23*, 527–557. doi:10.1108/S1571-5027(2010)00000230028

Nölke, A. (2015). *State permeated capitalism in large emerging markets*. Key note presentation at SVoC conference, Central Eastern Europe University, Budapest, Hungary.

Nölke, A., & Vliegenthart, A. (2009). Enlarging the Varieties of Capitalism: The Emergence of Dependent Market Economies in East Central Europe. *World Politics*, *61*(04), 670–702. doi:10.1017/S0043887109990098

Noreng, O. (1994). National oil companies and their government owners: The politics of interaction and control. *Journal of the Energy Division*, *19*(2), 197–226.

Nowiński, W. (2015). *Effects of Cross-Border Acquisitions by Polish MNEs*. Paper presented at the Conference of Academy of International Business Central and Eastern Europe Chapter (AIB-CEE Chapter) and Institute of Management.

Obłój, K., & Wąsowska, A. (2012). Strategiczne wybory polskich firm – motywy i kierunki budowania powiązań zewnętrznych drogą kapitałowego umiędzynarodowienia działalności. In W. Morawski (Ed.), *Powiązania zewnętrzne. Modernizacja Polski* (pp. 102–120). Warszawa: Wolters Kluwer.

OECD. (2004). *Comparative Report on Corporate Governance of State-Owned Enterprises*. Paris: OECD Publishing.

OECD. (2012). *Competitive Neutrality: Maintaining a Level Playing Field Between Public and Private Business*. Paris: OECD Publishing.

OECD. (2013). *International Investments by SOEs: Economic Trends and the Policy Landscape*. Unpublished OECD document, DAF/INV/WD(2013)14.

OECD. (2014). *The Size and Sectoral Distribution of SOEs in OECD and Partner Countries*. Paris: OECD Publishing.

OECD Business Survey 2014 on State Influence on Competition in International Markets. (n.d.). Retrieved 05 July 2016, from http://www.oecd.org/tad/tradedev/oecd-business-survey-state-influence-competition-international-markets.htm

Pargendler, M., Musacchio, A., & Lazzarini, S. G. (2013). In strange company: The puzzle of private investment in state-controlled firms. *Cornell International Law Journal*, *46*(3), 569–610.

Penrose, E. T. (1959). *The theory of the growth of the firm*. Oxford, UK: Oxford University Press.

PWC. (2015). *State-owned enterprises: Catalysts for public value creation?* PWC Report. Retrieved July 05, 2016, from https://www.pwc.com/gx/en/psrc/publications/assets/pwc-state-owned-enterprise-psrc.pdf

Ramasamy, B., Yeung, M., & Laforet, S. (2012). Chinas outward foreign direct investment: Location choice and firm ownership. *Journal of World Business*, *47*(1), 17–25. doi:10.1016/j.jwb.2010.10.016

Roguski, A., & Furman, T. (2013). *Zagraniczne przejęcia to domena spółek surowcowych*. Retrieved July 05, 2016, from http://www.rp.pl/artykul/1070528-Zagraniczne-przejecia-to-domena-spolek-surowcowych.html

Schweiger, Ch. (2014). *The EU and the Global Financial Crisis. New Varieties of Capitalism*. Cheltenham, UK: Edward Elgar Publishing.

Shapiro, D., & Globerman, S. (2009). *The international activities and impacts of state-owned enterprises*, Retrieved July 17, 2016, from http://dspace.africaportal.org/jspui/bitstream/123456789/26419/1/The%20International%20Activities%20and%20Impacts%20of%20State-Owned%20Enterprises.pdf

Tan, J., & Tan, D. (2005). Environment - Strategy Co-Evolution and Co-Alignment: A Staged Model of Chinese Soes under Transition. *Strategic Management Journal*, *26*(2), 141–157. doi:10.1002/smj.437

Textual Proposal Possible Provisions on Competition. (n.d.). Retrieved 05, July 2016, from http://trade.ec.europa.eu/doclib/docs/2015/january/tradoc_153030.pdf

The world's biggest public companies in 2011. (2012). Retrieved July 05 2016, from http://www.forbes.com/lists/2012/18/global2000_2011.html

Vernon, R. (1979). The International Aspects of State-Owned Enterprises. *Journal of International Business Studies*, *10*(3), 7–15. doi:10.1057/palgrave.jibs.8490790

Wan, W. P. (2005). Country resource environments, firm capabilities, and corporate diversification strategies. *Journal of Management Studies*, *42*(1), 161–182. doi:10.1111/j.1467-6486.2005.00492.x

Wan, W. P., & Hoskisson, R. E. (2003). Home country environments, corporate diversification strategies, and firm performance. *Academy of Management Journal*, *46*(1), 27–45. doi:10.2307/30040674

Wąsowska, A., & Obłój, K. (2013). Location Determinants of Polish Outward Foreign Direct Investment and the Impact of the Global Crisis. In M. Marinov & S. Marinova (Eds.), *Emerging Economies and Firms in the Global Crisis* (pp. 240–258). London: Palgrave Macmillan. doi:10.1057/9781137277473_10

Williamson, O. E. (1985). *The economic institutions of capitalism*. New York: Free Press.

Witt, M. A., & Lewin, A. Y. (2007). Outward foreign direct investment as escape response to home country institutional constraints. *Journal of International Business Studies*, *38*(4), 579–594. doi:10.1057/palgrave.jibs.8400285

Wooton, I. (2015). The transatlantic trade and investment partnership (TTIP): The devil will be in the detail. *Fraser of Allander Economic Commentary*, *39*(1), 64–71.

World Investment Report. (2009). *Transnational Corporations, Agricultural Production and Development*. UNCTAD.

World Investment Report. (2011). *Non-equity modes of international production and development*. UNCTAD.

Zimny, Z. (2013). Outward FDI from Poland and its policy context. In *Columbia FDI Profiles Country profiles of inward and outward foreign direct investment*. Vale Columbia Center on Sustainable International Investment.

KEY TERMS AND DEFINITIONS

Diversity of Capitalism and Varieties of State Capitalism: Classification of types of capitalism which among others accounts for the role played in the economy by the state. Besides differentiating between liberal market economy, capital market economy, it recognizes various models of state capitalism with diversified scale of state intervention ranging from the wholly state-owned enterprises to subtle state aid facilitating development.

Escape Motive: The need to reduce the dependency on the state as potentially perceived by SOMNEs which can materialise via conducting investment abroad.

Extraterritoriality Argument: Tendency revealed by SOMNEs to perceive OFDI as a way to export certain ideology, expand zone of influence.

Foreign Direct Investment: FDI - the most advanced form of internationalisation, implies the highest commitment in running the activity abroad as compared to export or joint venture. It can take the form of acquisition (M&A) or greenfield projects.

IDP - Investment Development Path: The pattern describing the evolution of foreign direct inflows and outflows of a given economy and tracing it against the GDP developments. This construct shows whether a country is rather a FDI (capital and know-how) recipient or donor.

International Investment Regime: Vast collection of arrangement, agreements, partnerships and treaties (mostly IIA – international investment agreements and BIT – bilateral investment treaties) which set the perimeters of international expansion usually by private entities. Though, the increasing role of SOEs in the process of internationalisation leads to new generation of treaties and partnerships being negotiated / concluded which cover also these class of investors and controversial issues pertaining to them.

Non-Business Argument: Inclination revealed by SOMNEs to get involved in economically less (no) feasible projects, to incur unjustified higher costs, to accept more risk when venturing abroad and hence be less profitable than private business or even bring losses.

State Owned Transnational Company / State-Owned Multinational Enterprise: SOTNCs / SOMNEs – state-owned company active abroad, with affiliates and activities be they upstream or downstream performed in foreign markets. SOMNE / SOTNC can be created via nationalisation of existing MNE/TNC or via internationalisation of SOE. Polish SOTNCs – firms constituting the case study of this paper; group of selected nine Polish firms who met the criteria of state involvement – at least 10%, are listed on Warsaw Stock Exchange and possess affiliates abroad.

State-Owned Enterprise: SOE - broad term defined diversely in the literature usually stands for the company controlled, owned or invested by the state – mostly by the Treasury. The ownership and control can be expressed in various ways. Such firms are believed to enjoy special treatment (see: advantages), though, suffer also from certain inefficiencies, inflexibilities, etc. (see: disadvantages).

ENDNOTES

1 UNCTAD (WIR, 2011) defines a *state-owned multinational (SOMNE)* as an organizational form that is both a multinational enterprise (MNE) (i.e., the firm has one or more foreign affiliates engaged in value- adding activities in one or more foreign countries) and a state-owned (or controlled) enterprise (i.e., the firm has a minimum of 10% government ownership). The 10% cut-off is high enough that the state likely influences corporate governance and thereby affects firm performance.

2 The prevalence of SOEs also varies considerably across industrial sectors. Statistics on SOE sales, assets and market value among the world 's largest companies have been used to calculate Sectoral SOE Shares (SSS).

3 Dependent variables: in the first regression the number of firm's domestic subsidiaries, in the second - the number of its foreign subsidiaries; and in a third - the ratio of foreign to domestic subsidiaries as a proxy for internationalization. As independent variables have served parent sales, profits, assets, market value and a dummy that equals one if the firm is an SOE and equals zero otherwise (Kowalski et al., 2013, p. 36).

4 2014 OECD Business Survey on State Influence on Competition in International Markets sheds additional light on concerns related to cross-border activities of state enterprises. It also summarizes key results from the OECD Database on National Practices and Regulations which contains information on national and international regulation with respect to state enterprises - announced in May 2015 as pilot project requiring refinements.

5 Forbes Global 2000 - SOE sales, profits, assets and market value as a % GNI.

6 Database on National Practices and Regulations with Respect to State Enterprises, http://qdd.oecd.org/subject.aspx?Subject=8f22ef7d-b780-4570-a4b1-7e0cb3ad7e04

7 The problem with obtaining the reliable and comparable data for Poland is similar to the OECD studies (Christiansen, Kim, 2014, p. 26).

8 An unprecedented step – commission releases TTIP negotiation proposal (Julien, Sohlberg, 2015).

9 Textual Proposal - the European Union's initial proposal for legal text on "Competition" in TTIP. It was tabled for discussion with the US in the negotiating round of 10-14 March 2014 and made public on 7 January 2015. The actual text in the final agreement will be a result of negotiations between the EU and US. Textual Proposal Possible Provisions on Competition, http://trade.ec.europa.eu/doclib/docs/2015/january/tradoc_153030.pdf

10 Special issue of the Journal of International Business Studies: Governments as Owners: Globalizing State-Owned Enterprises (2014) 45 (8), 919–942 contributes significantly to the so far rather limited research.

Chapter 8
Outward Foreign Direct Investment in Post-Transition Economy:
Poland's Experience

Tomasz Dorożyński
University of Lodz, Poland

Agnieszka Kłysik-Uryszek
University of Lodz, Poland

Anetta Kuna-Marszałek
University of Lodz, Poland

ABSTRACT

Recent two decades witnessed unprecedented changes in the economies of Central and Eastern Europe. Accelerated economic growth following systemic transformations, globalisation and liberalisation and EU integration visibly intensified international capital flows, including foreign direct investment (FDI). Intense internationalisation of an economy is usually perceived as a positive process, which – in general – gives an opportunity to accelerate growth and strengthen competitiveness. Therefore the authorities of an economy try to support FDI flows by implementing different incentives. The main goal of the chapter is to show the scale and scope of outward foreign direct investments (OFDI) of Polish companies in the light of economic transformation experience and authorities support. The chapter is organized as follows: first it presents Poland's path from centrally planned state to developed, competitive economy. Secondly, the focus is laid on support offered to companies undertaking OFDI ventures and finally on the scale and scope of Poland's outward investments.

INTRODUCTION

Foreign direct investment, its definitions, forms, motives and consequences have already been broadly discussed in scientific literature. However the problem itself is still very urgent and hot-debated issue because dynamic changes in global economy triggers few directions and forms of flows. Central and

DOI: 10.4018/978-1-5225-2345-1.ch008

Eastern European countries (CEECs), which have successfully overcame transition period, play growing role in this process. For many years they have been mostly recipients of foreign capital (in the form of FDI) while recently also companies originating form CEE economies start to internationalize actively.

It should also be stressed that the net benefits for the economy which come from inclusion into international capital flows are unquestionable. Therefore, legal authorities often implement numerous incentives and support solutions not only for inward FDI but for outward FDI as well. Poland seems to be a perfect example of that process, that is why the main goal of the chapter is to present and discuss the scale and scope of outward foreign direct investments (OFDI) of Polish companies in the light of economic transformation experience and authorities support.

The chapter is organized as follows: first it presents Poland's path from centrally planned state to developed, competitive economy. Secondly, the focus is laid on support offered to companies undertaking OFDI ventures and finally on the scale and scope of Poland's outward investments.

BACKGROUND

Nowadays, transition economies, with Central and Eastern European countries and Poland in particular, are becoming increasingly important players at international FDI markets. So far these countries were mainly FDI recipients but since their EU accession their OFDI significantly increased. It was made possible as a result of intense economic and systemic transformations launched after 1989. The main objective was to do away with centrally planned economy model and adopt a strategy to build up liberal, free market economy. Reconstruction of the market system in CEECs after several decades of central planning was difficult, exhausting, and time consuming. These countries, including Poland, underwent macroeconomic reforms, which at the beginning consisted in implementing a tight monetary policy and market-economy rules, necessary in view of the total macroeconomic imbalance at the outset of the transformation.

Comparing the experience of Poland and other countries in the region, e.g., the remaining Visegrad Group Countries (the Czech Republic, Slovakia, and Hungary), we may conclude that Poland was confronted with the most difficult conditions at the start of economic transformations. According to the EBRD study the initial conditions index[1] for Poland was 1.9 while for the Czech Republic it amounted to 3.5, for Slovakia 2.9, and for Hungary 3.3 (the higher the index the better initial conditions to implement market reforms) (Transition Report 2000, 2000, p. 21). In spite of this, economic transformation in Poland produced a more general model for other CEECs. Major assumptions were based on five pillars of economic transformation: (1) rapid transformation into a functioning private market economy; (2) liberalization of economic functions, especially in relation to foreign trade and foreign direct investment; (3) privatization of state-owned-enterprises; (4) construction of an effective social safety net by reforming the pension, education, health care, and social security systems; and (5) mobilization of international financial assistance to support the process (Hunter and Ryan 2005). These pillars of transformation were closely interrelated (Mickiewicz 2005, p. 26 and further). The program identified all steps necessary to ensure macroeconomic stabilization. These included, inter alia, the limiting of budget deficits, reducing inflation and establishing fully convertible currency with real exchange rate.

In order to accomplish the above assumptions, numerous concrete actions had to be undertaken, and the so called "shock therapy" started. It meant quick implementation of a radical and comprehensive economic program, which included macroeconomic stabilization, market liberalization, and fundamental institutional restructuring. To entrepreneurs systemic changes were of fundamental importance as entrepreneurship model changed. After 1989 everyone could start a business and many Poles took advantage of this opportunity. In the first decade of transformation, ownership changes that increased the share of the private sector in the economy and helped develop micro, small and medium-sized enterprises were very dynamic. A lot of new provisions entered into force that regulated economic activity, e.g. the commercial law, tax code and the banking law.

Micro and small enterprises, practically right from the outset of the transformation until to date, have accounted for the majority of firms in Poland. They are the core of the Polish economic transformation and nowadays play a critical role in the Polish economy. SMEs create employment and are the source of large part of value added. Besides, they shape foreign trade in Poland, its structure and dynamics. Their share in total exports was ca. 1/3rd and has not changed much since the beginning of the century (Central Statistical Office of Poland 2016). Developed markets, mainly of the EU Member States, were and still are the main partners of Polish foreign trade. They represent ca. 3/4th of all the SME exports.

Entrepreneurship development was facilitated by political decisions on the accession to the European Union structures. On February 1, 1994, Poland and the EU, signed the Europe Agreement giving Poland the status of an associated country. Accession negotiations were completed in 2003 and six months later Poland and nine other countries formally joined the EU. Within 10 years following the accession, they exported to the EU goods worth almost PLN 3.5 billion. This is twice the value of Poland's GDP (Poland's 10 years in the European Union 2014).

The membership in the European Union and the opening up of the Polish economy consequently pursued throughout more than two decades have given powerful development impulse to the Polish economy and contributed to its improved competitiveness. First of all, it opened up new opportunities of development to enterprises. We mean here better access to the EU funds and external sources of funding, higher demand for Polish products in the EU single market, better access to loans, and improved financial performance. Besides, we witnessed positive changes in the economy, e.g., increased share of services in the GDP with simultaneous drop in the share of agriculture, increased efficiency of the economy as a result of technological progress and intensified competitiveness in the internal market, higher production levels of medium- and highly processed goods, and an increased share in global trade (Poland's 10 years in the European Union 2014).

Transformation in Poland paved the way for systematic economic growth at a relatively high rate. Recession instigated by systemic transformations did not last long and was followed by dynamic growth, which substantially improved Poland's position in the group of transition economies (Jarmołowicz and Piątek 2013, p. 81). Economic recovery, which could be observed already in mid-1992, got stabilised and acquired solid foundations in 1994 (Leszczyński 2015). The foregoing was evidenced by lasting high GDP growth rate. (Figure 1).

Source: authors' own compilation based on GUS data.

Over the years 1992-2013 GDP per capita in Poland was growing at a rate that was twice high as the rate in the most developed EU member states (Gomułka 2014). World Bank data show that per capita GDP presented in terms of purchasing power parity increased from almost USD 6,000 in 1990 to USD 26,135 in 2015, i.e. slightly more than fourfold (www.data.worldbank.org 2016). In 2013 GDP per capita reached 62% of income of developed Western European countries (Eurozone), a natural point of reference for Poland and a benchmark for social aspirations, while back in 1992 it represented less than 30% (Piątkowski 2013). In 2011, for the first time ever, OECD and the World Bank changed the clas-

Figure 1. GDP dynamics (in constant prices) over the period 1989-2015 (preceding year =100) (in %)
GUS, 2016.

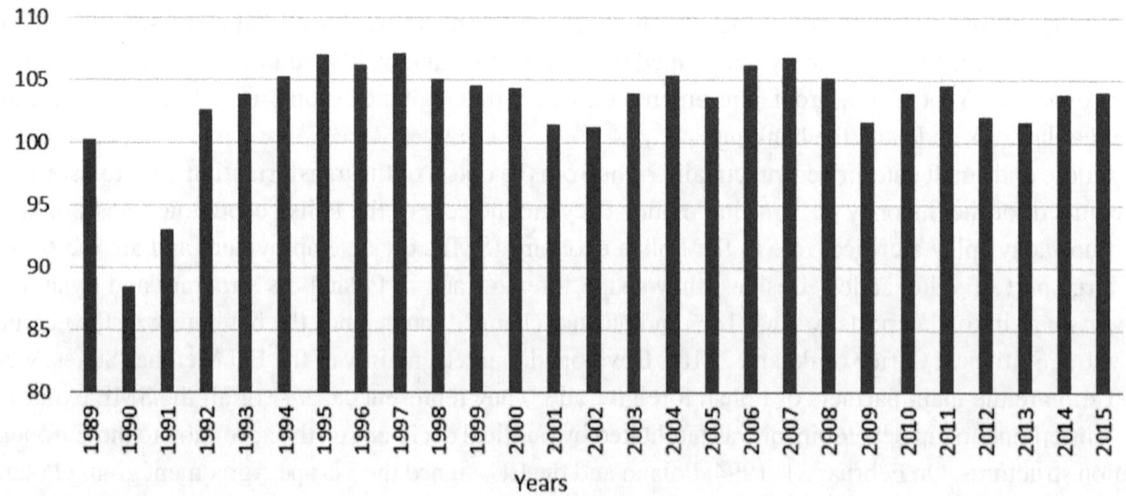

sification of Poland from an "upper middle income country" to a "high income country", which means that economic transformation has produced expected results.[2]

A range of changes was also reported in Poland's exports and imports after 1989. First of all, the volume of international trade increased and its geographic structure changed. Until the EU accession, exports (in USD) increased fivefold while Polish imports increased more than ninefold. Also per capita trade with other countries rapidly increased (per capita exports increased almost four times, imports almost seven times). All the above only confirms substantial opening of Polish economy in the 1990s (Chilimoniuk and Czarny 2005, p. 157). In the period of 2004–2012, the value of trade in Poland grew over two times – exports (in current prices, expressed in EUR), increased by 140%, and imports by 116% (Poland in the European Union … 2014, p. 55). Exports and imports dynamics over the years 1989-2015 is presented in Figure 2.

Figure 2. Exports and imports dynamics over the years 1989-2015
Source: authors' own compilation based on (GUS, 2016).

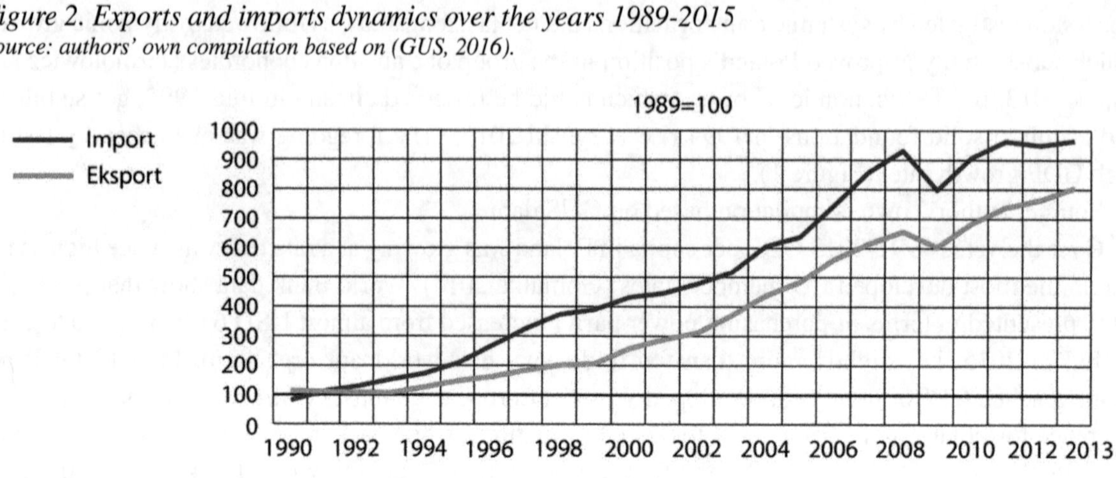

The structure of Polish foreign trade by SITC sections is similar to the overall structure of trade in the EU where both imports and exports are dominated by products from the section: "Machinery and transport equipment". Unfortunately, the share of high-tech products in Polish exports is low, which is not good for the economy. That is due to marginal importance of the manufacturing of high-tech goods in domestic enterprises and a very small share of foreign companies from high-tech sector in incoming FDI (Potencjał innowacyjny gospodarki… 2016).

As we have already mentioned, systemic transformation and liberalisation of trade policy did not remain neutral for geographic transformations in the structure of Polish foreign trade. These changes clearly reinforced the role of developed countries, in particular European ones. Additionally, changes in the structure of trade were encouraged by intensive inflow of foreign capital (including IFDI). Businesses with foreign capital account for almost 60% of Polish exports (Kłysik-Uryszek 2012). Thus, we may conclude that liberalisation of economic ties between Poland and the EU member states was one of the major factors that changed the structure of exports and imports of goods (Czubek and Molendowski 2005, p. 31).

The above effects have become visible in annual competitiveness rankings where Poland, slowly but systematically, improves its position. For example, between 2004 and 2016 Poland markedly improved its Global Competitiveness Index ranking from 60 to 41 (The Global Competitiveness Report 2015–2016, 2016). It is also considered as a country with development potential in the manufacturing sector, BPO/SSC services, and R&D. This potential is enhanced by the highest rate of absorption of EU resources (85%) among the new EU Member States (Economist Intelligence Unit 2015, p. 10).

In the case of Poland it is also stressed that recent improvements have been made in terms of institutions, infrastructure, and education, and that the flexibility of the labour market increased. These key achievements "are steps in the right direction to boost the country's competitiveness" (The Global Competitiveness Report 2014-2015, 2015, p. 24).[3] When analyzing the results of other leading international rankings, we may conclude that over the last several years, including the times of crisis and economic downturn, Poland (from among the CEECs) was one of the most preferred destinations for foreign investors. They were attracted mostly by cheap labour and a big, quickly developing market (the biggest in the CEECs, which as a result of integration and liberalisation has become a good place to further develop exports to the neighbouring countries). Investment promoting policy of the State (including establishing Special Economic Zones) was another factor favouring the location. All in all, Poland's attractiveness was created by legal and institutional conditions, such as (Kłysik-Uryszek 2010, pp. 20-21):

1. Economic, political and social stability, security, and predictability of legal and administrative regulations;
2. Tax policy, State aid, including investment incentives and allowances;
3. Regulations concerning market entry (i.e. equal treatment), operations, and protection of competition;
4. Efficiency of state administration and institutions involved in creating the business climate.

In the opinion of Ernst & Young experts (EY's attractiveness survey, Europe 2014) other countries are battling to replicate the Polish model of attracting investors. Poland ranks high also in the World Bank Group flagship report "*Doing Business*". It suffices to say, that in 2016 the country occupies 25th place in the ranking (Doing Business 2016, 2015), while in 2006 it ranked 54 (Doing Business 2006, 2006).

Poland is also appreciated in the UNCTAD ranking. Poland's competitive advantages are: a large and rapidly developing internal market, an educated and flexible workforce, stable banking system, access to international local markets, and the availability of suppliers and partners. Report for 2014 also stresses that Poland adopted the "Programme to support investments of high importance to the Polish economy for 2011-2020", with the aim of increasing innovation and the competitiveness of the economy by promoting FDI in high-tech sectors (World Investment Report 2014, p.113). Most probably the above mentioned factors gave Poland a place in the group of the top 15 attractive FDI locations in recent years (World Investment Report 2010-2015).

The above-presented considerations show that the assessment of Poland's investment attractiveness has always been high. We can read it not only in reports of international institutions but, primarily, in the value of FDI incoming to Poland. Surely, attracting foreign investment into the exporting sector (manufacturing) and services (banks, large format retail trade, telecommunication and hotels) was a success, although invested amounts were relatively modest (in 1995-2008 they represented ca. 10% of all investment) but they focused on neglected sectors of economy. With the benefit of hindsight, we can say that they were crucial for the growth of exports and services (Gomułka 2014).

Systemic transformation and the EU accession not only improved Poland's investment attractiveness but also very much intensified the involvement of Polish enterprises in investment projects abroad. Polish enterprises have invested their capital in almost 100 countries, however, a detailed analysis of the geographical breakdown of their investments clearly indicates that European markets, in particular those in neighbouring countries, were especially attractive to Polish enterprises. Almost 85% of all foreign affiliates are based in Europe (and ca. 88–90% of affiliates owned by manufacturing companies) while over a half of foreign affiliates of Polish non-financial companies (and slightly more than 60% of manufacturing companies) were located in our immediate neighbourhood (Germany, the Czech Republic, Slovakia, Ukraine, Belarus, Lithuania, and Russia) (Buczkowski et al. 2015, pp. 98-99).

INSTRUMENTS TO SUPPORT INVESTORS IN ACTIVE INTERNATIONALISATION

Economic Rationale behind Support to OFDI

Generally, FDI may prove to be either advantageous or disadvantageous to the receiving economy (e.g. Moran, Graham and Blomström 2005; Tytel and Yudaeva 2006; Herzer 2012; Temiz and Gökman, 2014). In the developing or (post) transition countries they are usually seen as a reliable and cheap source of capital, technology, and management skills and an easy way to access international markets.

Many researchers have also relatively thoroughly discussed and studied effects of outward FDI at the macro- and micro-economic level in developed and developing countries (e.g. Globerman 2012; Wiliński 2013; Globerman and Shapiro 2008; Gorynia, Nowak and Wolniak 2009). Numerous studies confirm that FDI impact upon economic performance of multinational enterprises (MNEs) depends on various factors, among which we should list their size, motivation behind FDI and expansion strategy, industry, experience in operating in international markets, the quality of institutions in the home and host countries, time horizon, etc. Obviously, the multiplicity of potential determinants, which may be interpreted in various ways, makes conclusions drawn by individual researchers, as well as research methods and assumptions strongly context-dependant (Gorynia and Trąpczyński 2014).

The assessment of effects of outward FDI to the home country is often ambiguous. Controversies intensify when OFDI effects are assessed not just from the viewpoint of the investing entity, but in a wider context considering the home economy of FDI, which includes also other enterprises, central budget or economic environment. However, in general positive opinions prevail. Active policy pursued by public authorities in support of foreign investment, inward as well as outward, seems to be economically justified. It also explains why various types of investment incentives are applied (Buczkowski et al. 2015).

Principal objective of investment incentives addressed to foreign investors is to attract capital that will help modernise production assets and technology. Such support can be offered at all three levels of government: central, regional, and local. The role of incentives designed to attract inward FDI and economic rationale behind them have been usually analysed at the two first levels. To the best of our knowledge, outward foreign direct investment incentives have not generated much interest among researchers, which could well be explained by the difficulties in access to reliable data on OFDI support tools and by poor portfolio of instruments available to local authorities.

There is a broad consensus that resources inflowing to host countries as inward FDI produce positive outcomes and hence efforts made to attract them are seen as positive. However, such consensus has not been so strong over OFDI, which is why until quite recently supporting outward FDI has often been avoided. But approaches to OFDI are changing fast and many countries have come to believe that incentives to OFDI are appropriate and efficient. This new attitude encourages governments, as well as regional and sub-regional authorities to be much more active in this field also because countries have realized that domestic companies need to be competitive in the global economy (Investment Incentives 2013).

OFDI Support Instruments

James (2009) defines investment incentives as measurable economic advantages that public institutions provide to specific companies or groups of firms, to steer investment into favoured sectors or regions or to influence the character of such investments projects.

Thomas (2007) describes investment incentives in a more unambiguous way and interprets them as a financial support given to affect the location of investment. The aim may be to enhance new investment projects or to retain an existing facility. As a general rule, wherever the system of investment incentives is in place, it exerts significant impact upon the investment climate in a given economy. This support also enhances investment attractiveness of the host country.

We may list various forms of investment incentives (Tavares-Lehmann et al. 2016, Investment Incentives 2013, OECD 2003):

1. **Regulatory:** E.g. exemptions from specific regulations binding in the host country (connected with the environment, labour market, social insurance);
2. **Financial:** E.g. providing physical infrastructure (e.g. roads, railways, harbours) or communication tailored to meet the needs of the investors; assistance in training workers where skilled labour is not available; relocation and expatriation support; administrative assistance; temporary wage subsidies; credits to investors; government preferential insurance; assistance in acquiring real estate (land or property sold below market prices);
3. **Fiscal:** E.g. reduced taxes (tax holidays, reduced rates of corporate income tax, special tax-privileged zones); incentives for capital formation (special investment allowances, investment tax credits, reduced impediments to cross-border operation, withholding tax);
4. **Technical:** They usually focus on technical matters relating to dissemination of information on investment opportunities and procedures and providing special services, and "aftercare" once an investor has already invested.

In the case of incentives offered as home country measures (HCMs) designed to intensify internationalisation of domestic entities through OFDI, classification of instruments (OFDII) slightly differs from the above presented catalogue. Hence OECD (2003) divided OFDII into three main categories:

1. Fiscal,
2. Financial,
3. Regulatory.

Economou and Sauvant (2013) proposed modified and extended OFDII classification, which encompasses:

1. Institutional framework,
2. Information services,
3. Financial measures,
4. Fiscal measures.

The Authors of Investment Incentives (2013) proposed 5 categories of OFDII, pointing at the same time to principal differences with regard to incentives intended for inward FDI (Table 1.).

Table 1. OFDII classification

No.	Type of OFDII	Typical Forms	(Potential) Differences Compared to Inward FDII
1.	Financial	Money transfers, subsidies, grants, soft loans, capital holdings in investment projects	Obvious differences in the objective. Preferential financial support may be helpful, e.g., in acquisitions.
2.	Fiscal	Tax allowances, exemptions, deferrals, reduction of rates, losses brought forward to the next accounting periods, accelerated depreciation	Tax allowances and exemptions are much more popular for inward FDI, although tax instruments may also be used as incentives that support active internationalisation of domestic enterprises.
3.	Information and technical services	Scope of information and advisory support is wide and diverse. In general, these services are addressed to selected foreign markets, where enterprises are established and developed, including, e.g., the analysis of economic indicators, institutional and legal environment, competitors, suppliers, subcontractors, clients, R&D capacity, human resources and advisory services in investment procedures	Such incentives are relevant for both inward and outward investments. Apparently, from the viewpoint of domestic authorities the need to support domestic entities who invest abroad prevails over the need to support foreign investors.
4.	Risk-minimizing measures	These incentives include primarily guarantees and insurances connected with risks involved in operating abroad. They may be linked with both political (conflicts, unfavourable changes in legislation, etc.) and economic (delayed payments, unreliable suppliers, clients, etc.) risks.	These incentives target OFDI only. International treaties and agreements (bilateral and multilateral) are important. A country, who is a signatory to such agreements usually offers more security to foreign investors.
5.	Regulatory	All regulations and agreements connected, e.g., with taxation or restricting procedures that facilitate or encourage investing abroad.	Completely different than for inward FDI when the authorities of the host country may create favourable investment climate through adequate regulations. In supporting OFDI it is much more difficult as it depends mainly on foreign partners.

Source: Investment Incentives (2013).

The above summary demonstrates that public administration has got rather substantial possibilities to support active internationalisation of enterprises. The scope of support is close to that of incentives addressed to foreign investors, although the objectives are completely different.

OFDI Support Instruments in Poland

Poland is one among the countries, which actively support various forms of internationalisation of domestic enterprises, also through foreign direct investment. Such support must be granted lawfully, based on detailed the EU and domestic regulations.

From the point of view of the EU law, which regulates some aspects of support to foreign investment, there are two key areas, i.e., regulations concerning bi- and multilateral investment agreements and regulations on State aid and competition.

In the first case, negotiating and concluding international agreements belongs to the so called the EU exclusive competences and pursuant to the Treaty on the Functioning of the European Union (TFEU) is subject to the rules of common trade policy. These common regulations are designed, first and foremost, to secure investors' interest in two points of time: when they enter a third country market and when investment project has already been launched. Moreover, they ensure equal treatment of the EU investors in third countries, irrespective of the country of origin of capital and potential differentiation of the scope of bilateral agreements (between an the EU Member State and a third country) (Art. 206-207 TFEU).

In the second case, incentives (financial and non-financial) granted by entities from the public finance sector at various levels must comply with competition and State aid rules. The same applies to Poland, who – as a EU member, must also observe State aid rules stipulated in Art. 107 and 108 of the Treaty on the Functioning of the European Union [4] when granting aid to domestic and foreign investors. Pursuant to Art. 107.1, State aid is banned in general when it is granted selectively and favours only certain enterprises or the production of certain goods by which it distorts or threatens to distort competition and when it impacts trade among the EU Member States.

Art. 107.2 enumerates some automatic exemptions from general ban on granting State aid; besides, there are also conditional exemptions, which make aid acceptable in accordance with Art. 107.3. These conditional exemptions enable public administration bodies to assist enterprises directly, as well as indirectly by creating favourable climate for business development.

In domestic law harmonised with *acquis communautaire*, provisions on foreign direct investment made by Polish enterprises are included in the Act on Foreign Exchange Law (Journal of Laws of 2002, No. 141, item 1178). In accordance with the wording of Art. 7. of the Act on Foreign Exchange Law, minister responsible for public finances issues general foreign exchange permits by way of a regulation. Permits may be granted to all entities or to a certain category of entities, as well as to all kinds of activities or to a certain type of activities. Moreover, by issuing an administrative decision the Governor of the National Bank of Poland grants individual foreign exchange permits outside of the scope of general foreign exchange permit (Art. 8.1.of the Act).

Considering all legal limitations, Poland exploits a variety of possibilities related to investment incentives. Obviously, these efforts are dominated by measures applied by governments at different levels to attract and retain operators with foreign capital in Poland. By joining the EU Poland gained access to Structural Funds distributed under Operational Programmes. These funds have become the main source of State aid available to all companies operating in Poland. In some aspects, incentives designed to attract new foreign investors may put additional burden on the central budget, as well as on the budgets of local governments. Special economic zones (SEZs), Programme for the support of investments of considerable importance for Polish economy (Support programme), and property tax allowances are examples of such incentive arrangements. Besides, the Polish Information and Foreign Investment Agency (Polish abr. PAIiIZ) promotes Poland as a good location for FDI. The Agency runs Regional Investor Assistance Centres in provinces and Regional Investor Assistance Offices in various cities. PAIiIZ offers services free of charge. It helps select investment sites in Poland, organises tailor-made investor visits to Poland, provides information on legal and economic environment and on available investment incentives, facilitates contacts with central and local authorities, identifies suppliers and contractors, and takes care of existing investors (to support reinvestments in Poland) (Dorożyński et al. 2014).

Although much less popular, incentives that target Polish enterprises who export FDI are offered by public administration responsible for support to entrepreneurship and internationalisation of Polish economy (Table 2).

Table 2. Examples of OFDII in Poland

No.	Type of Incentives	Source and Scope of Support	Responsible Institutions
1.	Financial	Foreign Expansion Fund FIZAN (Firms may benefit from financing that takes the form of capital, mezzanine and borrowings secured by foreign project assets without redress to the Polish company. The share of Foreign Expansion Fund in project funding will typically reach between several to several dozen million PLN but it will not exceed 50% of the total investment).	Investment Fund Company BGK S.A
2.	Financial	EU Structural Funds, in particular Operational Programme Smart Growth and regional operational programmes financed with the European Regional Development Fund (e.g., co-funding of innovative projects, internationalisation of enterprises and clusters)	Minister responsible for regional development and local authorities at provinces, which manage regional operational programmes
3.	Fiscal	No special incentives but provisions of the Act on Corporate Income Tax (CIT) prefer certain countries as investment host countries, i.e., EU, EEA, and Switzerland. Operators, who invest in these countries may expect more favourable tax regulations, including tax allowances in the host country.	Minister responsible for public finances, tax chambers and offices
4.	Risk-minimising instruments	Insurance of foreign direct investment, such as: • Acquisition of a foreign enterprise or an organised part thereof, • Establishing and running an enterprise abroad (also an affiliate or representative office), • Outlays intended to expand an already existing enterprise, • Capital injections and borrowings made by partners, • Acquisition of real estate and other fixed assets. • Insurance protection covers losses suffered in relation with a foreign direct investment that result from actions undertaken by the host country, such as: • Changes in legal regulations (the so called regulatory risk), • Expropriation, • Inability to transfer receivables (e.g. dividend), • Total depravation of rights related to the investment. Compensation is also paid if the investment gets damaged as a result of force majeure, e.g., earthquake, flood, fire or war.	Export Credit Insurance Corporation Joint Stock Company (Polish company whose shareholders are State Treasury represented by the Minister of Development and Bank Gospodarstwa Krajowego. The only one insurance company in Poland to offer export insurance guaranteed by the State Treasury)
5.	Information and advisory services	Provision of information about foreign markets, conditions of economic operations abroad; facilitates business relations; advisory services; assistance in taking part in fairs and economic missions abroad.	Ministry of Development, Polish Agency for Enterprise Development, Polish Information and Foreign Investment Agency, Departments of Trade Promotion and Investment, Regional Investor and Exporter Assistance Centres

Source: Buczkowski et al. 2015, Świerkocki 2015, https://tfibgk.com.pl/fundusz-ekspansji-zagranicznej-fizan (accessed on 11.10.2016), www.poir.gov.pl (accessed on 11.10.2016), http://www.kuke.com.pl/dla-firm/ubezpieczenie-inwestycji-za-granica (accessed on 11.10.2016).

The system of OFDI support instruments in Poland is not fully comprehensive and coherent yet. Most of the above mentioned incentives have been implemented relatively recently and are still largely limited by the EU and international legal restrictions, ie. competition policy or common trade policy. Therefore, as for now within the whole system of support tools those of information and promotion in nature (thus – less quantitative) prevail. Moreover, support is offered in many forms by different organizations which makes the whole system blurred and not holistic or complementary enough – it may thus be hard and laborious for investors to get familiar with all solutions and available to choose the best option.

That all makes any attempts to assess the effectiveness of Poland's OFDI support system difficult and limited. However, it should be expected that in the coming years the list of support instruments will be not only topped up and complemented but also tailored to the needs and expectations of entrepreneurs, so that their effects and effectiveness will be more visible (and measurable).

Poland's OFDI: Statistical Approach

Over the years of systemic transformation Poland became an interesting location for foreign direct investment. Its dynamics had been steadily growing since the 1990s while stable economic growth, gradual liberalisation of regulations, and preparations to the EU membership accelerated the process. Parallel, economic growth and the fostering of the position of Poland in international environment resulted in an increasing number of Polish enterprises who successfully entered foreign markets. Although Poland remains a net receiver of FDI, especially after 2004, the stream of OFDI has been continuously increasing.

Changes in the value of Polish OFDI over 1995-2014 can be observed in Figure 3. As we can see, dynamic increase in the involvement of Polish enterprises into OFDI started after Poland has joined the EU.

However, it is worth stressing that in the period covered by the study FDI classification changed twice. First, since 2010 FDI flows started to cover intercompany loans (i.e. flows of capital between sister companies within capital group). It considerably increased OFDI to almost USD 57.4 bn at the end of 2012 – mainly in "other capital" category (intercompany capital flows accounted for ca. USD 26.7 bn at the end of 2012). It also demonstrates relatively strong position of Polish enterprises in the times of crisis meaning, paradoxically, that Polish economy became the source of capital loans for all affiliates (subsidies, but also parent companies and associates).

The second – more substantial change – took place in 2013 and was consistent with OECD guidelines included in the Benchmark Definition of Foreign Direct Investment 4th ed. (BD4). As mentioned above, earlier classification (in line with International Investment Position statistics) of OFDI included also flows between Polish investor and other entities in capital group irrespectively of where the dominant entity in the group is based. Since 2013 this kind of loans has no longer been included into OFDI flows in cases where Polish investor is controlled by a foreign MNE (this kind of flows is now considered a part of IFDI). Substantial reduction in "other capital" value confirms high proportion of intercompany loans granted to related entities within international holdings.

All in all, when analysing the international expansion of Polish enterprises attention should be paid predominantly to the value of primary investment ("equity and reinvested profits") rather than "other capital". Firstly, primary investment tells us how much have the enterprises got involved into manufacturing and service operations abroad; secondly, its definition and classification into FDI flows remains relatively unchanged.

Figure 3. Polish foreign direct investment (cumulated value) in the years 1995-2014 in USD mio
Source: Authors' own compilation based on (NBP [National Bank of Poland] 2016).

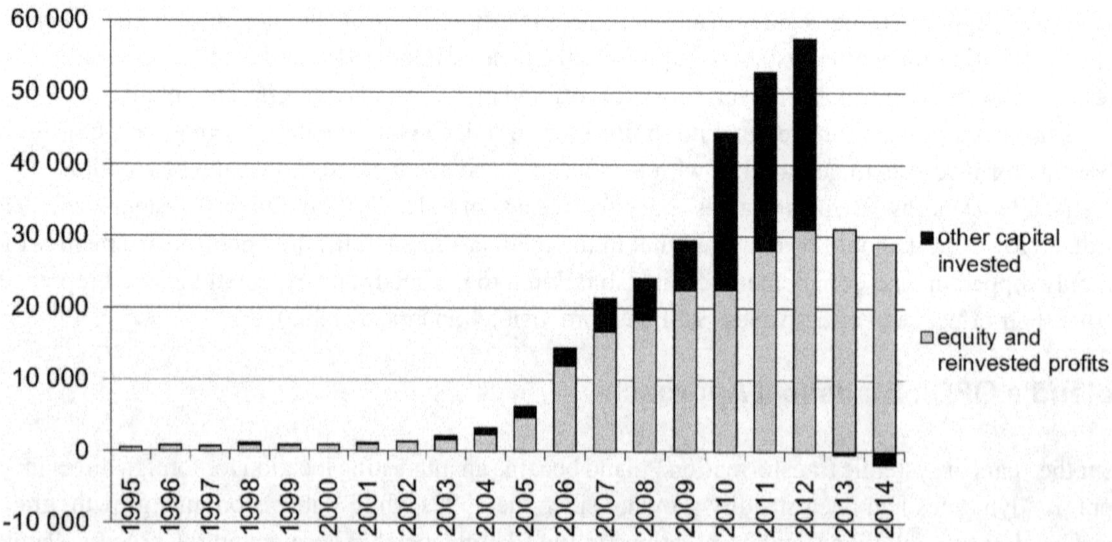

The flow of primary investment is largely dominated by investments in new foreign equity acquisition. Until 2009 reinvested profits represented not more than 10% of all equity investment. In subsequent years proportions slightly changed, mainly as a result of reduced involvement of Polish enterprises in new foreign undertakings, which was due to the crisis. In general, the primacy of new investment projects was an expected tendency, typical of the initial stage of internationalisation of enterprises, when they have just started developing a network of related foreign affiliates by investing in production assets.

The entire period was dominated by investments made by companies from the service sector; at the end of 2014 their share reached almost 80%. Major role was played by enterprises active in financial intermediary services or managerial consultancy. Their total investment ranged from 56% up to even 94% of FDI from the service industry. Only in 2008 the share was lower, ca. 35%. At the end of 2014 the proportion of investments generated by financial companies represented 50% of cumulated value of Polish OFDI, while head offices operations, managerial consulting, as well as (increasingly important in FDI flows) administration and business support activities – ca. 14% each. (see also Table 3.). The later can be associated mainly with business optimisation at international scale: tax optimisation, raising financial capital in international markets through special purpose vehicle companies, etc.

Investments made by manufacturing companies generated on average ca. 20% - 30% of total FDI of Polish companies after 2004. However, their share in the structure of Poland's OFDI was systematically decreasing. At the end of 2014 it amounted to only ca. 14%, which was not positive as it testified to the weakening manufacturing position of Polish companies, their decreasing competitiveness, even vis-à-vis service companies. On top of that, we may also suppose that Polish companies have started to approach international market as a place where they can optimise business rather than production processes. Little international involvement of manufacturing companies is an evidence of underused potential of international location-related assets, including cost reduction capabilities.

Table 3. Poland's OFDI at the end of 2014 broken down by economic activity of the direct investment in USD mio

	Total	Of Which:	
		Equity and Reinvested Profits	Other Capital
Total	27 155.0	28 881.6	-1 726.6
Industry	3 469.0	3 002.1	466.9
Manufacturing	3 832.8	2 559.4	1 273.4
Food products; beverages and tobacco products	268.7	200.0	68.8
Wood. paper & their products; printing and reproduction	216.9	132.6	84.4
Coke and refined petroleum products	784.0	701.4	82.6
Chemicals and chemical products and basic pharmaceutical products	400.3	121.9	278.4
Basic metals and fabricated metal products. except machinery & equipment	658.6	575.2	83.4
Motor vehicles. trailers and semitrailers	913.3	448.3	464.9
Construction	-280.2	126.7	-406.9
Services	21 392.5	23 591.2	-2 198.7
Wholesale and Retail Trade	1 777.7	1 099.2	678.5
Transportation and Storage	328.4	349.9	-21.6
Accommodation and Food Service Activities	-62.0	86.9	-149.0
Information and Communication	-2 982.1	-885.6	-2 096.5
Financial and Insurance Activities	13 680.2	14 890.1	-1 209.9
Activities of holding companies	10 585.6	11 136.8	-551.3
Real Estate Activities	316.7	-396.9	713.6
Professional. Scientific and Technical Activities	3 904.8	4 105.3	-200.4
Activities of head offices	2 648.2	2 335.0	313.2
Management consultancy act	1 135.0	1 680.2	-545.2
Administrative and Support Service Activities	3 816.5	3 794.8	21.7

Source: Authors' compilation based on (NBP, 2016).

Throughout the entire period covered by the study manufacturers of coke and refined petroleum products enjoyed the biggest share in investments made by industrial companies (20% in 2014). Moreover, these projects were, first and foremost, primary investment, which means they included the development of new assets abroad. We may thus consider that these companies have the biggest competitive advantages (ownership advantages) among all Polish manufacturing companies and best tap into opportunities offered by the international market. That is not surprising as – against hopes vested in intensive economic growth – Polish economy still rests on traditional industries.

Next in a row were investments made by companies manufacturing motor vehicles, trailers and semi-trailers (which exceeded investments made by manufacturers of coke and refined petroleum products only in 2014) and chemicals and pharmaceuticals. Opposite to the previous – these were made largely as intercompany loans. Similar situation was observed for manufacturers of metal and metal products, which may be attributed to the facts that in those branches many Polish investors in belong to foreign MNEs. In general terms, a large chunk of investments made by these entities may be attributed to their mother-companies intention to inject capital into all foreign affiliates within the group rather than "classical" manufacturing expansion resulting from decisions and advantages of Polish companies.

Polish investments targeted mainly European countries. Their share in outflows of Polish capital over the period covered by the study amounted to more than 95% (see Table 4.). In principle, there are three groups of countries, to which capital was directed: 1) countries, which hosted financial investments and investments connected with optimisation of business processes: Luxembourg, Cyprus and Switzerland; 2) Poland's neighbouring countries similar in their Slavonic culture: Ukraine, Russia, the Czech Republic, Lithuania; 3) countries that have invested the most (in IFDI form) in Poland: Germany and the Netherlands.

Luxembourg, Cyprus and Switzerland were the biggest recipients of Polish capital in the period covered by the study. Their share was systematically increasing. At the end of 2011 these countries received in total ca. 35% of the total value of Polish investment, including over 24% addressed to Luxembourg alone. At the end of 2014, total share of these countries reached ca. 60%, out of which more than 30% of capital targeted Cyprus. Luxembourg, similarly to Switzerland, hosts many international funds, as well as investment and financial organisations. All shares (i.a. shares of stock or certificates) acquired by Polish residents (including minimum of 10% of shares in a given entity) are classified as FDI. Ad-

Table 4. Poland's OFDI at the end of 2014 broken down by host country in USD mio

	Total	Equity and Reinvested Profits	Other Capital
Total	27 155.0	28 881.6	-1 726.6
Europe	25 090.8	27 516.9	-2 426.1
Euro Zone (17 countries)	20 367.7	20 114.0	253.7
EU-27	19 390.5	23 545.1	-4 154.7
Germany	1 134.8	749.8	385.0
Netherlands	2 786.9	1 926.7	860.3
Great Britain	981.1	927.6	53.5
Czech Republic	1 735.6	1 083.1	652.5
Lithuania	959.8	624.7	335.2
Cyprus	8 610.2	8 639.0	-28.7
Luxemburg	7 316.4	7 344.7	-28.3
Switzerland	3 256.4	3 153.9	102.5
Russia	721.3	434.2	287.0
Ukraine	56.8	161.2	-104.3
Turkey	258.1	-27.9	286.0
USA	635.1	463.5	171.6
Africa	196.0	168.1	27.9
Asia	978.0	670.2	307.9

Source: Authors' compilation based on (NBP, 2016).

ditionally, investors willingly establish special purpose vehicles (SPV) to get access to loan capital in local capital markets.

High value of investment into Cypriot economy is mainly due to some unique, favourable tax arrangements. Many companies, especially after the financial crisis started in 2008, decided to move their principal places of business or established their affiliates (also SPV) in Cyprus because it helped considerably reduce the average tax burden of all the company.

Manufacturing and trade-related investment projects headed mainly in the neighbouring countries - similar to Poland when it comes to their economic development, social and cultural environment. That is typical of the first stages of internationalisation of the economy. Such location facilitates "acclimatization" of a company in a new location, better understanding of market mechanisms, business environment institutions, and – the most important in business – interpersonal relations. The mechanism is explained by, e.g., the Uppsala model positively validated for Polish circumstances (Witek-Hajduk 2010, Kłysik-Uryszek and Kuna-Marszałek 2015).

Finally, we should pay attention to the period 2010-2012 when statistics showed the scale of loan support granted by Polish companies to related entities within capital groups. Significant share of loans granted within a group could be observed not only in Europe, but also in America or Asia. In Europe most countries used capital borrowed from Polish entities (usually ca. 65-75% of all Polish FDI cumulated in given economies). The highest values were reported for: Portugal (98%), Greece (97%), Finland (96%), Italy (95%), United Kingdom (90%), Germany (82%) or Hungary (81%). It proves again that Poland, who relatively little suffered from the crisis, has become the source of financial support to enterprises from countries that struggle with post-crisis difficulties. Average values of the discussed indicator both for Europe and for EU-27 amounted to ca. 45%, which was predominantly due to low share of capital flows in Luxembourg (ca. 20%) and in Cyprus (ca. 3,5%).

FUTURE RESEARCH DIRECTIONS

Further studies could develop along two major lines. Firstly, it would be worthwhile to examine the efficiency with which support instruments available to entrepreneurs who expand abroad within the OFDI framework are used. While in literature we can come across a variety of studies that discuss this very issue in the context of developed countries (te Velde 2007; Bannò, Piscitello and Varum 2014), very few such studies can be found in relation to the emerging markets or transition economies (Buczkowski et al. 2015). The problem, however, seems relevant as it refers to the efficiency of spending public funds and the outcomes of studies in field are ambiguous. On the one hand, some authors question the rationale behind offering assistance schemes to investors, while on the other hand we can hear voices that point to positive aspects of such schemes and their favourable impact upon the involvement of entrepreneurs into OFDI. Such studies could be particularly useful for the central government and for lower levels of administration, which increasingly often play a vital role in developing economic policy. This knowledge is important for managers and politicians responsible for commercial policy especially in the light of a rather common global practice of offering government support to domestic FDI (Sauvant et al. 2014).

The assessment of if and how the enterprises involved in foreign direct investment influence the economy of their home country and brought changes in, e.g., in local employment and jobs quality, or in collaboration level with R&D centres also seems interesting. The same can be said about studying the spillover effects for other domestic firms or business partners. By the same token we could demonstrate how OFDI from Poland or from other emerging markets impact economic development, at local, regional or national levels. So far literature on the subject is rather scarce and most researchers focus on developed economies (Globerman and Shapiro 2008; Sunesen, Jespersen and Thelle 2010). Effects of FDI exports to emerging economies are far less known (Gorynia i in. 2014).

CONCLUSION

Intensive international capital expansion of Polish enterprises which can be observed recently is the evidence of successful economic development and efficient market transformations that have taken place in Polish economy since the early 1990s. Gradual liberalisation of capital flows, opening up of the economy to the inflow of foreign direct investment and integration processes have made Polish enterprises capable of effectively competing not only in the domestic but also in international markets. With the support of own experience gained on national, but highly opened market they are becoming active players also at the international level.

Growing support (in the form of different OFDI incentives) is provided also by national and regional public institutions. Unfortunately, due to the short period of their presence on the market, as well as the substantial restrictions put by EU legal regulations, the fully effective and comprehensive system of OFDI support have not been settled down yet, and therefore investors do not use these incentives broadly. However, the dynamics of OFDI flows as well as its cumulated value show the increasing interest in internationalization process of firms. It will probably trigger the expansion of support instruments more and more custom-fitted to the companies' needs.

Sectoral structure of Poland's OFDI suggests the domination of the service sector, in which financial and advisory services play the major role. It is not surprising because financial markets and capital flows are among the most mobile ones. Besides, it is much easier to relocate financial and advisory activities or head offices in a group than to relocate manufacturing. It also shows that enterprises are not seeking only traditional resources or increased sales in foreign markets but also sources of higher effectiveness.

Investments in industry focus mainly on traditional, technologically little advanced sectors. It demonstrates comparative advantages of the economy, which – although experiences structural transformations – is still not particularly competitive in modern and technologically advanced production.

REFERENCES

Act on Foreign Exchange Law. (2002). Journal of Laws of 2002. No. 141, item 1178.

Bannò, M., Piscitello, L., & Varum, C. A. (2014). The Impact of Public Support on SMEs Outward FDI: Evidence from Italy. *Journal of Small Business Management*, *52*(1), 22–38. doi:10.1111/jsbm.12029

Buczkowski, B., Kłysik-Uryszek, A., Kuna-Marszałek, A., & Świerkocki, J. (2015). *Poland's Outward Foreign Direct Investment. Experiences of enterprises from the Łódź region*. Łódź: Łódź University Press.

Central Statistical Office of Poland. (2016). Retrieved from www.stat.gov.pl

Chilimoniuk, E., & Czarny, E. (2005). Otwieranie gospodarki polskiej w okresie transformacji systemowej. In E. Czarny (Ed.), *Gospodarka polska na przełomie wieków. Od A do Z* (pp. 153–188). Warsaw: NBP.

Consolidated version of the Treaty on the Functioning of the European Union (TFEU). (2010). *Official Journal of the European Union, 53.*

Czubek, H., & Molendowski, E. (2005). Zbliżanie się struktur wymiany handlowej krajów CEFTA z krajami UE. w okresie przygotowań do członkostwa. *Wspólnoty Europejskie, 11*(168), 27–32.

Doing Business 2006. (2006). The World Bank.

Doing Business 2016. (2015). The World Bank.

Dorożyński, T., Świerkocki, J., & Urbaniak, W. (2015). Incentives for attracting FDI: The case of the Lodz Region. *Gospodarka Narodowa, 1*(275), 147–169.

Globerman, S. (2012). *Canadian Outward Foreign Direct Investment and Its Implications for the Canadian Economy*. The Conference Board of Canada.

Globerman, S., & Shapiro, D. M. (2008). Outward FDI and the economic performance of emerging markets. In K.P. Sauvant (Ed.), The Rise of Transnational Corporations from Emerging Markets. Threat or Opportunity? (pp. 229-271). Cheltenham, UK: Edward Elgar. doi:10.4337/9781848441460.00023

Gomułka, S. (2014). Transformacja gospodarczo-społeczna Polski 1989-2014 i współczesne wyzwania. *Nauka, 3*, 7-16.

Gorynia, M., Nowak, J., & Wolniak, R. (2009). Motives and Modes of FDI, Firm Characteristics and Performance: Case studies of Foreign Subsidiaries in Poland. In M. Gorynia (Ed.), *International Business in Transition* (pp. 239–268). Warsaw: Difin.

Gorynia, M., & Trąpczyński, P. (2014). Determinanty efektywności zagranicznych inwestycji bezpośrednich. *Ekonomista, 5*, 663–684.

Herzer, D. (2012). How Does Foreign Direct Investment Really Affect Developing Countries Growth? *Review of International Economics, 20*(2), 396–414. doi:10.1111/j.1467-9396.2012.01029.x

Hunter, R. J., & Ryan, L. V. (2005). A Transitional Analysis of the Polish Economy: After Fifteen Years, Still a Work in Progress. *Global Economy Journal, 5*(2), 1–17. doi:10.2202/1524-5861.1061

Investment Incentives. The good, the bad and the ugly. (2013). Background Paper for the Eight Columbia International Investment Conference. Vale Columbia Center On Sustainable International Investment, Columbia University.

James, S. (2009). *Incentives and Investments: Evidence and Policy Implications.* ICAS of the World Bank Group.

Jarmołowicz, W., & Piątek, D. (2013). Polska transformacja gospodarcza. In S. Owsiak & A. Pollok (Eds.), *W poszukiwaniu nowego ładu ekonomicznego* (pp. 71–89). Warsaw: PTE.

Kłysik-Uryszek, A. (2010). *Bezpośrednie inwestycje zagraniczne w gospodarce regionu. Teoria i praktyka.* Warsaw: CeDeWu.pl.

Kłysik-Uryszek, A., & Kuna-Marszałek, A. (2015). Doświadczenia procesu internacjonalizacji przedsiębiorstw regionu łódzkiego. Próba weryfikacji modelu uppsalskiego. *Studia i Prace WNEiZ, 41*, 283–295. doi:10.18276/sip.2015.41/2-24

Leszczyński, D. (2015). Przeobrażenia gospodarcze w Polsce w latach 1989-2016. *Refleksje, 12*, 27–45.

Mickiewicz, T. (2005). *Economic Transition in Central Europe and the Commonwealth of Independent States*. Palgrave MacMillan. doi:10.1057/9780230504349

Moran, T. H., Graham, E. M., & Blomström, M. (Eds.). (2005). *Does Foreign Direct Investment Promote Development?* Washington, DC: Institute for International Economics.

OECD. (2003). *Checklist for Foreign Direct Investment Incentive Policies*. Paris: OECD.

OECD Benchmark Definition of Foreign Direct Investment. (2008). OECD.

Piątkowski, M. (2013). Poland's new golden age: shifting from Europe's periphery to its center. *The World Bank Working Papers. Policy Research Working Paper 6639*, 1-36.

Poland's 10 years in the European Union. (2014). Warsaw: Ministry of Foreign Affairs.

Potencjał innowacyjny gospodarki: uwarunkowania, determinanty, perspektywy. (2016). Warsaw: NBP.

Sauvant, K., Economou, P., Gal, K., Lim, S., & Wilinski, W. (2014). *Trends In FDI, Home Country Measures And Competitive Neutrality*. Retrieved November 18, 2016, from http://ccsi.columbia.edu/files/2014/03/Yb-12-13-ch.-1-8-Nov-13-stand-alone-final-for-website.pdf

Sunesen, E., Jespersen, S., & Thelle, M. (2010). *Impacts of EU Outward FDI*. Copenhagen Economics Final Report.

Świerkocki, J. (2015). Elementy polityki wobec polskich inwestycji zagranicznych. *Studia Prawno-Ekonomiczne, 95*, 345–368.

Tavares-Lehmann, A. T., Toledano, P., Johnson, L., & Sachs, L. (Eds.). (2016). *Rethinking Investment Incentives, Trends and Policy Options*. New York: Columbia University Press.

Te Velde, D. W. (2007). Understanding Developed Country Efforts to Promote Foreign Direct Investment to Developing Countries: The Example of the United Kingdom. *Transnational Corporations, 16*(3), 83–104.

Temiz, D., & Gökman, A. (2014). FDI Inflow as an International Business Operation by MNCs and Economic Growth: An Empirical Study on Turkey. *International Business Review, 23*(1), 145–154. doi:10.1016/j.ibusrev.2013.03.003

Thomas, P. K. (2007). *Investment incentives: Growing use, uncertain benefits, uneven controls*. Geneva: Global Subsidies Initiative, International Institute for Sustainable Development.

Transition Report 2000. (2000). London: European Bank for Reconstruction and Development.

Tytel, I., & Yudaeva, K. (2006). The Role of FDI in Eastern Europe and New Independent States: New Channels for the Spillover Effect. *Centro Studi Luca d'Agliano Development Studies Working Papers, 217*, 1-35.

Wiliński, W. (2013). *Polityka gospodarcza państw wysoko rozwiniętych i rozwijających się w zakresie wspierania krajowych spółek inwestujących poza granicami kraju*. Warsaw: SGH.

Witek-Hajduk, M. K. (2010). *Strategie internacjonalizacji polskich przedsiębiorstw w warunkach akcesji Polski do Unii Europejskiej*. Warsaw: SGH.

World Bank. (n.d.). Retrieved from www.data.worldbank.org

Zsoldos, I., & Zadornova, A. (2008). *New EU Member States – a Fifth BRIC?*. Goldman Sachs Global Economics Paper 173.

KEY TERMS AND DEFINITIONS

Central and Eastern Europe: For the needs of this publication we adopted the most commonly used scope of Central and Eastern Europe including: Poland, the Czech Republic, Slovakia, and Hungary (Visegrad Group), Baltic States (Lithuania, Latvia, and Estonia), countries of the former Yugoslavia, Romania, Bulgaria, and Albania.

Economic Transformation: Change of economic system, in particular shifting from centrally planned to market economy, based on a functioning free market, competition and private business. Centrally planned economy was the system in most of the Central and East European countries until the end of the 1980s. It made the economy fully dependent on the decisions of central authorities. Private business was limited to the minimum, production assets were fully owned by the state, there was not any financial or capital market, market mechanism did not work, prices were decided by officials, and competition was replaced with a monopoly. Trade with third countries was regulated.

FDI: Foreign direct investment (outward – OFDI; inward – IFDI), the most advanced form of internationalisation of companies; FDI are undertaken to exercise a long-term capital supervision over an entity located abroad (branches or subsidiaries).

Intercompany Loans: Are perceived as part of FDI flow, as long as the debt concerns entities belonging to one international group or MNE.

Internationalization of a Company: A process, through which a firm moves from operating in a domestic marketplace to international markets.

Primary Investment: Part of FDI flows that consist of equity investments. They precede the other parts of FDI flows – reinvested earnings and intercompany loans.

State Aid: Any action undertaken by state authorities consisting in granting aid, in any form whatsoever, to an individual entrepreneur or to a group of entities, which distorts competition on the market. In the EU State aid is regulated in Art. 107 and 108 TFEU. The following premises must be met (jointly) to decide, that we are dealing with incompatible State aid: 1. A measure is an aid to an undertaking; 2. Aid is granted by the State or from the State resources; 3. Aid favors certain undertakings or the production of certain goods; 4. Aid distorts competition or threatens to distorts it; 5. Aid distorts trade among member states; 6. Aid is not covered by any of the Treaty exemptions. An example of aid covered by the Treaty exemption and, as such, compatible with the EU market, is aid to promote economic development of areas where the standard of living is abnormally low or where there is serious underemployment. State aid consists in granting direct financial or in-kind advantages to the beneficiary, e.g. subsidies, grants for equipment. State aid may also consist in the reduction of public and legal liabilities of the beneficiary, e.g., liabilities write-off.

ENDNOTES

1 To calculate the index account was taken of: weighted average of measures for the level of development, trade dependence on the Council for Mutual Economic Assistance, macroeconomic disequilibria, distance to the EU, natural resource endowments, market memory and state capacity (Transition Report 2000, 2000, p. 21).

2 Investment bank Goldman Sachs foresees that until 2030 Poland (and other CEECs) should grow by at least 2 percentage points annually faster than the EU-15.It means that until 2050 GDP per capita in Poland would be by only 15% lower than in the most developed EU member states but higher than, e.g., in Spain (Zsoldos and Zadornova 2008).

3 Besides strengths, the report also highlights barriers faced and observed by foreign investors in Poland. The following dimensions have been assessed as poor in the ranking: transport infrastructure, some institutional aspects, such as the regulatory burden, rather inefficient legal framework for settling business disputes, and difficulties in obtaining information on government decisions for business. To bolster its innovative capacity, more attention should be paid to reinforcing its innovation ecosystem in close collaboration with the private sector.

4 Consolidated version of the Treaty on the Functioning of the European Union, 30 March 2010.

Chapter 9
The Role of Inward FDI for Economic Growth at the Time of Downturn:
The Case of Russia

Anatoly Zhuplev
Loyola Marymount University, USA

Mikhail Kuznetsov
National Association of Corporate Directors, Russia

ABSTRACT

The chapter explores FDI trends and patterns in Russia. FDI global framework includes multiple stakeholders with diverse interests, expectations, and political attitudes toward foreign investment. Conceptual RDI framework in the chapter is supported by examining Russia's FDI profile, patterns, and dynamics across major economic sectors and regions. Russia's performance in the Global Competitiveness Report 2015-2016 is used to analyze the nation's FDI attractiveness compared to other countries. Further discussion focuses on Russia's macro-economic structure in the FDI context that includes sectorial and regional aspects. Specifically, the chapter concentrates on examining FDI in the Greater Moscow and Greater St. Petersburg, Russia's leading economic regions. These regions receive significant FDI inflows and make substantial contribution to the nation's economic output and trade. The chapter culminates in exploring FDI dynamics in Russia under the current economic crisis and strategies for survival and revival on the regional, sectorial, and company level.

INTRODUCTION[1]

Foreign direct investments (FDI), their trends and dynamics are integral to a nation's political-economic system. FDI also affect this system in numerous ways. In a broad sense, the political-economic system of a nation is an amalgam of interacting interdependable economic, legal, and political components and forces. Within the frameworks of specific political-economic formations, such as capitalism, socialism

DOI: 10.4018/978-1-5225-2345-1.ch009

or communism, a nation's predominant political and popular cultural attitudes toward FDI vary. They range from an all-encompassing support under the free market system to fundamentally rejecting the idea altogether on ideological grounds or because of self-imposed isolation under the command economy of a host country.[2]

The dissolution of the USSR in the early 1990s and broad retreat of communism have made the attitude of an outright rejection of FDI as a tool for domestic socio-economic development less appealing across the world. To date, perhaps only N. Korea and – to a lesser extent - Cuba remain the last disciples of this type of political-economic platform, with the latter showing subtle signs of change lately. On the opposite side of the spectrum, the free market "Anglo-Saxon" model of laissez-faire capitalism has its own constraints. It appears, in its pure form, to have limited national appeal and acceptance of FDI on social, environmental, ideological, or cultural grounds. Numerous countries in Europe, Asia or South/ Central America, where governments play a significant role, may serve as a case in point.

Over the past few decades, many nations have been adopting pragmatic nationalism, driven by a selective approach when facilitating FDI inflows to the benefit of their domestic industries, regions, social groups, or top priority political and personal interests. This selective attitude toward FDI translates into such forms as national industrial policy, agricultural policy, or innovation policy and often borders with political-economic protectionism. Realizing the benefits of incoming FDI for domestic socio-economic development and growth, pragmatic nationalist governments pursue policies designed to maximize associated benefits and minimize costs. According to this view, FDI should be allowed only if the benefits in their entirety outweigh the costs (Hill & Hult, 2017).

On a broader political-economic scale, FDI-related economic drivers and dynamics are often closely intertwined with foreign policy and domestic politics. Moreover, it is not uncommon for politics to trump economics in FDI-related decisions, especially in nations characterized by centralized political systems and a dominant government role in domestic economies stemming from limited accountability in governance.[3] To complicate the picture, FDI involves stakeholders who often have diverse interests and expectations and whose roles and power in the decision making process differ. For instance, a host country's government, in its effort to attract FDI, may be driven by the need for job creation or a technology transfer in key segments of the national economy. However, a foreign investor's primary priority may lie in a high return on investment with a minimal infusion of technological know-how. Major groups of stakeholders in the FDI process generally include: home/host countries, represented by their respective government institutions and agencies, private companies, national and international interest groups with business developmental, social, environmental or other type of agenda, international institutions, such as the IMF or World Bank, regional banks, such as the European Bank for Reconstruction and Development, and national banks, such as the Russia-based Bank for Development and Foreign Economic Affairs [Vnesheconombank]. These stakeholders act as FDI sources, intermediaries, regulators, lobbyists, or the end recipients of FDI in the form of private entities and government agencies on a national, regional, or municipal level. Each institutional part of the above systems makes decisions on its FDI-related strategic mission, goals benefits, costs and associated risks.

In the eye of a stakeholder, FDIs, an alternative form of international business, are often contrasted in their attractiveness in the benefit-cost-risk context with other alternatives, such as foreign portfolio investments, trade (exporting/importing) and foreign licensing.

From the standpoint of the host country (FDI recipient), the main benefits and expectations associated with attracting FDI inflows lie in the: -resource transfer effects (technology, know-how, financial transfers, gaining access to foreign markets, etc.), -employment effects (improvements in workforce quality, training and development, work attitudes, etc.), -balance of payment effects, and various positive impacts on the host country's competitiveness and economic growth. Possible costs and adverse effects associated for a host country with incoming FDI may involve: -weakening national competitiveness, -negative effects on the balance of payments, and -losses in national sovereignty and political-economic autonomy. These costs and adverse impacts may be anticipated calculated and factored in a business/ political decision or come unexpectedly from unintended consequences, with reasons ranging from force majeure to lack of knowledge and incompetence.

From the standpoint of the home country (FDI source), the benefit-cost-risk landscape may look different.

From the investing company's standpoint, FDI tends to be favored over exporting and foreign licensing as a long-term strategic option when transportation costs or trade barriers in the host country make exporting unattractive, when the foreign-based parent company (the headquarter) wishes to maintain control over its technological know-how, or over its operations and business strategy, or when the firm's capabilities are simply not amenable to licensing.

Another FDI driver is strategic behavior. According to the strategic behavior theory, FDI patterns and flows result from strategic rivalry between firms in the global marketplace: companies in the same, often oligopolistic, industry tend to undertake FDI around the same time and tend to direct their investment activities towards certain attractive global locations. A critical competitive feature of such oligopolistic industries is the interdependence of the major players: what one firm does can have an immediate impact on the major competitors, forcing a response in kind.

Yet another acclaimed theory explaining and rationalizing the drivers and global patterns of FDI is the eclectic paradigm championed by John Dunning. Dunning argues that, in addition to the above conditions, companies in their outward FDI decisions are driven by location-specific advantages (arising from using resource endowments or assets that are tied to a particular location and that a firm finds valuable to combine with its own unique assets) and externalities (knowledge spillovers that occur when companies in the same industry are located in the same area). Thus, location-specific advantages and externalities are also of considerable importance in explaining the rationale for and the direction of foreign direct investment (Hill & Hult, 2017).

The chapter begins by examining the role of FDI in the nation's political-economic system and FDI-related general framework. This conceptual examination of an FDI-related framework and issues is followed by analysis of the Russia's FDI profile, patterns, and dynamics across major economic sectors and regions. One specific important aspect of this analysis in the chapter is a review of the Russia's global competitiveness dynamics in the FDI-grounded framework of the annual Global Competitiveness Report (Schwab, 2016). This analysis reveals that Russia's current strategic competitive advantages lie in its relatively large market size, infrastructure, and higher education and training. Its strategic weaknesses are institutions, financial markets and goods market efficiency. These strengths and weakness in the chapter are placed in a contrasting perspective with Russia's fellow "peer" BRIC countries (Brazil, China, and India) and U.S.A. and Germany selected for the purpose of comparison as "aspirational comparators."

Regaining momentum after the 1998 economic crisis Russia has registered robust performance in FDI inflows, outflows, and stock, reflecting strong interest in Russia on the part of global investors, particularly prominent among Russia's domestically based investors with much of the capital returning to Russia from their offshore accounts in the form of FDI. Over the past few years, however, FDI dynamics have worsened notably. As patterns of FDI inflows tend to correlate with trends in a nation's general economic structure, the chapter provides a concise macroeconomic assessment across Russia's major economic sectors and regions.

The big picture and internal dynamics in the Russian leading economic sectors, agriculture, industry, and services, highlight the paramount economic role of the industry sector, as well as its relatively higher efficiency and global competitiveness, in contrast to the agricultural and service sectors. The chapter argues that although some Russian industries appear to be FDI-attractive due to their sheer economic size and market potential, there are multiple administrative barriers and other non-economic factors that may complicate a foreign entity's strategic entry into these industries.

Across Russia's complex regional politico-economic system (46 provinces, 21 republics, 4 autonomous okrugs, 9 krais, 2 federal cities, and 1 autonomous oblast as independent federal subjects enjoying separate jurisdictions) the Central Federal District is clearly the economic leader. Central Federal District includes two major federal cities, Moscow, the national capital, and St. Petersburg. The chapter explores FDI-related economic potential and dynamics of the leading and lagging regional entities across Russia in a comparative domestic and international perspective.

Industry/sectorial analysis and regional analysis of Russia's economic dynamics in the FDI context in the chapter is followed by discussion of the current economic crisis and FDI impacts. These trends and dynamics have been considerably affected by the unfolding crisis. Oil and gas sector, Russia's main hard currency earner, large employer, contributor to the federal and regional budgets, as well as a critical lever of Russia's foreign policy, has been hit particularly hard.

Over the past few decades oil and gas have played an extraordinary role in domestic socio-economic developments and foreign policy. In the 2000s, Russia has taken notable advantage of skyrocketing global energy prices and resulting spectacular financial windfalls. After peaking at 151 USD per barrel of crude oil in June 2008, global oil prices have been on decline. In 2014, they abruptly plunged to their lowest recent levels. Natural gas prices, peaking at 13.42 USD per million of British thermal units (Btu) in October 2005, plunged to just 1.92 USD per million of Btu in May 2016. Russia's energy dependent economy has suffered severe blows. Deprived of the petrodollars, Russia has continued to experience large scale investment needs to maintain and develop its ageing oil and gas infrastructure as well as other economic sectors. In contrast, investment climate across economic sectors and regions remained difficult despite some recent improvements in the nation's global business ratings. That has fueled large scale capital flight and deterioration in the FDI inflows to Russia. Russia's involvement in several regional conflicts and disputes in the neighboring countries has caused imposition of multiple rounds of political-economic sanctions on Russia by the West; Russia has responded with countersanctions. Additionally, some long-standing political-economic disagreements and disputes with European countries and the EU as a whole have reached new levels. This triggered a range of political-economic steps hurting Russia's oil and gas sector. Meanwhile, over the past few years Russia has been shifting its own strategic orientation of energy-related commerce and investment relationships from the West (Europe) to the East, particularly China (Zhuplev & Shtykhno 2015). These developments are analyzed in the chapter in the FDI context.

The chapter culminates in examination of emerging FDI-related strategic scenarios, responses, and alternatives in Russia on the regional, sectorial and company level. Specifically, the authors discuss crisis-related regional situations and strategic responses in Moscow and St. Petersburg. Under the unfolding economic slump, the City of Moscow is implementing a special anti-crisis plan emphasizing improvements in investment climate. The plan includes provisions to postpone an introduction of certain regulatory initiatives concerning advertising billboards, environmental control of the freight transport, transition to a free market rate mechanism for the Moscow city government owned property leases, and regulatory requirements for agricultural markets. In particular, the anti-crisis plan pursues three goals specifically designed for improvements to the investment climate: -improving investment climate and institutions, -reduction of administrative barriers to business, and -the formation of a transparent competitive environment. St. Petersburg has also set long-term transformation goals in addition to anti-crisis measures. A general objective of the Development Strategy of St. Petersburg is to ensure consistent progress in the quality of life of its citizens and improve St. Petersburg's global competitiveness on the basis of implementation of the national development priorities, sustained economic growth and use of the results of innovation and technological activities.

The sectorial level of the FDI/crisis-related analysis in the chapter includes the Russian automotive sector and oil and gas sector. Prior to 2014, the Russian automotive industry was on the rise. Its strategic development and growth that attracted serious FDI inflows. The economic crisis hit the Russian automotive industry especially hard: in 2015 industry sales plunged almost 50% below the 2012 peak. The chapter examines how the two largest automotive manufactures, AvtoVAZ (cars) and KAMAZ (heavy tracks) cope with the crisis in the FDI development context.

The chapter analysis also includes Gazprom, the national champion and a global major in the natural gas production and distribution, part of the Russian oil and gas sector. Although in its recent corporate statement Gazprom made a pronouncement that as the national leader of the industry, it is poised to meet the challenges of the unfavorable macroeconomic situation and sanctions, it may be a daunting task: over the last 5 years, its production dropped 17%, although sales increased 68%, with net profitability weakening due to financing challenges. As the company remains profitable, paying dividends regularly, the economic recession becomes the driver for many reforms in the company – in terms of efficiency, new technologies, and localization of most of the supplying goods of the Russian plants. The role of FDI will be crucial.

The main goal of the chapter is to explore the role of FDI in economic growth and transformation of the Russian economy in a context of the current socio - economic and political turbulence, to outline emerging scenarios for change in the national economy. A discussion in the chapter relies on array of empirical supporting information and factual illustrations on the national, sectorial, and regional level in the international comparative context.

BACKGROUND

The origins, evolution, concepts, theories and patterns of international trade and FDI have received extensive coverage in the literature ranging from Adam Smith (1776) to John Dunning (1988, 1998), Rugman and Verbeke (2004), Shenkar (2014), Slaughter and May (2012), and Ietto-Gillies (2012)

International business has been promulgated by advances in transportation, enabling intercontinental travel and commercial shipments, and industrial revolution, boosting productivity and innovations and providing economic surplus for international trade and investment. Early FDI concepts were based on classical theories of trade in which the motive behind trade was a result of the difference in the costs of production of goods between two countries, focusing on the low cost of production as a motive for a firm's foreign activity (Ietto-Gillies, 2012). International trade and FDI, the two major forms of international business, take place as alternative modes and/or complementary forms, depending on the balance of comparative strategic benefits, costs and risks in the eyes of stakeholders in this economic process (Birkinshaw and Hood, 1998). In a pursuit of economic mission corporations strive to realize their economic benefits while minimizing costs and mitigating risks of doing business. Depending on the balance and tradeoffs between these often conflicting criteria, corporations in their international expansion decisions may lean toward either trade or FDI. Knickerbocker (1973) examined the relationship between FDI and rivalry in oligopolistic industries (industries composed of a limited number of large firms) and suggested that FDI flows are a reflection of strategic rivalry between firms in the global marketplace that translate in a multipoint global competition. Vernon (1966) argued that firms undertake FDI at particular stages in the life cycle of a product they have pioneered; as a result of changes in the balance of strategic benefits, costs and risks companies in developed nations may shift from exporting to relocating their manufacturing operations overseas, and their foreign subsidiaries may eventually get involve in importing products into their home countries. Dunning (1988, 1998) developed the concept of eclectic paradigm of international production. According to Dunning's concept, from a corporate standpoint, FDI in the corporate eyes is motivated by two driving forces: -location-specific advantages that emanate from using resource endowments of assets associated with a particular location in a host country that the company finds strategically valuable to assimilate with its own assets; -externalities that materialize in knowledge spillovers accruing to companies in the same industry that tend to locate their facilities in the same geographic area or country. Djankov and Hoekman in their widely cited article (2000) analyzed firm-level data for the Czech Republic to show that during 1992–1996 FDI had the predicted positive impact on total factor productivity growth of recipient firms. Together, joint ventures and FDI appear to have a negative spillover effect on firms that do not have foreign partnerships. However, with FDI alone, the magnitude of the spillover becomes much smaller and loses significance. This result, in conjunction with the fact that joint ventures and FDI account for a significant share of total output in many industries, suggests that further research is required to determine the extent of knowledge diffusion from firms that have foreign links to those that do not.

Russia is a special point in case of FDI. Due to its geographically remote position relative to major global markets and political-economic philosophy and history Russia has been less exposed to FDI compared to major nations worldwide. With the advent of the Bolshevik Revolution in 1917 private property (and by extension FDI) has been essentially banned. Government ownership and centralized planning and control became a political-economic foundation during the Soviet time for more than seven decades till the abolition of the U.S.S.R. in 1991. The nation's political-economic autarky has become particularly conspicuous after WWII when the Soviet Union and several Eastern European countries formed the Soviet political-economic-military alliance (arguments in support of Russia's limited propensity for internationalization can be found in Zhuplev, 2008). Beyond political-economic boundaries, limited role of FDI in the Soviet system was a result of constraints imposed by the Communist ideology and national security concerns. Limited FDI inflows designated for selected priority industries, regions or selected FDI projects have been decided on a case by case basis. The advent of post-Soviet capitalism in Russia induced radical changes in the role of FDI in the political-economy of Russia. Since Russia regained its prominence as a sovereign nation after the abolition of the U.S.S.R. in 1991, FDI has played important role in its economic prosperity and growth. Driven by political-economic pragmatism, government attitudes toward FDI in Russia over time tend to oscillate between positive in difficult economic times and negative when the economy improves (Zhuplev, 2008; Russia. Special Report, 2016).

RUSSIA: FDI PROFILE, PATTERNS, AND DYNAMICS ACROSS MAJOR ECONOMIC SECTORS AND REGIONS

Playing a crucial developmental role in the intersection of natural factors (climate, landscape, strategic location in global geography, demographics, etc.) and manmade factors (political-economic system, social fabric, macro and microeconomic forces, technology, innovation, etc.), FDI dynamics show great diversity and variations across nations.

According to the United Nations Conference on Trade and Development (UNCTAD), the key components of regulatory framework for FDI in a country or economy include (National Framework, 2016):

- Corporate law, including accounting and reporting regulations,
- Incentives for, and restrictions on, FDI,
- Forms of establishment mergers and acquisitions,
- Securities,
- Taxation (mainly corporate and individual income tax),
- Transfer of technology,
- Industrial/intellectual property.

By a broader extension, investment attractiveness in a comparative context can be also judged by analyzing the dynamics and rankings of the nation's performance in global competitiveness[4] as a proxy.

Russia's current global competitiveness profile, as reported in the Global Competitiveness Report (Schwab, 2016), is presented in Figure 1 and Table 1. All of the metrics included in the Global Competitiveness Index (GCI) in Table 1 are fundamentally important for attracting and retaining FDI. Over the past few years, Russia's global competitiveness, as reported in the GCI, has been improving. The nation's ranking in the latest GCI 2015 - 2016 scorecard stood at 45/140 compared to 53/144 in the previous GCI 2014 – 2015 scorecard, an 8-point improvement. Russia's major global competitive strengths in FDI attractiveness relative to other countries lie in its large market size, infrastructure, as well as higher education and training. Among its major comparative weaknesses are institutions, financial markets, and goods market efficiency. The word "relative" is important in the FDI context since the stakeholders in the global FDI-related environment have alternative choices in their investment decisions and are driven by the host nations' relative (comparative) FDI attractiveness in the respective benefit-cost-risk (BCR) balance. Nations enjoying strong BCR balances tend to outperform nations characterized by weak BCR balances in attracting and sustaining the inflows and stock of FDI from investors worldwide. For instance, U.S.A. and Germany, Russia's "aspirational" comparators, have high global competitiveness ranks, #3/140 and #4/140 accordingly. In contrast, Russia's fellow BRIC countries rank as follows: Brazil – 75/140, variable GCI dynamics over the past few years with a 20-point drop in the latest GCI 2015-2016 rank; India – 55/100, variable GCI dynamics over the past few years with a 20-point improvement in the latest 2015-2016 rank; and China – 28/140, flat GCI dynamics over the past few years. All other things equal, by extension and market competition aside, countries with higher global competitiveness tend to be more attractive for incoming FDI.

It should be noted that international cross-country comparisons of FDI-related trends, patterns and dynamics have methodological limitations: nations differ considerably in the strategic role and interplay of their natural factors, political, economic, social, technological and other conditions that together constitute their respective FDI-related business environments. Table 2 profiles Russia vs. comparator

Figure 1. Russia's global competitiveness profile
Source: Schwab, 2016, p. 306.

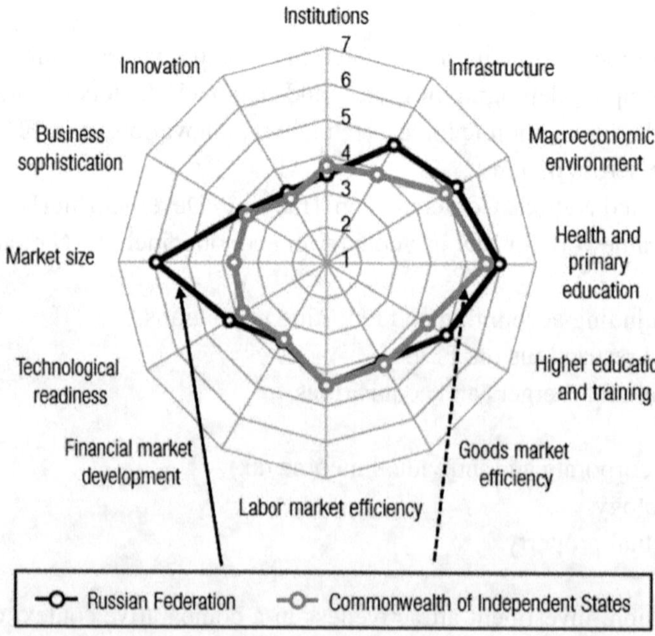

Table 1. Russia's Global Competitiveness Index (GCI)

	Rank (Out of 140)	Score (1–7)
GCI 2015–2016	45	4.4
GCI 2014–2015 (out of 144)	53	4.4
GCI 2013–2014 (out of 148)	64	4.2
GCI 2012–2013 (out of 144)	67	4.2
Basic requirements (30.2%)	47	4.9
1st pillar: Institutions	100	3.5
2nd pillar: Infrastructure	35	4.8
3rd pillar: Macroeconomic environment	40	5.3
4th pillar: Health and primary education	56	5.9
Efficiency enhancers (50.0%)	40	4.5
5th pillar: Higher education and training	38	5.0
6th pillar: Goods market efficiency	92	4.2
7th pillar: Labor market efficiency	50	4.4
8th pillar: Financial market development	95	3.5
9th pillar: Technological readiness	60	4.2
10th pillar: Market size	6	5.9
Innovation and sophistication factors (19.8%)	76	3.5
11th pillar: Business sophistication	80	3.8
12th pillar: Innovation	68	3.3

Source: Schwab, 2016, p. 306.

countries, "aspirational" comparators, and transitional economies and world. These FDI metrics for Russia fluctuate from year to year. They also tend to differ between countries not only within the developed vs. less developed countries' dichotomy but also within the group of Russia's fellow BRIC countries.

Table 2. FDI profile: Russia vs. BRIC countries, "aspirational" comparators, transitional economies and world

FDI Flows	Millions of Dollars					As a Percentage of Gross Capital Formation			
	2005-2007 (Pre-Crisis Annual Average)	2012	2013	2014	2015	2005-2007 (Pre-Crisis Annual Average)	2013	2014	2015
Russia									
Inward	35,579	30,188	53,397	29,152	9,825	18.1	11.8	6.7	3.4
Outward	30,145	28,423	70,685	64,203	26,558	15.3	15.7	14.8	9.1
Brazil									
Inward	22,824	76,098	53,060	73,086	64,648	11.5	10.1	14.9	20.1
Outward	12,595	-5,301	-1,180	2,230	3,072	6.4	-0.2	0.5	1.0
China									
Inward	76,214	121,080	123,911	128,500	135,610	6.9	2.9	2.8	3.0
Outward	18,800	87,804	107,844	123,120	127,560	1.7	2.5	2.7	2.8
India									
Inward	17,766	24,196	28,199	34,582	44,208	5.6	4.8	5.5	7.0
Outward	11,501	8,486	1,679	11,783	7,501	3.6	0.3	1.9	1.2
USA									
Inward	185,953	188,427	211,501	106,611	379,894	6.0	6.6	3.2	10.8
Outward	211,035	318,197	307,927	316,549	299,969	6.8	9.7	9.4	8.5
Germany									
Inward	61,105	28,181	11,671	880	31,719	10.0	1.6	0.1	4.7
Outward	120,181	62,164	40,362	106,246	94,313	19.6	5.5	13.7	14.0
Transition Economies**									
Inward	58,906	64,786	85,500	56,468	34,988	19.6	13.0	8.9	7.3
Outward	32,461	33,193	75,784	72,164	31,112	11.0	12.3	12.4	7.4
World									
Inward	1,418,164	1,510,918	1,427,181	1,276,999	1,762,155	11.6	7.8	6.7	9.9
Outward	1,445,276	1,308,820	1,310,618	1,318,470	1,474,242	11.8	7.2	7.0	8.3
FDI stock	Millions of dollars					As a percentage of GDP			
Russia									
Inward	5,601*	438,194	471,474	284,100	258,402	1.7	21.1	14.0	19.5
Outward	3,346*	332,834	385,321	303,349	251,979	1.0	17.3	14.9	19.0

continued on following page

Table 2. Continued

FDI Flows	Millions of Dollars					As a Percentage of Gross Capital Formation			
	2005-2007 (Pre-Crisis Annual Average)	2012	2013	2014	2015	2005-2007 (Pre-Crisis Annual Average)	2013	2014	2015
Brazil									
Inward	47,886*	675,533	644,837	615,179	485,998	6.1	26.2	25.5	27.4
Outward	44,474*	204,253	204,192	175,727	181,447	5.7	8.3	7.3	10.2
China									
Inward	101,098*	832,882	956,793	1,085,903	1,220,903	13.8	10.1	10.4	11.1
Outward	17,778*	531,941	660,478	882,642	1,010,202	2.4	6.9	8.5	9.2
India									
Inward	5,641*	224,985	226,549	252,817	282,273	1.5	12.2	12.4	13.5
Outward	495*	118,072	119,838	131,524	138,967	0.1	6.4	6.4	6.6
USA									
Inward	1,005,726*	3,915,538	4,954,713	5,390,081	5,587,969	13.1	29.7		31.1
Outward	1,363,792*	5,222,873	6,291,370	6,285,320	5,982,787	17.8	37.8	36.2	33.3
Germany									
Inward	312,576*	1,077,019	1,088,690	1,089,569	1,121,288	12.0	29.1	28.1	33.3
Outward	505,692*	1,571,548	1,611,910	1,718,157	1,812,469	19.5	43.0	44.3	54.0
Transition Economies									
Inward	10,972*	760,550	821,605	633,856	601,389	2.6	27.0	22.7	31.2
Outward	3,634	378,165	434,212	357,852	307,764	0.9	14.8	13.4	16.9
World									
Inward	3,565,318*	22,639,110	24,532,733	25,112,800	24,983,214	11.2	31.9	31.8	33.6
Outward	3,992,701*	22,701,815	24,664,815	24,809,704	25,809,704	12.9	32.3	31.7	34.0

Source: Authors' compilation from the World Investment Report, 2016.

*Data for 1995.

**Under the UN classification, the group of economies in transition includes countries of South-Eastern Europe (Albania, Bosnia and Herzegovina, Montenegro, Serbia, the former Yugoslav Republic of Macedonia) and the Commonwealth of Independent States and Georgia (Armenia, Azerbaijan, Belarus, Georgia (Georgia officially left the Commonwealth of Independent States in 2009, but its performance is discussed in the context of this group of countries for reasons of geographic proximity and similarities in economic structure), Kazakhstan, Kyrgyzstan, Moldova, Moldova, Russia, Tajikistan, Turkmenistan, Ukraine, and Uzbekistan).

Regaining momentum following the national economic crisis and government default in 1998, Russia has registered robust FDI performance with the inflows and outflows' yearly averages exceeding the thirty billions USD benchmark during 2005-2007, years preceding the latest global recession. At that time, Russia's FDI inflows have markedly outstripped outflows by an 18% margin, reflecting strong global investment interest in Russia, particularly prominent among Russia's domestically based investors with much of the capital returning to Russia from their offshore accounts in the form of FDI.

Over the past few years, however, Russia's share of FDI as a percentage of gross capital formation in the nation has declined in relative terms, compared to the levels of pre-crisis annual averages of 2005-

2007. After reaching a peak of 53.9 billion USD in 2013, Russia's inward FDI inflows abruptly plunged more than five-fold to 9.8 billion USD in 2015. In contrast with this drastic decline in the inward FDI flows, Russia's outward FDI in 2015 decelerated by only by 59% to 26.6 billion USD. This trend is also reflected in Russia's FDI flow levels as a percentage of the nation's gross capital formation. Another distinctive feature of Russia's FDI flows as a percentage of gross capital formation trend is its higher levels of FDI outflows compared to inflows: in 2015 the share of FDI outflows, as a percentage of gross capital formation, exceeded the share of inflows three-fold.

Similar trends can be observed in the dynamics of Russia's FDI stock both in value terms and as a percentage of GDP (the lower part of Table 2), albeit yearly variations for this indicator tend to be less drastic as the nature of the FDI stock indicator suggests in contrast to annual FDI flows.

As of 2015, Russia's stock of FDI at home reached 360.9 billion USD (December 2015 est.), placing the nation at #20 in country comparison worldwide. At the same time, Russia's FDI stock abroad reached 404.4 billion USD, #19 in country comparison worldwide (World Factbook, 2016).

Since patterns of FDI inflows tend to correlate with trends in a nation's general economic structure, the next section provides concise macroeconomic assessment across Russia's major economic sectors and regions. As of December 2015, Russia's GDP had the following composition by sector of origin: services – 59.7%, industry – 35.8%, and agriculture – 4.4% (World Factbook, 2016).

Within services, Russia's largest economic sector, the leading subsectors are: wholesale and retail trade, repair of motor vehicles, motorcycles and personal and household goods (together accounting for 17% of the nation's GDP), public administration, real estate, renting and business activities (together comprising 12% of GDP), transport and communications (comprising 9% of GDP), and education, health and social work (together comprising 7% of GDP) (Russia` 2015 Statistical Pocketbook, 2015).

The agriculture sector's share in Russia's GDP is relatively small. The sector employs an estimated 5.9% of the workforce nationwide. Although the soil is fertile, unfavorable general weather conditions and years of neglect mean that yields are just a third of those in Western Europe. Farmers are ill prepared to meet the goal of self-sufficiency that national leaders and government officials have scrambled to impose in response to western sanctions. For example, up to half of the fruit production from small farms and 20% of industrial vegetable production is lost to spoilage each year.

Russia's manufacturing sector accounts for 14.4% of GDP and – proportionally - employs 13.2% of the workforce nationwide. Several international automobile firms operate production facilities in Russia but the industry has been hit hard by negative market dynamics and sanctions. Car sales fell by more than a third in 2015. GM shut most its Russian operations in 2015. The food and chemical industry is gaining market share after Russia restricted western imports but many other industries are struggling. Investment in manufacturing has been anemic, though loans from China provide some support.

There are massive mineral deposits and forest resources with iron ore, coal, copper, aluminum, manganese, salt and precious metals being produced, though facilities are in need of modernization. Raw materials, such as oil, natural gas, and metals make up more than two-thirds of all export revenues. South Korean, Japanese and Chinese investors hope to move into the Russian market to secure stable supplies of coal and other energy resources. Mining output grew by 4.7%, in real terms, during 2015.

According to Euromonitor/Passport, services make up 61.8% of GDP, slightly higher than the CIA's World Factbook's estimate. Just two large banks (Sberbank and VTB) dominate the Russian banking market with 60-70% of deposits. Unsecured credit growth poses an increasing financial risk. The real value of tourist receipts rose by 6.9% in 2015 and gains of 1.8% are forecast for 2016. Retail sales fell by 10% in 2015 and have continued to slow in 2016.

Between 2000 and 2012, Russia's per capita income rose remarkably - from 33% to 51% of the OECD average. Rising oil prices and increasing use of spare resources were the main drivers during this period. The economy contracted during the Great Recession but a fiscal stimulus, valued at about 14% of nominal GDP, boosted growth in 2011 and 2012. However, another slowdown occurred in 2013 and virtually no growth was recorded in 2014. Business investment contracted, productivity fell and the ruble lost more than half of its value against the dollar as sanctions were intensified and oil prices plummeted. In 2015, the economy contracted by 3.3%. This was the steepest decline in six years (Russia, Country Profile, 2016).

Within industry, manufacturing is Russia's second largest economic sector after services: it comprises 15% of the total Russian GDP. Mining/quarrying and construction, the most important industry segments, contribute to the GDP 10% and 7%, respectively (Federal State Statistics Service, 2015). Russia has a range of mining and extractive industries producing coal, oil, gas, chemicals, and metals; all forms of machine building from rolling mills to high-performance aircraft and space vehicles; defense industries (including radar, missile production, advanced electronic components), shipbuilding; road and rail transportation equipment; communications equipment; agricultural machinery, tractors, and construction equipment; electric power generating and transmitting equipment; medical and scientific instruments; consumer durables, textiles, foodstuffs, and handicrafts.

Table 3 contrasts the origins of Russian GDP with that of its fellow BRIC and "inspirational comparators," Germany and the U.S.A. In this perspective, Russia looks less reliant on agriculture compared to other BRICs, but its agricultural share of GDP is markedly higher than that of Germany and the U.S.A. Russia's industrial share in GDP is lower than that of China, but still considerably higher than in both its BRIC peers and "inspirational comparators." Accordingly, while Russia's share of services in GDP trails that of Brazil, Germany, and the U.S.A., it is slightly higher than India's and considerably higher than China's.

The big picture and internal sectorial dynamics in the Russian sectors of agriculture, industry, and services highlight a paramount economic role of the industry sector, as well as its relatively higher efficiency and global competitiveness, in contrast to the agricultural and service sectors.

For an outside observer with limited experience some Russian industries appear to be FDI-attractive due to their sheer economic size and market potential. However, there are multiple administrative bar-

Table 3. GDP origins: Russia vs. BRIC and "aspirational comparators", percent share, 2015 est.

	GDP Origins		
	Agriculture	**Industry**	**Services**
Brazil	5.9	22.2	71.9
China	8.9	42.7	48.4
Germany	0.7	30.2	68.9
India	16.1	29.5	54.4
Russia	4.4	35.8	59.7
U.S.A.	1.6	20.8	77.6

Source: World Factbook, 2016.

riers and other non-economic factors that may complicate a foreign entity's strategic entry into these industries. Entry and operational impediments include burdensome regulatory regimes, issues with intellectual property rights, protection and enforcement, widespread corruption and inadequate rule of law, inconsistent application of laws and regulations, lack of transparency, and a non-level playing field for competition due to the continued presence of large state-owned or state-controlled enterprises dominating strategic sectors of the economy. Investments in the wide-ranging list of "strategic sectors" of the Russian economy are subject to Russian Government control[5] (U.S. Commercial Service, 2016. Doing Business in Russia, 2015; U.S. Department of State. Russia Investment Climate Statement, 2016).

Another important dimension of Russia's FDI-related economic landscape is its regional structure. Russia's current governing-administrative system and regional subdivisions have come a long way, emanating from the nation's complex geography, history, political economy, socio-cultural and military developments.

As of 2016, there were numerous federal administrative subjects as constituent members of the Russian Federation.[6] Russia's federal subjects are categorized as follows: 46 provinces (oblastey, singular - oblast), 21 republics (respublik, singular - respublika), 4 autonomous okrugs (avtonomnykh okrugov, singular - avtonomnyy okrug), 9 krays (krayev, singular - kray), 2 federal cities (goroda, singular - gorod), and 1 autonomous oblast (avtonomnaya oblast') (World Factbook, 2016). Apart from these federal subjects, Russian regional structure is comprised of nine federal districts,[7] twelve economic regions,[8] four military districts[9] and a multitude of municipal divisions. Additionally, there are 29 special economic zones set up to facilitate foreign investment through tax breaks, insurance privileges, relaxed customs regimes, ready to use infrastructure and other incentives (Special Economic Zones of the Russian Federation, 2011).

Until recently, regional governance and development on the federal level had been under the jurisdiction of the Ministry of Regional Development of Russia (Министерство регионального развития Российской Федерации – Минрегион России). In September 2014, the Ministry of Regional Development was abolished and its responsibilities redistributed across other ministries. The task of facilitating foreign investments in Russia was assigned to the newly created federal Russian Investment Agency, Invest in Russia (2016) (Российское инвестиционное агентство).[10]

Depending on the nature of a contemplated FDI, comparative attractiveness of Russian regions may vary widely in terms of their business potential, costs and risks.

Table 4 characterizes Russian leading economic regions and major federal subjects selected on the basis of their largest regional contribution to the national GDP. Table 4 suggests that the Central Federal District, which includes the city of Moscow and Moscow oblast (Moscow oblast is used interchangeably with Moscow region), clearly emerges as the national economic leader.

Central Federal District, the most economically developed one, compared to other administrative districts, accounted in 2015 for only 3.8% of the Russian territory, but was home to 27% of the nation's total population. In 2013, the Central Federal District controlled 32.1% of the total fixed capital formation and contributed 35.0% to the Russian GDP nationwide. In addition, The Central Federal District's share in the national manufacturing output reached 14.56% in extracting industries, 33.94% in manufacturing industries, and 29.96% in generation and distribution of electric power, natural gas and water.

The city of Moscow and Moscow oblast combined registered less than 1% of the country's territory nationwide, but their population was 13.2% of the national total. In contrast, together they generated 26% of the national GDP, 23.6% of the fixed capital formation, 13.02% output in extracting industries,

Table 4. Russia's economic regions and federal subjects with the greatest regional GDP, percent*

	Area	Population as of Jan 1 2015	Regional GDP, 2013	Fixed Capital Formation, (Actual Book Value at Year's End)	Regional Output by Extracting and Manufacturing Industries		
					Extraction	Manufacturing	Generation and Distribution of Electric Power, Natural Gas and Water
Russian Federation	100	100	100	100	100	100	100
Central Federal District	3.8	27.0	35.0	32.1	14.56	33.94	29.96
Moscow oblast	0.3	4.9	4.5	4.1	0.10	5.87	5.51
City of Moscow	0.01	8.3	21.5	19.5	12.92	15.34	12.19
North-West Federal District	9.8	9.5	10.3	10.9	6.03	14.16	12.02
City of St. Petersburg	0.01	3.5	4.6	3.3	0.14	6.94	3.79
South Federal District	2.5	9.6	6.5	6.4	1.88	6.10	6.26
Krasnodar krai	0.4	3.7	3.0	2.9	0.21	2.20	2.06
North Caucasus Federal District	1.0	6.7	2.4	2.4	0.21	1.08	2.47
Privolzhsky (Volga) Federal District	6.1	20.3	16.0	14.1	14.32	20.98	18.43
Republic of Bashkorstan	0.8	2.4	2.3	1.4	1.64	2.97	2.33
Republic of Tatarstan	0.4	2.6	2.9	2.4	3.59	3.93	2.67
Ural Federal District	10.6	8.4	14.1	18.3	36.66	11.64	12.67
Sverdlovsk oblast	1.1	3.0	2.9	3.2	0.51	4.46	3.63
Tyumen oblast. Including:							
Khanty-Mansi autonomous okrug-Yugra	3.1	1.1	5.2	6.5	23.36	1.32	4.39
Yamalo-Nenets Autonomous Okrug	4.5	0.4	2.5	5.4	11.15	0.52	1.06
Tyumen oblast without the autonomous okrugs	0.9	1.0	1.6	1.1	1.27	1.76	0.92
Siberian Federal District	30.0	13.2	10.2	9.0	12.75	10.39	12.19
Krasnoyarsk krai	13.8	2.0	2.3	1.7	3.10	2.58	2.85
Far East Federal District	36.1	4.2	5.4	6.3	13.55	1.71	5.60

Source: Adopted from Zhuplev, 2016.

*The table includes selected federal subjects of Russia with their regional share in the national GDP equal or higher that 2 percent.

21.21% output in manufacturing, and an 17.7% contribution to the national output in generation and distribution of electric power, natural gas and water. Additionally, the Moscow oblast, and, especially, the city of Moscow, enjoys a wide-margin comparative advantage in employee compensation. For example, in 2014 the average nominal monthly monetary labor compensation in the city of Moscow stood at 61,208 rubles compared to only 39,945 rubles in the Central Federal District and even the lower amount of 32,495 rubles for Russian Federation nationwide. In the Moscow oblast, the 2014 average monetary compensation stood at 38,598 rubles or 63% of the city of Moscow level and 119% of the Russian Federation overall level (Регионы России 2015).

Higher salaries tend to translate into a greater regional purchasing power and boost Moscow's potential attractiveness as a marketplace. Moscow's higher salaries, sophisticated life styles and better quality of life also tend to attract qualified workforce, thus providing favorable opportunities for foreign companies looking to recruit local talent in starting or running their investment-based business operations in Russia.

According to the 2016 World Investment Report (UNCTAD 2016), in 2015 Russia received 9.8 billion USD in foreign direct investment inflows, a sharp drop compared to 29.2 billion USD in 2014). In 2014 the Central Federal District registered 12.5 billion USD or 55% of the total inflows of foreign direct investments in Russia. Out of the Central Federal District's 12.5 billion USD total, the city of Moscow in 2014 attracted 11 billion USD or 16% of the total foreign direct investment inflows in Russia. The Central Federal District and Moscow's role as the nation's leading business hub and marketplace is also evident from Table 5 containing Russia's international trade statistics: in 2014, the Central Federal District accounted for 51% of all Russian national exports and 61% of imports. Moscow alone, as part of Central Federal District, accounted for a stunning 46% of the Russian national exports and 49% of imports (Регионы России 2015).

On the opposite end of the Russian regional economic spectrum are such federal entities as South Federal District, North Caucasus Federal District, Privolzhsky (Volga) Federal District, and Siberian Federal District: their shares of contribution to the national GDP are notably lower relative to their population size. Not surprisingly, these districts lag behind in attracting FDI, with the exception of the Privolzhsky (Volga) Federal District (in 2014 it received 1.2 billion USD of foreign direct investment inflows), each of the federal districts in the laggard group attracted less than one billion dollars in FDI and generated substantially lower amount of international trade in contrast to the Central Federal District and the city of Moscow (Регионы России 2015).

As Russia's economy continues to experience headwinds, the country's 83 regions are under pressure to compete with one another for outside investment. The quest for funding was a popular theme at the recent St. Petersburg International Economic Forum (2016), where regional governments and corporations tried to woo foreign partners and financiers. Some regions have focused their campaigns on Asia and Europe: The Kaluga and Kaliningrad provinces, for example, have signed investment deals with Bavaria, and Kaluga's governor visited Vietnam earlier in the year seeking funding. But four of Russia's Muslim republics -- Tatarstan, Bashkortostan, Chechnya and Dagestan — have set their sights on Muslim states in the Middle East and Southeast Asia (Russia's Muslim Regions 2016).

As mentioned earlier, the recent creation of the new Russian Investment Agency "Invest in Russia" was intended to facilitate incoming foreign investments. Given Russia's large economic size, complexity and substantial differences characterizing its regional entities, each of them possessing varying potential for investment and economic development, now almost every region has its own local affiliate agency charged with attracting investments (regional investment agencies can be accessed through the Invest in Russia (2016) entry point).

Table 5. Russian regions-leaders in foreign trade, actual prices, millions of US dollars

	2012				2014			
	With the Countries of "Far Abroad"*		With NIS** Countries		With the Countries of "Far Abroad"		With NIS Countries	
	Exports	Imports	Exports	Imports	Exports	Imports	Exports	Imports
Russian Federation	445,478	272,323	79,258	44,941	433,850	253,864	63,984	32,806
Central Federal District	199,703	167,740	37,955	25,342	221,053	154,218	34,299	19,600
Moscow oblast	3,101	30,776	2,473	1,898	2,569	22,991	3,173	2,323
City of Moscow	182,416	118,531	29,071	14,214	205,016	114,830	25,426	10,808
North-West Federal District	49,000	56,013	6,571	1,750	51,082	51,939	4,669	2,592
City of St. Petersburg	19,330	35,249	4,053	1,105	19,592	29,309	2,735	1,561
South Federal District	17,159	8,628	3,507	3,213	17,177	8,624	3,038	2,424
Krasnodar krai	8,741	4,356	1,069	.585	9,641	4,704	559	585
North Caucasus Federal District	937	1,421	356	596	797	1,598	489	479
Privolzhsky (Volga) Federal District	53,705	12,967	15,501	3,415	52,848	14,508	10,880	3,132
Republic of Bashkorstan	10,345	1,008	2,764	372	12,439	932	1,416	255
Republic of Tatarstan	18,896	2,968	3,262	649	16,595	3,601	1,511	607
Ural Federal District	69,846	6,865	9,012	3,571	31,943	6,552	5,793	2,132
Sverdlovsk oblast	9,004	3,073	1,725	940	6,478	2,933	2,050	773
Tyumen oblast. Including:	56,894	1,809	4,995	614	22,281	1,948	1,357	129
Khanty-Mansi autonomous okrug-Yugra	22,114	997	1,883	43	19,416	1,238	1,062	44
Yamalo-Nenets Autonomous Okrug	3,044	360	30	70	507	157	0,5	52
Tyumen oblast without the autonomous okrugs	31,736	452	3,082	501	2,358	552	294	34
Siberian Federal District	31,274	8,129	4,239	2,370	30,373	5,848	4,597	2,225
Krasnoyarsk krai	8,037	1,694	279	265	7,266	1,038	466	442
Far East Federal District	25,688	10,487	270	61	28,483	10,436	198	217

Source: Регионы России. Внешняя торговля. (2015).

* The unofficial term "far abroad" ("дальнее зарубежье") was coined after the abolition of the U.S.S.R. in the early 1990s. It signifies the nations not included in the Newly Independent States (NIS). Despite geography, the "far abroad" category also incorporates countries having common border with Russia - Finland, Norway, Poland, Mongolia, PRC (mainland China), North Korea, and sometimes the Baltic countries (Latvia, Lithuania and Estonia).

** NIS stands for Newly Independent States.

Russian Investment Agency (2016) performs the following key functions:

- Building systemic relations with foreign investment agencies and investors;
- Providing foreign investors with reliable and up-to-date information;
- Assisting and supporting foreign investors at all stages of cooperation;
- Developing and providing recommendations to the Government of the Russian Federation, to the investment ombudsman and investment officials in Federal Districts for the improvement of the investment climate;
- Interacting with regional administrations and agencies of regions of the Russian Federation in the sphere of attracting investments.

To perform the functions listed above, the Invest in Russia and its regional affiliates provide information and assistance that can become a starting point in foreign company's strategic analysis and decision. Additionally, the Invest in Russia portal houses reports prepared by premier global consultancies and the Russian Direct Investment Fund designated for specific economic sectors and industries in which Russia claims to have investment potential. The list of priority industries include: pharmaceutical and medical, real estate, innovations and technology, infrastructure, aluminum, lead, iron and steel, platinum-group metals, precious metals, nickel, copper, zinc, coal, telecommunications, transportation, agriculture and food as well as gas industry (Russian Investment Agency, 2016).

As an example, Table 6 presents comparative investment profiles for four regional entities: the city of Moscow, the city of St. Petersburg and the surrounding Moscow region and Leningrad region.[11]

ECONOMIC CRISIS AND FDI DYNAMICS

Oil and gas price volatility has played an extraordinary role in domestic socio-economic developments and foreign policy. Russia has taken notable advantage of skyrocketing global energy prices in the 2000s and resulting spectacular financial windfalls. After peaking at 151 USD per barrel of crude oil in June 2008, global oil prices have been declining. In 2014, they abruptly plunged to their lowest recent levels and are hovering currently (June 2016) around 47 USD per barrel. Natural gas prices peaked at 13.42 USD per million of British thermal units (Btu) in October 2005 and plunged to 1.92 USD per million of Btu in May 2016. Russia's energy dependent economy has suffered severe blows that sharply depleted government coffers. Deprived of the petrodollar bonanza, Russia has still continued to experience large scale investment needs to maintain and develop its ageing oil and gas infrastructure as well as other economic sectors. In contrast, investment climate across economic sectors and regions remained difficult despite some improvements in the nation's global ratings. That has driven large scale capital flight and deterioration in the FDI inflows to Russia.

As Russia strives to re-establish itself as a superpower in the post-Soviet international arena, an additional factor has been the nation's involvement in several regional conflicts and political disputes in the neighboring countries - Georgia (2008), Ukraine (2014). Altogether, that led to deterioration of the relationships with the West and imposition of multiple rounds of political-economic sanctions on Russia by the West and countersanctions by Russia. Part of these Western sanctions was intended to cut off Russia from access to some advanced technologies and limit its access to global (Western) financial markets in order to curb Russia's financial borrowing capability and cumulatively complicate its domestic

Table 6. Investment profiles: city of Moscow, city of St. Petersburg, Moscow region, and Leningrad region, 2014

	Moscow	St. Petersburg	Moscow Region	Leningrad Region
Key Macroeconomic Indicators				
GRP*, RUB billion	8,248	1,431	1,645.7	383.3
GRP dynamics, percent vs. previous year	123	109	127	105
Equity investments per capita, RUB thousand	86.7	81.4	69.5	98.0
Registered unemployment rate, percent of economically active population (as at the end of the period)	n/a	2	0.7	0.9
Foreign direct investments, USD thousand	8,611,964	1,373,650	2,243,273	438,110
Geography				
Region population size, thousand people	11,282	4,568	6,958	1,695
Regional center population size, thousand people	11,282	4,568	n/a	4568.1
Shortest highway distance to the nearest border crossing, km	440	163	480	n/a
Shortest highway distance to the nearest sea port, km	720	0 km	710	14
Highway distance from regional center to the nearest million-plus population city, km /population size in million-plus population city, million people	0 /12.11	0 km, St Petersburg, 5 mln people	12 / 12.11	0/5.0
Transportation and Energy Infrastructure				
Number of international airports	3	1	3	n/a
Railway freight transportation, MT	7	7.6	15	39.7
Motor transport freight turnover, MT/km	5,451	5,089	5,697	1,791
Electricity generation/consumption, %	75.6	77.3	75.6	101
Domestic market size				
Income per capita, RUB thousand	31.9	16.9	19.0	11.6
Retail sales turnover, RUB bn	2,365	576	887	131
Products shipped in manufacturing sector, RUB mln	2,129,463	721,113	1,069,302	316
Labor Market				
Average monthly salary, RUB thousand	30.5	22.47	21.5	17.5
Average monthly salary in manufacturing sector, RUB thousand	23.8	21.98	21.1	19.8
Economically active population, thousand people	6369	2808.8	3900	961.3
Human Capital				
Number of students per 10 thousand people (at the last reporting date)	1,164	956	248	107
Mortality of working age (per 100 thousand people of working age - 3-year average)	415	514	686	693
Migration balance (3-year average) per thousand people	99	155	149	123

Source: Russian Investment Agency, 2016.

*Great regional product.

economic dynamics. Part of the Russian political and strategic response was the initiation of a range of import substitution policies in agriculture and some industry sectors, particularly those associated with defense, IT, and high technologies.

On the top of that, some long-standing political-economic disagreements and disputes between Russia, numerous European countries, and the European Union as a whole involving trade, strategic investments, as well as strategic marketing and management practices related to Russian oil and gas have reached new threshold levels. This triggered a range of political-economic steps on the European national and EU level in devising technological solutions and strategies alternative to Russian oil and gas, including Europe's shift toward alternative global energy suppliers, renewable sources, liquefied natural gas, fracking shale oil and gas, etc. In contrast, over the past few years Russia has engaged in its own strategic reorientation of energy-related commerce and investment relationships from the West (Europe) to the East, particularly China.

As mentioned earlier, a host country's economic benefits from attracting FDI inflows can accrue from the resource transfer effects (technology, know-how, financial transfers, gaining access to foreign markets, etc.) and employment effects (improvements in workforce quality, training and development, work attitudes, etc.) (Hill & Hult, 2017). FDI can play a particularly prominent role in increasing productivity, fostering innovation and boosting the export capacity of Russian firms – all critical factors in maintaining and advancing national competitiveness in the global arena.

According to the World Bank (Russia: Economic Report, 2016), prior to 2014 Russia's inbound FDI levels were comparable to those of the other BRICS countries, though "round-tripping" was notably common. Between 2007 and 2012 as much as one-third of Russia's inbound FDI was in fact Russian capital channeled through offshore tax havens. Correcting for round-tripping, inbound FDI hit its post-2008 peak during the first quarter of 2013, when net inflows reached 69 billion USD. However, during 2014 net FDI plunged by two-thirds. The most severe declines were observed in the third and fourth quarters, when aggregate net inbound FDI turned negative across all sectors of the economy, indicating widespread capital flight (Figure 2).

Figure 2. Net FDI inflows to Russia
Source: Central Bank of Russia.

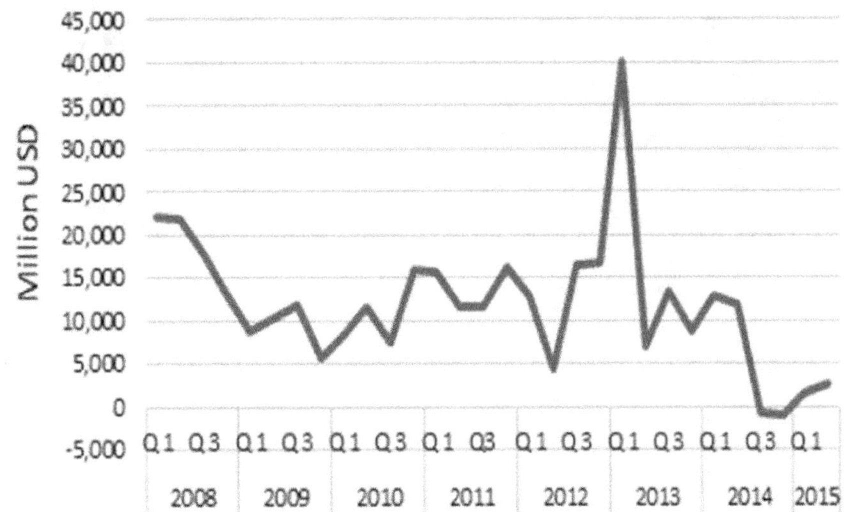

A feeble recovery began during the first half of 2015, though net FDI inflows remained far lower than in previous years. Round-tripping, which has always been more prevalent in Russia than in other fellow BRIC countries, has intensified since 2014 (Figure 3) causing a strategic and financial concern. Some Russian companies tend to engage in round-tripping schemes driven by three major factors. First, unpredictable changes in the national business environment, investment climate, uneven or arbitrary enforcement of property rights and financial laws drive some Russian companies and FDIs overseas in their quest for tax advantages, risk avoidance and safe havens, which they often find in foreign offshore centers. Second, legal loopholes, corruption and other weaknesses in the legal system allow for offshore capital transfers under various schemes. And third, apart from selected global business success stories in raw materials (oil, natural gas, coal, and timber), grain, metals, chemicals and fertilizers, IT and few other industries as well as investment in real estate, Russian companies have limited exposure and managerial expertise in international operations. Since round-tripped FDI is not authentically a foreign capital, but rather domestic capital reentering the country, it is less likely to generate strategic benefits in innovations, technology transfer, productivity growth, and other areas associated with genuine FDI (Russia: Economic Report, 2016).

The external economic sanctions set in motion in 2014 intended to restrict FDI inflows to Russia by targeting financial transactions in general and investments in the oil sector in particular. The economic sanctions regime has inhibited the international operations of Russia's largest banks, preventing Russian firms from acquiring international debt or making cross-border financial transactions. They have also partially blocked the oil sector from acquiring new technology and equipment, and some prospective FDI projects have been frozen. As of late, Russia's oil sector was the country's primary destination for inbound FDI, and by targeting the oil sector the economic sanctions regime has had an immediate and deeply negative impact on FDI inflows (Russia: Economic Report, 2016).

Figure 3. Sources of Russian net incoming FDI
Source: Central Bank of Russia.

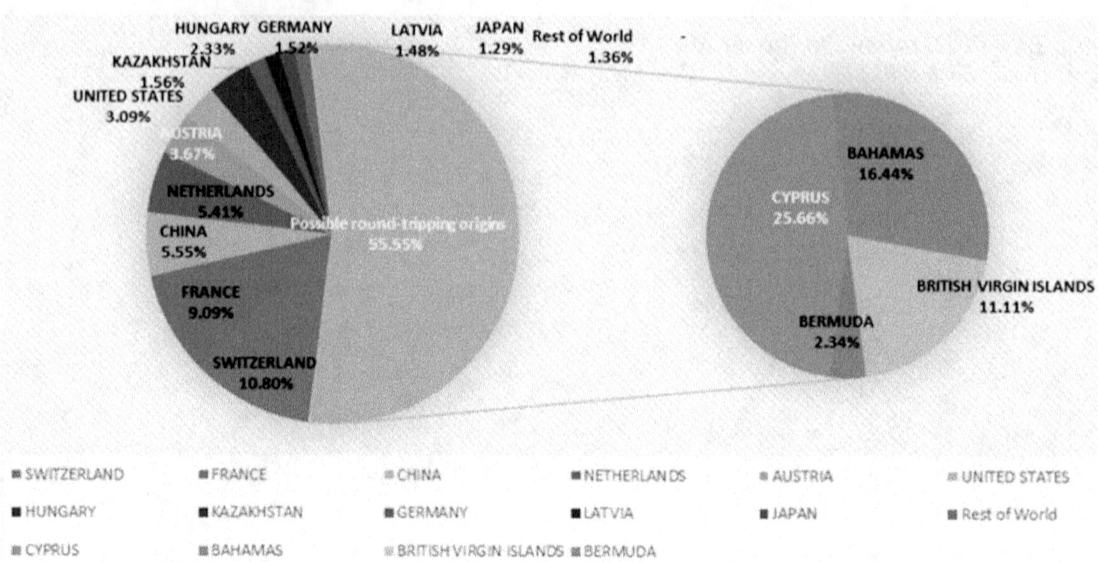

Prior to 2012, FDI rates were increasing fastest in high-tech manufacturing, utilities, construction and financial intermediation, sectors that are strongly associated with positive technological spillovers. Foreign auto manufacturers broadened a range of affordable and high-quality cars in the domestic market. Rising FDI in the chemicals sector leveraged Russia's absolute advantage in fossil fuels, and foreign chemical firms expanded into the domestic pharmaceutical subsector. Foreign firms also diversified the range of available construction services. The minority participation of foreign investors in Russia's telecommunications subsector accelerated technology transfer despite an especially large share of round-tripped FDI.

Net outflows of foreign capital since 2014 affected all sectors of the Russian economy simultaneously, particularly during the third quarter of 2014. A modest rebound in FDI, focused largely on the oil and gas sectors, began in the first half of 2015. Unless FDI inflows continue to recover, the government is unlikely to achieve its ambitious medium-to-long-term plans to enhance the export competitiveness of Russian firms. Constrained FDI inflows are not only slowing Russia's overall growth, but also have significant negative implications for regional development. Russia's regions have benefitted differently from FDI, and regional development patterns illustrate the important links between foreign investment, export performance and economic growth (Russia: Economic Report, 2016).

Survival and Revival: Strategic Scenarios, Responses, and Emerging Alternatives on the Regional, Sectorial, and Company Level

- **Regional Strategies for Survival and Growth:** The current economic downturn has several implications for Russian regions, affecting the level of economic growth, demand, debt level, real monetary income. As follows from the charts below, comparing and contrasting Moscow and St. Petersburg, national leaders, with the Russian Federation as a whole, the influence of the economic recession on the regional level has been acute and uneven.

On the one hand, the nominal domestic product per capita continues to grow. The debt level is decreasing (although staying at high level in most of the regions, except in Moscow and St. Petersburg) due to the austerity budget policy, imposed on all levels. At the same time, monetary income per capita, which is increasing in all regions in nominal value, is significantly influenced by inflation, and the real monetary income decreases in Moscow (92.8% 2014 to 2013) and other regions, except St. Petersburg (103.7%). This decrease, exacerbated by high interest rates and relatively high level of household debt (with about

Figure 4. GDP per capita, thousand Rub
Source: Federal State Statistics Service.

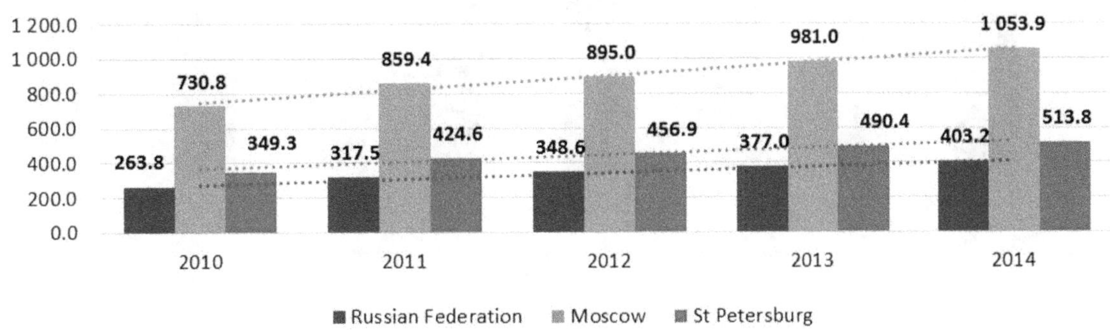

Figure 5. Debt level, debt to regional income, percent
Source: Federal Treasury of Russia.

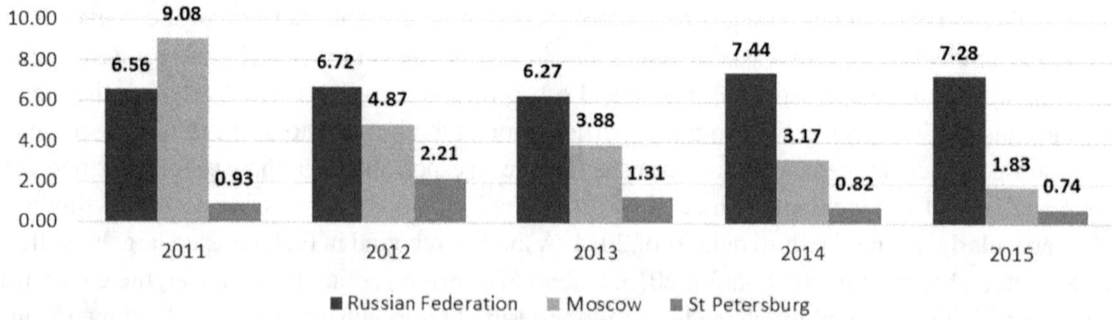

Figure 6. Monetary income, Rub per capita
Source: Federal State Statistics Service.

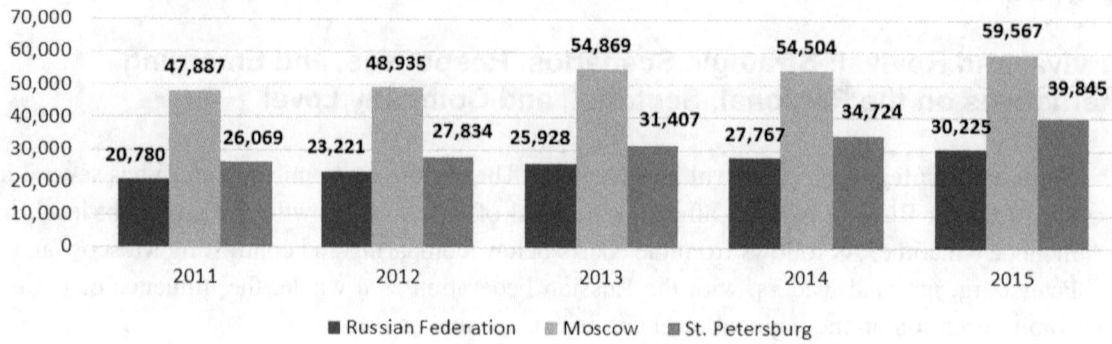

Figure 7. Real monetary income, percent of previous period
Source: Federal State Statistics Service.

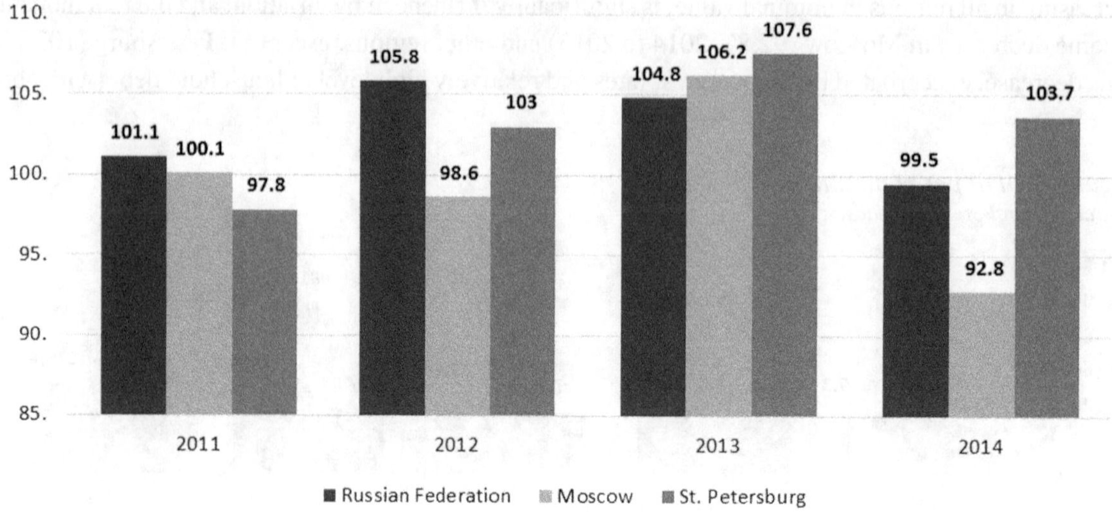

20% debt-to income ratio in most households, according to the Central Bank of Russia statistics), is pushing consumer confidence and consumer spending down to the level of the 2009 economic crisis (Figures 8 and 9) and inhibit FDI.

Under these challenging dynamics and constraints, regional governments strive to develop different strategies to adapt their respective regional economies to the challenges posed by the crisis. For example, the City of Moscow, the national capital and leader among economic regions, is implementing a special anti-crisis plan emphasizing improvements in investment climate. The plan includes provisions to postpone an introduction of certain regulatory initiatives concerning advertising billboards, environmental control of the freight transport, transition to a free market rate mechanism for the Moscow city government owned property leases, and regulatory requirements for agricultural markets. In particular, the anti-crisis plan pursues three goals specifically designed for improvements to the investment climate:

Figure 8. Russia: consumer confidence
Sources: Trading Economics, Federal Statistics Service.

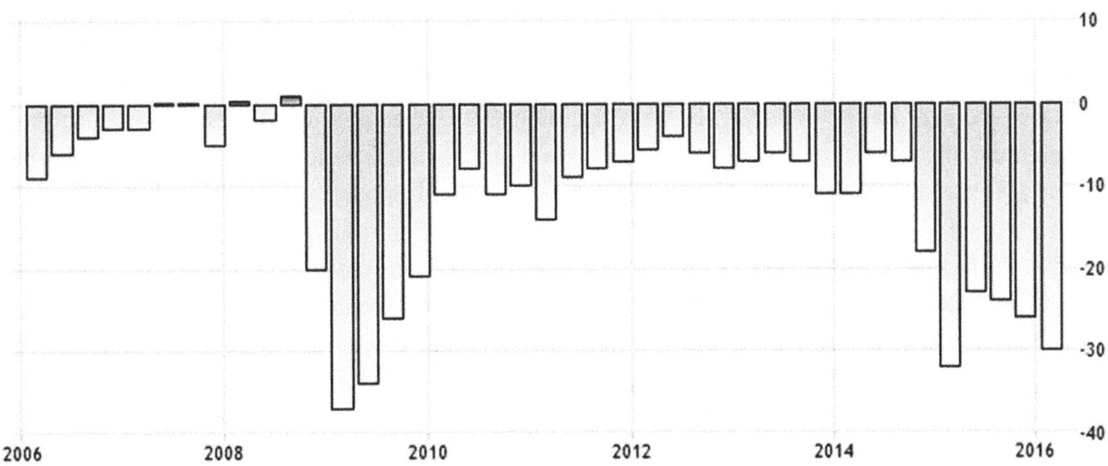

Figure 9. Russia: consumer spending
Sources: Trading Economics, Federal Statistics Service.

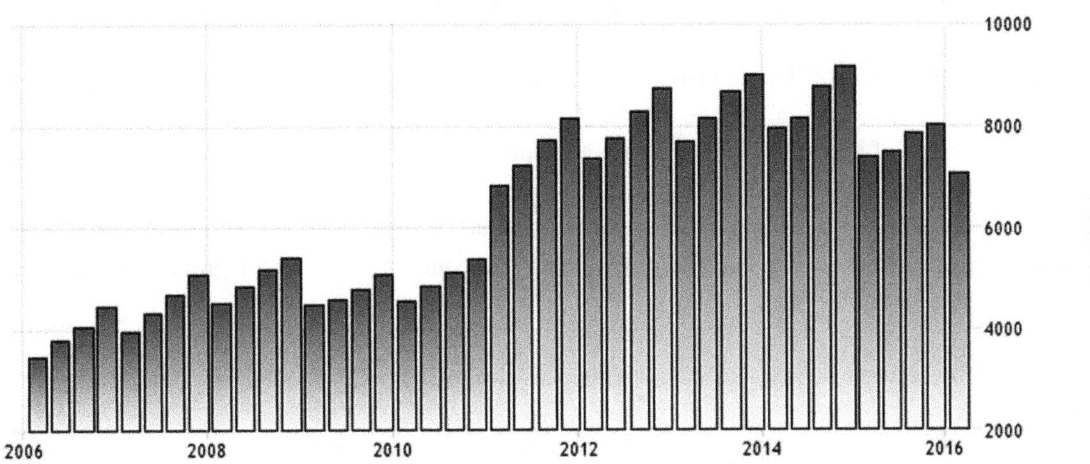

-improving investment climate and institutions, -reduction of administrative barriers to business, and -the formation of a transparent competitive environment.[12]

St. Petersburg has also set long-term transformation goals in addition to anti-crisis measures. A general objective of the Development Strategy of St. Petersburg is to ensure consistent progress in the quality of life of its citizens and improve St. Petersburg's global competitiveness on the basis of implementation of the national development priorities, sustained economic growth and use of the results of innovation and technological activities. [13]

In relative terms, Moscow and St. Petersburg, Russia's leading economic regions have developed their long-term vision for transforming these regions from national champions into global leaders, driven by improved business infrastructure and investment climate, opportunities for a creative and healthy life, advanced education, and innovations.

Strategies for Survival and Growth on the Industry and Corporate Level

The impacts of economic downturn across sectors and industries of the Russian economy vary widely, depending on the dynamics of supply and demand, currency position, intensity of competition within the industry, competitive strengths and strategies of the main industry players, and level of their corporate debt. Our further discussion in this chapter focuses on the automotive industry and oil & gas sector. The automotive industry has been one of the main recipients of FDI in previous years; the oil & gas sector has been the main contributor to the national economy and a critical national source of export earnings. Both the automotive industry and oil & gas sector exert critical impacts on the Russian economy.

- **The Automotive Industry:** Prior to 2014, the Russian automotive industry was on the rise. It was projected that more than 10 billion USD would be committed to upgrading facilities and expanding capacity through 2020, making the auto industry one of the leaders in and drivers of the Russian economy Russia, thus attracting serious levels of FDI, with projected growth into the largest European car market - and the 4th largest globally—with annual sales of 4.4 million vehicles[14].

However, the Russian automotive industry was hit hard by the economic crisis. The industry had its second straight year of precipitous decline in 2015; sales were almost 50% below the 2012 peak. Since 2014, several reasons contributed to the shrinking of sales and profits in the automotive industry:

- Significant decrease of the effective demand due to uncertainty and shrinking real incomes on a wide scale.
- Sharp increase of the car loan interest rates combined with conservative banking policy, exacerbating negative effects of dwindling sales.
- Companies involved in a large scale importation of automotive accessories have suffered a severe exchange rate shocks when the ruble lost half of its value against major global currencies after collapse of global oil prices.

Altogether these trends have caused a significant decrease in car production and sales (Table 7, Figure 10).

Table 7. Car production in Russia

	2014	2015	% Change
Cars produced, units	1,887,193	1,384,399	-26,60%

Source: The International Organization of Motor Vehicle Manufacturers, 2016.

Figure 10. Car sales volumes in Russia, units
Sources: The International Organization of Motor Vehicle Manufacturers.

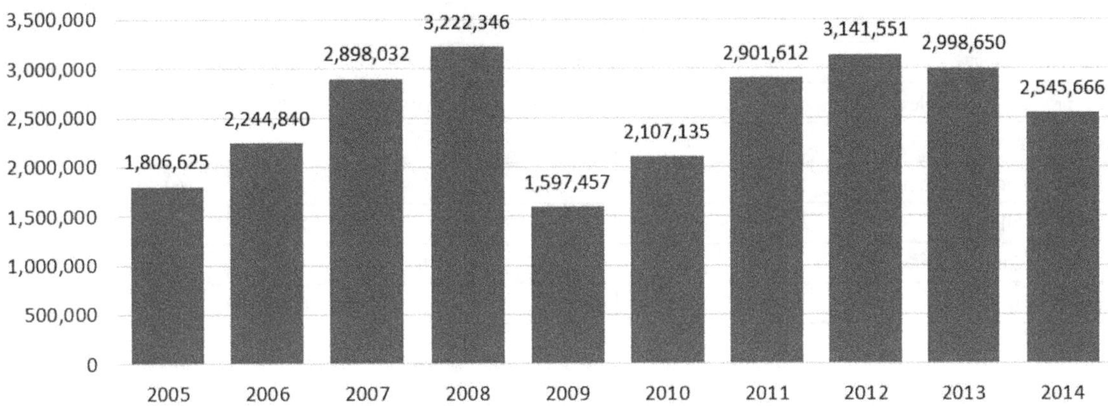

Under these trends and dynamics, the projected market growth and production have not materialized. That's why several foreign car producers and trendsetters are leaving Russia. Some experts estimate that anywhere from three to six automotive plants out of the existing 24 could shut down temporarily or permanently.[15] Global car manufacturers could start losing their strategic interest in Russia and instead look at other emerging markets, for example China and India.

In 2015, General Motors GM decided to idle its Opel plant in Russia. Now the Detroit-headquartered auto maker has no assembly line at all in the country. Korea's SsangYong suspended its export program in Russia in 2015 because of the weak ruble. And Russian automaker Sollers canceled its planned rollout with Toyota of the Land Cruiser Prado back in August[16].

To complicate things for the industry, foreign car manufactures operating in Russia are not deeply integrated with local partners and suppliers. That jeopardizes their position due to currency volatility.

What are strategic options under the current negative environmental developments, most notably shrinking demand, volatile currency, and high costs of operation in Russia? Some industry experts argue that Russia could become an export hub, using weak currency as an advantage for localizing production and then exporting cars to the neighboring markets, such as the Middle East and Central Asia, thus reducing dependence on Russia's problematic domestic market. However, with all the necessary strategic and operational steps - certification, adaptation, promotion, sales networks, and the formation of strategic partnerships - involved in the development of new markets, positive results appear to be a long way off.

AvtoVAZ, one of the largest Russian domestic car producers,[17] is an illustration reflective of the overall controversial situation in the automotive industry.

Table 8. Key performance indicators, AvtoVAZ, 2010-2014

Years	2010	2011	2012	2013	2014
Operational Indicators					
Auto sales, cars	549,650	613,151	592,367	501,465	538,985
In Russia	505,811	557,131	522,586	402,199	362,475
Export	43,839	56,020	69,781	78,440	51,791
Special cars	-	-	-	20,826	124,719
Production of cars	545,450	593,296	587,610	516,331	511,894
Financial Indicators					
Sales, million rubles	137,027	174,846	183,217	175,152	189,370
Gross profit, million rubles	15,034	20,192	1,770	10,092	9,406
Gross margin, %	11	12	10	6	5
Profit from sales, million rubles	4,599	4,659	1,846	-6,640	-5,658
Sales profitability, %	3%	3%	1%	-4%	-3%
Net profit, million rubles	2,472	3,106	211	-6,899	-25,411
Net profitability, %	2	2	0,1	-4	-13

Source: AvtoVAZ, 2016.

As seen from the main indicators, under current circumstances the company production and sales are stagnating, and profitability suffers significantly, largely due to the high level of dollar-nominated imported accessories. A recent former president of the company, Bo Andersson, was heavily criticized for the low level of localization, as well as severe social policy in the company. The new president has to face all the challenges, along with the unfavorable economic environment. The company's latest strategy is outlined in Table 9[18]:

As follows from Table 9, the company's strategy still pursues ambitious growth: it envisions the doubling of its production by 2020 and at the same time is trying to transform its old and inefficient production capacities, increasing productivity and market potential of the company's products.

KAMAZ is another key player in the Russian automobile industry[19] included in a discussion in this chapter: its performance profile is summarized in Table 10.

As seen from Table 10, KAMAZ' sales were hit hard by the crisis, especially on the domestic market. However, in 2014, the crisis year, the company's exports increased 6% due to the weak ruble. The macroeconomic situation has influenced the company's financial position: from a historical maximum of 5.1% net profitability plunged to 0.2%. Yet the company is still profitable and has not lost its position in the prime markets.

KAMAZ' Top International Strategic Development Priorities Include:

- Key market - Russia, dominance in the CIS markets, presence in attractive markets of Eurasia; Africa and South America;
- Positioning in the middle price segment;
- Integration in the Global Automotive Industry

Table 9. AvtoVAZ: strategy till 2020

Main Goals	Key Initiatives
Retaining leadership in the automotive market in Russia	• Price advantage. • Sales plan till 2020 - 1 million cars, including export - 100 thousand cars.
Procurement reform	• The creation of "AvtoVAZ - Renault –Nissan" joint purchasing organization. • Optimization of the supplier base and strategic supplier selection panel. • Transition from component to module assembly. • Optimization of the volume and frequency of delivery orders. • Consolidation of the volume of purchases from Renault and Nissan, in Vol. H. The use of global Renault and Nissan partners (exchange rates, terms, etc.). • Optimization and standardization of procurement processes in accordance with Renault and Nissan standards.
The development of sales system Increased productivity	• Development of the dealer network. • Qualitative development of dealers (KPI). • The introduction of modern sales methods of control. • Increased corporate sales due to competitive price positioning, as well as by modern corporate policy. • Improving the efficiency of personnel directly engaged in the sale. • Improved internal processes, such as custom car dealers, car service, as well as improvement of IT-systems. • Effective marketing. Implementation of programs to improve production efficiency has a direct impact on the growth of the efficiency and productivity and allows to: • Reveal hidden losses in manufacturing (overproduction, the loss due to defects, losses associated with poor workplace organization, logistics loss, etc.); • Achieve maximum efficiency in the use of available resources (staff, production facilities); • Identify all types of working time losses with further exception, to achieve increased employment of staff; • Exclude the diversion of workers on work not covered by the employment contract; • Optimize the applied shift schedules; and • Reduce the level of absenteeism.
The development strategy of AvtoVAZ in the field of quality	• Produce high-quality products, fully adapted to the requirements of the Russian consumer; • Improve the level of customer service at dealerships; • Continuously improve production processes; • Achieve the required quality indicators in new projects for their timely launch; and • Ensure high quality suppliers.

Source: AvtoVAZ, 2016e.

Table 10. KAMAZ: Key performance indicators, 2010-2014

	2010	2011	2012	2013	2014
Operational Indicators					
Sales of trucks, cars	32,300	45,288	45,471	43,832	38,655
In Russia	28,260	39,122	39,142	38,089	32,566
Export	4,040	6,166	6,329	5,743	6,089
Sales of buses	858	549	687	897	535
Sales of trailers	4,587	7,904	7,762	5,812	3,974
Financial Indicators					
Sales, million rubles	73,773	109,995	118,510	114,317	110,599
Gross profit, million rubles	10,476	15,370	19,984	16,901	14,589
Gross margin, %	14.2	14	16.9	14.8	13.2
Profit from sales, million rubles.	1,886	3,983	8,378	5,695	2,243
Sales profitability, %	2.6	3.6	7.1	5	2
Net profit, million rubles	-652	2036	6,056	4,267	211
Net profitability, %	-0.9	1.9	5.1	3.7	0.2

Source: KAMAZ, 2016.

KAMAZ' Development Trends:

- Integration with Daimler, a strategic partnership on components, and the development of supplier park;
- Boosting exports, setting up KAMAZ assembly production abroad, expanding to new markets. Modernization and reengineering of production;
- Entering the Euro 5, 6 class line vehicle manufacturing. Development of vehicles and buses on gas fuel; Production of a new range of vehicles. Development of the KAMAZ-2020; and
- Expansion of the product range, the development of leasing and financial services, upgrading of the dealer network, the development of after-sales services.

Meanwhile, both AvtoVAZ and KAMAZ are looking at the export markets, targeting CIS countries, Asia and Africa. So, for both companies the economic crisis becomes not only the main challenge due to the weakening of the local market, but also provides several opportunities for foreign expansion and facilitates a drive for internal transformation and greater efficiency.

- **The Oil and Gas Industry:** Energy sector, and oil & gas in particular play an extraordinary role in the Russian political-economic system (Zhuplev & Shtykhno, 2015; Russia, European Commission, 2016). As demand growth slowed down and markets became over-saturated, 2015 saw a further decrease in oil prices, following the previous year's drop. The renewed EU and

US sanctions against Russia put energy companies in an even more challenging environment, both financially and technologically. Nonetheless, oil production in Russia grew in 2015, mostly due to the increased levels of oil recovery from conventional fields and the exploration of new deposits, including reserves that are hard to recover. Indeed, Russia set a historic record last with daily oil production at 10.7 mbpd.[20]

Experts who participated in the most recent Oil & Gas Outlook survey largely agree that declining oil prices are pushing the upstream sector toward improving profitability of oil fields in 2016, including upticks in the production efficiency of the extensively depleted fields. At the same time, the overwhelming majority of the survey respondents anticipate a significant growth in capital needs across the industry in 2016, while only 18% predict more investment: an opinion shared by the most experts states that investment in oil and gas is likely to decrease or at best, remain at the same level.[21]

Under these circumstances, the biggest players try to balance their priorities between the need to raise efficiency, invest in development, pay dividends to shareholders, and attract new capital and preserve financial stability under sanctions.

Some recent research data[22] points out that restricted access to capital is becoming one of the main challenges across the industry.

Gazprom's key strategic priorities till 2020 include: Maintaining its leadership in the global gas industry in the long term. In a pursuit of diversification of Russian natural gas exports as Gazprom Group's important strategic pillar the company is transitioning from the European to Eurasian global strategy.

In the Russian market, Gazprom intends to maintain its current position, both in terms of gas supply volumes and its reliability, including during the heating season. On traditional European gas markets, the company intends to keep its share and further strengthen its position, should the market environment become favorable. Gazprom seeks to grow its share of North-East Asia markets in the longer term.

Figure 11. Problems facing oil and gas companies
Source: Russian Oil and Gas Outlook Survey.

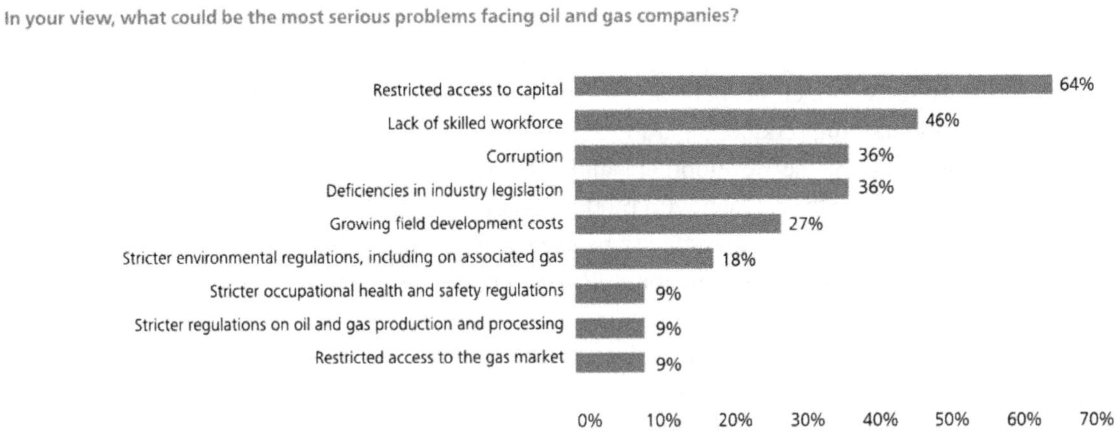

Table 11. Gazprom: Key performance indicators and the strategy, 2010-2014[23]

	2010	2011	2012	2013	2014	2015
Operational Indicators						
Gas production in Russia, km3	508,6	513,2	487	487,4	443,9	418,5
Condensate production in Russia, million tons	11,3	12,1	12,8	14,7	14,5	15,3
Oil production in Russia, million tons	32	32,3	33,3	33,8	35,3	36
Financial Indicators						
Sales, billion rubles	3597	4637	4766,5	5250	5589,8	6073,3
Profit from sales, billion rubles	1113,8	1656,8	1350,7	1587,2	1310,4	1228,3
Net profit, billion rubles	968,6	1307	1224,5	1139,3	159	787,1
Net profitability, %	31	35,7	28,3	30,2	23,4	20,22

Source: Gazprom, 2016, company annual reports.

To these ends, Gazprom plans to achieve a number of strategic steps toward enhancing its operations in Russia.

- In gas exploration and production, the development of new gas production centers in the Yamal Peninsula, on the continental shelf, in Eastern Siberia, and the Russian Far East will continue in parallel with sustaining production at the existing fields.
- In gas transportation, the development and refurbishment of the Unified Gas Supply System (UGSS) will continue to go along with production growth and diversification of gas export routes. The existing infrastructure is expected to be used as extensively as possible to ensure reliable supplies. The gas transportation expansion in Russia's eastern regions and building up of gas storage and LNG production capacities will continue.
- In gas processing and gas chemical production, the company development will be driven by the increasing extraction of valuable components from natural gas and associated petroleum gas (APG) and their effective utilization for further processing into marketable high value-added (HVA) products. Gas processing and gas chemical plants are to be upgraded or constructed from scratch, including in Eastern Siberia and the Russian Far East.
- Gazprom also intends to continue its expansion outside of Russia. In November 2015, the Company's Management Committee approved the Growth Strategy for PJSC Gazprom's Foreign Operations whereby all foreign operations should be focused on:
  - Establishing integrated value added chains, from exploration and production to the end consumer;
  - Tailoring the foreign project portfolio to corporate requirements to economic efficiency;
  - Enhancing interfaces with foreign strategic partners and implementation of joint projects aimed to strengthening and developing new competencies; and
  - Eliminating competition of the company's foreign supplies with Russian gas.
- In gas marketing, the company plans to expand its presence in the more promising markets, including the Asia-Pacific Region, and increase the LNG share in Gazprom's export portfolio.

Although in its recent corporate outlook statement Gazprom has made a pronouncement that as the national leader of the industry, it is poised to meet the challenges of the unfavorable macroeconomic situation and sanctions, it may be a daunting task: over the last 5 years, its production dropped 17%, although sales increased 68%, with net profitability weakening due to financing challenges. As the company remains profitable, paying dividends regularly, the economic recession becomes the driver for many reforms in the company – in terms of efficiency, new technologies, and localization of most of the supplying goods of the Russian plants.

SOLUTIONS AND RECOMMENDATIONS

After regaining the pre-crisis level in 2012, Russia's FDI inflows peaked at 53.4 billion USD in 2013 and went into a tailspin afterwards: in 2015 Russia registered a 9.8 billion USD inflow. Since 2014, negative FDI net outflows have affected all sectors of the Russian economy simultaneously, particularly during the third quarter of 2014. A modest rebound in FDI, largely in the oil and gas sector, began in the first half of 2015. Unless FDI inflows continue to recover, the government is unlikely to achieve its ambitious medium-to-long-term plans to enhance the export competitiveness of Russian firms. Constrained FDI inflows are not only slowing Russia's overall growth, but also have negative implications for regional socio-economic development. As Russia's economy continues to experience headwinds, straining the flows of government economic support for each of the country's 83 federal subjects, the regions come under pressure to compete with one another for outside investment.

Under these pressures and strategic constraints, regional governments strive to develop strategies to adapt their respective regional economies to the challenges imposed by the crisis. Regional strategic response ranges from adopting special anti-crisis plans emphasizing improvements in investment climate and relaxing certain regulatory initiatives (the City of Moscow) to setting up long-term transformation goals in addition to anti-crisis measures (the city of St. Petersburg). In relative terms, Moscow and St. Petersburg, Russia's leading economic regions have developed their long-term vision for transforming these regions from national champions into global leaders, driven by improved business infrastructure and investment climate, opportunities for a creative and healthy life, advanced education, and innovations.

The impacts of economic downturn and survival strategies across sectors and industries of the Russian economy also vary widely, depending on the dynamics of supply and demand, currency position, intensity of competition within the industry, competitive strengths and strategies of the main industry players, and level of their corporate debt. Examination in the chapter includes two illustrative cases in point: the automotive industry and oil & gas sector. Both of them meet certain challenges because of the drop in demand, financing difficulties, sanctions. At the same time, the leading companies in these industries are using this challenging time to transform their business processes, increase efficiency and find new markets abroad, taking advantage of weak local currency and price advantage at the momentum.

The company level survival strategies are illustrated by the cases of AvtoVAZ and KAMAZ, two leaders in the Russian automotive industry, and Gazprom, a national champion and global leader in oil and natural gas production and distribution. Examination in the chapter of sectorial/ industry and company level FDI-related survival strategies under the current economic downturn in Russia has revealed inconclusive trends and patterns. With a significant degree of government control and involvement, politics, and support dependency, these industries and companies' success in attracting and retaining FDI in these industries and their leading companies will ultimately depend on political decisions and macroeconomic developments involving domestic and international variables.

FURTHER RESERCH DIRECTIONS

Highly complex, politicized and sensitive to changes in geo-regional political-economic climate, the topic of FDI in Russia is widely opened for research. Under these conditions the scope and directions of research engaged in this publication will remain in demand in the short to mid-range perspective.

Authors propose the following specific directions for future research on FDI in Russia.

- Inward and outward FDI trends, dynamics and impacts: macro (national, regional, sectorial/industry) and microeconomic (company) level.
- FDI: cross-country attractiveness on the geo-regional and global level.
- FDI and their role in Russia's domestic socio-economic and foreign policy.
- Inward and outward FDI trends, dynamics across economic sectors and industries nationwide.
- Inward and outward FDI trends, dynamics across regions nationwide.

- FDI and their impacts on Russia's global competitiveness.
- FDI and their impacts on Russia's innovation potential and developments.
- The dynamics of regulatory environment, investment climate and their impacts of FDI.
- Evolving FDI-related policies and strategies under economic downturn: national, regional, sectorial/industry, and company level.
- FDI-related impacts on employment, technology transfer, the development of regional institutions and infrastructure.

CONCLUSION

In the age of globalization FDI plays vital role in domestic social-economic growth and global competitiveness of the nation. From the host country (FDI recipient) standpoint the main benefits associated with attracting FDI lie in the resource transfer effects, employment effects, balance of payment effects, and various positive impacts on the host country's competitiveness and economic growth. Possible adverse effects associated for a host country with incoming FDI may involve weakening national competitiveness, negative effects on the balance of payments, and losses in national sovereignty and political-economic autonomy.

Over the past few years, Russia's attractiveness as an FDI recipient and its comparative global competitiveness in this regard has been improving. The nation's major global competitive strengths in FDI attractiveness relative to other countries lie in its large market size, infrastructure, as well as higher education and training. Among its major weaknesses are institutions, financial markets, and goods market efficiency.

After the national economic crisis and government default in 1998, Russia has registered robust FDI performance with the yearly averages in inflows and outflows exceeding 30 billion USD during 2005-2007, the pre-crisis time span. At that time, Russia's FDI inflows outstripped outflows by an 18% margin, reflecting robust global investment interest in Russia. Over the past few years, Russia's share of FDI as a percentage of gross capital formation in the nation has declined in relative terms, compared to 2005-2007. After reaching a peak of 53.9 billion USD in 2013, Russia's FDI inflows abruptly plunged in 2015 five-fold to 9.8 billion USD. In contrast, Russia's FDI outflows in 2015 decelerated only by 59% to 26.6 billion USD. This trend is also reflected in Russia's FDI inflows as a share of the nation's gross capital formation dynamics. Russia has registered higher levels of FDI outflows compared to inflows: in 2015 the share of FDI outflows, as a percentage of gross capital formation, exceeded the share of inflows three-fold. Similar trends can be observed in the dynamics of Russia's FDI stock both in value terms and as a percentage of GDP.

FDI patterns and dynamics tend to correlate with trends in a nation's general economic structure. Russia's GDP composition by sector of origin is as follows: services – 59.7%, industry – 35.8%, and agriculture – 4.4%. In this perspective, Russia looks less reliant on agriculture compared to other BRICs, but its agricultural share of GDP is markedly higher than that of Germany and the U.S.A. Russia's industrial share in GDP is lower than that of China, but still considerably higher than in both its BRIC peers and "inspirational comparators." Accordingly, while Russia's share of services in GDP trails that of Brazil, Germany, and the U.S.A., it is slightly higher than India's and considerably higher than China's.

The big picture and internal sectorial dynamics in the Russian sectors of agriculture, industry, and services highlight paramount economic role and high FDI potential of the industry sector, as well as its relatively higher efficiency and global competitiveness, in contrast to the agricultural and service sectors. For an outside observer with limited experience some Russian industries may appear to be FDI-attractive due to their sheer economic size and market potential. However, there are multiple administrative barriers and other non-economic factors that may complicate a foreign entity's strategic entry into these industries. The Russian economy is currently struggling from the economic downturn, not only from the current political context, but also from historical economic misbalances and resource dependency.

Regional structure is an important dimension of Russia's FDI-related economic landscape. Russia's governing-administrative system and regional subdivisions emanate from the nation's complex geography, history, political economy, socio-cultural and military developments. Depending on the nature of specific FDI project, comparative attractiveness of Russian regions may vary widely in terms of their business potential, costs and risks. The Central Federal District, with the city of Moscow and Moscow oblast as the national economic leader. Having 2.3% of the total geographic area and being home to 27% of population nationwide, The Central Federal District contributes 35% of the GDP, enjoys 32.1% of the fixed capital formation and contributes significant shares to the national output in some main extracting and manufacturing industries. The leading economic role of Moscow and Moscow Oblast as part of the Central Federal District is even more pronounced. In 2014, prior to the most recent economic drop, the Central Federal District received 55% of the total FDI inflows in Russia, with the city of Moscow claiming 16% of the total FDI inflows nationwide. In 2014, the Central Federal District accounted for 51% of all Russian national exports and 61% of imports. Moscow alone accounted for 46% of the Russian national exports and 49% of imports.

REFERENCES

России, Р. Социально-экономические показатели [Regions of Russia. Socio-economic factors]. (2015). *Федеральная служба государственной статистики* [Federal State Statistics Service – Rosstat]. Retrieved May 28, 2016 from http://www.gks.ru/bgd/regl/b15_14s/Main.htm

AvtoVAZ. (2016). Retrieved September 26, 2016 from http://company.avtovaz.ru/en/

Azzimonti, M., & Sarte, P. G. (2007). Barriers to foreign direct investment under political instability. *Economic Quarterly*, *93*(3), 287–315.

Bank of Russia Annual Report for 2014. (n.d.). Retrieved from http://www.cbr.ru/Eng/publ/God/ar_2014_e.pdf

Birkinshaw, J., & Hood, N. (1998). Multinational subsidiary evolution: Capability and charter change in foreign-owned subsidiary companies. *Academy of Management Review*, *23*(4), 773–795.

Consumer Lifestyles in Russia. (2016, January 13). Retrieved June 9, 2016, from Global Market Information Database (GMID by Euromonitor).

Djankov, S., & Hoekman, B. (2000). Foreign Investment and Productivity Growth in Czech Enterprises. *The World Bank Economic Review*, *14*(1), 49–64. doi:10.1093/wber/14.1.49

Doing Business in the Russian Federation. (2016). Retrieved September 26, 2016 from http://www.doingbusiness.org/data/exploreeconomies/~/media/giawb/doing%20business/documents/profiles/country/RUS.pdf?ver=3

Dunning, J. (1988, March). The eclectic paradigm of international production: A restatement and some possible extensions. *Journal of International Business Studies, 19*(1), 1–31. doi:10.1057/palgrave.jibs.8490372

Dunning, J. (1998). Location and the multinational enterprise: A neglected factor? *Journal of International Business Studies, 29*(1), 45–66. doi:10.1057/palgrave.jibs.8490024

Federal State Statistics Service. (2016). Retrieved September 26, 2016 from http://www.gks.ru/wps/wcm/connect/rosstat_main/rosstat/en/main/

Hill, C. W., & Hult, G. T. (2017). *International Business: Competing in the Global Marketplace* (11th ed.). Irwin/McGraw-Hill.

Hochberg, N., Klick, J., & Reilly, E. (2015). What companies have learned from losing billions in emerging markets. *Harvard Business Review*. Available at https://hbr.org/2015/09/what-companies-have-learned-from-losing-billions-in-emerging-markets

Hoskisson, R., Eden, L., Lau, C., & Wright, M. (2000). Strategy in emerging economies. *Academy of Management Journal, 43*(3), 249–267. 39

Ietto-Gillies, G. (2012). Transnational Corporations and International Production: Concepts, Theories and Effects (2nd ed.). London: Edward Elgar Publishing. Retrieved from http://www.e-elgar.com/shop/transnational-corporations-and-international-production?___website=uk_warehouse

IMD World Competitiveness Yearbook. (n.d.). Retrieved June 14, 2016, from http://www.imd.org/wcc/research-methodology/

KAMAZ. (2016). Retrieved August 28, 2016 from http://kamaz.ru/en/

Knickerbocker, F. (1973, Spring). Oligopolistic reaction and multinational enterprise. *Thunderbird International Business Review, 15*(2), 7–9.

London, T., & Hart, S. (2004). Reinventing strategies for emerging markets: Beyond the transnational model. *Journal of International Business Studies, 35*(5), 350–370. doi:10.1057/palgrave.jibs.8400099

Makino, S., Isobe, T., & Chan, C. M. (2004). Does country matter? *Strategic Management Journal, 25*(10), 1027–1043. doi:10.1002/smj.412

National Framework. (2016). *United Nations Conference on Trade and Development (UNCTAD)*. Retrieved June 9, 2016, from http://unctad.org/en/Pages/DIAE/National-Framework.aspx

Rugman, A., & Verbeke, A. (2004). A perspective on regional and global strategies of multinational enterprises. *Journal of International Business Studies, 35*(1), 3–18. doi:10.1057/palgrave.jibs.8400073

Russia 2013: Shaping Russia's Future. (n.d.). Retrieved May 12, 2015, from Ernst & Young Attractiveness Survey website: http://www.ey.com/Publication/vwLUAssets/2013-Russia-attractiveness-survey-Eng/$FILE/2013-Russia-attractiveness-survey-Eng.pdf

Russia 2015 Statistical Pocketbook (Statistical Pocketbook). (2015). Retrieved May 28, 2016, from http://www.gks.ru/free_doc/doc_2015/rus15_eng.pdf

Russia. (2016, April 29). *European Commission.* Retrieved June 3, 2016, from http://ec.europa.eu/trade/policy/countries-and-regions/countries/russia/

Russia Country Commercial Guide. (2015, October 16). Retrieved May 29, 2016, from http://www.export.gov/ccg/russia090879.asp

Russia: Country Profile. (2016, April 15). Retrieved June 9, 2016, from Global Market Information Database (GMID/Euromonitor/Passport).

Russia, Country Profile. (2016). *Euromonitor/Passport.* Retrieved April 30, 2016 from http://www.euromonitor.com/russia-country-profile/report

Russia: Economic Report: The Long Journey to Recovery. (2016, April). *World Bank Group,* (35). Retrieved May 29, 2016, from http://www.worldbank.org/eca/pubs/rer35_ENG.pdf

Russia Investment Climate Statement 2016. (n.d.). U.S. Department of State. Retrieved July 9, 2016, from http://www.state.gov/e/eb/rls/othr/ics/investmentclimatestatements/index.htm#wrapper

Russia. Special Report. (2016). *The Economist.* Retrieved November 13, 2016, from http://www.economist.com/printedition/2016-10-22

Russia's Muslim Regions Turn to the Gulf for Help. (2016). *STRATFOR.* Retrieved July 18, 2016 from https://www.stratfor.com/analysis/russias-muslim-regions-turn-gulf-help?utm_source=paidlist-a&utm_medium=email&utm_campaign=07/18/2016&utm_content=Daily+Intelligence+Brief%3A-+July+18%2C+2016&id=be1ddd5371&uuid=e05332c9-d7fd-449e-9a97-4c4ce2d9b8bf

Russian Investment Agency. (2016). Retrieved September 10, 2016 from http://invest-rf.com/

Santangelo, G., & Meyer, K. (2011). Extending the internationalization process model: Increases and decreases of MNE commitment in emerging economies. *Journal of International Business Studies, 42*(7), 894–909. doi:10.1057/jibs.2011.25

Schwab, K. (n.d.). The Global Competitiveness Report 2015–2016. *Insight Report.* Retrieved June 11, 2016, from http://www3.weforum.org/docs/gcr/2015-2016/Global_Competitiveness_Report_2015-2016.pdf

Shenkar, O. (2004). One more time: International business in a global economy. *Journal of International Business Studies, 35*(2), 161–171. doi:10.1057/palgrave.jibs.8400074

Smith, A. (1776). *An Inquiry into the Nature and Causes of the Wealth of Nations.* Library of Economics and Liberty. Retrieved November 7, 2016 from http://www.econlib.org/library/Smith/smWN.html

Special Economic Zones of the Russian Federation. (2011). Retrieved September 25, 2016 from http://www.ved.gov.ru/eng/investing/sez/

St. Petersburg International Economic Forum. (2016). Retrieved September 11, 2016 from https://www.forumspb.com/en

The International Organization of Motor Vehicle Manufacturers. (2016). Retrieved September 26, 2016 from http://www.oica.net/

The Russian Evolution: How can foreign businesses prepare to prosper?. (2013). Retrieved April 15, 2016, from https://www.pwc.com/us/en/forensic-services/publications/assets/marketmap-russia.pdf

U.S. Commercial Service in Russia. (2016). Retrieved September 26, 2016 from http://2016.export.gov/russia/

Vernon, R. (1966). International investment and international trade in the product life cycle. *The Quarterly Journal of Economics*, *80*(May), 190–207. doi:10.2307/1880689

World Factbook Russia. (2016). Retrieved May 29, 2016, from https://www.cia.gov/library/publications/the-world-factbook/geos/rs.html

World Investment Report. (2016). *Russian Federation Country Fact Sheet 2016*. Retrieved June 8, 2016, from http://unctad.org/en/Pages/DIAE/World Investment Report/Country-Fact-Sheets.aspx

Zhuplev, A. (2008, January). Economic Internationalization of Russia: Roots, Trends, and Scenarios. *International Political Science Review*, *29*(1), 99–119. doi:10.1177/0192512107083449

Zhuplev, A. (2016). *Doing business in Russia: a Concise Guide*. Retrieved from http://www.businessexpertpress.com/authors/anatoly-zhuplev

Zhuplev, A., & Shtykhno, D. (2015). Energy and Sustainability in the European Region: The Russian Factor. In Handbook of Research on Sustainable Development and Economics. IGI Global.

KEY TERMS AND DEFINITIONS

Capital Flight: A large-scale exodus of financial assets and capital from a nation due to political or economic instability, currency devaluation, the imposition of capital controls or other negative impacts, uncertainties and risks. Capital flight may be legal, as is the case when foreign investors repatriate capital back to their home country, or illegal, which occurs in economies with capital controls that restrict the transfer of assets out of the country.

FDI Drivers and Dynamics: Investment decisions are motivated by strategic benefits, costs, and risks. A decision in a pursuit or refrain of FDI rests on a balance of potential pros and cons associated with this decision. Major financial drivers associated with FDI are profitability and return in investment. In a broader context, FDI-related decisions often integrate such factors as global market share, branding, competitiveness, and other. An interaction between investor's FDI activities and business environment in the host country creates FDI patterns, trends and outcomes collectively categorized as FDI dynamics.

FDI Regulatory Framework (UNCTAD): The United Nations Conference on Trade and Development (UNCTAD) regulatory framework for FDI in a country or economy include the following key components: Corporate law, including accounting and reporting regulations; Incentives for, and restrictions on, FDI, Forms of establishment mergers and acquisitions; Securities; Taxation (mainly corporate and individual income tax); Transfer of technology; and Industrial/intellectual property.

Industry/Sectorial FDI Composition: Industry/sectorial FDI composition in the large and diverse Russian economy is an important characteristic showing a distribution of FDI flows and stock across economic sectors and industries.

Pragmatic Nationalism: Pragmatic nationalism is an attitude toward FDI exercised by a host (recipient) country government. It is driven by a selective approach in facilitating FDI inflows to the benefit of their domestic industries, regions, social groups, or top priority political and personal interests. Realizing the benefits of incoming FDI for socio-economic development and growth, pragmatic nationalist governments pursue policies designed to maximize benefits and minimize costs associated with incoming FDI. According to this view, FDI should be allowed only if the benefits in their entirety outweigh the costs.

Regional FDI Composition: Regional FDI Composition in the large and regionally diverse Russia is an important characteristic showing a distribution of FDI flows and stock across economic regions.

Round Tripping: Round-tripping, also known as round-trip transactions, is a form of barter that involves a company selling "an unused asset to another company, while at the same time agreeing to buy back the same or similar assets at about the same price." In international scenarios, round tripping is used for tax evasion and money laundering, often involving offshore banking centers.

Russian Investment Agency: Federal Russian Investment Agency "Invest in Russia" has a mission to facilitate incoming foreign investments. Prior to the establishment of the Agency there was no single framework integrating all regional development corporations across Russia (there are 85 federal subjects in Russia). The Agency became a federal level platform for the "investors –regions" cooperation and a tool to provide support for foreign companies in entering the Russian market. The main task of the Agency is to function as a single customer center, which serves for foreign investors as a source of relevant information about the investment potential of the Russian regions, ongoing projects, success stories, new investment opportunities.

ENDNOTES

1 Authors express gratitude to Ekaterina Sheliga, MBA Research Assistant at the College of Business Administration, Loyola Marymount University, for her outstanding editorial support.

2 A reference to the Mao quote, "If you open the window, some flies naturally get in" can serve as an illustration for this type of ideological attitudes toward foreign influences in a host country.

3 A recent example of this kind was an imposition of countersanctions on some western countries' imports and incoming investments by Russian government in response to western sanctions on Russia following conflicts around Ukraine, and some other developments in the Russian "near abroad". Russian countersanctions have had negative impacts on Russia and western countries.

4 Two authoritative methodological frameworks and competitiveness rankings are published in the annual Global Competitiveness Report by the Swiss based World Economic Forum and the World Competitiveness Yearbook (WCY) by the Swiss-based IMD World Competitiveness Center. The Global Competitiveness Report's framework (Schwab, 2016) incorporates 12 criteria ("pillars") of competitiveness organized into 3 groups of factors weighted in their overall impact on competitiveness: 4 pillars in the Basic Requirements category (30.2/100% weight), 6 pillars in the Efficiency Enhancers category (50/100% weight), and 2 pillars in the Innovation and Sophistication category (19.8/100% weight). The WCY competitiveness framework divides the national environment into four main factors: Economic Performance, Government Efficiency, Business Efficiency, and Infra-

structure. In turn, each of these factors is divided into 5 sub-factors which highlight every facet of the areas analyzed. Altogether, the World Competitiveness Yearbook features 20 such sub-factors (IMD World Competitiveness Center, 2016)

5 Most sectors of the Russian economy are open to foreign investment, though there are ownership restrictions in strategic sectors. The Strategic Sectors Law (FZ-57) stipulates 45 activities for which foreign investment requires government approval (see Limits on Foreign Control below). Foreign ownership in air transportation, financial services, insurance, media, and agricultural land is also restricted.

6 Two of these Russian federal subjects until recently were part of Ukraine.

7 Each federal district is administered by a Presidential envoy. Federal districts' envoys serve as liaisons between the federal subjects and the federal government and are primarily responsible for overseeing the compliance of the federal subjects with the federal laws.

8 Economic regions and their parts sharing common economic trends are in turn grouped into economic zones and macro zones.

9 Each military district operates under the command of the district headquarters, headed by the district commander, and is subordinated to the General Staff of the Armed Forces of the Russian Federation.

10 National Investment Agency "Invest in Russia" was established in December 2013 under the auspices of the Ministry of Regional Development of the Russian Federation and in cooperation with the World Association of Investment Agencies (WAIPA). From May 1st, 2014 the Agency operates under the new name – Russian Investment Agency "Invest in Russia." Its primary objectives are attracting foreign investment in the Russian economy by facilitating foreign investors in entering the Russian market and promotion of investment opportunities and business image of Russia by the efficient system of communication and interaction with the international investment community. Working closely with regional investment agencies, the Agency creates a platform for "investor -region" interaction at the federal level as well as forms a unique center of information on all regions, ongoing projects and investors interested in projects in the Russian Federation. The main task of the Agency is to function as a single Customer Center, which serves for foreign investors as a source of extensive information about the investment potential of Russian regions, ongoing projects, new investment opportunities, as well as a tool to create favorable conditions for foreign companies to enter the Russian market. More information about the Agency and its functions and services can be obtained at http://invest-rf.com/.

11 In 1914 the name of the city was changed from Saint Petersburg to Petrograd (Петроград), in 1924 to Leningrad (Ленинград), and in 1991, back to Saint Petersburg. Currently, the Greater St. Petersburg area is comprised of two administrative-economic entities: the city of St. Petersburg and Leningrad oblast/region named after Vladimir Lenin that retains its name to date.

12 Vedomosti, 26.03.2015

13 Strategy for the socio-economic development of St. Petersburg till 2030. St. Petersburg, 2014.

14 Transforming Russia automotive industry: from recovery to growth. BCG, 2013.

15 Russia's Incredibly Shrinking Auto Industry. Forbes, May, 10, 2016.

16 Russia's Incredibly Shrinking Auto Industry. Forbes, May, 10, 2016.

17 AvtoVAZ (Russian: АвтоВАЗ) is the Russian automobile manufacturer formerly known as VAZ: Volzhsky Avtomobilny Zavod (ВАЗ, Во́лжский автомоби́льный заво́д, or Volga Automobile Plant), but better known to the world under the trade name Lada. The current company name is

"AvtoVAZ". AvtoVAZ's majority owner is Alliance Rostec Auto BV with 74.5%, which is a joint venture of the Renault-Nissan Alliance with 67.1% and Russian company Rostec with the remainder. AvtoVAZ produces nearly one million cars a year. The VAZ factory is the largest car manufacturer in Russia and Eastern Europe and one of the largest in the world, with over 90 miles (140 km) of production lines; it is unique in that most of the components for the cars are made in-house. The company was established in the late 1960s in cooperation with Fiat as a collaboration between Italy and the Soviet Union and built on the banks of the Volga River in 1966.

18 www.avtovaz.com

19 KAMAZ Group of Companies is the largest automobile corporation in the Russian Federation. KAMAZ PTC ranks 11-th among the world's leading heavy duty truck producers. February 16-th 1976 witnessed the first truck produced on the banks of the Kama River roll off the assembly line of the Truck Assembly Plant. The Year 1988 had seen the one millionth truck come off the final assembly line of the Truck Assembly Plant since production began. In February 2008, the final assembly line of KAMAZ-Diesel OJSC turned out the 2.5-millionth engine. On February15-th 2012, KAMAZ produced its 2-millionth truck. By mid-December 2015, KAMAZ Truck Assembly Plant had built more than 2 million 170 thousand finished trucks since production began (KAMAZ, 2016).

20 2016 Russian Oil & Gas Outlook Survey, Deloitte.

21 Ibid.

22 2016 Russian Oil & Gas Outlook Survey, Deloitte.

23 The company web site: http://www.gazprom.com/

Chapter 10
Trade and FDI Between the Czech Republic and Portugal:
Analysis of the 2000–2015 Period

Lenka Novotná
University of Aveiro, Portugal

Inês Martins
University of Aveiro, Portugal

António Carrizo Moreira
University of Aveiro, Portugal

ABSTRACT

With the collapse of communism, some former communist States of Eastern Europe managed to muddle through their way to a market economy and entered the European Union. This brought about the acceleration of Foreign Direct Investment (FDI) among the European economies and accelerated the globalization process. Although there is plenty of research on FDI and trade among countries, the aim of this chapter is to analyze how trade between Portugal and the Czech Republic have evolved over form 2000 until 2015. The chapter seeks to complement previous studies on FDI and trade as Portugal and the Czech Republic are part of the European Union, but have had different historical, cultural, and economic paths. The main conclusion of the chapter is that trade between both countries has grown significantly. The main reason affecting trade between both countries is the economic unrest Portugal has been through since 2008.

INTRODUCTION

Although FDI and the analysis of trade have been extensively researched among scholars, as well as their effects for both home and host countries, far less attention has been placed on how countries that historically had hardly any trade between them – as they belonged to different economic blocs – have evolved over time, as is the case of the Czech Republic and Portugal, that entered the European Union

DOI: 10.4018/978-1-5225-2345-1.ch010

(EU) in, 2004 and 1986, respectively. As such the purpose of this article is to analyze the commercial trade between the Czech Republic and Portugal between 2000 and 2015, who are the main players participating in this process, and how this has impacted on the Czech firms investing in Portugal and on Portuguese firms investing in the Czech Republic.

The chapter begins with the literature review on Foreign Direct Investment (FDI) and on how Czech firms have managed to internationalize. Afterwards, it is presented a brief presentation of both countries, Portugal and the Czech Republic, economically and culturally. For this the chapter contextualizes the analysis based on the EU context. The third section contains the main factors of trade. The fourth and fifth sections compare both countries historically and economically and evaluate both countries with an analysis of the evolution of the mutual trade during 15 years. Within the analysis two main events are introduced: 2004, when the Czech Republic joined the EU and 2008, when the global economic crisis started. The sixth section presents the main Czech companies operating and investing in Portugal and the main Portuguese companies operating and investing in the Czech Republic. The final section presents the conclusions.

BACKGROUND

Studies about international trade, internationalization and FDI are abundant. Analyzing how the theories about internationalization have evolved, Ribau, Moreira, and Raposo (2015) conclude that for decades theories analyzed how trade and FDI between countries occurred. Subsequently, there was a huge focus on multinational firms, and only after the 1980s onwards focus on internationalization shifted to Small and Medium-sized firms (SMEs) and how important they are to international business.

International trade can be defined as the exchange of goods and services that connect people, businesses, and countries along international borders in global processes of production and consumption influencing, directly and indirectly, the way everybody lives live.

As a result of international trade, FDI has become one of the most significant factors for economic development, as it allows the international flow of goods among countries, enabling the recovery and / or modernization of the economies (Razin & Sadka, 2007). FDI is one of the results and, at the same time, one of the major drivers of international trade, where multinational and small and medium-sized enterprises (SMEs) started to play a leading role.

FDI allows not only the flow of goods but also the creation of jobs. One consequence of this increasing flow of FDI is that countries seek to implement economic policy measures to attract investment flows (Chenaf-Nicet & Ronjier, 2016). Moreover, as FDI embodies technology and know-how, there are potential benefits that are not very explicitly exposed as technology transfers, productivity gains, managerial and know-how transfers, and access to broader markets (Blomström & Kokko, 1998).

Hanson (2001) supports that FDI generates positive spillovers for host countries. However, Lipsey (2002) finds that there is no consistent relation between the size of inward FDI and GDP or growth. Markusen and Venables (1999) defend that FDI could harm local industry.

Moreira (2008) defends that there are positive effects from FDI as there are positive technology accumulation among SMEs supplying their multinational clients. Görg and Greenway (2004) support that spillovers from foreign to domestically owned firms are mostly negative. Although there appears to be no consensus among scholar about the externalities of FDI, most countries are looking forward to increasing their international trade, as well as their share of FDI activities.

The lack of policy making supporting the internationalization of SMEs led Moini, Kalouda, and Tesar (2008) to propose that government policy makers in the Czech Republic need to understand the necessary linkages between their SMEs foreign market entry modes and the country's future economic growth. For the Czech Republic to improve its economic status in the European Union, it is mandatory to support Czech SMEs in order to underpin their competitiveness in the global marketplace.

Fink, Harms, and Kraus (2008) conclude that 40% of Czech firms enter the German market, followed by the Slovakian market (12%), and the Polish market (11%). Taking into account the different language skills of the old and new generations in the Czech Republic – as the older generation was used to learn only Russian as a second language and the new generation is more akin of learning English or German – they claim that the greatest obstacle for firms to penetrate in foreign markets is the language barrier (Fink, Harms, & Kraus, 2008), as German was selected as the most popular language in terms of international trade in this study, which might explain why Germany is the largest and the most attractive neighbor for the Czechs. Fink, Harms, and Kraus (2008) conclude that that self-commitment is particularly important in international business cooperation, as self-commitment positively influences the performance of both cooperating firms. As such trust-based relationships in the firms' internationalization process is a promising alternative particularly for SMEs.

Musteen and Datta (2011), when analyzing how Czech manufacturing SMEs learn about foreign markets, reinforce the importance of role of knowledge of prospective managers when developing a good understanding of the international markets. The better the improved understanding of the main factors to compete in foreign markets, the better entrepreneurs and SME managers perform in international markets.

Based on a qualitative study among entrepreneurs in the Saxon-Czech border area, Zanger, Hodicová, and Gaus (2008) conclude that entrepreneurs on both sides of the border experience feelings of foreignness towards the corresponding neighboring country, which limits the entrepreneurs' willingness to cooperate with companies from the neighboring country.

Cieślik, Michałek, Michałek, and Mycielski (2015) investigated the determinants of export activity comparing firms from the Baltic States and Central European Countries for three years: 2002, 2005, and 2009. They conclude that the results for both groups of countries are not different as firms' export performance was positively related to the level of productivity, firm size, the share of university graduates in productive employment, investment on R&D activities, and the internalization of firms measured by foreign ownership. Moreover, there are some differences among countries, namely the level of productivity was significant for the Czech Republic. Similarly, they also conclude that it would be advisable to formulate policy recommendations for the development of export promotion strategies as export performance could be improved by attracting export-oriented FDI, which can generate positive spillovers to domestic firms.

Based on the analysis of data collected in interviews with managers and founders of 67 Czech entrepreneurs, Zapletalová (2012) concludes that most of the firms follow a typical stage approach of outward internationalization. Moreover, very few firms follow the "rapid internationalization" approach followed by born-globals, which is a clear indication that internationalization is still a leapfrogging process for most SMEs. Based on the analysis of questionnaire-based research that involved 297, Zapletalová (2015) concludes that the historical context of centrally planned economy in the Czech Republic until 1989 is still affecting negatively the internationalization process of Czech firms, as their degree and level of internationalization is still significantly low.

The lack of language skills of key employees before entering foreign markets, the lack of employee experience with foreign market expansion, the time that elapses between the opening of the business and foreign market expansion, the lack of explicit objectives for export activities, the unclear definition of the strategy to be implemented abroad, and the lack of clear market segment focus are the main difficulties of Czech SMEs when expanding abroad (Kubíčková & Procházková, 2014).

According to Moini, Kalouda, and Tesar (2008), when compared to their non-exporting counterparts, exporting SMEs in the Czech Republic (a) tend to be larger, and more motivated in systematically exploring export opportunities, (b) utilize a larger percentage of their production capacity, and (c) have fewer problems in obtaining financial services. Exporting firms tend to face three major challenges when embracing international business activities: a financial burden, unknown foreign marketing practices, and locating prospective clients.

Símová (2010) follows an inward internationalization perspective and studied how the retailing industry in the Czech Republic went through dramatic changes from the early 1990s to mid-2000s. She concludes that there have been dramatic changes, quantitatively and qualitatively, as the Czech retailing industry has achieved a relatively high level of concentration and internationalization, as many international firms entered the Czech market.

Foreign direct investment in Portugal was analyzed by Moreira and Dias (2008), who concluded that Portugal went through several phases, and FDI skyrocketed since Portugal joined the EU.

The literature on internationalization of Portuguese SMEs is also abundant. For example, Lisboa, Skarmeas, and Lages (2011) explore the importance of innovation as a means for developing firm-specific advantages abroad. Moreira and Alves (2016) claim that internationalization is difficult for SMEs even when small psychic distances between countries are present. Carvalheira and Moreira (2016) support the idea that even artisanal firms can internationalize when opportunities arise. However, no single study was found regarding Portuguese SMEs internationalizing to the Czech Republic.

One can conclude that, on the one hand, the perspective towards FDI is multifaceted and, on the other hand, that there is no single study regarding foreign direct investment or trade analyzing how Portugal and the Czech Republic are interrelated. Moreover, the studies on Czech SMEs are almost unanimous referring the difficulties in internationalizing.

BRIEF PRESENTATION OF THE CZECH REPUBLIC ECONOMY

The Czech Republic is a small central European country (about 79,000 km^2). As of 2015, it had around 10.5 million inhabitants (EuroStat, 2016a). The Czech currency is the Czech Koruna (CZK) and the GDP in 2015 was €163,948 million (€16,600/per capita) (Countryeconomy.com, 2016). The country's human development index (HDI) (used by the United Nations to measure the progress of a country), was 0.870 points in 2014. As such, the Czech Republic is in the 28th place among 188 countries (CountryEconomy.com, 2016). The Czech Republic holds the 36th position of the Doing Business ranking (The World Bank, 2016).

After joining the EU in 2004, the Czech economy has continuously grown. However, this significant boost was affected by the economic crisis in 2008 and although the Czech economy has recovered quite fast, it has not been able to follow up with the previous, pre-crisis pace. Since joining the EU, the rate of the Czech export within the EU has doubled (81% from all the export) and the surplus of the trade has quintupled. The Czech Republic's main import and export partners are Germany, Slovakia and Poland. Although the Czech and German industries are strongly linked, the Czech economy is very dependent on the German one. Since joining the EU, the Czech Republic has been considered as a recipient of foreign direct investment from the EU. In comparison with the other Central European countries, the Czech Republic has the strongest share of Foreign Direct Investments inflows (Rusnok, 2014).

According the Eurocentrum Praha seminar, that was held in December of 2014 and where were discussed among others the economic models that would be the most suitable for the Czech Republic, Mr. Ales Chmelar – the Chief Economist at the European Section of the Czech Office of Government – presented various forecasts of economic development, which echoed since 1989. The development of the Czech economy was, as mentioned above, primarily influenced by inflow of foreign investment. The inflow peaked around the time of the entry into the EU in 2004. However, after the last economic crisis broke out, the Czech economy felt a steep fall in 2008. As such, the main objective of the Czech economic policies is the support of a long-term productivity growth (Government of the Czech Republic, 2015).

According to the Economic and Financial Affairs of the European Commission from 2015, the Czech economy returned to growth in 2014, following two years of contraction, and unemployment has been on a declining trend. The return to growth has been largely driven by domestic demand, with investment growing particularly strongly.

The Czech Republic's public finance outturns have improved markedly, but some issues remain in the areas of taxation, fiscal sustainability, and fiscal framework. The country continues to suffer from a relatively high level of tax evasion, although efforts are being made to fight this problem.

There is an overall high level of employment but certain disadvantaged groups remain underrepresented in the labor market. These groups include parents with young children, low-skilled workers, people with disabilities and gypsies.

The general government deficit has improved significantly since 2009 and the Czech public finances do not appear to face sustainability risks in the short term.

Real GDP growth is expected to strengthen further in 2016, although developments in the external environment might have a negative effect (European Commission, 2015).

BRIEF PRESENTATION OF THE PORTUGUESE ECONOMY

Portugal is a small country (around 92,000 km^2) situated on the West coast of Europe. Its territory includes two autonomous regions: Azores and Madeira. It is one of the oldest countries in the world. Portugal has a population of around 10.3 million inhabitants (EuroStat, 2016a). Portugal's currency is the Euro (€). The country's GDP (nominal) in 2014 was of €174,385 million (€16,800/per capita). The service sector is the main contributor to the economy.

The human development index (HDI) (used by the United Nations to measure the progress of a country) was 0.830 points in 2014, 43rd place out of 187 countries. As for the Doing Business Ranking, Portugal occupies the 23rd place (The World Bank, 2016).

The majority of Portugal's commercial trade and foreign direct investment flow happens within the European Union. In 2015, 72.7% of exported goods and 76.4% of imported goods were traded with UE countries. Spain, Germany, and France stand out as the main partners both in terms of imports and exports. Regarding foreign direct investment, the Netherlands and Spain represent both the biggest percentage of inflow and outflow (AICEP, 2016a).

Regarding the most recent members (Bulgaria, Slovakia, Slovenia, Estonia, Hungary, Latvia, Lithuania, Poland, Czech Republic, and Romania), despite the increases caused by their entry in the European

Union, they still account for a small part of Portugal's imports and exports (INE, 2008). The Czech Republic and Poland stand out as the main partners amongst this group.

The Portuguese economy has been severely affected by the international economic crisis. However, from 2008 to 2013, it has shown visible signs of international dynamic. Commercial trade and foreign direct investment have both increased. In 2013, exports surpassed imports for the first time in this period, forming 40% of the GDP (€67,000 million in goods and services). Spain, Germany, France, Angola, and the United Kingdom, Portugal's most important partners have seen their percentage in the total export/import reduced (see Table 1), which suggests a tendency to look for new markets.

Portugal has been increasing its investments in foreign countries, although it remains a bigger receiver than investor. As of 2012, Portugal occupied the 9th place amongst the UE27 countries in the FDI intensity index (INE, 2014).

Portuguese technological companies have also developed cooperative actions: 96% of them with national partners, 45% with UE27 partners and 9% with the USA (INE, 2014).

THE MAIN FACTORS OF TRADE

In order to understand trade between Portugal and the Czech Republic, it is important first to understand the common market these countries are part of. Both countries have joined the European Union, Portugal in 1986 and the Czech Republic in 2004. This allows for both countries, as well as all countries in the single EU market, to take advantage of the free circulation of goods, capital, people, and services. It also allows goods to travel internally without being subject to customs duties, discriminatory taxes or import quotas. Investment is also made easier.

Table 1. Percentage of Portugal's biggest partners in the total imported/exported goods

Country	2008	2009	2010	2011	2012	2013	2014	2015
% of Total Exported Goods								
Spain	27.9	27.2	27.0	24.9	22.5	23.6	23.5	25.0
Germany	12.8	13.0	13.0	13.5	12.4	11.6	11.7	11.8
France	11.8	12.4	12.0	12.2	11.8	11.6	11.7	12.1
Angola	5.8	7.1	5.1	5.4	6.6	6.6	6.6	4.2
United Kingdom	5.5	5.6	5.5	5.2	5.3	5.5	6.1	6.7
Total	63.8	65.3	62.6	61.2	58.6	58.9	59.6	59.8
% of Total Imported Goods								
Spain	30.8	32.8	32.1	32.3	32.0	32.3	32.6	32.8
Germany	13.4	13.2	13.9	12.3	11.4	11.4	12.3	12.9
France	8.1	8.3	7.2	6.8	6.6	6.8	7.1	7.4
Angola	5.4	5.8	5.7	5.4	5.2	5.2	2.7	1.9
Netherlands	4.7	5.3	5.1	4.8	4.8	5.0	5.1	5.1
Total	62.4	65.4	64.0	61.6	60.0	60.7	59.8	60.1

Source: Own preparation based on data from National Institute of Statistics (INE).

The Eurozone was created in 1999 (although not all member states joined) introducing a common currency, the Euro (€). This common currency eliminates fluctuations in the exchange rate providing predictability and safety and reducing transaction costs, which facilitates trade and capital movement. However, the Eurozone also has its disadvantages; the economy of a particular country might influence buyers and investors on their decision to buy Euro, thus affecting the Euro exchange rate (Geoghegan, 2014). While Portugal joined the Eurozone, the Czech Republic did not, which is a factor that surely affects trade between the two countries, which will be explored later on.

Various factors affect trade in Europe. While the EU facilitates trade, its member States do not all trade equally amongst themselves. Factors like direction of trade, distance, population, language, legal origins, currency, physical infrastructures, borders, and transport efficiency have an impact on trade between certain countries (Hanousek & Kočenda, 2014). As part of the analysis regarding goods, parts and components, capital goods, and consumer goods, this chapter summarizes them below, noting which factors may influence the trade between Portugal and the Czech Republic.

The direction of trade does matter and we reject the hypothesis of a zero effect. (…) The trade links among the old EU members have been long established (…). The majority of the trade flows in parts and components within the EU is carried along the East–West alignment, as is trade in capital and consumer goods. (Hanousek & Kočenda, 2014, p. 19)

The fact that most of Portugal's trade is carried out with old EU members can be explained by this factor. Commercial trade with its neighbors has been happening for a long time, and they are its biggest partners. Regarding the trade between Portugal and the Czech Republic, it is hard to understand to which extent this tendency affects trade; while Portugal does tend to import more from, than export to, the Czech Republic, the numbers are not so different as to confirm this trend.

Distance negatively affects trade in all four types of goods. (…) However, the economic significance of distance is relatively low. (Hanousek & Kočenda, 2014, p. 15)

While the geographic proximity of European countries is not very significant, it is important to note that most of Portugal's trade (within the EU) is with the countries closest to it like Spain; and Germany and France for the Czech's trade. This can lead us to believe that (cultural and geographic) distance might be one of the factors that explain the low levels of trade amongst the two countries.

Population as a factor exhibits a positive effect on all types of goods. The combined populations of the country pairs represent the size of the market. (Hanousek & Kočenda, 2014, p. 16)

Portugal and the Czech Republic have a similar number of inhabitants, around 10 million. While not the smallest, each country definitely has a small internal market. The sizes of both markets are one of the strongest reasons responsible for such a small interest in doing business with each other. Small markets can be often unattractive, especially in comparison with the bigger – in this case also closer – markets (Spain and Germany for example) that can provide economies of scale.

A common language does not seem to matter excessively for European trade, (Hanousek & Kočenda, 2014, p. 16), which is understandable as in the European context there is a large number of different languages and companies deal mostly in English with their European partners.

The effect of a common currency is largely statistically significant, but its economic impact is limited. (Hanousek & Kočenda, 2014, p. 17)

While Portugal adhered to the Eurozone, the Czech Republic did not. This means trade is subject to exchange rates, which can also influence the exchange of goods between the two countries. According to the statistics of the CNB (Czech National Bank) from 2015, the Czech Koruna since 2000 has been significantly strengthening against both Euro (see Table 2) and US Dollar (Mrázek, 2015). The effect of the exchange rate on businesses can depend on several factors, like elasticity of demand, economic growth in other countries, percentage of raw materials imported, reason of an appreciation/depreciation, inflation or fixed contracts (Pettinger, 2013).

The factor of hard physical infrastructure exhibits the lowest coefficients when compared with the rest of the infrastructure measures. (…) High level of physical infrastructure is (…) taken as a standard, despite existing differences between old and new EU countries. (Hanousek & Kočenda, 2014, p. 17)

European countries are generally equipped with good infrastructures. Portugal is equipped with one of the most developed road networks in Europe, 14,310 km long (in the mainland, of which 2,988 km are highways), a railway 2,544 km long, 15 airports (a high number due to the many islands of Azores and Madeira) and 20 ports (AICEP, 2016a).

The Czech Republic possesses one of the most advanced transport networks in Central and Eastern Europe. Its geographical position at the very centre of Europe makes it a natural crossroads for major transit corridors. An extensive network of transport routes serves not only the Czech Republic but also links the country to neighbouring and other European states, and the density of the transport network ranks the Czech Republic among the world's most advanced countries. (CzechInvest, 2013)

The Czech Republic features 9,435 km of railway, 10 airports and 127,693 km of highways.

ICT [Information and communications technology] exerts the most influence on trade in parts and components and in capital goods. (Hanousek & Kočenda, 2014, p. 17)

Table 2. CZK/EUR exchange rate: annual average

Year	2000	2002	2004	2006	2008	2010	2011	2012	2013	2014
CZK/EUR Exchange Rate	35.61	30.81	31.90	28.34	24.94	25.29	24.59	25.14	25.97	27.53

Source: Own preparation based on data from the Czech Statistical Office.

According to the ICT development index, which monitors and compares developments in information and communication technology across countries, Portugal (49th) and the Czech Republic (38th) are above the global average, while not reaching the European average (International Telecommunication Union, 2014). The two countries rank extremely close to each other. Considering parts and components are some of the most traded goods between both countries, this factor might be quite influential.

Border and transport efficiency is the most influential factor for trade in primary and consumer goods. (Hanousek & Kočenda, 2014, p. 18)

Shipping by sea has always been one of the most important means of transport that the goods exchange has been dependent on. In our case, this plays an inherent role for the Czech-Portuguese trade. The closest Czech ports are either Hamburg, Germany or Naples, Italy, which obviously makes shipping more complicated for the Czechs.

The effect of the business and regulatory environment is quite pronounced for the trade flows of primary goods. (Hanousek & Kočenda, 2014, p. 18)

This factor refers to indicators of irregular payments, favoritism, government transparency, and measures to combat corruption. The transparency index published, which measures how corrupt each country's public sector is perceived, shows that Portugal and the Czech Republic rank on 28th and on 37th position with similar values (Transparency International, 2016a; 2016b).

Clearly, there is no single factor influencing trade between both countries. However, market size, distance, and border and transport efficiency are the strongest arguments speaking against a bright future of the Czech-Portuguese trade.

COMPARING BOTH COUNTRIES. MAIN SIMILARITIES AND DIFFERENCES

Becoming aware of essential similarities and differences between the Czech Republic and Portugal is important to analyze what opportunities and cultural challenges need to be overcome in order to bring these countries together and stimulate trade. This section summarizes them below.

History

During last century both countries went through difficult times with Portugal being ruled by a right wing dictatorship during part of the century and Czech Republic being ruled by a communist dictatorship after the World War II.

Autocratic regimes suffered the influence of international actors that led Portugal to lose their former colonies, on one side, and the Czech Republic to break free from the tight control exercised by the former Soviet Union. With democracy both countries have managed to enter the European Union, and a process of Europeanization, in which the European Monetary Fund has played an important role in the institutional change and policy adjustments to their European counterparts (Petrovic & Solingen, 2005).

Historically, both countries have followed different paths. The Czech Republic has been part of the Duchy of Bohemia under the great Moravian Empire and afterwards of the Holy Roman Empire. In the sixteenth century it was gradually integrated into the Habsburg Monarchy. In the 1800s the Bohemian kingdom became part of the Austrian Empire. With the collapse of the Austro-Hungarian Empire after the World War I it became the Republic of Czechoslovakia in 1918. After the World War II it fell under the soviet influence until 1989 when the communist regime collapsed. In 1993 Czechoslovakia peacefully dissolved into two independent states: the Czech Republic and Slovakia. In 2004 the Czech Republic entered the European Union.

The Roman Empire had a strong influence in Portugal since the first century b. C. In the fifth century, with the decline of the Roman Empire, Iberia in general was influenced by Germans. In the eighth century Arabs occupied Iberia and Christians run away to the north of Iberia.

In 1139, with the Christian conquest, the Kingdom of Portugal was set up. Since 1297 Portugal is the European country that maintains its original frontiers.

As a result of an outward perspective during the XV and XVI Portugal expanded its borders abroad establishing the first global empire with foothold in Africa, South America, Asia and Oceania.

In 1990 a revolution ended the Portuguese monarchy and the first republic was set up. In 1926, due to social conflicts, a dictatorship was established that lasted until 1974, when a military coup ended the colonial war that was taking place since 1961. In 1986 Portugal entered the European Union (at that time European Economic Community).

The support of an industrial strong foothold allowed the Czech economy to withhold the changes it went through over time. Portugal was more outward oriented building an empire offshore which impeded the creation of an industrial network (Soares, 2015).

Economy

Table 3 summarizes the main economic indicators for both countries. Currently in Portugal there is a structural lack of competitiveness, low levels of cooperation and little flexibility in determining wages and productivity. Foreign investment in Portugal has been low. Although the Portuguese economy has been growing, its growth has been slow. As such, Portugal needs to create jobs, readjust social policies, review labor legislation, and bring academia and the business community closer (Valles, 2015).

Table 3. Comparing the Czech Republic and Portugal

Indicator	Year	Czech Republic	Portugal
GDP at current prices (10^6 €)	2014	154,929	174,384
GDP at current prices (€ per capita)	2014	14,700	16,800
Public Debt (% of GDP)	2013	45.7	128
FDI inflow	2013	4,990 Million USD	6,626 Million EUR
FDI outflow	2013	3,294 Million USD	6,199 Million EUR
Exports (10^6 €)	2014	130,808	48,168
Imports (10^6 €)	2014	114,594	58,708
Trade Balance (10^6 €)	2014	16,172	-10,605
Global Competitiveness Ranking	2016	37th	36th
Doing Business Ranking	2015	36th	23rd

Sources: Own preparation from EuroStat (2016b), INE (2014), CountryEconomy.com (2015; 2016).

Portugal and the Czech Republic present the same value in the Global Competitiveness Ranking (4.5). Taking a closer look to each country's specific evaluation, one can find that Portugal surpasses the Czech Republic in most basic requirements: institutions, infrastructure and health and primary education. It is, however, drastically surpassed by the Czech Republic on the macroeconomic environment requirement, occupying the 128th position compared to the Czech Republic's 40th. Most secondary indicators remain close, except for the financial market development requirement, where Portugal is in 104th place versus the Czech Republic's 44th. Furthermore, the countries also vary in labor market efficiency, with Portugal finding itself in 83rd place versus the Czech Republic's 62nd, and market size. While the domestic market size ranking is close for the two countries, foreign market size ranks Portugal in 48th versus the Czech Republic's 27th (World Economic Forum, 2015a; 2015b).

With a GDP per capita in purchasing power parity similar to Portuguese, the minimum wage in the Czech Republic is of 337€ (9200 Czk). Salaries are on average 30% lower in the Czech Republic than in Portugal. The weight of social security in GDP is around 20%, less 6% of recorded between Portuguese (Valles, 2015).

Although some features and indicators are common, currently there are some aspects that distinguish the situation of both countries, such as Portugal's public debt, which has presented levels above 125% of the GDP (AICEP, 2016a), as opposed to the Czech Republic, which maintains levels below 46% (AICEP, 2016b).

In terms of income of the families, while Portugal presents high levels of inequality in income distribution, the Czech Republic exhibits low inequality. However, both countries presented income in Purchasing Power Parity (PPP) per capita that is only slightly more than half of the EU average (INE, 2005, p. 113, 209).

Between 1995 and 2004, the unit labor costs fell 3.6% among the EU15.

While in the Czech Republic this indicator fell as well, Portugal was among the few European countries that saw these costs increased (INE, 2005, p. 220).

The unsustainability forecast of the social protection system has led the Czech government to a strict management of responsibilities and rights, significantly preventing the escalation of its weight in the economy. The contributions of employers, workers and pensioners are financing the system by about 75%. In Portugal, it does not exceed 45%, requiring of the state an additional effort of 12% of GDP. (Valles, 2015)

The contributions are proportionally higher in the Czech Republic (34% employer and 11% employee) than in Portugal (27% employer and 11% employee) (Valles, 2015).

Regarding education, essential to the economy of a country, while Portugal presented the second highest rate of school dropouts in the European Union (EU 25), 38.6% as of 2005, the Czech Republic had one of the best performances in this area, 4.3%. It also surpassed the EU15 average of the percentage of people aged 20-24 that has completed at least secondary education, topping this list (INE, 2005, p. 92). Czech policies are based on incentives to bring universities closer to business, avoiding scenarios where unemployment of young graduates is alarming. These policies aim to increase added value growth in innovation-driven areas where competitive factors are based on design, innovation, research, and development in an economy that started from a strong industrial base. In 2013, the percentage of 30 to 34 year olds who had completed tertiary education increased significantly in comparison to 2002 in both countries, from 13% to 29.2% in Portugal and 12.6% to 26.7%. In the same year, Portugal and the Czech Republic also registered two of the lowest rates of early school dropouts, 5.4% and 19.2%, respectively. The Czech Republic has fulfilled its 2020 national target for this indicator (EuroStat, 2014).

Regarding investment in research and development, Portugal presented a considerable growth in 2004, staying at a top position. However, the Czech Republic surpassed it regarding the percentage of GDP that this investment represented (INE, 2005).

Although, especially due to the crisis, Portugal belongs between the less developed economies of the EU, its economy is growing linearly with its potential. The significant role in Portuguese economy is held by small and middle enterprises that are involved by 80% on the employment creation and by 60% on the Portuguese export. This feature is obvious also on quite high amount of Portuguese FDI abroad. There is a quite high concentration of enterprises especially on the north of Portugal and then around Lisbon. The south of the country is more agricultural and also touristic.

Portugal's trade balance has been historically negative, although this deficit has been decreasing thanks to a growing dynamic of Portuguese exports (BusinessInfo, 2014). "With a vibrant automotive industry, the Czech Republic has established itself as an open and dynamic market economy" (The Heritage Foundation, 2015). The Czech Republic is also strongly characterized as a mature host country for FDI (CzechInvest, 2016).

The most prospective fields where both counties supplement each other very well are: construction/civil engineering, food industry, banking, telecommunications, car industry and tourism (BusinessInfo, 2014).

FDI

Table 4 shows stock of FDI between Portugal and the Czech Republic Million Dollars at current prices and current Exchange rate, between 2000 and 2015. Table 5 shows the stock of FDI in % of gross domestic product. One of the main conclusions is the difference between inward and outward foreign direct investment has grown faster for the Czech Republic than for Portugal. This means that, as outward FDI (OFDI) is larger in Portugal than in the Czech Republic, the Portuguese economy is more outwardly oriented, whereas the Czech economy is still more inwardly oriented with massive FDI from Holland and Germany.

When one analyzes OFDI from Czech Republic to Portugal, the total amount invested is 613 Million € highly concentrated between 2005 and 2007. However, the OFDI from Portugal to the Czech Republic is only 431 Million throughout 2001 and 2010, as such, it is possible to conclude that FDI between two countries still have a long margin to grow and that trade between both countries is strongly dependent on exporting activities.

Hofstede's Cultural Dimensions

Hofstede's cultural dimensions (Hofstede Centre, 2016a; 2016b) are important to compare both countries in a cultural and business perspective, as shown in Table 6.

Both countries rank extremely close on Power Distance and Indulgence. This means that there is a clear hierarchical order accepted by society in both countries. It also tells us that both societies are relatively restrained in that they respect social norms and do not focus on leisure time as other self-indulgent

Table 4. Stock of FDI, in US million dollars at current prices and current exchange rate

	Outward FDI from Czech Rep.	Outward FDI from CZ to PT	Inward FDI to Czech Rep.	IFDI-OFDI	Outward FDI from Portugal	Outward FDI form PT to CZ	Inward FDI to Portugal	IFDI-OFDI
2000	738	-	21,644	20,906	19,794	-	32,043	12,249
2001	1,136	-	27,092	25,956	22,091	1	38,188	16,097
2002	1,473	-	38,669	37,196	20,730	2	47,117	26,387
2003	2,284	18	45,287	43,003	33,914	147	64,589	30,675
2004	3,760	-	57,259	53,499	43,257	160	71,319	28,062
2005	3,610	167	60,662	57,052	40,927	15	66,697	25,770
2006	5,017	198	79,841	74,824	52,063	14	89,596	37,533
2007	8,557	230	112,408	103,851	67,726	22	119,682	51,956
2008	12,531		113,174	100,643	62,769	10	105,511	42,742
2009	14,805	-	125,827	111,022	66,988	22	118,299	51,311
2010	14,923	-	128,504	113,581	62,286	39	114,994	52,708
2011	13,214	-	120,569	107,355	64,767	-	103,481	38,714
2012	17,368	-	136,493	119,125	59,992	-	115,599	55,607
2013	20,627	-	134,085	113,458	61,960	-	123,727	61,767
2014	19,041	-	121,530	102,489	58,355	-	108,515	50,160

Source: Own preparation based on UNCTAD Database.

Table 5. Stock of FDI as % of the gross domestic product

	Outward FDI from Czech Rep.	Inward FDI to Czech Rep.	Outward FDI from Portugal	Inward FDI to Portugal
2000	1.2	35.21	16.72	27.07
2001	1.69	40.21	18.18	31.42
2002	1.8	47.33	15.44	35.1
2003	2.3	45.61	20.56	39.15
2004	3.16	48.13	22.86	37.7
2005	2.65	44.61	20.74	33.8
2006	3.23	51.44	24.96	42.96
2007	4.53	59.53	28.2	49.83
2008	5.33	48.12	23.96	40.27
2009	7.2	61.16	27.48	48.54
2010	7.21	62.07	26.14	48.26
2011	5.81	53.04	26.45	42.26
2012	8.4	66.02	27.52	53.03
2013	9.88	64.22	27.26	54.43
2014	9.27	59.14	25.15	46.76

Source: Own preparation based on UNCTAD Database.

Table 6. Portugal vs. Czech Republic scores

	Portugal	Czech Republic
Power Distance	63	57
Individualism	27	58
Masculinity	31	57
Uncertainty Avoidance	99	74
Long Term Orientation	28	70
Indulgence	33	29

Source: Own preparation based on data obtained from www.geert-hofstede.com.

countries. This can potentially help business between both countries since they can find a cultural connection and interact better while doing business. A common respect for the rules and the hierarchy of a company, for example, can help build trust and facilitate business.

Individualism, Masculinity and Long Term Orientation present the biggest difference between both countries. While the Czech Republic is closer to an individualistic society, Portugal is clearly collectivist. This could present an obstacle in a business context since Portugal focuses highly on relationship building and the group is more prevalent that the individual, while the Czech society expects the individual to take care of him/herself and those immediately close to them. In a business context, there might be clear differences as trust-commitment relationships might be much more prevalent for Portuguese firms than for Czech firms. Portugal, being a feminine country, values consensus and negotiation, while the Czech Republic, being a masculine country, focuses more on competitiveness and performance. Long Term Orientation is the dimension that polarizes the two countries the most. The Czech Republic is a pragmatic society that aims to achieve results, showing a better ability to adapt than Portugal, a country highly focused on its traditions and on maintaining them, where societal changes are seen with suspicion.

Both countries rank very high on Uncertainty Avoidance, with an extremely high score in Portugal. Both countries rely on rules and security and people focus on working hard. However, Portugal shows more prevalence in maintaining rigid codes of belief and in avoidance of unorthodox behavior.

EVOLUTION OF THE CZ-PT TRADE

The evolution of the trade between both countries from 2000 until 2014 is shown in Table 7.

Starting the analysis in 2000 allows a brief look at the years before the Czech Republic joined the EU. According to the annual reports on the Foreign Policy of the Czech Republic – published every year by the Ministry of Foreign Affairs of the Czech Republic – and annual statistics reports published by the Portuguese National Institute of Statistics (INE), it is possible to observe a positive, growing trend in the trade evolution between Portugal and the Czech Republic.

Years 2000 to 2004

In 2000, Portugal was holding an important position especially within the EU due to its chairing in the first half of the year. The attention that was paid to the mutual relationships has increased especially

Table 7. Evolution of trade between the Czech Republic and Portugal (in 10^6 €)

	Turnover	Imports	Exports	Balance
2000	187.5	62.5	124.9	62.4
2001	225.9	84.4	141.5	57.1
2002	254.7	98.1	156.6	58.6
2003	239.3	113.6	125.7	12.1
2004	289.5	131.5	158.0	26.5
2005	370.6	136.3	234.2	97.9
2006	467.8	180.3	287.5	107.2
2007	562.3	239.0	323.3	84.3
2008	560.4	230.8	329.6	98.9
2009	518.7	228.6	290.1	61.5
2010	682.0	302.8	379.2	76.4
2011	719.3	326.8	392.5	65.8
2012	676.0	331.7	344.3	12.6
2013	689.7	344.6	345.1	0.5
2014	799.2	372.4	426.8	54.5
2015	862.2	382.8	479.4	96.6

Source: Own preparation based on the Czech Statistical Office's External Trade Database.

because of the planned extension of the EU. This was mirrored in frequent visits (heading mainly to Portugal) and intensive political dialogues of representatives of both countries about intensification of mutual relationships and cooperation. During the year several visits were held in both countries. An important moment was a visit from the prime minister of the Czech Republic, Mr. Miloš Zeman. The evolution of the international trade between the Czech Republic and Portugal shows the growth of the Czech exports. The mutual turnover reached 187.5 million EUR. Czech exports amounted to 124.9 million EUR. Czech imports from Portugal have totaled 62.5 million EUR, which is an increase around 80% from the previous year. The most important Czech exported items were machines and means of transport (54.7% - especially SKODA cars) followed by export of market products (37.7%) and chemicals (4.2%). Among the Portuguese main exports are machines and transportation equipment (44%), market products (27.9%), chemicals (9.2%) and raw material (8.4%) (Ministry of Foreign Affairs, 2001).

In 2001, the level of Czech-Portuguese relationship had been influenced by the membership of both countries in the North Atlantic Treaty Organization (NATO). Moreover Portugal had been supporting the Czech Republic in its effort to enter the EU. Portugal considered the Czech Republic as its potential ally due to similar geographical and economical extension. One of the most important visits held in this year was an official visit of the Portuguese president Mr. J. Sampaio. The main export commodities from the Czech Republic were again machines, means of transport (30.4% of all export are SKODA cars), metallurgical products – especially concrete steel and rails, tires, machines and devices for energy production, fabric, chemicals and glass-making (Ministry of Foreign Affairs, 2002).

The main commodities imported from Portugal were cork and its products, linen thread and fabric, cloth wear and footwear, electro technical products (Ministry of Foreign Affairs, 2002)

The year 2002 witness an increase in the Czech-Portuguese relations as result of the membership of both countries in NATO, and the preparations of the Czech Republic to enter the EU. Portugal was considered a prospective partner of the Czech Republic in the Union. Due to parliamentary elections (held in both countries in 2002) there were no high-level bilateral visits.

The main imported commodities from the Czech Republic were, much like the previous year, cork and related products, clothing wear, footwear, ball bearings, electro technical products, linen threads, glass-making, chemicals and metalworking machines. Portuguese investors were active in the Czech Republic in several enterprises from the fields of metallurgy and construction industries. Nevertheless, there is room for potential improvements for mutual economic relations (Ministry of Foreign Affairs, 2003).

Czech-Portuguese relations recorded in 2003 a significant boost. Portugal was considered by the Czech Republic as a key partner within the euro-Atlantic alliance, also due to the similar perception of International Policy aspects, as a result of their similar geographical size and geopolitical importance.

Portugal and the Czech Republic kept long-term intensive economic relations and a significant reinforcement was to be expected after the Czech Republic joined the EU. The trade between both countries maintained the same flow of commodities.

Portuguese investors visited the Czech Republic on behalf of many common enterprises from fields of metallurgy and construction (Ministry of Foreign Affairs, 2004).

Years 2004 to 2008

The relationship between Portugal and the Czech Republic had been successfully developing on the bilateral and multinational level in the context of the EU and NATO. Intensive development had been noted also between governments and parliaments, also due to similar experience of both countries with a totalitarian regime, but also because of similar interest in good relationships with neighboring countries, close approach to the transatlantic connection and similar opinions about the arrangement of the EU. Czech-Portuguese relationships were also boosted by visits involving the highest political and diplomatic level.

Portugal and the Czech Republic have a long-term intensive economic relationship that increased significantly after the Czech Republic joined the EU. In 2004 a sharp increase of the Czech exports was registered (29%). Portugal held 33rd position of the foreign trade turnover of the Czech Republic. The main Czech export commodities did not changed and were: means of transport, metallurgical products, devices and mechanical tools, electronics, glass, plastic products, natural rubber, rubber-based products, and cotton.

Neither the main imported commodities from Portugal changed: TV and car radio components, motor cars, metallurgical products, natural rubber, cork, clothing, footwear, and pharmaceutical products. Following the 2003 trend, an increased interest for textile fibers and metalworking machines was registered (Ministry of Foreign Affairs, 2005)

In 2005, the relationship between the Czech Republic and Portugal, within the EU and the Euro-Atlantic alliance, kept successfully developing bilaterally as well as multilaterally, stimulating mutual communication and parliamentary dialogue. In May 2005, a new honorary Consulate of the Czech Republic started activity in Funchal – the capital of the autonomous region of Madeira. Mutual economic relations proved significantly dynamic, especially after the Czech Republic entered the EU. Both the Czech exports to Portugal and Portuguese exports to the Czech Republic significantly increased and the turnover doubled since the year 2000. The main Czech export commodities are still means of transport, manufactured goods classified by the type of the material, cars and their spare parts, metallurgical products, glass, textile, tires and metalworking tools. The main Portuguese import commodities also did not register significant changes (Ministry of Foreign Affairs, 2006)

In 2006, Portugal and the Czech Republic continued its important partnership, not only within the EU and NATO but also outside of it. The countries are connected by close opinions and positions about some of the European questions as they are for example important supporters of the principle of solidarity. Both countries are recipients of the funds from the Cohesion Fund and the Structural Funds of the EU. During the year 2006 a Bilateral Cultural agreement between Portugal and the Czech Republic was discussed and formed and its signing set out to enable more active cooperation in the area of education, science and research, for example. Mutual economical relationships kept dynamically growing and traded commodities did not change from the previous years (Ministry of Foreign Affairs, 2007).

In March 2007 during the official visit of the Czech Minister of the Interior to Portugal, a software and information about the application of the program 'SIS One 4All' was officially handed by Portugal. The program is related to the integration of the Czech Republic to the Schengen area. Portugal took an important part during enforcement of the enlargement of the Schengen area and supported the entrance of the Czech Republic.

During the second half of 2007 Portugal was holding the Presidency of the Council of the European Union. Within the Presidency there were official visits by the Czech Prime Minister and the Minister of Foreign Affairs to Portugal. Moreover several contacts at the ministry level were established. These bilateral meetings have strengthened the existing alliance between both countries. Also, discussions about the coordination procedures of the institutional reform of the EU were held, while in the end there was an obvious convergence of the positions of both countries.

Mutual economic relations have been growing. In 2007, Portugal held the 31st position of the Czech exports and 34th position of the Czech imports. The main commodities have not changed significantly. Traditionally the highest individual items of the Czech export were personal cars and their components. The radios and sound reproduction devices, chemically produced fibers, pharmaceutical products and wine enriched Portuguese exports (Ministry of Foreign Affairs, 2008).

Between January 2007 and June 2008 a growing tendency was found in the trade between Portugal and the Czech Republic. Regarding imports, these countries were responsible for 945.6 million euros in 2007, 1.7% of total imports. The Czech Republic (ranked at 27th globally) was the main partner then, despite accounting for less than 0.6%. Regarding exports, in 2007 these countries were responsible for 848.3 million euros, 2.3% of total exports. The Czech Republic (25th) was the second biggest receiver of goods.

In 2008 mutual business relations between the Czech Republic and Portugal were developing very well. Especially since 1997, the Czech Republic registered a surplus and trade balance. Portugal kept the 30th position of the Czech export and 36th position of the Czech imports. The main export commodities from the Czech Republic are among others still machines and transportation. The main exports commodities from Portugal to the Czech Republic are above all machines and transportation, market products, chemicals, raw material (Ministry of Foreign Affairs, 2009).

Years 2009 to 2015

In 2009 the business relations between Portugal and the Czech Republic were affected by the global downturn in economic activity. In regards to the Czech exports, Portugal has moved up from 30th to the 27th position, and from 36th to the 34th position regarding Czech import. The turnover has moved up from 34th to the 32nd position. Among the Czech export, to the commodities previously mentioned have been added products like telecommunications equipment, screens, projectors, devices for heating and cooling, musical instruments, papers and paperboards. The main Portuguese export commodities have been also enriched with products like tobacco, electronics, measuring instruments, metal and plastic products, waste paper, and cork products (Ministry of Foreign Affairs, 2010)

In 2010 trade increased significantly between Portugal and the Czech Republic. From 518.7 million EUR in 2009 the number has increased to 682.0 million EUR in 2010. The export and import commodities have been expanding and have started to vary more than in the past years. The previous Czech export commodities to Portugal have been enriched by the navigational aid apparatus, processing units, TVs, the steel parts of motor vehicles, brakes, tires, speedometers for vehicles, parts of electrical capacitors, seamless pipes. The main Portuguese import commodities to the Czech Republic were enriched as well by audio players for motor vehicles, tire materials, electric capacitors, radios with cassette recorders, bleached wood pulp (cellulose), parts of seats, brakes (Ministry of Foreign Affairs, 2011).

During the last 4 years, Portugal has been strengthening its position considering the Czech trade relations; from the 64th position in 1993 it has moved to the 33rd position (regarding total turnover) from in 2011. The year 2011 has registered a very high turnover of the trade between Portugal and the Czech Republic, 719.3 million EUR. The numbers have proven that the crisis has not affected the CZ-PT trade significantly. However, in 2013 the mutual trade has noticed just an infinitesimal growth, while the balance remained the same. This was a good sign for Portugal. The main commodities of Czech exports for 2013 were, much like previous years, cars (24.6%), electronics (24.3%), mechanical tools (17%), products from steel and iron (4%), metallic products (3.8%), tires and rubber products (3.7%), furniture (2.6%), plastic and its products (2.5%), toys and sport equipment (1.9%), aluminum and its products (1.2%). The main commodities of Portuguese export for 2013 were electronics (23.2%), cars (10.1%), high-strength textiles (9%), unmanufactured tobacco (8%), plastic products (6%), mechanical tools (5.8%), products from steel and iron (5.5%), pharmaceutical products (4.1%), tires and rubber products (3.1%) (BusinessInfo, 2014).

The year of 2014 has shown a significant increase of the Czech export. The turnover has reached the highest number, 799.0 million €, making it obvious that the trade between the Czech Republic and Portugal has been increasing and that the mutual relationships and economies resisted the crisis well. The increase is moderated without significant deflections. This can mean a good prognosis of the future trade between those two countries.

As of 2014, the Czech Republic ranked at 18th globally with 0.67% of total Portuguese exports, and at 22nd globally with 0.7% of total Portuguese imports.

For the first time in history, trade between both countries was above the threshold of 800 million EUR.

MAIN CZECH AND PORTUGUESE COMPANIES INVOLVED IN TRADE

Main Czech Companies Trading with Portugal

The main Czech companies operating in Portugal are Skoda Auto and Moravia Steel. Skoda, a Czech car company, founded in 1925, is one of the oldest of this branch in the world. In 1991, became a subsidiary of the Volkswagen Group. In 2015, the company expects to strengthen its presence in the Portuguese market by 50%. «In 2014 the brand sales were slightly above the market average: grew 36.5%, although it has maintained its share compared to 2013. The fleets channel represented approximately 65% of total sales, with special focus on the taxi business, where the Škoda managed to extend their presence by 40% (Rebelo, 2015).

Moravia Steel Iberia is a Czech metallurgical company operating in Portugal, since 1997, based in Lisbon. It trades stainless steel products.

There are several Czech firms working as intermediary between PT and CZ, such as: Likor, Portugalmarket, Kateřina Kročilová, Cerfis Wines, Café Portugal, and Um Porto. Excepting Café Portugal, all of them import Portuguese wines. Portugalmarket and Cerfis Wines also import Portuguese olive oil, and Café Portugal only imports coffee (Ministério dos Negócios Estrangeiros, 2012).

Main Portuguese Companies Trading with the Czech Republic

The main Portuguese companies operating in Czech Republic are Mota-Engil and EFACEC. Mota-Engil, a Portuguese industrial conglomerate, works with civil engineering and construction, energy, steel works, transport concessions, environment and services. It also deals with logistics, retail and warehousing. EFACEC is a Portuguese group working with electro mechanics and electronics; it is the biggest company in this industry.

As Portuguese business established in Czech Republic, there are Café Oliveira and Trindadent. Café Oliveira is a very traditional Portuguese style of café, serving Portuguese snacks and wine. Trindadent is a Portuguese dental office based in Prague (Ministério dos Negócios Estrangeiros, 2012)

In 2013, 850 Portuguese companies exported to the Czech Republic, a number that has escalated from 748 in 2010 (AICEP, 2016b).

SOLUTIONS AND RECOMMENDATIONS

One can describe those markets as economically similar but culturally different. The cooperation and exchange of goods have been significantly growing after the Czech Republic entered to the European Union. However, the 2008 crisis disturbed the dynamic economic trade growth between both countries. Still, after a small decrease and stagnation of the trade between those two countries, the last years have registered a slow recovery and the prognosis seems to be positive. However, if Portuguese and Czech authorities desire to increase trade and foreign direct investment between the two countries at a more accelerated pace, it is necessary to promote trade fairs among potential investors in order to overcome cultural and economic barriers, as well as the strong feelings of foreignness between both countries.

FUTURE RESEARCH DIRECTIONS

It would be interesting to understand how Portuguese firms are evolving in the Czech Republic and how Czechs firms are evolving in Portugal after their investment abroad. This would be important to understand how foreignness has affected their economic path abroad.

Taking into account the new important roles that have been given to economic diplomacy, it would be important to address how diplomats and economic players of both countries are deploying their strategies, and what resources are using to increase exports and trade.

CONCLUSION

One of the main conclusions is that trade has been increasing over time. Although exports from Portugal to the Czech Republic show an almost constant growth, exports from the Czech Republic to Portugal show several fluctuation, as a result of the economic unrest Portugal has gone through since 2008 financial crisis, which is reflected on the trade balance constant ups and downs favoring the Czech Republic.

Another important conclusion is that despite the heavy historical, cultural and economic differences Portugal and Czech Republic are improving their trade rankings. However, despite their growing trend their main economic partners are the same: Spain, and Germany for Portugal, and Germany, Slovakia, and Poland for the Czech Republic.

As supported in the literature review (Fink, Harms, & Kraus, 2008; Zanger, Hodicová, & Gaus, 2008; Zapletalová, 2012; Kubíčková, & Procházková, 2014), Czech firms still follow a traditional sequential path when internationalizing their activities, showing strong feelings of foreignness and lack of understanding of foreign markets. As such, as most of the internationalization of Czech firms is to neighbor countries, the feeling of foreignness and the lack of understanding of foreign markets might be aggravated to far distant countries like Portugal, with which the Czech have more dissimilar cultural attributes.

Another conclusion is that despite this fruitful cooperation, both markets are too small, and possibly unattractive for a huge deeper future cooperation. Clearly, history plays a heavy role: Portugal is still concentrated in its former colonies, with a small psychic distance, common language, and close cultural gap, while the Czech Republic is still concentrated in its close neighbors, with whom they have close affinities.

One thing is clear, joining the EU was an important step for both countries to deepen their relationships. Future policy intervention is necessary to increase trade between both countries, as small and medium-sized firms may find it difficult to overcome their historical and cultural differences. This is tuned with what was proposed by Moini, Kalouda, and Tesar (2008) and by Cieślik, Michałek, Michałek, and Mycielski, (2015) who propose the formulation of export promotion strategies for SMEs and the attraction of export-oriented FDI.

There are several areas, such as heavy industries or electronics, which would possibly be attractive and interesting for investments or trade of both countries. For Portugal the wine industry, cork, celluloses and paper, or agricultural (fruits, fish, seafood) products could represent a sizeable source of future income.

For the Czech Republic, as an industrial country, metallic parts, cars, and heavy industries are still representing the most important source of income. However, IT and pharmaceutical industries have good perspectives for growth.

At firm level it is important to emphasize that it is necessary that firms embrace more assertive modes of entry (as foreign direct investment and franchising) in order to control distribution of goods in the recipient country, as for example Skoda is doing in Portugal.

REFERENCES

AICEP. (2016a). *Portugal – Ficha País Março 2016*. Retrieved 3 July, 2016 from http://www.portugal-global.pt/PT/Biblioteca/Paginas/Detalhe.aspx?documentId=50f511f4-d2ea-4f9f-90e4-d47bde498c50

AICEP. (2016b). *Républica Checa – Síntese País*. Retrieved 3 July, 2016 from http://www.portugalglobal.pt/PT/Internacionalizar/SobreMercadosExternos/Documents/Perfil/95.pdf

Blomström, M., & Kokko, A. (1998). Multinational corporations and spillovers. *Journal of Economic Surveys*, *12*(3), 247–277. doi:10.1111/1467-6419.00056

BusinessInfo. (2014). *Portugalsko: Základní podmínky pro uplatnění českého zboží na trhu*. Retrieved April 4, 2015, from http://www.businessinfo.cz/cs/clanky/portugalsko-zahranicni-obchod-zeme-19426.html

Carvalheira, A., & Moreira, A. C. (2016). Searching for opportunities and trust in internationalization markets. entrepreneurial perspective of a traditional industry SME. In L. C. Carvalho (Ed.), *Handbook of Research on Entrepreneurial Success and its Impact on Regional Development* (pp. 675–701). Hershey, PA: IGI Global. doi:10.4018/978-1-4666-9567-2.ch028

Chenaf-Nicet, D., & Rougier, E. (2016). The effect of macroeconomic instability on FDI flows: A gravity estimation of the impact of regional integration in the case of Euro-Mediterranean agreements. *Inter Economics*, *145*, 66–91. doi:10.1016/j.inteco.2015.10.002

Cieślik, A., Michałek, A., Michałek, J., & Mycielski, J. (2015). Determinants of export performance: Comparison of central European and Baltic firms. *Czech Journal of Economics and Finance*, *65*(3), 211–229.

Countryeconomy.com. (2015). *Portugal*. Retrieved 12 April, 2015 from http://countryeconomy.com/countries/Portugal

Countryeconomy.com. (2016) *Czech Republic*. Retrieved 3 July, 2016 from http://countryeconomy.com/countries/czech-republic

CzechInvest. (2013). *Transport Infrastructure*. Retrieved March 10, 2015, from http://www.czechinvest.org/data/files/fs-16-transport-infrastructure-80-en.pdf

CzechInvest. (2016) *Why Invest in the Czech Republic*. Retrieved 3 July, 2016 from http://www.czech-invest.org/en/why-invest-in-the-czech-republic

European Commission. (2015). *Country Report Czech Republic 2015*. Brussels: European Commission.

EuroStat. (2014). *Share of Young Adults Having Completed Tertiary Education up to 37%*. Retrieved 19 April, 2015 from http://ec.europa.eu/eurostat/documents/2995521/5178598/3-11042014-AP-EN.PDF/4e01669e-2c2e-4c0e-a16b-487753183826?version=1.0

EuroStat. (2016a). *Population and Employment*. Retrieved 21 April, 2015 from http://appsso.eurostat.ec.europa.eu/nui/show.do?dataset=namq_10_pe&lang=en

EuroStat. (2016b). *Gross Domestic Product at Market Prices*. Retrieved 3 July, 2016 from http://ec.europa.eu/eurostat/tgm/refreshTableAction.do?tab=table&plugin=1&pcode=tec00001&language=en

Fink, M., Harms, R., & Kraus, S. (2008). Cooperative internationalization of SMEs: Self-commitment as a success factor for International Entrepreneurship. *European Management Journal, 26*(6), 429–440. doi:10.1016/j.emj.2008.09.003

Geoghegan, S. (2014). *The Euro: Advantages and Disadvantages of a Single Currency*. Retrieved 15 April, 2015 from http://www.currencysolutions.co.uk/news/the-euro-advantages-and-disadvantages-of-a-single-currency.html

Görg, H., & Greenaway, D. (2004). Much ado about nothing? Do domestic firms really benefit from foreign direct investment? *The World Bank Research Observer, 19*(2), 171–197. doi:10.1093/wbro/lkh019

Government of the Czech Republic. (2015). *What Economic Model Does the Czech Republic Need?* Retrieved March 15, 2015, from http://www.vlada.cz/en/evropske-zalezitosti/aktualne/eurocentrum-seminar-what-economic-model-does-the-czech-republic-need--125936

Hanousek, J., & Kočenda, E. (2014). Factors of trade in Europe. *Economic Systems, 38*(4), 518–535. doi:10.1016/j.ecosys.2014.06.001

Hanson, G. (2001). *Should Countries Promote Foreign Direct Investment?* G-24 Discussion Paper 9.

Hofstede Centre. (2016a). *What about Czech Republic*? Retrieved April 23, 2016, from http://geert-hofstede.com/czech-republic.html

Hofstede Centre. (2016b). *What about Portugal*? Retrieved April 23, 2016, from http://geert-hofstede.com/portugal.html

INE. (2005). *Anuário Estatístico De Portugal 2004*. Retrieved 20 March, 2015 from https://www.ine.pt/xportal/xmain?xpid=INE&xpgid=ine_destaques&DESTAQUESdest_boui=73471&DESTAQUESmodo=2

INE. (2008). *Estatísticas Do Comércio Internacional Junho De 2008*. Retrieved 20 March, 2015 from https://www.ine.pt/xportal/xmain?xpid=INE&xpgid=ine_destaques&DESTAQUESdest_boui=10938023&DESTAQUEStema=55448&DESTAQUESmodo=2

INE. (2014) *Estatísticas Da Globalização 2008-2013*. Retrieved 20 March, 2015 from https://www.ine.pt/xportal/xmain?xpid=INE&xpgid=ine_destaques&DESTAQUESdest_boui=209999963&DESTAQUESmodo=2

International Telecommunication Union. (2014). *Measuring the Information Society Report 2014*. Geneva: International Telecommunication Union.

Kubíčková, L., & Procházková, L. (2014). Success evaluation of small and medium-sized enterprises in terms of their participation in the internationalization process. *Ekonomie a Management, 17*(2), 131–145. doi:10.15240/tul/001/2014-2-010

Lipsey, R. E. (2002). *Home and Host Country Effects of FDI*. NBER Working Paper 9293.

Lisboa, A., Skarmeas, D., & Lages, C. (2011). Entrepreneurial orientation, exploitative and explorative capabilities, and performance outcomes in export markets: A resource-based approach. *Industrial Marketing Management, 40*(8), 1274–1284. doi:10.1016/j.indmarman.2011.10.013

Markusen, J., & Venables, A. (1999). Foreign direct investment as a catalyst for economic development. *European Economic Review*, *43*(2), 335–356. doi:10.1016/S0014-2921(98)00048-8

Ministério dos Negócios, E. (2012). *Portugal na República Checa*. Prague. Retrieved 19 April, 2015 from http://www.embportugal.cz/pt/portugal-na-republica-checa.html

Ministry of Foreign Affairs. (2001). *Report on the Foreign Policy of the Czech Republic Jan- Dec 2000*. Prague: Decibel Production.

Ministry of Foreign Affairs. (2002). *Report on the Foreign Policy of the Czech Republic Jan-Dec 2001*. Prague: Decibel Production.

Ministry of Foreign Affairs. (2003). *Report on the Foreign Policy of the Czech Republic Jan-Dec 2002*. Prague: Decibel Production.

Ministry of Foreign Affairs. (2004). *Report on the Foreign Policy of the Czech Republic Jan-Dec 2003*. Prague: Decibel Production.

Ministry of Foreign Affairs. (2005). *Report on the Foreign Policy of the Czech Republic Jan-Dec 2003*. Prague: Decibel Production.

Ministry of Foreign Affairs. (2006). *Report on the Foreign Policy of the Czech Republic Jan-Dec 2005*. Prague: Decibel Production.

Ministry of Foreign Affairs. (2007). *Report on the Foreign Policy of the Czech Republic Jan-Dec 2006*. Prague: Decibel Production.

Ministry of Foreign Affairs. (2008). *Report on the Foreign Policy of the Czech Republic Jan-Dec 2007*. Prague: Decibel Production.

Ministry of Foreign Affairs. (2009). *Report on the Foreign Policy of the Czech Republic Jan-Dec 2008*. Prague: Decibel Production.

Ministry of Foreign Affairs. (2010). *Report on the Foreign Policy of the Czech Republic Jan-Dec 2009*. Prague: Decibel Production.

Ministry of Foreign Affairs. (2011). *Report on the Foreign Policy of the Czech Republic Jan-Dec 2010*. Prague: Decibel Production.

Moini, H., Kalouda, K., & Tesar, G. (2008). Foreign market entry: The case of SMEs in the Czech republic. *Journal of East-West Business*, *14*(1), 41–65. doi:10.1300/J097v14n01_03

Moreira, A. C. (2008). Upstream linkages between TNCs and local suppliers: Evidences from Portugal. *World Review of Science. Technology and Sustainable Development*, *5*(1), 28–48.

Moreira, A. C., & Alves, C. (2016). Commitment-Trust dynamics in the internationalization process: a case study of market entry in the Brazilian market. In M. Garita & J. Godinez (Eds.), *Business Development Opportunities and Market Entry Challenges in Latin America* (pp. 224–255). Hershey, PA: IGI Global. doi:10.4018/978-1-4666-8820-9.ch011

Moreira, A. C., & Dias, A. A. (2008). O investimento directo do estrangeiro em Portugal. Uma perspectiva histórica. *Global Economics and Management Review*, *13*(1), 23–42.

Mrázek, J. (2015). Inflation in the Czech Republic and European Union between 2000-2014. Paper presented at the Tiksová Conference, Prague, Czech Republic.

Musteen, M., & Datta, D. K. (2011). Learning about foreign markets: A study of Czech SMEs. *Journal of International Entrepreneurship*, *9*(2), 91–109. doi:10.1007/s10843-010-0067-5

Petrovic, B., & Solingen, E. (2005). Europeanisation and Internationalisation: The Case of the Czech Republic. *New Political Economy*, *10*(3), 281–303. doi:10.1080/13563460500203391

Pettinger, T. (2013). *Effect of the Exchange Rate on Business*. Retrieved April 7, 2015, from http:// www.economicshelp.org/blog/9328/business/effect-exchange-rate-business

Razin, A., & Sadka, E. (2007). *Foreign Direct Investment*. Princeton, NJ: Princeton University Press.

Rebelo, R. (2015). *Em 2015, a Škoda quer crescer 50% em Portugal*. Retrieved 20 April, 2015 from http://www.fleetmagazine.pt/2015/01/29/skoda-vendas-frotas/

Ribau, C. P., Moreira, A. C., & Raposo, M. (2015). Internationalisation of the firm theories: A schematic synthesis. *International Journal of Business and Globalisation*, *15*(4), 528–554. doi:10.1504/IJBG.2015.072535

Rusnok, J. (2014). *Aktuální vývoj a perspektivy české ekonomiky v širším kontextu 10 let členství v EU*. Czech National Bank. Retrieved April 28, 2014, from http://www.cnb.cz/miranda2/export/sites/www.cnb.cz/cs/verejnost/pro_media/konference_projevy/vystoupeni_projevy/download/rusnok_20140428_univerzita_pardubice.pdf

Soares, P. (2015). *República Checa: um mercado laboral competitivo – Uma comparação para o futuro*. PricewaterhouseCoopers International Limited. Retrieved April 20, 2015, from http:// pwc.pt/pt/temas-actuais/pcn/republica-checa.html

The Heritage Foundation. (2015) *2015 Index of Economic Freedom - Czech Republic*. Retrieved 15 April, 2015 from http://www.heritage.org/index/country/czechrepublic

The World Bank. (2016). *Doing Business 2016. Measuring Regulatory Quality and Efficiency*. Washington, DC: International Bank for Reconstruction and Development.

Transparency International. (2016a). *Corruption by Country / Territory Czech Republic*. Retrieved July 5, 2016, from http://www.transparency.org/country#CZE

Transparency International. (2016b). *Corruption by Country / Territory Portugal*. Retrieved July 5, 2016 from http://www.transparency.org/country#PRT

Valles, R. (2015). *República Checa: um mercado laboral competitivo – Um exemplo a seguir e que se destaca nos indicadores de eficiência do mercado laboral*. PricewaterhouseCoopers International Limited. Retrieved April 20, 2015, from http:// pwc.pt/pt/temas-actuais/pcn/republica-checa.html

World Economic Forum. (2015a). *Czech Republic*. Retrieved 7 July, 2016 from http://reports.weforum.org/global-competitiveness-report-2014-2015/economies/#indexId=GCI&economy=CZE

World Economic Forum. (2015b). *Portugal*. Retrieved 7 July, 2016 from http://reports.weforum.org/global-competitiveness-report-2014-2015/economies/#indexId=GCI&economy=PRT

Zanger, C., Hodicová, R., & Gaus, H. (2008). Psychic distance and cross-border cooperation of SMEs: An empirical study on Saxon and Czech entrepreneurs' interest in cooperation. *Journal of East European Management Studies*, *13*(1), 40–62.

Zapletalová, Š. (2012). Přístupy k internacionalizaci podnikatelských aktivit a českých podniků. *Ekonomie a Management*, *4*, 84–96.

Zapletalová, Š. (2015). Models of Czech companies internationalization. *Journal of International Entrepreneurship*, *13*(2), 153–168. doi:10.1007/s10843-015-0145-9

KEY TERMS AND DEFINITIONS

Balance of Trade (BOT): The difference between a country's imports and its exports. When a country imports more than it exports, one can say that it has a trade deficit. When a country exports more than it imports, one can say that it has a trade surplus.

Culture: Considered the collective programming of the mind. The main consequence of this collective programming is that members of groups, categories, or countries will tend to behave homogeneously among them, bet heterogeneously between them. Culture is important in business as firms operating in different countries need to be aware of those differences. Several dimensions – Power Distance Index (PDI), Individualism versus Collectivism (IDV), Masculinity versus Femininity (MAS), Uncertainty Avoidance Index (UAI), Long Term Orientation versus Short Term Normative Orientation (LTO), Indulgence versus Restraint (IND) – have been put forward to meaningfully compare counties.

European Single Market: Established by 12 countries in 1993 to ensure the so-called four freedoms: the movement of goods, services, people and money. With the European single market, EU citizens can study, live, shop, work, and retire in any EU country.

European Union (EU): A group of 27 countries (Austria, Belgium, Bulgaria, Cyprus, the Czech Republic, Denmark, Estonia, Finland, France, Germany, Greece, Hungary, Ireland, Italy, Latvia, Lithuania, Luxembourg, Malta, the Netherlands, Poland, Portugal, Romania, Slovakia, Slovenia, Spain, Sweden, and the United Kingdom) that operates as a cohesive economic and political block. It was formed in 1993 with the purpose of achieving political and economic integration. Nineteen of the countries use the euro as their official currency.

Exports: An export is a function of international trade whereby goods produced in one country are shipped to another country for future sale or trade. Exports contribute to the producing nation's gross output.

Foreign Direct Investment: A foreign direct investment (FDI) is an investment made by a company or entity based in one country, into a company or entity based in another country. It normally includes mergers and acquisitions, building new facilities, reinvesting profits earned from overseas operations and intra company loans.

Imports: A good or service brought into one country, but produced in another country. The higher the value of imports entering a country, compared to the value of exports, the more negative that country's balance of trade becomes.

International Trade: The exchange of goods and services that connect people, businesses and countries along international borders in global processes of production and consumption.

SMEs: Abbreviation of small and medium-sized enterprises. Although there are plenty of definitions across the world, the working definition used in this document is the one that was created by the European Commission, to permit a coherent and effective access of SMEs to European community funds.

Section 3

OFDI in Emerging Economies:

Case Studies from Asia

Chapter 11
The Determinants of Foreign Direct Investment Outflows from Turkey

Raif Cergibozan
Kırklareli University, Turkey

Caner Demir
Kırklareli University, Turkey

ABSTRACT

The aim of this study is to specify the determinants of the outward Foreign Direct Investment (FDI) flows from Turkey. For this purpose, the ARDL Bounds Test is used in order to observe the possible relation between these flows and define potential factors that might have an effect on them. The evidences of the empirical analysis reveal that the destination countries' market size, the home country's development level, trade openness and wage rate are positively related to outward FDI while the home country's interest rate shows a negative relationship. Turkey's outward FDI is significantly determined by the opportunities of the foreign markets as well as the outstanding home country factors.

INTRODUCTION

Foreign direct investment (FDI) flows have made an important impact on the globalization process. Since 1980's, the volume of FDI inflows has shown a substantial increase especially in developing countries. Even though the impact of FDI inflows on developing economies is still discussed by various perspectives in the literature, main findings state that it is hard to ignore the long run benefits of these types of investments for many developing countries. Nowadays, many firms or investors from developing countries seek to invest in abroad. This type of investment, which is termed the outward foreign direct investment (OFDI), reveals that the investors from developing world intend to compete in foreign countries. However, economic development performance of countries is not the only motivation for firms and investors to make a decision on investing abroad. There might be some other factors determining the outward foreign

DOI: 10.4018/978-1-5225-2345-1.ch011

direct investment flows. From this point of view, the analysis of this chapter attempts to investigate the determinants of the FDI outflows from an important emerging market and developing country; Turkey.

Since the foundation of the Republic of Turkey in 1923, Turkish Economy has passed through several policy periods. During the first decade of the republic, the government had promoted the private sector and also established some public enterprises to provide the necessary inputs for the private sector. Despite these public interventions, until the great depression the main objective of the Turkish economic policies was forming an open economy model that advanced the country to an industrialized stage. As from the 1930's, the Turkish Economy had been considerably affected by the great depression. Moreover, the incentives given in the previous decade did not serve the purpose of the open economy. In order to change the course of economic developments, the government applied state-oriented economic policies and changed its exchange rate regime to the fixed system. In 1930s, the Central Bank of the Republic of Turkey was also established. In the late 1940's and 1950's Turkey shifted to liberal economic policies. In 1947, Turkey became a member of the International Monetary Fund (IMF) and World Bank. Also some foreign economic supports, such as under the Marshall Plan, were received to help rebuild the development process. Likewise in 1950's, foreign capitals were encouraged to come to Turkey for the purpose of contributing to the development process of the country. Besides, the means of credit were expanded and credit volume was increased particularly with the infrastructural investments. However, the inflation problem that showed itself later left behind the initial benefits. As a result, the paradigm of the Turkish economic policy was again changed to the planning mentality. Between 1960 and 1980, Turkey had been aiming to limit the volume of import and raise the exports. The oil shock in the mid 1970's influenced Turkish economy in a unfavorable way and the high prices in energy damaged the industrialization process. During the 1970's the country also faced with some internal and external political issues. Even if the economic administration had tried to overcome the emergent economic issues, their efforts could not succeed. In the beginning of 1980's, the economy was upgraded to a new stage which might be called as a transition stage to a free market economy. In 1980's the main economic policies were as followings; encouraging foreign investment inflows, limiting the public interventions and ensuring the economic stability (Boratav, 2009; Eğilmez and Kumcu, 2015).

The financial liberalization process of the Turkish Economy in the late 1980's was accompanied by the commercial deregulation process; and thus the free movement of both goods and capital became possible. Since then, the great deal of foreign direct investment has been flowing into Turkey and making the economy more integrated with the world. The obvious effects of this transformation have been being observed since the early 1990's. In the same time, the outward FDI flows have shown significant increase. To be able to investigate these investment developments, econometric time series analysis methods on the outward FDI flows from the Turkish Economy are used over the period 1992-2015.

In 2015, the volume of the outward foreign direct investment flows from Turkey was worth about USD 5.3 billion. Figure 1 provides information about the destinations of these investments for the period of 2005-2015. 54% of these flows go only towards three countries; Netherlands, Azerbaijan and USA. Of the total outward FDI from Turkey, Germany, U.K., Malta, Luxemburg and Russia receive 6%, 5%, 4%, 3% and 3%, respectively. Thanks to its largely liberal economic structure and conveniences for foreign investors, Netherlands is one of the most attractive countries for the global FDI flows. Like many other investors around the world, Turkish investors also mostly invest in Netherlands. Due to the fact that both countries have a long historical and cultural relationship, Azerbaijan is the second biggest destination

Figure 1. The destinations of outward FDI flows from Turkey (2005-2015 total)
Source: The Central Bank of the Republic of Turkey.

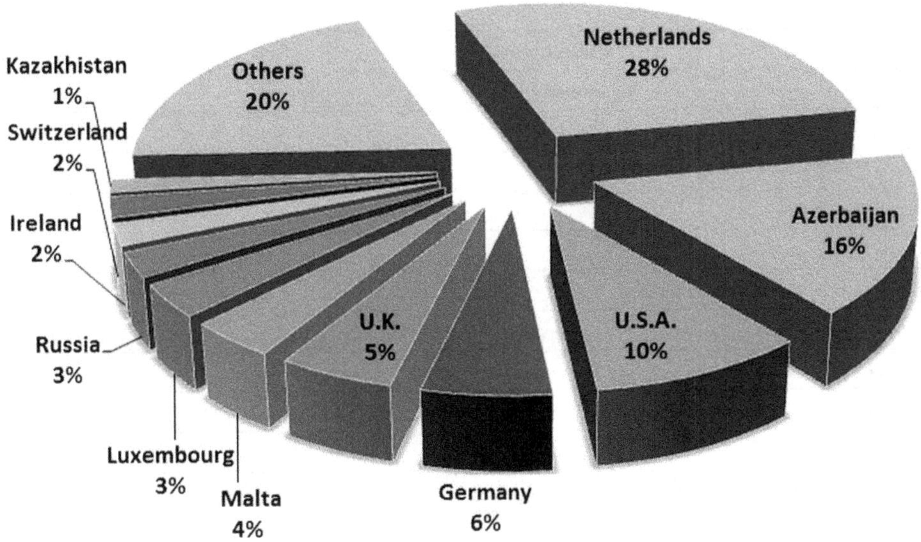

for the Turkish outward foreign direct investments. As for the USA, being the land of opportunity and providing remarkable conveniences for investors, it comes after Azerbaijan by getting 10% of the total outward foreign direct investments from Turkey.

Table 1 shows the share of the outward Turkish foreign direct investments by sectors and presents the tendency of the Turkish investors over the period 2005-2015. The outward Turkish FDI mainly consists of industrial and service sector, 57% and 42%, respectively. The data states that mining, food production, textile production and non-metallic mineral production are the outstanding industrial sector for the outward FDI flows while financial and insurance activities, information and communication services, construction, transportation and real estate activities are the major activities in service sector. It is also observed that the total amount of the industrial outward FDI flows is about 1.5 fold greater than that of services. This is an expected symptom for a developing country that is still pursuing its industrialization process. For sure, it is hard to claim that there is an absolute positive relationship between economic development and the share of the services sector in the total outward FDI. Today, many highly industrialized countries' industrial sectors progressively invest in abroad while their services sectors mainly chose to stay in domestic market.

The developments of the outward foreign direct investment flows from Turkey are shown on Figure 2. As the data clearly exhibits, since 2001 the outward FDI flows from Turkey have shown a dramatic increase. At the first part of 1990's, the yearly volume of the flows was about less than USD 500 million while it reached USD 5 billion in 2015. Although the Turkish Economy has integrated with foreign countries since a long time ago, the yearly total flows did not surpass the level of USD 1 billion until 2000. It may imply that even if the Turkish Economy has opened its gates to foreign countries since 1980, its impacts on the outward FDI could be seen only after 2000's.

Table 1. Turkey's outward foreign direct investment flows by sectors (2005-2015 total)

Sectors	Amount (Million $)
Agriculture	**98**
Industrial	**18540**
Mining and Quarrying	8517
Manufacturing	9444
Manufacture of Food Products	4272
Manufacture of Textiles and Textile Products	1141
Manufacture of Leather and Leather Products	6
Manufacture of Wood and Wood Products	241
Manufacture of Pulp	84
Manufacture of Coke	63
Manufacture of Chemicals	504
Manufacture of Rubber and Plastic Products	102
Manufacture of Other Non-Metallic Mineral Products	1175
Manufacture of Basic Metals and Fabricated Metal Products	385
Manufacture of Machinery and Equipment	648
Manufacture of Computers	434
Manufacture of Transport Equipment	175
Manufacturing n.e.c.	214
Electricity	575
Water Supply	4
Services	**13736**
Construction	1569
Wholesale and Retail Trade	522
Transportation and Storage	1390
Accommodation and Food Service Activities	458
Information and Communication Services	1743
Financial and Insurance Activities	5951
Real Estate Activities	1426
Professional	216
Administrative and Support Service Activities	34
Public Administration and Defense	8
Education	24
Human Health and Social Work Activities	95
Arts	16
Other Service Activities	281
Activities of Households as Employers	0
Activities of Extra-Territorial Organizations and Bodies	3
Total	32374

Source: The Central Bank of the Republic of Turkey.

Figure 2. Outward FDI flows from Turkey (million, USD)
Source: The Central Bank of the Republic of Turkey.
**Note: To avoid monthly fluctuations, the figure is displayed by transforming the monthly data to yearly.*

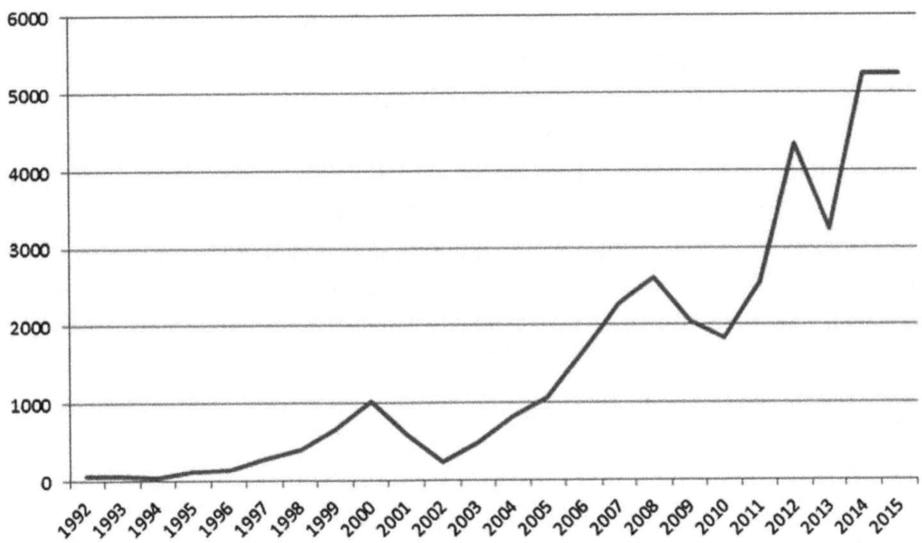

The outward foreign direct investment of a country may follow different paths and might be affected by various factors. Firms or investors may decide to invest in abroad due to the following main reasons;

- If the potential market size of their home country is insufficient (i.e. FDI by rich firms or investors of developing world).
- If the return on investment in the home country is relatively lower than investing in abroad (i.e. FDI from developed world).

With this study, it is tried to determine these factors and compare their impacts on investment decision in abroad. Undoubtedly, two main reasons which are mentioned above could be composed of many sub factors. For instance, the first reason implies factors such as low population and low household income level while the second reason implies factors such as high labor and production costs and low market share caused by extreme competition. For sure, the home country's conditions are as important as the conditions of the host country are important for the determinants of the outward FDI. In the literature, there are several studies which investigate the outward FDI flows between two or limited number of countries. In such analyses, it is possible to analyze both home and host country. However, in this study, the total outward FDI flows from Turkey is examined and this makes it impossible to measure the conditions of each host country. Thus, only the home country determinants of the outward foreign direct investment flows from Turkey have been focused.

BACKGROUND

To present a brief literature survey, several studies from the existing theoretical and empirical literature have been composed. Unlike many topics in the economics literature, the number of studies focused on the outward foreign direct investment is relatively low. However, in this section some significant studies in the relevant literature either in a general view or in a country-specific view on the outward FDI will be presented.

For sure, it would not be rational to think the outward FDI by dissociating it from the global FDI flows. The logic is simple; the outward FDI of a country is the inward FDI of another one. Therefore, also the conditions of the destinations countries might be important determinants of home country's outward FDI. So, by keeping this fact in mind let us start with some early studies in the outward foreign direct investment literature that have focused on the investment flows between the U.S. and European Economic Community (EEC). Scaperlanda and Mauer (1969) have investigated the determinants of U.S. direct investments in the E.E.C for the 1952-1966 period. The evidences obtained from their least squares regressions reveal that the *market size* of the destination country (or countries) is the prominent and the most significant determinant of US direct investment. Although their analysis contains some other indicators such as openness, the volume of the export between the two regions and within the EEC, growth rates of countries, the estimation results do not yield significant coefficient for these variables. Also Lunn (1980) has examined the determinants of US outward FDI in the EEC for the 1957-1970 period. Beside the basic determinants, his model specification allowed to observe the impact of growth of the market for the US affiliates and their net plant and equipment expenditures in the destination country which are estimated significantly via the regression analysis. Scaperlanda and Balough (1983) have revisited some previous studies including Scaperlanda and Mauer (1969) and Lunn (1980) papers by making some changes in the model structure and extending the time series which covers 1953-1977 period. The results of the newer study support the market size finding of the former studies and reveal that the market size of the destination country positively affects the US outward FDI. Moreover, the findings also show that the growth of the market for the US affiliates attract the potential US foreign direct investments. However, in the same issue of the same journal, Lunn (1983) has responded again to Scaperlanda and Balough (1983) and defended his (1980) paper in some aspects. Lunn (1983) has estimated the base theoretical model of Lunn (1980) by using the variable used by Scaperlanda and Balough (1983) for the 1957-1970 period. The findings are similar to the results of the Lunn (1980) paper and Lunn (1983) has annotated also some critics for the former study; such as the estimated model specifications and the period of the analysis covered. Lunn (1983) has stated that 1970's contain many national and global structural breaks that might have influence on the results and the period that has been extended to 1977 by Scaperlanda and Balough (1983) could lead to biased results.

Some other studies have focused on the home country determinants of outward direct investment. Kyrkilis and Pantelidis (2003) have investigated the country-specific determinants of the outward FDI for the 1977-1997 period of five European-Union and four non-European Union countries. The results vary across countries. However, as it is understood from the evidences, the reel GNP level of the home country is an important determinant of OFDI almost for all countries in the analysis. Secondly, the effective exchange rate and interest rate are estimated significantly for some countries even though some unexpected signs are observed for the exchange rate coefficients. These kinds of defects are possibly caused by the simple estimation method of the analysis which is ordinary least squares regression. Similarly, Kueh et al. (2010) have made a country-specific analysis and dealt with the macroeconomic determinants of Singapore's outward FDI. The empirical findings of their cointegration analysis that covers the 1975-2007 period reveal that the income of the home country, trade openness and interest rate are positively correlated with the FDI outflows of Singapore.

Kalotay and Sulstarova (2010) have investigated the determinants of Russian outward FDI for the 1993-2007 period. Despite the authors have used both home and host countries' factors such as home country's GDP, host country's GDP, policy change, natural resources of the host country, ratio of services to GDP, geographical distance, exchange rates and patents, only the GDP levels of countries and natural resource variables are significantly estimated. Besides the justification of the previous literature's evidence on GDP levels (both for the *home* and the *host*), this study's finding on the natural resources of the host country is a remarkable evidence. Yet another study focused on the impact of natural resources is Kolstad and Wiig (2012) which has estimated the impacts of the host country factors on Chinese outward FDI. Unsurprisingly, also this study's first evidence show that host country's market size is the most significant determinant of the outward FDI. The second and interesting evidence of the study has been observed via the interactive structure of its model. In the main model of the study, the impacts of institutions and natural resources has been estimated interactively (with an explanatory variable created by multiplying natural resources and institutions) that implies the interpretations of these factors are not independent of each other. The sign of the interactive variable has been estimated significantly and negative which has been interpreted by the authors as follows; "The worse the institutions are in the host country, the greater Chinese investment is attracted by natural resources." (Kolstad and Wiig, 2012: 32).

Goh and Wong (2011) have analyzed the impacts of market size and government policy on outward FDI flows of Malaysia over the 1999-2008 period. The evidences of the study reveal that Malaysian outward foreign direct investment is positively associated with the market size of the destination country, trade openness, reel effective exchange rate and international reserves held by the Malaysian Central Bank.

Mihci et al. (2011) have examined the home country determinants of FDI outflows of 12 European Union countries for the 1997-2003 period via a panel data analysis. Their findings reveal firstly that cost related factors such as interest rates, environmental sensitivity index and real labor cost (even if the last one was estimated as insignificant) have positive impacts on FDI outflows. As distinct from studies that measure the impacts of the market size of the destination country, Mihci et al. (2011) have employed the growth of the domestic market size and observed that the growth of the domestic market size is negatively associated with the FDI outflows.

As it has been clearly inferred from the existing literature some factors such as home and destination countries' market size, interest rate, production costs and openness come to the fore. Therefore, to examine whether there is any significant relationship, in the empirical analysis of the study these variables or appropriate proxies of them are used.

DATA AND METHODOLOGICAL FRAMEWORK

The aim of this study is to investigate the determinants of outward FDI in the Turkish economy both in the short and the long-run, over the 1992Q1 - 2015Q2 period by using the ARDL bound testing approach. Due to the important trade and financial liberalization process undertaken during the 1980s that radically transformed the Turkish economy and the data constraints for outward direct investments, the sample period stars from 1992Q1. All the data are obtained from IMF International Financial Statistics (*IFS*), Republic of Turkey Ministry of Development-Economic and Social Indicators and The Central Bank of the Republic of Turkey (*CBRT*). All the variables in the data set are transformed into natural logarithms for econometric estimation. Based on the theoretical discussions and previous studies, the following model is suggested;

$$OFDI = f(RGDP, INT, OPEN, WAGE, MARKET) \quad (1)$$

where *OFDI* is Turkey's outward *FDI*, *RGDP* is real *GDP* which stands for the development level of the home country, *INT* is nominal interest rate in the home country, *OPEN* is openness indicator (foreign trade amount of the home country, % of *GDP*), *WAGE* is wage rate which stands for the labor costs of the home country investors, *MARKET* is market size of the destination countries. Expected impacts (signs) of the variables on the outward *FDI* are as follows:

$$\frac{\partial OFDI}{\partial WAGE} > 0, \frac{\partial OFDI}{\partial INT} < 0, or > 0, \frac{\partial OFDI}{\partial OPEN} > 0, \frac{\partial OFDI}{\partial GDP} < 0 \; or > 0, \frac{\partial OFDI}{\partial MARKET} > 0 \quad (2)$$

Theoretically, increases in wage rate, trade openness and market size are expected to raise outward FDI. The expected signs of real GDP, nominal interest rate could be negative or positive. The definition and sources of all variables used in this study are shown in Table 2.

The long run relationship among outward FDI, real GDP, nominal interest rate, openness indicator, wage rate and market is investigated by applying the ARDL Bounds testing approach. The ARDL bounds testing approach of cointegration is developed by Pesaran and Shin (1999) and Pesaran et al. (2001). The ARDL cointegration approach has numerous advantages compared to other cointegration methods such as Engle and Granger (1987), Johansen (1988), and Johansen and Juselius (1990). The existence of a long run relationship among the variables used in the econometric model are performed, regardless of their order of integration contrary to Engle and Granger (1987), Johansen (1988, 1991), and Johansen and Juselius (1990) cointegration methods. Furthermore, ARDL bounds testing approach

Table 2. Variables: definitions and sources

Notation	Definition	Source
OFDI	Turkish Outward Foreign Direct Investment	CBRT
RGDP	Real Gross Domestic Product Index (2010=100)	IMF
INT	Nominal Interest Rate	IMF-IFS
OPEN	(Exports of goods and services + Imports of goods and services) / Gross Domestic Product	IMF-IFS
WAGE	Nominal Unit Wage Index (2010=100)	CBRT, ESI
MARKET	This variable is constructed as a weighted average of real foreign incomes of Turkey's major partners, each country receiving a weight equal to its share in Turkey's OFDI. $MARKET = \sum_i w_i GDP_i^*$ where w_i: share of country i in Turkey's OFDI, Y^*: Real GDP Index of *i* country (2010=100), *i*: Netherlands, Azerbaijan, United States, Germany, United Kingdom and Switzerland (these 6 countries constitute two-thirds of total market of the Turkish OFDI).	IMF-IFS, Datastream

Note: ESI: Republic of Turkey Ministry of Development-Economic and Social Indicators.

providing that the variables have different optimal lags and the estimation results are consistent in small sample size allows to estimate the long and short run parameters of econometric model (Panopoulou and Pittis, 2004; Baek and Kim, 2013).

The F and t-statistics are essential for ARDL bounds testing approach. The asymptotic distributions of these statistics are non-standard under the null hypothesis that there exists no level relationship, irrespective of whether the variables are I(0) or I(1). However, if the order of integration of any of the variables is greater than one (i.e. I(2)) then the critical bounds provided by Pesaran et al. (2001) are not valid. Thus, before proceeding to the estimation stage the integrating properties of variables must be checked. Two sets of asymptotic critical values are provided; when all variables are I(1) and when they all are I(0). These two sets of critical values provide a band covering all possible classifications of the variables into I(0), I(1) or mutually cointegrated (Pesaran et al., 2001).[1] For econometric estimation, the following ARDL model is employed:

$$\begin{aligned}\Delta OFDI &= \alpha_0 + \sum_{i=1}^{p} \alpha_1 \Delta OFDI_{t-i} + \sum_{i=0}^{p} \alpha_2 \Delta RGDP_{t-i} + \sum_{i=0}^{p} \alpha_3 \Delta INT_{t-i} + \sum_{i=0}^{p} \alpha_4 \Delta OPEN_{t-i} \\ &+ \sum_{i=0}^{p} \alpha_5 \Delta WAGE_{t-i} + \sum_{i=0}^{p} \alpha_6 \Delta MARKET_{t-i} + \lambda_1 OFDI_{t-1} + \lambda_2 RGDP_{t-1} + \lambda_3 INT_{t-1} \\ &+ \lambda_4 OPEN_{t-1} + \lambda_5 WAGE_{t-1} + \lambda_6 MARKET_{t-1} + \varepsilon_t\end{aligned} \tag{4}$$

where the terms from λ_1 to λ_6 indicates the long-run relationship among the variables, while the expression from α_1 to α_6 with the summation signs corresponds to the short-run dynamics of variables. Moreover, α_0 stands for the constant term, Δ is the first difference operator, and ε_t is the Gaussian white noise.

The complete results for short and long-run dynamics through ARDL Bounds testing are obtained through two steps. In the first step, Eq. (4) is estimated by using OLS method employing an optimal lag selection criterion such as Akaike Information Criterion (AIC) and Schwarz Information Criterion (SIC). The existence of a long-run relationship among the variables is examined by applying the F-test which indicates the joint significance of the coefficients at their one period lagged level of the time series variables in Equation 4. The null hypothesis of no cointegration

$$H_0 : \lambda_1 = \lambda_2 = \lambda_3 = \lambda_4 = \lambda_5 = \lambda_6 = 0$$

is tested against the alternative of cointegration

$$H_1 : \lambda_1 \neq \lambda_2 \neq \lambda_3 \neq \lambda_4 \neq \lambda_5 \neq \lambda_6 \neq 0.$$

The calculated F-statistics value is then compared with upper and lower critical values which are given by Pesaran et al. (2001). The calculated F-statistics value is greater than upper critical value obtained from Pesaran et al. (2001), indicating that the null hypothesis of no-cointegration is rejected irrespective of whether the regressors are I(0) or I(1).

$$\Delta OFDI_i = \beta_0 + \sum_{i=1}^{p} \delta_i \Delta OFDI_{t-i} + \sum_{i=0}^{p} \phi_i \Delta RGDP_{t-i} + \sum_{i=0}^{p} \phi_i \Delta INT_{t-i} + \sum_{i=0}^{p} \phi_i \Delta OPEN_{t-i} + \sum_{i=0}^{p} \phi_i \Delta WAGE_{t-i} + \sum_{i=0}^{p} \phi_i \Delta MARKET_{t-i} + \alpha ECT_{t-1} + u_t \quad (5)$$

where Δ is the first difference operator and u_t represents residual terms that are assumed to be identically, independently, and normally distributed. α is the speed of adjustment parameter and ECT is the error correction term. The statistical significance of lagged error correction term ECT_{t-1} with negative sign validates the established long-run relationship between the variables and its coefficient indicates the proportion by which deviations from the long-run equilibrium in the dependent variable are eliminated or corrected in in each period (Yusoff, 2010).

Finally, the cumulative sum (CUSUM) and cumulative sum of squares (CUSUMSQ) tests are employed to investigate the stability of the short and long run parameters of the model. Ignoring structural breaks in econometric models might lead to model misspecification and inconsistent estimation results of model parameters. In these methods, staying within the critical bounds of CUSUM and CUSUMSQ statistics implies that long and short run parameters are stable over the time.

EMPIRICAL FINDINGS

Before estimating the econometric model, the stationarity of the time series was checked by unit root tests in order to avoid *spurious regression problem* suggested by Granger and Newbold (1974). In the literature, there are different unit root tests such as Dickey-Fuller, Augmented Dickey-Fuller, Phillips-Perron and KPSS to investigate integrating properties of variables.[2] In this study, Augmented Dickey-Fuller (ADF) and Phillips-Perron (PP) unit root tests were used to evaluate the order of integration. Table 3 provides results from unit root tests for all variables used in the model. According to these results, all variables are non-stationary at level but stationary at their first difference. In other words, they are integrated of order one I(1). Hence, the ARDL Bound Testing Approach can properly be used in the model.

Table 3. Unit root test results

Variable	ADF Unit Root Test		PP Unit Root Test	
	T-Statistic (Level)	T-Statistic (First Difference)	T-Statistic (Level)	T-Statistic (First Difference)
OFDI	-1.685	-13.120***	-2.032	-13.909***
RGDP	-0.186	-3.706***	-2.635*	-14.882***
INT	-3.079	-5.775***	-2.870	-8.997***
OPEN	-1.892	-3.745***	-1.143	-13.810***
WAGE	-2.430	-4.355***	-1.632	-10.598***
MARKET	-1.999	-3.697***	-2.427	-5.686***

Note: The superscripts ***, ** and * denote the significance at 1%, 5% and 10% level, respectively.

The selection of optimal lag length is essential for the ARDL bounds testing approach. To determine the optimal lag length for the econometric analysis Schwarz Information Criterion (SIC) is employed. Based on SIC results, it is found that lag 0 is appropriate for trade openness, while lag 1 is fitting for outward FDI, real GDP, interest rate, wage rate, and market size. The estimation results of the ARDL are shown in Table 4. F-statistics for

$$F\left(OFDI \mid RGDP, INT, OPEN, WAGE, MARKET\right)$$

greater than the upper critical value, thus there is a long-run relationship between outward FDI, trade openness, real GDP, interest rate, wage rate, and market size at 5% significance level.

After investigating the existence of cointegration among the series, the long-run and short-run relationship between outward FDI, trade openness, real GDP, interest rate, wage rate, and market size are examined. The results of ARDL bounds test are given in Table 5 and all variables' expected sign are statistically significant at 1% level except for market size. The long run elasticity of market size is significant at 5% level. According to the estimation results, in the long run, real GDP is positively related to outward FDI, suggesting that 1% increase in real GDP raises outward FDI by 0.82%. The relationship between interest rate and outward FDI is negative and an increase of a 1% in interest rate decreases outward FDI by 0.83%. The effect of trade openness on outward FDI is positive and 1% increase in trade openness raises outward FDI by 0.68%. The long run elasticity of wage rate is positive, implying that a 1% increase in wage rate raises outward FDI by 0.24%, ceteris paribus. The impact of market size on outward FDI is also positive, indicating that an increase in market size raises outward FDI by 0.70%.

At this point, it might be useful to debate over the evidence on the relationship between the interest rate and outward FDI. Let it be known that there is not a single, commonly-held impact of interest rate on outward direct investment. The classical view on the interaction between foreign direct investment and interest rate is so obvious; lower interest rates induce foreign direct investment. If one thinks a country's outward FDI as the inward FDI of another country, it might be clearly suggested that higher home country interest rates cause the domestic investors to escape through foreign countries with lower interest rates. The logic here is simple; investors always pursue lower cost of capital. However, to specify the determinants of outward direct investment, one should primarily consider that getting into foreign markets requires a considerable amount of capital. As Kyrkilis and Pantelidis (2003) has stated, for a firm which has not got into foreign markets yet, capital accumulation is directly in association with the home country interest rate. In such a condition, lower home country interest rates raise the capital abundance of the domestic firms and pave the way for getting into foreign markets.

Table 4. The results of ARDL cointegration test

	Optimal Lag Length	F-Statistics	Critical Values %5		Critical Values %10	
			I(0)	I(1)	I(0)	I(1)
F(OFDI I RGDP, INT, OPEN, WAGE, MARKET)	(1, 1, 1, 0, 1, 1)	9.13	2.62	3.79	2.26	3.35

Notes: The critical values for the lower I(0) and upper I(1) bounds are taken from Pesaran et al. (2001).

Table 5. Long and short run analysis

Dependent Variable: OFDI	Coefficients	
Regressors	**Short Run Coefficients**	**Long Run Coefficients**
RGDP	0.484 (3.487)***	0.818 (7.341)***
INT	-0.340 (-4.053)***	-0.833 (-9.793)***
OPEN	0.113 (4.047)***	0.675 (3.045)***
WAGE	0.409 (3.765)***	0.237 (3.350)***
MARKET	0.810 (7.696)***	0.701 (1.886)*
Constant		5.236 (1.981)**
ECT(-1)	-0.167 (-11.182)***	
Diagnostic Tests		**p Value**
χ^2 (Serial correlation)		0.17
χ^2 (Heteroskedasticity)		0.13
χ^2 (Normality)		0.11
χ^2 (Functional form)		0.28

Note: The superscripts ***, ** and * denote the significance at 1%, 5% and 10% level, respectively. Parentheses are t-statistics.

As it can be seen from Table 5, the ECT_{t-1} has a negative expected sign and this is statistically significant at %1, suggesting that there is a long-run relationship between the variables in Turkey over the 1992-2015 period. The short run deviations from the long run equilibrium are corrected by 17% towards long-run equilibrium path each year. The diagnostic test results are reported in Table 5 showing that there is no diagnostic problem in the econometric model.

Finally, the cumulative sum (CUSUM) and cumulative sum of squares (CUSUMSQ) tests are used to check stability of long run and short run parameters of the econometric model. The result presents that the estimated coefficients lie within the critical bounds of 5% significance. It means that the estimated parameters are stable over the sample period.

SOLUTIONS AND RECOMMENDATIONS

As it has been clearly mentioned in the previous sections, the main goal of the study is to determine the main factors of the outward foreign direct investment flows from Turkey. In this context, some potential determinants have been presumed in a theoretical framework and estimated in via an econometric model. Before the empirical analysis, it has been stated that the openness rate of the home country, the wage rate of the home country and the market size of the destination countries are expected to have positive impacts on the outward foreign direct investment flows of Turkey. However, it was indicated that the

Figure 3. Plot of cumulative sum of recursive residuals
Note: The dashed-lines show critical bounds at 5% significance level.

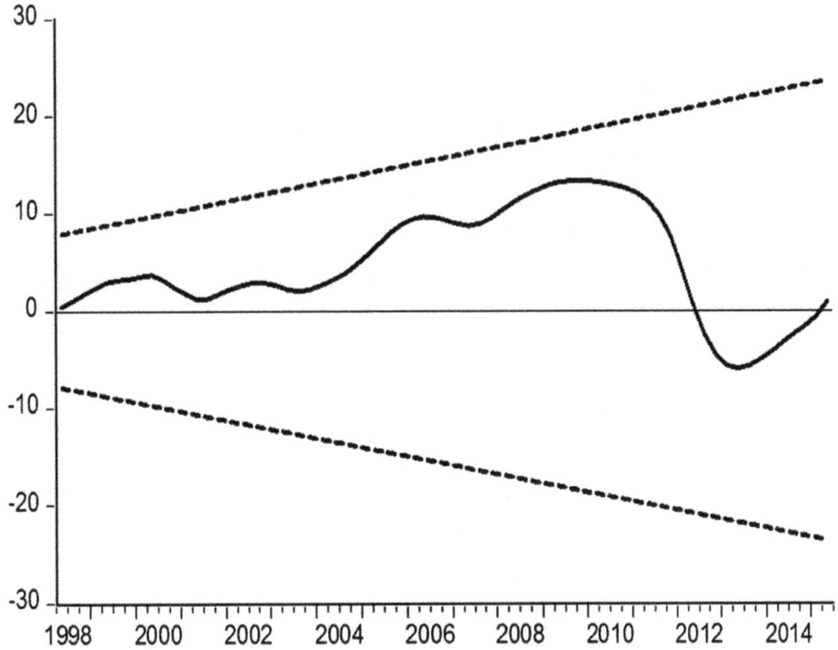

Figure 4. Plot of cumulative sum of squares of recursive residuals
Note: The dashed-lines show critical bounds at 5% significance level.

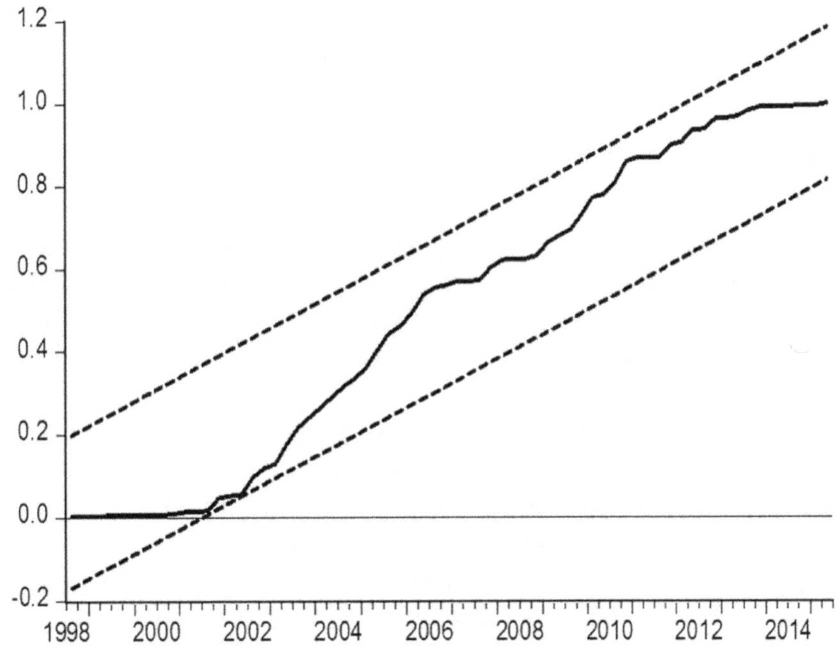

development level and the interest rate of the home country could have either positive or negative impacts. Higher development levels may bring about higher domestic market size and this may keep the investor in domestic market. On the impact of the domestic country's interest rate, the issue is more complicated. Higher home country interest rates may cause domestic investors to escape through foreign countries with lower interest rates. But there is another possibility; since moving into markets in abroad requires a considerable amount of capital, lower home country interest rates may raise the capital abundance of the investors and make it easier to branch out.

Since Turkey is still in the developing stage, firms and investors still need capital accumulation for great decisions; such as investing in abroad. The empirical finding that suggests the domestic interest rate negatively affects Turkey's outward FDI caused by this fact. We may also suggest that in the further development paths, this impact might become reversed.

FUTURE RESEARCH DIRECTIONS

Even though the findings obtained in this study reveal significant and considerable results, there are still some deficiencies and improvable points. Firstly, the analysis includes five variables in addition the outward FDI variable. For sure, there might be many other factors and variables that have an impact on Turkish OFDI. In this study, due to the data limitations a model with only these five variables has been employed. Future analyses may extend the model used. Secondly, in the analysis of this study, a destination country market size variable has been calculated by considering the share of Turkey's OFDI to these countries and their GDP levels. Although defining the market size of the destination countries with such a methodology is a useful way, it also has some disadvantages. Each destination country has different economic, geographical, historical and cultural relationship with Turkey (*or with any home country*). For instance, the underlying reasons of Turkey's outward FDI flowing into Netherlands and Azerbaijan are probably different from each other. Thus, to overcome this issue, applying country-by-country analyses (*i.e. gravity models*) might give more explicit results.

CONCLUSION

International capital movements and foreign investments have an important role on today's globalizing world. Since 1980's, with the speed-up of globalization around the world, capital holders and investors have been seeking for profitable areas out of national borders. In this study, the determinants of outward foreign direct investment flows are investigated for Turkey, which is an important emerging country in global economy.

The detailed data on the outward direct investment flows from Turkey shows that about 60% of the total investment flows from Turkey are shared by Netherlands, Azerbaijan, USA and Germany which implies that these four countries constitute an important part of the market for the Turkey's outward FDI. Correspondingly, to be able to create a proxy variable for market size, two more countries (U.K. and Switzerland which induce %5 and %2 of Turkish OFDI respectively) have been added to this group of countries and attained a ratio of %67 which makes two-thirds of the total flows. In addition to this variable, also the impacts of home country's real GDP level, interest rate, openness and wage rate have been estimated via the ARDL bounds test approach. The results of the analysis show that all the variables used are significantly associated with the outward foreign direct investment flows from Turkey. However, the signs of the estimated coefficients vary across variables. All the other variables are in a positive relationship with Turkish outward foreign direct investment while the home country interest rate has a negative impact on it.

The evidences reveal that, higher development level of the home country, higher rate of openness in the home country, higher labor cost in the home country and higher market size of the destination countries encourage outward foreign direct investment tendency for Turkish investors while higher interest rates in the home country discourages them. Within the observed evidences of the present study one may suggest that these five variables might be counted as significant determinants of Turkish outward foreign direct investment.

REFERENCES

Baek, J., & Kim, H. S. (2013). Is economic growth good or bad for the environment? Empirical evidence from Korea. *Energy Economics*, *36*, 744–749. doi:10.1016/j.eneco.2012.11.020

Boratav, K. (2009). *Türkiye İktisat Tarihi*. Ankara: İmge.

Dickey, D. A., & Fuller, W. A. (1979). Distribution of the estimators for autoregressive time series with a unit root. *Journal of the American Statistical Association*, *74*(366a), 427–431.

Eğilmez, M., & Kumcu, E. (2015). *Ekonomi Politikası: Teori ve Türkiye Uygulaması, 20. Baskı*. İstanbul: Remzi.

Engle, R. F., & Granger, C. W. (1987). Co-integration and error correction: Representation, estimation, and testing. *Econometrica*, *55*(2), 251–276. doi:10.2307/1913236

Goh, S. K., & Wong, K. N. (2011). Malaysias outward FDI: The effects of market size and government policy. *Journal of Policy Modeling*, *33*(3), 497–510. doi:10.1016/j.jpolmod.2010.12.008

Granger, C. W., & Newbold, P. (1974). Spurious regressions in econometrics. *Journal of Econometrics*, *2*(2), 111–120. doi:10.1016/0304-4076(74)90034-7

Johansen, S. (1988). Statistical analysis of cointegration vectors. *Journal of Economic Dynamics & Control*, *12*(2), 231–254. doi:10.1016/0165-1889(88)90041-3

Johansen, S. (1991). Estimation and hypothesis testing of cointegration vectors in Gaussian vector autoregressive models. *Econometrica*, *59*(6), 1551–1580. doi:10.2307/2938278

Johansen, S., & Juselius, K. (1990). Maximum likelihood estimation and inference on cointegration—with applications to the demand for money. *Oxford Bulletin of Economics and Statistics*, *52*(2), 169–210. doi:10.1111/j.1468-0084.1990.mp52002003.x

Kalotay, K., & Sulstarova, A. (2010). Modelling Russian outward FDI. *Journal of International Management*, *16*(2), 131–142. doi:10.1016/j.intman.2010.03.004

Kolstad, I., & Wiig, A. (2012). What determines Chinese outward FDI? *Journal of World Business*, *47*(1), 26–34. doi:10.1016/j.jwb.2010.10.017

Kueh, J. S. H., Puah, C. H., & Liew, K. S. (2010). *Selected macroeconomic determinants of foreign direct investment outflow of Singapore* (MPRA Working Paper No.25940). Munich: Munich Personal RePEc Archive.

Kwiatkowski, D., Phillips, P. C., Schmidt, P., & Shin, Y. (1992). Testing the null hypothesis of stationarity against the alternative of a unit root: How sure are we that economic time series have a unit root? *Journal of Econometrics*, *54*(1-3), 159–178. doi:10.1016/0304-4076(92)90104-Y

Kyrkilis, D., & Pantelidis, P. (2003). Macroeconomic determinants of outward foreign direct investment. *International Journal of Social Economics*, *30*(7), 827–836. doi:10.1108/03068290310478766

Lunn, J. (1980). Determinants of US direct investment in the EEC: Further evidence. *European Economic Review*, *13*(1), 93–101. doi:10.1016/0014-2921(80)90048-3

Lunn, J. (1983). Determinants of US direct investment in the EEC: Revisited again. *European Economic Review*, *21*(3), 391–393. doi:10.1016/0014-2921(83)90099-5

Mıhcı, H., Çağatay, S., & Koska, O. A. (2011). The determinants of foreign direct investment outflows from the European Union countries.''. *Economic Bulletin*, *31*(3), 2653–2666.

Panopoulou, E., & Pittis, N. (2004). A comparison of autoregressive distributed lag and dynamic OLS cointegration estimators in the case of a serially correlated cointegration error. *The Econometrics Journal*, *7*(2), 585–617. doi:10.1111/j.1368-423X.2004.00145.x

Pesaran, M. H., & Shin, Y. (1999). An Autoregressive Distributed Lag Modelling Approach to Cointegration Analysis. In S. Strom (Ed.), *Econometrics and Economic Theory in 20th Century: The Ragnar Frisch Centennial Symposium*. Cambridge, UK: Cambridge University. doi:10.1017/CCOL521633230.011

Pesaran, M. H., Shin, Y., & Smith, R. J. (2001). Bounds testing approaches to the analysis of level relationships. *Journal of Applied Econometrics*, *16*(3), 289–326. doi:10.1002/jae.616

Phillips, P. C., & Perron, P. (1988). Testing for a unit root in time series regression. *Biometrika*, *75*(2), 335–346. doi:10.1093/biomet/75.2.335

Scaperlanda, A., & Balough, R. S. (1983). Determinants of US direct investment in the EEC: Revisited. *European Economic Review*, *21*(3), 381–390. doi:10.1016/0014-2921(83)90098-3

Scaperlanda, A. E., & Mauer, L. J. (1969). The determinants of US direct investment in the EEC. *The American Economic Review*, *59*(4), 558–568.

Yusoff, M. B. (2010). The effects of real exchange rate on trade balance and domestic output: A case of Malaysia. *The International Trade Journal*, *24*(2), 209–226. doi:10.1080/08853901003652377

KEY TERMS AND DEFINITIONS

ARDL Bounds Testing Approach: It is a cointegration test providing that the existence of a long run relationship among the variables used in the econometric model are performed, regardless of their order of integration contrary to the other cointegration methods.

Cointegration: It is known that if two or more time series are not stationary but some linear combinations of them are stationary, hence the time series are said to be cointegrated.

Foreign Direct Investment (FDI): A kind of investment made in one country by an investor in another country.

Home Country: The country that is the origin of the investors that make OFDI.

Host (Destination) Country: The country that is the destination and the target of the investors that make OFDI.

Market Size: The intensity of demand in the destination country.

Outward Foreign Direct Investment (OFDI): The flowed FDI that has been counted for the home country.

ENDNOTES

1 See Pesaran et al. (2001) for further details on ARDL bounds testing approach.

2 See Dickey and Fuller (1979), Phillips and Perron (1988) and Kwiatkowski et al., (1992) for detailed information on unit root tests.

Chapter 12
Outward Foreign Direct Investment in Emerging Economies:
A Case of Turkey

Ahmet Oğuz Demir
Istanbul Commerce University, Turkey

Muhammad Moiz
Istanbul Commerce University, Turkey

ABSTRACT

Outward Foreign Direct Investment (OFDI) has been utilized by developed economies to enter developing markets for competitive advantages. However, recent boom in OFDI from emerging economies has prompted the question as to why these economies are investing abroad? A modest amount of literature exists regarding China and India, however, Turkey being an emerging economy has been largely untapped when it comes to determinants of OFDI. This study uses the Global Competitiveness Index (GCI) to find host and home country factors which have led to OFDI from Turkey to their top 10 investment destinations for the past 10 years. The host country factors found to be significantly correlated with Turkish OFDI are innovation (Netherlands and Russia), technological readiness (Russia and UK), labor market efficiency (Netherlands), infrastructure (Netherlands), domestic market size (Germany), and exports (UK). The home factors found to be significantly correlated with Turkish OFDI are infrastructure and domestic competition.

INTRODUCTION

Foreign Direct Investment (FDI) is an important factor for economic growth especially within developing economies. Generally the flow of FDI has been from developed towards developing economies, however in recent history there has been a shift in the outward foreign direct investment (OFDI). Emerging economies have been increasingly investing abroad sparking the question of how FDI outflows or OFDI impacts the home country and why are companies in emerging economies engaging in more OFDI today?

DOI: 10.4018/978-1-5225-2345-1.ch012

Outward FDI refers to companies investing abroad through various tools such as Green field investments, Brown field investments, and expansion of existing foreign facilities. Since the year 2000, there has been a surge in the OFDI from developing economies around the globe. The OFDI figures for all developing economies combined have increased exponentially. According to United Nations Conference on Trade and Development (UNCTAD, 2016; UNCTAD), FDI Outflows from developing economies increased from an estimated $88.63 billion to an estimated $377.94 billion from the year 2000 to 2015 respectively. The proportion of FDI outflows from developing economies to all FDI outflows from the world has also increased immensely, changing from 7.62% in 2000 to 25.64% in 2015. Whereas, the OFDI stock from developing economies increased from $734.81 billion (9.88% of global OFDI stock) in 2000 to $5, 296.35 billion (21.15% of global OFDI stock) in 2015.

Turkey holds a geographical advantage due to its location forming a connection between Asia and Europe. Turkey is also one of the fastest growing economies around the globe, growing almost three fold since the year 2000; the GDP of Turkey grew from $266 billion in 2000 to $798 billion in 2014. The increasing foreign direct investment has helped the Turkish economy grow over time, while there has been growth in FDI inflows there has also been an increase in FDI outflows. Turkish organizations are looking to take their business abroad and invest in different regions. But the question arises as to why Turkish companies are going abroad? Why invest in the international market rather than the domestic market? This study is undertaken in order to find the OFDI determinants among Turkish organizations.

The rest of the paper is divided into the following sections: Section 2, Turkey's Current Outward Foreign Direct Investment Overview; Section 3, Literature Review; Section 4, Methodology; Section 5, Results; Section 6, Conclusion.

TURKEY'S CURRENT OUTWARD FOREIGN DIRECT INVESTMENT OVERVIEW

Turkey's OFDI flows have been increasing over the years improving the OFDI stock to over $40 billion. Turkish firms are looking to go abroad and have recently had major mergers and acquisitions. OFDI not only helps these Turkish firms reach new markets, resources, and technology but also provides employment to thousands of people in host countries. Several surveys completed over the years show the number of foreign workers which are employed by Turkish MNEs; in 2007 the top 12 Turkish MNEs employed over 72, 000 workers abroad (KHU-DEIK-VCC, 2009), in 2009 the top 19 Turkish MNEs employed over 90, 000 workers abroad (KHU-DEIK-KPMG-T-VCC, 2012), and in 2012 the top 29 Turkish MNEs employed over 115, 000 workers aboard (KHU-DEIK-VCC, 2014). Turkish MNEs continue to invest abroad and increase their foreign affiliates and assets. Turkish OFDI Stock had crossed the $40 billion mark in the year 2014 over double its size in 2008 (estimated $17.85 billion). UNCTAD (2015) data on Turkish OFDI shows that Turkish investors have substantially increased their investments abroad after the 2008 global financial crisis.

Geographical Breakdown

A breakdown of the geographical OFDI is important because it helps us analyze the regions in which Turkey's investors hold interest. Europe has always been a close trading partner of Turkey especially after the Customs Union agreement between European Union and Turkey in 1996. Customs Union strengthened the trade relationship between EU and Turkey paving the way for higher volumes of trade

Table 1. Turkey's outward foreign direct investment (1990-2014)

Turkey's OFDI Figures Millions of U.S. Dollars		
Year	**FDI Outflows**	**FDI Outward Stock**
1990	-16.0	1150.32
1991	27.0	1177.32
1992	65.0	1242.32
1993	14.0	1256.32
1994	49.0	1305.32
1995	113.0	1418.32
1996	110.0	15[illegible]
1997	251.0	1779.32
1998	367.0	2146.32
1999	645.0	2791.32
2000	870.0	3668.0
2001	497.0	4581.0
2002	143.0	5847.0
2003	480.0	6138.0
2004	780.0	7060.0
2005	1064.0	8315.0
2006	924.0	8866.0
2007	2106.0	12210.0
2008	2549.0	17846.0
2009	1553.0	22250.0
2010	1469.0	22509.0
2011	2330.0	27681.0
2012	4106.0	30968.0
2013	3527.0	33373.0
2014	6658.33	40088.0

Source: UNCTAD (2015).

Figure 1. Depiction of Turkey's outward foreign direct investment over the years

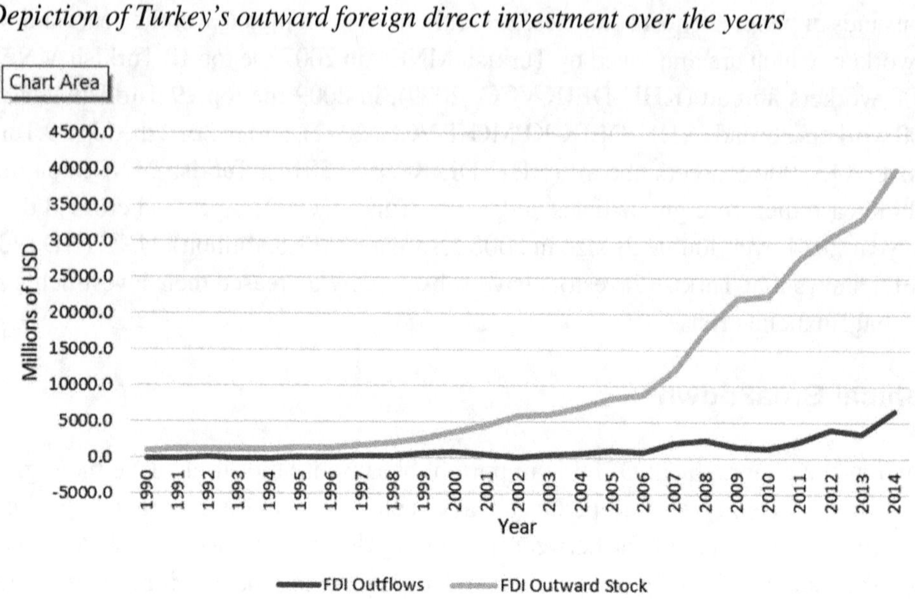

and FDI. This is evident from the amount of money Turkish investors have been investing in Europe. A majority of the Turkish OFDI have been directed towards Europe. Since 2002, 63% of all OFDI flows have been to Europe whereas only 25% have been to Asia, 10% to America, and a mere 2% to Africa.

Surveys of top Turkish MNEs completed by KHU-DEIK-VCC (2009, 2011, and 2014) also show that the majority of their affiliates are located in Europe. Furthermore, these surveys also found drivers for foreign investments by Turkish MNEs. A survey of top 19 Turkish MNEs (KHU-DEIK-KPMG-T-VCC, 2012) revealed that Turkish MNEs target Europe to acquire technology and skills, Africa and Asia for low cost labor, and Central Asian Turkic Countries for natural resources. Through a survey of top 29

Table 2. Turkey's outward FDI according to region (2002-2015)

Turkey's Regional Foreign Direct Investments Abroad (Millions USD)														
	2002	2003	2004	2005	2006	2007	2008	2009	2010	2011	2012	2013	2014	2015*
Europe	199	166	315	504	1,104	1,621	1,370	1,537	1,254	1,879	3,502	2,138	2,207	3,217
Africa	0	4	1	5	15	86	211	36	41	38	50	69	44	24
America**	43	69	46	22	40	83	533	73	58	54	176	251	485	1,360
Asia	4	240	452	504	518	485	490	394	470	569	600	768	2,483	581
Oceania and Polar Regions	0	0	0	30	0	0	0	0	0	2	6	0	0	0
Unclassified	5	7	1	0	0	0	0	0	0	0	0	0	15	58
Total	**251**	**486**	**815**	**1,065**	**1,677**	**2,275**	**2,604**	**2,040**	**1,823**	**2,542**	**4,334**	**3,226**	**5,234**	**5,240**

*Provisional

**America includes both North and South America

Source: Data obtained from Central Bank of the Republic of Turkey's online database.

Figure 2. Graphical representation of Turkey's Regional OFDI (2002-2015)

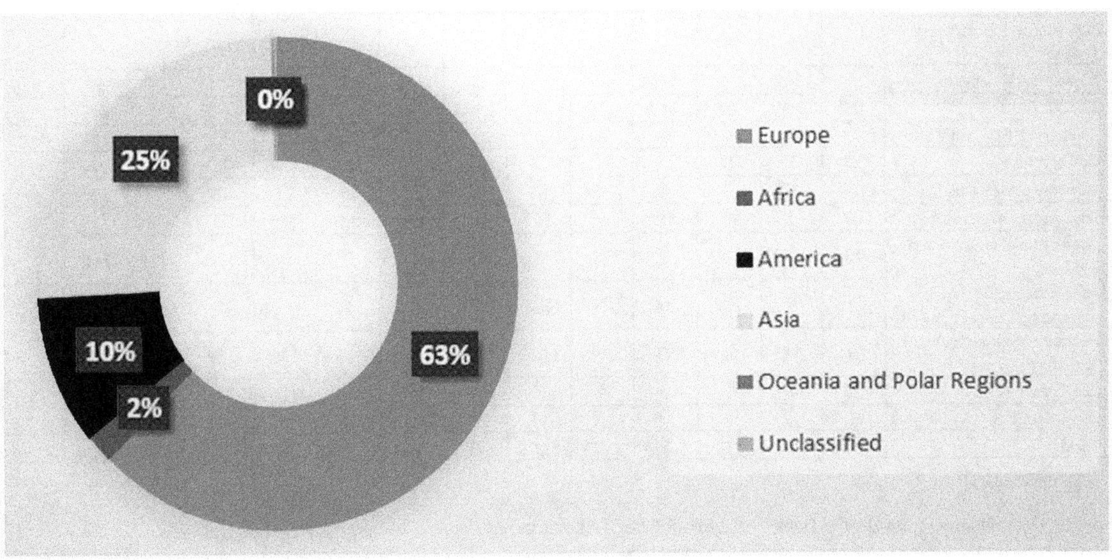

Turkish MNEs (KHU-DEIK-VCC, 2014), respondents were asked to identify drivers of investments abroad; these drivers include new markets and market diversification (75%), sustainable growth (60%), managing risk (50%), and access to natural resources and low costs (almost 40%). The same study also identified that the Turkish Government has been assisting investors through the opening of new embassies in Africa. Furthermore, the Government of Turkey has adopted an expansion policy by opening trade and investment offices in new regions, increasing flight destinations of Turkish Airlines, and increasing development assistance by Turkish Co-operation and Co-ordination Agency (TIKA). OFDI flows trends towards Europe determine that Turkish MNEs are looking to move towards developed markets which can provide them with high technology and highly skilled labor. Africa is still an untapped market for Turkish investors however, the government of Turkey is trying to push Turkish investors to invest in the African region.

Industry Breakdown

Through the industrial breakdown, a recent surge in OFDI in the Mining and Quarrying sector can be observed. This could be associated with recent large pipeline projects which Turkey has undertaken in neighboring countries. OFDI in Manufacturing has always been attractive since Turkish firms are going abroad in search for better technology which they have done by mostly acquiring firms in other nations. The financial sector of Turkey has also been very successful, various Turkish banks have opened offices in neighboring countries expanding their markets.

Table 3. Turkey's outward foreign direct investment by industry (2002-2015)

Turkey's Foreign Direct Investments Abroad by Industry (Millions USD)														
	2002	2003	2004	2005	2006	2007	2008	2009	2010	2011	2012	2013	2014	2015*
Agriculture, Forestry and Fishing	0	0	0	1	0	2	8	3	53	19	0	2	4	6
Mining and Quarrying	9	246	472	506	456	343	264	254	233	298	471	750	2,985	1,869
Manufacturing	83	99	60	419	810	230	1,382	281	444	517	2,742	1,086	667	852
Electricity, Gas, and Water	2	5	4	0	0	0	2	17	21	129	52	83	158	117
Construction	10	3	25	11	54	75	94	122	158	150	72	211	296	322
Wholesale and Retail Trade	9	17	25	8	42	21	20	22	35	21	48	101	123	69
Transportation and Storage	29	6	9	19	9	100	211	63	63	586	32	141	127	38
Accommodation and Food Services	13	1	2	6	2	0	14	7	3	14	194	20	148	44
Information and communication services	0	0	151	28	78	125	362	245	110	17	45	69	7	656
Financial and Insurance Activities	91	81	66	52	202	1,352	175	694	549	590	379	487	507	801
Real Estate Activities	0	0	0	1	1	12	13	267	66	114	217	199	130	389
Other Services	5	28	1	14	23	15	59	65	88	87	82	77	82	77
Total	**251**	**486**	**815**	**1,065**	**1,677**	**2,275**	**2,604**	**2,040**	**1,823**	**2,542**	**4,334**	**3,226**	**5,234**	**5,240**

*Provisional

Source: Data obtained from Central Bank of the Republic of Turkey's online database.

LITERATURE REVIEW

Research on outward foreign direct investment from emerging economies picked up pace after the turn of the 21st Century. Various studies have been conducted on OFDI from emerging economies ranging from the determinants of OFDI to the benefits of OFDI for home and host countries. Evidence from various emerging economies suggest that motives for OFDI from these economies have changed over time and vary among regions and industries. Dunning (1993) explained that firms invest abroad for three reasons: foreign-market seeking FDI, efficiency-seeking FDI, and resource-seeking FDI. Emerging economies also look for asset acquisition when investing abroad (Hill & Jongwanich, 2014), especially acquiring of assets in western economies. It is possible that these emerging economies are trying to acquire assets in countries with sounder institutional environment. However, in general emerging economies look to invest in countries which have relatively close or weaker institutions, moreover, institutional distance is diminished given that the host country has natural resources which are required by the home country (Athukorala & Hill, 2010; Aleksynska & Havrylchyk, 2012). Investment in natural resource rich areas can also explained by the fact that emerging East Asian countries are generally investing abroad through Sovereign Wealth Funds (SWFs) hence their aim for acquiring natural resources (Hill & Jongwanich, 2014). According to Andreff (2015), Russian Multinational Corporations (MNCs) are targeting industries in U.S., Canada, Italy, Switzerland, and South Africa for natural resources.

Emerging economies are also investing abroad in order to acquire technological assets which are not available in their domestic market (Dunning et al., 2008). Further motivations for OFDI include large surpluses, to gain competitive advantage (strengthen R&D and increase knowledge of regionally close markets), to seek markets (in case there are high trade barriers), and due to unfavorable domestic investment climate (Hill & Jongwanich, 2014). Stoian and Mohr (2016) find various motives for firms investing abroad due to avoidance of home country regulative voids. They find that OFDI from firms in emerging economies is a result of high protectionism, high corruption, high bureaucracy, and missing or inadequacy of rules and regulations which aren't enforced. They suggest that firms in emerging economies engage in escapist OFDI in order to avoid competitive disadvantages which may result from regulative voids. However, escapist OFDI does not have positive effects on the home country since firms are leaving due to shortcomings in the domestic market. Hill (2012) In Stoian and Mohr (2016) explains that bureaucracy, corruption, and protectionism all lead to negative consequences for the home country which hamper the economic growth. Similarly, Luo and Tung (2007) state that MNCs in emerging economies expand internationally in order to escape institutional and market constraints within domestic markets because these constraints lead to competitive disadvantages for emerging economy MNCs. A large number of studies on emerging economies and their determinants for OFDI have been done on China and India hence the OFDI patterns from these two economies are studied in-depth in this literature review. Furthermore, past studies on OFDI behavior from Turkey are examined.

In the case of India, one of the fastest growing economies in the world today, OFDI was motivated through learning and knowledge acquired from multinational corporations (Matthews, 2002). According Pradhan (2008), Indian multinational corporations (MNCs) go abroad in order to avoid a stagnant domestic market as well as policies which restrict firm growth such as the Foreign Exchange Regulations Act, licensing, regulations, and the Monopoly & Trade Restrictive Practices Act. Likewise, Andreff (2015) states that Indian MNCs go abroad in order to reduce dependency on the local market and business cycle. Indian MNCs have also been targeting Western Europe and U.S. in an attempt to improve their research and development, strategic assets, and skill structure (Andreff, 2015).

Other motivations of Indian MNCs include attaining global size and status as well as combining international economy with the low cost labor market at home (Andreff & Balcet, 2013). Furthermore, Nayyar (2008) conducted a survey of Indian MNCs and their motives for investing abroad; the survey found that market access (51% respondents) was the top motive for Indian MNCs going abroad, other motives were efficiency seeking (22%), resource seeking (13%), and created asset seeking (14%). In the case of India, liberalization of investments policies according to the changing preferences of the Indian companies have helped these companies increase their investments abroad (Anupam, Rani, & Kumar, 2014). Government policies are very important when it comes to FDI and OFDI, the government of India has been able to facilitate investors looking to go abroad. Pradhan (2011) found several drivers for Indian multinationals investing abroad, these include attraction towards countries with larger population and GDP per capita and countries which hold bilateral investment agreements (BIT) with India. These factors show that Indian MNCs like to target bigger markets and are willing to invest in countries where they have favorable investment policies in place through a BIT.

China is the largest emerging economy in the world. The rapid economic growth of China has also led to a rapid growth in OFDI from China. According to Ye Gang (1992), the first foreign investments of China were made in 1979 when Chinese companies began creating subsidiaries in an attempt to open up to new export markets. The early growth in OFDI from China has been due to FDI spillovers which resulted in technology transfers from MNCs towards local firms (Andreff, 2015). The rapid growth of OFDI after 2001 is due to the "go global" strategy adopted in 2001 as well as China's accession into the World Trade Organizations (Chen, n.d.). Chinese OFDI is directed towards natural resources in countries with poor institutions which explains higher investment by the Chinese in African nations (Kolstad & Wiig, 2012).

Additionally, Zhang and Daly (2011) conducted a panel data analysis of China's top importing countries from 2003 to 2009 in order to find the determinants for OFDI from China. They found that China's OFDI is attracted towards regions in which China has large exports, high GDP growth, high GDP per capita, large natural resources, and open economic nations. Similarly, Chang (2014) studied the characteristics and determinants of China's OFDI using the spatial gravity model for the same time period of 2003-2009. Chang found that OFDI characteristics for China include a focus on extraction of natural resources from developing and developed nations such as Kazakhstan, Australia, and African nations and investment in technology-intensive firms in developed nations. Chang identified determinants for China's OFDI as host country's GDP, vertical OFDI opportunities, a common language, fuel exports of host nations, and an export platform in the case of petroleum exporting nations. These results reveal the preferences of the Chinese OFDI towards natural resources and specifically towards petroleum rich nations.

It is important to note that OFDI from China is dominated by state owned firms which are controlled by the central government (Chen, n.d.) therefore the determinants of these firms would be aligned with the government policies unlike other emerging nations where MNCs are the major players in OFDI. This is evident due to the Chinese government providing subsidies to state owned firms which have invested in energy such as zero percent loan to China National Oil Corporation when bidding for a U.S. oil company (Xiao & Sun, 2005) and preferential interest rates to Chinalco bidding on an Australian mining company (Yao, Sutherland, & Chen, 2010). This also provides evidence that Chinese OFDI is directed towards strategic assets which align with China's strategic needs (Deng, 2007). Some motivations for OFDI from China's state owned firms include bypassing host country trade barriers, securing natural resources, gaining managerial expertise, acquiring technology, and gaining strategic assets (Wei & Alon, 2010). Whereas, provincial firms (which are mostly non-state owned) in addition to the determinants mentioned earlier, look for gaining knowhow, management skills, expansion of marketing networks, and increased competition at home leads to these firms seeking OFDI opportunities (Chen, n.d.).

Turkey is also a fast growing emerging economy which along with its economic growth has also increased in its OFDI although not as fast as other emerging economies such as China, Brazil, India, and Russia. To our knowledge there are only a handful of studies which have been conducted on the OFDI behavior of Turkey. These studies include a study of OFDI drivers for Turkish MNEs (Erdilek, 2008), determinants of OFDI from Turkey (Kayam & Hisarcikcilar, 2009; Onder & Karal, 2013), the impact of unfavorable home environment on Turkish Manufacturing firms' FDI (Kaya, 2009), and determinants of OFDI from Turkey towards Europe (Uray, Vardar, & Nacar, 2012; Gubbi & Sular, 2015). Erdilek (2008) conducted a case based study of MNEs in Turkey consisting of six SMEs and two large corporations. Several motives were found for OFDI from Turkey including ease of regulations, home environment (push factors such as high competition and exit costs), access to new markets, and host country environment (pull factors such as international brands, and access to natural resources). Similarly, considering Turkish manufacturing firms Kaya (2009) found utility costs, political instability, instability of exchange rate, and high inflation to be push factors for OFDI.

Kayam and Hisarcikcilar (2009) conducted an empirical study in order to find the determinants for Turkish OFDI using data of 11 countries from 1999 to 2005. They found the major determinants for Turkey's OFDI to be market seeking, substituting foreign markets for domestic markets, higher corruption index of host country, an increase in Turkish GDP decreases OFDI, and Turkish firms tend to produce low quality alternatives for higher quality products in host countries. Increase of Turkey's GDP has a negative impact on OFDI because Turkish firms are substituting domestic markets for foreign ones hence an increase in GDP per capita means that the buying power of domestic consumers are increasing leading to higher purchasing power motivating firms to focus on domestic markets. Uray, Vardar, and Nacar (2012) find that Turkish firms have invested in developed nations in order to attain technology and innovation. Furthermore, Turkish firms investing in Eastern European countries aim to change the country of origin in order to be more appealing toward the European customers (Uray, Vardar, & Nacar, 2012; Gubbi & Sular, 2015). Another important factor for investing in European countries is favorable tax policies for foreign investors (Gubbi & Sular, 2015). Literature shows that Turkish firms are investing abroad in order to expand their market, gain access to technology, present themselves are European firms (in the case of investment in Europe), gain product innovation, and avoid instability in the home environment.

METHODOLOGY

The researchers applied a preliminary data analysis approach in order to narrow down the determinants for investing in a specific region and the determinants for leaving the domestic market. The Global Competitiveness Report was used to analyze a list of determinants which were deemed fit in the case of OFDI. The Global Competitiveness Report is published yearly by the World Economic Forum, the purpose of the report is to assess the competitiveness of economies around the globe. Currently the Global Competitiveness Index (GCI) comprises of 12 pillars divided into three sub-indices including basic requirements subindex (institutions, infrastructure, macroeconomic environment, health and primary education), efficiency enhancers subindex (higher education and training, goods market efficiency, financial market development, technological readiness, market size), innovation and sophistication factors subindex (business sophistication, innovation).

Global Competitiveness Report for 2015-2016 consisted of 140 countries within which 14, 000 business executives were surveyed about the dimensions mentioned above. The executives chosen for this survey are investment decision makers hence their ability to provide accurate information on the business environment of an economy. Furthermore, the data for analyzing a business environment is difficult to gather hence surveying business executives seems to be a good alternative. The researchers chose a few questions from within this survey to analyze the top 10 countries in which Turkish investors have invested over the past 10 years. A few questions from the survey were also chosen to analyze the business environment of Turkey. These factors would help assess the host and home country factors which motivate Turkish investment abroad. A period of 10 year is analyzed through GCI from 2006-2007 to 2015-2016. A preliminary analysis is conducted on these questions by analyzing the correlation between indicators and Turkish OFDI patterns over the years. This analysis facilitates understanding of whether if the GCI is a good fit for analyzing business environment factors which impact the decision making for Turkish investors.

RESULTS

The analysis only showed meaningful results for several home and host country factors for a few countries (Appendix A and B). Through preliminary analysis it was found that only Germany, Netherlands, Russia, and UK showed significant results in some of their business environment factors. Similarly, correlation analysis for Turkey also showed that some home factors were significantly correlated to its OFDI patterns. Turkey's OFDI patterns show correlation with domestic competition and infrastructure. The Pearson correlation coefficient for OFDI and domestic competition is 0.882, which is statistically significant ($p < 0.01$ for a 2-tailed test). The Pearson correlation coefficient for OFDI and infrastructure is 0.690, which is also statistically significant ($p < 0.05$ for a 2-tailed test). The rest of the factors did not show any significant correlation. The relationships between domestic competition and OFDI from Turkey is interesting because the domestic competition has been increasing over the years which means that firms may be investing abroad in order to counter the competition at home. In the case of host countries, Turkish investors have invested the most in Netherlands with an OFDI stock of over $9 billion. Turkey's OFDI patterns towards Netherlands showed correlation with three market factors. Following are the results of Turkey's FDI in Netherlands. The Pearson correlation coefficient for Turkey's FDI and Labor Market Efficiency is 0.784, which is significant ($p < 0.01$ for a 2-tailed test). The Pearson correlation coefficient for Turkey's FDI and Infrastructure is 0.668, which is significant ($p < 0.05$ for a 2-tailed test). The Pearson correlation coefficient for Turkey FDI and Innovation is 0.738, which is significant ($p < 0.05$ for a 2-tailed test).

Germany receives the fourth highest FDI from Turkey having an OFDI stock of almost $2 billion since 2002. In the case of Germany we found only one factor to have significant results. The Pearson correlation coefficient for Turkey's FDI and Domestic Market Size is 0.856, which is significant ($p < 0.01$ for a 2-tailed test). The Pearson r shows a high correlation between Turkey's FDI to Germany and the German Market Size which could possibly mean that Turkish firms are investing there to capture a larger market. In the case of United Kingdom, which receives the fifth highest FDI from Turkey with an OFDI stock of over $1.5 billion since 2002, there are two factors which have been found significant when correlated with FDI from Turkey. The Pearson correlation coefficient for Turkey's FDI and Technological Readiness is 0.741, which is significant ($p < 0.01$ for a 2-tailed test). The Pearson correlation coefficient for Turkey's FDI and Exports to UK is 0.778, which is significant ($p < 0.01$ for a 2-tailed test). This shows the Turkish firms willingness to go to the UK market for technology. Finally, two factors were found to be significantly correlated with the Russian market. Russia receives the 8th highest FDI from Turkey with an OFDI stock of about $835 million since 2002. The Pearson correlation coefficient for Turkey's FDI and Technological Readiness is 0.643, which is significant ($p < 0.05$ for a 2-tailed test). The Pearson correlation coefficient for Turkey's FDI and Innovation is -0.716, which is significant ($p < 0.05$ for a 2-tailed test). This is interesting because there is a negative correlation between Turkey's FDI to Russia and their innovation level. We would have to look into this further to understand this relationship. The rest of the top 10 FDI locations for Turkish investors did not show any significant relations in terms of their business environment and Turkey's FDI into that region. Although the results of the current study only showed significant relations with only a few dimensions and Turkey's OFDI, we believe that the Global Competitive Index can be helpful in predicting the OFDI host and home country indicators.

CONCLUSION

Outward Foreign Direct Investment from emerging economies has been increasing since the 1990s and began to multiply greatly after the turn of the 21st Century. Studies on this topic have also been limited greatly due to a lack of data from within these emerging economies. We have found this to be true especially in the case of Turkey where data from primary sources was difficult to attain. Therefore, we tried a different approach by using several dimensions within the Global Competitive Index in order to determine the host and home country factors for OFDI. Although our results were not significant for many of the dimensions, we found there to be some significantly correlated factors for Turkish FDI towards various countries. The host country factors which were found to be significantly correlated with Turkish FDI were innovation (Netherlands and Russia), technological readiness (Russia and UK), labor market efficiency (Netherlands), infrastructure (Netherlands), domestic market size (Germany), and exports (UK). The home factors found to be significantly correlated with Turkish FDI were infrastructure and domestic competition. Data was a major limitation for this research since it was difficult to attain primary data which would have provided us with better results. However, for future research the researchers propose working with the Global Competitiveness Index to test the investment factors for other emerging economies such as China, India, Russia, Brazil, Indonesia, etc. because the researchers believe that the GCI can help provide much needed data for this topic which is difficult to attain otherwise.

REFERENCES

Aleksynska, M., & Havrylchyk, O. (2013). FDI from the South: The role of institutional distance and natural resources. *European Journal of Political Economy*, *29*, 38–53. doi:10.1016/j.ejpoleco.2012.09.001

Andreff, W. (2015). Outward Foreign Direct Investment from BRIC countries: Comparing strategies of Brazilian, Russian, Indian and Chinese multinational companies. *The European Journal of Comparative Economics*, *12*(2), 79.

Andreff, W., & Balcet, G. (2013). Emerging countries' multinational companies investing in developed countries: At odds with the HOS paradigm? *The European Journal of Comparative Economics*, *10*(1), 3.

Anupam, M., Rani, S., & Kumar, D. (2014). FDI Outflows Trends and Patterns of Indian Companies. *International Journal of Research*, *1*(5), 119–126.

Central Bank of the Republic of Turkey. (n.d.). *Türkiye Cumhuriyet Merkez Bankası*. Retrieved June 7, 2016, from http://www.tcmb.gov.tr/wps/wcm/connect/TCMB EN/TCMBEN/MainMenu/STATISTICS/Balance of Payments and Related Statistics/Balance ofPaymentsStatisticss/Data

Chang, S. C. (2014). The determinants and motivations of Chinas outward foreign direct investment: A spatial gravity model approach. *Global Economic Review*, *43*(3), 244–268. doi:10.1080/1226508X.2014.930670

Chen, C. Determinants and motives of outward foreign direct investment from China's provincial firms. *Transnational Corporations, 23*(1).

Deng, P. (2007). Investing for strategic resources and its rationale: The case of outward FDI from Chinese companies. *Business Horizons*, *50*(1), 71–81. doi:10.1016/j.bushor.2006.07.001

Erdilek, A. (2008). Internationalization of Turkish MNEs. *Journal of Management Development*, *27*(7), 744–760. doi:10.1108/02621710810883634

Gubbi, S. R., & Sular, S. A. (2015). *Why Do the Turkish Firms Invest in Mainland Europe? In Emerging Economies and Multinational Enterprises* (pp. 441–470). Emerald Group Publishing Limited. doi:10.1108/S1571-502720150000028019

Hill, C. W. L. (2012). International business: competing in the global market place. New York: McGraw-Hill Higher Education.

Hill, H., & Jongwanich, J. (2014). Emerging East Asian Economies as Foreign Investors: An Analytical Survey. *The Singapore Economic Review*, *59*(03), 1450019. doi:10.1142/S0217590814500192

Kadir Has University (KAH), Foreign Economic Relations Board (DEIK), KPMG Turkey (KPMG-T), Vale Columbia Center on Sustainable International Investment (VCC). (2011). *Turkish MNEs steady on their course despite crisis, survey finds*. Author.

Kadir Has University (KAH), Foreign Economic Relations Board (DEIK), Vale Columbia Center on Sustainable International Investment (VCC). (2009). *Survey provides the first ever ranking of Turkish multinationals investing abroad*. Author.

Kadir Has University (KAH), Foreign Economic Relations Board (DEIK), Vale Columbia Center on Sustainable International Investment (VCC). (2014). *Turkish OFDI Continues to Grow*. Author.

Kaya, H. (2009). Unfavorable business environment and foreign direct investment activities of Turkish manufacturing firms. *Journal of BRSA Banking and Financial Markets*, *3*(1), 101–118.

Kayam, S., & Hisarciklilar, M. (2009). *Determinants of Turkish FDI abroad*. Academic Press.

Kolstad, I., & Wiig, A. (2012). What determines Chinese outward FDI? *Journal of World Business*, *47*(1), 26–34. doi:10.1016/j.jwb.2010.10.017

Luo, Y., & Tung, R. L. (2007). International expansion of emerging market enterprises: A springboard perspective. *Journal of International Business Studies*, *38*(4), 481–498. doi:10.1057/palgrave.jibs.8400275

Nayyar, D. (2008). The internationalization of firms from India: Investment, mergers and acquisitions. *Oxford Development Studies*, *36*(1), 111–131. doi:10.1080/13600810701848219

Onder, G., & Karal, Z. (2013). Determinants of Foreign Direct Investments Outflow From a Developing Country: The Case of Turkey.*Business. Management in Education*, *11*(2), 241.

Pradhan, J. P. (2008). The evolution of Indian outward foreign direct investment: Changing trends and patterns. *International Journal of Technology and Globalisation*, *4*(1), 70–86. doi:10.1504/IJTG.2008.016188

Pradhan, J. P. (2011). Emerging multinationals: A comparison of Chinese and Indian outward foreign direct investment. *Institutions, Etc.*, *3*(1), 113–148.

Stoian, C., & Mohr, A. (2016). Outward foreign direct investment from emerging economies: Escaping home country regulative voids. *International Business Review*, *25*(5), 1124–1135. doi:10.1016/j.ibusrev.2016.02.004

UNCTAD. (2015). World Investment Report 2015. *United Nations Conference on Trade and Development.* Available at: http://unctad.org/en/pages/DIAE/World%20Investment%20Report/WIR-Series.aspx

UNCTAD. (2016). World Investment Report 2015. *United Nations Conference on Trade and Development.* Available at: http://unctad.org/en/pages/PublicationWebflyer.aspx?publicationid=1555

Uray, N., Vardar, N., & Nacar, R. (2012). International marketing-related outward FDI motives: Turkish MNCs' experience in the EU. New Policy Challenges for European Multinationals (Progress in International Business Research, Volume 7). *Emerald Group Publishing Limited*, *7*, 305–338.

Wei, W. X., & Alon, I. (2010). Chinese outward direct investment: a study on macroeconomic determinants. *International Journal of Business and Emerging Markets,* 2(4), 352-369.

Xiao, J., & Sun, F. (2005). Challenges Facing Outbound Chinese M& (and) A. *Int'l Fin. L. Rev.*, *24*, 44.

Yao, S., Sutherland, D., & Chen, J. (2010). Chinas Outward FDI and Resource-Seeking Strategy: A Case Study on Chinalco and Rio Tinto. *Asia-Pacific Journal of Accounting & Economics*, *17*(3), 313–325. doi:10.1080/16081625.2010.9720868

Ye, G. (1992). Chinese transnational corporations. *Transnational Corporations*, *1*(2), 125–133.

Zhang, X., & Daly, K. (2011). The determinants of Chinas outward foreign direct investment. *Emerging Markets Review*, *12*(4), 389–398. doi:10.1016/j.ememar.2011.06.001

APPENDIX 1

Pearson's Correlation analysis was conducted between Turkey's OFDI and Business Environmental Factors of the top 10 countries towards which Turkish investors invest. The OFDI to each country was correlated with various business environmental factors to find the significance of these factors with the OFDI from Turkey. The results are given in the table below.

Table 4. Correlation between Turkey's OFDI and business environmental factors in partner countries

Correlations Among Host Country OFDI from Turkey and Business Environment Factors

		OFDI	Infrastructure	Quality of Education System	Domestic Competition	Foreign Competition	Labor Market Efficiency	Financial Market Development	Technology Readiness	Domestic Market Size	Innovation	Exports	Imports
OFDI Azerbaijan	Pearson Correlation	1	.361	.166	.369	-.383	-.299	-.148	.390	.196	-.069	.487	.179
	Sig. (2-tailed)		.305	.647	.294	.274	.402	.684	.265	.588	.849	.153	.621
	N	10	10	10	10	10	10	10	10	10	10	10	10
OFDI Germany	Pearson Correlation	1	-.103	.229	.203	-.274	.050	.287	-.212	.856**	.270	-.243	-.133
	Sig. (2-tailed)		.778	.525	.573	.443	.891	.421	.557	.002	.451	.499	.714
	N	10	10	10	10	10	10	10	10	10	10	10	10
OFDI Ireland	Pearson Correlation	1	.057	-.600	-.609	.048	-.165	-.339	-.027	-.239	-.408	-.424	-.251
	Sig. (2-tailed)		.876	.066	.061	.896	.648	.338	.941	.507	.242	.222	.484
	N	10	10	10	10	10	10	10	10	10	10	10	10
OFDI Luxembourg	Pearson Correlation	1	.219	.226	.406	.111	.307	-.379	.320	-.152	.108	-.397	-.049
	Sig. (2-tailed)		.544	.530	.244	.760	.388	.280	.368	.675	.766	.256	.894
	N	10	10	10	10	10	10	10	10	10	10	10	10
OFDI Malta	Pearson Correlation	1	-.402	-.222	-.227	-.471	-.254	.289	-.585	-.249	-.221	-.111	-.165
	Sig. (2-tailed)		.250	.537	.529	.169	.478	.418	.076	.489	.539	.760	.649
	N	10	10	10	10	10	10	10	10	10	10	10	10
OFDI Netherlands	Pearson Correlation	1	.668*	.590	-.020	.620	.784**	-.376	.262	-.131	.738*	.373	.404
	Sig. (2-tailed)		.035	.073	.956	.056	.007	.285	.464	.718	.015	.289	.247
	N	10	10	10	10	10	10	10	10	10	10	10	10
OFDI Russia	Pearson Correlation	1	.497	-.400	-.142	.315	-.430	-.568	.643*	.311	-.716*	.608	.468
	Sig. (2-tailed)		.144	.252	.695	.375	.215	.087	.045	.381	.020	.062	.173
	N	10	10	10	10	10	10	10	10	10	10	10	10
OFDI Switzerland	Pearson Correlation	1	.538	-.027	.227	-.174	-.220	.020	-.142	-.357	-.387	.081	.293
	Sig. (2-tailed)		.109	.942	.528	.631	.541	.956	.696	.311	.269	.823	.411
	N	10	10	10	10	10	10	10	10	10	10	10	10
OFDI UK	Pearson Correlation	1	.357	.390	.404	.295	-.142	-.384	.741*	-.515	.464	.778**	.314
	Sig. (2-tailed)		.311	.265	.248	.409	.695	.273	.014	.128	.177	.008	.377
	N	10	10	10	10	10	10	10	10	10	10	10	10
OFDI USA	Pearson Correlation	1	.055	.130	.291	-.240	-.380	.290	.562	.[a]	-.147	.596	.077
	Sig. (2-tailed)		.880	.721	.415	.504	.278	.416	.091		.685	.069	.833
	N	10	10	10	10	10	10	10	10	10	10	10	10

**. Correlation is significant at the 0.01 level (2-tailed).

*. Correlation is significant at the 0.05 level (2-tailed).

APPENDIX 2

Pearson's Correlation analysis was conducted on Turkey's OFDI and their home business environmental factors. Table 5 shows the results.

Table 5. Correlation between OFDI from Turkey and home country factors

Correlation between OFDI from Turkey and Home Country Factors

		OFDI	Ethics and Corruption	Undue Influence	Government Efficiency	Infrastructure	Domestic Competition	Labor Market Efficiency	Foreign Competition	Financial Market Development	Innovation
OFDI Turkey	Pearson Correlation	1	.623	-.438	.621	.690*	.882**	-.121	-.395	.149	.592
	Sig. (2-tailed)		.054	.205	.055	.027	.001	.738	.258	.681	.072
	N	10	10	10	10	10	10	10	10	10	10

*. Correlation is significant at the 0.05 level (2-tailed).

**. Correlation is significant at the 0.01 level (2-tailed).

Chapter 13
Foreign Direct Investment in Indian Market

Manoj Kumar
Mother Parwati Education Services, India

ABSTRACT

A number of recent studies examine technology transfer from foreign direct investment (FDI) to India's domestic industrial enterprises. This study goes further by investigating the implications of institutions for the nature of technology spillovers during 2004 - 2013. We examine three institutional features that comprise aspects of India's "special characteristics": (1) the different sources of FDI, where FDI is nearly evenly divided between mostly Organization for Economic Co-operation and Development (OECD) countries and Mauritius; (2) India's heterogeneous ownership structure, involving state- (SOEs) and non-state owned (non-SOEs) enterprises; and (3) industrial promotion via tariffs or through tax holidays to foreign direct investment. We find robust positive and significant spillovers (as measured by total factor productivity) to domestic firms via backward linkages (the contacts between foreign buyers and local suppliers). Our results suggest varied success with industrial promotion policies. Final goods tariffs as well as input tariffs are negatively associated with firm-level productivity. However, we find statistically significant evidence of stronger productivity spillovers associated with firms that received tax breaks, suggesting that tax holidays were more successful than tariffs as an instrument to promote productivity growth in India.

INTRODUCTION

Since opening its economy to the outside world in late 1991, India has absorbed an increasing amount of FDI. It is now among the world's second largest hosts for foreign investment, and has consistently ranked number two as the largest developing country recipient of FDI inflows in recent years. Potential technology transfer is likely to have been an important rationale behind the Indian government's aggressive efforts over the past two decades to attract foreign investment to India (Hu and Jefferson (2002)). Indeed, the Indian government has intervened extensively to promote industrialization in India, relying on a range of policy instruments. These instruments include tariffs, tax subsidies, and promotion of foreign investors in key sectors.

DOI: 10.4018/978-1-5225-2345-1.ch013

One typical justification for subsidizing incoming foreign investment is an externality in the form of technology spillovers. Technology spillovers can be defined to take place when the entry or presence of multinationals increases the productivity of domestic firms who do not have any foreign equity participation. If such spillovers occur, then multinationals do not fully internalize the value of these benefits. It defines intra-industry spillovers (also called horizontal spillovers) as occurring when domestic firm productivity is affected by foreign corporations located in the same sector, while inter-industry spillovers (vertical spillovers)occur when domestic firms are affected by foreign firms in the upstream (forward linkage) or downstream sectors (backward linkages).

There have been a number of recent papers that test for technology spillovers from foreign investment. Most of these studies, such as papers by Haddad and Harrison (2010) on Morocco, Aitken and Harrison (1999) on Venezuela, and Konings (2001) on Bulgaria, Romania and Poland, either failed to find evidence of horizontal spillovers or reported negative horizontal spillover effects. More recently, Brecher and Carlos (2012) argued that since multinationals may simultaneously have an incentive to prevent information leakage that would enhance the performance of their local competitors, while at the same time possibly benefitting from transferring knowledge to their local suppliers or clients, spillovers from FDI are more likely to be negative along the horizontal dimension and positive along the vertical dimension. Brecher and Carlos (2012) uses firm-level data from Lithuania to show that positive FDI spillovers take place through backward linkages (between foreign affiliates and their local suppliers in upstream sectors); however, there is no robust evidence of positive spillovers occurring through either the horizontal or the forward linkage channel. One recent manuscript that investigates both horizontal and vertical FDI spillovers in China is Lin (2009). In contrast to Brecher and Carlos (2012), Lin (2009) finds evidence of forward positive spillovers, but no significant backward linkages.

There are also a set of theoretical studies demonstrating that positive FDI spillovers are more likely to operate at the inter-industry rather than the intra-industry level. For instance, there are studies on the choice by multinationals to use FDI as a model of market penetration. These studies emphasize efforts to minimize the probability of imitation, especially under imperfect intellectual property rights in the host country. As Markusen and Venables (2008) point out, proximity to potential domestic competitors with absorptive capacity to reverse engineer proprietary technology would be detrimental to a multinational, thus motivating it to set up its subsidiaries where potential rivals cannot erode its market share. By contrast, the multinational can benefit from knowledge diffusion when it reaches downstream clients and upstream suppliers, which will encourage vertical flows of generic knowledge that lead to inter-industry spillovers.

This study goes further by investigating the implications of the institutional context for the nature of spillovers. In particular, we examine three institutional features that comprise aspects of India's "special characteristics": the different sources of FDI, which are nearly evenly divided between mostly OECD countries and Mauritius (The Mauritius route is a channel used by foreign investors to invest in India, Mauritius is the main provider of foreign direct investment to India and also the preferred jurisdiction for Indian outward investments into Africa. In fact 39.6% of foreign direct investment to India came from Mauritius during 2001-2011. Hence, this country is treated separately for India); India's extraordinarily heterogeneous ownership structure, involving state and non-state ownership, and tax incentives such as income tax subsidies. Many foreign investors in India over the last ten years have faced much lower corporate tax rates; before 2014, foreign investors received a 15 percent corporate tax rate while domestic enterprises faced a regular 33percent corporate tax rate. This policy of promoting foreign investors and other favored firms in India was only discontinued in 2014.

In addition to exploring the differential effects of foreign investment linkages across special characteristics in explaining productivity performance, we also control for the impact of intermediate and final good tariffs. Until 1997, average tariffs on manufacturing in India were as high as 50 percent. There is a rich literature which examines the impact of trade liberalization on productivity, although there are fewer studies that disentangle the effects of input and output tariffs. One example is Amiti and Konings (2007), who use Indonesia manufacturing census data to show that the effect of reducing input tariffs significantly increases productivity, and that this effect is much higher than reducing output tariffs. For China, Borensztein *et al.* (2008) focus specifically on the impact of trade liberalization on productivity. Using Chinese firm-level data (1998-2005), they suggest that a ten percentage point reduction in final good output tariffs results in an increase in TFP of 0.42 percent.

This chapter results suggest varied outcomes from promoting domestic productivity growth through these different instruments. The benefits via vertical linkages from foreign investment have been significant and positive, but the impact of tariffs on total factor productivity growth has been negative. It finds some horizontal externalities from foreign direct investment (FDI), although the positive effects are not robust across specifications. It finds strong evidence of positive and significant vertical linkages to domestic firms via forward linkages (the contacts between foreign affiliates and their local clients in downstream sectors) and backward linkages (the contacts between foreign buyers and local suppliers).

Unlike previous studies on foreign investment in India, it finds strong evidence of backward linkages. One reason for this finding may be that previous studies did not have sufficiently differentiated sector level price deflators; this evidence suggests that foreign firms have exerted significant downward pressure on prices through vertical linkages, which would appear as lower vertical productivity effects if not properly accounted for.

This chapter also shows that firm ownership and sources of FDI significantly affect the magnitude of FDI spillovers. After it recalculates sector-level FDI based on its origin, it finds that investors from Mauritius and those from the rest of the world, largely the OECD region, generate completely different horizontal linkages for domestic firms. That is, OECD investors do help domestic firms located in the same industry whereas investors from Mauritius hurt their domestic counterparts or have no impact.

For trade policy, this paper results suggest a negative, significant effect of final goods tariffs on domestic productivity growth. It also tests for the effects of input tariffs on productivity, and find negative and significant effects of input tariffs on productivity growth. Finally, it explores the rationale for tax subsidies bestowed on foreign investors. If the India government correctly targets, through tax concessions, those firms with greater potential for capturing spillovers, we would expect stronger linkages associated with tax breaks. It finds statistically significant evidence of stronger productivity externalities associated with firms that received tax breaks.

Our empirical strategy follows Brecher and Carlos (2012). First, it uses Brecher and Carlos (2012) empirical strategies to calculate *Backward* and *Forward* linkages and follow her estimation models to test whether there are vertical FDI spillovers in the manufacturing sector in India. It addresses the endogeneity of inputs by applying the strategy proposed by OP. It also applies a variety of specifications to take into account firm-specific fixed effects, and find that our results are robust to these alternative approaches.

The rest of chapter is organized as follows. Section 2 describes the basic framework and the data used in this chapter. We also review broad trends for the 2004 through 2013 period. Section 3discusses the econometric issues and presents the empirical results. Section 4 concludes.

BASIC FRAMEWORK AND DATA

Section 2.A describes the analytical framework, estimation equation, and measures for constructing the key spillover variables that we use. Section 2.B describes the key features of our firm-level panel data set and the summary statistics for our sample period.

Basic Framework

To examine the impact of intra- and inter-industry FDI spillovers and trade policy across various institutional dimensions on firm productivity, we employ the following basic model, inspired by Aitken and Harrison (1999) and Brecher and Carlos (2012):

$$\ln Y_{ijt} = \alpha + \beta_1 \ln K_{ijt} + \beta_2 \ln L_{ijt} + \beta_3 \ln M_{ijt} + \beta_4 ForeignShareMA_{ijt} + \beta_5 ForeignShareFR_{ijt} \\ + \beta_6 StateShare_{ijt} + \beta_7 Horizontal_{jt} + \beta_8 Backward_{jt} + \beta_9 Forward_{jt} + \alpha_i + \alpha_t + \varepsilon_{ijt} \quad (1)$$

Y_{ijt} is the quantity produced by firm i in sector j at time t. It is calculated by deflating the output value (quantities*prices)by the sector-specific ex-factory price index of industrial products in order to separately identify quantity. K_{ijt}, capital, is defined as the value of fixed assets, which is deflated by the fixed assets investment index, and L_{ijt} is the total number of employees. M_{ijt} represents the intermediate inputs purchased by firms to use for production of final products, which is deflated by the intermediate input price index. *ForeignShare* MA_{ijt}, *ForeignShare* FR_{ijt} and $StateShare_{ijt}$ are defined as the share of the firm's total equity owned by Mauritius investors, foreign investors, and the state respectively. The omitted share, the non-state domestically-owned share, is represented by the constant term. By construction, these three firm-level controls are continuous variables and range from 0 to 1 in value.

The motivation for separating foreign share into two types is two-fold. First, we would like to see whether some types of foreign investment are more likely to result in technology spillovers than others. Second, anecdotal evidence suggests large quantities of so-called foreign investors in India are actually domestic investors who channel investment through Mauritius in order to take advantage of special treatment for foreign firms (so-called "round tripping"). If this is the case, then we would expect that foreign investment of this type might have a smaller impact on domestic firms.

Following Brecher and Carlos (2012), it define three sector-level FDI variables. First, $Horizontal_{jt}$ captures the extent of foreign presence in sector *j* at time *t* and is defined as foreign equity participation averaged over all firms in the sector, weighted by each firm's share in sectoral output. In other words,

$$Horizontal_{jt} = \left[\sum_{iforalli \in j} ForeignShare_{it} * Y_{it} \right] / \sum_{iforalli \in j} Y_{it} , \quad (2)$$

where $ForeignShare_{it}$ is the sum of $ForeignShareMA$ and $ForeignShareFR$. Second, $Backward_{jt}$ captures the foreign presence in the sectors that are supplied by sector j. Therefore, $Backward_{jt}$ is a measure for foreign participation in the downstream industries of sector j. It is defined as

$$Backward_{jt} = \sum_{kifk \neq j} \alpha_{jk} Horizontal_{kt} \quad (3)$$

The value of α_{jk} is taken from the 2009 input-output table representing the proportion of sector j's production supplied to sector k. Finally, $Forward_{jt}$ is defined as the weighted share of output in upstream industries of sector j produced by firms with foreign capital participation. As Brecher and Carlos (2012) points out, since only intermediates sold in the domestic market are relevant to the study, goods produced by foreign affiliates for exports (X_{it}) should be excluded. Thus, the following formula is applied:

$$Forward_{jt} = \sum_{mifm \neq j} \delta_{jm} \left[\left[\sum_{iforalli \in m} ForeignShare_{it} * (Y_{it} - X_{it}) \right] / \left[\sum_{iforalli \in m} (Y_{it} - X_{it}) \right] \right] \tag{4}$$

The value of δ_{jm} is also taken from 2009 input-output table. Since $Horizontal_{jt}$ already captures linkages between firms within a sector, inputs purchased within sector j are excluded from both $Backward_{jt}$ and $Forward_{jt}$.

Data and Broad Trends

The dataset employed in this paper was collected by the Indian National Bureau of Statistics. The Statistical Bureau conducts an annual survey of industrial plants, which includes manufacturing firms as well as firms that produce and supply electricity, gas, and water. It is firm-level based, including all state-owned enterprises (SOEs), regardless of size, and non-state-owned firms (non-SOEs) with annual sales of more than 5 million rupees. We use a ten-year unbalanced panel dataset, from 2004 to 2013.The number of firms per year varies from a low of 162,033 in 2005 to a high of 336,768 in 2013.The sampling strategy is the same throughout the sample period (all firms that are state-owned or have sales of more than 5 million rupees are selected into the sample); the variation of numbers of enterprises across years may be driven by changes in ownership classification or by increases (or reductions) in sales volume in relation to the 5 million rupees threshold. However, the data show that 5 million rupees is not a strict rule. Among non-SOEs, about 6 percent of the firms report annual sales of less than 5 million rupees in 2004; this number rises to 8 percent by 2005 and falls after 2009. In 2013, only 1 percent of non-SOEs have annual sales below 5 million rupees. In terms of the full sample, the percent of firms with sales less than 5 million rupees stays at the same level for 2004 and 2005 and starts falling in 2006. In 2013, around 2 percent of the sample consists of firms with annual sales less than 5 million rupees.

The original dataset includes 2,226,104 observations and contains identifiers that can be used to track firms over time. Since the study focuses on manufacturing firms, it eliminates non-manufacturing observations. The sample size is further reduced by deleting missing values, as well as observations with negative or zero values for output, number of employees, capital, and the inputs, leaving a sample size of 1,842,786. Due to incompleteness of information on official output price indices, three sectors are dropped from the sample. Thus, our final regression sample size is 1,545,626.

The dataset contains information on output, fixed assets, total workforce, total wages, intermediate input costs, foreign investment, Mauritius investment, sales revenue, and export sales. These are the key variables from which we obtain measures of firm-level foreign asset shares and the FDI spillover variable, which are discussed in detail in the next section. In this paper, to test the impact of FDI spillovers on domestic firm productivity, we use the criterion of zero foreign ownership to distinguish domestic firms and foreign owned firms, that is, domestic firms are those with zero foreign capital in their total assets. In the dataset, 1,197,597 observations meet the criterion.

Table 1. Summary statistics for all years, 2004-2013

	Levels	Mean	Std. Dev.	Growth Rates	Mean	Std. Dev.
	Number of Observations			Number of Observations		
logY	1,545,626	10.015	1.343	1,086,616	0.135	0.563
logL	1,545,626	4.808	1.152	1,086,616	0.013	0.503
logK	1,545,626	8.468	1.719	1,086,616	0.107	0.753
logM	1,545,626	9.534	1.378	1,086,616	0.094	0.661
Foreign share (contributed by Mauritius investors)	1,545,626	0.089	0.267	1,086,616	0.012	0.377
Foreign share (contributed by other investors)	1,545,626	0.079	0.249	1,086,616	0.0003	0.146
Stateshare	1,545,626	0.089	0.272	1,086,616	-0.007	0.147
Horizontal	1,545,626	0.254	0.142	1,086,616	0.004	0.046
Backward	1,545,626	0.077	0.046	1,086,616	0.002	0.015
Forward	1,545,626	0.103	0.173	1,086,616	0.004	0.066
Tariff	1,545,626	12.691	6.600	1,086,616	-0.869	2.295
Tariff_backward	1,545,626	8.191	3.769	1,086,616	-0.319	1.611
Tariff_forward	1,545,626	9.185	4.064	1,086,616	-0.359	2.066

Table 1 reports the summary statistics for the main variables used in the regressions. The summary statistics indicate the mean of the ratios, which is different than weighted means which would give more weight to larger firms. The first three columns report means for levels and the last three columns report means for growth rates of the key variables used in the analysis.

The statistical means highlight the remarkable growth rates exhibited by the manufacturing sector during this period, with average output growing 13.5 percent a year, and the net capital stock growing 10.7 percent per year. Labor input grew significantly slower, with average annual increases of only 1.3 percent per year. The means also document that on average foreign-invested assets have been almost evenly split between sources in Mauritius, and foreign investment originating in other locations. The state continues to play an important role in manufacturing, with a mean asset share of 8.9 percent during the sample period; over the sample period the share of total foreign investment in manufacturing is significantly larger, at 16.8 percent. For the sample as a whole, the average state share during this period fell by approximately 0.7 percentage point per year.

In Tables 2, 3, 4, and 5, we provide summary statistics for the four sets of spillover variables. Table 2 shows that the share of foreign-invested assets at the sector level, the horizontal foreign share, increased over the sample period from 20.4 to 26.7 percent.

To take into account the sources of FDI for sectoral spillovers, we re-calculate sector-level FDI variables from two broad geographic categories. To explore the importance of the source of foreign investment within the firm for productivity, we calculate firm-level foreign investment, horizontal foreign shares, and vertical foreign shares for Mauritius FDI, and for foreign investment originating in other locations, i.e. principally the OECD countries. Table 2 shows basic summary statistics for these two sets of sectoral spillover variables. The basic summary statistics show that the two sets have exhibited different

Table 2. Summary statistics for spillover variables

Year	Number of Observations	Horizontal		Backward		Forward	
		Mean	Std. Dev.	Mean	Std. Dev.	Mean	Std. Dev.
2004	96,135	0.204	0.125	0.059	0.034	0.068	0.103
2005	104,253	0.220	0.132	0.066	0.038	0.077	0.120
2006	102,745	0.233	0.134	0.071	0.040	0.085	0.136
2007	114,735	0.240	0.135	0.071	0.041	0.089	0.142
2008	122,464	0.242	0.132	0.073	0.042	0.090	0.143
2009	138,377	0.250	0.139	0.075	0.044	0.099	0.166
2010	202,735	0.270	0.146	0.082	0.049	0.109	0.180
2011	194,274	0.273	0.149	0.083	0.049	0.117	0.199
2012	217,062	0.275	0.146	0.085	0.048	0.120	0.201
2013	255,042	0.267	0.143	0.083	0.048	0.119	0.199

Table 3. Summary statistics for spillover variables that are calculated based on sources of FDI

Year	Number of Obs	Horizontal_MA		Backward_MA		Forward_MA		Horizontal_FR		Backward_FR		Forward_FR	
		Mean	Std. Dev.	Mean	Std. Dev.	Mean	Std. Dev.	Mean	Std. Dev.	Mean	Std. Dev.	Mean	Std. Dev.
2004	96,135	0.097	0.068	0.026	0.015	0.033	0.037	0.059	0.069	0.033	0.021	0.037	0.059
2005	104,253	0.106	0.070	0.030	0.016	0.036	0.041	0.075	0.073	0.036	0.023	0.041	0.075
2006	102,745	0.112	0.072	0.033	0.018	0.038	0.048	0.089	0.077	0.038	0.024	0.048	0.089
2007	114,735	0.114	0.070	0.033	0.017	0.038	0.049	0.095	0.086	0.038	0.026	0.049	0.095
2008	122,464	0.112	0.070	0.032	0.018	0.041	0.052	0.097	0.082	0.041	0.026	0.052	0.097
2009	138,377	0.117	0.073	0.033	0.018	0.042	0.057	0.113	0.089	0.042	0.029	0.057	0.113
2010	202,735	0.116	0.067	0.034	0.019	0.048	0.065	0.126	0.102	0.048	0.033	0.065	0.126
2011	194,274	0.115	0.068	0.034	0.020	0.048	0.071	0.135	0.102	0.048	0.031	0.071	0.135
2012	217,062	0.114	0.067	0.034	0.019	0.051	0.074	0.144	0.104	0.051	0.032	0.074	0.144
2013	255,042	0.109	0.063	0.033	0.018	0.050	0.074	0.139	0.103	0.050	0.031	0.074	0.139

trends over time.FDI shares for, Mauritius investment steadily increased over the period of 1998-2003. In contrast, FDI from other regions shows an even faster and steadily increasing pattern of growth over the entire time period, with more than a doubling of foreign investment shares. It is clear from Table 3 that most of the increase in foreign investment over 1998-2007 originated outside of Japan.

Table 4 reports trends in subsidized and non-subsidized foreign investment. While the standard tax rate across all firms during the sample period was 33 percent, a large share of foreign-owned firms were granted tax subsidies, thus facing tax rates that were significantly lower. In the left three columns of Table 4, we redefine our sector-level foreign share variables by restricting them to only those foreign firms who paid less than the statutory tax rate. In the right three columns of Table 4, we redefined sector-level foreign share to restrict it to those firms who paid the full rate. The trends show a steady increase

Table 4. Summary statistics for subsidized and non-subsidized spillover variables (calculated based on income tax)

Year	Number of Obs	Subsidized						Non-Subsidized					
		Horizontal		Backward		Forward		Horizontal		Backward		Forward	
		Mean	Std. Dev.	Mean	Std. Dev.	Mean	Std. Dev.	Mean	Std. Dev.	Mean	Std. Dev.	Mean	Std. Dev.
2004	96,135	0.076	0.060	0.022	0.015	0.024	0.047	0.112	0.068	0.033	0.018	0.038	0.050
2005	104,253	0.083	0.067	0.025	0.018	0.027	0.056	0.125	0.069	0.040	0.020	0.046	0.064
2006	102,745	0.096	0.072	0.029	0.020	0.033	0.070	0.130	0.070	0.041	0.021	0.049	0.068
2007	114,735	0.102	0.075	0.031	0.020	0.034	0.057	0.130	0.067	0.039	0.021	0.052	0.083
2008	122,464	0.107	0.080	0.035	0.025	0.041	0.091	0.128	0.066	0.037	0.018	0.047	0.059
2009	138,377	0.110	0.078	0.034	0.023	0.042	0.083	0.131	0.069	0.039	0.021	0.053	0.080
2010	202,735	0.132	0.090	0.041	0.027	0.054	0.110	0.129	0.063	0.038	0.020	0.051	0.070
2011	194,274	0.132	0.096	0.041	0.028	0.055	0.110	0.131	0.064	0.039	0.021	0.058	0.092
2012	217,062	0.138	0.094	0.043	0.028	0.057	0.101	0.126	0.061	0.039	0.020	0.057	0.097
2013	255,042	0.138	0.089	0.044	0.026	0.062	0.111	0.119	0.061	0.036	0.021	0.054	0.086

Table 5. Summary statistics for subsidized and non-subsidized spillover variables (calculated based on value added tax)

Year	Number of Obs	Subsidized						Non-Subsidized					
		Horizontal		Backward		Forward		Horizontal		Backward		Forward	
		Mean	Std. Dev.	Mean	Std. Dev.	Mean	Std. Dev.	Mean	Std. Dev.	Mean	Std. Dev.	Mean	Std. Dev.
2004	96,135	0.053	0.062	0.014	0.011	0.009	0.018	0.151	0.078	0.045	0.024	0.059	0.085
2005	104,253	0.049	0.056	0.013	0.012	0.007	0.012	0.169	0.089	0.052	0.027	0.069	0.107
2006	102,745	0.049	0.053	0.013	0.011	0.009	0.019	0.182	0.094	0.058	0.030	0.076	0.118
2007	114,735	0.049	0.050	0.013	0.011	0.008	0.017	0.187	0.095	0.057	0.029	0.080	0.123
2008	122,464	0.063	0.064	0.017	0.014	0.008	0.016	0.178	0.088	0.055	0.028	0.081	0.127
2009	138,377	0.070	0.075	0.018	0.018	0.013	0.038	0.177	0.083	0.056	0.027	0.085	0.130
2010	202,735												
2011	194,274	0.061	0.058	0.017	0.015	0.014	0.035	0.207	0.102	0.064	0.034	0.101	0.162
2012	217,062	0.054	0.054	0.015	0.014	0.015	0.045	0.214	0.103	0.069	0.034	0.102	0.153
2013	255,042	0.047	0.056	0.013	0.015	0.012	0.038	0.214	0.097	0.068	0.032	0.105	0.159

in subsidized foreign investment between 1998 and 2007. By the end of the sample period, the majority of foreign investors received some form of a tax subsidy.

Figure 1 shows the distribution of taxes paid by different types of enterprises for the year 2004. The top left-hand side quadrant shows that a large share of firms paid the 33 percent tax rate. This was particularly true for non-foreign, non-SOE enterprises. However, only a small minority of foreign-invested

Figure 1.

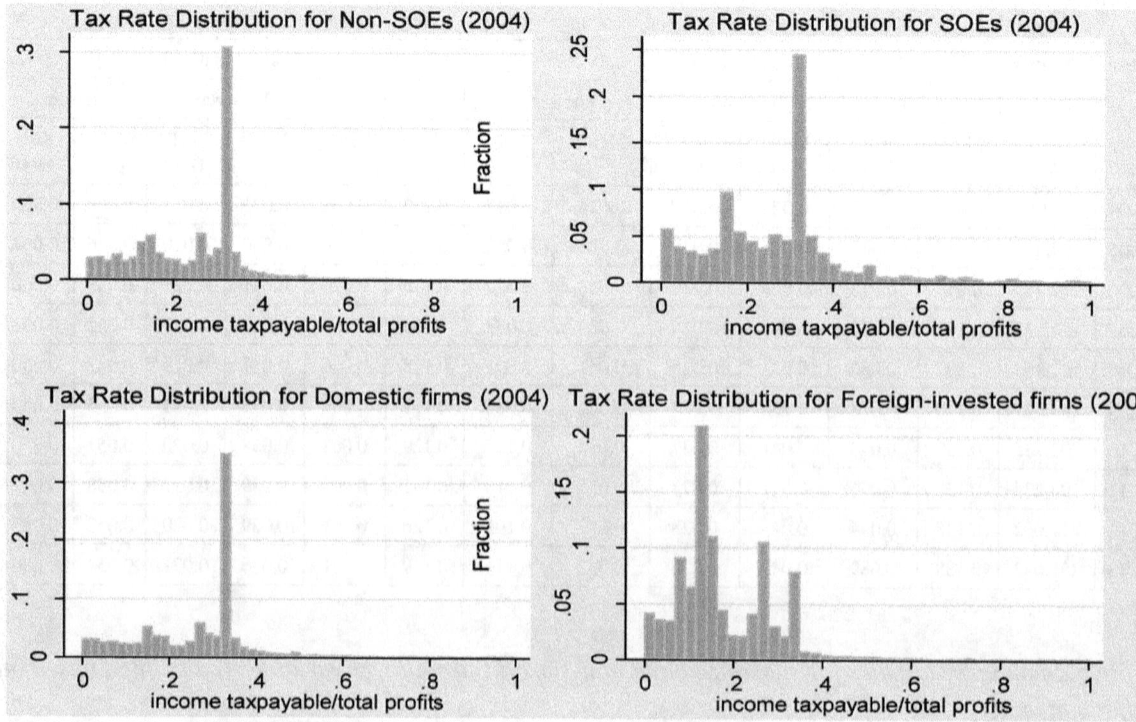

firms paid the statutory rate, as indicated by the bottom right-hand side quadrant. In 2004, 7 percent of foreign-invested firms paid the statutory rate, compared to almost 40 percent for domestically-owned enterprises.

Table 5 reports the percentage of firms who were subsidized based on value-added taxes, which are reported separately from income taxes on profits. Fewer firms receive subsidies in the form of exemptions on value-added taxes. These exemptions increased until 2003, then declined. It is clear from these tables that income tax holidays were a more pervasive form of incentives until the 2008 tax reform.

ESTIMATION AND RESULTS

Baseline Results

We begin the analysis by estimating the model described in equation (1) using ordinary least square (OLS) with and without firm fixed effects Columns (1) and (2) of Table 3 are estimated with the dependent variable as the log of the firm's deflated output. To study the impact of FDI spillovers on the performance of domestic firms, we are interested in how FDI invested in other firms affect the domestic firms located in the same sector. Therefore, the key parameters in the above specification are β_7, β_8 and β_9.

One possibility that has not been explored in the literature on vertical and horizontal linkages is that foreign investment shares are proxy for different trade policies across sectors. Protected sectors

Table 6. OLS and Olley-Pakes regression with contemporaneous spillover variables with tariff controls: with vs. without firm-fixed effects (sample: all firms)

	Dependent Variable: logY		Dependent Variable: lnTFP	
LogL	0.0914***	0.0755***		
	(0.0036)	(0.0041)		
LogK	0.0278***	0.0347***		
	(0.0016)	(0.0024)		
LogM	0.766***	0.865***		
	(0.0069)	(0.0042)		
Foreignshare(by Mauritius)	-0.0018	-0.0018	-0.00353	0.0231***
	(0.0031)	(0.0052)	(0.0031)	(0.0049)
Foreignshare (by other countries)	0.0076**	0.0644***	0.0054*	0.115***
	(0.0032)	(0.0057)	(0.0032)	(0.0089)
Stateshare	-0.0168***	-0.0586***	-0.0201***	-0.126***
	(0.0036)	(0.0060)	(0.0032)	(0.0108)
Horizontal	0.162*	0.128	0.164*	0.0771
	(0.088)	(0.116)	(0.0871)	(0.110)
Backward	0.813***	0.956***	0.807***	1.096***
	(0.259)	(0.331)	(0.256)	(0.328)
Forward	0.163*	0.185	0.160*	0.190
	(0.0869)	(0.114)	(0.0865)	(0.119)
lnTariff	-0.0385**	0.00198	-0.0381**	-0.0129
	(0.0150)	(0.0319)	(0.0151)	(0.0319)
lnTariff_backward	-0.0276	-0.0061	-0.0289	-0.0236
	(0.0188)	(0.0312)	(0.0189)	(0.0319)
lnTariff_forward	-0.0064	-0.0396**	-0.0066	-0.0410**
	(0.0080)	(0.0173)	(0.0079)	(0.0178)
Constant	1.921***	0.956***	1.721***	1.749***
	(0.0704)	(0.123)	(0.0577)	(0.118)
Firm-fixed effect	Yes	No	Yes	No
Observations	1,545,626	1,545,626	1,545,626	1,545,626
R-squared	0.831	0.949	0.179	0.237

may be more likely to receive foreign investment as these firms may be motivated to relocate in order to circumvent tariff or non-tariff barriers ("tariff-jumping" foreign investment, which leads to effects as modeled by Caves (2012)). In this case, the gains from foreign investment could be under-estimated due to omitted variable bias.

To control for the effects of trade policies, it has created a time series of tariffs, obtained from the World Integrated Trading Solution (WITS), maintained by the World Bank. It aggregated tariffs to the same level of aggregation as the foreign investment data, using output for 2003 as weights. It also created forward and backward tariffs, to correspond with our vertical FDI measures. Table 1 and Table A-6 show basic summary statistics for these tariff variables. During the sample period, average tariffs fell nearly 9 percentage points, which is a significant change over a short time period. While the average level of tariffs during this period, which spans the years before and after WTO accession, was nearly 13 percent, this average masks significant heterogeneity across sectors, with a high of 41 percent in grain mill products and a low of 4 percent in railroad equipment.

It initially pools the data to include both firms with and without foreign investment, reporting results with and without firm fixed effects. The first column of Table 3, with the application of fixed effects, shows that firm productivity levels are higher for firms with participation from other (OECD) investors than those from Mauritius, and lower for firms with state-owned assets. There are no significant horizontal spillovers, but backward vertical linkages are positive and statistically significant. Final goods tariffs are negative and significantly associated with productivity in the fixed effect specifications, but not in the fixed effect specifications. This suggests that tariffs are imposed in sectors where productivity is lower, but the association between changes in tariffs and changes in productivity across all firms is weak. It will see that the negative significance of tariffs is stronger when we split the sample based on ownership differences later in the paper.

Comparing the fixed effects results in the first column with the second column (where firm fixed effects are omitted), the results are consistent across the two specifications. As expected, the coefficient on capital's output elasticity is attenuated with the fixed effect estimator. While foreign-invested firms are much more efficient and state-invested enterprises are much less efficient than the non-state-domestically-invested enterprises that represent the reference, once firm fixed effects are controlled for the differences are much smaller. Such differences suggest important differences between productivity levels and growth rates of state owned and foreign enterprises versus other types of enterprises.

Also using the entire sample, the third and fourth columns of Table 3 compare OLS and fixed effect estimates using Brecher and Carlos (2012) to correct for the potential endogeneity of input choice. The earlier literature on production function estimation shows that the use of OLS is inappropriate when estimating productivity, since this method treats labor, capital and other input variables as exogenous. As Globerman (2011) argue, inputs should be considered endogenous since they are chosen by a firm based on its productivity. Firm-level fixed effects will not solve the problem, because time-varying productivity shocks can affect a firm's input decisions.

Using OLS will therefore bias the estimations of coefficients on the input variables. To solve the simultaneity problem in estimating a production function, we employ the procedure suggested by Brecher and Carlos (2012) (henceforth OP), which uses investment as a proxy for unobserved productivity shocks. OP addresses the endogeneity problem as follows. Let us consider the following Cobb-Douglas production function in logs:

$$y_{it} = \beta_k k_{it} + \beta_l l_{it} + \beta_m m_{it} + \omega_{it} + \varepsilon_{it} \tag{5}$$

y_{it}, k_{it}, l_{it}, and m_{it} represent log of output, capital, labor, and materials, respectively. ω_{it} is the productivity and ε_{it} is the error term (or a shock to productivity). The key difference between ω_{it} and ε_{it} is that ω_{it} affects firm's input demand while the latter does not. OP also makes timing assumptions regarding the input variables. Labor and materials are free variables but capital is assumed to be a fixed factor and subject to an investment process. Specifically, at the beginning of every period, the investment level a firm decides together with the current capital value determines the capital stock at the beginning of the nest period, i.e.

$$k_{it+1} = (1-\sigma)k_{it} + i_{it} \tag{6}$$

The key innovation of OP estimation is to use firm's observable characteristics to model a monotonic function of firm's productivity. Since the investment decision depends on both productivity and capital, OP formulate investment as follows,

$$i_{it} = i_{it}(\omega_{it}, k_{it}) \tag{7}$$

Given that this investment function is strictly monotonic in ω_{it}, it can be inverted to obtain

$$\omega_{it} = f_t^{-1}(i_{it}, k_{it}) \tag{8}$$

Substituting this into the production function, we get the following,

$$\begin{aligned} y_{it} &= \beta_k k_{it} + \beta_l l_{it} + \beta_m m_{it} + f_t^{-1}(i_{it}, k_{it}) + \varepsilon_{it} \\ &= \beta_l l_{it} + \beta_m m_{it} + \varphi_t(i_{it}, k_{it}) + \varepsilon_{it} \end{aligned} \tag{9}$$

In the first stage of OP estimation, the consistent estimates of coefficients on labor and materials as well as the estimate of a non-parametrical term (φ_t) are obtained. The second step of OP identifies the coefficient on capital through two important assumptions. One is the first-order Markov assumption of productivity, ω_{it} and the timing assumption about k_{it}. The first-order Markov assumption decomposes ω_{it} into its conditional expectation at time *t*-1, $E\left[\omega_{it} \mid \omega_{it-1}\right]$, and a deviation from that expectation, ζ_{it}, which is often referred to the "innovation" component of the productivity. These two assumptions allow it to construct an orthogonal relationship between capital and the innovation component in productivity, which is used to identify the coefficient on capital.

The biggest disadvantage of applying the OP procedure is that many firms report zero or negative investment. To address this problem, we also explore the robustness of our results to using the Levinsohn and Petrin (2003) approach. With the Brecher and Carlos (2012) correction, it can get an unbiased estimate of the firm's productivity. Therefore, the independent variable then becomes total factor productivity (TFP) instead of the log of output. Specifically, this is a two-stage estimation procedure when using TFP as the dependent variable. The first step is to use OP to obtain unbiased coefficients on input variables and then calculate TFP (residual from the production function). Estimates of input coefficients from the first step using both OLS with firm fixed effects as well as the Brecher and Carlos (2012) procedure are reported in Appendix Table A-2. The second step is to regress TFP on firm-level controls and FDI variables.

Moulton showed that in the case of regressions performed on micro units that also include aggregated market (in this case industry) variables, the standard errors from OLS will be underestimated. As Moulton demonstrated, failing to take account of this serious downward bias in the estimated errors results in spurious findings of the statistical significance for the aggregate variable of interest. To address this issue, the standard errors in the paper are clustered for all observations in the same industry.

As a robustness check, we also employed the procedure suggested by Levinsohn and Petrin (2003), which uses intermediate inputs as a proxy for unobserved productivity shocks. With LP's correction, the estimation procedure is also two-stage. In the first stage, it obtain input shares and calculate the firm's total factor productivity (TFP) (i.e., the residuals from production function). In the second stage, it regress TFP on the remaining independent regressors in this initial specification. However, to save on space we only report the results using the OP, and not the LP procedure. The results are qualitatively similar using both approaches.

The results in the last two columns of Table 3 present the pooled estimates using the OP method. Consequently, it cannot distinguish between spillovers to domestic firms or cluster effects for foreign enterprises. In all the results which follow, it separate firms into foreign-invested firms, those with some positive foreign ownership and domestically-owned firms, defined as enterprises with zero foreign ownership.

The baseline results, which incorporate firm fixed effects, are presented in Table 4. Comparing the results across three different samples (all, foreign-invested, and domestic firms) shows differences in the patterns of FDI spillovers across different groups. Horizontal spillovers are significantly positive only for domestic firms. Backward linkages are large in magnitude and positive for domestic firms, indicating that domestic enterprises benefit from foreign investors through acting as suppliers to foreign firms. Foreign-invested enterprises benefit from other foreign investment through both backward and forward linkages, indicating benefits to foreign firms from purchasing inputs from other foreign firms. The magnitudes of the vertical linkages are generally larger for foreign-invested firms, suggesting that firms with foreign participation are even more likely to benefit from being near other foreign firms.

The F-tests listed at the bottom of the Table 4 identify whether these differences are statistically significant. As reported in the F-tests, the magnitudes are significantly larger for foreign-invested firms' vis-à-vis forward linkages but not significantly different with regards to backward linkages. This implies that foreign firms benefit more than domestically-invested firms from interacting with upstream foreign suppliers. Due to these significant differences, in the rest of the paper we separately report the effects of horizontal and vertical spillovers on firms according to their degree of foreign asset participation.

Our results show that positive externalities are operating via horizontal, forward and backward linkages. The positive forward linkages imply that enterprises benefit from foreign firms that are upstream to their operations. The evidence is also consistent with strong backward linkages, suggesting that enterprises benefit from foreign firms that are downstream, who may use domestic firms as input suppliers.

This paper results differ significantly from Brecher and Carlos (2012) and other studies of vertical linkages through foreign investment; all previous studies find significant and positive coefficients for "Backward"but not for"Forward", and they explain that the vertical spillovers occurred through contracts between multinational consumers and domestic suppliers. In our case, an additional linkage occurs; vertical spillovers take place through contracts between domestic firms who source inputs from multinational suppliers as well.

One possible explanation is that the foreign participation in the upstream sectors may increase the variety of inputs and provide more sources of inputs to the downstream firms and thus lead to a higher productivity in downstream firms. Ethier (2012) provides theoretical support for this argument, showing that access to a greater variety of inputs results in a higher productivity of downstream industries. Brecher and Carlos (2012) also show that FDI can improve the performance of downstream firms by increasing

Table 7. Olley and Pakes regressions with contemporaneous spillover variables and tariff controls: all firms, foreign-invested, domestic firms with zero foreign investment

	All Firms	Foreign-Invested Firms	Domestic Firms (0 Foreign Share)
Foreignshare (by Mauritius)	-0.0035	0.003	
	(0.0031)	(0.0048)	
Foreignshare (by other countries)	0.0054*	0.0132***	
	(0.0032)	(0.0049)	
Stateshare	-0.0201***	0.0023	-0.0193***
	(0.0032)	(0.0075)	(0.0034)
Horizontal	0.164*	0.115	0.191**
	(0.0871)	(0.0991)	(0.0883)
Backward	0.807***	0.860***	0.801***
	(0.256)	(0.276)	(0.268)
Forward	0.160*	0.246***	0.0920
	(0.0865)	(0.0876)	(0.0920)
lnTariff	-0.0381**	-0.0241	-0.0417**
	(0.0151)	(0.0182)	(0.0164)
lnbwTariff	-0.0289	-0.0167	-0.0350
	(0.0189)	(0.0176)	(0.0211)
lnfwTariff	-0.0066	-0.0203*	-0.0027
	(0.0079)	(0.0116)	(0.0072)
Constant	1.721***	2.002***	2.053***
	(0.0577)	(0.0598)	(0.0416)
Observations	1,545,626	348,029	1,197,597
R-squared	0.179	0.204	0.166
Horizontal*dummy		-0.124***	
		(0.046)	
F-stat (Horizontal*dummy=0)		7.14	
Prob >*F*		0.010	
Backward*dummy		0.011	
		(0.009)	
F-stat (Backward*dummy=0)		0.62	
Prob >*F*		0.433	
Forward*dummy		-0.011*	
		(0.006)	
F-stat (Forward*dummy=0)		19.81	
Prob >*F*		0	
F-stat (interaction term jointly zero)		7.76	
Prob >*F*		0.0002	

Notes: Robust clustered standard errors are presented in parentheses. The dependent variable lnTFP. Each regression includes firm-fixed effects and year dummies. The bottom of the table reports the results of tests, which compares whether three sector-level FDI variables are different across the two sub-samples of foreign-invested firms and domestic firms. The dummy is defined as 1 if firm i has non-zero foreign share at period t, 0 otherwise.

the range of intermediate inputs available. Since costs of intermediate inputs account for a much larger share of output than is typically the case in other countries, it is not surprising that access to lower cost or higher quality inputs has such a significant impact on domestic firm productivity.

Backward linkages are also significant. It cannot distinguish between productivity increases that occur when domestic firms learn to comply with the higher standards for the goods and services required by multinationals, from the additional competition that leads to lower prices when foreign suppliers enter the input market. In any case, the technological gap between domestic firms and foreign enterprises that might have created a significant barrier for effective technological diffusion, limiting the establishment of backward linkages between domestic firms and multinationals seems not to be a problem for the firms in our sample.

While Brecher and Carlos (2012) found evidence of backward linkages for Lithuania, previous efforts to identify backward linkages for India have been unsuccessful. In contrast, it finds evidence of highly significant and large backward linkages. One possible reason may be that we are careful to deflate output with sector-level price deflators. To the extent that foreign investors induced additional competition among supplying enterprises, we would expect that foreign firms would have led to downward pressure on prices in those sectors where backward linkages are greatest. Without proper deflators, this would have appeared as falling productivity in those sectors, with falling prices being misinterpreted as falling output instead.

One way to test if this possibility is correct is to examine whether sector-level prices during the sample period were systematically related to foreign activity. Appendix Table A-3 shows that this is indeed the case. Price levels fell significantly in sectors where foreign firms exerted a significant downward pressure via backward linkages. This suggests that one important vehicle through which foreign firms played a key role was by exerting downward pressure on prices of domestic suppliers. The evidence on the competition effect induced by foreign firms on prices of input suppliers reported in Table A-3 is also useful in another respect. It illustrates the importance of using sector-specific price deflators (or prices) when identifying the spillovers from foreign investment, and explains why previous work on India failed to identify backward spillovers. Previous work did not take into account the lower prices associated with backward spillovers, which resulted in under-estimating the productivity gains since the lower prices and revenues were misinterpreted as lower productivity.

With the sample of all and domestic firms, the coefficient on the state's share in equity in Table 4 is negative and statistically significant, indicating that increases (decreases) in state-invested shares are associated with falling (increasing) productivity. The results on the state share are consistent with rising productivity for privatizing enterprises. The coefficients on the final goods tariff measures are generally negative and statistically significant. These results are somewhat different from Borensztein *et al.*(2008), who fail to find a significant relationship between tariffs and total factor productivity for Indian enterprises.

There are several reasons why the negative impact of input or final goods tariffs on productivity may be under-estimated. A large fraction of firms are granted exemptions from paying tariffs; without additional information on which firms are subjected to tariffs, it is difficult to identify the negative effect of tariffs on inputs. Second, average tariffs may be imposed for a number of reasons. If tariffs are successfully imposed in sectors where there are externalities in production, then the average effect of tariffs reflects both (beneficial) targeting and (harmful) disincentives associated with x-inefficiency. Third, to the extent that Moulton (2010) is correct, then many of the productivity gains associated with trade reform occur through reallocation of production towards more efficient firms, rather than within-firm productivity increases associated with greater exposure to international competition.

In Table A-2, we compare the coefficient estimates using OLS with firm fixed effects and the Brecher and Carlos (2012) approach. Brecher and Carlos (2012), as well as Levinsohn and Petrin (2003) predict, after implementing these two-stage procedures, that the coefficient on L should decrease, the coefficient on intermediate inputs should decrease and the coefficient on capital should increase. The results are generally consistent with these predictions across ownership classes. The coefficient on capital inputs is higher using OP across all specifications. It also generally finds that the coefficient on the labor shares and material shares are lower with OP. What is unusual across all specifications is that the labor share is very low, compared to estimates for other countries. While the coefficient for input costs is very high. As a robustness check, we performed two tests. First, it calculated the share of labor expenditures in total output, the labor share in output according to the data. Under certain plausible restrictions (i.e., Cobb-Douglas production function, perfect competition) the coefficients on the factor inputs in our estimating equations should equal the factor shares. Imposing these restrictions, the estimate of labor's share over the sample period is around 10 percent (reported in column (5) of Table A-1), which is similar to the underlying OLS fixed effect estimates reported in Table A-2. Second, we compare the implied average wages from our sample (calculated by dividing total wages by the number of employees with average wages reported in the Indian Statistical Yearbook for 2004 through 2013. The results are listed in Appendix Table A-1. From Table A-1, we can see that the average wages from the dataset are close to that from the statistical yearbook, although there are some differences. It also compute in column (6) of Table A-1the ratio of both wages and non-wage costs to total output, and the average is not much different than 10 percent. While labor's share could be too low and the share of intermediate inputs too high, it feel confident that the factor shares implied by the OLS and OP coefficient estimates are broadly consistent with the factor shares in our data as well as external evidence.

We note that while the coefficient estimates for our OLS fixed effect and OP specifications are plausibly close to the computed factor shares; this is only the case if one takes into account firm fixed effects in the estimation. In unreported results it model the fixed effect at the industry, and not the firm level, which yields OLS estimates with coefficient estimates which are even smaller for labor and implausibly high for material inputs. This bias is also evident if we compare the coefficient estimates with and without firm fixed effects, as reported in Table 3. It believes that this is the primary reason why the coefficient estimates presented in Lin (2009) are so different. Because they model the fixed effect at the industry and not the firm level, their labor coefficient is half the size of ours and their material input coefficient is significantly larger.

The Effects of Different Sources of Foreign Investment

In many FDI spillover studies, all domestic firms are assumed to benefit equally from FDI. However, different indigenous firms have varying absorptive capacities and the effectiveness of technology diffusion depends on technological capacities of indigenous firms as well as the characteristics of the foreign investors. To provide insights into the effect of this externality of FDI spillovers, we divide sector-level FDI variables into two groups based on their sources. The results are reported in Table 8.

The results point to significant and large differences in vertical as well as horizontal linkages which depend on the origin of the foreign investors. While horizontal linkages, which are not differentiated by country of ownership of the foreign investors, are sometimes insignificant, this average hides signifi-

Table 8. Olley and Pakes regressions with contemporaneous spillover variables and tariff controls: all firms, foreign-invested, and domestic firms with zero foreign investment (sector-level FDI are calculated based on sources of FDI)

	All Firms	Foreign-Invested Firms	Domestic Firms (0 Foreign Investment)
Foreign share (Mauritius)	-0.0028	0.00312	
	(0.003)	(0.0047)	
Foreign share (by other countries)	0.0059*	0.013***	
	(0.0032)	(0.0048)	
Horizontal_MA	-0.0198	0.0143	-0.0647
	(0.099)	(0.106)	(0.105)
Backward_MA	0.570	0.339	0.697
	(0.580)	(0.581)	(0.659)
Forward_MA	-0.227	-0.241	-0.162
	(0.177)	(0.154)	(0.217)
Horizontal_FR	0.284**	0.183	0.350***
	(0.132)	(0.149)	(0.131)
Backward_FR	0.872*	1.110**	0.764*
	(0.445)	(0.522)	(0.437)
Forward_FR	0.332**	0.457***	0.214
	(0.148)	(0.116)	(0.179)
lnTariff	-0.0263*	-0.00987	-0.0313*
	(0.0154)	(0.0180)	(0.0165)
lnTariff_backward	-0.0379	-0.0265	-0.0413*
	(0.0231)	(0.0259)	(0.0245)
lnTariff_forward	-0.0037	-0.0153	-0.0008
	(0.0078)	(0.0118)	(0.0071)
Constant	1.715***	1.997***	2.046***
	(0.0638)	(0.0703)	(0.0440)
Observations	1,545,626	348,029	1,197,597
R-squared	0.180	0.205	0.167
F-stat (HMA=HFR)	3.01	0.80	5.42
Prob>*F*	0.088	0.374	0.023
F-stat (BMA=BFR)	0.11	0.61	0
Prob>*F*	0.736	0.438	0.944
F-stat (FMA=FFR)	3.61	10.63	1.02
Prob>*F*	0.062	0.002	0.32
F-stat (three conditions jointly)	4.64	6.99	4.16
Prob>*F*	0.006	0.004	0.009

Notes: Robust clustered standard errors are presented in parentheses. The dependent variable for each regression is lnTFP. Each regression includes firm-fixed effects and year dummies. HMA = Horizontal (by Mauritius investors), HFR = Horizontal (by other countries). BMA = Backward (by Mauritius investors), BFR = Backward (by other countries). FMA = Forward (by Mauritius investors), FFR = Forward (by other countries).

cant and contrasting effects. Horizontal linkages are negative but not significant for sectors with large shares of foreign investors originating in Mauritius, suggesting that these firms act as competitors for domestically-owned firms. In contrast, horizontal linkages are positive and significant for foreign investment originating in other countries, suggesting that there are positive linkages within the same sector for foreign investment coming from further afield.

The results are also different for vertical linkages. There are strong, positive and significant backward and forward linkages for foreign investors originating outside of Mauritius. These differences are statistically significant for horizontal and vertical forward linkages, as indicated by the formal tests of equality reported at the bottom of Table 8. These results point to clear differences in the pattern of technology transfer originating with foreign investment. Foreign firms coming from nearby regions act as competition in the same industry. Firms coming from further away are not direct competitors and convey positive horizontal and vertical externalities.

The Effect of State Ownership

In India, state-owned firms include firms that are formally classified as state-owned enterprises (SOEs), state-owned jointly operated enterprises and wholly state-owned companies. Non-state-owned enterprises (non-SOEs) include collectively- and privately-owned firms. Compared to non-SOEs, SOEs are typically larger and often technically competitive but less market-oriented; they also face softer budget constraints and limited access to private financial capital. Indigenous Indian firms of different ownership typically behave differently with respect to imitation, innovation and competition, and have different technological capabilities for knowledge absorption from the presence of foreign firms (Lin, 2009).

In Table 9, we divide the sample of all, foreign-invested, and domestic firms into two groups, SOEs and non-SOEs, to test whether the formal ownership structure and the composition of asset ownership matter for FDI spillover effects and trade policies. In columns (1) and (2), which present the results from OLS regressions with firm fixed effects, both enterprises with and without foreign equity participation are included in the analysis together. Columns (3) and (4) show the results using the sample of foreign-invested firms, and columns (5) and (6) present the results using the sample of purely domestic firms, defined as enterprises with zero foreign equity participation. All specifications allow for firm-specific effects and year effects.

The first two columns allow us to compare the impact of firm-level equity participation by foreign investors on the productivity of SOEs relative to non-SOEs. The coefficient on foreign participation from foreign investors outside of Mauritius for SOEs is 0.098 relative to 0.0052 for non-SOEs. This suggests that foreign equity participation is associated with an improvement in productivity which is twenty times greater for SOEs. The much larger and statistically significant coefficient associated with foreign equity participation in SOEs is consistent with the hypothesis that foreign firms have played an important role in improving the performance of some SOEs.

There is also evidence that SOEs benefit more from vertical linkages, as the magnitudes on backward as well as forward linkages are greater for SOEs. The coefficients are larger for SOEs, suggesting that foreign investment has played a particularly large role in transferring technology to SOEs, including those without foreign equity participation. The only exception is with horizontal spillovers. Horizontal spillovers are restricted to privately owned enterprises, suggesting that SOEs may not be able to benefit from any demonstration effects from foreign firms located in the same sector.

Table 9. Olley and Pakes regressions with contemporaneous spillover variables and tariff controls: non-SOEs vs. SOEs (with the sample of all firms, foreign-invested, and domestic firms with zero foreign share)

	All Firms		Foreign-Invested Firms		Domestic Firms (Zero Foreign Share)	
	Non-SOEs	**SOEs**	**Non-SOEs**	**SOEs**	**Non-SOEs**	**SOEs**
Foreign share (by Mauritius)	-0.0037	0.0348	0.0033	-0.0734		
	(0.003)	(0.0545)	(0.0048)	(0.0663)		
Foreign share (by other countries)	0.0052	0.098**	0.013***	0.082		
	(0.0031)	(0.0393)	(0.0049)	(0.0692)		
State share	-0.0016	-0.0256***	0.0037	0.0172	-0.0017	-0.0259***
	(0.0030)	(0.0041)	(0.0078)	(0.0305)	(0.0033)	(0.0041)
Horizontal	0.164*	0.109	0.117	-0.506	0.194**	0.111
	(0.088)	(0.100)	(0.099)	(0.444)	(0.089)	(0.100)
Backward	0.785***	1.027***	0.850***	2.893***	0.765***	1.005***
	(0.253)	(0.349)	(0.275)	(0.844)	(0.262)	(0.350)
Forward	0.162*	0.166	0.245***	0.483**	0.0867	0.169
	(0.0851)	(0.128)	(0.0875)	(0.219)	(0.0882)	(0.132)
lnTariff	-0.0349**	-0.0526**	-0.0237	-0.0676**	-0.0375**	-0.0519**
	(0.0154)	(0.0198)	(0.0183)	(0.0312)	(0.0171)	(0.0198)
lnTariff_backward	-0.0285	-0.0163	-0.0169	0.00579	-0.0354*	-0.0159
	(0.0185)	(0.0337)	(0.0176)	(0.0705)	(0.0207)	(0.0338)
lnTariff_forward	-0.0086	0.0065	-0.0205*	0.0705***	-0.0046	0.006
	(0.0082)	(0.0077)	(0.0115)	(0.0245)	(0.0074)	(0.0077)
Constant	1.721***	2.545***	1.913***	1.413***	1.663***	2.550***
	(0.0576)	(0.0690)	(0.0723)	(0.118)	(0.0598)	(0.0701)
Observations	1,418,632	126,994	345,631	2,398	1,073,001	124,596
R-squared	0.186	0.078	0.204	0.222	0.173	0.077
Horizontal*ownership	-0.184**		-0.030		-0.201**	
	(0.091)		(0.193)		(0.095)	
F-stat (Horizontal * ownership = 0)	4.06		0.02		4.4	
Prob>*F*	0.048		0.879		0.04	
Backward*ownership	-0.018		-0.236		-0.042	
	(0.220)		(0.350)		(0.233)	
F-stat (Backward * ownership = 0)	0.01		0.46		0.03	
Prob>*F*	0.934		0.502		0.857	
Forward*ownership	0.007		-0.100		0.043	
	(0.064)		(0.109)		(0.065)	
F-stat (Forward * ownership = 0)	0.01		0.85		0.44	
Prob>*F*	0.915		0.36		0.51	
F-stat (interaction terms jointly zero)	6.55		1.46		6.68	
Prob>*F*	0.001		0.235		0.001	

We also find different responses across SOEs and non-SOES to trade policy. Higher final goods tariffs are associated with significantly lower productivity for SOEs, relative to non-SOEs. The point estimates on final goods tariffs, which is -0.0676 for SOEs with foreign investment and -0.0519 for those with no foreign assets, suggests that a 1 percent fall in tariffs would increase productivity growth by 0.05 to 0.07percent. Since average tariffs during the period fell over 10 percentage points (see Appendix), this suggests a gain in productivity of 0.5 to 0.7 percentage points associated on average with trade reforms for the SOEs. One possible interpretation of the larger effect of final goods tariffs on SOE performance is the greater importance of international competition for SOEs, which were traditionally supported by the government.

The Effects of Tax Incentives for FDI

In Tables 10a and 10b it explore the extent to which subsidized foreign investment is more likely to convey spillovers relative to unsubsidized foreign investment. While the standard tax rates across all firms during the sample period was 33 percent, a large share of foreign-owned firms were granted tax subsidies and faced tax rates that were significantly lower. Indeed, the means reported in Tables 4 and 5 suggest that the majority of foreign investment in India during the sample period benefited from income tax subsidies and a significant fraction benefited from subsidies on value-added taxes. To the extent that the Indian government was able to target successfully firms more likely to convey positive externalities, it would expect different effects for these subsidized firms.

To test for this possibility, it split our sector-level foreign share variables into two groups: one is calculated based on foreign investment being subsidized (those paid less than the statutory tax rate) and the other one is computed based on non-subsidized foreign investment. The results based on income tax incentives are presented in Table 7.

There is strong evidence that foreign firms receiving tax subsidies are more likely to generate positive externalities than other kinds of foreign firms. While the coefficients on backward linkages are positive and statistically significant for foreign firms which received incentives in the form of lower income taxes, the coefficients on backward linkages for other types of foreign firms are negative. These differences are significant for backward linkages but not for forward or horizontal linkages, where the formal F-tests fail to reject that the effects are the same.

In Table 8, it tests whether the results are different when it explores tax holidays on value-added taxes as a form of fiscal incentive instead. It defines firms as subsidized when they were exempted from paying value-added taxes altogether. The results in Table 8 are consistent with differences in the effects of foreign investment based on income tax incentives. In particular, forward linkages are significantly stronger when foreign investors received tax incentives in the form of exemptions on value-added taxes.

Robustness Tests

Since its dependent variable is firm-level productivity and the focus of the analysis is on how sector-level foreign investment affects domestic firm productivity, endogeneity is less likely to be an issue. It is difficult to make a case that firm-level productivity affects sector-level foreign investment, particularly upstream and downstream foreign investment. To the extent that foreign ownership could be attracted to sectors where suppliers or users are more productive, this is accounted for by the use of firm-level fixed effects. However, some critics might argue that foreign investors are drawn to sectors where they expect

Table 10a. Olley and Pakes regressions for grouped data with contemporaneous subsidized and non-subsidized spillover variables (constructed based on income tax) and tariff controls: non-SOEs vs. SOEs (all firms, foreign-invested, and domestic firms with zero foreign investment

	All Firms		Foreign-Invested Firms		Domestic Firms (0 Foreign Investment)	
	Non-SOEs	SOEs	Non-SOEs	SOEs	Non-SOEs	SOEs
Foreign share (by Mauritius)	-0.00381	0.0363	0.00368	-0.0766		
	(0.00302)	(0.0543)	(0.00484)	(0.0675)		
Foreign share (by other countries)	0.00522	0.0986**	0.0137***	0.0807		
	(0.00313)	(0.0388)	(0.00498)	(0.0690)		
State share	-0.00174	-0.0254***	0.00420	0.0180	-0.00206	-0.0257***
	(0.00290)	(0.00420)	(0.00767)	(0.0307)	(0.00331)	(0.00421)
Hor_subsidized	0.117	0.103	0.0512	-0.595	0.163	0.103
	(0.107)	(0.133)	(0.109)	(0.511)	(0.111)	(0.134)
Bw_subsidized	2.189***	2.833***	2.065***	3.203***	2.286***	2.822***
	(0.644)	(0.611)	(0.475)	(0.986)	(0.799)	(0.628)
Fw_subsidized	0.165	0.203	0.238***	0.526**	0.0817	0.213
	(0.107)	(0.151)	(0.0859)	(0.259)	(0.141)	(0.158)
Hor_non_subsidized	0.189*	-0.0729	0.179*	-0.429	0.188	-0.0702
	(0.104)	(0.117)	(0.103)	(0.355)	(0.114)	(0.119)
Bw_non_subsidized	-0.934	-1.173**	-0.649	2.287*	-1.051	-1.175**
	(0.623)	(0.464)	(0.474)	(1.239)	(0.749)	(0.471)
Fw_non_subsidized	0.184**	0.222**	0.261***	0.403**	0.132	0.221**
	(0.0885)	(0.105)	(0.0683)	(0.163)	(0.122)	(0.110)
lnTariff	-0.0346**	-0.0458**	-0.0262*	-0.0712**	-0.0366**	-0.0451**
	(0.0144)	(0.0184)	(0.0155)	(0.0329)	(0.0163)	(0.0185)
lnTariff_backward	-0.0170	0.00734	-0.00343	0.0123	-0.0249	0.00716
	(0.0179)	(0.0305)	(0.0175)	(0.0727)	(0.0200)	(0.0306)
lnTariff_forward	-0.00981	0.00613	-0.0211*	0.0695***	-0.00610	0.00561
	(0.00782)	(0.00679)	(0.0110)	(0.0233)	(0.00716)	(0.00680)
Constant	1.728***	2.499***	1.920***	1.431***	1.673***	2.504***
	(0.0531)	(0.0632)	(0.0654)	(0.118)	(0.0577)	(0.0645)
Observations	1,418,632	126,994	345,631	2,398	1,073,001	124,596
R-squared	0.187	0.079	0.205	0.223	0.174	0.078
F-stat (HS=HNS)	0.28	0.96	0.98	0.42	0.03	0.88
Prob>F	0.596	0.332	0.327	0.518	0.862	0.351
F-stat (BS=BNS)	6.72	19.12	10.39	0.42	5.01	18.02
Prob>*F*	0.012	0.0001	0.002	0.52	0.029	0.0001
F-stat (FS=FNS)	0.02	0.02	0.14	0.74	0.06	0
Prob>*F*	0.882	0.889	0.705	0.394	0.813	0.955
F-stat (three conditions jointly)	2.61	7.46	3.92	0.32	1.99	6.85
Prob>*F*	0.06	0.0003	0.013	0.808	0.126	0.0005

Table 10b. Olley and Pakes regressions for grouped data with contemporaneous subsidized and non-subsidized spillover variables (constructed based on income tax) and tariff controls: non-SOEs vs. SOEs (all firms, foreign-invested, and domestic firms with zero foreign investment

	Domestic Firms		
	Non-SOEs	**SOEs**	**Non-SOEs**
Foreign share (by Mauritius)	-0.0041	-0.0765	
	(0.0031)	(0.0716)	
Foreign share (by other countries)	0.0050*	0.0829	
	(0.0026)	(0.0698)	
State share	-0.001	0.0312	0.0007
	(0.0033)	(0.0318)	(0.0035)
Hor_subsidized	0.0398	-0.683	0.0662
	(0.0871)	(0.416)	(0.0963)
Bw_subsidized	0.831	2.560***	0.636
	(0.534)	(0.793)	(0.574)
Fw_subsidized	1.068***	0.785***	0.943***
	(0.130)	(0.183)	(0.147)
Hor_non_subsidized	0.240**	-0.518	0.255**
	(0.0928)	(0.497)	(0.0978)
Bw_non_subsidized	0.765**	2.763**	0.842*
	(0.376)	(1.109)	(0.456)
Fw_non_subsidized	-0.0597	0.408	-0.105
	(0.102)	(0.258)	(0.0990)
lnTariff	-0.0394**	-0.0408	-0.0424**
	(0.0165)	(0.0355)	(0.0187)
lnTariff_backward	-0.0324	0.0151	-0.0361
	(0.0198)	(0.0737)	(0.0223)
lnTariff_forward	-0.00487	0.0568**	-0.0017
	(0.0079)	(0.0242)	(0.0072)
Constant	2.074***	1.390***	1.672***
	(0.0401)	(0.127)	(0.0666)
Observations	1,225,481	2,323	926,304
R-squared	0.205	0.213	0.185
F-stat (HS=HNS)	6.36	0.34	4.14
Prob>F	0.014	0.563	0.046
F-stat (BS=BNS)	0.01	0.04	0.05
Prob>*F*	0.932	0.848	0.823
F-stat (FS=FNS)	29.45	1.9	26.52
Prob>*F*	0	0.173	0
F-stat (three conditions jointly)	13.49	1.14	10.22
Prob>*F*	0	0.341	0

higher productivity growth in the future. To address this unlikely but nevertheless potential source of endogeneity, we apply instrumental variables (IV) techniques. It uses future tariffs (tariffs at time t+1) as instruments. For instance, *lnTariff* (at time t+1) is used to instrument *HorizontalFDI*; *lnTariff_backward* (at time t+1) is used to instrument *Backward*; and *lnTariff_forward* (at time t+1) is used to instrument *Forward*. Since our tariff data is from 2004-2013, it loses one year of observations when it apply future tariff as instruments. All identification tests show that the equations are exactly identified.

The results are reported in Table A-4. The point estimates are magnified for backward linkages, confirming the importance of the linkages between domestic suppliers and foreign-owned buyers of their inputs. However, the coefficients for non-SOE domestic enterprises on both forward and horizontal linkages become negative and statistically significant. The negative and significant coefficient on the horizontal variable confirms previous work by Aitken and Harrison (1999) and others suggesting that foreign firms in the same sector act as competitors for domestic enterprises. The switch in sign for the coefficient on horizontal FDI calls into question the positive coefficient for horizontal FDI in other specifications reported elsewhere in this paper, but confirms the positive vertical linkages between domestic suppliers and foreign users of their products.

In Table A-5, it explores how vertical and horizontal linkages vary over the ten-year sample period. With India's entry into the WTO in the middle of the sample period, domestic content rules became illegal and tariffs were significantly reduced. The results in Table A-5 suggest that vertical linkages were strengthened during the second half of the sample period, when tariffs were lowered and domestic content restrictions relaxed. Backward linkages only become large in magnitude and significant with India's entry into the WTO. Forward linkages also become significant and positive later in the sample period.

Solutions and Recommendation

There is a need to increase investment inflows in light manufacturing sector and also in Small and Medium Enterprises (SMEs) sector which can enhance domestic production and increase employment. Since employment elasticity in manufacturing sector is high, so Iran in order to reduce unemployment problems should attract FDI in this sector. Also, the approval process needs to be simplified in order to make it more efficient. More FDI is needed in sub-sectors of manufacturing like OEMs, food processing, packaging, textile, clothing and leather, cellulose industries (wood and paper), printing and publishing, basic metal industries, recycling, and medical device industries. Across a variety of specifications, and controlling for firm and year effects, it finds that positive productivity spillovers from FDI take place through contacts between foreign affiliates and their local clients in upstream (backward) or downstream sectors (forward linkages). It also finds evidence that positive productivity spillovers occur through horizontal foreign investment, but these types of spillovers are less robust, and become negative when we instrument for FDI. It is also highlights the different effects played by the sources of sectoral foreign direct investment on domestic firm productivity. While at the firm level foreign equity participation is generally associated with higher productivity, this is not the case for foreign equity participation that originates in Mauritius. There are several possible explanations for this. One major reason could be that such investments actually originate in India, and are simply rechanneled through nearby locations to take advantage of special incentives offered to foreign investors. Another possible explanation is that nearby foreign investors are not sufficiently different technologically during the last decade for which we have data. Finally, it also takes into account trade policies and tax policies. Controlling for differential tariffs across sectors is useful because some foreign investors may have invested in India in order to access protected domestic markets, which could have led to a bias in estimating the effects of foreign investment linkages on firm productivity. It finds that tariffs are associated with negative and significant effects on firm productivity. Finally, it also explores the extent to which foreign investors who were targeted via special tax incentives generated different effects on domestic firms than others. It finds significantly higher effects of targeted FDI on productivity growth relative to other kinds of FDI. In several respects the Indian experience has been different. This paper results indicate that the institutional framework is critical for understanding the presence as well as the magnitude of such gains. The example of how foreign investment originating from Mauritius, is associated with zero spillovers, while foreign investment from other regions generates significant vertical and horizontal linkages is one vital example of the important role of this institutional analysis. FDI policy should be prepared and made available to investors in such a way that clearly guides them in areas where investments are not welcomed and areas where investments are on priority list.

FUTURE RESEARCH DIRECTIONS

The future research will explore how different patterns of interventions are associated with productivity outcomes. Nunn and Trefler (2006) hypothesize that interventions oriented towards skill-intensive sectors are more likely to generate productivity growth, while Lin (2009) suggests that promotion of sectors where a country has a latent comparative advantage is more likely to be successful. The evidence presented here has several implications for the direction of future research on FDI spillovers. First, it suggests that the focus of the debate should shift from attempting to generalize whether or not FDI spillovers exist to determining the conditions under which they are likely to do so. The nature and magnitude of FDI spillovers depends on the conditions in the host country, which determine both the type of FDI inflows as well as the extent to which local firms are likely to be affected (positively, negatively, or both) by foreign entry. Examining FDI spillovers in the context of one country at a time is unlikely to be very productive. What is needed is a multi-country study based on comparable high-quality, firm-level panel data. Such data would allow for examination of host country characteristics as determinants of both FDI inflows and spillovers from FDI. Conducting a meta-study focusing on the host country business environment and level of development could be another promising avenue for future research. Second, more effort should be directed at understanding the exact mechanisms behind the observed patterns. Rather than correlating the performance of host country firms with the presence of multinationals in their or other sectors, researchers should look at the flows of workers between the two types of firms, identify domestic suppliers of foreign customers, consider the effect of foreign presence on the entry of new firms and their characteristics, and ask firms detailed questions about the sources of innovation. Some researchers have already pursued this line of study, but more work is needed. While it creates new challenges in terms of finding appropriate econometric strategies, collecting data, and overcoming the fear of relying on surveys, this area of research probably has the greatest potential. Third, the scope of investigations should be extended to encompass the service sector. Anecdotal evidence suggests that the movement of service industry professionals to executive positions in other firms may constitute an important spillover channel to other service firms and to the manufacturing industry. Moreover, because the nature of the sector and trade barriers limit cross-border trade in services, opening service industries to foreign providers may constitute an important channel of spillovers to downstream manufacturing.

CONCLUSION

In this chapter, it explores the role played by foreign investors in generating technology transfer via horizontal and vertical linkages, as well as their role in promoting the reform of state enterprises through joint venture activity. It also explores the impact on productivity growth at the firm level of protection through tariffs and explore whether the India government's targeting through the selective imposition of tax subsidies to attract foreign investors is consistent with larger externalities. Given the intensive interest in FDI as a vehicle through which developing countries learn about new technology, many firm-level studies have examined FDI spillovers. However, due to the lack of accessibility of firm-level data, few studies test for FDI spillovers in India. This chapter, based on a rich firm-level dataset from India for the 2004-2013 period, tests for vertical and horizontal spillovers from FDI. Unlike previous studies of the Indian experience, it finds significant backward linkages. It believes that this is because it takes into account the downward pressure induced by foreign firms on prices in supplying sectors. Taking account of the heterogeneity of sectoral FDI as well as the heterogeneity of firms' absorptive capacities, it also explores different institutional factors in explaining the role of foreign investment in promoting technology transfer in India. It focuses on three institutional factors in particular: the source of foreign investment, the structure of domestic firm ownership, and the role of tax concessions.

This is the first study to examine whether fiscal incentives in the form of tax subsidies are associated with stronger linkages from foreign firms to domestic enterprises. It finds strong evidence that subsidized foreign investment generates greater productivity spillovers than unsubsidized firms.

REFERENCES

Aitken, B. J., & Harrison, A. E. (1999). Do domestic firms benefit from direct foreign investment? evidence from Venezuela. *The American Economic Review*, *89*(3), 605–618. doi:10.1257/aer.89.3.605

Aitken, B. J., Harrison, A. E., & Lipsey, R. (1996). Wages and foreign ownership. A comparative study of Mexico, Venezuela and the United States. *Journal of International Economics*, *40*(1), 345–371. doi:10.1016/0022-1996(95)01410-1

Amiti, M., & Konings, J. (2007). Trade libralization, intermediate inputs and productivity. *The American Economic Review*, *97*(5), 1611–1638. doi:10.1257/aer.97.5.1611

Blomstrom, M. (2011). Foreign investment and productive efficiency: The case of Mexico. *The Journal of Industrial Economics*, *35*(1), 97–110. doi:10.2307/2098609

Borensztein, E., Gregorio, J. D., & Lee, J. W. (2008). How does foreign direct investment affect economic growth? *Journal of International Economics*, *45*(1), 115–135. doi:10.1016/S0022-1996(97)00033-0

Brecher, R., & Carlos, D. A. (2012). Tariffs, foreign capital and immiserizing growth. *Journal of International Economics*, *7*(1), 317–322.

Caves, R. E. (2012). Multinational firms, competition and productivity in host country markets. *Economica*, *41*(1), 176–193.

Ethier, W. (2012). National and international returns to scale in the model theory of international trade. *The American Economic Review*, *72*(1), 389–405.

Globerman, S. (2011). Foreign direct investment and spillover efficiency benefits in Canadian manufacturing industries. *The Canadian Journal of Economics. Revue Canadienne dEconomique*, *12*(1), 42–56. doi:10.2307/134570

Haddad, M., & Harrison, A. E. (2010). Are there positive spillovers from direct foreign investment? Evidence from panel data for Morocco. *Journal of Development Economics*, *42*(1), 51–74. doi:10.1016/0304-3878(93)90072-U

Hu, A., & Jefferson, G. (2002). FDI impact and spillover: Evidence from Chinas electronic and textile industries. *World Economy*, *25*(8), 1063–1076. doi:10.1111/1467-9701.00481

Kokko, A. (2009). Technology, market characteristics and spillovers. *Journal of Development Economics*, *43*(1), 279–293.

Konings, J. (2001). Effects of foreign direct investment on domestic firms. *Economics of Transition*, *9*(3), 619–633. doi:10.1111/1468-0351.00091

Levinsohn, J., & Petrin, A. (2003). Estimating production functions using inputs to control for unobseravbles. *The Review of Economic Studies*, *70*(1), 317–341. doi:10.1111/1467-937X.00246

Lin, J. (2009). *Economic development and transition: Thought, strategy, and viability*. Cambridge, UK: Cambridge University Press. doi:10.1017/CBO9780511805622

Markusen, J., & Venables, A. (2008). Multinational firms and the new trade theory. *Journal of International Economics*, *46*(2), 183-203.

Moulton, B. R. (2010). An illustration of a pitfall in estimating the effects of aggregate variables on micro units. *The Review of Economics and Statistics*, *72*(2), 334–338. doi:10.2307/2109724

Smarzynska-Javorcik, B. (2004). Does foreign direct investment increase the productivity of domestic firms? In search of spillovers through backward linkages. *The American Economic Review*, *94*(3), 605–627. doi:10.1257/0002828041464605

KEY TERMS AND DEFINITIONS

Foreign Direct Investment: A foreign direct investment is an investment in the form of a controlling ownership in a business in one country by an entity based in another country. It is thus distinguished from foreign portfolio investment by a notion of direct control.

International Trade: International trade is the exchange of capital, goods, and services across international borders or territories. It is the exchange of goods and services among nations of the world.

Internationalization: Internationalization is the process of increasing involvement of enterprises in international markets, although there is no agreed definition of internationalization. There are several internationalization theories which try to explain why there are international activities.

Open Economy: An open economy is an economy in which there are economic activities between the domestic community and outside. People and even businesses can trade in goods and services with other people and businesses in the international community, and funds can flow as investments across the border. Trade can take the form of managerial exchange, technology transfers, and all kinds of goods and services.

Productivity: Productivity is an average measure of the efficiency of production. It can be expressed as the ratio of output to inputs used in the production process, i.e. output per unit of input. When all outputs and inputs are included in the productivity measure it is called total productivity.

Technology Assessment: Technology assessment is a scientific, interactive, and communicative process that aims to contribute to the formation of public and political opinion on societal aspects of science and technology.

Technology Transfer: Technology transfer is the process of transferring (disseminating) technology from the places and in groups of its origination to wider distribution among more people and places.

APPENDIX

Table 12. Average wages comparison

Year	(1) Mean of Average Wages from the Data	(2) Average Wages from the National Statistical Yearbook (for the Manufacturing Industry)	(3) Average Wages from the National Statistical Yearbook (for SOEs Manufacturing Firms)	(4) Mean of Average Wages and Non-Wage Cost from the Data	(5) The Ratio of Total Wages to Output Value	(6) The Ratio of Total Cost on Labor (Wages and Non-Wage Cost) to Output Value
2004	9,795	7,064	6,981	11,654	0.118	0.146
2005	8,072	7,794	7,611	9,653	0.122	0.151
2006	9,038	8,750	8,554	13,556	0.120	0.147
2007	10,329	9,774	9,590	11,858	0.130	0.150
2008	10,586	11,001	10,876	12,181	0.105	0.123
2009	11,002	12,496	12,601	12,602	0.101	0.116
2010	13,588			16,543	0.098	0.123
2011	14,087	15,757	16,963	17,472	0.087	0.108
2012	16,925	17,966	20,317	21,069	0.090	0.112
2013	19,957	20,884	23,913	24,720	0.083	0.100

Notes: Wages are measured in yuan/year for one person. To obtain means of average wages of the sample, we first calculate the average wage for each firm in each year by dividing total wages by the number of total employees then take the means of these averages. The official information on average wage is missing for the year of 2010, therefore we leave them with blank. In column (3) and (4), we calculate the total cost of wage and non-wage and get the mean of average cost for each year. For the year of 2004-2009, non-wage cost includes unemployment insurance and other welfare. Starting from the year of 2010, information on medical insurance and housing subsidies becomes available; therefore we include these two additional costs when we calculate the non-wage cost for the year of 2010-2013. In column (5), we calculate the ratio of total wages to output value (at current price, both wages and output value are in nominal term). To take non-wage cost into account, we re-calculate the ratio using the sum of wages and non-wage cost as the numerator, which are shown in column (6).

Table 13. Summary of estimated elasticities of input variables

Coefficients on Input Variables Estimated by OLS with firm Fes and time dummies									
	(1) Full	(2) FIE	(3) Domestic	(4) Full_nonSOEs	(5) Full_SOEs	(6) FIE_nonSOEs	(7) FIE_SOEs	(8) Domestic_nonSOEs	(9) Domestic_SOEs
logL	0.0918***	0.122***	0.0818***	0.0920***	0.0828***	0.122***	0.0798***	0.0809***	0.0820***
	(0.00413)	(0.00765)	(0.00336)	(0.00434)	(0.00575)	(0.00772)	(0.0207)	(0.00360)	(0.00593)
logK	0.0278***	0.0374***	0.0249***	0.0285***	0.0193***	0.0374***	0.0303*	0.0255***	0.0182***
	(0.00159)	(0.00266)	(0.00152)	(0.00157)	(0.00311)	(0.00267)	(0.0152)	(0.00156)	(0.00306)
logM	0.766***	0.732***	0.776***	0.768***	0.742***	0.732***	0.844***	0.781***	0.740***
	(0.00683)	(0.00709)	(0.00735)	(0.00732)	(0.0107)	(0.00713)	(0.0359)	(0.00811)	(0.0110)
Obs	1,545,626	348,029	1,197,597	1,418,632	126,994	345,694	2,403	1,073,001	124,596
Coefficients on Input Variables Estimated by Olley and Pakes Regression									
	(1) Full	(2) FIE	(3) Domestic	(4) Full_nonSOEs	(5) Full_SOEs	(6) FIE_nonSOEs	(7) FIE_SOEs	(8) Domestic_nonSOEs	(9) Domestic_SOEs
logL	0.0888***	0.153***	0.068***	0.0951***	0.012**	0.154***	0.0231	0.0743***	0.012**
	(0.0019)	(0.0035)	(0.0019)	(0.0022)	(0.005	(0.004)	(0.0245)	(0.0022)	(0.005)
logK	0.0436***	0.0427***	0.044***	0.0464***	0.0205***	0.0428***	0.0644*	0.0473***	0.0202***
	(0.0018)	(0.003)	(0.0016)	(0.0015)	(0.004)	(0.0024)	(0.027)	(0.0018)	(0.004)
logM	0.771***	0.725***	0.785***	0.770***	0.772***	0.725***	0.836***	0.786***	0.771***
	(0.004)	(0.006)	(0.005)	(0.0048)	(0.010)	(0.007)	(0.046)	(0.005)	(0.009)
Obs	779,148	192,146	587,002	724,371	54,777	191,006	1,140	533,365	53,637

Table 14. FDI effect on price level

Dependent Variable: Log of Price Index		
Horizontal	0.008	-0.008
	(0.017)	(0.014)
Backward	-0.097**	-0.097**
	(0.046)	(0.045)
Forward	-0.024	-0.024
	(0.016)	(0.015)
Robust Standard Error	No	Yes
Year Dummies	Yes	Yes
Industry fixed effect	Yes	Yes
Number of observations	610	610
R-squared	0.58	0.58

Table 15. Robustness tests for Table 6 (instrumental variable estimation)

	All		Foreign-Invested Firms		Domestic Firms	
	Non-SOEs	SOEs	Non-SOEs	SOEs	Non-SOEs	SOEs
Foreign share (by Mauritius)	-0.0011	-0.205	-0.0011	-0.0351		
	(0.0035)	(0.772)	(0.0056)	(0.149)		
Foreign share (by other countries)	0.0060	0.103	0.0072	0.0344		
	(0.0039)	(0.221)	(0.0056)	(0.120)		
State share	-0.0063*	-0.0441	0.0032	0.0175	-0.0080*	-0.0312*
	(0.0037)	(0.0516)	(0.0090)	(0.0455)	(0.0042)	(0.0168)
Horizontal	-0.744**	9.953	0.420	4.683	-0.682**	5.830
	(0.296)	(19.16)	(0.594)	(11.85)	(0.318)	(6.988)
Backward	3.469***	-39.11	1.201	-2.416	3.042***	-19.10
	(0.755)	(100.4)	(1.466)	(16.56)	(0.715)	(41.75)
Forward	-0.479***	-18.06	0.101	-2.951	-1.156***	-11.18
	(0.0899)	(35.40)	(0.166)	(7.440)	(0.154)	(14.08)
lnTariff	-0.209***	-1.064	-0.0383	-0.491	-0.191***	-0.679
	(0.0246)	(1.802)	(0.0490)	(0.752)	(0.0207)	(0.670)
lnTariff_backward	-0.0507***	-0.304	-0.0579*	0.00305	-0.112***	-0.343*
	(0.0133)	(0.239)	(0.0296)	(0.304)	(0.0196)	(0.187)
lnTariff_forward	0.0791***	0.290	0.00983	0.257	0.109***	0.213
	(0.0135)	(0.422)	(0.0112)	(0.394)	(0.0173)	(0.175)
Observations	915,545	83,453	241,372	1,490	661,978	81,570
R-squared	0.098	-4.630	0.194	-0.597	0.046	-1.598

Table 16. Robustness tests for Table 6 continued (exploration of time effects)

	All		Foreign-Invested Firms		Domestic Firms	
	Non-SOEs	SOEs	Non-SOEs	SOEs	Non-SOEs	SOEs
Foreign share (by Mauritius)	-0.00444	0.0389	0.00610	-0.0477		
	(0.00287)	(0.0564)	(0.00483)	(0.0671)		
Foreign share (by other countries)	0.00418	0.107***	0.0159***	0.0844		
	(0.00300)	(0.0376)	(0.00499)	(0.0713)		
State share	-0.00351	-0.0252***	0.00191	0.0155	-0.00320	-0.0255***
	(0.00289)	(0.00440)	(0.00827)	(0.0307)	(0.00331)	(0.00439)
Hor_interact1	0.199**	0.0630	0.296***	-0.731	0.119	0.0676
	(0.0815)	(0.112)	(0.0787)	(0.528)	(0.0895)	(0.112)
Hor_interact2	0.158**	0.0463	0.186**	-0.719	0.126	0.0479
	(0.0781)	(0.0948)	(0.0772)	(0.526)	(0.0832)	(0.0946)
Hor_interact3	0.216***	0.123	0.170**	-0.561	0.217***	0.121
	(0.0699)	(0.0779)	(0.0656)	(0.550)	(0.0721)	(0.0767)
Hor_interact4	0.158**	0.0866	0.0992	-0.820	0.157**	0.0889
	(0.0744)	(0.0708)	(0.0735)	(0.542)	(0.0750)	(0.0699)
Hor_interact5	0.0835	0.0422	0.0217	-0.344	0.0862	0.0480
	(0.0782)	(0.0974)	(0.0730)	(0.480)	(0.0789)	(0.0955)
Hor_interact6	0.0598	0.0217	-0.0145	-0.424	0.0884	0.0238
	(0.0801)	(0.0887)	(0.0753)	(0.496)	(0.0821)	(0.0890)
Hor_interact7	0.188*	0.0596	0.142	0.386	0.200*	0.0476
	(0.104)	(0.134)	(0.0969)	(0.422)	(0.113)	(0.134)
Hor_interact8	0.196	0.0872	0.171	0.148	0.216	0.0741
	(0.123)	(0.143)	(0.118)	(0.359)	(0.130)	(0.142)
Hor_interact9	0.244*	0.118	0.263**	0.423	0.253*	0.106
	(0.129)	(0.164)	(0.131)	(0.456)	(0.133)	(0.163)
Hor_interact10	0.289*	0.227	0.322**	0.176	0.309*	0.207
	(0.163)	(0.186)	(0.151)	(0.491)	(0.175)	(0.184)
Back_interact1	-0.251	-0.162	-0.644***	1.473*	0.0298	-0.229
	(0.225)	(0.380)	(0.179)	(0.841)	(0.304)	(0.389)
Back_interact2	-0.236	-0.278	-0.376**	1.411	-0.0847	-0.333
	(0.194)	(0.326)	(0.164)	(0.974)	(0.243)	(0.330)
Back_interact3	-0.0749	-0.111	-0.104	1.526	0.0289	-0.168
	(0.153)	(0.229)	(0.134)	(0.970)	(0.174)	(0.230)
Back_interact4	0.194	0.0457	0.155	2.234**	0.327*	-0.0218
	(0.165)	(0.220)	(0.152)	(1.043)	(0.188)	(0.219)
Back_interact5	0.415**	0.262	0.509***	1.298	0.432**	0.205
	(0.167)	(0.287)	(0.155)	(0.885)	(0.185)	(0.282)
Back_interact6	0.602***	0.602**	0.662***	1.928**	0.665***	0.555**
	(0.184)	(0.242)	(0.158)	(0.842)	(0.213)	(0.248)

continued on following page

Table 16. Continued

	All		Foreign-Invested Firms		Domestic Firms	
	Non-SOEs	SOEs	Non-SOEs	SOEs	Non-SOEs	SOEs
Back_interact7	0.769***	1.183***	0.721***	0.496	0.841***	1.228***
	(0.234)	(0.338)	(0.201)	(0.768)	(0.272)	(0.345)
Back_interact8	0.836***	1.314***	0.798***	1.465**	0.902***	1.355***
	(0.269)	(0.407)	(0.232)	(0.642)	(0.314)	(0.414)
Back_interact9	0.761**	1.460***	0.685**	1.543*	0.825**	1.462***
	(0.295)	(0.487)	(0.265)	(0.840)	(0.340)	(0.502)
Back_interact10	0.820**	1.706***	0.769**	1.641**	0.879**	1.757***
	(0.371)	(0.487)	(0.319)	(0.810)	(0.430)	(0.497)
For_interact1	-0.0176	-0.00245	-0.0459	-0.0493	0.0266	0.0126
	(0.0873)	(0.149)	(0.0801)	(0.269)	(0.105)	(0.159)
For_interact2	0.0180	0.0423	0.0135	0.107	0.0458	0.0686
	(0.0723)	(0.109)	(0.0580)	(0.283)	(0.0877)	(0.110)
For_interact3	0.00939	0.0250	0.0412	0.0764	0.00315	0.0423
	(0.0423)	(0.0737)	(0.0307)	(0.278)	(0.0541)	(0.0759)
For_interact4	0.0672	0.109	0.0901**	0.260	0.0720	0.117*
	(0.0500)	(0.0659)	(0.0417)	(0.286)	(0.0571)	(0.0685)
For_interact5	0.136***	0.140**	0.173***	0.0465	0.123**	0.152**
	(0.0494)	(0.0686)	(0.0437)	(0.271)	(0.0586)	(0.0705)
For_interact6	0.167***	0.134**	0.211***	0.161	0.146**	0.143**
	(0.0467)	(0.0518)	(0.0402)	(0.260)	(0.0566)	(0.0546)
For_interact7	0.143**	0.201**	0.200***	-0.00693	0.0887	0.216**
	(0.0629)	(0.0885)	(0.0514)	(0.221)	(0.0762)	(0.0912)
For_interact8	0.133*	0.153	0.203***	0.0120	0.0632	0.170
	(0.0776)	(0.115)	(0.0601)	(0.178)	(0.0960)	(0.121)
For_interact9	0.154*	0.169*	0.217***	0.00373	0.0841	0.180*
	(0.0781)	(0.0999)	(0.0638)	(0.218)	(0.0949)	(0.104)
For_interact10	0.163*	0.163*	0.227***	0.178	0.0860	0.180*
	(0.0911)	(0.0922)	(0.0718)	(0.236)	(0.111)	(0.0957)
lnTariff	-0.0200	-0.0322*	-0.00861	-0.0332	-0.0241	-0.0321*
	(0.0172)	(0.0177)	(0.0148)	(0.0431)	(0.0190)	(0.0179)
lnbwTariff	-0.0267	-0.00377	-0.0126	0.00929	-0.0334*	-0.00161
	(0.0172)	(0.0283)	(0.0136)	(0.0711)	(0.0200)	(0.0284)
lnfwTariff	-0.00712	0.00314	-0.0150**	0.0910***	-0.00488	0.00220
	(0.00780)	(0.00735)	(0.00711)	(0.0160)	(0.00795)	(0.00727)
Constant	1.740***	2.393***	1.927***	1.221***	1.682***	2.394***
	(0.0561)	(0.0644)	(0.0511)	(0.144)	(0.0652)	(0.0656)
Observations	1,418,632	126,994	345,631	2,398	1,073,001	124,596
R-squared	0.190	0.083	0.212	0.274	0.175	0.082

Table 17. Summary statistics on tariff (by sectors)

Industry Names	Tariff		Tariff_backward	Tariff_forward
	Mean	Diff b/w 2004 and 2013	Mean	Mean
1. Grain mill products	41.002	-18.29 (means fall by 18 percentage)	11.410	19.799
2. Forage	13.501	-7.87	19.654	1.932
3.Vegetable oil refining	19.85	-21.77	2.752	8.796
4. Sugar manufacturing	37.101	10.710	5.837	14.656
5. Slaughtering and meat processing	18.949	-4.510	10.705	15.193
6. Fish and fish products	16.052	-12.419	12.196	10.698
7. All other food manufacturing	22.206	-13.238	17.262	12.642
8.Wines, spirits and liquors	27.569	-34.290	16.811	4.384
9. Soft drink and other beverages	28.916	-20.560	16.372	1.328
10. Tobacco products	49.584	-24.000	4.275	
11.Cotton textiles	14.96	-13.88	4.168	14.558
12. Woolen textiles	14.96	-13.88	7.638	11.505
13. Hemp textiles	14.96	-13.88	5.044	8.632
14. Textiles products	17.674	-15.005	12.643	12.958
15. Knitted and crocheted fabrics and articles	20.082	-17.936	12.841	13.452
16. Wearing apparel	21.997	-16.212	14.651	11.568
17. Leather, fur, down and related products	19.176	-8.271	7.629	3.691
18. Products of wood, bamboo, cane, palm, straw	8.849	-8.346	4.591	8.130
19. Furniture	11.7	-18.51	10.835	12.740
20. Paper and paper products	11.975	-12.734	4.862	13.265
21. Printing, reproduction of recording media	13.584	-14.950	10.897	15.092
22. Stationary and related products	18.112	-5.306	11.426	9.624
23. Toys, sporting and athletic and recreation products	12.120	-14.198	11.291	1.494
24. Petroleum and nuclear processing	6.499	-0.930	6.647	11.159
25. Coking	5.479	-0.080	9.099	7.447
26. Basic chemicals	6.848	-3.13	5.342	10.513
27. Chemical fertilizers	7.511	3.15	8.390	2.418
28. Chemical pesticides	8.974	-2.07	7.906	1.169
29. Paints, varnishes and similar coatings, printing ink	9.242	-3.71	6.644	10.096
30. Man-made chemical products	10.043	-6.108	6.844	11.981
31. Special chemical products	12.661	-5.804	6.906	10.784
32. Chemical products for daily use	16.088	-11.882	9.763	7.675
33. Medical and pharmaceutical products	6.535	-4.599	6.911	1.817
34. Chemical fibers	9.825	-12.423	6.639	11.829
35. Rubber products	16.167	-3.752	8.967	12.782
36. Plastic products	12.583	-8.299	7.137	12.860
37. Cement, lime and plaster	11.811	-2.741	10.929	9.913

continued on following page

Table 17. Continued

Industry Names	Tariff		Tariff_backward	Tariff_forward
	Mean	Diff b/w 2004 and 2013	Mean	Mean
38. Glass and glass products	15.457	-4.890	7.790	10.669
39. Pottery, china and earthenware	18.236	-12.03	9.899	6.928
40. Fireproof materials	9.777	-3.671	9.550	7.751
41. Other nonmetallic mineral products	10.030	-2.355	7.801	8.187
42. Iron-smelting	6.601	-3.76	6.809	7.720
43. Steel-smelting	6.601	-3.76	7.538	9.424
44. Steel pressing	6.601	-3.76	6.700	11.368
45. Alloy iron smelting	6.601	-3.76	6.318	6.282
46. Nonferrous metal smelting	6.189	-2.382	5.554	7.897
47. Nonferrous metal pressing	5.63	-2.33	6.356	11.921
48. Metal products	12.788	-4.814	6.043	12.599
49. Boiler, engines and turbine	10.081	-4.635	7.551	10.693
50. Metalworking machinery	10.978	-5.201	8.875	8.637
51. Other general industrial machinery	10.869	-6.203	7.562	11.131
52. Agriculture, forestry, animal husbandry and fishing machinery	8.253	-5.070	9.018	1.163
53. Other special industrial equipment	9.871	-5.426	8.575	9.798
54. Railroad transport equipment	4.082	-1.34	8.528	2.403
55. Motor vehicles	29.126	-26.921	11.348	7.771
56. Parts and accessories for motor vehicles and their engines	17.584	-18.57	6.907	13.769
57. Ship building	7.365	-1.151	9.258	2.488
58. Other transport equipment	25.944	-9.094	8.338	3.349
59. Generators	10.725	-6.465	9.211	9.195
60. Household electric appliances	18.441	-7.963	9.438	7.640
61. Other electric machinery and equipment	15.103	-5.202	8.425	12.144
62. Telecommunication equipment	10.992	-13.480	6.546	4.279
63. Electronic computer	8.422	-14.87	6.629	5.235
64. Other computer peripheral equipment	8.352	-14.828	6.780	7.261
65. Electronic element and device	4.912	-7.01	7.641	10.988
66. Radio, television and communication equipment and apparatus	21.374	-13.97	8.162	5.635
67. Other electronic and communication equipment	9.528	-5.450	8.450	5.169
68. Instruments, meters and other measuring equipment	10.097	-5.150	8.621	8.603
69. Cultural and office equipment	10.460	-9.548	8.647	4.231
70. Arts and crafts products	16.980	-7.374	10.600	6.483
71. Other manufacturing products	19.324	-5.036	10.777	9.855
Average (all sectors)	12.691	-8.862	8.191	9.185

Table 18. Summary statistics on foreign investment (by sectors)

Industry Names	Mean of Firm-Level Foreign Share (Range from 0 to 1)	Diff b/w 2004 and 2013	Mean of Horizontal (Range from 0 to 1)	Diff b/w 2004 and 2013
1. Grain mill products	1.5	0.2	4.0	-2.0
2. Forage	8.3	1.2	20.1	-10.7
3. Vegetable oil refining	4.8	1.3	28.1	13.4
4. Sugar manufacturing	3.4	2.9	7.7	5.3
5. Slaughtering and meat processing	5.7	1.3	16.9	4.9
6. Fish and fish products	19.7	7.6	19.7	3.4
7. All other food manufacturing	16.6	4.8	28.8	2.2
8. Wines, spirits and liquors	6.4	3.5	15.3	1.2
9. Soft drink and other beverage	15.0	1.6	41.2	8.2
10. Tobacco products	1.1	1.1	0.2	-0.1
11. Cotton textiles	10.0	0.7	14.4	1.7
12. Woolen textiles	15.6	-2.8	21.9	0.7
13. Hemp textiles	5.9	3.1	8.7	4.6
14. Textiles products	20.3	4.7	24.7	3.4
15. Knitted and crocheted fabrics and articles	26.0	-3.3	31.4	-2.2
16. Wearing apparel	32.1	-1.4	36.0	-2.6
17. Leather, fur, down and related products	30.9	0.3	42.3	-0.9
18. Products of wood, bamboo, cane, palm, straw	12.0	-2.9	17.2	-7.6
19. Furniture	24.5	4.1	39.6	8.4
20. Paper and paper products	11.8	3.8	24.6	8.0
21. Printing, reproduction of recording media	9.5	3.0	22.4	1.9
22. Stationary and related products	25.3	6.1	34.6	12.2
23. Toys, sporting and athletic and recreation products	42.0	-1.5	54.4	3.2
24. Petroleum and nuclear processing	7.2	2.8	7.5	4.2
25. Coking	2.2	1.0	5.1	5.1
26. Basic chemicals	6.2	2.4	9.7	9.7
27. Chemical fertilizers	3.1	3.3	3.1	3.1
28. Chemical pesticides	5.5	3.7	8.8	2.0
29. Paints, varnishes and similar coatings, printing ink	17.5	8.0	30.3	16.8
30. Man-made chemical products	18.6	6.5	25.3	12.8
31. Special chemical products	10.0	2.1	18.3	9.8
32. Chemical products for daily use	20.4	8.8	48.3	18.9
33. Medical and pharmaceutical products	10.4	3.1	16.8	4.4
34. Chemical fibers	14.9	0.9	18.5	0.7
35. Rubber products	17.0	6.8	27.9	8.1
36. Plastic products	21.7	0.5	33.0	1.0
37. Cement, lime and plaster	5.3	2.8	9.4	3.7

continued on following page

Table 18. Continued

Industry Names	Mean of Firm-Level Foreign Share (Range from 0 to 1)	Diff b/w 2004 and 2013	Mean of Horizontal (Range from 0 to 1)	Diff b/w 2004 and 2013
38. Glass and glass products	12.4	0.6	18.4	5.9
39. Pottery, china and earthenware	17.1	-0.1	23.5	-1.1
40. Fireproof materials	4.8	3.0	7.4	2.7
41. Other nonmetallic mineral products	7.9	2.7	13.5	0.5
42. Iron-smelting	3.2	-0.3	5.6	-4.5
43. Steel-smelting	4.7	1.6	6.7	6.8
44. Steel pressing	6.3	4.0	10.9	8.0
45. Alloy iron smelting	2.5	-0.2	4.8	-2.2
46. Nonferrous metal smelting	5.8	1.5	6.1	0.3
47. Nonferrous metal pressing	9.5	3.9	15.7	4.5
48. Metal products	15.2	2.6	25.9	2.2
49. Boiler, engines and turbine	5.6	3.6	11.1	0.9
50. Metalworking machinery	10.8	5.4	12.6	5.0
51. Other general industrial machinery	10.1	4.4	20.9	5.7
52. Agriculture, forestry, animal husbandry and fishing machinery	3.3	6.3	3.8	6.2
53. Other special industrial equipment	14.2	10.6	18.6	14.7
54. Railroad transport equipment	3.7	4.9	2.9	4.3
55. Motor vehicles	6.7	3.1	24.0	3.9
56. Parts and accessories for motor vehicles and their engines	13.3	10.8	27.9	21.4
57. Ship building	12.6	0.9	12.0	4.9
58. Other transport equipment	13.4	3.0	19.0	2.3
59. Generators	15.3	6.0	25.5	10.5
60. Household electric appliances	22.9	4.6	31.5	7.5
61. Other electric machinery and equipment	23.0	4.2	36.2	3.6
62. Telecommunication equipment	27.6	10.4	55.5	16.3
63. Electronic computer	43.5	22.1	81.8	54.2
64. Other computer peripheral equipment	59.5	11.9	85.8	14.5
65. Electronic element and device	44.3	10.2	68.7	27.1
66. Radio, television and communication equipment and apparatus	46.1	10.8	54.4	19.4
67. Other electronic and communication equipment	35.7	5.2	59.6	10.3
68. Instruments, meters and other measuring equipment	23.7	3.0	36.5	7.7
69. Cultural and office equipment	45.8	8.9	85.7	9.0
70. Arts and crafts products	25.9	3.7	30.7	1.1
71. Other manufacturing products	25.6	4.0	36.1	-3.8
Overall (all sectors)	15.9	3.8	25.3	6.0

Chapter 14
Incentives to Attract Foreign Direct Investment in Emerging Economies:
A Causality Analysis for the Indian Case

Ishita Ghoshal
Symbiosis International University, India

Ishita Ghosh
Symbiosis International University, India

ABSTRACT

The study delves into a diagnostic check for macroeconomic factors that may cause and explain outward FDI flows to India as a representative of the emerging economies. The seventeen top investing economies to India across the period from 2008-14 reveal that overall FDI outflows, inflation, exchange rate and growth of the economy affect FDI outflows to India in the long run where only exchange rate has a causal effect. Also, the above-mentioned variables except growth along with the size of the economy has significant effect on the extent of FDI flows to India from the economies considered for the study.

INTRODUCTION

Foreign Direct Investments (FDI), a key component of foreign private capital flows, has been an important means to financing investments and growth in the emerging economies. Such inflows often exceed official sectoral financing within the economy and have continued to remain an important engine of growth in a majority of the Emerging Market Countries (EMC) of the current global economy. Foreign private capital flows, and in particular short-term flows, can, however, be unpredictable as is evident from the recent financial crises. In this light, it has become imperative to understand the trends in FDI flows to EMCs. Insights into investment decisions and structural changes that may affect the trends and direction of such flows have become the prevailing pointers in recognising net private flows to emerging

DOI: 10.4018/978-1-5225-2345-1.ch014

markets and can possibly be a source of negotiating economic stability at times of volatility in global capital markets (The World Bank, 2003).

China and India are the largest emerging markets in the current global economy (Jain, 2006). Around the mid-2015, the World Bank estimated that while China was the leading Emerging Market Country (EMC), India will be poised to overtake China with a 7.5 per cent projected growth rate (Times of India, 2015). The World Bank also anticipated that China would grow at 7.1 per cent while other EMCs would grow by 4.4 per cent in 2015, with a likely rise to 5.2 per cent in 2016, and 5.4 per cent in 2017. Although the "carefully managed" slowdown would continue in China, the oil importing Indian economy would move ahead because reforms helped in stimulating the market confidence and falling oil prices reduced economic liabilities (World Investment Report, 2015).

In 2015, the World Bank Chief Economist, Kaushik Basu opined that

... slowly but surely the ground beneath the global economy is shifting. China has avoided the potholes skillfully for now and is easing to a growth rate of 7.1 per cent; Brazil, with its corruption scandal making news, has been less lucky, dipping into negative growth; growth in South Asia is expected to continue firming to 7.1 per cent this year, led by a cyclical recovery in India and supported by a gradual strengthening of demand in high-income countries. (Times of India, 2015)

India's gain from the declining global oil prices has enabled the country to improve its fiscal and trading accounts. Implementation of subsidy reforms and the easing of monetary policy has helped the country raise business and investor confidence, thereby attracting new capital inflows. The "Make in India" initiative since late 2014 has been a vital impetus to the inflow of funds and boosting economic growth (The Economist, 2014).

Regional studies pertaining to Asia submit that India is poised to be the next economic super-power, surpassing China soon (Thirlwell, 2004). Whether this prediction holds any water, is a matter of time. However, it is undeniable that the importance of the Indian economy as a key driver in the global economic growth will remain a force to reckon with (Chandler & Zainulbhai, n.d.) (Asia House, 2013) (Sanghoee, 2015) (Forbes, 2015) (LSE IDEAS, 2012). It is in this light, that the chapter aims to investigate the determinants of inward FDI in India from its highest investing partners.

The chapter is divided into two main parts – a) the importance of India in the global economy and how investment inflows will help the economy grow b) the empirical analysis to understand short run and long run relationships amongst the variables considered and estimate the extent of the effects.

BACKGROUND

In the last few years, the global economy has slowed down considerably. Foreign Direct Investment (FDI) in 2014 recorded a decline of 16 per cent (approximately, 1.2 trillion). The decline has been fraught with economic and geopolitical instability, creating various policy driven uncertainties for investors world-wide; large disinvestments have also off set new global investments. New investments were also offset by some large divestments. The drop in FDI flows was particularly concerning when compared to the global growth in GDP, trade, gross fixed capital formation and employment. However, since 2015, an upward trend in FDI has been noted. In fact, the current FDI flows are responsible for almost 40 percent of external development finance to developing and transition economies. The UNCTAD predicts FDI flows to touch $1.4 trillion in 2015 and further on at $1.5 trillion in 2016 and $1.7 trillion in 2017, respectively. Some cited reasons are growth prospects in the United States, the demand-side stimulation in the economies because of the recent spiraling down of oil prices and various macroeconomic and trade policies that have been relaxed and reformulated to accommodate trade and investment liberalization and promotion between trading partners. The current macroeconomic forecasts for the world economy estimate that multinational corporations (MNCs) will have a wave of profitability and cash reserves in the forthcoming years of the current global business cycle. This expectant outlook will also fuel higher FDI flows. However, the recent instabilities surrounding the European Union (namely, the BREXIT and its aftermath), other geopolitical insecurities and susceptibilities in emerging economies may soon dampen this optimism in the near future for the world investment climate (World Investment Report, 2015) (World Investment Report, 2016).

A cursory look at FDI inflows by geography clearly indicates that developed nations have continued to receive record high investments in 2014, while developing and emerging nations fell flat as far as this economic variable goes. Remarkably, it was noticed that while the developing regions of Asia drove the inflows to the developed nations (where FDI reached a record high of USD 681 billion in 2014), FDI flows to Asia grew by 9 per cent (USD 465 billion in 2014). East, South-east and South Asia – all witnessed a surge in FDI inflows. It is notable that economic giants of this region, China and India, both enjoyed considerable rise in FDI inflows. While China's inflows went up by 4 per cent in 2014, India's went up by a significant 22 per cent. However, given the geopolitical insurgencies in West Asia, there was a downward trend in the FDI inflows for the sixth consecutive year.

In terms of regional groupings, FDI is essentially determined by larger global macroeconomic trends, economic performances of the members in the partnership among themselves and vis-à-vis the world economy and other geopolitical factors. Increasing long term cooperation and supporting a common climate for foreign investments, do augment the inflows, as well. Extra-regional FDI is also attracted by a larger and unified market size that such regions offer. In spite of these inherent merits, it was noticed that most economic clusters experienced a fall in inflows till around 2014. However, notably, the Association of Southeast Asian Nations (ASEAN), witnessed a 5 per cent increase in inflows, and the Regional Comprehensive Economic Partnership (RCEP), an increase of 4 per cent. Also, while the share of intra and extra regional FDI is largely dependent on the particular characteristics of the regions themselves, total inflow of FDI in the developing and emerging clusters are still very low. In comparison, ASEAN has shown a significant pull in the inflow of FDIs. The APEC economies reached $652 billion in 2014, accounting for more than half of global FDI flows, while intra-APEC FDI flows and stocks are significant, at about 40 per cent of inward stock that was noted during 2009–2011.

Top Investors and Invested Sectors in India

Table 1 provides estimates published by the Reserve Bank of India (RBI) in the latter part of 2015. Various aggregated values provided here may be different from the figures specified by the World Investment Reports. This is due to methodological differences.

Some cursory observations from this data and other more recent developments, show the following:

- In the last decade, Mauritius, Singapore and USA have consistently remained the top three investors in India (The Reserve Bank of India, 2016).

- While the trend in inflows have gone up, there has been a dip in the inward FDI in the years 2011-12 and 2012-13. This was possibly due to the political uncertainties and policy changes anticipated with a change in Government (The Reserve Bank of India, 2015).
- It is interesting to note that in spite of the various bilateral and regional trading agreements that India has engaged in with other nations (some of the significant ones being SAFTA, EU-India, ASEAN-India), barring Singapore, Mauritius and Japan, so far the inflows have not been very robust from these trading partners ("Department of Commerce, Government of India", 2016).
- With the launch of the "Make in India" initiative in the late 2014, there seems to be an upswing in the inflows with new trade and investment policies in place ("Economic Survey 2015-16", 2016) ("Department of Commerce, Government of India", 2016).
- There are some 18 trade partnership negotiations underway with India and another nine that have been recently made operational. The improvement in the inflows may well be considerably high in the long run, other economic factors remaining conducive ("Department of Commerce, Government of India", 2016).
- As recently as February 2016, the Economic Survey of India (2015-16) declared that FDI inflows in India increased by 31 per cent to USD 24.8 billion between April-November, 2014. The survey also pointed out that more than 60 per cent of the FDI equity inflows of USD 24.8 billion during 2015-16 (April-November) came from Singapore and Mauritius. Since the launch of the "Make in India" initiative in September 2014, there has been a 40 per cent increase approximately in FDI inflows between October 2014 and June 2015, vis-à-vis the analogous period of the previous financial year. With the aim to open up and streamline the FDI policy while boosting the ease of doing business climate in the country, the government has undertaken various reforms, since. It has also been noted that after the introduction of the initiative, FDI inflows have consistently increased into sectors like computer software and hardware, services, trading, automobile industry, construction activities, chemicals and telecommunications. Over this development, countries such as Japan, China, France and South Korea have confirmed their intent of substantially investing in India in various industrial and infrastructure projects in the offing.

Another important observation is that India's services sector has remained the most significant in terms of its contribution to the FDI inflows into the country. Almost 66.1 per cent of the country's gross value added growth in 2015-16 has been attributed to FDI inflows from this sector. Regardless of the economic slump in the post crisis period of 2010-14 India showed the fastest growth in its services sector, recording a Compound Annual Growth Rate (CAGR) of 8.6 per cent and just tipping over the Chinese who were at 8.4 per cent. Also, India's services sector growth in 2014 was at 10.3 per cent while the Chinese were at 8.0 per cent (DNA, 2016) (Live Mint, 2016) (The Economic Times, 2016) ("Foreign Direct Investment", 2016).

MAIN FOCUS OF THE CHAPTER

Drivers of FDI Inflow and Outflow: A Literature Review

The determinants of FDI inflows have been empirically tested in many studies, so far. The broad classification of variables that were set out by UNCTAD and used by (Walsh & Yu, 2010) are market size,

Table 1. Foreign direct investment flows to India: country-wise and industry-wise (in millions of USD)

Source/Industry	2010-11	2011-12	2012-13	2013-14	2014-15 P
1	2	3	4	5	6
Total FDI	14,939	23,473	18,286	16,054	24,748
Country-Wise Inflows					
Mauritius	5,616	8,142	8,059	3,695	5,878
Singapore	1,540	3,306	1,605	4,415	5,137
U.S.A	1,071	994	478	617	1,981
Cyprus	571	1,568	415	546	737
Japan	1,256	2,089	1,340	1,795	2,019
Netherlands	1,417	1,289	1,700	1,157	2,154
United Kingdom	538	2,760	1,022	111	1,891
Germany	163	368	467	650	942
UAE	188	346	173	239	327
France	486	589	547	229	347
Switzerland	133	211	268	356	292
Hong Kong	209	262	66	85	325
Spain	183	251	348	181	401
China	2	73	148	121	505
Malaysia	40	18	238	113	219
South Korea	136	226	224	189	138
Luxembourg	248	89	34	539	204
Others	1,142	892	1,154	1,015	1,250
Sector-Wise Inflows					
Manufacturing	4,793	9,337	6,528	6,381	9,613
Construction	1,599	2,634	1,319	1,276	1,640
Financial Services	1,353	2,603	2,760	1,026	3,075
Real Estate Activities	444	340	197	201	202
Electricity and other Energy Generation, Distribution & Transmission	1,338	1,395	1,653	1,284	1,284
Communication Services	1,228	1,458	92	1,256	1,075
Business Services	569	1,590	643	521	680
Miscellaneous Services	509	801	552	941	586
Computer Services	843	736	247	934	2,154
Restaurants and Hotels	218	870	3,129	361	686
Retail & Wholesale Trade	391	567	551	1,139	2,551
Mining	592	204	69	24	129
Transportation	344	410	213	311	482
Trading	156	6	140	0	228
Education, Research & Development	56	103	150	107	131
Others	506	419	43	293	232
P: Provisional.					

Source: RBI, 2015.

Note: Includes FDI through Secretariat of Industrial Assistance (SIA)/Foreign Investment Promotion Board (FIPB) and Reserve Bank of India (RBI) routes only.

Table 2. FDI determinants (as given by UNCTAD)

Determining Variables	Examples
Policy variables	Tax, trade, privatization and macroeconomic policies
Business variables	Investment incentives
Market related economic determinants	Market size, growth and structure
Resource related economic determinants	Raw materials, labour costs and productivity
Efficiency related economic determinants	Transport and communication costs and labour

Source: United Nations Conference on Trade and Development, 2015.

labour cost, trade openness, infrastructural facilities, gross capital formation, labour force, macroeconomic stability, growth prospects, etc. The following table summarizes the nature of determinants and variables that could be responsible for FDI inflows.

The spurt in FDI in the last decade has given rise to a few generalized theories that determine the global flow of funds between nations. One, the heterogeneous methods to understanding international production (Dunning, 1986) and the classical model for determinants of FDI stems from the formerly done research by Dunning (1981) which provide an extensive analysis based on ownership, location and the internationalization (OLI) paradigm. In 1993, Dunning had put forward that FDIs are driven by access to income generating assets, early mover entry, internalization of net benefits necessitated by the costs of transactional market failures being higher than administrative costs of operating a foreign branch, and the location of production advantages such as access to capital, access to skilled and abundant labor, control over transfer price, reduction in exchange risks, lag and lead payments, and so on, which will remain attractive as long as there are gains to be made from operating in different locations. All these advantages must be favorable enough to outweigh the costs of setting up and operating from a foreign operation (Penrose, 1994) (Dunning, 2001) (Dunning, 2009) (Al-sadiq, 2013).

Two, according to the theory of internationalization (Rugman & Dunning, 1973) (Rugman, 1987), FDI takes place because Multi-National Corporations (MNCs) want to substitute external markets with internal markets that are more efficient (such as, intra-firm transactions). This helps them avoid difficulties that arise with differences in transaction costs, time lags, bargaining and buyer uncertainties, and other externalities in the goods and factors markets. The movement of funds continue till marginal benefits and costs equalize (Horstmann & Markusen, 1995) (Kindleberger, 2002).

Three, according to several experts, FDI is an outcome from the imperfections that exist in the market structure of the world – concentration and agglomeration of firms and economies of scales that come into being because of competition and comparative advantage. FDIs may also be an outcome of the firms' specific competencies stemming from managerial skills, brand name, superior marketing distribution, bargaining and political power, access to raw materials, and patent-protected technology. Kindleberger (1969), Hymer (1972) and Horaguchi and Toyne (1990) have worked observing such market imperfections and conclude that the movement of investments may substantially depend on these factors.

According to Arbatli (2011), cross-country and over-time variations in FDI inflows can be split into two categories, namely, global push factors and country-specific pull factors. Many studies have established that global push factors are central to the explaining of capital flows to EMCs, hence making the regulation of their outcomes important in the purview of domestic policies. The importance of global economic conditions has also gained importance with the recent global economic crisis and the subsequent decline in FDI inflows.

The country-specific pull factors that are usually classified as a) fixed or structural factors such as whether the country is an oil exporter or not, its location and the average level of education; b) political factors including existence of conflict, labour strikes, and/or protests; c) macroeconomic factors such as inflation, the share of exports, and the real exchange rate; and d) economic policy variables including corporate tax rates, tariff rates, exchange rate policy, and whether there are capital account restrictions.

1. **Global Push Factors:**
    a. Growth in capital exporting countries on FDI flows to EMCs have been somewhat ambiguous. While higher income growth in developed nations allow for expansions into other markets and are associated with easier internal financing conditions, it may also make investment in the domestic economy relatively more attractive. Usually, 3 to 4-year moving averages of real GDP growth account for lag effects due to implementation and planning times associated with FDI.
    b. International liquidity helps in understanding the effects of credit conditions in advanced countries on FDI flows. Lower interest rates are expected to increase FDI flows, making it easier for firms to finance investment projects.
    c. Risk environment indicate the global risk appetite is also a common push factor that could affect FDI flows to EMCs.
2. **Country Specific Pull Factors:**
    a. **Fixed or Structural Factors:**
        i. The size of the domestic market can play a role in drawing FDI, where firms decide to invest in the host country to capture a share of the domestic market. This variable is also related to the capital-to-labor ratio and, hence, the productivity of capital. Countries with a low level of per capita income might invite more inflows, consistent with a higher marginal product of capital.
        ii. Several studies have established a strong empirical correlation between educational level in the host country and FDI inflows. Policies encouraging investments in human capital, augmenting skill sets and generic education usually attract FDI. A certain level of educational fulfilment is vital to a country's ability to draw FDI and to maximise the human capital spill overs that take place due to the presence of MNCs in the host country. The minimum level of education required will depend on the industries present in the host country and according to other characteristics of the host country's enabling environment. By its self, education unlikely to make FDI inflows attractive but it remains a vital variable in determining inflows when considered in tandem with other key macroeconomic concerns (Usman, 2014) (Bellak, Leibrecht, Stehrer 2009) (OECD, 2003). Lipsey (2000) also captures a positive effect of FDI on growth and has a strong interaction with the level of schooling in the host country.
        iii. Oil importing nations are affected by the global prices of oil and this can affect the nation's trading account (and GDP) significantly.
        iv. Most studies that have used the Gravity equation to determine FDI, have traditionally used location (distance between the home and host countries). Amongst a host of variables that can be added to the augmented gravity model, the fundamental variables are size and distance – the crux of the model (Podda, 2016) (Marku, 2014) (Pagano & Volpin, 2004) (Shatz, 2000).

b. **Political Environment and Institutions:** Many studies have shown a negative relationship with FDI inflows and political uncertainties and corruption. While quantifying and measuring such risks can be vague, biased and difficult, there are indices that rank countries according to political stability, domestic and conflicts, law and order norms (even labour laws), ease of doing business, global competiveness and bureaucracy (Arbatli, 2011) (Bénassy-Quéré, Coupet & Mayer, 2007) (Rose-Ackerman & Tobin, 2003) (Henisz 2000). A study by Bevan and Estrin (2000, 2004) that measured determinants of FDI inflows to transition economies, namely, the central and eastern parts of Europe, considered factors such as country risk, labour cost, host market size and gravity factors for the duration 1994 to1998. The investigation concluded that country risks are influenced by private sector and industrial development, government balance, reserves and corruption. A dummy variable employed for capturing the key announcements of progress in the EU agreement seemed to directly affect the FDI inflows.

c. **The Macroeconomic Environment:** The macroeconomic environment and policies in EMCs have improved consistently over the last decade. This can clarify the overall positive trend and the sharp rise in inflows in the 2000s. However, an important concern that remains is examining the effects of macroeconomic variables on FDI and the feedback effect from FDI to macroeconomic variables, especially in the case of economic growth.

    i. In a review done by (Ghosh & Chakrabarti, 2016), it was noted that many empirical studies reported that market size indicates potential for consumption and hence, trade. It can be measured by Gross Domestic Product (GDP), GDP per capita income, and size of the middle class population. These are expected to be positive and significant determinants of FDI flows. Literature made available through studies undertaken by Lankes and Venables (1996), Resmini (2000), Bevan et al. (2000), Garibaldi et al. (2002), Nunes, Oscategui, and Peschiera (2006), and Sahoo (2006) – all point towards the same findings. In contrast, Holland and Pain (1998) and Asiedu (2006) have found out that growth and market size are insignificant determinants of FDI flow (Narayanamurthy, Perumal, & Kode Chandra, 2010). It has also been empirically observed that the rate of growth and FDI inflows are positively related. There can also be feedback effects from FDI (both current and past) on economic growth in return (Arbatli, 2011). Also, Duran (1999) found that some of the key variables that drive FDI were the market size, the growth rate of the economy, the country's wealth and savings, its macroeconomic stability and trade openness, among others. Dunning's work (the OLG paradigm), as mentioned earlier, is seminal in the case of determinants of FDI. Therefore, FDI tends to flow to the countries with larger market size and higher economic growth rates in which larger economies of scale could be provided for FDI to exploit their ownership advantages (Culem, 1988). Also, a country which has a stable macroeconomic condition with high and sustained growth rates will receive more FDI inflows than a more volatile economy. The proxies measuring growth rate are GDP growth rates, industrial production index, interest rates, inflation rates (Amaya & Rowland, n.d.) (Dadush, Dasgupta, & Ratha, 2000).

    ii. Low inflation rate is makes FDI inflows more attractive. Domestic inflation will affect the net returns and hence the investment decisions of the MNCs. It is a safe assumption to say that inflation rates and FDI inflows are inversely related. In 2010, Dabla-Norris et. al., found results in their study that are concurs with this relationship (International Monetary Fund, 2010).

iii. Many studies have reported that the effect of export orientation on FDI inflows may be indefinite since it would be differently dependent on horizontal and vertical FDI. International trade tends to boost and support FDI. Much of FDI is export oriented and may also require the import of complementary, intermediate and capital goods. Most MNCs are now trading through Global Value Chains (GVC). In either case, volume of trade is augmented, thereby increasing trade openness (Lankes & Venables, 1996; Sahoo, 2006). Trade openness can be proxied as the ratio of the total trade by GDP (Nunes et al., 2006).

iv. The exchange rates levels and their volatility can affect FDI inflows significantly, as well as, the total amount of foreign direct investment that takes place and the allocation of this investment spending across a range of countries. When a currency depreciates (say in the host country), it can be advantageous in terms of FDI inflows in two ways. One, it lowers the domestic wages and production costs relative to the home country. Keeping all other factors constant, the country undergoing the real currency depreciation has improved "locational advantage" or attractiveness as a location for receiving productive capacity investments. Two, with this new-found "relatively" lower wage situation, the exchange rate depreciation improves the overall rate of return for the host country. Also, the change in the real exchange rate can help assess the effects of competitiveness on FDI flows. This may be more important if the investment is oriented towards the export market (Goldberg & Kolstad 1994) (Abbott, Cushman, & Vita, 2012). (Goldberg & Klein, 1997) (Udoh & Egwaikhide, 2010).

v. Gross capital formation is a strong determinant of FDI receipts (Ranjan & Agrawal, 2011) (Sridharan, Vijayakumar & Rao, 2009). Krkoska (2001) and Lipsey (2000) found that there was no significant impact on FDI with an increasing rate of capital formation. This finding is purely from the dataset that they used for the study. However, a positive or negative and significant relationship between FDI and capital formation is anticipated.

vi. The host country's infrastructural quality plays a significant role in attracting FDI receipts. Loree and Guisinger (1995) assessed the determinants of FDI by United States towards developed nations from 1977 to 1982 and concluded that the host country policy related variables are significant in developed countries and infrastructure seems to be an important determinant for all the regions. Similar studies have been conducted by for developing and emerging economies and show similar results – quality of infrastructure in the host country is a vitally important factor for FDI inflows (Rehman, Ilyas, Alam & Akram, 2011) (Subramanian, Chakrabarti, Sairam & Kuntluru, 2012) (Shah, 2014).

vii. Yeyati (1996) and later, Torre, L. D., Schmukler and Yeyati (2002) have examined the extent of business cycles and interest rate cycles of developed countries and their impact on FDI inflows for the period 1980 to 1990. They considered the determinants of bilateral FDI using the Gravity model and found that FDI flows from US and Europe move counter cyclical to the business cycle in the home country, while the interest rate cycles are the important determinants of FDI inflows. Jansen and Stokman (2004) found that countries that have comparatively intensive FDI relations, also have more synchronized business cycles during 1995–2001. Before 1995, they found a positive association between FDI linkages and output co-movement, but this may partly reflect the effects of trade relations. Moreover, more intensive FDI links were also associated with a greater vulnerability to lagged output spill overs from abroad, whereas trade links are not. Policy implications of this study were a) that there is an underlying tendency for business cycles to exhibit greater co-movement in the future, and b) that policy makers need to incorporate the FDI linkage among economies in their models and analytical framework for policy analysis.

viii. In two independent studies for Ghana and Malaysia, Andinuur (2013) and Roslan (2013), have respectively found out that while there exists a unidirectional causal link for GDP and FDI to inflation, there was no such relationship for inflation to GDP and FDI. Also, a unidirectional causality was discovered running from GDP to inflation and all causality observed were statistically significant. In another study for the ASEAN 5, it was observed through VAR techniques that there was a clear negative relationship with inflation rates and FDI receipts (Siddiqui & Aumeboonsuke, 2014). In an IMF working paper of 2002, Garibaldi et al. studied the FDI and Portfolio investment flows to 26 EMCs in Eastern Europe including the former Soviet Union from 1990 to 1999. The estimates from the study indicated that the FDI flows are well explained by standard economic fundamentals, including inflation.

ix. Higher the labour costs in the home country, more likely it is to seek a destination for FDI, while the higher the labour force participation rate (LFPR) is, it will increase the GDP and lead the nation to investing abroad. FDI often takes a form of capital flows from a parent company to its foreign affiliate by relocating technical factors from one region to another and substituting capital movement with labour mobility in host regions while profiting from domestic markets. Ethier (1986) suggests that one more driving force could be uncertainty and asymmetric information (Latorre, 2008).

d. **Economic Policies:** According to Arbatli (2011), trade policy and agreements, capacity of the home country and capability of undertaking outward investments, costs and returns on investments, exchange rate classifications, restrictions in capital account transactions related to FDI, corporate tax rates and other taxes, etc., are also key factors in attracting FDI[1].

Methods and Materials

Ideally a comprehensive set of macroeconomic and policy variables are required to understand their effects on FDI inflows. Data non-availability and disparity in the time frame and intensity of reforms, policies and trade agreements across countries pose a big challenge for such analysis.

Based on the above discussion, the study concentrates on the following variables:

- Annual foreign direct investment flows from the 17 home countries to India over the years (outward FDI from the 17 countries into India)
- Annual trade as a ratio of GDP of the home countries (to capture trade openness)
- Annual GDP at market prices of the home country (to capture the market size of the home country)
- Net outflows of annual foreign direct investment of the home country in current US$
- Annual percentage growth rate of the home country
- Annual percentage of consumer price index (to capture inflation)
- Labour force participation rate as a percentage of the total population aged above 15 years (modelled ILO estimate) (to capture the capacity of the home country)

- Annual gross fixed capital formation as a percentage of GDP of the home country (to capture the capacity of the home country)
- Real effective exchange rate index (2010 = 100) of the home country

It was not feasible to include infrastructure index, ease of doing business, corruption index, political stability, business cycles, trading policies, etc. as determining factors of outward FDI due to paucity of data and difficulty in measurement for the countries considered in the study. Also, the existence of trading agreement between India and the individual home countries could not be considered. The countries selected for the study account for the highest FDI inflows to India despite many of them not having any trade agreement with India currently. Trade agreements with many of these countries are under negotiation.

Model

For empirical analysis, the following linear equation is estimated using country-wise data for 2008-2014. As per the nature of the data, the study has used the panel data estimation technique to estimate the following model to show the impact of various macroeconomic indicators of the home countries on FDI inflows into India from these countries.

$$\log\left(FDI_{it}^{India\ Inflows}\right) = a + b_1 Trade_{it}^{Ratio} + b_2 \log\left(GDP_{it}\right) + b_3 \log\left(FDI_{it}^{Outflows}\right) + b_4 \log\left(Growth_{it}^{Rate}\right)$$
$$+ b_5 Inflation_{it} + b_6 \log\left(LFPR_{it}\right) + b_7 \log\left(Capital_{it}^{Fixed}\right) + b_8 REER_{it} + \varepsilon_{it}$$

where, $\log\left(FDI_{it}^{India\ Inflows}\right)$. is the log of the annual foreign direct investment flows from the 17 home countries to India over the years; $Trade_{it}^{Ratio}$ is the annual trade as a ratio of GDP of the home countries; $\log\left(GDP_{it}\right)$ is the annual GDP at market prices of the home country; $log\left(FDI_{it}^{Outflows}\right)$ is the log of net outflows of annual foreign direct investment of the home country in current US$; $\log\left(Growth_{it}^{Rate}\right)$ is the annual percentage growth rate of the home country; $Inflation_{it}$ is the annual percentage of consumer price index; $\log\left(LFPR_{it}\right)$ is the logf the labour force participation rate as a percentage of the total population aged above 15 years (modelled ILO estimate); $\log\left(Capital_{it}^{Fixed}\right)$ is the log of annual gross fixed capital formation as a percentage of GDP of the home country; $REER_{it}$ is the real effective exchange rate index (2010 = 100) of the home country.

Data

Data for the above mentioned variables were collected from World Development Indicators provided by the World Bank. Panel data for 17 countries ranging from 2008-2014 has been used for the analysis.

Tools and Tests

The authors have used panel data estimation methods to find the relationship defined above. The following illuminates the methodology used for the study.

Panel Data Unit-Root Tests

The authors have used panel data unit root tests to check whether the variables are stationary or not. Several statistical methods (Levin, Lin and Chu 2002; Im, Pesaran and Shin, 2003; Choi, 2001; Breitung, 2000; and Hadri, 2000) are constructed to test for unit roots in panel data. Among those the study has employed Levin-Lin-Chu test and Im-Pesaran-Shin tests to check for stationarity in the variables.

Levin-Lin-Chu (LLC) Test

The model is:

$$y_{i,t} = \alpha_i + \rho_i y_{i,t-1} + \varepsilon_{it}, \text{ t} = 1, 2, \ldots, \text{T; i} = 1, 2, \ldots, \text{N}$$

It proposes a panel based ADF test which restricts ρ_i by keeping them identical across cross sections as follows:

$$\Delta y_{i,t} = \alpha_i^* + \rho_i^* y_{i,t-1} + \sum_{j=1}^{\rho_i} \theta_{ij} \Delta y_{i,t-j} + \varepsilon_{it}$$

The null and alternative hypotheses are defined as:

H$_0$: $\rho_i = \rho = 0$ for all i, against
H$_A$: $\rho_1 = \rho_2 = \ldots = \rho < 0$ for all i, with test based on statistics: $t_\rho = \hat{\rho} / SE(\hat{\rho})$

The LLC unit root test suggests that both the variables are stationary at first difference in the case of developing as well as developed countries.

Im-Pesaran-Shin (IPS) Test

The model is: $y_{i,t} = \alpha_i + \rho_i y_{i,t-1} + \varepsilon_{it}$, t = 1, 2, . . ., T
The null and alternative hypotheses are defined as:

H$_0$: $\rho_i = 1$, i = 1, 2, . . ., N i.e. each series in the panel contains a unit root for all i
H$_A$: $\rho_i < 1$, for at least one i

They use separate unit root tests for the N cross-section units.
The DF regression:

$$y_{i,t} = \alpha_i + \rho_i y_{i,t-1} + \varepsilon_{it}$$

or the ADF regression:

$$\Delta y_{i,t} = \alpha_i + \rho_i y_{i,t-1} + \sum_{j=1}^{\rho_i} \theta_{ij} \Delta y_{i,t-j} + \varepsilon_{it}$$

is estimated and the t-statistic for testing ρi = 1 is computed. Let $t_{i,T}$ (i = 1, 2, . . ., N) denote the t-statistic for testing unit roots in individual series i, and let $E(t_i,T) = \mu$ and $V(t_i,T) = \sigma^2$.

Then $\bar{t}_{N,T} = \frac{1}{N}\sum_{j=1}^{N} t_i, T$ and $\overline{W} = \sqrt{\frac{N\left(\bar{t}_{N,T} - \mu\right)}{\sigma}} \Rightarrow N\left(0,1\right)$

$\overline{W}$ converges in distribution to a standard normal variate sequentially, as T→ ∞ first and then N→ ∞. The IPS test is a way of combining the evidence on the unit root hypothesis from N unit root tests performed on N cross-section units. The test assumption is that T is the same for all cross-section units and hence *E (ti,T)* and *V (ti,T)* are the same for all *i*, so the IPS test is applied only for balanced panel data. In the case of serial correlation, IPS test proposes using the ADF t-test for individual series.

Panel Cointegration

Pedroni's Residual Cointegration Test

To test the cointegration relationship, Pedroni's method (1999, 2004) which extends the idea of residual based cointegration, proposed by Engle and Granger (1987) is used. Pedroni's formulation allows for the heterogeneity across the cross-sections by permitting individual specific fixed effect, slopes and deterministic time trend for each cross-section. To test the cointegration, following bi-variate regression equation is estimated:

$$Y_{jt} = a_j + \delta_{jt} + b_t + \beta_j X_{jt} + e_{jt}$$

Under the null hypothesis of no cointegration in heterogeneous panels i.e. e_{it} is non-stationary, Pedroni develops seven different test statistics based on the estimated error term e_{it} in equation. These are divided in two groups. The first group, "within dimensions" contains four test statistics termed as panel-v, panel-p, panel-t non parametric (PP) and panel-t parametric (ADF). The second group "between dimensions" contains three test statistics termed as group-p, group-t non parametric (PP) and group-t parametric (ADF).

The estimated statistic will be the average of the individual statistics. The rejection of null of no cointegration indicated that the cointegration holds at least for one individual. After the calculation of the panel cointegration test statistics, Pedroni shows that the standardized statistic is asymptotically normally distributed as follows:

$$K = \frac{\left(K_{N,T} - \mu\left(N\right)^{\frac{1}{2}}\right)}{\left(V\right)^{\frac{1}{2}}} \Rightarrow N\left(0,1\right)$$

He reports the critical values for μ and v for different values of number of regressors in cointegration relationship.

Johansen Cointegration Test for Two Variables (Fischer-Type Test)

Johansen (1988) proposes two different approaches; one of them is the likelihood ratio trace statistics and the other one is maximum Eigen value statistics, to determine the presence of cointegration vectors in non-stationary time series. The trace statistics and maximum eigenvalue statistics have shown in equation below:

$$\lambda_{trace}\left(r\right) = -\mathrm{T}\sum_{i=r+1}^{N} \ln\left(1-\hat{\lambda}_i\right)$$

$$\lambda_{max}\left(r, r+1\right) = -\mathrm{T}\ln\left(1-\hat{\lambda}_{r+1}\right)$$

where T is the sample size. For the trace test tests the null hypothesis of at most r cointegration vector against the alternative hypothesis of full rank r = n cointegration vector, the null and alternative hypothesis of maximum eigenvalue statistics is to check the r cointegrating vectors against the alternative hypothesis of r+1 cointegrating vectors.Using Johannsen's (1988) test for cointegration, Maddala and Wu (1999) consider Fisher's (1932) suggestion to combine individual tests, to propose an alternative for testing for cointegration in the full panel by combining individual cross-sections tests for cointegration.

If π_i is the p-value from an individual cointegration test for cross-section i, then under the null hypothesis for the whole panel,

$$-2\sum_{i=1}^{N} ln\left(\pi_i\right)$$

is distributed as χ^2_{2N}.A big benefit is that the test can handle unbalanced panels. EViews reports χ^2-value based on MacKinnon-Haug-Michelis (1999) p-values for Johansen's cointegration trace test and maximum eigenvalue test.

Further, to estimate the long run relationship between the heterogeneous cointerated panels, Panel Fully Modified Least Square (FMOLS) method is used. This methodology allows consistent and efficient estimation of cointegrating vector and also addresses the problem of simultaneous bias. The cointegrated regression for estimation is:

$$Y_{it} = a_i + bX_{it} + e_{it}; \quad X_{it} = X_{i,t-1} + e_{it}$$

Panel Causality for a Pair of Variables

Granger causality is checked in both the panels to analyze the causality hypotheses explained in section 1. In case of long-run relationship, panel Vector Error Correction Model (VECM) is used while panel

Vector Auto Regression (VAR) method is used in case of no cointegration. The conventional Granger causality tests raise two critical issues for a panel data case, both dealing with the potential heterogeneity of the individual cross sections. The first source of heterogeneity is cross sectional variation due to the distinctive intercepts; such heterogeneity may be addressed with a fixed effects model (i.e. it is controlled by introduction of individual effects in the model). The more crucial case is where heterogeneous slope coefficients should be considered (i.e. should be controlled by introducing individual dimension for regression slopes in the model). The second source of heterogeneity affects the causality relationships. For instance, for some individuals the introduction of past values of may improve the forecast on, whereas for others there may be no improvement. Therefore, we should distinguish two subgroups of individuals according to the causality relationships between and. If this heterogeneity is not considered, the test of causality hypothesis may lead to a fallacious conclusion concerning the relative size of the two subgroups. In a nutshell, the Granger causality for panel data sets should consider the different sources of heterogeneity of the data-generating. A newly suggested theory of Granger Causality in Panel by Hurlin and Venet (2001) is used here to test causality which controls for both sources of heterogeneity. The procedure has three main steps, which are related to the homogeneous non-causality (HNC), homogeneous causality (HC) and heterogeneous non-causality (HENC) hypotheses. Following model is estimated:

$$\Delta \ln energy_{it} = \sum_{k=1}^{p} a_k \Delta \ln energy_{i,t-k} + \sum_{k=1}^{p} b_k \Delta \ln gdp_{i,t-k} + \lambda_i + \mu_{it}$$

$$\Delta \ln gdp_{it} = \sum_{k=1}^{p} a_k \Delta \ln gdp_{i,t-k} + \sum_{k=1}^{p} b_k \Delta \ln energy_{i,t-k} + \lambda_i + \mu_{it}$$

Homogeneous Non Causality hypothesis refers to the case in which there is no linear causality between dependent variable and explanatory variable for any cross section (the null hypothesis states non-existence of causal relationships across all cross sections, N).

$\mathbf{H_0}$: $b_k^i = b_k^j = 0 \ \forall_i \epsilon [1, N], \ \forall_k \epsilon [1, p]$

$\mathbf{H_1}$: $b_k^i \neq 0 \ \exists [1, k]$

To test these Non-linear restrictions, the following Wald statistic is computed:

$$F_{HNC} = \frac{\left(RSS_1 - RSS_\mu\right) / N_p}{RSS_\mu / \left[NT - N\left(1+p\right) - p\right]}$$

where, RSS1 denotes the sum of squared residuals obtained under the null hypothesis, RSS_u denotes the sum of squared residuals produced by unrestricted model. If the HNC hypothesis is not accepted, Homogeneous Causality hypothesis is tested which says that there exists causality between per capita GDP and per capita energy consumption for all cross sections (the null hypothesis states existence of causal relationships across all cross sections, N).

$$\mathbf{H_0}: b_k^i = b_k^j \forall_i \epsilon [1, N], \forall_k \epsilon [1, p]$$
$$\mathbf{H_1}: b_k^i \neq b_k^j \exists [i, j, k]$$

with the F-statistic being:

$$F_{HNC} = \frac{\left(RSS_2 - RSS_\mu\right) / \left[\left(N-1\right)p\right]}{RSS_\mu / \left[NT - N\left(1+p\right) - p\right]}$$

where RSS2 denotes the sum of squared residuals under the null hypothesis. If the HC hypothesis is also rejected, Heterogeneous Non Causality hypothesis is tested which means that least one cross section unit does not indicate a causality relationship between two variables (the null hypothesis states non-existence of causal relationship for each cross section unit).

$$\mathbf{H_0}: b_k^i = 0 \ \forall_i \epsilon [1, N], \forall_k \epsilon [1, p]$$
$$\mathbf{H_1}: b_k^i \neq 0 \ \forall_i \epsilon [1, N], \forall_k \epsilon [1, p].$$

with the F-statistic being:

$$F_{HENC} = \frac{\left(RSS_{3,i} - RSS_\mu\right) / p}{RSS_\mu / \left[NT - N\left(1+2p\right) - p\right]}$$

where RSS3,i denotes the sum of residual squares obtained from model when one imposes $b_k^i = 0$ for all k ϵ [1,p], for each i. These N cross-sectional tests allow to us to identify the individuals for which there are no causality relationships.

Panel Vector Error Crection Model (VECM)

In case of long-run relationship, panel VEC method is used to get the direction of causality between the variables. Following are the steps to conduct this analysis:

Step 1: Estimate $Y_{it} = a_i + b_t X_{it} + e_{it}$ and obtain residuals;
Step 2: Estimate Granger causality model with a dynamic error correction term (residuals obtained from step 1)

$$\Delta Y_{it} = a_{1j} + \sum_{k=1}^{m} a_{11ik} \Delta Y_{it-k} + \sum_{k=1}^{m} a_{12ik} \Delta X_{it-k} + b_{1i} ect_{it-1} + \mu_{it} \tag{1}$$

$$\Delta X_{it} = a_{2j} + \sum_{k=1}^{m} a_{21ik} \Delta X_{it-k} + \sum_{k=1}^{m} a_{22ik} \Delta Y_{it-k} + b_{2i} ect_{it-1} + \mu_{it} \tag{2}$$

where Δ is first difference, m is the lag length, eit-1 is error correction term and b is speed of convergence parameter for each individual. Sources of causation can be identified by testing for significance of the coefficients on the lagged variables in Equations (A) and (B). First, by testing H0: $a_{12ik} = 0$ for all *i* in Equation (A) or H_0: $a_{22ik} = 0$ for all i in Equation (B), Granger weak causality is evaluated. Masih and Masih (1996) and Adjaye (2000) interpreted the weak Granger causality as 'short run' causality in the sense that the dependent variable responds only to short-run shocks to the stochastic environment. Another possible source of causation is the Error Correction Term (ECT) in Equations (A) and (B). In other words, through the ECT, an error correction model offers an alternative test of causality (or weak exogeneity of the dependent variable). The coefficients on the ECTs represent how fast deviations from the long run equilibrium are eliminated following changes in each variable. If, for example, b1i is zero, then Y does not respond to a deviation from the long run equilibrium in the previous period. It is also desirable to check whether the two sources of causation are jointly significant, in order to test Granger causality. This can be done by testing the joint hypotheses H0: a12ik = 0 and b1i = 0 for all i in Equation (A) or H0: a22ik = 0 and b2i = 0 for all i in Equation (B). This is referred to as a strong Granger causality test. The joint test indicates which variable(s) bear the burden of short run adjustment to re-establish long run equilibrium, following a shock to the system (Adjaye, 2000). If there is no causality in either direction, the 'neutrality hypothesis' holds.

Panel Vector Auto Regression (VAR)

To check for causality in case of no long-run relationship, panel VAR is used. Following fixed effects model is estimated:

$$\Delta Y_{it} = \sum_{k=1}^{p} a_k \Delta Y_{it-k} + \sum_{k=1}^{p} b_k \Delta X_{it-k} + \lambda_i + \mu_{it}$$

$$\Delta X_{it} = \sum_{k=1}^{p} a_k \Delta X_{it-k} + \sum_{k=1}^{p} b_k \Delta Y_{it-k} + \lambda_i + \mu_{it}$$

where, p= lag length, λ_i: country fixed effects-controls the potential heterogeneity of cross sections.

Panel ARDL Approach: Multivariate Analysis

To test for panel unit roots in multivariate analysis, the study have used LLC and IPS tests again to check whether the variables are stationary or not. Let us consider the following AR(1) processfor panel data:

$$y_{it} = \rho_i y_{i(t-1)} + X_{it}\delta_i + \varepsilon_{it}$$

where i=1,2,...N cross-section units or series, that are observed over periods t=1,2,...T. The X_{it} represent the exogenous variables in the model, including any fixed effects or individualtrends, ρi are the autoregressive coefficients, and ε_{it} the errors are assumed to bemutually independent idiosyncratic disturbance. If $|\rho i| < 1$, yi is said to be weakly (trend) stationary. On the other hand, if $|\rho_i| = 1$ then y_i contains a unit root. For purposes of testing, there are two assumptions that we can make about the ρi .First, one can assume that the persistence parameters are common across cross-sections so that $\rho_i = \rho$ for all i. The Levin-Lin-Chu (LLC), Breitung and Hadri tests all employ this assumption. Alternatively, one can allow pi to vary freely across cross-sections. The Im-Pesaran-Shin (IPS), and Fisher-ADF and Fisher-PP tests are of this form.

After determining the level of integration of all variables, the study proceeds to the application of panel ARDL to estimate the long-run and short-run relationships between regression variables. Autoregressive Distributed Lag (ARDL) models are standard least squares regressions which include lags of both the dependent variable and independent variables as regressors (Greene, 2008). Although, ARDL models have been used in econometrics for decades,they have gained popularity in recent years as a method of examining long-run and cointegrating relationships between variables (Pesaran and Shin, 1999). In panel settings with individual effects, standard regression estimation of ARDL models is problematic due to bias caused by correlation between the mean-differenced regressors and the error term. This bias only vanishes for large numbers of observations T, and cannot be corrected by increasing the number of cross-sections, N. To address this problem, a number of small T–large N, dynamic panel data GMM estimators have been developed (for example, Arellano-Bond, 1991). In large datasets, these assumptions underlying dynamic GMM are often inappropriate, and the estimator breaks down. In these cases, a popular alternative is the Pooled Mean Group (PMG) estimator of Pesaran, Shin and Smith (PSS, 1999). This model takes the cointegration form of the simple ARDL model and adapts it for a panel setting by allowing the intercepts, short-run coefficients and cointegrating terms to differ across cross-sections. The model can be written as:

$$\Delta y_{i,t} = \phi_i EC_{i,t} + \sum_{j=0}^{q-1} \Delta X_{i',t-j'} \beta_{i,j} + \sum_{j=1}^{p-1} \lambda_{i,j} \Delta y_{i,t-j} + \varepsilon_{i,t}$$

where

$$EC_{i,t} = y_{i,t-1} - X_{i,t'} \theta$$

It is assumed that both the dependent variable and the regressors have the same number of lags in each cross-section. For notational convenience, it is also assumed that the regressors X, have the same number of lags q in each cross-section, but this assumption is not strictly required for estimation. The following log-likelihood function is then derived:

$$l_t(\varphi) = -\frac{T_i}{2} \sum_{i=1}^{N} \log\left(2\pi\sigma_i^2\right) - \frac{1}{2} \sum_{i=1}^{N} \frac{1}{\sigma_i^2} \left(\Delta Y_i - \phi_i EC_i\right)' H_i \left(\Delta Y_i - \phi_i EC_i\right)$$

where

$$\Delta Y_i = \left(\Delta y_{i,1}, \Delta y_{i,2}, \ldots\ldots \Delta y_{i,T_i}\right)'$$

$$EC_i = \left(EC_{i,1}, EC_{i,2}, \ldots\ldots EC_{i,T_i}\right)'$$

$$H_i = \left(I_{T_i} - W_i \left(W^{'W_i}\right)^{-1} W_i'\right)^{-1}$$

$$W_i = \left(\Delta Y_{i,-1}, \Delta Y_{i,-p+1}, \Delta X_i, \Delta X_{i,-1} \ldots\ldots \Delta X_{i,-q+1}\right)$$

$$\Delta X_i = \left(\Delta X_{i,1}, \Delta X_{i,2}, \ldots\ldots \Delta X_{i,T_i}\right)'$$

where the jth lags of ΔY_i and ΔX_i as $\Delta Y_{i,-j}$ and $\Delta X_{i,-j}$, respectively. This log-likelihood can be maximized directly. However, there exists an iterative procedure. Initial least squares estimates of θ based on the regression $Y_t = \theta X_t$ (where Y_t and X_t are the stacked forms of $y_{i,t}$ and $x_{i,t}$) are used to compute estimates, using the first-derivative relationships, of Φ_i and σ_i^2. These estimates are then used to compute new estimates of θ, and the process continues until convergence. Given the final estimates of θ, Φ_i and σ_i^2, estimates of $\beta_{i,j}$ and $\lambda_{i,j}$* may be computed.

Panel Causality through Panel Granger Test

In the pairwise causality tests with the stationarised data, the bivariate regressions in a panel data context take the following form:

$$x_{i,1} = \alpha_0 + \alpha_{1,i} x_{i,t-1} + \ldots + \alpha_{l,i} x_{i,t-1} + \beta_{1,i} y_{i,t-1} + \ldots + \beta_{1,i} y_{i,t-1} + \varepsilon_{i,t}$$

where t denotes the time period dimension of the panel, and i denotes the cross-sectional dimension. The different forms of panel causality test differ on the assumptions made about the homogeneity of the coefficients across cross-sections. The first is to treat the panel data as one large stacked set of data, and then perform the Granger Causality test in the standard way, with the exception of not letting data from one cross-section enter the lagged values of data from the next cross-section. This method assumes that all coefficients are same across all cross-sections, i.e.:

$$\alpha_{0,i} = \alpha_{0,j}, \alpha_{1,i} = \alpha_{1,j}, \ldots\ldots\ldots \alpha_{l,i} = \alpha_{l,j} \forall i, j$$

$$\beta_{1,i} = \beta_{1,j}, \ldots\ldots\ldots\ldots \beta_{l,i} = \beta_{l,j} \forall i, j$$

A second approach adopted by Hurlin and Dumitrescu (2012) makes an extreme opposite assumption, allowing all coefficients to be different across cross-sections:

$$\alpha_{0,i} \neq \alpha_{0,j}, \alpha_{1,i} \neq \alpha_{1,j}, \ldots\ldots\ldots \alpha_{l,i} \neq \alpha_{l,j} \forall i, j$$

$$\beta_{1,i} \neq \beta_{1,j}, \ldots\ldots\ldots\ldots \beta_{l,i} \neq \beta_{l,j} \forall i, j$$

This test is calculated by simply running standard Granger Causality regressions for each cross-section individually. The next step is to take the average of the test statistics, which are termed the $\overline{W}$ statistic. They show that the standardized version of this statistic, appropriately weighted in unbalanced panels, follows a standard normal distribution. This is termed the $\overline{Z}$ statistic. The authors have relied on the first version of the test. The p-values of the statistic are reported below.

Analysis

The empirical results with data of 17 developed and developing countries across 2008-2014 is reported below.

Unit Root Tests

The first step is to check for presence of unit roots in all the variables using LLC and IPS tests. The results are shown in Table 3.

The results of Table 3 help us to specify the order of integration for each variable. The same is reported in Table 4.

Table 3. Unit root tests

Variable	Im-Pesaran-Shin			Levin-Lin-Chu
	p-Value			
	Level	1st Diff	2nd Diff	Level
Trade GDP ratio	0.0050*			0.0000
ln(FDI Outflow)	0.4362	0.0046*		0.0000
Growth rate	0.2113	0.0110*		0.0000
lnGDP	0.0409*			0.0000
ln(K)	0.1498	0.1765	0.0000*	0.0000
ln(LFPR)	0.3326	0.1717	0.0000*	0.0000
Inflation	0.2579	0.0304*		0.0000
ln(India inflows)	0.4095	0.0496*		0.0000
REER	0.4549	0.0000*		0.0000

Source: Authors' calculations.

Table 4. Order of integration

Variable	Im-Pesaran-Shin	Levin-Lin-Chu
Trade GDP ratio	*I(0)*	*I(0)*
ln(FDI Outflow)	*I(1)*	*I(0)*
Growth rate	*I(1)*	*I(0)*
lnGDP	*I(0)*	*I(0)*
ln(K)	*I(2)*	*I(0)*
ln(LFPR)	*I(2)*	*I(0)*
Inflation	*I(1)*	*I(0)*
ln(India inflows)	*I(1)*	*I(0)*
REER	*I(1)*	*I(0)*

Source: Authors' calculations.

As per the results of the unit root tests, FDI Outflow, Growth Rate, Inflation, Inflows to India and REER are stationary at first difference, i.e. integrated of first order. Capital formation and LFPR are stationary at second difference, i.e. integrated of second order. Only Trade GDP Ratio and GDP are stationary at level, i.e. integrated of zero order.

Cointegration

As explained earlier, if two variables are stationary at first difference, i.e., integrated of first order, then there may exist a long-run relationship between them. To check the same, cointegration results for FDI Inflows to India with each of the other 3 variables that are integrated of one order are given in Table 5.

The results show that FDI Outflow, Growth rate, Inflation and REER are cointegrated with FDI Inflows to India, i.e., these variables have long-run relationships with FDI Inflows to India.

Further, to estimate the long-run relationship between the heterogeneous cointegrated panels in case of developing countries, Panel Fully Modified Least Square (FMOLS) method is used. The result is given as follows:

$$\log\left(FDI_{it}^{India\ Inflows}\right) = 5.002\log\left(FDI_{it}^{Outflows}\right) - 5.505\log\left(Growth_{it}^{Rate}\right)$$
$$-31.414 Inflation_{it} + 15.246 REER_{it} + \varepsilon_{it}$$

The above result explains that if FDI Outflows of the home country increases by 1 percent then FDI Inflows to India increases by 5.002 percent; if Growth Rate of the home country increases by 1 percent then FDI Inflows to India decreases by 5.5 percent; if Inflation of the home country increases by 1 unit then FDI Inflows to India decreases by 31.4 percent; and if the REER of the home country increases by 1 unit then FDI Inflows to India increases by 15.24 percent.

Table 5. Pedroni residual cointegration test

Variable		Statistic	Probability
ln(FDI Outflow)	Panel v-Statistic	-0.759332	0.7762
	Panel rho-Statistic	1.080445	0.8600
	Panel PP-Statistic	-5.810855	0.0000
	Panel ADF-Statistic	-5.446056	0.0000
	Group rho-Statistic	3.294467	0.9995
	Group PP-Statistic	-5.369382	0.0000
	Group ADF-Statistic	-3.944702	0.0000
Growth rate	Panel v-Statistic	-4.149884	1.0000
	Panel rho-Statistic	1.858189	0.9684
	Panel PP-Statistic	-14.87355	0.0000
	Panel ADF-Statistic	-8.086718	0.0000
	Group rho-Statistic	3.321937	0.9996
	Group PP-Statistic	-15.91766	0.0000
	Group ADF-Statistic	-8.631667	0.0000
Inflation	Panel v-Statistic	-2.729841	0.9968
	Panel rho-Statistic	1.742754	0.9593
	Panel PP-Statistic	-8.19909	0.0000
	Panel ADF-Statistic	-6.475082	0.0000
	Group rho-Statistic	3.543013	0.9998
	Group PP-Statistic	-6.42158	0.0000
	Group ADF-Statistic	-4.948385	0.0000
REER	Panel v-Statistic	-1.765	0.9613
	Panel rho-Statistic	1.878	0.9699
	Panel PP-Statistic	-10.065	0.0000
	Panel ADF-Statistic	-5.859	0.0000
	Group rho-Statistic	3.119	0.9991
	Group PP-Statistic	-8.394	0.0000
	Group ADF-Statistic	-4.923	0.0000
Kao Residual Cointegration Test			
Variable		**Statistic**	**Probability**
ln(FDI Outflow)	ADF Statistic	-2.1181	0.0171*
Growth rate	ADF Statistic	-2.1262	0.0167*
Inflation	ADF Statistic	1.7306	0.0418*
REER	ADF Statistic	-1.7934	0.0365*

Source: Authors' calculations.

Causality

The pair-wise causality results for FDI Inflows to India and all the other variables under scrutiny are reported in Table 6.

The results show that only REER of the home country causes FDI Inflows to India. The rest of the variables, i.e., ln (FDI Outflow), Growth rate, Inflation, Trade GDP ratio, ln(GDP), ln(K) and ln(LFPR) do not show any causal relationship towards FDI Inflows to India.

Estimation

In order to estimate the relationship running from all the I(1) and I(0) variables to FDI Inflow to India, an ARDL model is constructed. Capital formation and LFPR are not included in the model since they are I (2) and therefore, cannot be fit into an ARDL model. Prior to that it was necessary to ascertain the optimal lag length to be used for estimation. Models were estimated with various possible lag lengths and the model with lag 1 demonstrated the minimum AIC and BIC values. Hence, we restricted ourselves to estimate the ARDL model with lag 1. The residuals from this model were collected (which

Table 6. Panel causality test results

Serial No.	Hypothesis	F-Statistics	P-Value
1	ln(FDI Outflow) does not Granger Cause ln(India inflows)	0.3075	0.8652
	ln(India inflows) does not Granger Cause ln(FDI Outflow)	0.5916	0.6785
2	Growth rate does not Granger Cause ln(India inflows)	0.3456	0.8401
	ln(India inflows) does not Granger Cause Growth rate	0.8473	0.5332
3	Inflation does not Granger Cause ln(India inflows)	1.9407	1.97E-01
	ln(India inflows) does not Granger Cause Inflation	0.0511***	0.9941
4	Trade GDP ratio does not Granger Cause ln(India inflows)	0.4725	0.7554
	ln(India inflows) does not Granger Cause Trade GDP ratio	4.0635	0.0436
5	Ln(GDP) does not Granger Cause ln(India inflows)	1.1821	3.88E-01
	ln(India inflows) does not Granger Cause ln(GDP)	0.9982	0.4617
6	ln(K) does not Granger Cause ln(India inflows)	1.0909	0.4228
	ln(India inflows) does not Granger Cause ln(K)	0.1803	0.9422
7	ln(LFPR) does not Granger Cause ln(India inflows)	0.7388	0.5912
	ln(India inflows) does not Granger Cause ln(LFPR)	0.3902	0.8103
8	REER does not Granger Cause ln(India inflows)	4.3475	0.0918***
	ln(India inflows) does not Granger Cause REER	1.8834	0.2774

Source: Authors' calculations.

Notes: *, ** and *** represent the coefficient is significant at 1, 5 and 10 percent respectively.

will represent the long run relationship in the ARDL model). Two models were constructed, one with the lagged values of the explanatory variables only and the other with lagged values as well as current values of the explanatory variables. The results are reported below:

$$\begin{aligned}
&lnindiainflowsd1 = -1.1142 - 0.0071 * growthrated1(-1) + 0.1401 * inflationd1(-1) \\
&+0.0126 * lnfdioutflowd1(-1) + 0.0495 * lngdp(-1) + 0.0027 * reerd1(-1) \\
&-0.0001 * trade_gdp_ratio(-1) + 1 * ect
\end{aligned}$$

where, Inflation and the error correction term are statistically significant, showing that in the short run only inflation of the home country has significant effect on FDI outflows to India and there is a significant long run relationship running from all the explanatory variables of the home country to FDI outflows to India. The significant error correction term explains that the disequilibrium in FDI outflows to India is being adjusted annually towards its final equilibrium.

$$\begin{aligned}
&lnindiainflowsd1 = -0.6918 - 0.0005 * lnfdioutflowd1(-1) - 0.0394 * growthrated1(-1) \\
&+0.1027 * inflationd1(-1) - 9.5780 * lngdp(-1) - 0.0167 * reerd1(-1) \\
&-0.0003 * trade_gdp_ratio(-1) + 0.0138 * growthrated1 - 0.1333 * inflationd1 \\
&-0.0186 * lnfdioutflowd1 + 9.6041 * lngdp - 0.0828 * reerd1 \\
&-0.0002 * trade_gdp_ratio + 1.0212 * ect
\end{aligned}$$

where, past values of growth rate, inflation, GDP, current values of inflation, FDI outflows, GDP, REER and the error correction term are statistically significant. This shows that current growth rate of the home country, past values of FDI Outflows and REER, both current and past values of inflation and GDP affect FDI inflows to India significantly in the short run. Also all of these variables affect FDI inflows to India significantly in the long run. The significant error correction term explains that the short run disequilibrium in FDI outflows to India is being adjusted annually towards its final equilibrium.

Summary of Results

The results above show that FDI Outflow, Growth rate, Inflation and REER affect the FDI outflows from the home countries to India in the long-run. However, only REER causes the FDI outflow. The estimation of the model reveals that when only the past values of the macroeconomic indicators are considered, only inflation affect outward FDI significantly in the short run. The adjustment of FDI outflows to its long run equilibrium from the short run fluctuations are seen to occur in a significant manner. When the model is estimated with past as well as current values of the indicators, current growth rate of the home country, past values of FDI Outflows and REER, both current and past values of inflation and GDP affect FDI outflows from the selected countries to India. In this model too, the adjustment from short run fluctuations to the long run equilibrium occurs significantly.

Current growth rate of the home country has adverse effect on FDI inflows to India because higher growth rate is associated with more developed economies. The more developed the economy becomes, it may choose to invest in other developed economies rather than in a developing economy like India.

Previous year's FDI outflows shows a negative impact on outflows to India. This may be due to the expectation of a cyclical behaviour of overall FDI outflows. A rise in the previous year's outflows may lead to believe that in the current period flows should fall following the cyclical nature of the variable. A rise in the past value of REER leads to fall in outflows to India since rise in the exchange rate depreciates the local currency making investment in terms of USD more expensive than before which may make the country reluctant towards outward FDI. Anticipation of stickiness in the average exchange rate may be the triggering factor in such a scenario. A rise in previous period's inflation leads to a rise in the dependent variable, however, current inflation shows negative impact. Higher current inflation will make the currency weaker making it disadvantageous for the economy to invest abroad. Past GDP displays negative relation while current GDP shows positive effect. If the current size of the economy increases it would imply that the markets have expanded as well as capacity, making it conducive to invest in other countries. In both the models, the adjustment component being statistically significant, it may be said that the short run ups and downs of outward FDI flows from these economies get nullified rapidly and takes the variable closer to the equilibrium value implying a naturally stable mechanism.

SOLUTIONS AND RECOMMENDATIONS

Between 2010 and 2014, there has been a lot of criticism that India has faced about its inward FDI situation. In spite of its large market size, affordable labour costs, abundance of work force and a promising growth path, India could not capitalize on these positives. Large tariff and non-tariff barriers (high import tariffs and exit barriers for firms, stringent labour laws, inferior infrastructure, centralised decision-making, and a limited number of export-processing zones, etc.) dampened the impetus to bring in the FDI receipts that the nation had potential for. In November 2011, India's central government announced retail reforms for both multi-brand stores and single-brand stores and paved the way for retail innovation and competition with multi-brand retailers such as Walmart, Carrefour and Tesco. It also allowed single brand majors such as IKEA, Nike, and Apple to participate in such innovation. However, most MNCs interested in setting up shop in India still seek clarifications on clauses like sourcing from Indian SMEs and infrastructure investments by them in India (Wall Street Journal, 2011).

India continues to be far behind China and the other nations of the BRICS, in the ease of "Doing Business" rankings of 2016 (Doing Business, 2016). Although India is better off than China in the Corruption Perceptions Index (CPI) of 2015 (Corruption Perceptions Index, 2015), the rankings are paltry in the "Global Enabling Trade Index" of 2014 (Global Enabling Trade Index, 2014) and the "Global Competitiveness Index" rankings of 2015-16, as well (Global Competitiveness Index, 2016)

However, in spite of these dismal figures and circumstances, India has recently beaten China[2] as the top FDI destination (Times of India, 2016). The FDI Intelligence Report 2016, said that with $63 billion of FDI announced in 2015, India has taken the top rank in the list of countries in terms of Greenfield capital investments, specifically across the coal, oil and natural gas and renewable energy sectors (*The FDI Report*, 2016). Additionally, according to the report, India's project numbers increased by 8% to 697, although they still lagged behind China's 789 projects. The report also said that "for the first time in many years, China was a laggard on regional FDI growth rather than an engine: it saw a 23 per cent decline in capital investment and a 16 per cent drop in FDI projects due to plateauing economic growth and rising costs" (Financial Times, 2016) (Smart Investor, 2016).

On April 11, 2016, the RBI has also declared that FDI in the country increased to USD 42 billion during April-February in 2015-16, up 27.45 per cent from the inflows in the corresponding period of the previous financial year, and as of today India saw a record 53 per cent increase in FDI in last two years as the investment climate brightened due to steps taken to foster growth, price stability and fiscal prudence which also improved the overall macroeconomic stability (First Post, 2016).

From struggling to be an attractive FDI destination to "pipping China at the post", it has been a hard but a fast faced and worthwhile journey for India. Measures taken by the government to foster economic growth, price stability and fiscal prudence have improved the overall macroeconomic stability and brightened the investment climate in the country over the last two years. The global economic indices and rakings that have been a poor show for India will gradually make a turn-around, as well. The Finance Minister of India has been on record saying that "Improving the ease of doing business is a "work in progress", and adding measures have also been initiated to ensure that the system itself is more transparent" (Times of India, 2016).

India is projected to require around USD 1 trillion in the 12th Five-Year Plan (2012–17), to fund infrastructure growth covering sectors such as highways, ports and airways. This would require support from FDI flows. As mentioned earlier, during 2014, foreign investment was witnessed in sectors such as services, telecommunications, computer software and hardware, construction development, power, trading, and automobile, among others, with services taking the lead (Foreign Direct Investment, 2016). According to the "World Employment and Social Outlook: Trends 2015" report published by the International Labour Organisation (ILO), job creation in the coming years will mainly stem from the services sector. This also is another reason for India to look forward to an economically positive future (World Employment and Social Outlook Trends, 2015).

With a philosophy based on the four principles of new processes, new infrastructure, new sectors and a new mind-set, the "Make in India" initiative aims at making India a global hub of manufacturing, design and innovation, has been taken by the government. The initiative is set to boost entrepreneurship, not only in manufacturing but in relevant infrastructure and service sectors as well. The Department of Industrial Policy and Promotion (DIPP), in consultation with various central ministries, state governments, industry leaders, and other stakeholders, has formulated a strategy for increasing the contribution of the manufacturing sector to 25 per cent of the GDP by 2020; while, an exhaustive plan of action has been drawn out to improve "ease of doing business" (indiabudget.nic.in, 2016). With all the buzz that the economy has created in the last couple of years, India should record a robust growth rate from all the investments (among others) that in the offing.

FUTURE RESEARCH DIRECTIONS

This study does not capture a robust time period post the implementation of the "Make in India" initiative. While India is on its path to take a giant economic leap, at least in terms of FDI receipts, there are many socio economic factors that still need addressing and overhauling. Formal investigations involving trade agreements, trade policies, socio-economic and geo-political factors – all put together to build a comprehensive panel causality study that considers a time frame between 2006 to 2026 (say) – should provide a 360-degree view and a more wide-ranging understanding of how the factors responsible for inward FDI work in India, specifically. It will also help in determining if the new wave of trade and investment reforms have truly made the desired substantial and sustainable impact on the economy or not; and whether complementary economic factors and policy measures can be further introduced or refitted to augment the flow of FDI into the nation.

CONCLUSION

India is standing at the gateway to a new wave of economic success. With a young and educated working population, there is a huge talent pool and human capital to tap from. India is also endowed with vast natural resources. If the gaps between the demand and supply sides of the economy can be filled in skilfully, there is very little that can actually stop India from becoming the next economic super-power.

REFERENCES

Abbott, A., Cushman, D. O., & Vita, G. D. (2012). Exchange Rate Regimes and Foreign Direct Investment Flows to Developing Countries. *Review of International Economics*, *20*(1), 95–107. doi:10.1111/j.1467-9396.2011.01010.x

Agarwal, V., & Bahree, M. (2011, December 8). *India Retreats on Retail* [Online posting]. Retrieved July 30, 2016, from http://www.wsj.com/articles/SB10001424052970204903804577083343062468240

Al-sadiq, A. (2013). Outward Foreign Direct Investment and Domestic Investment: The Case of Developing Countries. *IMF Working Papers, 13*(52), 1. 10.5089/9781475517934.001

Andinuur, J. (2013). *Inflation, Foreign Direct Investment and Economic Growth in Ghana* (M.Phil. dissertation). Legon, Ghana: University of Ghana.

Arbatli, E. (2011). Economic Policies and FDI Inflows to Emerging Market Economies. *IMF Working Papers, 11*(192), 1. 10.5089/9781462306251.001

Arellano, M., & Bond, S. (1991). Some Tests of Specification for Panel Data: Monte Carlo Evidence and an Application to Employment Equations. *The Review of Economic Studies*, *58*(2), 277–297. doi:10.2307/2297968

Banga, R. (2003). *Government Policies and FDI Inflows of Asian Developing Countries: Empirical Evidence*. Economic Reform in Developing Countries; doi:10.4337/9781781007655.00013

Bellak, C., Leibrecht, M., & Stehrer, R. (2009). The role of public policy in closing foreign direct investment gaps: An empirical analysis. *Empirica*, *37*(1), 19–46. doi:10.1007/s10663-009-9107-6

Bénassy-Quéré, A., Coupet, M., & Mayer, T. (2007). Institutional Determinants of Foreign Direct Investment. *The World Economy World Economy*, *30*(5), 764–782. doi:10.1111/j.1467-9701.2007.01022.x

Bevan, A. A., & Estrin, S. (2000). *The Determinants of Foreign Direct Investment in Transition Economies*. University of Michigan William Davidson Institute DP 342.

Bevan, A. A., & Estrin, S. (2004). The determinants of foreign direct investment into European transition economies. *Journal of Comparative Economics*, *32*(4), 775–787. doi:10.1016/j.jce.2004.08.006

Blomstrom, M., & Kokko, A. (1998). Multinational Corporations and Spillovers. *Journal of Economic Surveys J Economic Surveys*, *12*(3), 247–277. doi:10.1111/1467-6419.00056

Bose, T. K. (2012). Advantages and Disadvantages of FDI in China and India. *IBR International Business Research*, *5*(5). doi:10.5539/ibr.v5n5p164

Breitung, J. (2000). The Local Power of Some Unit Root Tests for Pane Data. In B. H. Baltagi (Ed.), *Nonstationary Panels, Panel Cointegration, and Dynamic Panels* (pp. 161–177). Amsterdam: Elsevier. doi:10.1016/S0731-9053(00)15006-6

Canton, N. (2013). *Will India Become Asia's Next Superpower?* Asia House. Retrieved from http://asiahouse.org/will-india-become-asias-next-superpower/

Chandler, C. & Zainulbhai, A. (2013). *Reimagining India*. Reimagining India: Unlocking the Potential of Asia's Next Superpower.

Choi, I. (2001). Unit Root Tests for Panel Data. *Journal of International Money and Finance*, *20*(2), 249–272. doi:10.1016/S0261-5606(00)00048-6

Corruption Perceptions Index. (2015). Transparency International. Retrieved from http://www.transparency.org/cpi2015/results

Department of Commerce, Government of India. (2016). Retrieved 21 July 2016, from http://commerce.nic.in/trade/international_ta.asp?id=2&trade=i

DNA. (2016). *FDI inflows in India increases 40per cent in April-December 2015*. Retrieved from http://www.dnaindia.com/money/report-fdi-increases-40-in-april-december-2015-2183359

Doing Business. (2016). World Bank Group. Retrieved from http://www.doingbusiness.org/data/exploreeconomies/india/

Dunning, J. (1981). Explaining the international direct investment position of countries: Towards a dynamic or developmental approach. *Weltwirtschaftliches Archiv*, *117*(1), 30–64. doi:10.1007/BF02696577

Dunning, J. (1986). The investment development cycle revisited. *Weltwirtschaftliches Archiv*, *122*(4), 667–676. doi:10.1007/BF02707854

Dunning, J. (2001). The Eclectic (OLI) Paradigm of International Production: Past, Present and Future. *International Journal of the Economics of Business*, *8*(2), 173–190. doi:10.1080/13571510110051441

Dunning, J. (2009). Explaining Changing Patterns of International Production: In Defence of the Eclectic Theory. *Oxford Bulletin of Economics and Statistics*, *41*(4), 269–295. doi:10.1111/j.1468-0084.1979.mp41004003.x

Durán, J. E. (1999). *Los determinantes de la ied en los países de américa latina y el caribe: su impacto sobre el comercio y la integración regional*. ECLAC, Mimeo.

Economic Survey 2015-16: Services Sector remains the key driver of Economic Growth contributing almost 66.1per cent in 2015-16. (2016). Retrieved 13 July 2016, from http://pib.nic.in/newsite/PrintRelease.aspx?relid=136868

Employment, W., & Trends, S. O. (2015). (Rep.). Geneva: International Labour Office. Retrieved from http://www.ilo.org/wcmsp5/groups/public/@dgreports/@dcomm/@publ/documents/publication/wcms_337069.pdf

Engle, R. F., & Granger, C. W. J. (1987). Co-Integration and Error Correction: Representation, Estimation, and Testing. *Econometrica*, *55*(2), 251–276. doi:10.2307/1913236

Ethier, W. (1986). The Multinational Firm. *The Quarterly Journal of Economics*, *101*(4), 805. doi:10.2307/1884179

FDI inflows jump 53% in last two years, says Jaitley in Lok Sabha. (2016, July 29). Retrieved July 30, 2016, from http://www.firstpost.com/politics/fdi-inflows-jump-53-in-last-two-years-says-jaitley-in-lok-sabha-2922554.html

Fingar, C. (2016, April 28). *India knocks China from top of FDI league table*. Retrieved July 30, 2016, from http://www.ft.com/cms/s/3/94351bda-0620-11e6-a70d-4e39ac32c284.html#axzz4FpRzwwK

Forbes, S. (2015). How Modi Can Make India A Global Superpower. *Forbes*. Retrieved from http://www.forbes.com/sites/steveforbes/2015/06/18/how-modi-can-make-india-a-global-superpower/#31bcb3173406

Foreign Direct Investment. (2016, June). Retrieved July 29, 2016, from http://www.ibef.org/economy/foreign-direct-investment.aspx

Foreign Direct Investment, India Brand Equity Foundation. (2016). Retrieved 25 July 2016, from http://www.ibef.org/economy/foreign-direct-investment.aspx

Ghosh, I., & Chakrabarti, S. (2016). Inward and Outward Foreign Investments of the Asian Economies in Transition and India: Determinants of FDI and India's Prospects in CLMV. In V. Erokhin (Ed.), *Global Perspectives on Trade Integration and Economies in Transition* (pp. 212–237). Hershey, PA: IGI Global; doi:10.4018/978-1-5225-0451-1.ch011

Global Competitiveness Index. (2016). World Economic Forum. Retrieved from http://reports.weforum.org/global-competitiveness-report-2015-2016/competitiveness-rankings/

Global Enabling Trade Report. (2014). World Economic Forum. Retrieved from https://www.weforum.org/reports/global-enabling-trade-report-2014/

Goldberg, L., & Klein, M. (1997). *Foreign Direct Investment*. Trade and Real Exchange Rate Linkages in Developing Countries. doi:10.3386/w6344

Goldberg, L., & Kolstad, C. (1994). *Foreign Direct Investment*. Exchange Rate Variability and Demand Uncertainty. doi:10.3386/w4815

Greene, W. H. (2008). *Econometric Analysis*. Prentice Hall.

Hadri, K. (2000). Testing for Stationarity in Heterogeneous Panel Data. *The Econometrics Journal*, *3*(2), 148–161. doi:10.1111/1368-423X.00043

Henisz, W. (2000). The institutional environment for multinational investment. *Journal of Law Economics and Organization*, *16*(2), 334–364. doi:10.1093/jleo/16.2.334

Horaguchi, H., & Toyne, B. (1990). Setting the Record Straight: Hymer, Internationalization Theory and Transaction Cost Economics. *Journal of International Business Studies, 21*(3), 487–494. doi:10.1057/palgrave.jibs.8490830

Horstmann, I., & Markusen, J. (1995). *Exploring New Markets: Direct Investment.* Contractual Relations and the Multinational Enterprise. doi:10.3386/w5029

Hurlin, C., & Dumitrescu, E. (2012). *Testing for Granger Non-causality in Heterogeneous Panels.* Retrieved from https://halshs.archives-ouvertes.fr/halshs-00224434/document

Hurlin, C., & Venet, B. (2001). *Granger Causality Tests in Panel Data Models with Fixed Coefficients.* Retrieved from http://basepub.dauphine.fr/bitstream/handle/123456789/6159/3F117993d01.pdf?sequence=1

Hymer, S. (1972). The Internationalization of Capital. *Journal of Economic Issues, 6*(1), 91–111. doi:10.1080/00213624.1972.11503013

Im, K. S., Pesaran, M. H., & Shin, Y. (2003). Testing for Unit Roots in Heterogenous Panels. *Journal of Econometrics, 115*(1), 53–74. doi:10.1016/S0304-4076(03)00092-7

India overtakes China as top FDI destination: Report. (2016, April 22). Retrieved July 30, 2016, from http://smartinvestor.business-standard.com/market/Marketnews-379712-Marketnewsdet-India_overtakes_China_as_top_FDI_destination_Report.htm#.V5uypmh97Dc

India pips US, China as No. 1 foreign direct investment destination. (2015, September 30). Retrieved July 30, 2016, from http://timesofindia.indiatimes.com/india/India-pips-US-China-as-No-1-foreign-direct-investment-destination/articleshowprint/49160838.cms?null

Industrial, C., & Performance, I. (2016). Delhi: Indiabudget.nic.in. Retrieved July 30, 2016, from http://indiabudget.nic.in/es2015-16/echapvol2-06.pdf

International Monetary Fund. (2010). FDI Flows to Low-Income Countries: Global Drivers and Growth Implications. *IMF Working Papers, 10*(132), 1. 10.5089/9781455201150.001

Is foreign direct investment (FDI) included in gross fixed capital formation? (n.d.). Retrieved July 29, 2016, from https://datahelpdesk.worldbank.org/knowledgebase/articles/195312-is-foreign-direct-investment-fdi-included-in-gro

Jain, S. (2006). *Emerging economies and the transformation of international business.* Cheltenham, UK: Edward Elgar. doi:10.4337/9781847202987

Jansen, W. J., & Stokman, A. C. (2004). *International Business Cycle Comovement: Trade and Foreign Direct Investment.* SSRN Electronic Journal SSRN Journal. doi:10.2139/ssrn.1940278

Johansen, S. (1988). Statistical Analysis of Cointegrating Vectors. *Journal of Economic Dynamics & Control, 12*(2-3), 231–254. doi:10.1016/0165-1889(88)90041-3

Kindleberger, C. (1969). American business abroad. *The Int. Exec., 11*(2), 11–12. doi:10.1002/tie.5060110207

Kindleberger, C. P. (2002). Stephen Hymer and the Multinational Corporation. *Contributions to Political Economy, 21*(1), 5–7. doi:10.1093/cpe/21.1.5

Latorre, M. (2008). *Multinationals and Foreign Direct Investments: Main Theoretical Strands and Empirical Effects*. Madrid: Universidad Complutense de Madrid. Retrieved November 1, 2015, from http://estudiosestadisticos.ucm.es/data/cont/docs/12-2013-02-06-CT06_2008.pdf

Levin, A., Lin, C. F., & Chu, C.-S. J. (2002). Unit Root Tests in Panel Data: Asymptotic and Finite Sample Properties. *Journal of Applied Econometrics*, *108*(1), 1–22. doi:10.1016/S0304-4076(01)00098-7

Lipsey, R. (2000). *Interpreting Developed Countries' Foreign Direct Investment*. doi:10.3386/w7810

London School of Economics. IDEAS. (2012). *India: The Next Superpower?* London: LSE IDEAS. Retrieved from http://www.lse.ac.uk/IDEAS/publications/reports/pdf/SR010/LSE%20IDEAS%20India%20Superpower.pdf

Loree, D. W., & Guisinger, S. E. (1995). Policy and Non-Policy Determinants of U.S. Equity Foreign Direct Investment. *Journal of International Business Studies J Int Bus Stud*, *26*(2), 281–299. doi:10.1057/palgrave.jibs.8490174

MacKinnon, J. G., Haug, A., & Michelis, L. (1999). Numerical Distribution Functions of Likelihood Ratio Tests for Cointegration. *Journal of Applied Econometrics*, *14*(5), 563–577. doi:10.1002/(SICI)1099-1255(199909/10)14:5<563::AID-JAE530>3.0.CO;2-R

Maddala, G. S., & Wu, S. (1999). A Comparative Study of Unit Root Tests with Panel Data and a New Simple Test. *Oxford Bulletin of Economics and Statistics*, *61*(s1S1), 631–652. doi:10.1111/1468-0084.61.s1.13

Marku, M. (2014). The Gravity Model on EU Countries – An Econometric Approach. *European Journal of Sustainable Development EJSD*, *3*(3), 149–158. doi:10.14207/ejsd.2014.v3n3p149

Mint, L. (2016). *FDI inflows rise 40per cent on Make in India initiative: Economic Survey*. Retrieved from http://www.livemint.com/Politics/sYFaCzUi4paE9UCajwYjuO/FDI-inflows-rise-40-on-Make-in-India-initiative-Economic-S.html

Mora, N., Sahay, R., Zettelmeyer, J., & Garibaldi, P. (2002). What Moves Capital to Transition Economies? *IMF Working Papers*, *2*(64), 1. doi:10.5089/9781451848571.001

OECD. (2003). Foreign Direct Investment for Development: Maximising Benefits, Minimising Costs. *Attracting International Investment for Development OECD Global Forum on International Investment*, 55-90. doi:10.1787/9789264101944-5-en

Pagano, M., & Volpin, P. F. (n.d.). Securitization, Transparency and Liquidity. *SSRN Electronic Journal SSRN Journal*. doi:10.2139/ssrn.1337898

Pedroni, P. (1999). Critical Values for Cointegration Tests in Heterogeneous Panels with Multiple Regressors. *Oxford Bulletin of Economics and Statistics*.

Pedroni, P. (2004). Panel Cointegration: Asymptotic and Finite Sample Properties of Pooled Time Series Tests with an Application to the PPP Hypothesis. *Econometric Theory*, *20*(03), 597–625. doi:10.1017/S0266466604203073

Penrose, E. (1994). Multinational Enterprises and the Global Economy. By John H. Dunning. *Business History Review*, *68*(03), 437–438. doi:10.2307/3117185

Pesaran, M. H., Shin, Y., & Smith, R. J. (1999). *Bounds Testing Approaches to the Analysis of Long-run Relationships*. Cambridge Working Papers in Economics. No. 9907. University of Cambridge.

Podda, P. A. (2016). The impact of Institutional Distance on FDI inflows in the Czech Republic. *Acta Oeconomica Pragensia, 2016*(1), 3-14. doi:10.18267/j.aop.495

Ranjan, V., & Agrawal, G. (2011). FDI Inflow Determinants in BRIC countries: A Panel Data Analysis. *IBR International Business Research*, *4*(4). doi:10.5539/ibr.v4n4p255

Rehman, C. A., Ilyas, M., Alam, H. M., & Akram, M. (2011). The Impact of Infrastructure on Foreign Direct Investment: The Case of Pakistan. *IJBM International Journal of Business and Management*, *6*(5). doi:10.5539/ijbm.v6n5p268

Rose-Ackerman, S., & Tobin, J. (2003). *Foreign Direct Investment and the Business Environment in Developing Countries: The Impact of Bilateral Investment Treaties*. SSRN Electronic Journal SSRN Journal. doi:10.2139/ssrn.557121

Roslan, F. N. (2013). *A Study on the Dynamic Relationship between Inflation, Foreign Direct Investment, International Trade and Economic Growth in Malaysia*. SSRN Electronic Journal SSRN Journal. doi:10.2139/ssrn.2276765

Rugman, A. (1987). Strategies for national competitiveness. *Long Range Planning*, *20*(3), 92–97. doi:10.1016/0024-6301(87)90076-8

Rugman, A., & Dunning, J. (1973). The Multinational Enterprise. *Southern Economic Journal*, *40*(1), 156. doi:10.2307/1056315

Sanghoee, S. (2015). India: The next superpower? *Fortune*. Retrieved from http://fortune.com/2015/01/25/india-the-next-superpower/

Shah, M. H. (2014). The Significance of Infrastructure for FDI Inflow in Developing Countries. *Journal of Life Economics Jlecon*, *1*(2), 1–1. doi:10.15637/jlecon.37

Siddiqui, H., & Aumeboonsuke, V. (2014, July/August). Role of Interest Rate in Attracting the FDI: Study on Asean 5 Economy. *International Journal of Technical Research and Applications*, *2*(3), 59–70. Retrieved from http://www.ijtra.com/special-issue-view/role-of-interest-rate-in-attracting-the-fdi-study-on-asean-5-economy.pdf

Sridharan, P., Vijayakumar, N., & Rao, K. C. S. (2009). Causal Relationship between Foreign Direct Investment and Growth: Evidence from BRICS Countries. *IBR International Business Research*, *2*(4). doi:10.5539/ibr.v2n4p198

Subramanian, K., Chakrabarti, R., Sairam, S., & Kuntluru, S. (2012). *Infrastructure and FDI: Evidence from District-Level Data in India*. SSRN Electronic Journal SSRN Journal. doi:10.2139/ssrn.1712185

The Economic Times. (2016). *Economic Survey 2016: FDI 31per cent at $24.8 billion during April-November*. Retrieved from http://economictimes.indiatimes.com/news/economy/finance/economic-survey-2016-fdi-up-31-per-cent-at-24-8-billion-during-april-november/articleshow/51154824.cms

The fDi Report. (2016). Retrieved July 30, 2016, from http://forms.fdiintelligence.com/report2016/

The Reserve Bank of India. (2016). *Annual Report of the RBI*. Mumbai: Reserve Bank of India. Retrieved from https://www.rbi.org.in/Scripts/AnnualReportPublications.aspx?Id=1110

The World Bank. (2003). *Foreign direct investment in emerging market countries*. Washington, DC: The World Bank. Retrieved from https://www.imf.org/external/np/cmcg/2003/eng/091803.pdf

Thirlwell, M. (2004). India: The Next Economic Giant. *Lowy Institute Paper*, (1). Retrieved from http://www.lowyinstitute.org/files/pubfiles/India_webFINALsml.pdf

Times of India. (2015). *India leads emerging economies in growth chart: World Bank*. Retrieved from http://timesofindia.indiatimes.com/business/india-business/India-leads-emerging-economies-in-growth-chart-World-Bank/articleshow/47631863.cms

Torre, L. D., Schmukler, S., & Yeyati, L. E. (2002). *Financial Globalization: Unequal Blessings*. Policy Research Working Papers. doi:10.1596/1813-9450-2903

Udoh, E., & Egwaikhide, F. (2010). Exchange Rate Volatility, Inflation Uncertainty and Foreign Direct Investment in Nigeria. *Botswana Journal of Economics*, *5*(7). doi:10.4314/boje.v5i7.60304

UNCTAD. (2015). Retrieved from http://unctad.org/en/PublicationsLibrary/wir2015_en.pdf

UNCTAD. (2016). Retrieved from http://unctad.org/en/PublicationsLibrary/wir2016_en.pdf

Usman, S. (2014). Higher Education, Infrastructure and Foreign Direct Investment in Pakistan. *IOSR Journal of Business and Management IOSRJBM*, *15*(6), 54–59. doi:10.9790/487X-1565459

Vallejo, H., & Aguilar, C. (2002). *Regional Integration and Foreign Direct Investment: The Case of Latin America*. SSRN Electronic Journal SSRN Journal. doi:10.2139/ssrn.393920

Vallejo, H., & Aguilar, C. (2002). *Regional Integration and Foreign Direct Investment: The Case of Latin America*. SSRN Electronic Journal SSRN Journal. doi:10.2139/ssrn.393920

Walsh, J., & Yu, J. (2010). *Determinants of Foreign Direct Investment: A Sectoral and Institutional Approach*. Washington, DC: International Monetary Fund.

Why India is doing better than most emerging markets. (2014). *The Economist*. Retrieved from http://www.economist.com/blogs/economist-explains/2014/11/economist-explains-11

Wilson, N., & Cacho, J. (2007). *Linkage Between Foreign Direct Investment, Trade and Trade Policy*. OECD Trade Policy Papers. doi:10.1787/18166873

Yeyati, E. L. (1996). Investment in Inflationary Economies. *IMF Working Papers, 96*(105), 1. doi:10.5089/9781451947571.001

ADDITIONAL READING

Bartels, F. L., & De Crombrugghe, S. A. (2009). FDI Policy Instruments: Advantages and Disadvantages. *Research and Statistics Branch, UNIDO*. Retrieved July 29, 2016, from https://www.unido.org/fileadmin/user_media/Publications/RSF_DPR/WP012009_Ebook.pdf

Blomström, M., & Kokko, A. (1998). Foreign Investment as a Vehicle for International Technology Transfer. *Creation and Transfer of Knowledge,* 279-311. doi:10.1007/978-3-662-03738-6_14

Elfakhani, S., & Mackie, W. (2015). An analysis of net FDI drivers in BRIC countries. *Competitiveness Review, 25*(1), 98–132. doi:10.1108/CR-05-2013-0053

Erokhin, V. (2016). *Global Perspectives on Trade Integration and Economies in Transition* (pp. 1–407). Hershey, PA: IGI Global; doi:10.4018/978-1-5225-0451-1.ch001

IMF. (2015). *World Economic Outlook April 2015: Uneven Growth: Short- and Long-Term Factors.* Washington, D.C.: International Monetary Fund.

Singh, H., & Jun, K. (1995). Some new evidence on determinants of foreign direct investment in developing countries. Policy Research Working Paper No. 1531, World Bank, Washington, DC.

United Nations. (2015). *World Economic Situation and Prospects 2015. Update as of mid-2015.* New York: United Nations.

WIR06. World Investment Report 2006 : FDI from Developing and Transition Economies: Implications for Development. New York and Geneva: United Nations.

WIR14. World Investment Report 2014 : Investing in the SDGs: An Action Plan. New York and Geneva: United Nations.

KEY TERMS AND DEFINITIONS

Causation: Indicates that one event is the result of the occurrence of the other event; i.e. there is a causal relationship between the two events. This is also referred to as cause and effect.

Emerging Economies: An emerging market economy is a nation's economy that is progressing toward becoming advanced, as shown by some liquidity in local debt and equity markets and the existence of some form of market exchange and regulatory body. Emerging markets are not as advanced as developed countries but maintain economies and infrastructures that are more advanced than frontier market countries.

FDI Outflows/Inflows: FDI net inflows are the value of inward direct investment made by non-resident investors in the reporting economy. FDI net outflows are the value of outward direct investment made by the residents of the reporting economy to external economies.

Foreign Direct Investment (FDI): FDI takes place when there is an existence of a controlling proprietorship in a business enterprise in one country by an entity based in another country.

Gross Capital Formation: Capital accumulation/formation refers to the stock of capital and/or its growth, usually by augmenting saving and investment at the macroeconomic level. The gross measurement of capital formation is usually calculated before deduction depreciation.

Horizontal and Vertical FDI: Horizontal FDI, where multi-plant firms duplicate roughly the same activities in multiple countries, has been distinguished from vertical FDI, where firms locate different stages of production in different countries.

Host/Home Country: A country where a company that is based in another country has business activities.

Inward Foreign Direct Investment (FDI): When a foreign entity invests in a local economy by purchasing another business or establishing new operations for an existing business.

Market Size: In economic terms, a proxy for the potential market size can be expressed as Gross Domestic Product (GDP). The confines of a market (in the context of the chapter) are the economic size of the concerned country trying to attract FDI.

Mergers and Acquisitions (M&A): A general term that refers to the consolidation of companies or assets. While there are several types of transactions classified under the notion of M&A, a merger means a combination of two companies to form a new company, while an acquisition is the purchase of one company by another in which no new company is formed.

MNCs/MNEs: A multinational corporation (MNC) or enterprise (MNE) is an organization that owns or controls production of goods or services in one or more countries other than their home country. It can also be referred as an international corporation, a "transnational corporation", or a stateless corporation.

Panel Data: This term is used in Econometrics and Statistics, for multi-dimensional data frequently involving measurements over time. Time series and cross-sectional data are special cases of panel data that are in one dimension only (one panel member or individual for the former and one-time point for the latter).

Real Exchange Rate: R is defined as the ratio of the price level abroad and the domestic price level, where the foreign price level is converted into domestic currency units via the current nominal exchange rate (E). Formally, R= (E.P*)/P, where the foreign price level is denoted as P* and the domestic price level as P.

Trade Openness: The inward and/or outward orientation of an economy to trade with other countries. Some determinants of trade openness are trade barriers, import-export, infrastructure, technologies, scale economies, and market competitiveness.

ENDNOTES

1 The authors have not considered economic policies in the model and hence, have not elaborated upon the section.

2 China was neck and neck with USA in terms of inward FDI flows and second in ranking for such receipts, till India recently beat China at around mid-2016.

Chapter 15
The Nexus Between Institutional Quality and Foreign Direct Investments (FDI) in South Asia:
Dynamic Heterogeneous Panel Approach

Mohammad Ashraful Ferdous Chowdhury
Shahjalal University of Science and Technology, Bangladesh

ABSTRACT

South Asia is one of the world's fastest growing regions, averaging 6.7 percent annual increases in real GDP over the past decade. However, South Asia's FDI inflows as a share of GDP are the lowest of all developing regions, averaging less than 2 percent in 2000-11(World Bank, 2013). Institutional quality is one of the factors that determine the volume of FDI inflow in any country. This study covers the data of three sampled countries of South Asia provided by the World Bank for the period 2003-2014. By using both static and dynamic models, this study reveals that regulatory quality and the political stability have significantly positive impact on the FDI inflow into each of the three countries. For Robustness, this study also employs dynamic heterogeneous panel approaches like Pool Mean Group (PMG) and found that institutional quality factors are significantly relevant to the FDI. As a policy implication, the regression results indicate that during the process of reform, the relation between FDI and institutional quality warrants a certain amount of attention.

INTRODUCTION

The role of foreign direct investment (FDI) as a key driver of economic development has been proved by many researchers (Borensztein et al., 1995). It contributes to economic development through raising capital accumulation, increasing production capacity, enhancing technology, transferring knowledge, creating employment opportunities, improving management practices, enhancing competitiveness and fostering macroeconomic stability. The United Nations Conference on Trade & Development (UNCTAD) in their 2013 World Investment Report states that developing countries take the lead in foreign

DOI: 10.4018/978-1-5225-2345-1.ch015

direct investment (FDI). In 2012 developing economies received a higher inflow of FDI than developed countries. Also, Aizenmann, J. (2003) sees an increase in FDI in emerging economies. Thus, based on the increase of FDI it seems like companies are more interested in investing in emerging markets. However, investing in developing economies is not without risk. Ghemawat & Khanna (1998) argue that doing business in emerging economies is challenging due to information asymmetry and uncertainties. Political and economic risks are also significant risks. Institutions, both formal and informal, provide rules and procedures that reduce uncertainties involved in economic exchange. Informal institutions such as codes of conduct or conventions can trim down these uncertainties. Formal institutions via rules and regulations, laws, effective judicial systems and other institutions can reduce the uncertainties and provide effective enforcement mechanism. Codes of Institutional quality can be helpful by creating a more stable environment and accordingly reduce risks for multinationals associated with investing in developing countries.

However, for most of the countries, success in attracting sufficient amount of FDI inflows is not an easy job. Because of diversity in nature of factors affecting FDI inflows between countries, it is difficult to assess all these factors provided some of them are related to government political system. Governance indicators are identified by many researchers as significant determinants of FDI. The research acknowledges the gap in literature on the relationship between Institutional quality indicators and FDI flows particularly with respect to the Sub continental countries namely Bangladesh, India, and Pakistan.

Due to deep-rooted corruption, weak political and institutional structure, subcontinent is a very interesting region for case studies. Sahoo (2006) believes that there is a gap between policies and their implementations in this regions due to its dysfunctional institutional quality. Therefore, it may be worthwhile to provide strong foundation for a policy formulation through exploring the relationship between FDI and institutions based on country specific analysis. Subcontinent is a very interesting case study, because it is one of those regions which has experienced political turmoil in one form or the other, wide spread corruption, worse law and order situations, etc., which seem to be hurdles in attracting FDI in this region. The objective of the study is to find the impact of institutional quality on FDI(both inward and outward) of these three south Asian countries.

PRESENT STATUS OF FDI IN SELECTED SOUTH ASIAN COUNTRIES

Like many other developing countries, South Asian nations have been experiencing increased FDI inflows over the past decade as developing countries get a larger share of cross-border investments once sent to developed countries. Nonetheless, South Asia's FDI inflows remain the lowest relative to GDP among developing country regions. Of the inflows that do reach South Asia, India dominates, with much of the inflow reaching the service sector and very little going into industry, agriculture, or mining.

This series shows in Figure 1 net inflows (new investment inflows less disinvestment) in the reporting economy from foreign investors, and is divided by GDP. Foreign direct investment are the net inflows of investment to acquire a lasting management interest (10 percent or more of voting stock) in an enterprise operating in an economy other than that of the investor. It is the sum of equity capital, reinvestment of earnings, other long-term capital, and short-term capital as shown in the balance of payments.

Foreign direct investment refers to direct investment equity flows in the reporting economy. Broadly, It is the sum of equity capital, reinvestment of earnings, and other capital. Direct investment is a category of cross-border investment associated with a resident in one economy having control or a significant

Figure 1. FDI percentage to GDP in subcontinents
Source: World Bank.

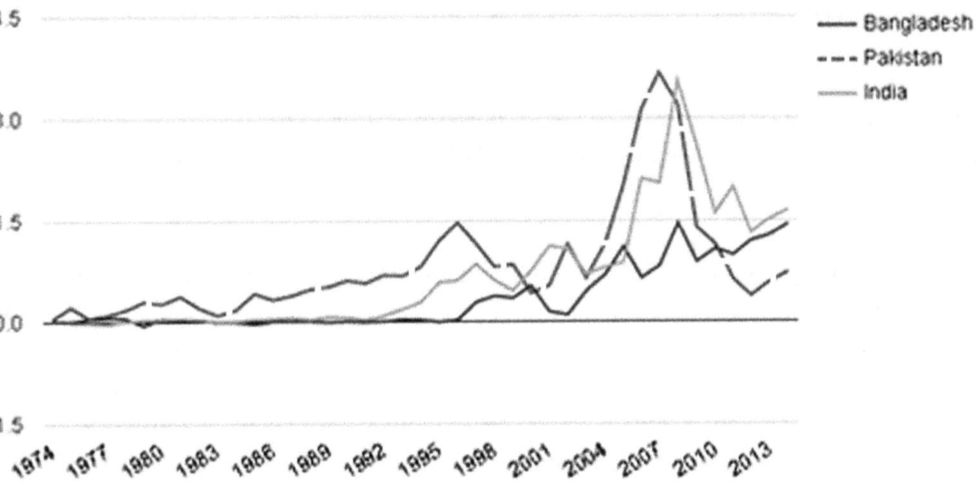

degree of influence on the management of an enterprise that is resident in another economy. Ownership of 10 percent or more of the ordinary shares of voting stock is the criterion for determining the existence of a direct investment relationship. According to the Figure 2, India leads regional inflow of FDI in south Asia accounting for $34 billion investment during 2014 and the upward trend is likely to continue in the upcoming years.

South Asia has seen FDI increases in the past decade and reaped their benefits; however, the region lags the rest of the other developing nations. Weak fundamentals have prevented more FDI flows into South Asia. The composition of FDI is heavily focused on the service industry, which may reflect the

Figure 2. FDI in subcontinents (billion USD)
Source: World Bank.

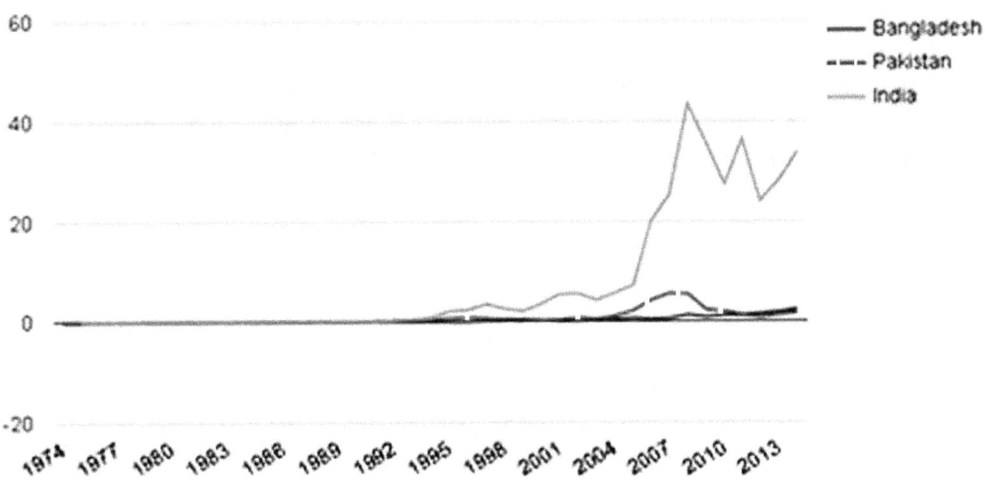

region's comparative advantage in this sector, but also may indicate that FDI into other sectors, such as manufacturing, is low due to insufficient infrastructure and cumbersome regulations discourage FDI inflows to these industries more than into services.

INSTITUTIONAL QUALITY AND ITS PRESENT STATUS IN SELECTED SOUTH ASIAN COUNTRIES

Institutional quality entails a guidance process that is institutionally and technically structured, that is, based on principles, norms, procedures and practices to collectively decide about common goals for coexistence and about how to coordinate and cooperate for the achievement of decided objectives. There are as many definitions of the term Institutional quality as there are contributors to the theoretical discourse. Available literature indicates that definition of the term varies from situation to situation as well as from party to party. For example, to the development actors such as the World Bank, the term bears a meaning completely different from the meaning understood by the Civil Society; in the case of public enterprises or social institutions meaning of the term tends to be completely different from the meaning it bears when applied for the profit-seeking organizations. And day after day the variations in meaning continue to increase.

In the light of its definition, the World Bank (2003) explicitly recognizes six dimensions of Institutional quality for measurement in countries as part of a research project in support of its assistance activities:

1. Voice and accountability;
2. Political stability and absence of violence;
3. Government effectiveness;
4. Regulatory quality;
5. Rule of Law; and
6. Control of corruption.

1. Rule of Law

The rule of law specially defined as the existence of a set of formal rules and enforcement mechanism has been regarded as the basic condition for economic development. Better rule of law desire large economic growth. But in subcontinent countries rule of law is not in not preferable. Graphically it is shown in Figure 3 that, from 2004 to 2008, the rule of law in India was pretty good. Lately, from 2008, it became negative.

In 2011, it was in –0.11% while in 2012 and 2013 it was in –0.10%. At last in 2014, it was in –0.09%. The present condition of Bangladesh and Pakistan is not up to mark. In 2005, it was –0.97% and during 2014, it was 0.72%. Pakistan's rule of law in 2008 was in its extremely tremendous point –0.98%, though it was –0.78% in 2008 which represents the laggard rule of law in Pakistan. This graph indicates that the rule of law ratio in subcontinent is not so good for the economy

Figure 3. Rule of law index in subcontinents
Source: World bank global database.

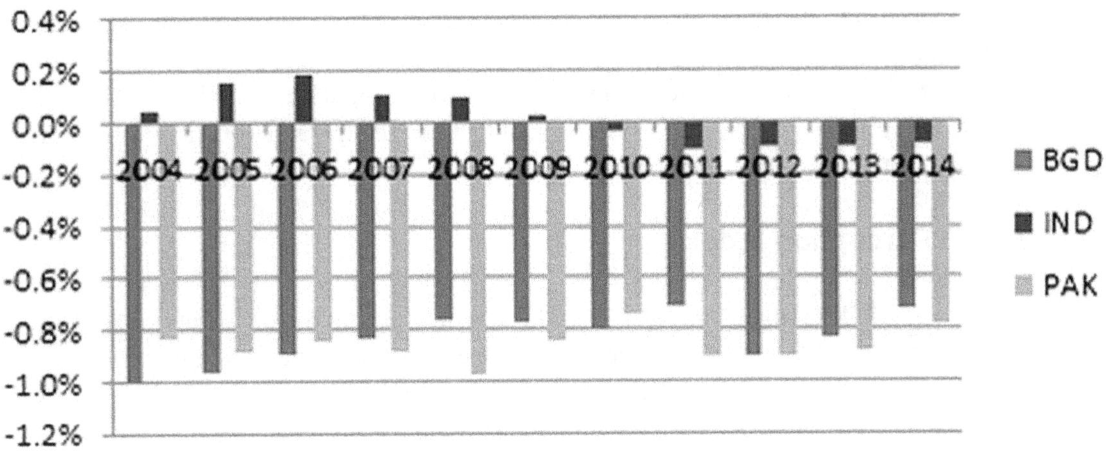

2. Political Stability

Political instability adversely affect in the economic growth by lowering the rates of productivity. It is regarded by economist as serious malaise to economic performance.

Our collected data shows in Figure 4 that, political stability was unsteady in the subcontinent. The status of political stability was inferior. Out of the three countries, the situation of Pakistan was dangerous. In 2011, Pakistan's political stability rate was −2.81%, which is its most adverse level. Bangladesh's political stability was −1.39% and India's political stability was −1.30% at the same time. From last ten years' political stability of Bangladesh, India and Pakistan as figured in sum, which is figured as −15.87%, −12.77% and −26.20% respectively that clearly shows the political imbalance of the three countries.

Figure 4. Rule of law index in subcontinents
Source: World bank global database.

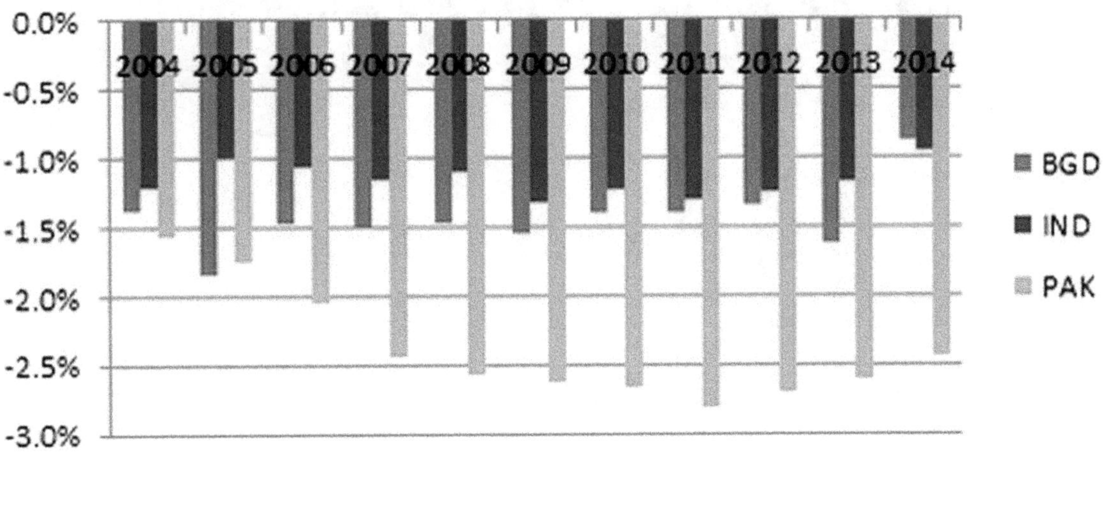

3. Regulatory Quality

The regulatory quality indicates the efficiency of the legal and operational institutional performances of the country. It can also reflect the bureaucratic situation of a country. Normally the scale of regulatory quality ranges from -2.5(weak) to 2.5(strong). In our estimation in Figure 5, it has been found that none of these south Asian countries scores positive sign meaning that the regulatory quality of these sampled countries are lower than the average.

4. Corruption Perception Index

Corruption perception index ranges from 0 to 100. The common perception of corruption in this region is not satisfactory at all. Although India is comparatively performing better than Bangladesh and Pakistan but the growth rate of higher perception is still lower. According to Figure 6, in 2004 the average score of corruption perception index score was around 30 in India and it increases only up to around 38 in 2014. The similar trend exists from Bangladesh and Pakistan.

5. Voice and Accountability

The voice and accountability is one of the most important institutional quality factors which ensures the human rights and legal situations of a country. The index of voice and accountability ranges from -2.5 to 2.5. Other than India, both Bangladesh and Pakistan scores negative scores in terms of voice and accountability shown in Figure 7.

Figure 5. Regulatory quality index in subcontinents
Source: World bank global database.

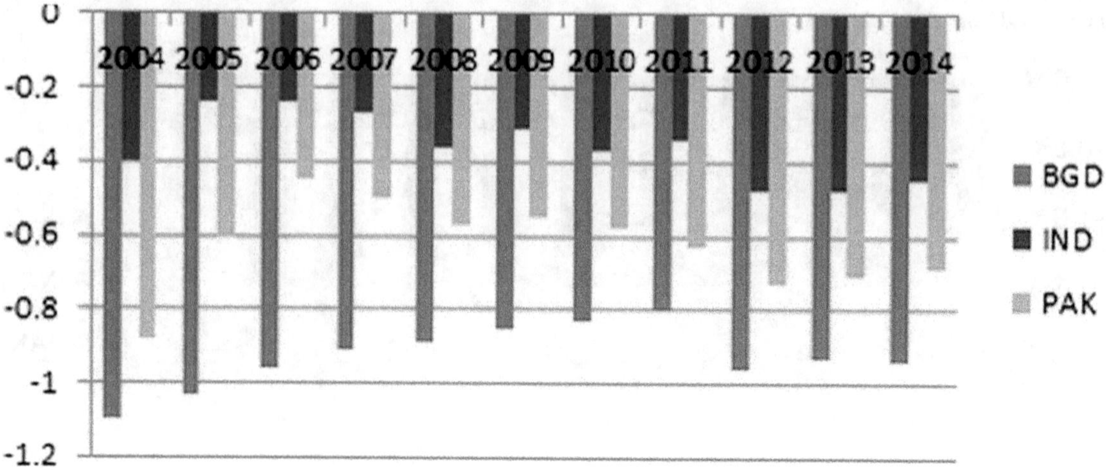

Figure 6. Corruption perception index in subcontinents
Source: World bank global database.

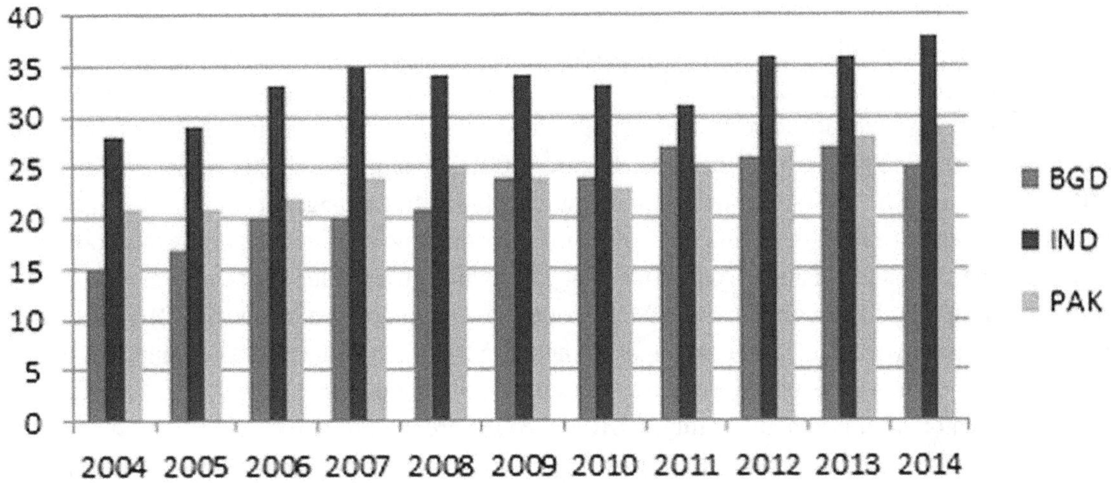

Figure 7. Voice and accountability index in subcontinents
Source: World bank global database.

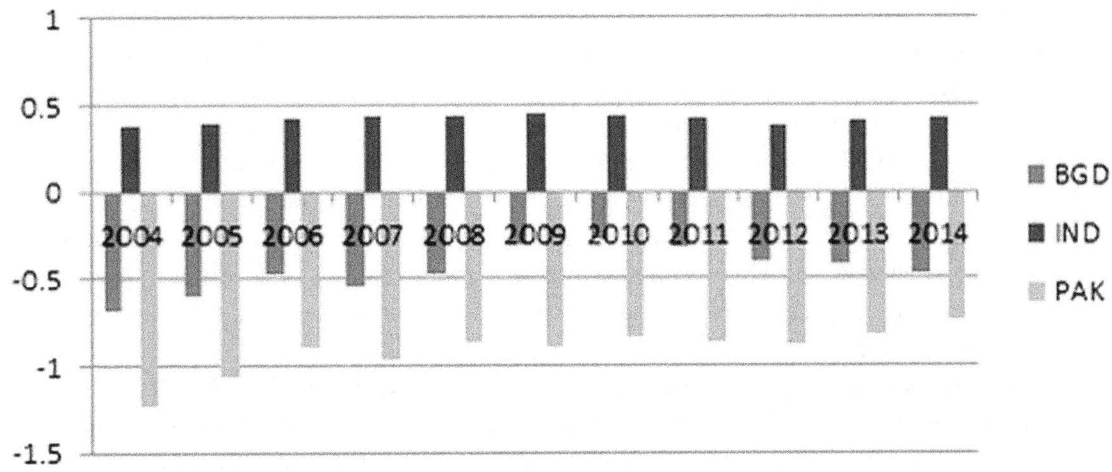

LITERATURE REVIEW

Kaufman, Kraay and Zoido-Lobaton (1999) have aggregated a database of hundreds of cross-country governance indicators into six fundamental indicators: voice and accountability (VACR), political stability and absence of violence (PSR), government effectiveness (GER), regulatory quality (RQE), rule of law (RLR) and control of corruption (CCR). The VACR indicator is about political freedom of government selection and freedom of media while the PSR indicator reflects the likelihood of government maintaining order in case of destabilization by unconstitutional means. Further, the GER indicator reveals the quality of public and civil services, and the policy formulation and credibility. Furthermore, the RQE indicator represents policies and regulations that permit and promote private sector development. The

RLR indicator illustrates agents' confidence in and abidance by the rules of society. Finally, CCR shows the extent of using public power for private gain (Kaufmann et al., 1999a, b).

However, the relationship between Institutional quality indicators and FDI remained debatable in empirical research for a long period of time. Some of the studies focused on only one indicator such as political stability, corruption, RLR and RQE while the others examined all the six indicators. Investigation of this relationship is given in La Porta et al. (1999), Edwards (1990), Jaspersen et al. (2000), Hausmann and Fernandez-arias (2000), Globerman and Shapiro (2002), Asiedu (2002, 2011), Samimi and Ariani (2010), Ahmad et.al (2014). While some of these studies failed to find significant relationship between governance indicators and FDI, the majority of them confirmed the significance of the relationship. For instance, Globerman and Shapiro (2002) find that improving governance attracts foreign capital and creates conducive conditions under which MNCs operate. Gangi and Abdrazak (2012) investigate the impact of governance on FDI flows using a panel data of 50 African countries. They find that three out of the six World Bank's governance indicators are statistically significant: VACR, GER and RLR. The rest of the indicators (i.e. political stability, CCR and RQE) are insignificant.

With regard to the relationship between Institutional quality and FDI, the prevailing view is that countries with Institutional quality tend to attract more FDI because in the absence of Institutional quality, investment cannot be protected (Globerman and Shapiro 2002) and poor governance increases costs and uncertainty (Cuervo-Cazurra 2008a). Due to the relatively irreversible nature of FDI, foreign investors are keen to minimize unnecessary risks resulting from poor governance. Although poor governance may influence the entire economy, it may act as a deterrent to foreign firms. For example, the low level of 'bureaucratic quality', which involves extensive regulation, discretion rather than rule, red-tape, lack of skilled personnel, administrative inefficiency, unfair tax system, complicated rules to establish a firm, lack of transparency and weak protection of property rights, may generate opportunities for rent-seeking and cause inefficiencies. The unpredictable and low quality of government services may increase firms' exposure to additional risks and their operational costs (Drabek and Payne 1999). The high levels of bureaucratic quality also act as a shock absorber and tend to minimize the risk associated with drastic revisions of policy when governments change and there are interruptions in government services. The lack of transparency can increase information cost and lead to corruption. Weak property rights may increase risks and reduce investment.

Laws could be restrained or governments could overturn court decisions for political reasons. Weak legal provisions and the lack of effective legal enforcement could result in high levels of corruption. The lack of law and order may create conditions in which corruption can easily thrive. Random interpretation and enforcement of laws and regulations can create uncertainties that civil servants can take advantage of in their corrupt activities (Johnson and Dahlström 2004). The transaction costs such as negotiation costs, search costs, surveillance costs and enforcement costs can be higher in poorly governed countries. According to North (1990), reducing the transaction costs by constraining the behavior of economic agents and reducing the risk of opportunistic behavior is the main function of institutions.

Zhu (2007) argues that foreign firms are heterogeneous in dealing with poor governance and strategically adjust to the local environment in order to get business contracts. In a Institutional quality environment with well-developed laws, courts, democratic institutions and property rights protection, the firms play the game according to the rules as misbehavior would cost them heavily in terms of legal sanctions as well as reputation. However, in a poor governance environment where foreign firms compete with both domestic and other foreign firms, they adjust to the local business climate, and pay bribes in order to get business contracts that magnify the problems of poor governance in target countries. Therefore

Zhu (2007) states that 'in more democratic and developed countries, increasing FDI inflows are likely to contribute to reduction of corruption, while in non-democratic and less developed countries, a rise in FDI inflows is associated with a higher level of corruption'.

Zhu (2007) also suggests that in a poor governance environment, foreign firms would have few incentives to try to improve governance. Those firms that benefit from poor governance through paying bribes would obviously have no incentives to speak out against it. Those firms that lose business contract because of corruption may prefer to remain silent for two reasons. First, speaking out or prosecution often fails because of the weak legal system and the strong relationship between the winner and the courts. Second, business is a repeated game and losers in a single business contract may not want to damage their relation with local authorities given the opportunities to get contracts next time. Complaining about poor governance is likely to create more hostility and reduce opportunities to get future contracts.

In the case of corruption, the literature is richer compared with the other governance indicators. The dominant 'sand the wheels' view suggests that corruption deters FDI as it is a sign that the government is malfunctioning, which adds costs to foreign investment. Many researchers have argued that high corruption levels deter FDI in the transition countries (Resmini 2000; Hellman, Jones and Kaufmann 2002; Cuervo-Cazurra 2006). This implies that FDI should be lower with corruption in a country with relatively high quality of governance. In this case, corruption entails costs and has no distortions to grease. Although limited, a few empirical studies have found no negative link between corruption and FDI in non-transition countries (Moskalev 2007) which question the overall validity of the 'sand the wheels' argument.

Finally, it cannot rule out the possibility that poor governance itself may be a source of better investment opportunities for MNCs. Poor governance may be a source of rent not only for corrupt politicians and policy makers in the target countries but also for large MNCs. As Li (2005) argues, in a relation-based system, the political system tends to be dominated by powerful rulers and policies tend to favor big business, which provides fertile ground for large MNCs that have large sources to finance their rent seeking activities. Such arguments are not new. Many scholars have argued that undemocratic and authoritarian regimes in developing countries provide investors with higher returns and attract more FDI (Bellos & Subasat 2012).

Furthermore, recognizing that FDI as a key factor for economic growth and important tool for bringing technology to recipient countries, it has received great attention from many economists in recent literature. The literature on FDI can be categorized into three main groups: the first group investigates the effect of FDI on macroeconomic indicators, such as economic growth, exchange rate, rates of inflation, balance of payments and rates of unemployment. The second group examines the impact of FDI on different factors such as technology transfer to recipient countries, management practices by national firm and labor skill and productivities in hosting countries. The third group focuses on the determinants of FDI and the main driving forces for its inflow and outflows to different countries. This topic remains a hot issue for researchers from different disciplines for a long period of time. Their main concern has been to identify the key variables that cause variation in FDI and hence can be used as instruments for economic policies conducive for FDI attractiveness. This group can be subdivided into two sub-groups: the first sub-group undertaken at country level using time-series data. In these studies determinants of FDI were examined for individual countries over specific period of time. The variables identified by these studies include, GDP growth, GDP level, degree of openness measured by balance of trade, real exchange rate, political stability, market size measured by per capita income and size of population, domestic investment, the return or cost of capital rate as variable reflecting the costs of production in the host countries. The second subgroup undertaken across a set of country level over specific period of time using panel data an example of which includes Samimi and Ariani (2010).

In the literature there were no studies that examined the relation between Institutional quality and FDI flows especially to the Sub continental countries. However, the impacts of some of the Institutional quality indicators on FDI flows were examined as part of the determinants of FDI. Because of that, our review of the literature concentrated on the empirical studies that were related to the determinants of FDI. This can help identify the main factors that cause variation in FDI flows to different countries and at the same time investigate the relation between Institutional quality indicators and FDI flows. It has been apparent from the foregoing literature review that although there is no dearth of research done on various aspects of governance and FDI, no work done on the nexus between Institutional quality and FDI especially in India, Pakistan and Bangladesh. To this end, the prime focus of this paper to find the impact of Institutional quality on FDI inflow for the sampled countries.

DATA AND METHODOLOGY

Data

In this part of the paper the impact of Institutional quality on FDI using panel data analysis is explored. Empirical analysis is performed on sample 3 South Asian countries namely Bangladesh, India and Pakistan in the period between 2003 and 2014. All Institutional quality indicators such as corruption control, Political stabilities, regulatory quality, startup procedure, startup time and startup cost etc. have been taken from the Heritage Foundation, the database of World Bank.

Methodology

This research is conducted to econometrically analyze the relationship between FDI and Institutional quality factors. The methodologies applied in this study are both static and dynamic.

Static Models (Fixed and Random Effects)

The panel data is used in analyzing the FDI determinants. In the panel data, the used model consists n cross-sectional units, denoted n=1, ...,N, observed at each of T time periods, t=1, ...,T. In data set, the total observation is n × T. The basic framework for the panel data is defined as per the following regression model:

$$Ynt= \alpha+\beta Xnt+ \varepsilon nt \quad (1)$$

In functional form, FDI = *f (Institutional variables, Macro-economic Variables)*
Econometric specifications:

$$FDI= \alpha+\beta 1COR+ \beta 5GDP+ \beta 9PS+ \beta 9REQ+ \beta 9\ SP+ \beta 9\ SC+\beta 9\ INF+ \varepsilon \quad (2)$$

Here, Y represents the dependent variable FDI,

Independent variables:

FDI = Foreign Direct Investment
COR = Control of Corruption
GDP = Gross Domestic Products
PS = Political Stability
REQ = Regulatory Quality
SP =Startup Procedure
SC = Startup cost
INF = Inflation

Dynamic Models

This study employs the pooled mean group (PMG) estimators to address to estimate non-stationary dynamic panels in which the parameters are heterogeneous across groups Taking into account that analyzed 3 economies are different with the respect to their economic policy, the two mentioned dynamic panel models are estimated. Since, the focus of this paper is the impact of regulatory quality on FDI in the long and in the short- run, in order to capture that relationship empirically, the following equation is estimated:

$$FDI_{it} = \gamma_{0i} + \gamma_{1i}GDP_{it} + \gamma_{2i}CORs_{it} + \gamma_{3i}PS_{it} + \gamma_{4i}RQ_{it} + \ell_{it}, \; i = 1, 2, ..., N; \; t = 1, 2, ..., T \quad (3)$$

where FDI is the Foreign Direct Investment, *gdp_growth* is the annual percentage GDP growth rate, *COR* is the Control of Corruption, PS is the political stability and RQ represents the regulatory quality. Error term capturing the effects of unexpected shocks to *FDI* is denoted by ℓ_{it}. The subscripts *i* and *t* denote country and time respectively, suggesting an unbalanced panel. Since FDI differs across countries in the short-run, this assumption is hereby implemented by using conventional statistical criteria and determining lag length of each variable. Furthermore, an important issue that needs to be dealt with in econometric analysis is the dynamic structure of FDI model, assuming that certain economic aspects prevent immediate adjustment of FDI to changes in its fundamental determinants. Accordingly, the first and foremost step of the empirical analysis was to choose the lag order of ARDL model by applying the Schwarz information criterion (SBC). Even though there was no clear evidence of a most common representation, after choosing a country specific lag order of the ARDL model by applying the SBC information criterion, the preferred specification for the whole sample of analyzed countries was an autoregressive distributed lag ARDL (1,0,0,0,0) model:

$$FDI_{it} = Ł_i + \beta_{10i}GDP_{it} + \beta_{20i}COR_{it} + \beta_{30i}PS_{it} + \beta_{40i}RQ_{it} + \gamma_i FDI_{t-1} + \eta_{it}$$

That is, FDI is lagged once, whereas *COR (*Control of Corruption), PS is the (political stability) and RQ (regulatory quality), GDP are given in levels.

According to Engle and Granger (1987) if the variables are I(1) and co-integrated, the error term is an I(0) process for all countries (i). Furthermore, co-integrated variables show great responsiveness to any deviation from long-run equilibrium, so this feature implies an error correction re-parameterization of equation (2) such as:

$$\Delta FDI_{it} = Ni\,(FDI_{i,t-1} - \gamma_{0i} - \gamma_{1i}GDPt_{it}) - \beta_{11i}\Delta \mathrm{GDP}_{it} - \beta_{21i}\Delta COR_{it} - \beta_{31i}\Delta iPS_{it} - \beta_{41i}\Delta RQ_{t} + \eta_{it} \quad (4)$$

where,

$$\phi_i, = -(-1-\gamma_i), \gamma_{0i} = \delta_i / (1-\gamma_I)\gamma_{1i} = (\beta_{10i} + \beta_{11i}) / 1-\gamma_I$$

Parameter ϕ_i is the error-correcting speed of adjustment term, so we expect it to be significantly negative under the prior assumption that the variables of interest show a return to long-run equilibrium Here, the dependent variable is the Foreign Direct investment.

FINDINGS

Descriptive Statistics

To better understand the preliminary features of the data the descriptive statistics of all the variables selected are presented in Table 2. The average of our dependent variables, the FDI of 3 countries used in the study is 9.49 in natural logarithm form. The average GDP growth rate is 6.02%. The mean of all other independent variables are also positive except political stability and Regulatory quality. From the socioeconomic perspective, the negative mean of the PS and the RQ signifies that the political stability and the Regulatory Quality of these 3 countries are less than the standard level.

Correlation Matrix

The correlation matrix between the selected variables is presented in table 6. From the main variables of our study, socioeconomic determinants, all the variables are positively related to the FDI except the startup time. From the macroeconomic perspectives, the relationship between the GDP and the FDI is negatively correlated on the other hand Inflation has a negative relation to the FDI.

Table 1. Details of the independent variables

Variable	Definition	Descriptions
GDP	Annual GDP Growth rate	Taken from the World Bank Database
INF	Inflation	Taken from the World Bank Database
COR	Control of corruption	Ranges from -2.5 (weak) to 2.5(strong).
PR	Property Rights	The property rights index (0-100). Collected from The Heritage Foundation
PS	Political Stability	Ranges from -2.5 (weak) to 2.5(strong). Collected from the World Bank Database.
REQ	Regulatory Quality	Ranges from -2.5 (weak) to 2.5(strong).
SP	Startup Procedure	Taken from the World Bank Database
SC	Startup cost	Taken from the World Bank Database

Table 2. Descriptive statistics

	COR	LFDI	GDP	PS	REQ	SP	SC	INF
Mean	25.93939	9.492558	6.028949	-1.659769	-0.633968	10.40909	37.33636	35.70909
Median	25.00000	9.305781	6.177542	-1.482810	-0.610984	11.00000	38.90000	26.50000
Maximum	36.00000	10.63755	10.25996	-0.990955	-0.233571	13.00000	78.40000	81.00000
Minimum	13.00000	8.428597	1.606692	-2.811578	-1.095224	8.000000	5.800000	19.00000
Std. Dev.	5.910475	0.654387	2.193414	0.557226	0.257993	1.400081	21.80364	18.95398
Skewness	-0.056674	0.409362	-0.116222	-0.940517	-0.052406	0.163412	0.251330	1.199492
Kurtosis	2.504259	1.929466	2.573456	2.467078	1.706590	2.180813	1.773665	3.088132
Obs.	33	33	33	33	33	33	33	33

Notes 1: The dependent variables FDI is Foreign Direct investment, GDP indicate GDP growth rate, PS measures the political stability COR refers the Control of corruption, SP refers stratup procedure, SC refers the Startup cost, INF refers Inflation

Table 3. Correlation matrix

	COR	LFDI	GDP	PS	REQ	SP	SC	INF
COR	1							
LFDI	0.863	1						
GDP	0.318	0.367	1					
PS	0.268	0.313	0.722	1				
RQ	0.755	0.861	0.319	0.136	1			
SP	0.716	0.838	0.299	0.190	0.835	1		
SC	0.217	0.348	0.619	0.764	0.300	0.382	1	
INF	-0.257	-0.168	0.3791	0.449	-0.058	-0.239	0.499	1

Notes 1: The dependent variables FDI is Foreign Direct investment,. GDP indicate GDP growth rate, PS measures the political stability COR refers the Control of corruption, SP refers stratup procedure, SC refers the Startup cost, INF refers Inflation

As expected corruption of corruption and political stability favors the FDI in the courtiers but the late startup time causes the negative FDI in the sampled countries. Finally, since there is no value more than .85, we can say that there should not be any multicollinearity.

Model Estimations as a Whole

Static Model

In static relationship, the literature usually applied least square methods of fixed effects (FE) or random effects (RE). The FE estimator is the most restrictive of all. It imposes equality of all slopes coefficients (both short and long run) and equality of error variances across units or countries and only the intercept across units or countries are allowed to vary. On the contrary, Random effect estimator also imposes equality of all slope coefficients (both short and long run) but allows error variances and intercepts to differ across countries. It assumes random intercepts, the mean of which is captured by the constant term and the variances of which is captured by the variance of the error term. To find which model is superior, this study tested the Hausman test. Since the probability of Chi-square value (7.45) with P-value 0.019, it can be said that random effect model is comparatively more suitable than fixed effect model meaning that this study accepts the result of random effect model.

The analysis of the variables confirms with the findings of a numbers of the previous literature while providing some new ground for study. In both Static models such as the fixed effects and the Random Effects, the results of the analysis proved a number of variables have a significant impact on the FDI of the country. In all our analysis, it has been found that the institutional /socio-economic factors such as Regulatory quality, Control of Corruptions are positively correlated to the FDI.

Since the Hausman test has proven that in our case random effect is more suitable than fixed effect.[1] This paper will give more focus on random effect from the static model. As expected, high startup cost causes the negative FDI in the sampled countries. It has been found that 1% increases in the regulatory

Table 4. Result of static and dynamic models

Variables Dep. Variable : FDI	Static Model		Dynamic Model-PMG	
	Fixed	Random	Dependent Variable: FDI	PMG
Intercept	6.819 (.9325706) ***	8.239 (1.001599) ***	Convergence coefficient (ECT)	-.970959 (.2545973)***
FDI –lag of dep.Variable	———	———	GDP	.5387247 (.1957853)***
GDP	-0.006 (.0255069)	-0.0152 (.0308769)	RQ	.6714 (.091963) ***
RQ	1.0714 (.3919631) **	0.9185 (.3596054) ***	PS	-.1686112 (.1343574)
PS	-0.9837 (.1594826)	0.2341 (.1616658)	COR	.0518712 (.0042735)***
COR	0.0132 (.0143829)	0.0412 (.0131982) ***	dGDP	.0601597 (.0227681)***
SP	-0.3097 (.0731242) ***	-0.1268 (.0626947) ***	dRQ	.6714 (.091963) ***
SC	-0.0090 (.0037857) **	-0.0019 (.0037063)	dPS	-.6225866 (.1876477)***
INF	-0.016 (.00150)***	-0.0812 (.0269)***	dCOR	.0445079 (.0091942)***
R-squared	0.8320	0.8820	No. of countries:	3
F-stat/ Wald-χ^2	37.69***	194.42***	Log-likelihood	49.855
No of Obs.	33	33		

Notes 1: The dependent variables FDI is Foreign Direct investment, GDP indicates GDP growth rate, PS measures the political stability COR refers the Control of corruption, SP refers stratup procedure, SC refers the Startup cost, INF refers Inflation

Notes 2: The dependent variables FDI is Foreign Direct investment, is a proxy measure of size, calculated as a natural logarithm of total bank assets. GDP indicate GDP growth rate, PS measures the political stability COR refers the Control of corruption, SP refers stratup procedure, SC refers the Startup cost, ST startup time. D.FDI is Foreign Direct investment in differenced form. d.GDP indicate GDP growth rate in differenced form, d.PS measures the political stability in differenced form . d. COR refers the Control of corruption in differenced form, d.SP refers stratup procedure, d.SC refers the Startup cost, d. ST startup time in differenced form.

Notes 3: Estimations are performed using the PMG estimator of Pesaran et al. (1999); the reported short-run coeficients and the speed of adjustment are simple averages of country-speciic coeficients; all equations include a constant term; standard errors are in brackets

Notes 4: Values in parenthesis are t statistics, (***), (**), (*) indicates significance at 1, 5, and 10% level respectively.

quality can increase 1.07% in FDI. The Control of corruption can also bring positive outcome for the FDI. If there is 1% level of corruption control increase, it will increase 0.041% percent of FDI. The burucratic problems such as long stratup procedure and the startup cost decreseas FDI by -0.12% and -0.001% percent respectively. From the macroeconomic perspectives, it has been found that only inflation has inverse and statistically strong relationship with the FDI for these sampled countries.

Dynamic Heterogeneous Model

The Table 4 presents the results of the baseline model of FDI specified by the equation (iv). Furthermore, the Hausman test of long-run homogeneity of coefficients is employed in order to determine which estimator is more appropriate. According to Pesaran et al. (1999), the MG estimator provides consistent estimates of the mean of long-run coefficients, but these are inefficient if slope homogeneity assumption holds. However, if the slope coefficients are indeed homogeneous, then PMG estimator is consistent and efficient. That's why, this study employs PMG estimators.

According to results presented in Table-4, error correction mechanism is in place, since the adjustment coefficient has the correct negative sign and is statistically significant on 1% significance level. The average value of the error correction coefficient (according to PMG estimator) is -0.97 implying that equilibrium is reached in less than 1.5 years. In the above table, it can be seen that the GDP, Regulatory quality and the control of corruptions are positively related to the performance of FDI inflow in the long run. According to PMG model, 1% increases in the GDG growth rate increases FDI by 0.53%. Regulatory quality also effects positively on the growth of FDI. For example if there is 1% increases in the regulatory quality, 0.67% of FDI will be increased. The same trend exists in the control of corruption variable where 1% increases in the control of corruption bring 0.05% of FDI.

Furthermore, according to estimated model, all three control variables have statistically significant influence on FDI in the short run with economically meaningful signs, stressing a positive influence of those variables on FDI, with having the largest coefficient (0.67).

CONCLUSION AND FUTURE RESEARCH IMPLICATIONS

The importance of institutions can hardly be exaggerated. These are hallmarks of development. For strong institutions are often associated with good governance, transparency, accountability and integrity, while weak institutions breed poor governance, macroeconomic mismanagement, endemic corruption, and serious misallocation of resources. Evidently, developed countries have fairly strong institutions, while institutions are extremely weak, especially in least developed countries. Institutional quality is highly associated with FDI given the relative irreversible nature of this type of capital flows. Corruption, loss of public confidence in the government, likelihood of destabilization of the government by unconstitutional means, rent-seeking and uncertainties about law enforcement will all create a highly risky atmosphere for FDI. It has been found in the study that the Institutional quality indicators such as Regulatory quality, control of corruption have significantly positive impact on the performance of FDI for the long run for all the three countries. Since these two factors were found to be significant determinants of FDI inflow into the countries, policymakers should give proper focus onto these indicators in order to make the region an attractive destination for the potential foreign investors. As because each of the three countries put emphasis on sustainable growth of GDP and since contribution of FDI to GDP for all the three countries have been meager(less than 1.5%) the countries must ensure unhindered FDI inflow by addressing Institutional quality issues such as Control of corruption and Regulatory quality in policy making. In the absence of solid property rights, foreign firms may have very few incentives to engage in new investment as the return on their investment may be uncertain. 'Law and order' may be a major concern for foreign firms. The empirical analysis presented in this study offers a powerful set of factors as key contributors to FDI growth— regulatory quality, control of corruption, reduced trade protection, and greater investment openness.

REFERENCES

Ahmad, M. H., & Ahmed, Q. M. (2014). Does the Institutional Quality Matter to Attract the Foreign Direct Investment? An Empirical Investigation for Pakistan. *South Asia Economic Journal, 15*(1), 55–70. doi:10.1177/1391561414525708

Aizenman, J. (2003). Volatility, employment and the patterns of FDI in emerging markets. *Journal of Development Economics, 72*(2), 585–601. doi:10.1016/S0304-3878(03)00123-8

Alam, Q., Mian, M. E. U., & Smith, R. F. I. (2005). *The Impact Of Poor Governance On Foreign Direct Investment: The Bangladesh Experience.* Network of Asia-Pacific Schools and Institutes of Public Administration and Governance (NAPSIPAG) Annual Conference 2005, Beijing, China.

Arellano, M., & Bover, O. (1995). Another look at the instrumental variable estimation of error-components models. *Journal of Econometrics, 68*(1), 29–51. doi:10.1016/0304-4076(94)01642-D

Asiedu, E. (2002). On the determinants of foreign direct investment to developing countries: Is Africa different? *World Development, 30*(1), 107–119. doi:10.1016/S0305-750X(01)00100-0

Asiedu, E., & Lien, D. (2011). Democracy, foreign direct investment and natural resources. *Journal of International Economics, 84*(1), 99–111. doi:10.1016/j.jinteco.2010.12.001

Athanasoglou, P. P., Brissimis, S. N., & Delis, M. D. (2008). Bank-specific, industry-specific and macroeconomic determinants of bank profitability. *Journal of International Financial Markets, Institutions and Money, 18*(2), 121–136. doi:10.1016/j.intfin.2006.07.001

Azim, T., & Uddin, N. (2001). Environment of foreign direct investment in Bangladesh: an empirical assessment.Bangladesh Institute of International and Strategic Studies (BIISS) Journal, 22(3), 285-306.

Bellos, S., & Subasat, T. (2012). Governance and foreign direct investment: A panel gravity model approach. *International Review of Applied Economics, 26*(3), 303–328. doi:10.1080/02692171.2011.587110

Borensztein, E., De-Gregorio, J., & Lee, J. W. (1995). *How does Foreign Direct Investment. affect economic growth?* NBER Working Paper Series No. 5057. National Bureau of Economic Research, Inc.

Cuervo-Cazurra, A., & Genc, M. (2008). Transforming disadvantages into advantages: developing-country MNEs in the least developed countries. *Journal of International Business Studies, 39*(6), 957-979.

Drabek, Z., & Payne, W. (1999). *The impact of transparency on foreign direct investment.* Staff working paper, EAR 99–02. Geneva: World Trade Organisation.

Edwards, S. (1990). *Capital flows, Foreign Direct Investment, and debt-equity swaps in developing countries*. NBER Working Paper Series No. 3497. National Bureau of Economic Research, Inc.

Gangi, Y. A., & Abdulrazak, R. S. (2012). The impact of governance on FDI flows to African countries, World Journal of Entrepreneurship. *Management and Sustainable Development*, *8*, 162–169.

Ghemawat, P., & Khanna, T. (1998). The nature of diversified business groups: A research design and two case studies. *The Journal of Industrial Economics*, *46*(1), 35–61. doi:10.1111/1467-6451.00060

Globerman, S., & Shapiro, D. (2002). Global foreign direct investment flows: The role of governance infrastructure. *World Development*, *30*(11), 1899–1919. doi:10.1016/S0305-750X(02)00110-9

Hausmann, R., & Fernandez-arias, E. (2000). *Foreign Direct Investment: good cholesterol?* Inter-American Development Bank Working Paper No. 417.

Hellman, J. S., Jones, G., & Kaufmann, D. (2002). *Far from home: Do foreign investors import higher standards of governance in transition economies?* Available at SSRN 386900

Jaspersen, F., Aylward, A., & Knox, A. (2000) The effects of risk on private investment: Africa compared with other developing areas. In Investment and Risk in Africa. St. Martin's Press.

Jensen, N. (2003). Democratic governance and multinational corporations: Political regimes and inflows of foreign direct investment. *International Organization*, *57*(03), 587–616. doi:10.1017/S0020818303573040

Johnson, A., & Dahlström, T. (2004). *Bureaucratic corruption, MNEs and FDI Mimeo*. Jönköping International Business School.

Kaufmann, D., Kraay, A., & Mastruzzi, M. (2009). *Governance matters VIII: Aggregate and individual governance indicators*. World Bank Policy Research Working Paper, 4978.

Kaufmann, D., Kraay, A., & Zoido-Lobaton, P. (1999a). Aggregating governance indicators, World Bank Policy Research Working Paper No. 2195. Washington, DC: World Bank. Available at http://www.worldbank.org/wbi/governance/wp-governance.html

Kaufmann, D., Kraay, A., & Zoido-Lobaton, P. (1999b). Governance matters, World Bank Policy Research Working Paper No. 2196. Washington, DC: World Bank. Available at http://www. worldbank.org/wbi/governance/pubs/govmatters.html

La Porta, R., López de Silanes, F., & Shleifer, A. (1999). The quality of government. *Journal of Law Economics and Organization*, *15*(1), 222–279. doi:10.1093/jleo/15.1.222

Li, S. (2005). Why a poor governance environment does not deter foreign direct investment: The case of China and its implications for investment protection. *Business Horizons*, *48*(4), 297–302. doi:10.1016/j.bushor.2004.06.002

Mamatzakis, E., & Remoundos, P. (2003). Determinants of Greek commercial banks, 1989- 2000. *Spoudai*, *53*(1), 84–94.

Moskalev, S. (2007). *Governance and foreign direct investment.* Available at SSRN 959905

North, D. C. (1990). *Institutions, institutional change and economic performance*. Cambridge University Press. doi:10.1017/CBO9780511808678

Pesaran, M. H., Shin, Y., & Smith, R. P. (1999). Pooled mean group estimation of dynamic heterogeneous panels. *Journal of the American Statistical Association*, *94*(446), 621–634. doi:10.1080/01621459.1999.10474156

Resmini, L. (2000). The determinants of foreign direct investment in the CEECs: New evidence from sectoral patterns. *Economics of Transition*, *8*(3), 665–689. doi:10.1111/1468-0351.00060

Sahoo, P. (2006). *Foreign Direct Investment in South Asia: Policy, Trends, Impact and Determinants.* ADB Institute. Discussion paper No. 56.

Samimi, J. A., & Ariani, F. (2010). Governance and FDI in MENA region. *Australian Journal of Basic and Applied Sciences*, *4*, 4880–4882.

World Bank. (2005). *Bangladesh: Growth and Export Competitiveness.* Report No:31394-BD. Washington, DC: Author.

World Bank. (2013). Trends and Determinants of Foreign Direct Investment in South Asia. Report No: ACS4862. Washington, DC: Author.

Zhu, B. (2007). *Fortune or evil? The effects of inward foreign direct investment on corruption.* Paper presented for the Mini APSA Conference at the Department of Political Science, New York, NY.

KEY TERMS AND DEFINITIONS

ARDL: Autoregressive-Distributed Lag- A commonly used testing for the presence of long-run relationships between economic time-series.

FDI: Foreign direct investment (FDI) is an investment made by a company or individual in one country in business interests in another country.

Institutional Quality: Institutional quality is the comprehensive attributes that captures law, individual rights and high quality government regulation and services.

MNC: An enterprise operating in several countries but managed from one (home) country.

PMG: Pooled Mean Group (PMG) is the econometric techniques where long run coefficients to be should be identical, but allows the short run coefficients and error variances to differ across groups.

ENDNOTE

1 To find which model is superior, this study tested the Hausman test. Since the probability of Chi-square value (7.45) with P-value 0.73, so, this study accepts the result of random effect model.

Chapter 16
Factors Driving Firms from Emerging Countries into the Global Market:
The Case of Chinese SMEs Entering the North East of England

Rose Quan
Northumbria University, UK

Zhibin Lin
Northumbria University, UK

ABSTRACT

The purpose of this chapter is to identify the key factors that explain the decision of Chinese small and medium sized enterprises' (CSMEs) investment into the North East of England. The authors conducted 23 semi-structured interviews with key decision makers of Chinese SMEs that have business operations in the North East of England. It has been found that there are four major categories of factors that drive Chinese SMEs' investment into the North East of England: 1) resource-based factors; 2) home and host institutional factors; 3) network factors; and 4) international entrepreneurial factors. The findings have policy implications for both the governments of the UK and China, as well as managerial implications for future Chinese investors. This chapter provides fresh explanation of Chinese SMEs' investment into a developed economy.

INTRODUCTION

The UK has a long history of attracting East Asian investment (Garrahan & Ritchie, 1999). Within the UK, the North East England is ranked the second largest region in terms of the volume of inward foreign direct investment after London (Burghart & Rossi, 2009). Research on the phenomenon of Chinese outward foreign direct investment is still at infancy stage. While the motives of large Chinese state-owned

DOI: 10.4018/978-1-5225-2345-1.ch016

enterprises entering developed markets are becoming clear (asset seeking and home government support), why Chinese small and medium-sized enterprises (SMEs) expand their business into developed markets is not yet known. The literature is primarily developed on the basis of two theoretical frameworks: resource-based view and institution-based view. There are two limitations of the existing Chinese outward direct investment literature. First, most studies have focused on Chinese state-owned enterprises, such as Lenovo, Huawei, TCL and Haier. Despite the rapid growth of Chinese Small and Medium-sized Enterprises (SMEs) and their business activities in the international markets (Anderson et al., 2003; Clegg & Voss, 2012; Liu, Xiao, & Huang, 2008), only a few empirical studies have examined Chinese SMEs' overseas business venturing (Boisot & Meyer, 2008; Liu et al., 2008). Very little research has been conducted on Chinese SMEs' investment in the developed economies (Liu et al., 2008). Second, much of the literature is dominated by the theoretical approaches based on resource-based view and institution-based view with limited attention given to other key international management theories such as network and international entrepreneurship theories. This is surprising because network ties play a significant role in facilitating Chinese firms to venture overseas markets, particularly for Chinese SMEs (Lin, 2010; Zhou, 2007) and international entrepreneurship has also been identified as an important factor influencing Chinese SMEs' entry to international markets (Liu et al., 2008).

The aim of this chapter is to explore the factors that drive Chinese SMEs to invest in the Northeast of England. Specifically, the chapter uses a qualitative research method by interviewing business leaders from Chinese SMEs operating in the Northeast of England to explore potential driving factors such as resources, social network, institution, and international entrepreneurship. In the following sections, a review of the literature was conducted on the extant theories of firm internationalisation and international entrepreneurship. The next section outlines the methodology. Thereafter, research findings were presented. Finally, the chapter provides the managerial implications and suggestions for future research.

BACKGROUND

The extant international management literature is dominated with studies of mature multinational corporations, whereas research on the internationalisation of SMEs is only a recent endeavour (Ruzzier, Hisrich, & Antoncic, 2006). To build a holistic theoretical framework, a review of the major theories explaining firm's motivation for internationalisation was conducted: resource-based view, institution-based view, network theory, followed by a review of the international entrepreneurship theory, which is particularly relevant for the internationalisation of SMEs.

Resource-Based View and Social Network Theory

Resource-based view suggests that firms that possess resources that are valuable and rare would attain a competitive advantage (Barney, 2001). To sustain its advantages over time these resources must be inimitable and non-substitutable. It is the firm's distinctive competence in making better use of its resources that create competitive advantage (Mahoney & Pandian, 1992).

From resource-based view, Dunning (2001) advocates that ownership advantages (O-advantages) determine firms' internationalisation. These O-advantages, such as unique resources, can be exploited when entering foreign markets to support the firms' international activities. Based on the mainstream Western multi-national enterprises (MNEs)-based foreign direct investment (FDI) literature, four motivations can be identified: natural resources, market, efficiency and strategic asset seeking (Fetscherin, 2010). Firms' international capabilities, including knowledge accumulation, financial and physical resources and organisational capabilities are believed to be the main drivers of a firm's primary motivation of internationalisation. However, SMEs generally lack of these resources and suffer from liability of smallness, resource constrains and lack of ownership competences when venturing to developed economies (Boisot & Meyer, 2008), in addition to liability of foreignness (Yamakawa, Peng, & Deeds, 2008).

Networks provide additional ownership advantages, particularly for Chinese SMEs (Deng, 2012; Lin, 2010; Zhou, 2007). A network can be used as a mechanism to facilitate information exchange and resource flow between members of the network (Jean, Sinkovics, & Cavusgil, 2010). Different types of networks have been widely studied, including political network (connection with government) (Peng & Luo, 2000), business network (relationship with business partners) (Tang, 2011), and social network (interpersonal relationship) (Ellis, 2011). For resource-constrained SMEs, networks are essential in helping them to overcome barriers of lacking foreign market information and knowledge (Zahra, Korri, & Yu, 2005), and networks perform the role of substituting for external markets (Khanna & Palepu, 2004; Peng, 2003). For example, home country network ties are found to facilitate firms' internationalisation endeavours (Yiu, Lau, & Bruton, 2007), institutional networks help SMEs to better cope with the change of institutional environment (Zhou, 2007) and social networks help SMEs to successfully venture abroad early or quickly (Lin, 2010; Zhou, 2007).

Previous research has shown that Chinese firms investing abroad is both asset exploiting and asset augmenting (Luo & Rui, 2009). Boateng, Qian, and Tianle (2008) indicated that the major motives are market development, diversification, and seeking foreign advanced technology and other resources. Rui and Yip (2008) revealed that the main motives are to obtain strategic capabilities and to leverage unique ownership advantages. Mathews (2006) suggested that Chinese firms' international expansion is driven by resource linkage, leverage and learning. While Chinese MNEs are largely driven by acquiring strategic assets overseas (Rui & Yip, 2008), Chinese SMEs are usually driven by seeking relational assets to redress competitive disadvantage at home (Rugman & Li, 2007; Sethi, 2009).

Institution-Based View and International Entrepreneurship

Institution is defined as macro-level of 'rules of the game' (North, 1990, p. 7). It is 'the cultural-cognitive, normative and regulative elements' of a market (Scott, 2001, p. 48). Institutional theory emphasises the roles of institutional components in shaping a firm's behaviour (Peng, Wang, & Jiang, 2008). It is argued that imposed regulatory (formal) and social constrains (informal) have significant impact on firms' strategic decisions and managerial practices (Child & Tsai, 2005; Meyer et al., 2009). Previous studies have largely focused on host country institution factors (Peng et al., 2008), while firms' internationalisation from emerging economies to developed economies is influenced by 'two institutional frameworks' in both home and host countries (Yamakawa et al., 2008).

One of the well-known home institution factors for the firms in emerging economy are the centrally controlled political and economic systems (Meyer & Nguyen, 2005). Despite progress made in recent years, imposed regulatory constrains in many developed countries still are considered to be barriers for firms' growth which influence their internationalisation strategies (Meyer & Peng, 2005). Legal origin, investor protection and judicial efficiency (such as discrimination against SMEs) and government misbehaviour (such as state intervention in industrial policy, Luo, Xue, & Han, 2010) may push emerging economy-based firms to venture into developed countries (Child & Tse, 2001; Meyer & Nguyen, 2005) in order to transcend home-based limits to growth (Deng, 2012). In recent years, Chinese government has encouraged Chinese state-owned enterprises to 'go global' by providing cheaper finance at home (Buckley, Clegg, & Wang, 2007; Voss, Buckley, & Cross, 2010). Furthermore, market liberalisation in China may also provide stimulus for Chinese state-owned enterprises to pursue outward foreign direct investment (Yang et al., 2009). But for Chinese SMEs, investing into foreign countries is more likely to be driven by the motive of escaping the restrictive business environment in China than by state's financial stimulus (Child & Rodrigues, 2005; Wang, 2002).

Examining host country institutions, a number of studies revealed that Chinese firms are more likely to seek business opportunities in an environment that is similar with their home country (Alden & Davies, 2006). Buckley et al. (2007) suggest that similarities and familiarities of the host culture motivate Chinese firms entering foreign markets. This helps to explain why Chinese firms enter other emerging markets, but it cannot explain Chinese SMEs' investment into a culturally distant country and a developed market such as England. Liu et al. (2008) indicate that 'entrepreneurship' may play a role in determining Chinese SMEs' internationalisation into developed markets.

International entrepreneurship is defined as the process of creatively discovering and exploring new opportunities outside of entrepreneurs' home country (Zahra & George, 2002). International entrepreneurship research focuses on both new and established ventures that 'engaged in cross-border value-exchange processes' (Peiris, Akoorie, & Sinha, 2012, p. 287), from born global (Knight & Cavusgil, 2004) to international new venture (Oviatt & McDougall, 1994). The two core areas of the international entrepreneurship research are opportunity-seeking and entrepreneurial orientation (Chandra, Styles, & Wilkinson, 2009; Oviatt & McDougall, 2005). The extant international entrepreneurship literature suggests that entrepreneurs start their international expansion to exploit international opportunities (Oviatt & McDougall, 2005). Entrepreneurs' right mind-set (e.g. pro-activeness and learning orientation) and prior knowledge (e.g. education background) help them pursue business opportunities across national borders (Kyvik et al., 2013; Zahra et al., 2005). Several factors that influence the formation of a global mind-set, including international work experience, prior international knowledge, and personal characteristics in terms of propensity to interdisciplinary collaboration, cognitive flexibility, and networking capability (Kyvik et al., 2013). Yamakawa et al. (2008) argue that a high level of entrepreneurial orientation will motivate new ventures to internationalise from emerging markets to developed markets. However, many Chinese entrepreneurs, as Liu et al. (2008) indicate, have low levels of education and foreign linguistic capability and they lack of international experience, thus their entrepreneurship is 'bounded' when making international investment decisions. They tend to use domestic mind-sets to scan international opportunities (Deng, 2009).

METHODOLOGY

The study adopts a qualitative, interpretive methodological approach due to the exploratory nature of the research. Chinese SMEs' outward investment is a relatively new phenomenon and suitable secondary data is not available. Key decision makers of Chinese SMEs operating in the Northeast of England were recruited to participate in semi-structured interviews. The reason for choosing the UK as the host country is because the UK accounts 40% of all Chinese investment in Europe (Ernst and Young European Investment Monitor, 2007) and the Northeast of England has the second largest number of Chinese-invested firms, just behind Greater London (Burghart & Rossi, 2009). The sampled Chinese

SMEs are all small-sized, privately owned firms (with fewer than 250 employees) and cover a wide range of industries, including the jewellery industry, textile industry, food industry, computer industry (accessories and software design), as well as Chinese medicine and consultancy services. The period of time the sampled Chinese SMEs had been operating in the Northeast of England varied from 2 to 8 years. The length of interviews lasted from 60 to 120 minutes.

Thematic template analysis was used for coding and interpreting the interview data (King, 2004). As recommended by Ghauri and Grønhaug (2005) and Bryman (2004), the authors followed the four steps of ensuring high quality interview data: preparing interview (e.g. contact the interviewees, revise interview questions); pre-interview (e.g. plan the time, rehearse and practise); main interview (e.g. start small talk; time control; avoid leading-directing manner etc.) and post interview (e.g. send 'thank-you' letter and write interview memo etc.).

FINDINGS

The analysis revealed the categories of: 1) resource-based factors; 2) home and host institutional factors; 3) network factors; and 4) entrepreneurial factors.

Resource-Based Factors

In responding to the question '*Why did you decide to invest your business in this region*', some informants put more weight on firms' strategic objectives internally rather than concerns of external factors. For them, investing in the Northeast of England was to leverage their ownership capabilities via developing their marketing and managerial knowledge in the UK.

Manager Z expressed that he wanted to gather first hand market information when he decided to invest in the Northeast of England. He explained that:

Gaining efficient market knowledge of England can help us understand the Western business better and enhance our international business performance in other Western, developed European countries.

For other informants, they claimed that their initial intentions were to build up their international expertise for further international expansion from a long-term perspective. In his reflection, Manager M noted that

Setting business venture in England could improve and enhance our international knowledge and practical experience that reinforces our foreign customer services for now and in the future.

Manager M indicated that currently they had more than 400 employees in China, last year they recruited two foreign jewellery designers, one from Italy and another from South Korea. Their products, as manager M stated, have a great potential to sell well in the European markets.

We just moved a small step in our international business expanding at the moment. Invading the Western markets is one important goal for us. We want to prepare our own international expertise in a long-term commitment by investing in the North East of England markets. (Manager M)

According to informants' narratives, it became apparent that 'lack of ownership advantages' is a major concern for Chinese SMEs' growth in the future. Entering developed markets, like UK, helps them develop their market knowledge. Thus, strategic-asset seeking can be concluded to be an important motive in this case.

Institutional Factors

Home Country

Three home institutional factors emerged from Chinese SME managers' narratives: 1) relaxation of government control, 2) Chinese government supports and incentivise 'going abroad', 3) avoiding pressures of competitions from both Chinese and foreign companies in China.

Informants highlighted how important and powerful the role of the Chinese government plays in Chinese SMEs' international business activities. In order to control and govern Chinese SMEs' international activities, relevant regulations and policies are rigorously regulated. Managers' narratives reflected on their experiences of how the Chinese government interventions largely constrained Chinese SMEs' international activities. Although informants negatively recalled their experiences with the Chinese government's control of Chinese SMEs' internationalisation, they further suggested that the Chinese government has gradually moved from 'over-intervention' to 'liberalisation'. The Chinese government has relatively (not completely) relaxed some controls with respect to Chinese SMEs' international business activities. These managers indicated that this change has inspired their initial intention of 'going abroad' and they highlighted the motives of 'government incentives'.

Owner Manager T indicated that support from the Chinese government was a key factor that drove him to seek business opportunities overseas. He commented that the Chinese government launched a number of favourable foreign investment regulatory policies not only for inward FDI but also outward investments. For example, Manager T recalled, in 1999, the Chinese government carried out the 'going global' strategy to encourage both large Chinese firms and Chinese SMEs to integrate their business into international markets. By doing this, the Chinese government released a policy that reduced control over foreign currency exchange restrictions. Agreeing with Manager T, three other managers all asserted that tightly controlled foreign currency by the Chinese government had formerly been a large constraint factor for Chinese SME managers involved with international business in the past, especially the 'non-neighbour' countries (refer to the Western developed countries). Although some rules and regulations that constrain growth of Chinese SME's still exist, the incremental support and incentive of the Chinese government cannot be denied.

Another highly emphasized motive factor is 'competition pressure'. Every interviewee strongly addressed their concerns of fierce competitions from both foreign (mainly from developed countries) and domestic companies in China. This situation was described by informants as "*a nightmare*". They reinforced the necessity of going abroad for Chinese SMEs, especially entering developed countries as their China-based foreign competitors are mainly from developed countries (like USA, France, Germany, and the UK). To win the battle, they must be equipped with certain competitive advantages (e.g. higher quality products and services).

Host Country

While Chinese government supports are emphasized when investigating motives of Chinese MNEs in developed markets, host institutional effect is highlighted by informants in this study. British government support, as six informants described, especially from One North East, the regional development agency, is the main host country institutional factor that attracts Chinese SMEs' investment in the Northeast of England. Manager P confirmed, to attract more Chinese companies investing in the Northeast of England, One North East established their offices in Beijing and Shanghai, organised a series of workshops in China to introduce business environment and favourable FDI policies in the Northeast of England to potential Chinese investors. Importantly, One North East emphasised that, as a regional development agency, they would provide comprehensive supports to Chinese investors (e.g. cheaper rent, free business advice, even help with visa applications). These supports truly encouraged Chinese SME managers' intentions of investing in the North East of England. In early of this interview, manager P explained:

Before attending Mr. X's presentation (from One North East), we really debated over the choices between going abroad or staying…we made our decision knowing we would have comprehensive supports from One North East, they have an office in China so we can communicate with each other, this is crucial for us.

Three other managers from the manufacturing sector expressed their comments from same point of view:

For me, 'One –stop shopping' supports from One North East was true encouragement…for many Chinese SME managers, language and cultural barriers are obvious, these barriers affect many aspects of doing business overseas. Consider this, One North East assigned an alliance manager, who speaks both mandarin Chinese and English. From initial marketing investigation to business proposal, from accommodation to office rental, this manager provided us with great supports. (Owner Manager T)

Moreover, One North East works jointly with International Departments of local city councils to provide Chinese SME managers free basic legal and consultant services. In the early market investigating stage, the alliance manager gave us many supports and valuable advice. These 'superb services' from One North East really built up our confidence to pursue further investments in this region. (Owner Manager Q)

The majority of the interviewees confirmed that the better institutional environment in the UK did attract them to invest in UK markets, for example more transparent polices, and business-friendly enhancement procedures with clearer appeals mechanisms. Some managers studied at British universities and others confirmed that they had visited UK several times to conduct their pre-entry research. By learning about the UK business environment, they confirmed that in comparison to China, the investment conditions in the UK are more fair and show more transparency (e.g. policies).

Network Factors

Chinese SMEs entering the Northeast of England was a result of network relationship. Manager F from a Chinese textile company strongly expressed the 'trustful' personal relationship and emphasized that their company would not appear in the UK markets without the personal connection. In addition, other informants disclosed that their investments in the North East of England were driven by their business networks in the UK. Manager G indicated that to seek out more business opportunities in DE countries, in addition to attending international trade fairs in China, they also go to 2 large international trade fairs every year: the Frankfurt Trade Fair in Germany and the Birmingham Trade Fair in the UK. Via these trade fairs, these managers built up their business contacts and further developed their relationships to become business partners.

Manager G narrated:

... attending trade fairs abroad cost us money, but it was worth it... we built up our networks in the foreign countries (Germany and UK), and some of them became our customers later ... being closer to them enabled us to provide them with better services.

The manager's story from the jewellery company also illustrated how his international business activities triggered by their business networks in the UK.

The political network via personal ties (government official) was also discovered in motivating Chinese SMEs entering UK. During the interviews, an Asian liaison manager from One North East was mentioned a several times. This liaison manger, a native Chinese speaker, was mainly in charge of Asian companies' foreign investment in the Northeast of England. More than half of the interviewees knew him because he organised some 'investment in the Northeast of England' workshops in China on behalf of One North East. These managers called him a 'Chinese political actor'. Influenced heavily by Chinese 'Guanxi' business culture, these Chinese SME owners believed that building up a good relationship with the government is essential as firm-government networks can bring benefits for them, such as funding for development, licences and approvals for some business activities. One interviewee explained:

He (the liaison manager) is a nice person. I feel comfortable investing in the UK with his help. It is also very important that he works for the government...he speaks Chinese and understands the Chinese culture.

The interviewees widely believed that they could be proactive participants in the political system in the host country through this personally linked political network. This seemed to be a critical motive for Chinese SMEs entering the UK market because this trustful political actor can be a vehicle for information (political knowledge of the host country) and communication with the local government. This firm-government network driven by a political actor, particularly one speaking their native language, is regarded as a 'reliable external resource' helping them to overcome the liability of foreignness and mitigate various political hazards in the host country.

International Entrepreneurship Factors

Regarding entrepreneurship factors, several informants claimed that Chinese SME managers' strong personal preference (entrepreneurial orientation) of internationalising developed economies, like UK, was a key internal motivating factor. Manager T emphasised that external motives may lead Chinese SMEs to consider the possibility of launching business abroad, but they are not necessary conditions for entrepreneurs to entering the developed markets. Manager T's story clearly illuminated that Chinese SME managers may not consider investing their business at developed economies, even when a foreign business opportunity arises, if they have no intention of going abroad at all. Comparing the two generations of managers, entrepreneurs' risk-taking attitudes, owners/managers' personal visons and goals have significant influence on DE entry choice. Manager W's narratives also indicate that Chinese SMEs entering UK were not limited by liabilities of foreignness. To reinforce manager T and W's points, manager B affirmed that

I did not deny that some external forces do drive Chinese SME managers thinking about doing business internationally. However, you can take a horse to the water, but you cannot make it drink.

Another emerged theme is managers' intention of seeking entrepreneurial freedom combined with their Western education background. Manager P used to study in Switzerland. Her experience of living in the Western European country widened her view and made her feel that 'being an autonomy', not just institutionally but also socially, was of great significance for the new generation of entrepreneurs. She believed that the UK provides such an atmosphere. Manager W held same opinion. He also confirmed that doing business overseas gives him more opportunities to gain entrepreneurial freedom than in China. It is important to note, among these interviewed Chinese SME managers, more than half of them had previously either worked or studied in Western developed countries, such as the UK and Switzerland. Three managers obtained their business management degrees from foreign universities. According to a few informants, via studying at Western universities, they were not only able to absorb the knowledge of local social and business cultures and improve their English language ability, but they also developed their international mind-set. Their orientations (towards autonomy, innovativeness and risk taking) and spirit of 'true' entrepreneurship were changed after completing their studies in developed countries. Their knowledge acquired at developed countries offers a cognitive bridge for Chinese SMEs entering the UK market.

DISCUSSION

The main objective of this chapter is to investigate the motivations driving Chinese SMEs to enter the Northeast of England. Building upon the interview data, a set of factors are identified which can be categorised into resource-based factors, institutional factors, network factors and international entrepreneurship factors.

Resource-Based View and Strategic-Asset Seeking

Many existing Chinese outward FDI studies reveal that Chinese MNEs lack of ownership-advantages (apart from the state-ownership), moving to developed markets, for them, is to strengthen their ownership advantages (Buckley et al., 2007; Voss et al., 2010). In the context of Chinese SMEs, the study's findings are in line with the motives of Chinese MNEs. In general, Chinese SMEs are resource-constrained and lack managerial knowledge. With massive FDI inflows in China, cost-leadership strategy does not work profitably for Chinese SMEs in the long-term compared to their neighbours like Vietnam and the Philippines. To survive, they must prepare themselves to improve their competitive advantage by *leveraging* their ownership advantages *via learning* in developed markets (Mathews, 2006). Clearly, these Chinese SMEs have a focus on 'strategic-asset seeking' to strengthen their ownership advantages. It was found that the only difference between Chinese MNEs and Chinese SMEs in seeking strategic-assets, is that

Chinese SMEs attempt to familiarise themselves with UK market behaviours and managerial practices rather than obtaining advanced technology (Buckley et al., 2007; Child & Rodrigues, 2005).

Institutional-Based View

Both home-country and host-country institutional factors motivate Chinese SMEs internationalising UK markets. On one hand, the study's findings corroborate Rugman and Li's (2007) argument that economic changes, government power and market liberation play important roles in motivating both SMEs and MNEs' foreign investments. Although some Chinese government interventions still exist, many hurdles of foreign investments have been eliminated. Relaxation of control and support provide a favourable condition and create more opportunities for Chinese SME managers to invest in the Northeast of England. However, the level of support Chinese state-owned enterprises and Chinese SMEs received differs. Many Chinese MNEs, particularly state-owned enterprises, gain strong government support, such as substantial monetary support (Luo et al., 2010). Chinese SMEs' internationalisation appears as an outcome of 'changed policy' at the macro-level. Financial supports from the Chinese government are limited, and private sources are necessary for Chinese SMEs when entering overseas markets (Cardoza & Fornes, 2011). On the other hand, Chinese SMEs' business activities are still intervened by the government as China is an extreme case of a 'central government controlled' country (Buckley et al., 2007; Li, 2007; Meyer & Peng, 2005). Although one of the important Chinese economic reforms is to increase the autonomy of Chinese enterprises, inheritance from the planned economy makes it hard for Chinese SME managers to act entrepreneurially (Child & Tse, 2001).

Competition from foreign international companies in home markets is a push factor for SMEs to seek new markets. The competition from both foreign and domestic companies in China made it difficult for Chinese SMEs to survive. As this research exemplified, price-war and intensive competition in China make SMEs operate in a hostile environment, thus pushing them to consider other means of survival and look for foreign investment opportunities (Tang & Hull, 2012) in different regions in the world, such as the Northeast of England.

Finally, friendly institutional environment and formal institutional supports provided by One North East in the UK play a significant role in attracting Chinese SMEs to the Northeast of England. There are two main reasons for this. First, institutional environment in many emerging countries, like China, is a combination of social legacy, high context culture and transition economy (Peng & Luo, 2000). Institutional rules are often incomplete and ambiguous (Gibb & Li, 2003). The friendlier regulative environment in developed countries is more attractive for emerging country-based SMEs. Second, entering a new market, managers face tremendous uncertainties and challenges due to cultural and institutional differences. Government support, One North East in this case, appears highly important to lower the level of institutional and country risks when entering foreign countries (Welter & Smallbone, 2011). Host government support made Chinese SME investors feel well protected.

Networks

Networks have a central figure in triggering Chinese SMEs entering the Northeast of England. Networks shown in this study include entrepreneurs' interpersonal ties, professional networks and political network.

All three types of networks are believed by Chinese managers to be able to help Chinese SMEs overcome the liability of foreignness. In line with existing theories, dealing with resource restrains is inevitable for SMEs, especially when internationalising non-homogeneity markets. Networks not only benefit SMEs from synergistic effect of pooled resources (Chetty & Holm, 2000), by exchanging values of market knowledge and experiences, but also help SMEs reduce uncertainties, particularly by exposing more business opportunities (Ellis, 2011). The political network established via the political officer in One North East seems crucial. In the case of this study, the officer from One North East (the Asian liaison manager) played a crucial role in motivating Chinese SMEs entering the UK market. Based on the notion of Chinese high context culture (Peng, 2005), Chinese SMEs decision makers deeply believe that connection with the local government, due to its legitimate position in the host country, can help them gain more support. Here, links can be made between networks and the Chinese Guanxi culture. Finally, the study's network findings extended findings of the Fujita (1995) study suggesting that SMEs may be pulled into foreign markets by their business partners who are in larger firms. Indeed, different types of networks have positive impact on Chinese SMEs' investment in the Northeast of England.

Entrepreneur Factors

Evidence in this research suggests that entrepreneurs' attitudes towards risk-taking is a key driver which reflects Buckley and Casson (1998) who argue that investing in a foreign country is a result of entrepreneur foresight. Given the extraordinary liability of foreignness of Chinese SMEs, venturing from emerging market to developed market is a risk. Without risk-taking attitude, Chinese SMEs would stay in China and ignore international business opportunities. A numbers of scholars have claimed that internationalisation is preceded by opportunity recognition by entrepreneurs in order to exploit international opportunities (Oviatt & McDougall, 1994; Zahra et al., 2005). These opportunities may not be profit-seeking but rather knowledge and managerial skills seeking (Liu et al., 2008; Mathews, 2006). Seeking business opportunities is heavily influenced by the owner/founder's entrepreneurial attitudes, such as autonomy orientation. Moreover, seeking entrepreneurial freedom is considered important for Chinese SME managers. Although the Chinese government is gradually reducing control of Chinese SMEs activities, it seems that Chinese SME managers did not enjoy the entrepreneurial freedom as much as Western SME managers do in the developed markets.

Chinese SMEs decision makers' Western education background is factor to invest in a foreign country. Entrepreneurs of the older-generation Chinese SME founders/managers differ significantly from the young-generation in terms of entrepreneurial orientation (e.g. risk-taking). After three decades of adopting open door policy by the Chinese government, large number of Chinese students study in Western universities. In most cases, many of them possess cross-cultural communication skills and a global perspective. These entrepreneurial-advantages have caused young Chinese SMEs managers to have different entrepreneurial orientations in comparison with entrepreneurs who have not been educated in the Western countries (old-generation). To reach a deeper understanding of Chinese SMEs entrepreneurial impact on internationalisation, changes of entrepreneurial characteristics over time must be considered. Thus, context matters in studying entrepreneurs' internationalisation behaviour as 'it provides the basis for the subtext to operate'(Garud & Giuliani, 2013).

SOLUTIONS AND RECOMMENDATIONS

This study has several policy and managerial implications. First, from the home country's perspective, the Chinese government should realise the necessity of further reducing restrictions and obstacles, and providing more tailored support to Chinese SMEs' internationalisation (e.g. offer sufficient information of particular countries and international business training programs). For policy makers at the host country, a clear understanding of nature characteristics of emerging market-based SMEs (e.g. importance of political networks) is required. Second, this study strongly suggests that Chinese SMEs managers should not only account external factors but also consider entrepreneurial factors when venturing DE markets, and have a clear understanding of how their personal strengths or biases (attitude towards risk-taking, pro-activeness, etc.) affect their internationalisation process.

FUTURE RESEARCH DIRECTIONS

There are several limitations of this study which introduce opportunities for further research. First, the outcomes of this study are not generalizable to all Chinese SMEs' overseas investment, but are rather specific and context oriented. Thus the authors suggest further research could verify this study's findings to other contexts using large scale quantitative study. Second, due to the relatively small scale and availability of sampled Chinese SMEs in the Northeast of England, this study did not compare manufacturing firms with service ones. Researchers may consider investigating motives of Chinese SMEs investing into other European regions in a specific industry or sector. Finally, regarding the important role of decision makers' Western education background, greater specification of this certain group of entrepreneurs' international behaviours would be valuable and worth paying extra attention to in the future studies.

CONCLUSION

Previous research has shown that institutional-based theory and resource-based theory can be used to explain Chinese MNEs' motives of entering developed markets (Buckley et al., 2006; Voss et al., 2010; Mathews, 2006). In the Chinese SMEs context, this study adds to the understanding of the impact of networks and entrepreneurial factors on Chinese SMEs' motives of entering a developed market. This outcome is in line with Peng's (2006) argument that no single perspective is to be strong enough to explain SMEs internationalising from emerging markets to developed markets, it is a combination of different insights. In addition, the study made methodological contribution to existing studies. To the best of the authors' knowledge, this study is among the first conducting primary research in the context of Chinese SMEs investing in a particular developed market. Previous studies are largely based on secondary data that may lack of authenticity and include measurement error (Bernard & Ryan, 2009). Studies in the context of Chinese SMEs internationalisation (Cardoza & Fornes, 2011) do not differentiate specific country the investigated Chinese SMEs entered. This study moves the existing research forward by investigating Chinese SMEs' motives of entering particular developed market supported by valuable, first-hand qualitative data.

REFERENCES

Alden, C., & Davies, M. (2006). A profile of the operations of Chinese multinationals in Africa. *South African Journal of International Affairs, 13*(1), 83–96. doi:10.1080/10220460609556787

Anderson, A. R., Li, J. H., Harrison, R. T., & Robson, P. J. (2003). The increasing role of small business in the Chinese economy. *Journal of Small Business Management, 41*(3), 310–316. doi:10.1111/1540-627X.00084

Barney, J. B. (2001). Resource-based theories of competitive advantage: A ten-year retrospective on the resource-based view. *Journal of Management, 27*(6), 643–650. doi:10.1177/014920630102700602

Bernard, H. R., & Ryan, G. W. (2009). *Analyzing Qualitative Data: Systematic Approaches*. SAGE Publications.

Boateng, A., Qian, W., & Tianle, Y. (2008). Cross-border M&As by Chinese firms: An analysis of strategic motives and performance. *Thunderbird International Business Review, 50*(4), 259–270. doi:10.1002/tie.20203

Boisot, M., & Meyer, M. W. (2008). Which way through the open door? Reflections on the internationalization of Chinese firms. *Management and Organization Review, 4*(3), 349–365. doi:10.1111/j.1740-8784.2008.00116.x

Bryman, A. (2004). Qualitative research on leadership: A critical but appreciative review. *The Leadership Quarterly, 15*(6), 729–769. doi:10.1016/j.leaqua.2004.09.007

Buckley, P. J., & Casson, M. C. (1998). Models of the multinational enterprise. *Journal of International Business Studies, 29*(1), 21–44. doi:10.1057/palgrave.jibs.8490023

Buckley, P. J., Clegg, J., & Wang, C. (2007). Is the relationship between inward FDI and spillover effects linear? An empirical examination of the case of China. *Journal of International Business Studies, 38*(3), 447–459. doi:10.1057/palgrave.jibs.8400274

Burghart, N., & Rossi, V. (2009). *China's overseas direct investment in the UK.* Chatham House Programme Paper, 2009.

Cardoza, G., & Fornes, G. (2011). The internationalisation of SMEs from China: The case of Ningxia Hui autonomous region. *Asia Pacific Journal of Management, 28*(4), 737–759. doi:10.1007/s10490-009-9174-z

Chandra, Y., Styles, C., & Wilkinson, I. (2009). The recognition of first time international entrepreneurial opportunities: Evidence from firms in knowledge-based industries. *International Marketing Review, 26*(1), 30–61. doi:10.1108/02651330910933195

Chetty, S., & Holm, D. B. (2000). Internationalisation of small to medium-sized manufacturing firms: A network approach. *International Business Review, 9*(1), 77–93. doi:10.1016/S0969-5931(99)00030-X

Child, J., & Rodrigues, S. B. (2005). The Internationalization of Chinese Firms: A Case for Theoretical Extension? *Management and Organization Review, 1*(3), 381–410. doi:10.1111/j.1740-8784.2005.0020a.x

Child, J., & Tsai, T. (2005). The Dynamic Between Firms Environmental Strategies and Institutional Constraints in Emerging Economies: Evidence from China and Taiwan. *Journal of Management Studies*, *42*(1), 95–125. doi:10.1111/j.1467-6486.2005.00490.x

Child, J., & Tse, D. K. (2001). Chinas transition and its implications for international business. *Journal of International Business Studies*, *32*(1), 5–21. doi:10.1057/palgrave.jibs.8490935

Clegg, J., & Voss, H. (2012). *Chinese Overseas Direct Investment in the European Union*. Europe China Research and Advice Network London.

Deng, P. (2009). Why do Chinese firms tend to acquire strategic assets in international expansion? *Journal of World Business*, *44*(1), 74–84. doi:10.1016/j.jwb.2008.03.014

Deng, P. (2012). The Internationalization of Chinese Firms: A Critical Review and Future Research. *International Journal of Management Reviews*, *14*(4), 408–427. doi:10.1111/j.1468-2370.2011.00323.x

Dunning, J. H. (2001). The Eclectic (OLI) Paradigm of International Production: Past, Present and Future. *International Journal of the Economics of Business*, *8*(2), 173–190. doi:10.1080/13571510110051441

Ellis, P. D. (2011). Social ties and international entrepreneurship: Opportunities and constraints affecting firm internationalization. *Journal of International Business Studies*, *42*(1), 99–127. doi:10.1057/jibs.2010.20

Fetscherin, M. (2010). The determinants and measurement of a country brand: The country brand strength index. *International Marketing Review*, *27*(4), 466–479. doi:10.1108/02651331011058617

Fujita, M. (1995). Small and medium-sized transnational corporations: Trends and patterns of foreign direct investment. *Small Business Economics*, *7*(3), 183–204. doi:10.1007/BF01135364

Garrahan, P., & Ritchie, J. (1999). *East Asian Direct Investment in Britain*. Psychology Press.

Garud, R., & Giuliani, A. P. (2013). A narrative perspective on entrepreneurial opportunities. *Academy of Management Review*, *38*(1), 157–160. doi:10.5465/amr.2012.0055

Ghauri, P. N., & Grønhaug, K. (2005). *Research Methods in Business Studies: A Practical Guide*. London: Pearson Education.

Gibb, A., & Li, J. (2003). Organizing for enterprise in China: What can we learn from the Chinese micro, small, and medium enterprise development experience. *Futures*, *35*(4), 403–421. doi:10.1016/S0016-3287(02)00089-7

Jean, R.-J. B., Sinkovics, R. R., & Cavusgil, S. T. (2010). Enhancing international customer–supplier relationships through IT resources: A study of Taiwanese electronics suppliers. *Journal of International Business Studies*, *41*(7), 1218–1239. doi:10.1057/jibs.2010.4

Khanna, T., & Palepu, K. (2004). *Emerging giants: building world class companies from emerging markets.* Harvard Business School Working Papers.

Knight, G. A., & Cavusgil, S. T. (2004). Innovation, organizational capabilities, and the born-global firm. *Journal of International Business Studies*, *35*(2), 124–141. doi:10.1057/palgrave.jibs.8400071

Kyvik, O., Saris, W., Bonet, E., & Felício, J. A. (2013). The internationalization of small firms: The relationship between the global mindset and firms internationalization behavior. *Journal of International Entrepreneurship, 11*(2), 172–195. doi:10.1007/s10843-013-0105-1

Li, P. P. (2007). Toward an integrated theory of multinational evolution: The evidence of Chinese multinational enterprises as latecomers. *Journal of International Management, 13*(3), 296–318. doi:10.1016/j.intman.2007.05.004

Lin, X. (2010). State versus private MNCs from China: Initial conceptualizations. *International Marketing Review, 27*(3), 366–380. doi:10.1108/02651331011048023

Liu, X., Xiao, W., & Huang, X. (2008). Bounded entrepreneurship and internationalisation of indigenous Chinese private-owned firms. *International Business Review, 17*(4), 488–508. doi:10.1016/j.ibusrev.2008.02.014

Luo, Y., & Rui, H. (2009). An ambidexterity perspective toward multinational enterprises from emerging economies. *The Academy of Management Perspectives, 23*(4), 49–70. doi:10.5465/AMP.2009.45590140

Luo, Y., Xue, Q., & Han, B. (2010). How emerging market governments promote outward FDI: Experience from China. *Journal of World Business, 45*(1), 68–79. doi:10.1016/j.jwb.2009.04.003

Mahoney, J. T., & Pandian, J. R. (1992). The resource-based view within the conversation of strategic management. *Strategic Management Journal, 13*(5), 363–380. doi:10.1002/smj.4250130505

Mathews, J. A. (2006). Dragon multinationals: New players in 21st century globalization. *Asia Pacific Journal of Management, 23*(1), 5–27. doi:10.1007/s10490-006-6113-0

Meyer, K. E., Estrin, S., Bhaumik, S. K., & Peng, M. W. (2009). Institutions, resources, and entry strategies in emerging economies. *Strategic Management Journal, 30*(1), 61–80. doi:10.1002/smj.720

Meyer, K. E., & Nguyen, H. V. (2005). Foreign Investment Strategies and Sub-national Institutions in Emerging Markets: Evidence from Vietnam. *Journal of Management Studies, 42*(1), 63–93. doi:10.1111/j.1467-6486.2005.00489.x

Meyer, K. E., & Peng, M. W. (2005). Probing theoretically into Central and Eastern Europe: Transactions, resources, and institutions. *Journal of International Business Studies, 36*(6), 600–621. doi:10.1057/palgrave.jibs.8400167

North, D. C. (1990). *Institutions, Institutional Change and Economic Performance*. Cambridge University Press. doi:10.1017/CBO9780511808678

Oviatt, B. M., & McDougall, P. P. (1994). Toward a theory of international new ventures. *Journal of International Business Studies, 25*(1), 45–64. doi:10.1057/palgrave.jibs.8490193

Oviatt, B. M., & McDougall, P. P. (2005). Defining international entrepreneurship and modeling the speed of internationalization. *Entrepreneurship Theory and Practice, 29*(5), 537–554. doi:10.1111/j.1540-6520.2005.00097.x

Peiris, I. K., Akoorie, M. E., & Sinha, P. (2012). International entrepreneurship: A critical analysis of studies in the past two decades and future directions for research. *Journal of International Entrepreneurship*, *10*(4), 279–324. doi:10.1007/s10843-012-0096-3

Peng, M. W. (2003). Institutional transitions and strategic choices. *Academy of Management Review*, *28*(2), 275–296.

Peng, M. W. (2005). Perspectives - from China strategy to global strategy. *Asia Pacific Journal of Management*, *22*(2), 123–141. doi:10.1007/s10490-005-1251-3

Peng, M. W., & Luo, Y. (2000). Managerial ties and firm performance in a transition economy: The nature of a micro-macro link. *Academy of Management Journal*, *43*(3), 486–501. doi:10.2307/1556406

Peng, M. W., Wang, D. Y., & Jiang, Y. (2008). An institution-based view of international business strategy: A focus on emerging economies. *Journal of International Business Studies*, *39*(5), 920–936. doi:10.1057/palgrave.jibs.8400377

Rugman, A. M., & Li, J. (2007). Will Chinas multinationals succeed globally or regionally? *European Management Journal*, *25*(5), 333–343. doi:10.1016/j.emj.2007.07.005

Rui, H., & Yip, G. S. (2008). Foreign acquisitions by Chinese firms: A strategic intent perspective. *Journal of World Business*, *43*(2), 213–226. doi:10.1016/j.jwb.2007.11.006

Ruzzier, M., Hisrich, R. D., & Antoncic, B. (2006). SME internationalization research: Past, present, and future. *Journal of Small Business and Enterprise Development*, *13*(4), 476–497. doi:10.1108/14626000610705705

Scott, W. R. (2001). *Institutions and Organizations*. Thousand Oaks, CA: Sage.

Sethi, D. (2009). Are multinational enterprises from the emerging economies global or regional? *European Management Journal*, *27*(5), 356–365. doi:10.1016/j.emj.2009.04.009

Tang, Y. K. (2011). Influence of networking on the internationalization of SMEs: Evidence from internationalized Chinese firms. *International Small Business Journal*, *29*(4), 374–398. doi:10.1177/0266242610369748

Tang, Z., & Hull, C. (2012). An investigation of entrepreneurial orientation, perceived environmental hostility, and strategy application among Chinese SMEs. *Journal of Small Business Management*, *50*(1), 132–158. doi:10.1111/j.1540-627X.2011.00347.x

Voss, H., Buckley, P. J., & Cross, A. R. (2010). The impact of home country institutional effects on the internationalization strategy of Chinese firms. *Multinational Business Review*, *18*(3), 25–48. doi:10.1108/1525383X201000014

Wang, M. Y. (2002). The motivations behind Chinas government-initiated industrial investments overseas. *Pacific Affairs*, *75*(2), 187–206. doi:10.2307/4127182

Welter, F., & Smallbone, D. (2011). Institutional perspectives on entrepreneurial behavior in challenging environments. *Journal of Small Business Management*, *49*(1), 107–125. doi:10.1111/j.1540-627X.2010.00317.x

Yamakawa, Y., Peng, M. W., & Deeds, D. L. (2008). What drives new ventures to internationalize from emerging to developed economies? *Entrepreneurship Theory and Practice*, *32*(1), 59–82. doi:10.1111/j.1540-6520.2007.00216.x

Yang, X., Lim, Y., Sakurai, Y., & Seo, S. y. (2009). Internationalization of Chinese and Korean firms. *Thunderbird International Business Review*, *51*(1), 37–51. doi:10.1002/tie.20243

Yiu, D. W., Lau, C., & Bruton, G. D. (2007). International venturing by emerging economy firms: The effects of firm capabilities, home country networks, and corporate entrepreneurship. *Journal of International Business Studies*, *38*(4), 519–540. doi:10.1057/palgrave.jibs.8400278

Zahra, S. A., & George, G. (2002). International entrepreneurship: the current status of the field and future research agenda. In M. A. Hitt, R. D. Ireland, S. M. Camp, & D. L. Sexton (Eds.), *Strategic Entrepreneurship: Creating a New Mindset* (pp. 255–288). Oxford, UK: Blackwell Publishers.

Zahra, S. A., Korri, J. S., & Yu, J. (2005). Cognition and international entrepreneurship: Implications for research on international opportunity recognition and exploitation. *International Business Review*, *14*(2), 129–146. doi:10.1016/j.ibusrev.2004.04.005

Zhou, L. (2007). The effects of entrepreneurial proclivity and foreign market knowledge on early internationalization. *Journal of World Business*, *42*(3), 281–293. doi:10.1016/j.jwb.2007.04.009

KEY TERMS AND DEFINITIONS

Guanxi: A Chinese term that describes a social relationship and network. Guanxi is an informal relationship that is based on interpersonal reciprocal exchange of favors. The idea is widely accepted in Chinese society.

Institution-Based View: A theoretical perspective that emphasizes the roles of institutional components in shaping a firm's behavior. It is argued that imposed regulatory (formal) and social constrains (informal) have significant impact on firms' strategic decisions and managerial practices.

International Entrepreneurship: The process of creatively discovering and exploring new opportunities outside of entrepreneurs' home country. The key characteristics of entrepreneurship include innovativeness, proactive-ness, and risk-seeking.

Liability of Foreignness: The costs or difficulties that firms experience when they operate in a foreign market. These costs include the firm's limited knowledge of host market's political, socio-cultural and economic environments; the discriminatory attitudes from host country's institutions, competitors and consumers; and the difficulties of managing between headquarters and subsidiaries which are located in different countries.

Network Perspective: A theoretical perspective that sees markets as networks of relationship between firms. A network can be used as a mechanism to facilitate information exchange and resource flow between members of the network. For resource-constrained small and medium-sized companies, networks are essential in helping them to overcome barriers to enter a foreign market.

Ownership Advantages (O-Advantages): One of the three important factors of OLI-Model of foreign direct investment, originally proposed by John Dunning in 1979. The other two are location (L) and internalization (I) advantages. Ownership advantages refer to the unique resources that a firm can exploit when entering foreign markets, including resources such as patent, technology know-how, brand reputation, entrepreneurial skills and others.

Resource-Based View: A theoretical perspective that focuses on resources for creating and maintaining competitive advantage. It is believed that valuable and rare resources help a firm to attain a competitive advantage, but to sustain its advantages over time these resources must be inimitable and non-substitutable. Firm's competence in making use of resources is essential in the process of creating and maintaining competitive advantage.

Strategic Asset Seeking: A motive that drives a firm to expand to a foreign market. Strategic assets are those resources that enhance a firm's competitiveness, such as advanced technology, managerial know-how, brand equity and others. Other internationalization motives include: natural resource seeking, market seeking, and efficiency seeking.

Compilation of References

Abbott, A., Cushman, D. O., & Vita, G. D. (2012). Exchange Rate Regimes and Foreign Direct Investment Flows to Developing Countries. *Review of International Economics*, *20*(1), 95–107. doi:10.1111/j.1467-9396.2011.01010.x

Acemoglu, D., Johnson, S., & Robinson, J. A. (2001). The colonial origins of comparative development: An empirical investigation. *The American Economic Review*, *91*(5), 1369–1401. doi:10.1257/aer.91.5.1369

Act on Foreign Exchange Law. (2002). Journal of Laws of 2002. No. 141, item 1178.

Adamczyk, J. (2014). *Ekonomiczne i społeczne efekty spółek z udziałem skarbu państwa, Studia i Materiały*. Wydział Zarządzania i Administracji Uniwersytetu Jana Kochanowskiego w Kielcach.

Agarwal, V., & Bahree, M. (2011, December 8). *India Retreats on Retail* [Online posting]. Retrieved July 30, 2016, from http://www.wsj.com/articles/SB10001424052970204903804577083343062468240

Ahmad, M. H., & Ahmed, Q. M. (2014). Does the Institutional Quality Matter to Attract the Foreign Direct Investment? An Empirical Investigation for Pakistan. *South Asia Economic Journal*, *15*(1), 55–70. doi:10.1177/1391561414525708

AICEP. (2016a). *Portugal – Ficha País Março 2016*. Retrieved 3 July, 2016 from http://www.portugalglobal.pt/PT/Biblioteca/Paginas/Detalhe.aspx?documentId=50f511f4-d2ea-4f9f-90e4-d47bde498c50

AICEP. (2016b). *Républica Checa – Síntese País*. Retrieved 3 July, 2016 from http://www.portugalglobal.pt/PT/Internacionalizar/SobreMercadosExternos/Documents/Perfil/95.pdf

Aitken, B. J., & Harrison, A. E. (1999). Do domestic firms benefit from direct foreign investment? evidence from Venezuela. *The American Economic Review*, *89*(3), 605–618. doi:10.1257/aer.89.3.605

Aitken, B. J., Harrison, A. E., & Lipsey, R. (1996). Wages and foreign ownership. A comparative study of Mexico, Venezuela and the United States. *Journal of International Economics*, *40*(1), 345–371. doi:10.1016/0022-1996(95)01410-1

Aizenman, J. (2003). Volatility, employment and the patterns of FDI in emerging markets. *Journal of Development Economics*, *72*(2), 585–601. doi:10.1016/S0304-3878(03)00123-8

Alam, Q., Mian, M. E. U., & Smith, R. F. I. (2005). *The Impact Of Poor Governance On Foreign Direct Investment: The Bangladesh Experience*. Network of Asia-Pacific Schools and Institutes of Public Administration and Governance (NAPSIPAG) Annual Conference 2005, Beijing, China.

Alden, C., & Davies, M. (2006). A profile of the operations of Chinese multinationals in Africa. *South African Journal of International Affairs*, *13*(1), 83–96. doi:10.1080/10220460609556787

Aleksynska, M., & Havrylchyk, O. (2013). FDI from the South: The role of institutional distance and natural resources. *European Journal of Political Economy*, *29*, 38–53. doi:10.1016/j.ejpoleco.2012.09.001

Alfaro, L., Chandab, A., Kalemli-Ozcanc, Ş., & Sayek, S. (2004). FDI and economic growth: The role of local financial markets. *Journal of International Economics*, *64*(1), 89112. doi:10.1016/S0022-1996(03)00081-3

Aliber, R. Z. (1970). A theory of direct foreign investment. In C. P. Kindleberger (Ed.), *The International Corporation*. Cambridge, MA: MIT Press.

Alon, T., Hale, G., & Santos, J. (2010). *What Is China's Capital Seeking in a Global Environment?* Retrieved September 30, 2016, from http://www.frbsf.org/economic-research/files/el2010-09.pdf

Al-sadiq, A. (2013). Outward Foreign Direct Investment and Domestic Investment: The Case of Developing Countries. *IMF Working Papers, 13*(52), 1. 10.5089/9781475517934.001

Amiti, M., & Konings, J. (2007). Trade libralization, intermediate inputs and productivity. *The American Economic Review*, *97*(5), 1611–1638. doi:10.1257/aer.97.5.1611

Amnesty International. (2016). *Niger Delta: Government clean-up does not let Shell off the hook*. Retrieved July 12, 2016 from https://www.amnesty.org/en/latest/news/2016/06/niger-delta-government-clean-up-does-not-let-shell-off-the-hook/

Anderson, A. R., Li, J. H., Harrison, R. T., & Robson, P. J. (2003). The increasing role of small business in the Chinese economy. *Journal of Small Business Management*, *41*(3), 310–316. doi:10.1111/1540-627X.00084

Andinuur, J. (2013). *Inflation, Foreign Direct Investment and Economic Growth in Ghana* (M.Phil. dissertation). Legon, Ghana: University of Ghana.

Andreff, W. (2015). Outward Foreign Direct Investment from BRIC countries: Comparing strategies of Brazilian, Russian, Indian and Chinese multinational companies. *The European Journal of Comparative Economics*, *12*(2), 79.

Andreff, W., & Balcet, G. (2013). Emerging countries' multinational companies investing in developed countries: At odds with the HOS paradigm? *The European Journal of Comparative Economics*, *10*(1), 3.

Antras, P. (2003). Trade, Contracts, and Trade Structure. *The Quarterly Journal of Economics*, *118*(4), 1375–1418. doi:10.1162/003355303322552829

Antras, P. (2005). Incomplete Contracts and the Product Cycle. *The American Economic Review*, *95*(4), 1054–1073. doi:10.1257/0002828054825600

Antras, P. (2013). Grossman-Hart (1986) Goes Global: Incomplete Contracts, Property Rights, and the International Organization of Production. *Journal of Law Economics and Organization*, *30*(1), 1–58.

Antras, P., Desai, M., & Foley, F. C. (2009). Multinational Firms, FDI Flows and Imperfect Capital Markets. *The Quarterly Journal of Economics*, *125*(3), 1171–1219. doi:10.1162/qjec.2009.124.3.1171

Antras, P., & Helpman, E. (2004). Global Sourcing. *Journal of Political Economy*, *112*(3), 552–580. doi:10.1086/383099

Antras, P., & Helpman, E. (2008). Contractual Frictions and Global Sourcing. In E. Helpman, T. Verdier, & D. Marin (Eds.), *The Organization of Firms in a Global Economy* (pp. 9–54). Harvard University Press. doi:10.4159/9780674038547-001

Anupam, M., Rani, S., & Kumar, D. (2014). FDI Outflows Trends and Patterns of Indian Companies. *International Journal of Research*, *1*(5), 119–126.

Arbatli, E. (2011). Economic Policies and FDI Inflows to Emerging Market Economies. *IMF Working Papers, 11*(192), 1. 10.5089/9781462306251.001

Arellano, M., & Bond, S. (1991). Some tests of specification for panel data: Monte Carlo evidence and an application to employment equations. *The Review of Economic Studies*, *58*(2), 277–297. doi:10.2307/2297968

Arellano, M., & Bover, O. (1995). Another look at the instrumental variable estimation of error-components models. *Journal of Econometrics*, *68*(1), 29–51. doi:10.1016/0304-4076(94)01642-D

Arnott, S. (2010). *China's Geely buys Volvo for $1.5bn*. Retrieved September 20, 2016, from http://www.independent.co.uk/news/business/news/chinas-geely-buys-volvo-for-15bn-2041772.html

Asiedu, E. (2002). On the determinants of foreign direct investment to developing countries: Is Africa different? *World Development*, *30*(1), 107–119. doi:10.1016/S0305-750X(01)00100-0

Asiedu, E., & Lien, D. (2011). Democracy, foreign direct investment and natural resources. *Journal of International Economics*, *84*(1), 99–111. doi:10.1016/j.jinteco.2010.12.001

Athanasoglou, P. P., Brissimis, S. N., & Delis, M. D. (2008). Bank-specific, industry-specific and macroeconomic determinants of bank profitability. *Journal of International Financial Markets, Institutions and Money*, *18*(2), 121–136. doi:10.1016/j.intfin.2006.07.001

Augustynowicz, P., & Kwiatkowski, G. (2013). Przedsiębiorstwa państwowe na liście Fortune Global 500 w latach 2005–2012. *Przegląd Zachodniopomorski*, *3*(1), 21–35.

AvtoVAZ. (2016). Retrieved September 26, 2016 from http://company.avtovaz.ru/en/

Aysan, A. F., Nabli, M. K., & Véganzonès-Varoudakis, M. A. (2006). Governance and private investment in the Middle East and North Africa. *World Bank Policy Research Working Paper*, (3934), 1-65.

Azim, T., & Uddin, N. (2001). Environment of foreign direct investment in Bangladesh: an empirical assessment.Bangladesh Institute of International and Strategic Studies (BIISS) Journal, 22(3), 285-306.

Azzimonti, M., & Sarte, P. G. (2007). Barriers to foreign direct investment under political instability. *Economic Quarterly*, *93*(3), 287–315.

Baek, J., & Kim, H. S. (2013). Is economic growth good or bad for the environment? Empirical evidence from Korea. *Energy Economics*, *36*, 744–749. doi:10.1016/j.eneco.2012.11.020

Bain, J. S. (1956). Advantages of the large firm: Production, distribution, and sales promotion. *Journal of Marketing*, *20*(4), 336–346. doi:10.2307/1248235

Banga, R. (2003). *Government Policies and FDI Inflows of Asian Developing Countries: Empirical Evidence*. Economic Reform in Developing Countries; doi:10.4337/9781781007655.00013

Baniak, R. (2015). *Deputy of the Ministry of State Treasury*. Retrieved from http://www.polskatimes.pl/artykul/3813841,polskie-firmy-coraz-chetniej-inwestuja,id,t.html

Bank of Russia Annual Report for 2014. (n.d.). Retrieved from http://www.cbr.ru/Eng/publ/God/ar_2014_e.pdf

Bannò, M., Piscitello, L., & Varum, C. A. (2014). The Impact of Public Support on SMEs Outward FDI: Evidence from Italy. *Journal of Small Business Management*, *52*(1), 22–38. doi:10.1111/jsbm.12029

Bano, S., & Tabbada, J. (2015). Foreign Direct Investment Outflows: Asian Developing Countries. *Journal of Economic Integration*, *30*(2), 359–398. doi:10.11130/jei.2015.30.2.359

Barney, J. B. (2001). Resource-based theories of competitive advantage: A ten-year retrospective on the resource-based view. *Journal of Management*, *27*(6), 643–650. doi:10.1177/014920630102700602

Bartel, A., Lach, S., & Sicherman, N. (2005). *Outsourcing and Technological Change (National Bureau of Economic Research No. 11158)*. Cambridge, MA: National Bureau of Economic Research. doi:10.3386/w11158

Bass, A. E., & Chakrabarty, S. (2014). Resource security: Competition for global resources, strategic intent, and governments as owners. *Journal of International Business Studies*, *45*(8), 961–979. doi:10.1057/jibs.2014.28

Behbehani, M., & Al Hallaq, S. S. (2013). Impact of home country outward foreign direct investment on its economic growth: A case of Kuwait. *Asian Journal of Business and Management Sciences*, *3*(3), 19–33.

Bellak, C., Leibrecht, M., & Stehrer, R. (2009). The role of public policy in closing foreign direct investment gaps: An empirical analysis. *Empirica*, *37*(1), 19–46. doi:10.1007/s10663-009-9107-6

Bellak, Ch. (1998). The measurement of foreign direct investment: A critical review. *The International Trade Journal*, *12*(2), 227–257. doi:10.1080/08853909808523905

Bellos, S., & Subasat, T. (2012). Governance and foreign direct investment: A panel gravity model approach. *International Review of Applied Economics*, *26*(3), 303–328. doi:10.1080/02692171.2011.587110

Bénassy-Quéré, A., Coupet, M., & Mayer, T. (2007). Institutional Determinants of Foreign Direct Investment. *The World Economy World Economy*, *30*(5), 764–782. doi:10.1111/j.1467-9701.2007.01022.x

Bernard, A. B., Eaton, J., Jensen, J. B., & Kortum, S. (2003). Plants and Productivity in International Trade. *The American Economic Review*, *93*(4), 1268–1290. doi:10.1257/000282803769206296

Bernard, H. R., & Ryan, G. W. (2009). *Analyzing Qualitative Data: Systematic Approaches*. SAGE Publications.

Bevan, A. A., & Estrin, S. (2000). *The Determinants of Foreign Direct Investment in Transition Economies*. University of Michigan William Davidson Institute DP 342.

Bevan, A. A., & Estrin, S. (2004). The determinants of foreign direct investment into European transition economies. *Journal of Comparative Economics*, *32*(4), 775–787. doi:10.1016/j.jce.2004.08.006

Beyer, C. (2008). *Violent globalisms: conflict in response to empire*. Ashgate Publishing, Ltd.

Bickenbach, F., Liu, W. H., & Li, G. (2015) The EU-China Bilateral Investment Agreement in Negotiation: Motivation, Conflicts and Perspectives. *Kiel Policy Brief*, 95. Retrieved June 17, 2016, from https://www.ifw-kiel.de/wirtschaftspolitik/zentrum-wirtschaftspolitik/kiel-policy-brief/kpb-2015/kiel-policy-brief-95

Birkinshaw, J., & Hood, N. (1998). Multinational subsidiary evolution: Capability and charter change in foreign-owned subsidiary companies. *Academy of Management Review*, *23*(4), 773–795.

Blomstrom, M. (2011). Foreign investment and productive efficiency: The case of Mexico. *The Journal of Industrial Economics*, *35*(1), 97–110. doi:10.2307/2098609

Blomström, M., & Kokko, A. (1998). Multinational corporations and spillovers. *Journal of Economic Surveys*, *12*(3), 247–277. doi:10.1111/1467-6419.00056

Blundell, R., & Bond, S. (1998). Initial conditions and moment restrictions in dynamic panel data models. *Journal of Econometrics*, *87*(1), 115–143. doi:10.1016/S0304-4076(98)00009-8

Blyschak, P. M. (2016). State-Owned Enterprises in International Investment. *ICSID Review*, *31*(1), 5–11. doi:10.1093/icsidreview/siv048

Boateng, A., Qian, W., & Tianle, Y. (2008). Cross-border M&As by Chinese firms: An analysis of strategic motives and performance. *Thunderbird International Business Review*, *50*(4), 259–270. doi:10.1002/tie.20203

Boisot, M., & Meyer, M. W. (2008). Which way through the open door? Reflections on the internationalization of Chinese firms. *Management and Organization Review*, *4*(3), 349–365. doi:10.1111/j.1740-8784.2008.00116.x

Boratav, K. (2009). *Türkiye İktisat Tarihi*. Ankara: İmge.

Borensztein, E., De-Gregorio, J., & Lee, J. W. (1995). *How does Foreign Direct Investment. affect economic growth?* NBER Working Paper Series No. 5057. National Bureau of Economic Research, Inc.

Borensztein, E., Gregorio, J. D., & Lee, J. W. (2008). How does foreign direct investment affect economic growth? *Journal of International Economics*, *45*(1), 115–135. doi:10.1016/S0022-1996(97)00033-0

Borga, M. (2016). Not all foreign direct investment is foreign: the extent of round-tripping. *Columbia FDI Perspectives*, *172*, 1-3.

Bose, T. K. (2012). Advantages and Disadvantages of FDI in China and India. *IBR International Business Research*, *5*(5). doi:10.5539/ibr.v5n5p164

Bowen, H. R. (1953). *Social responsibilities of the businessman*. New York: Harper & Row.

Bozkurt, I., & Akman, E. (2016). Financial Integration Into EU: The Romanian Case. *Amfiteatru Economic*, *18*(42), 269–285.

BP. (2016). *Corporate Social Responsibility*. Retrieved October 13, 2016 from http://www.bp.com/en_ru/russia/csr.html

Brecher, R., & Carlos, D. A. (2012). Tariffs, foreign capital and immiserizing growth. *Journal of International Economics*, *7*(1), 317–322.

Breitung, J. (2000). The Local Power of Some Unit Root Tests for Pane Data. In B. H. Baltagi (Ed.), *Nonstationary Panels, Panel Cointegration, and Dynamic Panels* (pp. 161–177). Amsterdam: Elsevier. doi:10.1016/S0731-9053(00)15006-6

Bremmer, I. (2010). *The End of The Free Market. Who Wins the War Between States and Corporations*. New York, NY: Portfolio.

Breusch, T. S., & Pagan, A. R. (1980). The Lagrange multiplier test and its applications to model specification in econometrics. *The Review of Economic Studies*, *47*(1), 239–253. doi:10.2307/2297111

Brown, M. B., & Forsythe, A. B. (1974). Robust tests for equality of variances. *Journal of the American Statistical Association*, *69*(346), 364–367. doi:10.1080/01621459.1974.10482955

Bruton, G., Peng, V., Ahlstrom, D., Stan, C., & Xu, K. (2015). State-owned enterprises around the world as hybrid organizations. *The Academy of Management Perspectives*, *29*(1), 92–114. doi:10.5465/amp.2013.0069

Bryman, A. (2004). Qualitative research on leadership: A critical but appreciative review. *The Leadership Quarterly*, *15*(6), 729–769. doi:10.1016/j.leaqua.2004.09.007

Buckley, P. J., & Casson, M. C. (1976). *The Future of the Multinational Enterprise*. London: Homes and Meier. doi:10.1007/978-1-349-02899-3

Buckley, P. J., & Casson, M. C. (1998). Models of the multinational enterprise. *Journal of International Business Studies*, *29*(1), 21–44. doi:10.1057/palgrave.jibs.8490023

Buckley, P. J., Clegg, J., & Wang, C. (2007). Is the relationship between inward FDI and spillover effects linear? An empirical examination of the case of China. *Journal of International Business Studies*, *38*(3), 447–459. doi:10.1057/palgrave.jibs.8400274

Buckley, P. J., Clegg, L. J., Cross, A. R., Liu, X., Voss, H., & Zheng, P. (2007). The Determinants of Chinese Outward Foreign Direct Investment. *Journal of International Business Studies*, *38*(4), 499–518. doi:10.1057/palgrave.jibs.8400277

Buczkowski, B., Kłysik-Uryszek, A., Kuna-Marszałek, A., & Świerkocki, J. (2015). *Poland,s Outward Foreign Direct Investment. Experiences of enterprises from the Łódź region*. Łódź: Łódź University Press.

Buczkowski, B., Kłysik-Uryszek, A., Kuna-Marszałek, A., & Świerkocki, J. (2015). *Poland's Outward Foreign Direct Investment. Experiences of enterprises from the Łódź region*. Łódź: Łódź University Press.

Büge, M., Egeland, M., Kowalski, P., & Sztajerowska, M. (2013). *State-owned enterprises in the global economy: Reason for concern?* Retrieved June 17, 2016, from http://www.voxeu.org/article/state-owned-enterprises-global-economy-reason-concern

Bukari, P. A. (2016). *Foreign direct investment: How beneficial is it?* Retrieved May 5, 2016 from http://www.dundee.ac.uk/cepmlp/gateway/files.php?file=cepmlp_car17_36_983684938.pdf

Burghart, N., & Rossi, V. (2009). *China's overseas direct investment in the UK*. Chatham House Programme Paper, 2009.

Bürgi-Schmelz, A., Kozlow, R., Kitili, A., van Wersch, M., & Joisce, J. (2010). *Recent Progress in Measuring FDI in the Wake of Globalization*. Paper Prepared for the 31st General Conference of The International Association for Research in Income and Wealth, St. Gallen, Switzerland.

Business & Human Rights Resource Centre. (2016). *Search Topics*. Retrieved July 12, 2016 from https://business-humanrights.org/en/search-topics

BusinessInfo. (2014). *Portugalsko: Základní podmínky pro uplatnění českého zboží na trhu*. Retrieved April 4, 2015, from http://www.businessinfo.cz/cs/clanky/portugalsko-zahranicni-obchod-zeme-19426.html

Büthe, T., & Millner, H. V. (2008). The Politics of Foreign Direct Investment into Developing Countries: Increasing FDI through International Trade Agreements? *American Journal of Political Science*, *52*(4), 741–762. doi:10.1111/j.1540-5907.2008.00340.x

Byus, K., Deis, D., & Ouyang, B. (2010). Doing well by doing good: Corporate social responsibility and profitability. *SAM Advanced Management Journal*, *75*(1), 44–55.

Cahen, F. R. (2014). Internationalization of state-owned enterprises through foreign direct investment. *Revista de Administração de Empresas*, *55*(6), 645–659. doi:10.1590/S0034-759020150604

Canton, N. (2013). *Will India Become Asia's Next Superpower?* Asia House. Retrieved from http://asiahouse.org/will-india-become-asias-next-superpower/

Cantwell, J. (1992). The Methodological Problems Raised by the Collection of Foreign Direct Investment Data. *Scandinavian International Business Review*, *1*(1), 86–102. doi:10.1016/0962-9262(92)90038-8

Capobianco, A., & Christiansen, H. (2011). Competitive Neutrality and State-Owned Enterprises: Challenges and Policy Options. *OECD Corporate Governance Working Papers*, 1. 10.1787/5kg9xfgjdhg6-en

Cardoza, G., & Fornes, G. (2011). The internationalisation of SMEs from China: The case of Ningxia Hui autonomous region. *Asia Pacific Journal of Management*, *28*(4), 737–759. doi:10.1007/s10490-009-9174-z

Carroll, A. B. (1991, July-August). The Pyramid of Corporate Social Responsibility: Toward the Moral Management of Organizational Stakeholders. *Business Horizons*.

Carroll, A. B. (2015). Corporate social responsibility: The centerpiece of competing and complementary frameworks. *Organizational Dynamics*, *44*(2), 87–96. doi:10.1016/j.orgdyn.2015.02.002

Carvalheira, A., & Moreira, A. C. (2016). Searching for opportunities and trust in internationalization markets. entrepreneurial perspective of a traditional industry SME. In L. C. Carvalho (Ed.), *Handbook of Research on Entrepreneurial Success and its Impact on Regional Development* (pp. 675–701). Hershey, PA: IGI Global. doi:10.4018/978-1-4666-9567-2.ch028

Caseiro, L. C. Z., & Masiero, G. (2014). OFDI Promotion Policy in Emerging Economies: The Brazilian and Chinese Strategies. *Critical Perspectives on International Business*, *10*(4), 237–255. doi:10.1108/cpoib-03-2014-0023

Caves, R. E. (2012). Multinational firms, competition and productivity in host country markets. *Economica*, *41*(1), 176–193.

Central Bank of the Republic of Turkey. (n.d.). *Türkiye Cumhuriyet Merkez Bankası*. Retrieved June 7, 2016, from http://www.tcmb.gov.tr/wps/wcm/connect/TCMB EN/TCMBEN/MainMenu/STATISTICS/Balance of Payments and Related Statistics/Balance ofPaymentsStatisticss/Data

Central Statistical Office of Poland. (2016). Retrieved from www.stat.gov.pl

Chandler, C. & Zainulbhai, A. (2013). *Reimagining India*. Reimagining India: Unlocking the Potential of Asia's Next Superpower.

Chandra, Y., Styles, C., & Wilkinson, I. (2009). The recognition of first time international entrepreneurial opportunities: Evidence from firms in knowledge-based industries. *International Marketing Review*, *26*(1), 30–61. doi:10.1108/02651330910933195

Chang, S. C. (2014). The determinants and motivations of Chinas outward foreign direct investment: A spatial gravity model approach. *Global Economic Review*, *43*(3), 244–268. doi:10.1080/1226508X.2014.930670

Chen, C. Determinants and motives of outward foreign direct investment from China's provincial firms. *Transnational Corporations*, *23*(1).

Chen, W., Dollar, D., & Tand, H. (2015). *Why is China investing in Africa? Evidence from the firm level*. Retrieved September 25, 2016 from http://www.hwtang.com/uploads/3/0/7/2/3072318/odi_chen_dollar_tang_abstract.pdf

Chenaf-Nicet, D., & Rougier, E. (2016). The effect of macroeconomic instability on FDI flows: A gravity estimation of the impact of regional integration in the case of Euro-Mediterranean agreements. *Inter Economics*, *145*, 66–91. doi:10.1016/j.inteco.2015.10.002

Chen, C. (2015). Determinants and motives of outward foreign direct investment from Chinas provincial firms. *Transnational Corporations*, *23*(1), 1–28. doi:10.18356/6ba5ab37-en

Chetty, S., & Holm, D. B. (2000). Internationalisation of small to medium-sized manufacturing firms: A network approach. *International Business Review*, *9*(1), 77–93. doi:10.1016/S0969-5931(99)00030-X

Cheung, Y.-L., Kong, D., Tan, W., & Wang, W. (2014). Being Good When Being International in an Emerging Economy: The Case of China. *Journal of Business Ethics*, *130*(4), 805–817. doi:10.1007/s10551-014-2268-7

Chikán, A. (2003). *Vállalatgazdaságtan*. Budapest: Aula Kiadó.

Child, J., & Rodrigues, S. B. (2005). The Internationalization of Chinese Firms: A Case for Theoretical Extension? *Management and Organization Review*, *1*(3), 381–410. doi:10.1111/j.1740-8784.2005.0020a.x

Child, J., & Tsai, T. (2005). The Dynamic Between Firms Environmental Strategies and Institutional Constraints in Emerging Economies: Evidence from China and Taiwan. *Journal of Management Studies*, *42*(1), 95–125. doi:10.1111/j.1467-6486.2005.00490.x

Child, J., & Tse, D. K. (2001). Chinas transition and its implications for international business. *Journal of International Business Studies*, *32*(1), 5–21. doi:10.1057/palgrave.jibs.8490935

Chilimoniuk, E., & Czarny, E. (2005). Otwieranie gospodarki polskiej w okresie transformacji systemowej. In E. Czarny (Ed.), *Gospodarka polska na przełomie wieków. Od A do Z* (pp. 153–188). Warsaw: NBP.

Chiu, S. C., & Sharfman, M. (2016). Corporate Social Irresponsibility and Executive Succession: An Empirical Examination. *Journal of Business Ethics*, *17*(February), 1–17.

Choi, I. (2001). Unit Root Tests for Panel Data. *Journal of International Money and Finance*, *20*(2), 249–272. doi:10.1016/S0261-5606(00)00048-6

Choudhury, P., & Khanna, T. (2014). Toward resource independence - Why state-owned entities become multinationals: An empirical study of Indias public R&D laboratories. *Journal of International Business Studies*, *45*(8), 943–960. doi:10.1057/jibs.2014.20

Christiansen, H. (2011), The Size and Composition of the SOE Sector in OECD Countries, *OECD Corporate Governance Working Papers*, 5. 10.1787/5kg54cwps0s3-en

Christiansen, H., & Kim, Y. (2014), State-Invested Enterprises in the Global Marketplace: Implications for a Level Playing Field. *OECD Corporate Governance Working Papers*, 14. 10.1787/5jz0xvfvl6nw-en

Church, J., & Ware, R. (2000). *Industrial Organization: A Strategic Approach*. New York: Irwin McGraw-Hill.

Ciesielska, D. (2014). Polish Foreign Direct Investments – trends, patterns and determinants. *The Macrotheme Review*, *3*(1), 214-229.

Cieślik, A. (2000). *Nowa teoria handlu zagranicznego w świetle badań empirycznych*. Warsaw: PWN.

Cieślik, A. (2005). *Geografia inwestycji zagranicznych, przyczyny i skutki lokalizacji spółek z udziałem kapitału zagranicznego w Polsce*. Warsaw: Wyd. UW.

Cieślik, A., Michałek, A., Michałek, J., & Mycielski, J. (2015). Determinants of export performance: Comparison of central European and Baltic firms. *Czech Journal of Economics and Finance*, *65*(3), 211–229.

Clegg, J., & Voss, H. (2012). *Chinese Overseas Direct Investment in the European Union*. Europe China Research and Advice Network London.

Clifton, J., Comín, F., & Díaz-Fuentes, D. (2011). From national monopoly to multinational corporation: How regulation shaped the road towards telecommunications internationalisation. *Business History*, *53*(5), 761–781. doi:10.1080/00076791.2011.599588

Coase, R. H. (1937). The Nature of the Firm. *Economica*, *4*(16), 386–405. doi:10.1111/j.1468-0335.1937.tb00002.x

Cohn, T. H. (2011). *Global Political Economy* (6th ed.). Pearson.

Consolidated version of the Treaty on the Functioning of the European Union (TFEU). (2010). *Official Journal of the European Union, 53*.

Consumer Lifestyles in Russia. (2016, January 13). Retrieved June 9, 2016, from Global Market Information Database (GMID by Euromonitor).

Contessi, S. (2009). Foreign direct investment, productivity, and country growth: an overview. *Federal Reserve Bank of St. Louis Review,* (91), 61-78

Cook, R. D., & Weisberg, S. (1983). Diagnostics for heteroscedasticity in regression. *Biometrika*, *70*(1), 1–10. doi:10.1093/biomet/70.1.1

Corruption Perceptions Index. (2015). Transparency International. Retrieved from http://www.transparency.org/cpi2015/results

Costinot, A., Oldenski, L., & Rauch, J. (2011). Adaptation and the Boundary of Multinational Firms. *The Review of Economics and Statistics*, *93*(1), 298–308. doi:10.1162/REST_a_00072

Countryeconomy.com. (2015). *Portugal*. Retrieved 12 April, 2015 from http://countryeconomy.com/countries/Portugal

Countryeconomy.com. (2016) *Czech Republic*. Retrieved 3 July, 2016 from http://countryeconomy.com/countries/czech-republic

Cravino, J., & Levchenko, A. (in press). Multinational firms and international business cycle transmission. *The Quarterly Journal of Economics*.

Cuervo-Cazurra, A., & Genc, M. (2008). Transforming disadvantages into advantages: developing-country MNEs in the least developed countries. *Journal of International Business Studies, 39*(6), 957-979.

Cuervo-Cazurra, A., Inkpen, A., Musacchio, A., & Ramaswamy, K. (2014). Governments as owners: State-owned multinational companies. *Journal of International Business Studies*, *45*(8), 919–942. doi:10.1057/jibs.2014.43

CzechInvest. (2013). *Transport Infrastructure*. Retrieved March 10, 2015, from http://www.czechinvest.org/data/files/fs-16-transport-infrastructure-80-en.pdf

CzechInvest. (2016) *Why Invest in the Czech Republic*. Retrieved 3 July, 2016 from http://www.czechinvest.org/en/why-invest-in-the-czech-republic

Czubek, H., & Molendowski, E. (2005). Zbliżanie się struktur wymiany handlowej krajów CEFTA z krajami UE. w okresie przygotowań do członkostwa. *Wspólnoty Europejskie*, *11*(168), 27–32.

Damijan, J., Kostevc, Č., & Rojec, M. (2014). Outward FDI and company performance in CEECs. *GRINCOH Working Paper Series Papers 2.08*, 1-24.

Das, K. C. (2013). Home country determinants of outward FDI from developing countries. *Margin: The Journal of Applied Economic Research*, *7*(1), 93–116.

Database on National Practices and Regulations with Respect to State Enterprises. (n.d.). Retrieved November 2015 from http://qdd.oecd.org/subject.aspx?Subject=8f22ef7d-b780-4570-a4b1-7e0cb3ad7e04

Dau, L. (2012). Pro-market reforms and developing country multinational corporations. *Global Strategy Journal*, *2*(3), 262–276. doi:10.1111/j.2042-5805.2012.01033.x

Demuijnck, G., & Fasterling, B. (2016). The Social License to Operate. *Journal of Business Ethics*, *136*(4), 675–685. doi:10.1007/s10551-015-2976-7

Deng, P. (2007). Investing for strategic resources and its rationale: The case of outward FDI from Chinese companies. *Business Horizons*, *50*(1), 71–81. doi:10.1016/j.bushor.2006.07.001

Deng, P. (2009). Why do Chinese firms tend to acquire strategic assets in international expansion? *Journal of World Business*, *44*(1), 74–84. doi:10.1016/j.jwb.2008.03.014

Deng, P. (2012). The Internationalization of Chinese Firms: A Critical Review and Future Research. *International Journal of Management Reviews*, *14*(4), 408–427. doi:10.1111/j.1468-2370.2011.00323.x

Denisia, V. (2010). Foreign direct investment theories: An overview of the main FDI theories. *European Journal of Interdisciplinary Studies*, *2*(2), 104–110.

Department of Commerce, Government of India. (2016). Retrieved 21 July 2016, from http://commerce.nic.in/trade/international_ta.asp?id=2&trade=i

Desai, M., Foley, F., & Hines, J., Jr. (2005). Foreign Direct Investment and the Domestic Capital Stock. *NBER Working Paper 11075*, from www.nber.org/papers/w11075

Dharwadkar, R., George, G., & Brandes, P. (2000). Privatization in emerging economies: An agency theory perspective. *Academy of Management Review*, *25*, 650–669.

Dickey, D. A., & Fuller, W. A. (1979). Distribution of the estimators for autoregressive time series with a unit root. *Journal of the American Statistical Association*, *74*(366a), 427–431.

DiMaggio, P. J., & Powell, W. (1991). The new institutionalism in organizational analysis. Chicago: University of Chicago Press.

Djankov, S., & Hoekman, B. (2000). Foreign Investment and Productivity Growth in Czech Enterprises. *The World Bank Economic Review*, *14*(1), 49–64. doi:10.1093/wber/14.1.49

DNA. (2016). *FDI inflows in India increases 40per cent in April-December 2015*. Retrieved from http://www.dnaindia.com/money/report-fdi-increases-40-in-april-december-2015-2183359

Dodd, E. M. Jr. (1932). For Whom Are Corporate Managers Trustees? *Harvard Law Review*, *45*(7), 1145–1163. doi:10.2307/1331697

Doing Business 2006. (2006). The World Bank.

Doing Business 2016. (2015). The World Bank.

Doing Business in the Russian Federation. (2016). Retrieved September 26, 2016 from http://www.doingbusiness.org/data/exploreeconomies/~/media/giawb/doing%20business/documents/profiles/country/RUS.pdf?ver=3

Doing Business. (2016). World Bank Group. Retrieved from http://www.doingbusiness.org/data/exploreeconomies/india/

Dorey, D. J. (2011). The Transparent Supply Chain: From Resistance to Implementation at Nike and Levi-Strauss. *Journal of Business Ethics*, *103*(4), 587–603. doi:10.1007/s10551-011-0882-1

Dorożyński, T., Świerkocki, J., & Urbaniak, W. (2015). Incentives for attracting FDI: The case of the Lodz Region. *Gospodarka Narodowa*, *1*(275), 147–169.

Drabek, Z., & Payne, W. (1999). *The impact of transparency on foreign direct investment*. Staff working paper, EAR 99–02. Geneva: World Trade Organisation.

Driscoll, J., & Kraay, A. C. (1998). Consistent covariance matrix estimation with spatially dependent data. *The Review of Economics and Statistics*, *80*(4), 549–560. doi:10.1162/003465398557825

Dunning, J. (1998). Location and the multinational enterprise: A neglected factor? *Journal of International Business Studies*, *29*(1), 45–66. doi:10.1057/palgrave.jibs.8490024

Dunning, J. (2009). Explaining Changing Patterns of International Production: In Defence of the Eclectic Theory. *Oxford Bulletin of Economics and Statistics*, *41*(4), 269–295. doi:10.1111/j.1468-0084.1979.mp41004003.x

Dunning, J. H. (1973). The determinants of international production. *Oxford Economic Papers*, *25*, 289–336.

Dunning, J. H. (1977). Trade, location of economic activity and the MNE: A search for an eclectic approach. In B. Ohlin, P. O. Hesselborn, & P. M. Wijkman (Eds.), *The international allocation of economic activity* (pp. 395–418). London: Macmillan. doi:10.1007/978-1-349-03196-2_38

Dunning, J. H. (1980). Toward an eclectic theory of international production: Some empirical tests. *Journal of International Business Studies*, *11*(1), 9–31. doi:10.1057/palgrave.jibs.8490593

Dunning, J. H. (1981). Explaining the International Direct Investment Position of Countries: Towards a dynamic and development approach. *Weltwirtschaftliches Archiv*, *117*(1), 30–64. doi:10.1007/BF02696577

Dunning, J. H. (1986). The Investment Development Cycle Revisited. *Weltwirtschaftliches Archiv*, *122*(4), 667–677. doi:10.1007/BF02707854

Dunning, J. H. (1988). The eclectic paradigm of international production: A restatement and some possible extensions. *Journal of International Business Studies*, *19*(1), 1–31. doi:10.1057/palgrave.jibs.8490372

Dunning, J. H. (1993). *Multinational Enterprises and the Global Economy*. Addison-Wesley Publishing.

Dunning, J. H. (1997). *Alliance Capitalism and Global Business*. London: Routledge.

Dunning, J. H. (2001). The eclectic (OLI) paradigm of international production: Past, present and future. *International Journal of the Economics of Business*, *8*(2), 173–190. doi:10.1080/13571510110051441

Dunning, J. H., & Narula, R. (1996). The Investment Development Path Revisited: Some emerging issues. In J. H. Dunning & R. Narula (Eds.), *Foreign Direct Investment and Governments: Catalysts for economic restructuring*. London: Routledge.

Durán, J. E. (1999). *Los determinantes de la ied en los países de américa latina y el caribe: su impacto sobre el comercio y la integración regional*. ECLAC, Mimeo.

Duran, J. J., & Ubeda, F. (2001). The Investment Development Path: A new empirical approach and some theoretical issues. *Transnational Corporations*, *10*(2), 1–34.

Duran, J. J., & Ubeda, F. (2005). The Investment Development Path of Newly Developed Countries. *International Journal of the Economics of Business*, *12*(1), 123–137. doi:10.1080/1357151042000323076

E&Y. (2015) *European Attractiveness Survey 2015*. Retrieved January 22, 2016 from http://www.ey.com/GL/en/Issues/Business-environment/ey-european-attractiveness-survey-2015

Economic Survey 2015-16: Services Sector remains the key driver of Economic Growth contributing almost 66.1per cent in 2015-16. (2016). Retrieved 13 July 2016, from http://pib.nic.in/newsite/PrintRelease.aspx?relid=136868

Edwards, S. (1990). *Capital flows, Foreign Direct Investment, and debt-equity swaps in developing countries*. NBER Working Paper Series No. 3497. National Bureau of Economic Research, Inc.

Eğilmez, M., & Kumcu, E. (2015). *Ekonomi Politikası: Teori ve Türkiye Uygulaması, 20. Baskı*. İstanbul: Remzi.

Eicker, F. (1967). Limit theorems for regressions with unequal and dependent errors. In *Proceedings of the Fifth Berkeley Symposium on Mathematical Statistics and Probability*, (vol. 1, pp. 59–82). Berkeley, CA: University of California Press.

Ellis, P. D. (2011). Social ties and international entrepreneurship: Opportunities and constraints affecting firm internationalization. *Journal of International Business Studies*, *42*(1), 99–127. doi:10.1057/jibs.2010.20

Éltető, A., Ferenčíková, S., Götz, M., Hlušková, T., Jankowska, B., Kříž, E., & Sass, M. (2015). Outward FDI Policies in Visegrad Countries. *IZ Policy Papers*, 16. Retrieved September 10, 2016, from: http://www.iz.poznan.pl/news/1179_pp_16.pdf

Employment, W., & Trends, S. O. (2015). (Rep.). Geneva: International Labour Office. Retrieved from http://www.ilo.org/wcmsp5/groups/public/@dgreports/@dcomm/@publ/documents/publication/wcms_337069.pdf

Engle, R. F., & Granger, C. W. (1987). Co-integration and error correction: Representation, estimation, and testing. *Econometrica*, *55*(2), 251–276. doi:10.2307/1913236

Epstein, E. M. (2007). The Good Company. Rhetoric or Reality? Corporate Social Responsibility and Business Ethics Redux. *American Business Law Journal*, *44*(2), 207–222. doi:10.1111/j.1744-1714.2007.00035.x

Erdilek, A. (2008). Internationalization of Turkish MNEs. *Journal of Management Development*, *27*(7), 744–760. doi:10.1108/02621710810883634

Erenburg, S. J. (1993). The real effects of public investment on private investment. *Applied Economics*, *25*(6), 831–837. doi:10.1080/00036849300000137

Ethier, W. (2012). National and international returns to scale in the model theory of international trade. *The American Economic Review*, *72*(1), 389–405.

Ethier, W. J. (1986). Multinational Firm. *The Quarterly Journal of Economics*, *101*(4), 805–833. doi:10.2307/1884179

Etzioni, A. (2008). *Security first: for a muscular, moral foreign policy*. Yale University Press.

European Commission. (2011). *A renewed EU strategy 2011-14 for Corporate Social Responsibility*. Brussels: European Commission.

European Commission. (2015). *Country Report Czech Republic 2015*. Brussels: European Commission.

EuroStat. (2014). *Share of Young Adults Having Completed Tertiary Education up to 37%*. Retrieved 19 April, 2015 from http://ec.europa.eu/eurostat/documents/2995521/5178598/3-11042014-AP-EN.PDF/4e01669e-2c2e-4c0e-a16b-487753183826?version=1.0

EuroStat. (2016a). *Population and Employment*. Retrieved 21 April, 2015 from http://appsso.eurostat.ec.europa.eu/nui/show.do?dataset=namq_10_pe&lang=en

EuroStat. (2016b). *Gross Domestic Product at Market Prices*. Retrieved 3 July, 2016 from http://ec.europa.eu/eurostat/tgm/refreshTableAction.do?tab=table&plugin=1&pcode=tec00001&language=en

EY. (2016). *Corporate misconduct. Individual consequences. 14th Global Fraud Survey*. London: EYGM Limited.

FDI inflows jump 53% in last two years, says Jaitley in Lok Sabha. (2016, July 29). Retrieved July 30, 2016, from http://www.firstpost.com/politics/fdi-inflows-jump-53-in-last-two-years-says-jaitley-in-lok-sabha-2922554.html

Federal State Statistics Service. (2016). Retrieved September 26, 2016 from http://www.gks.ru/wps/wcm/connect/rosstat_main/rosstat/en/main/

Ferencikova, S., & Hluskova, T. (2015). Internationalization of Central and Eastern European companies – theory and its implications in the Slovak IT sector. *Journal for East European Management Studies*, *20*(4), 415–434.

Fetscherin, M. (2010). The determinants and measurement of a country brand: The country brand strength index. *International Marketing Review*, *27*(4), 466–479. doi:10.1108/02651331011058617

Fingar, C. (2016, April 28). *India knocks China from top of FDI league table*. Retrieved July 30, 2016, from http://www.ft.com/cms/s/3/94351bda-0620-11e6-a70d-4e39ac32c284.html#axzz4FpRzwwK

Fink, M., Harms, R., & Kraus, S. (2008). Cooperative internationalization of SMEs: Self-commitment as a success factor for International Entrepreneurship. *European Management Journal*, *26*(6), 429–440. doi:10.1016/j.emj.2008.09.003

Flores-Macias, F., & Musacchio, A. (2009). The Return of State-Owned Enterprises. *Harvard International Review*. Retrieved June 17, 2016, from http://hir.harvard.edu/the-return-of-state-ownedGuillén-enterprises

Forbes, S. (2015). How Modi Can Make India A Global Superpower. *Forbes*. Retrieved from http://www.forbes.com/sites/steveforbes/2015/06/18/how-modi-can-make-india-a-global-superpower/#31bcb3173406

Foreign Direct Investment, India Brand Equity Foundation. (2016). Retrieved 25 July 2016, from http://www.ibef.org/economy/foreign-direct-investment.aspx

Foreign Direct Investment. (2016, June). Retrieved July 29, 2016, from http://www.ibef.org/economy/foreign-direct-investment.aspx

Frączyk, J. (2014). *Państwowe giganty tracą miliardy za granicą. Wszystko naszym kosztem*. Retrieved June 17, 2016, from http://finanse.wp.pl/kat,1033747

Frees, E. W. (2004). *Longitudinal and Panel Data: Analysis and Applications in the Social Sciences*. New York: Cambridge University Press.

FRH. (2011). *Freedom in the world database*. New York: Freedom House.

Friedman, M. (1970, September 13). The Social Responsibility of Business is to Increase its Profits. *The New York Times Magazine*.

Fujita, M. (1995). Small and medium-sized transnational corporations: Trends and patterns of foreign direct investment. *Small Business Economics*, *7*(3), 183–204. doi:10.1007/BF01135364

Fujita, M. (2008). A critical assessment of FDI data and policy implications. *Transnational Corporations*, *17*(2), 107–126.

Gangi, Y. A., & Abdulrazak, R. S. (2012). The impact of governance on FDI flows to African countries, World Journal of Entrepreneurship. *Management and Sustainable Development*, *8*, 162–169.

Garcia-Herrero, A., Xia, L., & Casanova, C. (2015). *China's Outbound Foreign Direct Investment: How much goes where after round-tripping and offshoring?* BBVA Research, Working Paper 15/17.

Garrahan, P., & Ritchie, J. (1999). *East Asian Direct Investment in Britain*. Psychology Press.

Garud, R., & Giuliani, A. P. (2013). A narrative perspective on entrepreneurial opportunities. *Academy of Management Review*, *38*(1), 157–160. doi:10.5465/amr.2012.0055

Geng, X. (2004). *Round-Tripping Foreign Direct Investment and the People's Republic of China*. ADB Institute Research Paper Series 58.

Geoghegan, S. (2014). *The Euro: Advantages and Disadvantages of a Single Currency*. Retrieved 15 April, 2015 from http://www.currencysolutions.co.uk/news/the-euro-advantages-and-disadvantages-of-a-single-currency.html

Gersovitz, M. (1988). Saving and Development. In H. Chenery & T. N. Srinivasan (Eds.), *Handbook of Development Economics*. Amsterdam: Elsevier.

Ghauri, P. N., & Grønhaug, K. (2005). *Research Methods in Business Studies: A Practical Guide*. London: Pearson Education.

Ghemawat, P., & Khanna, T. (1998). The nature of diversified business groups: A research design and two case studies. *The Journal of Industrial Economics*, *46*(1), 35–61. doi:10.1111/1467-6451.00060

Ghosh, I., & Chakrabarti, S. (2016). Inward and Outward Foreign Investments of the Asian Economies in Transition and India: Determinants of FDI and India's Prospects in CLMV. In V. Erokhin (Ed.), *Global Perspectives on Trade Integration and Economies in Transition* (pp. 212–237). Hershey, PA: IGI Global; doi:10.4018/978-1-5225-0451-1.ch011

Giardini, C., & Ceretti, E. (2005). Implementation of an On-line Supervision System for Scheduling and Controlling a Production Plant. In *AMST'05 Advanced Manufacturing Systems and Technology:Proceedings of the Seventh International Conference* (*vol. 486*, pp. 347-356). Vienna: Springer. doi:10.1007/3-211-38053-1_33

Gibb, A., & Li, J. (2003). Organizing for enterprise in China: What can we learn from the Chinese micro, small, and medium enterprise development experience. *Futures*, *35*(4), 403–421. doi:10.1016/S0016-3287(02)00089-7

Global Competitiveness Index. (2016). World Economic Forum. Retrieved from http://reports.weforum.org/global-competitiveness-report-2015-2016/competitiveness-rankings/

Global Enabling Trade Report. (2014). World Economic Forum. Retrieved from https://www.weforum.org/reports/global-enabling-trade-report-2014/

Globerman, S. (2012). *Canadian Outward Foreign Direct Investment and Its Implications for the Canadian Economy*. The Conference Board of Canada.

Globerman, S. (2012). Canadian Outward Foreign Direct Investment and Its Implications for the Canadian Economy. The Conference Board of Canada. Report. May.

Globerman, S., & Shapiro, D. M. (2008). Outward FDI and the economic performance of emerging markets. In K.P. Sauvant (Ed.), The Rise of Transnational Corporations from Emerging Markets. Threat or Opportunity? (pp. 229-271). Cheltenham, UK: Edward Elgar. doi:10.4337/9781848441460.00023

Globerman, S. (2011). Foreign direct investment and spillover efficiency benefits in Canadian manufacturing industries. *The Canadian Journal of Economics. Revue Canadienne dEconomique*, *12*(1), 42–56. doi:10.2307/134570

Globerman, S., & Shapiro, D. (2002). Global foreign direct investment flows: The role of governance infrastructure. *World Development*, *30*(11), 1899–1919. doi:10.1016/S0305-750X(02)00110-9

Globerman, S., Shapiro, D., & Tang, Y. (2006). Foreign direct investment in emerging and transition European countries. *International Finance Review*, *6*(6), 431–459. doi:10.1016/S1569-3767(05)06017-6

Główny Urząd Statystyczny. (2016). *Statistics Database.* Retrieved June 30, 2016, from www.stat.gov.pl

Goh, S. K., & Wong, K. N. (2011). Malaysias outward FDI: The effects of market size and government policy. *Journal of Policy Modeling*, *33*(3), 497–510. doi:10.1016/j.jpolmod.2010.12.008

Goldstein, M., & Lardy, N. R. (2005). *China's Role in the Revived Bretton Woods System: Case of Mistaken Identity (Peterson Institute for International Economics No. 05-2).* Washington, DC: Peterson Institute for International Economics.

Golejowska, A. (2008). *Bezpośrednie inwestycje zagraniczne a procesy restrukturyzacji gospodarki*. Gdańsk: Wydawnictwo Uniwersytetu Gdańskiego.

Gomułka, S. (2014). Transformacja gospodarczo-społeczna Polski 1989-2014 i współczesne wyzwania. *Nauka, 3*, 7-16.

Görg, H., & Greenaway, D. (2004). Much ado about nothing? Do domestic firms really benefit from foreign direct investment? *The World Bank Research Observer*, *19*(2), 171–197. doi:10.1093/wbro/lkh019

Gorynia, M., Nowak, J., Trąpczyński, P., & Wolniak, R. (2015). *The Investment Development Path of Poland: a Current Assessment*. Paper presented at the 41st Annual Conference of the European International Business Academy (EIBA), Rio de Janeiro.

Gorynia, M. (Ed.). (2005). *Strategie firm polskich wobec ekspansji inwestorów zagranicznych*. Warsaw: PWE.

Gorynia, M., Nowak, J., Trąpczyński, P., & Wolniak, R. (2014). The internationalization of Polish firms: Evidence from a qualitative study of FDI behaviour. In *Internationalization of Firms from Economies in Transition* (pp. 39–68). Cheltenham, UK: Edward Elgar. doi:10.4337/9781783474707.00009

Gorynia, M., Nowak, J., & Wolniak, R. (2009). Motives and Modes of FDI, Firm Characteristics and Performance: Case studies of Foreign Subsidiaries in Poland. In M. Gorynia (Ed.), *International Business in Transition* (pp. 239–268). Warsaw: Difin.

Gorynia, M., Nowak, J., & Wolniak, R. (2010). Foreign direct investment of Central and Eastern European countries, and the investment development path revisited. *Eastern Journal of European Studies*, *2*(1), 23–25.

Gorynia, M., Nowak, J., & Wolniak, R. (2010). Investment Development Paths of Central European Countries: A Comparative Analysis. *Argumenta Oeconomica*, *1*, 65–87.

Gorynia, M., & Trąpczyński, P. (2014). Determinanty efektywności zagranicznych inwestycji bezpośrednich. *Ekonomista*, *5*, 663–684.

Gorynia, M., & Trąpczyński, P. (2014). Determinanty efektywności zagranicznych inwestycji bezpośrednich. *Ekonomista*, *5*, 663–684.

Götz, M. (2014). *Polskie bezpośrednie inwestycje za granicą. Metodologia teorii ugruntowanej*. Poznań: Wydawnictwo Instytutu Zachodniego.

Götz, M., & Jankowska, B. (2016). Internationalization by State-owned Enterprises (SOEs) and Sovereign Wealth Funds (SWFs) after the 2008 Crisis. Looking for Generalizations. *International Journal of Management and Economics*, *50*(1), 63–81. doi:10.1515/ijme-2016-0012

Government of the Czech Republic. (2015). *What Economic Model Does the Czech Republic Need?* Retrieved March 15, 2015, from http://www.vlada.cz/en/evropske-zalezitosti/aktualne/eurocentrum-seminar-what-economic-model-does-the-czech-republic-need--125936

Granger, C. W., & Newbold, P. (1974). Spurious regressions in econometrics. *Journal of Econometrics*, *2*(2), 111–120. doi:10.1016/0304-4076(74)90034-7

Greene, W. H. (2012). *Econometric Analysis*. Upper Saddle River, NJ: Pearson Education.

Gregorová, L. (2005). Foreign Direct Investment Statistics in the Czech Republic. Description of system and methodology. Balance of Payments Division. Czech National Bank.

Gubbi, S. R., & Sular, S. A. (2015). *Why Do the Turkish Firms Invest in Mainland Europe? In Emerging Economies and Multinational Enterprises* (pp. 441–470). Emerald Group Publishing Limited. doi:10.1108/S1571-502720150000028019

Haddad, M., & Harrison, A. E. (2010). Are there positive spillovers from direct foreign investment? Evidence from panel data for Morocco. *Journal of Development Economics*, *42*(1), 51–74. doi:10.1016/0304-3878(93)90072-U

Hadri, K. (2000). Testing for Stationarity in Heterogeneous Panel Data. *The Econometrics Journal*, *3*(2), 148–161. doi:10.1111/1368-423X.00043

Hanousek, J., & Kočenda, E. (2014). Factors of trade in Europe. *Economic Systems, 38*(4), 518–535. doi:10.1016/j.ecosys.2014.06.001

Hanson, G. (2001). *Should Countries Promote Foreign Direct Investment?* G-24 Discussion Paper 9.

Hasegawa, H., & Noonha, C. (Eds.). (2014). *Asian Business and Management. Theory, Practice and Perspectives* (2nd ed.). London: Palgrave Macmillen.

Hausman, J. A. (1978). Specification tests in econometrics. *Econometrica, 46*(6), 1251–1271. doi:10.2307/1913827

Hausmann, R., & Fernandez-arias, E. (2000). *Foreign Direct Investment: good cholesterol?* Inter-American Development Bank Working Paper No. 417.

Hellman, J. S., Jones, G., & Kaufmann, D. (2002). *Far from home: Do foreign investors import higher standards of governance in transition economies?* Available at SSRN 386900

Helpman, E. (1984). A Simple Theory of International Trade with Multinational Corporations. *Journal of Political Economy, 92*(3), 451–471. doi:10.1086/261236

Helpman, E. (1985). Multinational Corporations and Trade Structure. *The Review of Economic Studies, 52*(3), 443–457. doi:10.2307/2297663

Helpman, E., Melitz, M. J., & Yeaple, S. R. (2004). Export Versus FDI with Heterogeneous Firms. *The American Economic Review, 94*(1), 300–316. doi:10.1257/000282804322970814

Henisz, W. (2000). The institutional environment for multinational investment. *Journal of Law Economics and Organization, 16*(2), 334–364. doi:10.1093/jleo/16.2.334

Hennart, J. F. (1982). *A theory of multinational enterprise*. University of Michigan Press.

Hennchen, E. (2015). Royal Dutch Shell in Nigeria: Where Do Responsibilities End? *Journal of Business Ethics, 129*(1), 1–25. doi:10.1007/s10551-014-2142-7

Herzer, D. (2012). How Does Foreign Direct Investment Really Affect Developing Countries Growth? *Review of International Economics, 20*(2), 396–414. doi:10.1111/j.1467-9396.2012.01029.x

He, X., Eden, L., & Hitt, M. A. (2015). The Renaissance of State-Owned Multinationals. *Thunderbird International Business Review, 58*(2), 117–129. doi:10.1002/tie.21711

Hill, C. W. L. (2012). International business: competing in the global market place. New York: McGraw-Hill Higher Education.

Hill, C. W., & Hult, G. T. (2017). *International Business: Competing in the Global Marketplace* (11th ed.). Irwin/McGraw-Hill.

Hill, H., & Jongwanich, J. (2014). Emerging East Asian Economies as Foreign Investors: An Analytical Survey. *The Singapore Economic Review, 59*(03), 1450019. doi:10.1142/S0217590814500192

Hochberg, N., Klick, J., & Reilly, E. (2015). What companies have learned from losing billions in emerging markets. *Harvard Business Review*. Available at https://hbr.org/2015/09/what-companies-have-learned-from-losing-billions-in-emerging-markets

Hofstede Centre. (2016a). *What about Czech Republic*? Retrieved April 23, 2016, from http://geert-hofstede.com/czech-republic.html

Hofstede Centre. (2016b). *What about Portugal*? Retrieved April 23, 2016, from http://geert-hofstede.com/portugal.html

Holmstrom, B. (1979). Moral hazard and observability. *The Bell Journal of Economics*, *10*(1), 74–91. doi:10.2307/3003320

Horaguchi, H., & Toyne, B. (1990). Setting the Record Straight: Hymer, Internationalization Theory and Transaction Cost Economics. *Journal of International Business Studies*, *21*(3), 487–494. doi:10.1057/palgrave.jibs.8490830

Horstmann, I., & Markusen, J. (1995). *Exploring New Markets: Direct Investment*. Contractual Relations and the Multinational Enterprise. doi:10.3386/w5029

Hoskisson, R., Eden, L., Lau, C., & Wright, M. (2000). Strategy in emerging economies. *Academy of Management Journal*, *43*(3), 249–267. 39

Hu, A., & Jefferson, G. (2002). FDI impact and spillover: Evidence from Chinas electronic and textile industries. *World Economy*, *25*(8), 1063–1076. doi:10.1111/1467-9701.00481

Huang, H., & Zhao, Z. (2016). The influence of political connection on corporate social responsibility - evidence from Listed private companies in China. *International Journal of Corporate Social Responsibility*, *1*(9), 1–19.

Huang, X., & Zhu, Y. (2016). *Managing Chinese Outward Foreign Direct Investment: From Entry Strategy to Sustainable Development in Australia*. London: Palgrave Macmillan UK. doi:10.1057/9781137394606

Huber, P. J. (1967). The behavior of maximum likelihood estimates under nonstandard conditions. In *Proceedings of the Fifth Berkeley Symposium on Mathematical Statistics and Probability* (vol. 1, pp. 221–233). Berkeley, CA: University of California Press.

Hufbauer, G. C., & Cimino-Isaacs, C. (2015). *What You Need to Know about the Trans-Pacific Partnership*. Retrieved July 05 2016, from https://piie.com/commentary/op-eds/what-you-need-know-about-trans-pacific-partnership

Human Rights Watch. (2016). *Make Rules on Rights Binding for Businesses. ILO Should Create Treaty to Protect Workers*. Retrieved July 12, 2016 from https://www.hrw.org/news/2016/05/30/make-rules-rights-binding-businesses

Hunter, R. J., & Ryan, L. V. (2005). A Transitional Analysis of the Polish Economy: After Fifteen Years, Still a Work in Progress. *Global Economy Journal*, *5*(2), 1–17. doi:10.2202/1524-5861.1061

Hurlin, C., & Dumitrescu, E. (2012). *Testing for Granger Non-causality in Heterogeneous Panels*. Retrieved from https://halshs.archives-ouvertes.fr/halshs-00224434/document

Hurlin, C., & Venet, B. (2001). *Granger Causality Tests in Panel Data Models with Fixed Coefficients*. Retrieved from http://basepub.dauphine.fr/bitstream/handle/123456789/6159/3F117993d01.pdf?sequence=1

Hymer, S. (1976). The International Operations of Nation Firms: A Study of Foreign Direct Investment. Cambridge, MA: MIT Press.

Hymer, S. H. (1960). *The International Operation of National Firms: A Study of Direct Investment* (Ph.D. dissertation). M.I.T.

Hymer, S. (1972). The Internationalization of Capital. *Journal of Economic Issues*, *6*(1), 91–111. doi:10.1080/00213624.1972.11503013

ICRG. (2011). *International country risk guide*. New York: PRS Group.

Ietto-Gillies, G. (2012). Transnational Corporations and International Production: Concepts, Theories and Effects (2nd ed.). London: Edward Elgar Publishing. Retrieved from http://www.e-elgar.com/shop/transnational-corporations-and-international-production?___website=uk_warehouse

IFC. (2015). *Doing Business Index 2015*. Retrieved from http://www.doingbusiness.org/reports/global-reports/doing-business-2015

IMD World Competitiveness Yearbook. (n.d.). Retrieved June 14, 2016, from http://www.imd.org/wcc/research-methodology/

IMF. (2004). *Indirect FDI Relationships and Alternatives to the Fully Consolidated System*. BOPCOM-04/32. IMF.

Im, K. S., Pesaran, M. H., & Shin, Y. (2003). Testing for Unit Roots in Heterogenous Panels. *Journal of Econometrics*, *115*(1), 53–74. doi:10.1016/S0304-4076(03)00092-7

India overtakes China as top FDI destination: Report. (2016, April 22). Retrieved July 30, 2016, from http://smartinvestor.business-standard.com/market/Marketnews-379712-Marketnewsdet-India_overtakes_China_as_top_FDI_destination_Report.htm#.V5uypmh97Dc

India pips US, China as No. 1 foreign direct investment destination. (2015, September 30). Retrieved July 30, 2016, from http://timesofindia.indiatimes.com/india/India-pips-US-China-as-No-1-foreign-direct-investment-destination/articleshowprint/49160838.cms?null

Industrial, C., & Performance, I. (2016). Delhi: Indiabudget.nic.in. Retrieved July 30, 2016, from http://indiabudget.nic.in/es2015-16/echapvol2-06.pdf

INE. (2005). *Anuário Estatístico De Portugal 2004*. Retrieved 20 March, 2015 from https://www.ine.pt/xportal/xmain?xpid=INE&xpgid=ine_destaques&DESTAQUESdest_boui=73471&DESTAQUESmodo=2

INE. (2008). *Estatísticas Do Comércio Internacional Junho De 2008*. Retrieved 20 March, 2015 from https://www.ine.pt/xportal/xmain?xpid=INE&xpgid=ine_destaques&DESTAQUESdest_boui=10938023&DESTAQUEStema=55448&DESTAQUESmodo=2

INE. (2014) *Estatísticas Da Globalização 2008-2013*. Retrieved 20 March, 2015 from https://www.ine.pt/xportal/xmain?xpid=INE&xpgid=ine_destaques&DESTAQUESdest_boui=209999963&DESTAQUESmodo=2

Inoue, C. F. K. V., Lazzarini, S. G., & Musacchio, A. (2013). Leviathan as a minority shareholder: Firm level performance implications of equity purchases by the government. *Academy of Management Journal*, *56*(6), 1775–1801. doi:10.5465/amj.2012.0406

International Labor Organization. (2015). *World Employement Social Outlook. The Changing Nature of Jobs*. Geneva: International Labour Office.

International Monetary Fund. (2010). FDI Flows to Low-Income Countries: Global Drivers and Growth Implications. *IMF Working Papers, 10*(132), 1. 10.5089/9781455201150.001

International Monetary Fund. (2016). *Corruption: Cost and Mitigating Strategies*. Washington, DC: International Monetary Fund.

International Telecommunication Union. (2014). *Measuring the Information Society Report 2014*. Geneva: International Telecommunication Union.

International Trade Union Confederation (2016). *Scandal Inside the Global Supply Chains of 50 Top Companies. Frontlines Report 2016*. Brussels: International Trade Union Confederation.

Investment Incentives. The good, the bad and the ugly. (2013). Background Paper for the Eight Columbia International Investment Conference. Vale Columbia Center On Sustainable International Investment, Columbia University.

Ioannou, I., & Serafeim, G. (2014). *The Consequences of Mandatory Corporate Sustainability Reporting: Evidence from Four Countries*. Harvard Business School, Working Paper, 11-100, August 20, 2014. Retrieved July 12, 2016 from http://www.hbs.edu/faculty/Publication%20Files/11-100_7f383b79-8dad-462d-90df-324e298acb49.pdf

Irzyński, R. (2014). *Duże inwestycje mogą oznaczać duże straty. PKN Orlen i Lotos coś o tym wiedzą*. Retrieved July 05, 2016, from http://www.polskieradio.pl/42/1701/Artykul/1273885,Duze-inwestycje-moga-oznaczac-duze-straty-PKN-Orlen-i-Lotos-cos-o-tym-wiedza

Is foreign direct investment (FDI) included in gross fixed capital formation? (n.d.). Retrieved July 29, 2016, from https://datahelpdesk.worldbank.org/knowledgebase/articles/195312-is-foreign-direct-investment-fdi-included-in-gro

Jain, S. (2006). *Emerging economies and the transformation of international business*. Cheltenham, UK: Edward Elgar. doi:10.4337/9781847202987

James, S. (2009). *Incentives and Investments: Evidence and Policy Implications*. ICAS of the World Bank Group.

Jansen, W. J., & Stokman, A. C. (2004). *International Business Cycle Comovement: Trade and Foreign Direct Investment*. SSRN Electronic Journal SSRN Journal. doi:10.2139/ssrn.1940278

Jarmołowicz, W., & Piątek, D. (2013). Polska transformacja gospodarcza. In S. Owsiak & A. Pollok (Eds.), *W poszukiwaniu nowego ładu ekonomicznego* (pp. 71–89). Warsaw: PTE.

Jaspersen, F., Aylward, A., & Knox, A. (2000) The effects of risk on private investment: Africa compared with other developing areas. In Investment and Risk in Africa. St. Martin's Press.

Jean, R.-J. B., Sinkovics, R. R., & Cavusgil, S. T. (2010). Enhancing international customer–supplier relationships through IT resources: A study of Taiwanese electronics suppliers. *Journal of International Business Studies*, *41*(7), 1218–1239. doi:10.1057/jibs.2010.4

Jensen, N. (2003). Democratic governance and multinational corporations: Political regimes and inflows of foreign direct investment. *International Organization*, *57*(03), 587–616. doi:10.1017/S0020818303573040

Johansen, S. (1988). Statistical analysis of cointegration vectors. *Journal of Economic Dynamics & Control*, *12*(2), 231–254. doi:10.1016/0165-1889(88)90041-3

Johansen, S. (1991). Estimation and hypothesis testing of cointegration vectors in Gaussian vector autoregressive models. *Econometrica*, *59*(6), 1551–1580. doi:10.2307/2938278

Johansen, S., & Juselius, K. (1990). Maximum likelihood estimation and inference on cointegration—with applications to the demand for money. *Oxford Bulletin of Economics and Statistics*, *52*(2), 169–210. doi:10.1111/j.1468-0084.1990.mp52002003.x

Johnson, A., & Dahlström, T. (2004). *Bureaucratic corruption, MNEs and FDI Mimeo*. Jönköping International Business School.

Julien, C., & Sohlberg, M. (2015). *An unprecedented step – commission releases TTIP negotiation proposal*. Retrieved June 17, 2016, from http://www.internationallawoffice.com/Newsletters/International-Trade/European-Union/King-Spalding-LLP/An-unprecedented-step-commission-releases-TTIP-negotiation-proposals

Kadir Has University (KAH), Foreign Economic Relations Board (DEIK), KPMG Turkey (KPMG-T), Vale Columbia Center on Sustainable International Investment (VCC). (2011). *Turkish MNEs steady on their course despite crisis, survey finds*. Author.

Kadir Has University (KAH), Foreign Economic Relations Board (DEIK), Vale Columbia Center on Sustainable International Investment (VCC). (2009). *Survey provides the first ever ranking of Turkish multinationals investing abroad*. Author.

Kadir Has University (KAH), Foreign Economic Relations Board (DEIK), Vale Columbia Center on Sustainable International Investment (VCC). (2014). *Turkish OFDI Continues to Grow*. Author.

Kaldor, N. (1980). Public or private enterprise – The issue to be considered. In W. J. Baumol (Ed.), *Public and private enterprises in a mixed economy* (pp. 1–12). New York: St. Martin's. doi:10.1007/978-1-349-16394-6_1

Kalotay, K. (2010). The future of Russian outward foreign direct investment and the eclectic paradigm: What changes after the crisis of 2008-2009? *Competitio (University of Debrecen), 9*(1), 31-54. Retrieved April 02, 2016, from http://ssrn.com/abstract=1702829

Kalotay, K., & Sulstarova, A. (2010). Modelling Russian outward FDI. *Journal of International Management, 2*(16), 131–142. doi:10.1016/j.intman.2010.03.004

KAMAZ. (2016). Retrieved August 28, 2016 from http://kamaz.ru/en/

Kang, Y., & Jiang, F. (2012). FDI location choice of Chinese multinationals in East and Southeast Asia: Traditional economic factors and institutional perspective. *Journal of World Business, 47*(1), 45–53. doi:10.1016/j.jwb.2010.10.019

Karaszewski, W., Jaworek, M., Kuzel, M., Szałucka, M., Szóstek, A., & Kuczmarska, M. (2013). *Aktywność inwestycyjna polskich przedsiębiorstw za granicą. Czynniki i skutki*. Warsaw: PWN.

Kaufman, D., Kraay, A., & Mastruzzi, M. (2011). The worldwide governance indicators: Methodology and analytical issues. *Hague Journal on the Rule of Law, 3*(2), 220–246. doi:10.1017/S1876404511200046

Kaufmann, D., Kraay, A., & Mastruzzi, M. (2009). *Governance matters VIII: Aggregate and individual governance indicators*. World Bank Policy Research Working Paper, 4978.

Kaufmann, D., Kraay, A., & Zoido-Lobaton, P. (1999a). Aggregating governance indicators, World Bank Policy Research Working Paper No. 2195. Washington, DC: World Bank. Available at http://www.worldbank.org/wbi/governance/wp-governance.html

Kaufmann, D., Kraay, A., & Zoido-Lobaton, P. (1999b). Governance matters, World Bank Policy Research Working Paper No. 2196. Washington, DC: World Bank. Available at http://www. worldbank.org/wbi/governance/pubs/govmatters.html

Kawase, T. (n.d.). *Trans-Pacific Partnership negotiations and rulemaking to regulate state-owned enterprises*. Retrieved July 05, 2016, from http://www.voxeu.org/article/trans-pacific-partnership-negotiations-and-rulemaking-regulate-state-owned-enterprises

Kaya, H. (2009). Unfavorable business environment and foreign direct investment activities of Turkish manufacturing firms. *Journal of BRSA Banking and Financial Markets, 3*(1), 101–118.

Kayam, S., & Hisarciklilar, M. (2009). *Determinants of Turkish FDI abroad*. Academic Press.

Kayam, S. S. (2009). Home market determinants of FDI outflows from developing and transition economies. *MPRA Paper, 16781*, 1–19.

Khadaroo, A. J., & Seetanah, B. (2007, November). Transport Infrastructure and FDI: Lessons from Sub Saharan African Economies. In *African Economic Conference (AEC)* (pp. 15-17). Academic Press.

Khanna, T., & Palepu, K. (2004). *Emerging giants: building world class companies from emerging markets*. Harvard Business School Working Papers.

Kindleberger, C. (1969). American business abroad. *The Int. Exec., 11*(2), 11–12. doi:10.1002/tie.5060110207

Kindleberger, C. P. (2002). Stephen Hymer and the Multinational Corporation. *Contributions to Political Economy, 21*(1), 5–7. doi:10.1093/cpe/21.1.5

Kirca, A. H., Hult, G. T. M., Roth, K., Cavusgil, S. T., Perryy, M. Z., Akdeniz, M. B., & White, R. C. et al. (2012). Firm-specific assets, multinationality, and firm performance: A meta-analytic review and theoretical integration. *Academy of Management Journal, 54*(1), 47–72. doi:10.5465/AMJ.2011.59215090

Klimek, A. (2015). Institutions and outward foreign direct investment. *International Journal of Management and Economics, 46*(1), 101–119. doi:10.1515/ijme-2015-0023

Kłysik-Uryszek, A. (2010). *Bezpośrednie inwestycje zagraniczne w gospodarce regionu. Teoria i praktyka*. Warsaw: CeDeWu.pl.

Kłysik-Uryszek, A. (2013a). Skala i kierunki polskich bezpośrednich inwestycji zagranicznych. *Journal of Management and Finance, 11*(1), 293–305.

Kłysik-Uryszek, A. (2013b). Zagraniczna ekspansja kapitałowa polskich przedsiębiorstw. *Journal of Management and Finance, 11*(2), 161–173.

Kłysik-Uryszek, A., & Kuna-Marszałek, A. (2015). Doświadczenia procesu internacjonalizacji przedsiębiorstw regionu łódzkiego. Próba weryfikacji modelu uppsalskiego. *Studia i Prace WNEiZ, 41*, 283–295. doi:10.18276/sip.2015.41/2-24

Knickerbocker, F. (1973, Spring). Oligopolistic reaction and multinational enterprise. *Thunderbird International Business Review, 15*(2), 7–9.

Knickerbocker, F. T. (1973). *Oligopolistic reaction and the multinational enterprise*. Cambridge, MA: Harvard University Press.

Knight, G. A., & Cavusgil, S. T. (2004). Innovation, organizational capabilities, and the born-global firm. *Journal of International Business Studies, 35*(2), 124–141. doi:10.1057/palgrave.jibs.8400071

Knoerich, J. (2012) *The development dimension of outward foreign direct investment*. The Third Copenhagen Conference on Emerging Multinationals: OFDI from Emerging Economies, 25-26 October 2012, Copenhagen Business School, Denmark.

Knutsen, C. H., Rygh, A., & Hveem, H. (2011). Does state ownership matter? Institutions effect on foreign direct investment revisited. *Business and Politics, 13*(1), 1–33. doi:10.2202/1469-3569.1314

Kohler, W., & Smolka, M. (2009). *Global Sourcing Decisions and Firm Productivity: Evidence from Spain* (CESifo No. 2903). Munich: CESifo.

Kokko, A. (2009). Technology, market characteristics and spillovers. *Journal of Development Economics, 43*(1), 279–293.

Kolstad, I., & Wiig, A. (2012). What determines Chinese outward FDI? *Journal of World Business, 47*(1), 26–34. doi:10.1016/j.jwb.2010.10.017

Konings, J. (2001). Effects of foreign direct investment on domestic firms. *Economics of Transition, 9*(3), 619–633. doi:10.1111/1468-0351.00091

Kostova, T., & Zaheer, S. (1999). Organizational legitimacy under conditions of complexity: The case of the multinational enterprise. *Academy of Management Review, 24*(1), 64–81.

Kowalski, P., Büge, M., & Sztajerowska, M. (2013). State-Owned Enterprises, Trade Effects and Policy Implications. *OECD Trade Policy Papers*, 147. Retrieved July 05, 2016, from http://www.oecd-ilibrary.org/trade/state-owned-enterprises_5k4869ckqk7l-en

Kozlow, R. (2011). Multinational enterprises, foreign direct investment and related income flows. In *The Impact of Globalization on National Accounts* (pp. 27–38). New York: United Nations Economic Commission for Europe.

KPMG. (2013). *The KPMG Survey of Corporate Responsibility Reporting 2013.* Retrieved July 12, 2016 from https://www.kpmg.com/Global/en/IssuesAndInsights/ArticlesPublications/corporate-responsibility/Documents/corporate-responsibility-reporting-survey-2013-exec-summary.pdf

KPMG. (2014). *Breaking Through - How Corporate Social Innovation Creates Business Opportunity.* Retrieved July 12, 2016 from http://www.kpmg.com/Ca/en/IssuesAndInsights/ArticlesPublications/Documents/5441-KPMG-Social-Innovation-Report-FY14-web-Final.pdf

Krist, B., & Benka, S. (2013). *On a Collision Course: State Owned Enterprises and Free Trade.* Retrieved July 05, 2016, from http://americastradepolicy.com/new/#.ViJR5dZga9Y

Kubíčková, L., & Procházková, L. (2014). Success evaluation of small and medium-sized enterprises in terms of their participation in the internationalization process. *Ekonomie a Management*, *17*(2), 131–145. doi:10.15240/tul/001/2014-2-010

Kueh, J. S. H., Puah, C. H., & Liew, K. S. (2010). *Selected macroeconomic determinants of foreign direct investment outflow of Singapore* (MPRA Working Paper No.25940). Munich: Munich Personal RePEc Archive.

Kueh, J.S.H., Puah, C.H. & Liew, K.S. (2010). *Selected Macroeconomic Determinants of Foreign Direct Investment Outflow of Singapore.* MPRA Paper No.25940.

Kurucz, E., Colbert, B., & Wheeler, D. (2008). The business case for corporate social responsibility. In A. Crane, A. McWilliams, D. Matten, J. Moon, & D. Siegel (Eds.), *The Oxford handbook of corporate social responsibility* (pp. 83–112). Oxford, UK: Oxford University Press.

Kwiatkowski, D., Phillips, P. C., Schmidt, P., & Shin, Y. (1992). Testing the null hypothesis of stationarity against the alternative of a unit root: How sure are we that economic time series have a unit root? *Journal of Econometrics*, *54*(1-3), 159–178. doi:10.1016/0304-4076(92)90104-Y

Kyrkilis, D., & Pantelidis, P. (2003). Macroeconomic determinants of outward foreign direct investment. *International Journal of Social Economics*, *30*(7), 827–836. doi:10.1108/03068290310478766

Kyvik, O., Saris, W., Bonet, E., & Felício, J. A. (2013). The internationalization of small firms: The relationship between the global mindset and firms internationalization behavior. *Journal of International Entrepreneurship*, *11*(2), 172–195. doi:10.1007/s10843-013-0105-1

La Porta, R., López de Silanes, F., & Shleifer, A. (1999). The quality of government. *Journal of Law Economics and Organization*, *15*(1), 222–279. doi:10.1093/jleo/15.1.222

La Porta, R., Lopez-de-Silanes, F., Shleifer, A., & Vishny, R. W. (1997). Legal determinants of external finance. *The Journal of Finance*, *52*(3), 1131–1150. doi:10.1111/j.1540-6261.1997.tb02727.x

Latorre, M. (2008). *Multinationals and Foreign Direct Investments: Main Theoretical Strands and Empirical Effects.* Madrid: Universidad Complutense de Madrid. Retrieved November 1, 2015, from http://estudiosestadisticos.ucm.es/data/cont/docs/12-2013-02-06-CT06_2008.pdf

Ledyaeva, S., Karhunen, P., & Whalley, J. (2013). *Foreign Investment Is Not Foreign: Round-Trip Versus Genuine Foreign Investment In Russia.* CEPII Working Paper 2013-05.

Lentner, C., Szegedi, K., & Tatay, T. (2015). Corporate Social Responsibility in the Banking Sector. *Public Finance Quarterly*, *2015*(1), 95–103.

Leszczyński, D. (2015). Przeobrażenia gospodarcze w Polsce w latach 1989-2016. *Refleksje*, *12*, 27–45.

Levene, H. (1960). Robust tests for equality of variances. In I. Olkin, S. G. Ghurye, W. Hoeffding, W. G. Madow, & H. B. Mann (Eds.), *Contributions to Probability and Statistics: Essays in Honor of Harold Hotelling* (pp. 278–292). Menlo Park, CA: Stanford University Press.

Levin, A., Lin, C., & Chu, C. J. (2002). Unit Root Tests In Panel Data: Asymptotic And Finite-Sample Properties. *Journal of Econometrics*, *108*(1), 1–24. doi:10.1016/S0304-4076(01)00098-7

Levinsohn, J., & Petrin, A. (2003). Estimating production functions using inputs to control for unobseravbles. *The Review of Economic Studies*, *70*(1), 317–341. doi:10.1111/1467-937X.00246

Li, D. (2015). *The compressed development of Chinese OFDI and its impact on Chinese government investment policies*. Retrieved July 12, 2016 from http://www.victoria.ac.nz/chinaresearchcentre/publications/papers/The-Compressed-Development-of-Chinese-OFDI.pdf

Lin, J. (2009). *Economic development and transition: Thought, strategy, and viability*. Cambridge, UK: Cambridge University Press. doi:10.1017/CBO9780511805622

Lin, X. (2010). State versus private MNCs from China: Initial conceptualizations. *International Marketing Review*, *27*(3), 366–380. doi:10.1108/02651331011048023

Li, P. P. (2007). Toward an integrated theory of multinational evolution: The evidence of Chinese multinational enterprises as latecomers. *Journal of International Management*, *13*(3), 296–318. doi:10.1016/j.intman.2007.05.004

Lipsey, R. (2000). *Interpreting Developed Countries' Foreign Direct Investment*. doi:10.3386/w7810

Lipsey, R. E. (2002). *Home and Host Country Effects of FDI*. NBER Working Paper 9293.

Li, S. (2005). Why a poor governance environment does not deter foreign direct investment: The case of China and its implications for investment protection. *Business Horizons*, *48*(4), 297–302. doi:10.1016/j.bushor.2004.06.002

Lisboa, A., Skarmeas, D., & Lages, C. (2011). Entrepreneurial orientation, exploitative and explorative capabilities, and performance outcomes in export markets: A resource-based approach. *Industrial Marketing Management*, *40*(8), 1274–1284. doi:10.1016/j.indmarman.2011.10.013

Lista polskich przedsiębiorstw i eksporterów. (2015). Retrieved 13 July, 2016, from http://www.rp.pl/rankingi/lista_2000

Liu, X., Xiao, W., & Huang, X. (2008). Bounded entrepreneurship and internationalisation of indigenous Chinese private-owned firms. *International Business Review*, *17*(4), 488–508. doi:10.1016/j.ibusrev.2008.02.014

London School of Economics. IDEAS. (2012). *India: The Next Superpower?* London: LSE IDEAS. Retrieved from http://www.lse.ac.uk/IDEAS/publications/reports/pdf/SR010/LSE%20IDEAS%20India%20Superpower.pdf

London, T., & Hart, S. (2004). Reinventing strategies for emerging markets: Beyond the transnational model. *Journal of International Business Studies*, *35*(5), 350–370. doi:10.1057/palgrave.jibs.8400099

Loree, D. W., & Guisinger, S. E. (1995). Policy and Non-Policy Determinants of U.S. Equity Foreign Direct Investment. *Journal of International Business Studies J Int Bus Stud*, *26*(2), 281–299. doi:10.1057/palgrave.jibs.8490174

Lunn, J. (1980). Determinants of US direct investment in the EEC: Further evidence. *European Economic Review*, *13*(1), 93–101. doi:10.1016/0014-2921(80)90048-3

Lunn, J. (1983). Determinants of US direct investment in the EEC: Revisited again. *European Economic Review*, *21*(3), 391–393. doi:10.1016/0014-2921(83)90099-5

Luo, Y., & Rui, H. (2009). An ambidexterity perspective toward multinational enterprises from emerging economies. *The Academy of Management Perspectives*, *23*(4), 49–70. doi:10.5465/AMP.2009.45590140

Luo, Y., & Tung, R. L. (2007). International expansion of emerging market enterprises: A springboard perspective. *Journal of International Business Studies*, *38*(4), 481–498. doi:10.1057/palgrave.jibs.8400275

Luo, Y., Xue, Q., & Han, B. (2010). How emerging market governments promote outward FDI: Experience from China. *Journal of World Business*, *45*(1), 68–79. doi:10.1016/j.jwb.2009.04.003

Lyons, B. R. (2005). *Incomplete Contracts Theory and Contracts between Firms: A Preliminary Empirical Study (City College Norwich No. 01-1)*. Norwich: City College Norwich.

MacKinnon, J. G., Haug, A., & Michelis, L. (1999). Numerical Distribution Functions of Likelihood Ratio Tests for Cointegration. *Journal of Applied Econometrics*, *14*(5), 563–577. doi:10.1002/(SICI)1099-1255(199909/10)14:5<563::AID-JAE530>3.0.CO;2-R

Maddala, G. S., & Wu, S. (1999). A Comparative Study of Unit Root Tests with Panel Data and a New Simple Test. *Oxford Bulletin of Economics and Statistics*, *61*(s1S1), 631–652. doi:10.1111/1468-0084.61.s1.13

Mahoney, J. T., & Pandian, J. R. (1992). The resource-based view within the conversation of strategic management. *Strategic Management Journal*, *13*(5), 363–380. doi:10.1002/smj.4250130505

Makino, S., Isobe, T., & Chan, C. M. (2004). Does country matter? *Strategic Management Journal*, *25*(10), 1027–1043. doi:10.1002/smj.412

Mamatzakis, E., & Remoundos, P. (2003). Determinants of Greek commercial banks, 1989- 2000. *Spoudai*, *53*(1), 84–94.

Marku, M. (2014). The Gravity Model on EU Countries – An Econometric Approach. *European Journal of Sustainable Development EJSD*, *3*(3), 149–158. doi:10.14207/ejsd.2014.v3n3p149

Markusen, J., & Venables, A. (2008). Multinational firms and the new trade theory. *Journal of International Economics*, *46*(2), 183-203.

Markusen, J., & Venables, A. (1999). Foreign direct investment as a catalyst for economic development. *European Economic Review*, *43*(2), 335–356. doi:10.1016/S0014-2921(98)00048-8

Mathews, J. A. (2006). Dragon multinationals: New players in 21st century globalization. *Asia Pacific Journal of Management*, *23*(1), 5–27. doi:10.1007/s10490-006-6113-0

Mazzolini, R. (1980). The international strategy of state-owned firms: An organizational process and politics perspective. *Strategic Management Journal*, *1*(2), 101–118. doi:10.1002/smj.4250010202

Melitz, M. J. (2003). The Impact of Trade on Intra-industry Reallocations and Aggregate Industry Productivity. *Econometrica*, *71*(6), 1695–1725. doi:10.1111/1468-0262.00467

Melitz, M. J., & Ottaviano, G. (2008). Market Size, Trade, and Productivity. *The Review of Economic Studies*, *75*(1), 295–316. doi:10.1111/j.1467-937X.2007.00463.x

Mélypataki, G. & Szegedi, K. (in press). A vállalati társadalmi felelősségvállalás (CSR) és a jog kapcsolata. *Miskolci Jogi Szemle*. XI. évfolyam 2016 1. szám.

Meyer, K. E., Estrin, S., Bhaumik, S. K., & Peng, M. W. (2009). Institutions, resources, and entry strategies in emerging economies. *Strategic Management Journal*, *30*(1), 61–80. doi:10.1002/smj.720

Meyer, K. E., & Nguyen, H. V. (2005). Foreign Investment Strategies and Sub-national Institutions in Emerging Markets: Evidence from Vietnam. *Journal of Management Studies*, *42*(1), 63–93. doi:10.1111/j.1467-6486.2005.00489.x

Meyer, K. E., & Peng, M. W. (2005). Probing theoretically into Central and Eastern Europe: Transactions, resources, and institutions. *Journal of International Business Studies*, *36*(6), 600–621. doi:10.1057/palgrave.jibs.8400167

Michałek, J. J., Brzozowski, M., & Cieślik, A. (Eds.). (2012). *Wpływ Rozwoju Społecznego na Handel i Inwestycje Zagraniczne*. Warsaw: PWE.

Mickiewicz, T. (2005). *Economic Transition in Central Europe and the Commonwealth of Independent States*. Palgrave MacMillan. doi:10.1057/9780230504349

Mıhcı, H., Çağatay, S., & Koska, O. A. (2011). The determinants of foreign direct investment outflows from the European Union countries.''. *Economic Bulletin*, *31*(3), 2653–2666.

Ministério dos Negócios, E. (2012). *Portugal na República Checa*. Prague. Retrieved 19 April, 2015 from http://www.embportugal.cz/pt/portugal-na-republica-checa.html

Ministry of Foreign Affairs. (2001). *Report on the Foreign Policy of the Czech Republic Jan- Dec 2000*. Prague: Decibel Production.

Ministry of Foreign Affairs. (2002). *Report on the Foreign Policy of the Czech Republic Jan-Dec 2001*. Prague: Decibel Production.

Ministry of Foreign Affairs. (2003). *Report on the Foreign Policy of the Czech Republic Jan-Dec 2002*. Prague: Decibel Production.

Ministry of Foreign Affairs. (2004). *Report on the Foreign Policy of the Czech Republic Jan-Dec 2003*. Prague: Decibel Production.

Ministry of Foreign Affairs. (2006). *Report on the Foreign Policy of the Czech Republic Jan-Dec 2005*. Prague: Decibel Production.

Ministry of Foreign Affairs. (2007). *Report on the Foreign Policy of the Czech Republic Jan-Dec 2006*. Prague: Decibel Production.

Ministry of Foreign Affairs. (2008). *Report on the Foreign Policy of the Czech Republic Jan-Dec 2007*. Prague: Decibel Production.

Ministry of Foreign Affairs. (2009). *Report on the Foreign Policy of the Czech Republic Jan-Dec 2008*. Prague: Decibel Production.

Ministry of Foreign Affairs. (2010). *Report on the Foreign Policy of the Czech Republic Jan-Dec 2009*. Prague: Decibel Production.

Ministry of Foreign Affairs. (2011). *Report on the Foreign Policy of the Czech Republic Jan-Dec 2010*. Prague: Decibel Production.

Mint, L. (2016). *FDI inflows rise 40per cent on Make in India initiative: Economic Survey*. Retrieved from http://www.livemint.com/Politics/sYFaCzUi4paE9UCajwYjuO/FDI-inflows-rise-40-on-Make-in-India-initiative-Economic-S.html

Moini, H., Kalouda, K., & Tesar, G. (2008). Foreign market entry: The case of SMEs in the Czech republic. *Journal of East-West Business*, *14*(1), 41–65. doi:10.1300/J097v14n01_03

MOL Group. (2016). *About MOL Group*. Retrieved October 13, 2016 from https://molgroup.info/en/about-mol-group

Mora, N., Sahay, R., Zettelmeyer, J., & Garibaldi, P. (2002). What Moves Capital to Transition Economies? *IMF Working Papers, 2*(64), 1. doi:10.5089/9781451848571.001

Moran, T. H., Graham, E. M., & Blomström, M. (Eds.). (2005). *Does Foreign Direct Investment Promote Development?* Washington, DC: Institute for International Economics.

Moreira, A. C. (2008). Upstream linkages between TNCs and local suppliers: Evidences from Portugal. *World Review of Science. Technology and Sustainable Development*, *5*(1), 28–48.

Moreira, A. C., & Alves, C. (2016). Commitment-Trust dynamics in the internationalization process: a case study of market entry in the Brazilian market. In M. Garita & J. Godinez (Eds.), *Business Development Opportunities and Market Entry Challenges in Latin America* (pp. 224–255). Hershey, PA: IGI Global. doi:10.4018/978-1-4666-8820-9.ch011

Moreira, A. C., & Dias, A. A. (2008). O investimento directo do estrangeiro em Portugal. Uma perspectiva histórica. *Global Economics and Management Review*, *13*(1), 23–42.

Moskalev, S. (2007). *Governance and foreign direct investment.* Available at SSRN 959905

Moulton, B. R. (2010). An illustration of a pitfall in estimating the effects of aggregate variables on micro units. *The Review of Economics and Statistics*, *72*(2), 334–338. doi:10.2307/2109724

Mrázek, J. (2015). Inflation in the Czech Republic and European Union between 2000-2014. Paper presented at the Tiksová Conference, Prague, Czech Republic.

Musacchio, A., Lazzarni, S. G., & Aguilera, R. V. (2015). New varieties of state capitalism: Strategic and governance implications. *The Academy of Management Perspectives*, *29*(1), 115–131. doi:10.5465/amp.2013.0094

Musteen, M., & Datta, D. K. (2011). Learning about foreign markets: A study of Czech SMEs. *Journal of International Entrepreneurship*, *9*(2), 91–109. doi:10.1007/s10843-010-0067-5

Narula, R. (1996). *Multinational Investment and Economic Structure: Globalisation and Competitiveness*. London: Routledge.

National Framework. (2016). *United Nations Conference on Trade and Development (UNCTAD)*. Retrieved June 9, 2016, from http://unctad.org/en/Pages/DIAE/National-Framework.aspx

Navaretti, G. B., Venables, A., & Barry, F. (2004). *Multinational Firms in the World Economy*. Princeton, NJ: Princeton University Press.

Nayyar, D. (2008). The internationalization of firms from India: Investment, mergers and acquisitions. *Oxford Development Studies*, *36*(1), 111–131. doi:10.1080/13600810701848219

Newey, W. K., & West, K. D. (1987). A Simple, Positive Semi-Definite, Heteroskedasticity and Autocorrelation Consistent Covariance Matrix. *Econometrica*, *55*(3), 703–708. doi:10.2307/1913610

Newey, W. K., & West, K. D. (1994). Automatic Lag Selection in Covariance Matrix Estimation. *The Review of Economic Studies*, *61*(4), 631–653. doi:10.2307/2297912

Nielsen, B. B., & Nielsen, S. (2010). A multilevel approach to understanding the multinationality–performance relationship. *Advances in International Management*, *23*, 527–557. doi:10.1108/S1571-5027(2010)00000230028

Nölke, A. (2015). *State permeated capitalism in large emerging markets*. Key note presentation at SVoC conference, Central Eastern Europe University, Budapest, Hungary.

Nölke, A., & Vliegenthart, A. (2009). Enlarging the Varieties of Capitalism: The Emergence of Dependent Market Economies in East Central Europe. *World Politics*, *61*(04), 670–702. doi:10.1017/S0043887109990098

Noreng, O. (1994). National oil companies and their government owners: The politics of interaction and control. *Journal of the Energy Division*, *19*(2), 197–226.

North, D. C. (1990). *Institutions, institutional change and economic performance*. Cambridge University Press. doi:10.1017/CBO9780511808678

Nourbakhshian, M. R., Aghapour, A. H., & Gheshmi, R. (2012). The contribution of foreign direct investment into home country's development. *International Journal of Business and Social Science*, *3*(2), 275–287.

Nowiński, W. (2015). *Effects of Cross-Border Acquisitions by Polish MNEs*. Paper presented at the Conference of Academy of International Business Central and Eastern Europe Chapter (AIB-CEE Chapter) and Institute of Management.

Obłój, K., & Wąsowska, A. (2012). Strategiczne wybory polskich firm – motywy i kierunki budowania powiązań zewnętrznych drogą kapitałowego umiędzynarodowienia działalności. In W. Morawski (Ed.), *Powiązania zewnętrzne. Modernizacja Polski* (pp. 102–120). Warszawa: Wolters Kluwer.

OECD Business Survey 2014 on State Influence on Competition in International Markets. (n.d.). Retrieved 05 July 2016, from http://www.oecd.org/tad/tradedev/oecd-business-survey-state-influence-competition-international-markets.htm

OECD. (1999). *OECD Benchmark Definition of Foreign Direct Investment* (3rd ed.). OECD.

OECD. (2003). *Checklist for Foreign Direct Investment Incentive Policies*. Paris: OECD.

OECD. (2003). Foreign Direct Investment for Development: Maximising Benefits, Minimising Costs. *Attracting International Investment for Development OECD Global Forum on International Investment*, 55-90. doi:10.1787/9789264101944-5-en

OECD. (2004). *Comparative Report on Corporate Governance of State-Owned Enterprises*. Paris: OECD Publishing.

OECD. (2005). *Podręcznik wskaźników globalizacji ekonomicznej*. OECD.

OECD. (2008). *Benchmark Definition of Foreign Direct Investment* (4th ed.). Retrieved from https://www.oecd.org/daf/inv/investmentstatisticsandanalysis/40193734.pdf

OECD. (2012). *Competitive Neutrality: Maintaining a Level Playing Field Between Public and Private Business*. Paris: OECD Publishing.

OECD. (2013). *FDI Regulatory Restrictiveness Index*. Retrieved from http://www.oecd.org/investment/fdiindex.htm

OECD. (2013). *International Investments by SOEs: Economic Trends and the Policy Landscape*. Unpublished OECD document, DAF/INV/WD(2013)14.

OECD. (2014). *The Size and Sectoral Distribution of SOEs in OECD and Partner Countries*. Paris: OECD Publishing.

OECD. (2015a). *OECD Factbook 2015-2016 Economic, Environmental and Social Statistics*. Paris: OECD Publishing.

OECD. (2015b). *OECD Foreign Bribery Report: An Analysis of the Crime of Bribery of a Foreign Official*. Paris: Holman Fenwick Willan LLP.

Onder, G., & Karal, Z. (2013). Determinants of Foreign Direct Investments Outflow From a Developing Country: The Case of Turkey.*Business. Management in Education, 11*(2), 241.

Oviatt, B. M., & McDougall, P. P. (1994). Toward a theory of international new ventures. *Journal of International Business Studies, 25*(1), 45–64. doi:10.1057/palgrave.jibs.8490193

Oviatt, B. M., & McDougall, P. P. (2005). Defining international entrepreneurship and modeling the speed of internationalization. *Entrepreneurship Theory and Practice, 29*(5), 537–554. doi:10.1111/j.1540-6520.2005.00097.x

Pagano, M., & Volpin, P. F. (n.d.). Securitization, Transparency and Liquidity. *SSRN Electronic Journal SSRN Journal*. doi:10.2139/ssrn.1337898

Panopoulou, E., & Pittis, N. (2004). A comparison of autoregressive distributed lag and dynamic OLS cointegration estimators in the case of a serially correlated cointegration error. *The Econometrics Journal, 7*(2), 585–617. doi:10.1111/j.1368-423X.2004.00145.x

Pargendler, M., Musacchio, A., & Lazzarini, S. G. (2013). In strange company: The puzzle of private investment in state-controlled firms. *Cornell International Law Journal, 46*(3), 569–610.

Pedroni, P. (1999). Critical Values for Cointegration Tests in Heterogeneous Panels with Multiple Regressors. *Oxford Bulletin of Economics and Statistics*.

Pedroni, P. (2004). Panel Cointegration: Asymptotic and Finite Sample Properties of Pooled Time Series Tests with an Application to the PPP Hypothesis. *Econometric Theory, 20*(03), 597–625. doi:10.1017/S0266466604203073

Peiris, I. K., Akoorie, M. E., & Sinha, P. (2012). International entrepreneurship: A critical analysis of studies in the past two decades and future directions for research. *Journal of International Entrepreneurship, 10*(4), 279–324. doi:10.1007/s10843-012-0096-3

Peng, M. W. (2003). Institutional transitions and strategic choices. *Academy of Management Review, 28*(2), 275–296.

Peng, M. W. (2005). Perspectives - from China strategy to global strategy. *Asia Pacific Journal of Management, 22*(2), 123–141. doi:10.1007/s10490-005-1251-3

Peng, M. W., & Luo, Y. (2000). Managerial ties and firm performance in a transition economy: The nature of a micro-macro link. *Academy of Management Journal, 43*(3), 486–501. doi:10.2307/1556406

Peng, M. W., Wang, D. Y. L., & Jiang, Y. (2008). An institution-based view of international business strategy: A focus on emerging economies. *Journal of International Business Studies, 39*(5), 920–936. doi:10.1057/palgrave.jibs.8400377

Penrose, E. (1994). Multinational Enterprises and the Global Economy. By John H. Dunning. *Business History Review, 68*(03), 437–438. doi:10.2307/3117185

Penrose, E. T. (1959). *The theory of the growth of the firm*. Oxford, UK: Oxford University Press.

Pesaran, M. H., & Shin, Y. (1999). An Autoregressive Distributed Lag Modelling Approach to Cointegration Analysis. In S. Strom (Ed.), *Econometrics and Economic Theory in 20th Century: The Ragnar Frisch Centennial Symposium*. Cambridge, UK: Cambridge University. doi:10.1017/CCOL521633230.011

Pesaran, M. H., Shin, Y., & Smith, R. J. (1999). *Bounds Testing Approaches to the Analysis of Long-run Relationships*. Cambridge Working Papers in Economics. No. 9907. University of Cambridge.

Pesaran, M. H., Shin, Y., & Smith, R. J. (2001). Bounds testing approaches to the analysis of level relationships. *Journal of Applied Econometrics, 16*(3), 289–326. doi:10.1002/jae.616

Pesaran, M. H., Shin, Y., & Smith, R. P. (1999). Pooled mean group estimation of dynamic heterogeneous panels. *Journal of the American Statistical Association, 94*(446), 621–634. doi:10.1080/01621459.1999.10474156

Petrovic, B., & Solingen, E. (2005). Europeanisation and Internationalisation: The Case of the Czech Republic. *New Political Economy, 10*(3), 281–303. doi:10.1080/13563460500203391

Pettinger, T. (2013). *Effect of the Exchange Rate on Business*. Retrieved April 7, 2015, from http:// www.economicshelp.org/blog/9328/business/effect-exchange-rate-business

Phillips, P. C., & Perron, P. (1988). Testing for a unit root in time series regression. *Biometrika, 75*(2), 335–346. doi:10.1093/biomet/75.2.335

Piątkowski, M. (2013). Poland's new golden age: shifting from Europe's periphery to its center. *The World Bank Working Papers. Policy Research Working Paper 6639*, 1-36.

Piskalski, G. (2015): Corporate Social Responsibility in the Polish Reality. Theory and Practice. Warsaw: CentrumCSR.PL Foundation

Podda, P. A. (2016). The impact of Institutional Distance on FDI inflows in the Czech Republic. *Acta Oeconomica Pragensia, 2016*(1), 3-14. doi:10.18267/j.aop.495

Poland's 10 years in the European Union. (2014). Warsaw: Ministry of Foreign Affairs.

Potencjał innowacyjny gospodarki: uwarunkowania, determinanty, perspektywy. (2016). Warsaw: NBP.

Pradhan, J. P. (2008). The evolution of Indian outward foreign direct investment: Changing trends and patterns. *International Journal of Technology and Globalisation, 4*(1), 70–86. doi:10.1504/IJTG.2008.016188

Pradhan, J. P. (2011). Emerging multinationals: A comparison of Chinese and Indian outward foreign direct investment. *Institutions, Etc., 3*(1), 113–148.

Publica, P. (2008). *The World Wide Web of Siemens's Corruption*. Retrieved July 12, 2016 from https://www.propublica.org/special/the-world-wide-web-of-siemenss-corruption

PWC. (2015*). State-owned enterprises: Catalysts for public value creation?* PWC Report. Retrieved July 05, 2016, from https://www.pwc.com/gx/en/psrc/publications/assets/pwc-state-owned-enterprise-psrc.pdf

Ramasamy, B., Yeung, M., & Laforet, S. (2012). Chinas outward foreign direct investment: Location choice and firm ownership. *Journal of World Business, 47*(1), 17–25. doi:10.1016/j.jwb.2010.10.016

Rangan, V. K., Chase, L., & Karim, S. (2015). The Truth About CSR. *Harvard Business Review*, (January–February): 40–49.

Ranjan, V., & Agrawal, G. (2011). FDI Inflow Determinants in BRIC countries: A Panel Data Analysis. *IBR International Business Research, 4*(4). doi:10.5539/ibr.v4n4p255

Razin, A., & Sadka, E. (2007). *Foreign Direct Investment*. Princeton, NJ: Princeton University Press.

Rebelo, R. (2015). *Em 2015, a Škoda quer crescer 50% em Portugal*. Retrieved 20 April, 2015 from http://www.fleet-magazine.pt/2015/01/29/skoda-vendas-frotas/

Rehman, C. A., Ilyas, M., Alam, H. M., & Akram, M. (2011). The Impact of Infrastructure on Foreign Direct Investment: The Case of Pakistan. *IJBM International Journal of Business and Management, 6*(5). doi:10.5539/ijbm.v6n5p268

Resmini, L. (2000). The determinants of foreign direct investment in the CEECs: New evidence from sectoral patterns. *Economics of Transition, 8*(3), 665–689. doi:10.1111/1468-0351.00060

Ribau, C. P., Moreira, A. C., & Raposo, M. (2015). Internationalisation of the firm theories: A schematic synthesis. *International Journal of Business and Globalisation*, *15*(4), 528–554. doi:10.1504/IJBG.2015.072535

Rogers, W. H. (1993). sg17: Regression standard errors in clustered samples. Stata Technical Bulletin, 13, 19-23.

Roguski, A., & Furman, T. (2013). *Zagraniczne przejęcia to domena spółek surowcowych*. Retrieved July 05, 2016, from http://www.rp.pl/artykul/1070528-Zagraniczne-przejecia-to-domena-spolek-surowcowych.html

Roodman, D. (2009). How to do xtabond2: An introduction to difference and system GMM in Stata. *The Stata Journal*, *9*(1), 86–136.

Rose-Ackerman, S., & Tobin, J. (2003). *Foreign Direct Investment and the Business Environment in Developing Countries: The Impact of Bilateral Investment Treaties*. SSRN Electronic Journal SSRN Journal. doi:10.2139/ssrn.557121

Roslan, F. N. (2013). *A Study on the Dynamic Relationship between Inflation, Foreign Direct Investment, International Trade and Economic Growth in Malaysia*. SSRN Electronic Journal SSRN Journal. doi:10.2139/ssrn.2276765

Rugman, A. (1987). Strategies for national competitiveness. *Long Range Planning*, *20*(3), 92–97. doi:10.1016/0024-6301(87)90076-8

Rugman, A. M. (1980). Internalisation as a general theory of foreign direct investment. *Weltwirtschaftliches Archiv*, *116*(2), 365–279. doi:10.1007/BF02696864

Rugman, A. M., & Li, J. (2007). Will Chinas multinationals succeed globally or regionally? *European Management Journal*, *25*(5), 333–343. doi:10.1016/j.emj.2007.07.005

Rugman, A., & Dunning, J. (1973). The Multinational Enterprise. *Southern Economic Journal*, *40*(1), 156. doi:10.2307/1056315

Rugman, A., & Verbeke, A. (2004). A perspective on regional and global strategies of multinational enterprises. *Journal of International Business Studies*, *35*(1), 3–18. doi:10.1057/palgrave.jibs.8400073

Rui, H., & Yip, G. S. (2008). Foreign acquisitions by Chinese firms: A strategic intent perspective. *Journal of World Business*, *43*(2), 213–226. doi:10.1016/j.jwb.2007.11.006

Rusnok, J. (2014). *Aktuální vývoj a perspektivy české ekonomiky v širším kontextu 10 let členství v EU*. Czech National Bank. Retrieved April 28, 2014, from http://www.cnb.cz/miranda2/export/sites/www.cnb.cz/cs/verejnost/pro_media/konference_projevy/vystoupeni_projevy/download/rusnok_20140428_univerzita_pardubice.pdf

Russia 2013: Shaping Russia's Future. (n.d.). Retrieved May 12, 2015, from Ernst & Young Attractiveness Survey website: http://www.ey.com/Publication/vwLUAssets/2013-Russia-attractiveness-survey-Eng/$FILE/2013-Russia-attractiveness-survey-Eng.pdf

Russia 2015 Statistical Pocketbook (Statistical Pocketbook). (2015). Retrieved May 28, 2016, from http://www.gks.ru/free_doc/doc_2015/rus15_eng.pdf

Russia Country Commercial Guide. (2015, October 16). Retrieved May 29, 2016, from http://www.export.gov/ccg/russia090879.asp

Russia Investment Climate Statement 2016. (n.d.). U.S. Department of State. Retrieved July 9, 2016, from http://www.state.gov/e/eb/rls/othr/ics/investmentclimatestatements/index.htm#wrapper

Russia, Country Profile. (2016). *Euromonitor/Passport*. Retrieved April 30, 2016 from http://www.euromonitor.com/russia-country-profile/report

Russia. (2016, April 29). *European Commission.* Retrieved June 3, 2016, from http://ec.europa.eu/trade/policy/countries-and-regions/countries/russia/

Russia. Special Report. (2016). *The Economist.* Retrieved November 13, 2016, from http://www.economist.com/print-edition/2016-10-22

Russia: Country Profile. (2016, April 15). Retrieved June 9, 2016, from Global Market Information Database (GMID/Euromonitor/Passport).

Russia: Economic Report: The Long Journey to Recovery. (2016, April). *World Bank Group,* (35). Retrieved May 29, 2016, from http://www.worldbank.org/eca/pubs/rer35_ENG.pdf

Russian Investment Agency. (2016). Retrieved September 10, 2016 from http://invest-rf.com/

Russia's Muslim Regions Turn to the Gulf for Help. (2016). *STRATFOR.* Retrieved July 18, 2016 from https://www.stratfor.com/analysis/russias-muslim-regions-turn-gulf-help?utm_source=paidlist-a&utm_medium=email&utm_campaign=07/18/2016&utm_content=Daily+Intelligence+Brief%3A+July+18%2C+2016&id=be1ddd5371&uuid=e05332c9-d7fd-449e-9a97-4c4ce2d9b8bf

Ruzzier, M., Hisrich, R. D., & Antoncic, B. (2006). SME internationalization research: Past, present, and future. *Journal of Small Business and Enterprise Development, 13*(4), 476–497. doi:10.1108/14626000610705705

Saad, R. M., Noor, A. H. M., & Nor, A. H. S. M. (2014). Developing Countries Outward Investment: Push Factors for Malaysia. *Procedia: Social and Behavioral Sciences, 130*, 237–246. doi:10.1016/j.sbspro.2014.04.028

Sahoo, P. (2006). *Foreign Direct Investment in South Asia: Policy, Trends, Impact and Determinants.* ADB Institute. Discussion paper No. 56.

Samimi, J. A., & Ariani, F. (2010). Governance and FDI in MENA region. *Australian Journal of Basic and Applied Sciences, 4*, 4880–4882.

Sanghoee, S. (2015). India: The next superpower? *Fortune*. Retrieved from http://fortune.com/2015/01/25/india-the-next-superpower/

Santangelo, G., & Meyer, K. (2011). Extending the internationalization process model: Increases and decreases of MNE commitment in emerging economies. *Journal of International Business Studies, 42*(7), 894–909. doi:10.1057/jibs.2011.25

Sauvant, K., Economou, P., Gal, K., Lim, S., & Wilinski, W. (2014). *Trends In FDI, Home Country Measures And Competitive Neutrality*. Retrieved November 18, 2016, from http://ccsi.columbia.edu/files/2014/03/Yb-12-13-ch.-1-8-Nov-13-stand-alone-final-for-website.pdf

Scaperlanda, A. E., & Mauer, L. J. (1969). The determinants of US direct investment in the EEC. *The American Economic Review, 59*(4), 558–568.

Scaperlanda, A., & Balough, R. S. (1983). Determinants of US direct investment in the EEC: Revisited. *European Economic Review, 21*(3), 381–390. doi:10.1016/0014-2921(83)90098-3

Schwab, K. (n.d.). The Global Competitiveness Report 2015–2016. *Insight Report*. Retrieved June 11, 2016, from http://www3.weforum.org/docs/gcr/2015-2016/Global_Competitiveness_Report_2015-2016.pdf

Schweiger, Ch. (2014). *The EU and the Global Financial Crisis. New Varieties of Capitalism.* Cheltenham, UK: Edward Elgar Publishing.

Scott, W. R. (2001). *Institutions and Organizations*. Thousand Oaks, CA: Sage.

Sethi, D. (2009). Are multinational enterprises from the emerging economies global or regional? *European Management Journal*, *27*(5), 356–365. doi:10.1016/j.emj.2009.04.009

Shah, M. H. (2014). The Significance of Infrastructure for FDI Inflow in Developing Countries. *Journal of Life Economics Jlecon*, *1*(2), 1–1. doi:10.15637/jlecon.37

Shapiro, D., & Globerman, S. (2009). *The international activities and impacts of state-owned enterprises*, Retrieved July 17, 2016, from http://dspace.africaportal.org/jspui/bitstream/123456789/26419/1/The%20International%20Activities%20and%20Impacts%20of%20State-Owned%20Enterprises.pdf

Shenkar, O. (2004). One more time: International business in a global economy. *Journal of International Business Studies*, *35*(2), 161–171. doi:10.1057/palgrave.jibs.8400074

Siddiqui, H., & Aumeboonsuke, V. (2014, July/August). Role of Interest Rate in Attracting the FDI: Study on Asean 5 Economy. *International Journal of Technical Research and Applications*, *2*(3), 59–70. Retrieved from http://www.ijtra.com/special-issue-view/role-of-interest-rate-in-attracting-the-fdi-study-on-asean-5-economy.pdf

Smarzynska-Javorcik, B. (2004). Does foreign direct investment increase the productivity of domestic firms? In search of spillovers through backward linkages. *The American Economic Review*, *94*(3), 605–627. doi:10.1257/0002828041464605

Smith, A. (1776). *An Inquiry into the Nature and Causes of the Wealth of Nations*. Library of Economics and Liberty. Retrieved November 7, 2016 from http://www.econlib.org/library/Smith/smWN.html

Soares, P. (2015). *República Checa: um mercado laboral competitivo – Uma comparação para o futuro*. PricewaterhouseCoopers International Limited. Retrieved April 20, 2015, from http:// pwc.pt/pt/temas-actuais/pcn/republica-checa.html

Soltani, B. (2014). The Anatomy of Corporate Fraud: A Comparative Analysis of High Profile American and European Corporate Scandals. *Journal of Business Ethics*, *120*(2), 251–274. doi:10.1007/s10551-013-1660-z

Special Economic Zones of the Russian Federation. (2011). Retrieved September 25, 2016 from http://www.ved.gov.ru/eng/investing/sez/

Sridharan, P., Vijayakumar, N., & Rao, K. C. S. (2009). Causal Relationship between Foreign Direct Investment and Growth: Evidence from BRICS Countries. *IBR International Business Research*, *2*(4). doi:10.5539/ibr.v2n4p198

St. Petersburg International Economic Forum. (2016). Retrieved September 11, 2016 from https://www.forumspb.com/en

Statystyka bilansu płatniczego. Uwagi metodyczne. (2015). Departament Statystyki NBP. Warsaw.

Stoian, C. (2013). Extending Dunnings Investment Development Path: The role of home country institutional determinants in explaining outward foreign direct investment. *International Business Review*, *22*(3), 615–637. doi:10.1016/j.ibusrev.2012.09.003

Stoian, C., & Mohr, A. (2016). Outward foreign direct investment from emerging economies: Escaping home country regulative voids. *International Business Review*, *25*(5), 1124–1135. doi:10.1016/j.ibusrev.2016.02.004

Stuckey, J., & White, D. (1993). *When and when not to vertically integrate*. Retrieved August 20, 2016, from http://www.mckinsey.com/business-functions/strategy-and-corporate-finance/our-insights/when-and-when-not-to-vertically-integrate

Subasat, T., & Bellos, S. (2013). Governance and foreign direct investment in latin america: A panel gravity model approach. *Journal of Management and Sustainability*, *50*(1), 107–131.

Subramanian, K., Chakrabarti, R., Sairam, S., & Kuntluru, S. (2012). *Infrastructure and FDI: Evidence from District-Level Data in India*. SSRN Electronic Journal SSRN Journal. doi:10.2139/ssrn.1712185

Sunesen, E., Jespersen, S., & Thelle, M. (2010). *Impacts of EU Outward FDI.* Copenhagen Economics Final Report.

Sunesen, E., Jespersen, S., & Thelle, M. (2010). Impacts of EU Outward FDI. *Copenhagen Economics Final Report.* 20 May.

Surroca, J., Tribó, J. A., & Zahra, S. A. (2013). Stakeholder Pressure On MNEs and the Transfer of Socially Irresponsible Practices to Subsidiaries. *Academy of Management Journal, 56*(2), 549–572. doi:10.5465/amj.2010.0962

Sustainable Development Knowledge Platform. (2015). *Sustainable Development Goals.* Retrieved July 12, 2016 from https://sustainabledevelopment.un.org/sdgs

Svetlicic, M. (2007). Outward foreign direct investment by enterprises from Slovenia. *Transnational Corporations, 16*(1), 55-87.

Svetlicic, M. (2004). Transition economies multinationals – are they different from Third World multinationals? In C. Chakraborty (Ed.), *Proceedings of the 8th International Conference on Global Business and Economic Development.* Montclair State University.

Świerkocki, J. (2015). Elementy polityki wobec polskich inwestycji zagranicznych. *Studia Prawno-Ekonomiczne, 95,* 345–368.

Świerkocki, J. (Ed.). (2011). *Foreign Direct Investment. The Case of Lodz Region.* Łódź: Łódzkie Towarzystwo Naukowe.

Szegedi, K. (2010). The Concept and Development Tendencies of Corporate Social Responsibility. *Club of Economics in Miskolc. TMP, 5,* 67–74.

Szegedi, K., Fülöp, G., & Bereczk, Á. (2016). Relationships between Social Entrepreneurship, CSR and Social Innovation. *Theory and Practice. World Academy of Science, Engineering and Technology International Journal of Social, Behavioral, Educational, Economic. Business and Industrial Engineering, 10*(5), 1470–1475.

Tang, Y. K. (2011). Influence of networking on the internationalization of SMEs: Evidence from internationalized Chinese firms. *International Small Business Journal, 29*(4), 374–398. doi:10.1177/0266242610369748

Tang, Z., & Hull, C. (2012). An investigation of entrepreneurial orientation, perceived environmental hostility, and strategy application among Chinese SMEs. *Journal of Small Business Management, 50*(1), 132–158. doi:10.1111/j.1540-627X.2011.00347.x

Tan, J., & Tan, D. (2005). Environment - Strategy Co-Evolution and Co-Alignment: A Staged Model of Chinese Soes under Transition. *Strategic Management Journal, 26*(2), 141–157. doi:10.1002/smj.437

Tavares-Lehmann, A. T., Toledano, P., Johnson, L., & Sachs, L. (Eds.). (2016). *Rethinking Investment Incentives, Trends and Policy Options.* New York: Columbia University Press.

Te Velde, D. W. (2007). Understanding Developed Country Efforts to Promote Foreign Direct Investment to Developing Countries: The Example of the United Kingdom. *Transnational Corporations, 16*(3), 83–104.

Temiz, D., & Gökman, A. (2014). FDI Inflow as an International Business Operation by MNCs and Economic Growth: An Empirical Study on Turkey. *International Business Review, 23*(1), 145–154. doi:10.1016/j.ibusrev.2013.03.003

Textual Proposal Possible Provisions on Competition. (n.d.). Retrieved 05, July 2016, from http://trade.ec.europa.eu/doclib/docs/2015/january/tradoc_153030.pdf

The Economic Times. (2016). *Economic Survey 2016: FDI 31per cent at $24.8 billion during April-November.* Retrieved from http://economictimes.indiatimes.com/news/economy/finance/economic-survey-2016-fdi-up-31-per-cent-at-24-8-billion-during-april-november/articleshow/51154824.cms

The fDi Report. (2016). Retrieved July 30, 2016, from http://forms.fdiintelligence.com/report2016/

The Heritage Foundation. (2015) *2015 Index of Economic Freedom - Czech Republic*. Retrieved 15 April, 2015 from http://www.heritage.org/index/country/czechrepublic

The International Organization of Motor Vehicle Manufacturers. (2016). Retrieved September 26, 2016 from http://www.oica.net/

The Reserve Bank of India. (2016). *Annual Report of the RBI*. Mumbai: Reserve Bank of India. Retrieved from https://www.rbi.org.in/Scripts/AnnualReportPublications.aspx?Id=1110

The Russian Evolution: How can foreign businesses prepare to prosper?. (2013). Retrieved April 15, 2016, from https://www.pwc.com/us/en/forensic-services/publications/assets/marketmap-russia.pdf

The Wall Street Journal. (2010). *Panalpina Settlements Announced, With $236.5 Million in Penalties*. Retrieved July 12, 2016 from http://blogs.wsj.com/corruption-currents/2010/11/04/panalpina-settlements-announced-with-2365-million-in-penalties/

The World Bank. (1997). *Helping Countries Combat Corruption. The Role of the World Bank*. Washington, DC: World Bank Group.

The World Bank. (2003). *Foreign direct investment in emerging market countries*. Washington, DC: The World Bank. Retrieved from https://www.imf.org/external/np/cmcg/2003/eng/091803.pdf

The World Bank. (2016). *Doing Business 2016. Measuring Regulatory Quality and Efficiency*. Washington, DC: International Bank for Reconstruction and Development.

The world's biggest public companies in 2011. (2012). Retrieved July 05 2016, from http://www.forbes.com/lists/2012/18/global2000_2011.html

Thirlwell, M. (2004). India: The Next Economic Giant. *Lowy Institute Paper*, (1). Retrieved from http://www.lowyinstitute.org/files/pubfiles/India_webFINALsml.pdf

Thomas, P. K. (2007). *Investment incentives: Growing use, uncertain benefits, uneven controls*. Geneva: Global Subsidies Initiative, International Institute for Sustainable Development.

Tian, W., & Yu, M. (2015). *Distribution Outward FDI and Productivity Heterogeneity: Evidence from Chinese Firms*. Retrieved September 30, 2016, from http://www.econ.hit-u.ac.jp/~cces/HIAS_HP/paper/Miaojie_Yu.pdf

Times of India. (2015). *India leads emerging economies in growth chart: World Bank*. Retrieved from http://timesofindia.indiatimes.com/business/india-business/India-leads-emerging-economies-in-growth-chart-World-Bank/articleshow/47631863.cms

Timokhina, O. (2014). *Chinese foreign direct investment in Africa in corporate social responsibility context*. Maastricht School of Management, Working Paper No.2014/29. Retrieved July 12, 2016 from http://www.msm.nl/resources/uploads/2014/09/MSM-WP2014-29.pdf

Torre, L. D., Schmukler, S., & Yeyati, L. E. (2002). *Financial Globalization: Unequal Blessings*. Policy Research Working Papers. doi:10.1596/1813-9450-2903

Transition Report 2000. (2000). London: European Bank for Reconstruction and Development.

Transparency International. (2015a). *What is Corruption?* Retrieved July 12, 2016 from http://www.transparency.org/what-is-corruption/#define

Transparency International. (2015b). *Corruption Perception Index 2015.* Retrieved July 12, 2016 from http://www.transparency.org/cpi2015#downloads

Transparency International. (2015c). *Exporting Corruption. Assessing Enforcement of the OECD convention on Combating Foreign Bribery.* Retrieved July 12, 2016 from http://www.transparency.org/exporting_corruption

Transparency International. (2016). *Emerging market companies show low levels of transparency, allowing corruption to thrive.* Retrieved October 13, 2016 from http://www.transparency.org/news/pressrelease/emerging_market_companies_show_low_levels_of_transparency_allowing_corrupti

Transparency International. (2016a). *Corruption by Country / Territory Czech Republic.* Retrieved July 5, 2016, from http://www.transparency.org/country#CZE

Transparency International. (2016b). *Corruption by Country / Territory Portugal.* Retrieved July 5, 2016 from http://www.transparency.org/country#PRT

Trąpczyński, P. (2014). *Determinants of foreign direct investment performance in the internationalization of Polish companies.* unpublished doctoral thesis. Poznań: Uniwersytet Ekonomiczny w Poznaniu.

Tytel, I., & Yudaeva, K. (2006). The Role of FDI in Eastern Europe and New Independent States: New Channels for the Spillover Effect. *Centro Studi Luca d'Agliano Development Studies Working Papers, 217*, 1-35.

U.S. Commercial Service in Russia. (2016). Retrieved September 26, 2016 from http://2016.export.gov/russia/

Udoh, E., & Egwaikhide, F. (2010). Exchange Rate Volatility, Inflation Uncertainty and Foreign Direct Investment in Nigeria. *Botswana Journal of Economics*, *5*(7). doi:10.4314/boje.v5i7.60304

UNCTAD. (2006). *World Investment Report 2006. FDI from Developing and Transition Economies: Implications for Development.* New York: United Nations.

UNCTAD. (2011). *World Investment Report 2011. Non-Equity Modes of International Production and Development.* New York, NY: UNCTAD.

UNCTAD. (2014). *Bilateral FDI Statistics.* Retrieved from http://unctad.org/en/Pages/DIAE/FDI%20Statistics/FDI-Statistics-Bilateral.aspx

UNCTAD. (2015). Retrieved from http://unctad.org/en/PublicationsLibrary/wir2015_en.pdf

UNCTAD. (2015). *World Investment Report 2015. Reforming International Investment Governance.* Retrieved from http://unctad.org/en/pages/PublicationWebflyer.aspx?publicationid=1245

UNCTAD. (2015). World Investment Report 2015. *United Nations Conference on Trade and Development.* Available at: http://unctad.org/en/pages/DIAE/World%20Investment%20Report/WIR-Series.aspx

UNCTAD. (2015). *World Investment Report 2015: Reforming International Investment Governance.* Retrieved from http://unctad.org/en/PublicationsLibrary/wir2015_en.pdf

UNCTAD. (2016). Retrieved from http://unctad.org/en/PublicationsLibrary/wir2016_en.pdf

UNCTAD. (2016). *UNCTAD statistics.* United Nations. Retrieved March 17, 2016, from http://unctadstat.unctad.org/wds/ReportFolders/reportFolders.aspx?IF_ActivePath=P,5

UNCTAD. (2016). World Investment Report 2015. *United Nations Conference on Trade and Development.* Available at: http://unctad.org/en/pages/PublicationWebflyer.aspx?publicationid=1555

UNCTAD. (2016). World Investment Report. Investor Nationality: Policy Challenges. Geneva: UNCTAD.

UNEP Finance Initiative. (2015). *UNEP FI Membership around the world.* Retrieved August 28, 2015 http://www.unepfi.org/signatories/?tx_phpadd_pi1[sortby]=country

United Nations Conference on Trade and Development. (2012). *World Investment Report. Towards a New Generation of Investment Policies*. New York: United Nations.

United Nations Conference on Trade and Development. (2015). *World Investment Report. Reforming International Investment Governance*. New York: United Nations.

United Nations General Assembly. (1948). *The Universal Declaration of Human Rights*. Paris: United Nations General Assembly.

United Nations Global Compact. (2013). *Global Corporate Sustainability Report*. New York: United Nations Global Compact Office.

United Nations Global Compact. (2015a). *A Guide for Business How to Develop a Human Rights Policy* (2nd ed.). New York: United Nations Global Compact Office.

United Nations Global Compact. (2015b). *Our Participants*. Retrieved August 28, 2015 from https://www.unglobalcompact.org/what-is-gc/participants

United Nations Human Rights Office of the High Commissioner. (2011). *Guiding Principles on Business and Human Rights. Implementing the United Nations „Protect, Respect and Remedy" Framework*. New York: United Nations Human Rights Office of the High Commissioner.

United Nations Human Rights Office of the High Commissioner. (2016). *What are human rights?* Retrieved July 12, 2016 from http://www.ohchr.org/EN/Issues/Pages/WhatareHumanRights.aspx

Uray, N., Vardar, N., & Nacar, R. (2012). International marketing-related outward FDI motives: Turkish MNCs' experience in the EU. New Policy Challenges for European Multinationals (Progress in International Business Research, Volume 7). *Emerald Group Publishing Limited, 7*, 305–338.

Usman, S. (2014). Higher Education, Infrastructure and Foreign Direct Investment in Pakistan. *IOSR Journal of Business and Management IOSRJBM, 15*(6), 54–59. doi:10.9790/487X-1565459

Vallejo, H., & Aguilar, C. (2002). *Regional Integration and Foreign Direct Investment: The Case of Latin America*. SSRN Electronic Journal SSRN Journal. doi:10.2139/ssrn.393920

Valles, R. (2015). *República Checa: um mercado laboral competitivo – Um exemplo a seguir e que se destaca nos indicadores de eficiência do mercado laboral*. PricewaterhouseCoopers International Limited. Retrieved April 20, 2015, from http:// pwc.pt/pt/temas-actuais/pcn/republica-checa.html

Vermander, B. (2014): The Development of CSR in China. In The American Chamber of Commerce (Ed.), Shanghai Corporate Social Responsibility Ten Years Report 2004-2014. The American Chamber of Commerce.

Verma, R., & Brennan, L. (2013). An Analysis of the Macroeconomic Determinants of Indian Outward Foreign Direct Investment. In M. A. Marinov & S. T. Marinova (Eds.), *Emerging Economies and Firms in the Global Crisis* (pp. 137–153). New York: Palgrave Macmillan. doi:10.1057/9781137277473_6

Vernon, R. (1966). International investment and international trade in the product cycle. *The Quarterly Journal of Economics, 80*(2), 190–207. doi:10.2307/1880689

Vernon, R. (1979). The International Aspects of State-Owned Enterprises. *Journal of International Business Studies, 10*(3), 7–15. doi:10.1057/palgrave.jibs.8490790

Vigeo. (2015). *Paying the Penalty: The Cost of CSR Misconduct.* Paris: Vigeo. Retrieved July 12, 2016 from http://www.vigeo.com/csr-rating-agency/images/stories/formulaires/2015_05_Related_Sanctions_version_finale_ENG.pdf

von Westernhagen, N. (2002). *Systemic Transformation, Trade and Economic Growth: Developments Theoretical Analysis and Empirical Results.* Berlin: Springer-Verlag. doi:10.1007/978-3-642-57483-2

Voss, H., Buckley, P. J., & Cross, A. R. (2010). The impact of home country institutional effects on the internationalization strategy of Chinese firms. *Multinational Business Review, 18*(3), 25–48. doi:10.1108/1525383X201000014

Walsh, J., & Yu, J. (2010). *Determinants of Foreign Direct Investment: A Sectoral and Institutional Approach.* Washington, DC: International Monetary Fund.

Wang, M. Y. (2002). The motivations behind Chinas government-initiated industrial investments overseas. *Pacific Affairs, 75*(2), 187–206. doi:10.2307/4127182

Wan, W. P. (2005). Country resource environments, firm capabilities, and corporate diversification strategies. *Journal of Management Studies, 42*(1), 161–182. doi:10.1111/j.1467-6486.2005.00492.x

Wan, W. P., & Hoskisson, R. E. (2003). Home country environments, corporate diversification strategies, and firm performance. *Academy of Management Journal, 46*(1), 27–45. doi:10.2307/30040674

Wąsowska, A., & Obłój, K. (2013). Location Determinants of Polish Outward Foreign Direct Investment and the Impact of the Global Crisis. In M. Marinov & S. Marinova (Eds.), *Emerging Economies and Firms in the Global Crisis* (pp. 240–258). London: Palgrave Macmillan. doi:10.1057/9781137277473_10

Watts, P., & Holme, L. (2000). *Meeting changing expectations. Corporate Social responsibility.* World Business Council for Sustainable Development.

WDI. (2016). *World development indicators.* The World Bank. Retrieved March 17, 2016, from http://data.worldbank.org/data-catalog/world-development-indicators

Wei, W. X., & Alon, I. (2010). Chinese outward direct investment: a study on macroeconomic determinants. *International Journal of Business and Emerging Markets, 2*(4), 352-369.

Welter, F., & Smallbone, D. (2011). Institutional perspectives on entrepreneurial behavior in challenging environments. *Journal of Small Business Management, 49*(1), 107–125. doi:10.1111/j.1540-627X.2010.00317.x

WGI. (2016). *Worldwide governance indicators.* The World Bank. Retrieved March 17, 2016, from http://info.worldbank.org/governance/wgi/index.aspx#home

White, H. (1980). A heteroskedasticity-consistent covariance matrix estimator and a direct test for heteroskedasticity. *Econometrica, 48*(4), 817–838. doi:10.2307/1912934

Why India is doing better than most emerging markets. (2014). *The Economist.* Retrieved from http://www.economist.com/blogs/economist-explains/2014/11/economist-explains-11

Wiliński, W. (2013). *Polityka gospodarcza państw wysoko rozwiniętych i rozwijających się w zakresie wspierania krajowych spółek inwestujących poza granicami kraju.* Warsaw: SGH.

Williams, D. A. (2009). Determinants of Outward Foreign Direct Investments from Small Island Developing States. *American Journal of Economics and Business Administration, 1*(2), 47–56. doi:10.3844/ajebasp.2009.47.56

Williamson, N., Stampe-Knippel, A., & Weber, T. (2014). *Corporate Social Responsibility National Public Policies in the European Union.*Luxembourg: Publications Office of the European Union.

Williamson, O. E. (1985). *The economic institutions of capitalism*. New York: Free Press.

Wilson, N., & Cacho, J. (2007). *Linkage Between Foreign Direct Investment, Trade and Trade Policy*. OECD Trade Policy Papers. doi:10.1787/18166873

Witek-Hajduk, M. K. (2010). *Strategie internacjonalizacji polskich przedsiębiorstw w warunkach akcesji Polski do Unii Europejskiej*. Warsaw: SGH.

Witkowska, J. (1996). *Bezpośrednie inwestycje zagraniczne w Europie Środkowowschodniej. Próba interpretacji na gruncie teorii bezpośrednich inwestycji zagranicznych i teorii integracji*. Łódź: Wyd. UŁ.

Witt, M. A., & Lewin, A. Y. (2007). Outward foreign direct investment as escape response to home country institutional constraints. *Journal of International Business Studies*, *38*(4), 579–594. doi:10.1057/palgrave.jibs.8400285

Wooldridge, J. M. (2002). *Econometric Analysis of Cross Section and Panel Data*. Cambridge, MA: MIT Press.

Wooton, I. (2015). The transatlantic trade and investment partnership (TTIP): The devil will be in the detail. *Fraser of Allander Economic Commentary*, *39*(1), 64–71.

World Bank. (2003). *Better governance for development in the Middle East and North Africa. Mena Development Report*. Washington, DC: The World Bank.

World Bank. (2005). *Bangladesh: Growth and Export Competitiveness*. Report No:31394-BD. Washington, DC: Author.

World Bank. (2013). Trends and Determinants of Foreign Direct Investment in South Asia. Report No: ACS4862. Washington, DC: Author.

World Bank. (n.d.). Retrieved from www.data.worldbank.org

World Commission on Environment and Development. (1987). *Our Common Future*. Oxford, UK: Oxford University Press.

World Economic Forum. (2014). *White Paper on Business Sustainability: What it is and why it matters*. Geneva: World Economic Forum.

World Economic Forum. (2015). *Building Foundations Against Corruption. Recommendations on Anti-Corruption in the Infrastructure & Urban Development Industries*. Geneva: World Economic Forum.

World Economic Forum. (2015a). *Czech Republic*. Retrieved 7 July, 2016 from http://reports.weforum.org/global-competitiveness-report-2014-2015/economies/#indexId=GCI&economy=CZE

World Economic Forum. (2015b). *Portugal*. Retrieved 7 July, 2016 from http://reports.weforum.org/global-competitiveness-report-2014-2015/economies/#indexId=GCI&economy=PRT

World Economic Forum. (2016). *The Global Risks Report 2016* (11th ed.). Geneva: World Economic Forum.

World Factbook Russia. (2016). Retrieved May 29, 2016, from https://www.cia.gov/library/publications/the-world-factbook/geos/rs.html

World Investment Report. (2009). *Transnational Corporations, Agricultural Production and Development*. UNCTAD.

World Investment Report. (2011). *Non-equity modes of international production and development*. UNCTAD.

World Investment Report. (2016). *Russian Federation Country Fact Sheet 2016*. Retrieved June 8, 2016, from http://unctad.org/en/Pages/DIAE/World Investment Report/Country-Fact-Sheets.aspx

Wydmus, S., Bombińska, E., & Pera, B. (2012). *Bezpośrednie Inwestycje Zagraniczne a Konkurencyjność Eksportu Polski*. Warsaw: CEDEWU.

Xiao, J., & Sun, F. (2005). Challenges Facing Outbound Chinese M& (and) A. *Int'l Fin. L. Rev.*, *24*, 44.

Yamakawa, Y., Peng, M. W., & Deeds, D. L. (2008). What drives new ventures to internationalize from emerging to developed economies? *Entrepreneurship Theory and Practice*, *32*(1), 59–82. doi:10.1111/j.1540-6520.2007.00216.x

Yang, X., Lim, Y., Sakurai, Y., & Seo, S. y. (2009). Internationalization of Chinese and Korean firms. *Thunderbird International Business Review*, *51*(1), 37–51. doi:10.1002/tie.20243

Yao, S., Sutherland, D., & Chen, J. (2010). Chinas Outward FDI and Resource-Seeking Strategy: A Case Study on Chinalco and Rio Tinto. *Asia-Pacific Journal of Accounting & Economics*, *17*(3), 313–325. doi:10.1080/16081625.2010.9720868

Yeaple, S. R. (2005). A simple model of firm heterogeneity, international trade, and wages. *Journal of International Economics*, *65*(1), 1–20. doi:10.1016/j.jinteco.2004.01.001

Ye, G. (1992). Chinese transnational corporations. *Transnational Corporations*, *1*(2), 125–133.

Yeyati, E. L. (1996). Investment in Inflationary Economies. *IMF Working Papers*, *96*(105), 1. doi:10.5089/9781451947571.001

Yiu, D. W., Lau, C., & Bruton, G. D. (2007). International venturing by emerging economy firms: The effects of firm capabilities, home country networks, and corporate entrepreneurship. *Journal of International Business Studies*, *38*(4), 519–540. doi:10.1057/palgrave.jibs.8400278

Yusoff, M. B. (2010). The effects of real exchange rate on trade balance and domestic output: A case of Malaysia. *The International Trade Journal*, *24*(2), 209–226. doi:10.1080/08853901003652377

Zahra, S. A., & George, G. (2002). International entrepreneurship: the current status of the field and future research agenda. In M. A. Hitt, R. D. Ireland, S. M. Camp, & D. L. Sexton (Eds.), *Strategic Entrepreneurship: Creating a New Mindset* (pp. 255–288). Oxford, UK: Blackwell Publishers.

Zahra, S. A., Korri, J. S., & Yu, J. (2005). Cognition and international entrepreneurship: Implications for research on international opportunity recognition and exploitation. *International Business Review*, *14*(2), 129–146. doi:10.1016/j.ibusrev.2004.04.005

Zanger, C., Hodicová, R., & Gaus, H. (2008). Psychic distance and cross-border cooperation of SMEs: An empirical study on Saxon and Czech entrepreneurs' interest in cooperation. *Journal of East European Management Studies*, *13*(1), 40–62.

Zapletalová, Š. (2012). Přístupy k internacionalizaci podnikatelských aktivit a českých podniků. *Ekonomie a Management*, *4*, 84–96.

Zapletalová, Š. (2015). Models of Czech companies internationalization. *Journal of International Entrepreneurship*, *13*(2), 153–168. doi:10.1007/s10843-015-0145-9

Zhang, X., & Daly, K. (2011). The determinants of Chinas outward foreign direct investment. *Emerging Markets Review*, *12*(4), 389–398. doi:10.1016/j.ememar.2011.06.001

Zhou, L. (2007). The effects of entrepreneurial proclivity and foreign market knowledge on early internationalization. *Journal of World Business*, *42*(3), 281–293. doi:10.1016/j.jwb.2007.04.009

Zhu, B. (2007). *Fortune or evil? The effects of inward foreign direct investment on corruption*. Paper presented for the Mini APSA Conference at the Department of Political Science, New York, NY.

Zhuplev, A. (2016). *Doing business in Russia: a Concise Guide.* Retrieved from http://www.businessexpertpress.com/authors/anatoly-zhuplev

Zhuplev, A., & Shtykhno, D. (2015). Energy and Sustainability in the European Region: The Russian Factor. In Handbook of Research on Sustainable Development and Economics. IGI Global.

Zhuplev, A. (2008, January). Economic Internationalization of Russia: Roots, Trends, and Scenarios. *International Political Science Review*, *29*(1), 99–119. doi:10.1177/0192512107083449

Zimny, Z. (2013). Outward FDI from Poland and its policy context. In *Columbia FDI Profiles Country profiles of inward and outward foreign direct investment.* Vale Columbia Center on Sustainable International Investment.

Zsoldos, I., & Zadornova, A. (2008). *New EU Member States – a Fifth BRIC?*. Goldman Sachs Global Economics Paper 173.

России, Р. Социально-экономические показатели [Regions of Russia. Socio-economic factors]. (2015). *Федеральная служба государственной статистики* [Federal State Statistics Service – Rosstat]. Retrieved May 28, 2016 from http://www.gks.ru/bgd/regl/b15_14s/Main.htm

About the Contributors

Tomasz Dorożyński, Ph.D., is an Assistant Professor at Department of International Trade, Institute of Economics, Faculty of Economics and Sociology, University of Łódź (Poland). He is a member to several prestigious international organisations of researchers and experts in international economics and international business, such as: European International Business Academy, European Economics and Finance Society, Réseau Européen pour l'Insertion Sociale et Professionnelle des Personnes Défavorisées, Academy of International Business Central and Eastern Europe Chapter, EIBA Poland. His research achievements include ca. 90 reviewed publications (after 2008). Two of his publications were awarded by the Rector of the University of Lodz for their research content. So far he has been involved in 7 research projects, also as project manager, 3 of them were co-financed by the EU. On top of that, he received three grants for young research workers. Results of his studies have been presented on numerous occasions to domestic and international conferences, e.g., in the UK, Sweden, Germany, Brazil, France, Turkey, Spain, Greece, Denmark, Belgium, Hungary and Latvia. His research work focuses, inter alia, on the EU cohesion policy, regional development, internationalization and FDI. He has been the author and expert to several EC projects under, e.g., Competitiveness and Innovation Framework Programme, Leonardo da Vinci and Grundtvig programmes. Since 2015 he has been the partnership educational project manager with the EEA / Norway Grant, project manager with National Bank of Poland grant and Management Coordinator of the international project European Mobility Placements for Open Innovation (2015-2018). For many years he has been the expert for Enterprise Europe Network Centre (Foundation for Promotion of Entrepreneurship) within the Central Poland Business Support Network, co-financed by Competitiveness and Innovation Framework Programme and COSME 2014-2020. He lectured abroad (Portugal, Germany, Lithuania, Hungary, Estonia) under the ERASMUS (+) Programme.

Anetta Kuna-Marszałek, PhD is a senior lecturer at the Department of International Trade of the University of Łódź (Poland). She is a member to several prestigious international organisations including Polish European Community Studies Association and Association for the Study of East European Economies and Cultures. Her primary research interests focus on various aspects of contemporary economics, including research on internationalization of business activities, FDI, support instruments for exporters and the interlinks between trade liberalization and environmental policies. She is an author and co-author of over 60 papers, chapters and articles including the award-winning books about (1) Poland's outward foreign direct investments and (2) anti-dumping investigations as an instrument of contingent protection. She participated in several research projects, including projects co-financed by the EU and the National Science Centre.

***

Ádám Bereczk is an Assistant Lecturer of Business Economics at the Faculty of Economics, University of Miskolc, Hungary. His main research themes are business enterprises and resource management.

Raif Cergibozan is an assistant professor at the Kırklareli University and at the Center for European Studies. Earned his bachelor's degree from Marmara University, Department of Economics in 2009. Received a master's degree from Istanbul Technical University, Department of Economics in 2011. He completed his PhD in Economics at the Galatasaray University in 2015. Areas of special interest in economics: Financial Crises, Labor Markets, International Trade, Time Series Analysis and Macroeconometric Models.

Mohammad Ashraful Ferdous Chowdury is an Assistant Professor of the Department of Business Administration, Shahjalal University of Science & Technology (SUST), Sylhet, Bangladesh. He is a researcher graduated with a Bachelor degree in Finance and MBA in Finance & Banking from Shahjalal University of Science & Technology (SUST), Bangladesh. He also holds MSc degree in Islamic Finance from International Centre for Education in Islamic Finance (INCEIF), The Global University of Islamic Finance, a post-graduate university specializing in Islamic Finance, established by the Central Bank of Malaysia. He has managed to publish quite a number of articles in refereed international and local journals published by Inderscience, Emerald, Springer, Taylor and Francis etc. publishers. His main research interests are in the area of Islamic capital market, Islamic banking, Sustainable development, Ethical and socially responsible investments. Mohammad Ashraful Ferdous Chowdury is a financial economist with consulting, research and teaching experiences in development finance, money and capital markets, Islamic finance, corporate finance, investments.

Caner Demir is an Assistant Professor of Economics. He received his B.A. in Economics from Dokuz Eylul University, Turkey in 2009 and he holds a Ph.D. in Economics from Ege University, Turkey since 2015. He has been at the University of Massachusetts-Amherst, U.S.A. for a year during his doctoral studies. The main research area of Dr. Demir includes economic growth, the economics of intellectual property rights, innovation and international capital mobility.

Ahmet Oguz Demir is the Director of EU Research Center and Assistant Professor of Economics at Istanbul Commerce University since 2013. He holds a PhD on Economics from Istanbul University. He also worked at the Institute for Innovation, Creativity and Capital at the University of Texas at Austin in 2014 as a visiting scholar. He has developed and managed numerous research based and applied projects on economic and social development in several regions in Turkey. Added to these core tasks, he is also the Advisor to Chairman for Travel Agents' Union of Turkey and he is leading a think-tank named as The Economists' Association. He was also co-host of a live TV show in Bloomberg Turkey about economic and social development between the years 2010 – 2014. His main research interests are economic transformation, globalization, human capital, creativity and economic growth and EU integration of Turkey. He has 3 books and scholarly papers published.

Gyula Fülöp is a Professor of Business Economics at the Faculty of Economics, University of Miskolc, Hungary. His main research themes are corporate strategy and social responsibility, entrepreneurship and small business management.

Ishita Ghosh is a researcher and Ph.D. student and has been a faculty member associated with various academic institutions in Pune, especially with SIU and UoP. With over ten years of work experience, she has a Masters in Economics – specialized in Trade – and is UGC NET qualified. Ishita has worked on urban policy and planning for Maharashtra with special emphasis on Energy, Economic Policy, and Governance. Her Ph.D. focuses on trade in services and the latter day new-new trade theories. Currently, Ishita teaches Research Methodology, Trade, Macroeconomics, Economic Journalism, Public Finance and Econometrics and handles students' dissertations logistics and the Economic Journal, Oeconomica Scriptis. Ishita has also had a brief stint in the corporate prior to her full-time academic career.

Ishita Ghoshal is B.Sc. in Economics (Hons) with Mathematics and Statistics from Lady Brabourne College, University of Calcutta and M.A in Economics from Gokhale Institute of Politics and Economics, Pune. She is currently pursuing Ph.D. from Gokhale Institute of Politics and Economics. Her areas of interest are Macroeconomics, Applied Econometrics and International trade. Currently, she teaches Macro-Economics and Econometrics to M.Sc. and B.Sc. Economics students. She has published in reputed journals like Journal of Quantitative Economics, Global Economy Journal and Procedia - Economics and Finance.

Marta Götz, PhD., Associate Professor at Vistula University in Warsaw. Previously she has been research fellow at the Institute for Western Affairs (Instytut Zachodni) in Poznań and teaching assistant at Warsaw School of Economics in Warsaw. She has conducted individual and team projects granted by the National Science Centre and the Visegrad Fund. Her areas of expertise include: foreign direct investment, clusters, competitiveness and macroeconomics of the EU, economic transformations in reunified Germany.

Barbara Jankowska, Ph.D., is Associate Professor at the Poznan University of Economics and Business, Faculty of International Business and Economics, Head of Department of International Competitiveness and National Representative of Poland in the European International Business Academy. Her main research areas include international business (international competitiveness of firms and industries, strategy of the firm in international business, foreign direct investment) and business clustering. She is the author or co-author of more than 110 publications, among them six books in her area of expertise. She has participated in several national and international research and consultancy projects on the international competitiveness of enterprises in the context of European integration and economic crisis, strategies of local firms towards foreign investors, business clusters and their significance for the international competitiveness, innovativeness and internationalization of firms and foreign direct investment.

Rıfat Karakuş received his PhD degree in Business Administration from Kırıkkale University in Turkey. In 2009 he was hired as the Instructor by the Çankırı Karatekin University Technical College and is currently Assistant Professor in Faculty of Economic and Administrative Sciences Banking and Finance Department. He writes and presents widely on firm value, investing and related financial topics.

Manoj Kumar received his PhD in Mechanical Engineering from the Indian Institute of Technology, Delhi, India. He is presently working as Director, Mother Parwati Education Services. He has authored or co-authored over 80 research papers in journals and conferences. He has authored or co-authored 20 chapters of book. He is reviewer in 11 international research journal. His biographical note is published in Asia/pacific who's who (vol. XII)- 2013, Biography India-2014, Famous India: nation's who's who-2015.

Mikhail Kuznetsov is a Managing Director for the Moscow-based National Association of Corporate Directors in Russia. His educational and professional credentials include an Executive MBA degree from IE Business School (Spain), certification as a Chartered Director from the IoD (UK), and a PhD in Economics from the Samara State Economic University. In his current capacity as a Managing Director for the Moscow-based National Association of Corporate Directors Mikhail Kuznetsov spearheaded the creation of one of Russia's largest and most authoritative professional associations of corporate directors including more than 500 directors across 25 Russian regions. He is also a board member at the Credit Bank of Moscow, Russian 15th largest bank, and Energosetproject OJSC, the largest engineering institute in the Russian energy sector. As a Managing Partner at the Corporate Development Advisers Dr. Kuznetsov established a successful board advisory consulting company, contributed to the development of corporate governance systems at the leading Russian and CIS companies, including Gazprom, Rosneft, RZD, Rostelecom, MTS, Rosatom, KazMunayGas JSC. Earlier in his consulting career he served at the International Finance Corporation, an arm of the World Bank, as a regional project manager and financial analyst responsible for the "Corporate governance in Russia" project that facilitated investment in the development of Russian regional companies. During 2002-2005, he has been involved as a consultant in reforming corporate governance system in more than 30 regional companies across Russia. Mikhail Kuznetsov has more than ten years of experience at the boards of directors in finance, energy, transport, and food processing industries in Russia and the CIS.

Esra LaGro is a Jean Monnet Professor for EU Economic Governance, Professor of EU Studies; Vice-President of the CIRP International (an international think tank) - Director of CIRP European Studies Research Programme. She holds a PhD on Industrial Economics and an MA on Political Science. She speaks fluent English, German; has a working knowledge of Dutch and French. Prof. LaGro is holder of several international academic awards; and is the author of more than 155 publications on interdisciplinary and comparative basis related to the European Union, Turkey–EU economic and political relations, European politics, Europeanization, EU economic governance, EU economic policies, Horizon 2020, Industrial economics, Competitiveness and the Euro-Med Partnership among others. Her most recent books include; The EU for the World Leadership: Towards New Global Governance? (KalDer, 2004), and Turkey and the European Union: Prospects for a Difficult Encounter with Dr. K. E. Jorgensen (Palgrave-Macmillan, 2007), La Vida Es Sueno: Dialogues with a Prominent Intellectual on the EU and World Affairs (Istanbul, 2010). She has conducted comparative interdisciplinary post-doc research in several universities in Western Europe, and has been delivering conferences and seminars on different aspects of the EU as a guest professor in leading European universities and think tanks since 2004; has organized several high level international conferences and seminars on the EU related topics. She gives invited lectures and conferences in leading West European universities such as Science Po, Maastricht University, Amsterdam University, Aachen University among others, and, in the US, at Washington University. She is also a successful international business consultant for more than 22 years. She has been advising and still advises companies, sectoral associations, and (Prime Ministry and line Ministries) governments and also works for international organizations such as the EU Commission, UNDP, UN on regulatory reform, regulatory and business impact assessment, good governance, economic and political analyses, foreign direct investment, international trade, strategic management, institution building, capacity assessment and capacity building, competitiveness audits, and strategic communications issues among others. Apart from her academic and consultancy work, she has strong civil society involvement. She is member of several international scientific organizations; executive board member as well as EU advisor of leading organizations in Turkey. Prof. LaGro has several media appearances pertaining to the EU affairs. She writes invited columns on the EU governance, Euro crises, Turkey-EU affairs for leading newspapers at home and abroad, and has been a regular columnist for a national journal for several years. Most recently, she also has prepared and presented a live weekly TV programme on the EU affairs at Bloomberg TV in 2010-2011, enhancing awareness raising on the EU economic governance and the business world. She is invited frequently to speak as a keynote speaker at international business conferences in Turkey and abroad; has several media appearances nationally and internationally.

Zhibin Lin is a senior lecturer and research mentor at Newcastle Business School, Northumbria University, following his appointment at several leading UK universities including Universities of Bristol and Keele. He is also a Yunshan Chair Professor at Guangdong University of Foreign Studies, China. He has over 10 years of marketing management experience in China's airline industry before pursuing a career in academia. Dr Lin's main research area is customer loyalty, ethical consumerism and social media engagement. He has published over 30 academic articles in top-tier international journals and conferences. His work has appeared in Transportation Research, European Journal of Marketing, Computers in Human Behaviour, Current Issues in Tourism, Journal of Brand Management, and others.

Inês Martins obtained a Bachelor's degree in Languages and Business Relations from the University of Aveiro, Portugal. She is currently finishing a Master's degree in Languages and Business Relations from the University of Aveiro, Portugal.

Muhammad Moiz is a Master student at the Faculty of International Trade at Istanbul Commerce University, Turkey. He holds a Bachelor Degree in Business Administration from COMSATS Institute of Information Technology, Pakistan. He is also working as a Researcher at the Economists' Association, a leading think-tank in Turkey. He is currently doing research on the Economic Integration of Syrian Entrepreneurs in Turkey. His research interests include international trade, foreign direct investment, and migration economics.

António C. Moreira obtained a Bachelor's degree in Electrical Engineering and a Master's degree in Management, both from the University of Porto, Portugal. He received his PhD in Management from UMIST-University of Manchester Institute of Science and Technology, England. He is an Assistant Professor at the Department of Economics Management, Industrial Engineering, and Tourism at the University of Aveiro, Portugal, where he is the head of Management studies. He is member of GOV-COPP research unit.

Lenka Novotná obtained a Bachelor's degree in Foreign Languages for Business Purposes at the University of West Bohemia in Plzeň, the Czech Republic, and a Master's degree in Languages for Business Relations at the University of Aveiro, Portugal.

Rose Quan is Senior lecturer in International Business and Entrepreneurship at Northumbria University Newcastle, the United Kingdom. Her research interests are focused on internationalisation of SMEs; international entrepreneurship, international student and staff mobility. Before joining academia, she worked as a purchase manager and marketing manager in UK, China in both private and public sector.

Krisztina Szegedi is an Associate Professor of Business Economics at the Faculty of Economics, University of Miskolc, Hungary. Her main research themes are business ethics, corporate social responsibility and social enterprises.

Anatoly Zhuplev is a Professor of International Business and Entrepreneurship at Loyola Marymount University (Los Angeles, California). During the Soviet times, he taught for ten years at the Moscow Management Institute, and subsequently at the Advanced Training Institute of the State Committee for Printing and Publishing in Moscow. With the winds of globalization and change, he has been pursuing professional development and growth in the West since 1989. Teaching, as a visiting professor, at Northeastern University in Boston, Massachusetts, U.S.A. (1989-1990) was followed a dream job on the West Coast of the U.S.A. at Loyola Marymount University (LMU) in Los Angeles, California (1992-current). He currently teaches International Business, International Entrepreneurship and Doing Business in Emerging Markets at the undergraduate, MBA and executive MBA level. Work at LMU has given Anatoly Zhuplev ample opportunities for educational travel to over 40 countries across the world. He taught international business in various applications in Barcelona, Spain (2014, 2016); in Bonn, Germany (1994, 1998, and 2009); in Warsaw, Poland, as a Fulbright scholar (2005); in Paris, France (short programs, 2004-2007). As part of LMU's Comparative Management Systems (CMS) MBA program Anatoly Zhuplev participated in thirteen comparative strategic global industry studies ranging from hospitality to skin care, medical tourism, sustainability, fast food industry, and disruptive technologies in the hospitality sector. These studies resulted in numerous field trips and interviews with business professionals and executives in many global regions with a focus on Eurasia. His books, book chapters, and journal articles on global energy and European energy security in the Russian perspective, small business and entrepreneurship in Russia, economic internationalization of Russia, Russia's global competitiveness, international management, international entrepreneurship, international business, corporate governance and sustainability (around 100 overall) have been published in the U.S., Canada, Western Europe, Russia, and the former USSR. Anatoly Zhuplev is a former editor-in-chief at the Journal of East West Business and a member of editorial boards of two academic journals. He serves in an advisory capacity on the Council on Global Initiatives under the Los Angeles Chamber of Commerce in Los Angeles, California, U.S.A. Anatoly Zhuplev received his Ph.D. from the Moscow Management Institute, Russia, in 1981, and his B.S. from the Moscow Engineer-Economics Institute in 1974.

Index

G

H

I

K

L

M

N

O

P

R

S

T

U

V

www.ingramcontent.com/pod-product-compliance
Lightning Source LLC
LaVergne TN
LVHW060400300926
849162LV00006B/1310